WHERE ARE THE KAMITE KINGS?

WHERE ARE THE KAMITE KINGS?

FREDERICK MONDERSON

SUMON PUBLISHERS

FREDERICK MONDERSON

SuMon Publishers
PO Box 160586
Brooklyn, New York 11216

sumonpublishers.com@sumonpublishers.com
blackfolksbooks.com@blackfolksbooks.com
fredsegypt.com@fredsegypt.com
blackegyptbooks.com@blackegyptbooks.com

Copyright Frederick Monderson/SuMon Publishers, 2011, 2021. All Rights Reserved. No part of this book may be reproduced, stored in a retrieval system, or transmitted by any means without the written permission of the author.

ISBN - 978-1-61023-002-5
LCCN - 2010908037

In the **Tribute to Professor George Simmonds**, "**Unsung Hero**," Dr. Fred Monderson sat at the feet of his heroes, Brother X, Michael Carter, Dr. Leonard Jeffries, Elombe Brath, Dr. Arthur Lewis, Prof. George Simmonds, Dr. ben-Jochannan, Sister Camille Yarbrough, among others.

I dedicate this book - **Where are the Kamite Kings?** to **my son, Erik Monderson**, tragically lost at age 19, soon after his trip to Egypt, in 2018. The **Tour Guides** in Luxor, Egypt, jokingly informed he was a **Prince**; that is, after he indicated he would be staying at Old Cataract Hotel at Aswan on that leg of the trip!

WHERE ARE THE KAMITE KINGS?

James Spady begins the **AFTERWORD** to Cheikh Anta Diop's *The Cultural Unity of Black Africa: The Domains of Patriarchy and of Matriarchy in Classical Antiquity*, (Chicago: Third World Press, (1959) 1987) pp. 209-235) with a quote from Legrand H. Clegg, III "Ancient America: A Missing Link in Black History," *A Current Bibliography on African Affairs*, May, 1972, p. 308, with the following quote: "Ancient Egypt was stolen from Africa by nineteenth century Egyptologists whose doctrine was nourished by the African slave trade, the sugar empire, and the cotton Kingdom. Many scientists during this period were against associating Black folks with the human race, much less with civilization. Hence it was early determined that not only Black people be excluded from Egypt, but that Egypt itself, through ingenious anthropological manipulation, be excluded from Africa. Despite the testimony of ancient Hebrew, Greek and Roman eyewitnesses, who insisted that the ancient Egyptians were 'black and wooly-haired,' despite the myriads of sculptural and skeletal remains indicating the same, Western science turned a deaf ear, and to the world declared: 'The ancient Egyptians were white!' Never before or since has such a mockery been made under the auspices of anthropological pursuit. Science bowed before race prejudice and truth recoiled in panic. Today, however, we are indebted to Dr. Cheikh Anta Diop, John G. Jackson and others who have quietly re-established Egypt as an integral part of the Black past."

Falsification of history to mislead science and the reading public in general is not altogether new for *The Donation of Constantine* has been termed historical fraud as well as the effort of Le Gross Clarke, who, in the 1930's search for "Early man" misled the scientific community by "authenticating a fake skull" to show early man was of European extraction and the search for man had to wait some two decades until Louis and Mary Leakey discovered *Zinjanthropus-Boisie* in Africa in the post-World War II era. Hence, it is not surprising that so many people, even "respected" academics are misinformed about this ancient society. *Wikipedia* quotes Zahi Hawass that the ancient "Egyptians were not black!" Has he argued against the claim "The Egyptians were white?" What we do know, the ancient Egyptians were conquered by Hyksos, Persians, Assyrians, Greeks, Romans, Arabs, Mamelukes and then by French

FREDERICK MONDERSON

and British imperialists. Suffice to say, elsewhere in *Grassroots View of Ancient Egypt*, this writer discusses the issue of how ancient Africans of Egypt generally lost their culture. In relation to the ancient Gods, these Africans were instructed: "You worship and ritualize me and I will bless and protect you." Now, while this contract initially held with the successes of millennia of mental, moral, physical and spiritual blessings, the African then began to "backslide." As such, his social, cultural, spiritual and intellectual foundations were affected; weakened, he became a victim of foreigners who attacked and destroyed his creations, appropriated and utilized the good qualities for their benefit. They falsified the record, while denying his involvement in its creation and consigning him to the lowest rung of human development. Wade Nobles in *Kemet and the African Worldview* calls this "white vested interest." However, while Professor John H. Clarke has held, "The people who preached racism, colonized history" and "When Europe colonized the world, it colonized the world's knowledge" Nobles states: "This latter point is understood if one understands that the political control of knowledge is a necessary condition for white supremacy; and, that in this regard as Diop has pointed out, the common denominator characterizing the study of ancient Egypt by white Egyptologists has been their seemingly desperate pathological necessity and unrelenting attempt to refute ancient Africa's blackness. Consequently, information regarding ancient Africa has been destroyed, distorted, falsified, suppressed and intentionally made unclear." I should add also stolen and this is not simply modern but ancient also. George G.M. James in his *Stolen Legacy* (1954, New York Philosophical Society), pointed out, Aristotle appropriated much of the ancient knowledge attributing them to his own creation, while this was not so. He explained the volume of work Aristotle claims he wrote represents a period of some 5000 years of accumulated knowledge as opposed to some guy, within a decade, being able to write that volume of such profound thoughts.

A closer look at the cleverness of European-American scholarship shows how they dismiss the corpus of African and African American scholarship that has insisted the Egyptians were African and black. That is, the great black scholars starting with Martin Delaney, W.E.B. DuBois, Carter G. Woodson, Drusilla Dunjee, John Huggins, J.A. Rogers, John Jackson, John Henrik Clarke, Yosef ben-Jochannan, Jacob Carruthers, Ivan Van Sertima, Maulana Karenga, Molefi Asante, Asa Hillard, Wade Nobles, etc.,

WHERE ARE THE KAMITE KINGS?

have all asserted the ancient Egyptians were black. Yet, the racists were all wrong despite their unending research done in the light of day! Meanings, despite their spending sometimes a generation researching, writing, teaching, lecturing, etc., Afrocentrists arguments have been being dismissed. However, European scholarship, marauding in the 19th and 20th Centuries age of "naked imperialism" and "enlightened" as well as "intellectual imperialism," particularly, in that era of the "Rape of the Nile" and colonialism, these imperialists did pull off the falsification of history they are now accused of. Hence, the need for a corrective that future generations may know the truth becomes imperative.

Dr. Frederick Monderson displays his books offered for sale at Brooklyn Book Festival, September 2010 at Boro Hall.

ABOUT THE AUTHOR

Frederick Monderson is a retired college professor and school teacher who taught African History in the City University of New York and American History and Government in the New York public schools. He has written more than 1000 articles in the New York Black Press, *Daily Challenge*, *Afro Times* and *New American* newspapers. In this venture, Monderson lends his expertise as a

FREDERICK MONDERSON

historian, Egyptologist, journalist and author of several books including *Michael Jackson: The Last Dance, 50 on Point, Sonny Carson: The Final Triumph; Celebrating Dr. Ben-Jochannan; Black History Extravaganza: Honoring Dr. Ben-Jochannan; Let's Liberate the Temple; Black Nationalism: Alive and Well, Black Nationalism: Still Alive and Well, African Nationalist Poetry and Prose, Black History Everyday: Part One; Black History Everyday: Part Two; Barack Obama: Ready, Fit to Lead, Barack Obama: Master of Washington, D.C., Sonny Carson: The Final Triumph, Get Your Knee Off Our Necks, Who Speaks for the Black Vote in the Age of Trump,* and on ancient Egypt *Seven Letters to Mike Tyson on Egyptian Temples, 10 Poems Praising Great Blacks for Mike Tyson, Intrigue Through Time, Temple of Karnak: The Majestic Architecture of Ancient Kemet, Hatshepsut's Temple at Deir el Bahari, Abydos and Osiris, Temple of Luxor, Medinet Habu: Mortuary Temple of Rameses III, The Quintessential Book on Ancient Egypt: "Holy Land"* (A Novel on Egypt), *Research Essays on Ancient Egypt, The Majesty of Egyptian Gods and Temples* (a book of Egyptian Poems), *Egypt Essays on Ancient Kemet, Reflections On Ancient Egypt – Book One; Reflections on Ancient Egypt: Book Two; Ethiopians in Egypt- The Twenty Fifth Dynasty; Egyptian Synthesis: The Eternal House: The Egyptian Tomb; The Ramesseum: Mortuary Temple of Rameses II, The Colonnade: Then and Now, Reflections on Ancient Kemet, Ancient Egypt – Synthesis, Into the Egyptian Mind, Grassroots View of Ancient Egypt and Glory of the Ancestors: 19 Letters to O.J. Simpson on Ancient African History.* A student of the esteemed Dr. Yosef ben-Jochannan, Dr. Monderson conducts tours to Egypt.

For Tour information, please contact Orleane Brooks-Williams at Nostrand Travel, 730 Nostrand Avenue, Brooklyn, New York 11216. Phone Number 718-756-5300.

WHERE ARE THE KAMITE KINGS?

Where are the Kamite Kings Photo. Dr. Fred Monderson and son Erik atop the highlands of "Tombs of the Nobles" at Aswan, Egypt in 2018.

Where are the Where the Kamite Kings Photo. Two Geniuses, Champollion and Erik Monderson, together in the Cairo Museum of Egyptian Antiquities, 2018.

FREDERICK MONDERSON

Where are the Kamite Kings Photo. Erik Monderson stands in the Plaza entrance to Karnak Temple, Luxor Egypt.

Where are the Kamite Kings Photo. Kings wearing the Double Crown, White Crown and Nemes Headdress at Karnak Temple on the North-South Processional Way Axis in the "Cachette Court" with the Seventh Pylon at their rear. While Kings on the principal east/west axis face that axis, these statues face the east west axis not the processional axis on which they stand.

WHERE ARE THE KAMITE KINGS?

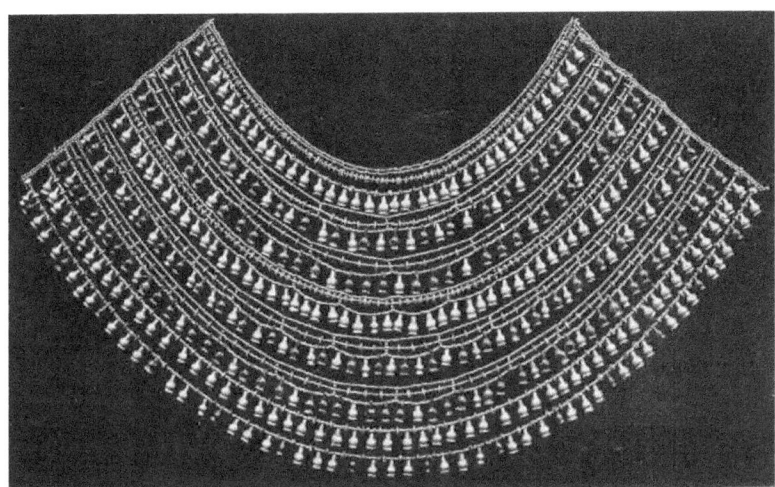

Where are the Kamite Kings Illustration. An intricately beautiful necklace worthy of being worn on a royal neck.

Where are the Kamite Kings Illustration. Menkaura and his Queen. Notice how she embraces him!

FREDERICK MONDERSON

Where are the Kamite Kings Illustration. Sekenenra, 17th Dynasty Theban King, father of Kamose and grandfather of Aahmes.

WHERE ARE THE KAMITE KINGS?

TABLE OF CONTENTS

	Preface	15
1.	Introduction	20
2.	Pre-Dynastic Kemet/Egypt	55
3.	The Archaic Period I	79
4.	The Archaic Period II	105
5.	Methodology I	147
6.	Methodology II	175
7.	The Old Kingdom	177
8.	First Intermediate Period	306
9.	The Middle Kingdom	321
10.	New Kingdom: Politics, Priesthood Culture and Architecture	431
11.	The New Kingdom and the Eighteenth Dynasty	472
12.	Nineteenth and Twentieth Ramesside Dynasties	561
13.	The Great Temple of Karnak	632
14.	The Temple of Luxor	641
15.	The Ramesseum: Temple of Rameses II	648
16.	Medinet Habu: Temple of Rameses III	659
17.	The Tomb of Seti I	677

FREDERICK MONDERSON

18. **The Tomb of Rekhmara**   **684**
19. **The Ethiopian Ascendancy**   **697**
20. **Tombs in Valley of the Kings**   **732**
21. **Table of Egyptian Dynasties**   **734**
22. **Chronology**   **735**
23. **The Alphabet**   **736**
24. **Index**   **738**

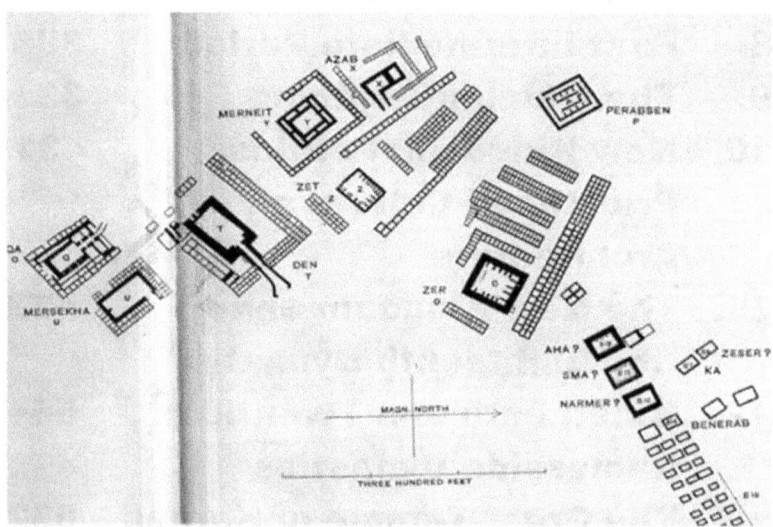

Where are the Kamite Kings Illustration. Tombs of the Archaic Kings at Abydos. *The Royal Tombs of The Earliest Dynasties* Part II by W.M. Flinders Petrie with a Chapter by F. Ll. Griffith, (1901).

WHERE ARE THE KAMITE KINGS?

Where are the Kamite Kings Photo. Enthroned monarch sits holding Ankh and Scepter before a vessel on a stand.

Where are the Kamite Kings Photo. Abu Simbel Temple of Rameses II. Four colossal seated statues of Rameses adorn the façade of his Temple while Ra-Horakhty is adored by miniature versions of the King and on the Cornice, baboons take the place of uraei.

FREDERICK MONDERSON

Where are the Kamite Kings Photo. Abu Simbel Temple of Rameses II. Close-up of two images of Rameses II paying tribute to the temple's titulary deity, Ra-Horakhty.

Where are the Kamite Kings Photo. Wall of the Heb Sed Court, shelter of the Colonnade and the Step-Pyramid in the rear at Sakkara.

WHERE ARE THE KAMITE KINGS?

Where are the Kamite Kings Illustration. The Celestial Cow with Divinities at work in the Heavens

Preface

Where are the Kamite Kings? In answer, besides the fact, the Kamite Kings mummies are in a second-floor room at the Cairo Museum of Egyptian Antiquities and visitors have to pay 100 Pounds Egyptian to view them, in addition to the regular Museum admission fee, this work is an attempt to identify places, in a chronological historical scheme, where Kings of Ancient Kemet/Egypt have left their names as recovered from excavations over the last two centuries. This attempt does not claim to identify all the names nor places for that matter, many are left out of this exercise for want of brevity and particularly as more and more evidence become available, through discovery and rediscovery. However, what this effort does is identify, for future research, such names, whether engraved or illustrated in religious structures, in tombs, on domestic and social projects as well as in wartime markings. In addition, on stele or stelae, in quarries, on papyrus, line drawings and where some of these artifacts can be located in today's world, is equally included the intent. There are many pieces located in museums all over the world, in private collections and particularly the Cairo Museum of Egyptian Antiquities, where artifacts from this glorious age of African historical contribution are housed in great abundance. Whether in their buildings, as commemorative erections or praise of noblemen for their sovereigns, the names have been preserved and this allows us to connect with these great Africans who left indelible impressions on the monuments, people and age during which they lived. The several hundred photographs and illustrations help to create a visual reinforcement of the culture, history and architecture of this ancient African assertion that is still a source of wonder and amazement to today's tourists and the academic community. However, these photographs are nor arranged in any particular order but are simply included to *reinforce the textual intent.*

In addition, Dr. Yosef ben-Jochannan was very instrumental in helping this writer as a young scholar to find himself at a critical juncture in his educational development. After reading his many books and having done several trips to Egypt with the "old master," two things seem to remain indelibly imprinted in my memory bank, thanks to "Doc Ben." The "old master teacher" has often remarked: "Now that you have been to Egypt, seen what you have seen, and gained the knowledge, 'What are you going to do with it?'" The second admonition Dr. Ben asserted is: "Get the oldest material you can find and work from there in your research." This is because many of the modern books on Egypt are much sanitized and "consciously and unconsciously" distort and omit the role of black Africans in the creation of this significant African civilization that rose on the banks of the Nile River when Europe and Asia were just beginning their long trek to civility. By virtue of anteriority, Egypt equally helped to mold the culture of Europe as it came into vogue.

Importantly, yet sadly, hardly a European scholar has the "marbles" to affirm that the ancient Egyptians were black! It is as if, despite the overwhelming evidence, they cling to the notion that the ancient Egyptians were "White Europeans," "Brown Europeans," "Red Europeans," Indo-Europeans and "I don't want to deal with it, Europeans," etc. In this vein, and because scholars from Europe and America were responsible for the significant archaeological and anthropological recovery of ancient Egypt from the bowels of mother Africa, in the aftermath of the ending of slavery, many of these workers colored their interpretations of the evidence because

WHERE ARE THE KAMITE KINGS?

they catered to audiences who were alien to Africa; and thus, these scholars were guilty of questionable scientific and intellectual integrity. At the time of the archaeological and anthropological excavation, recollection and analytic interpretation of the ancient evidence, the "penny press," and rapid disclosure of "finds" fed a particularly and intellectually hungry European and American audience, all enthralled with the glamour, mystique and fascination of discovery and acquisition of artifacts of antiquity. As such, many faulty interpretations of the historical record were presented and still, today, one has to read carefully to find the role of blacks in Egypt even though the same people created the culture and left evidence to underscore this. However, despite the many surviving and veiled references to Africans in Egypt much was destroyed in "The Rape of the Nile" phenomenon, doctored in museum basements and modern falsification of history and through intellectual dishonesty.

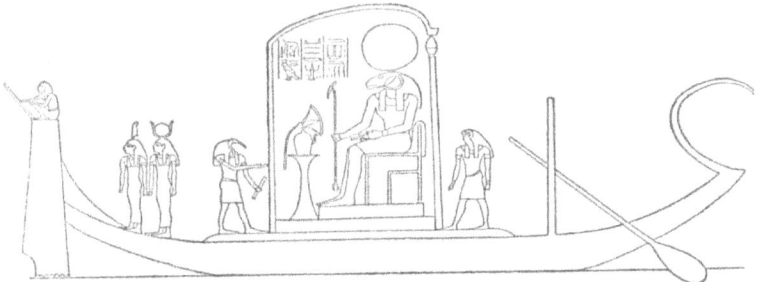

Where are the Kamite Kings Illustration. The Celestial Barque of the Sun-God with Ma'at and Hathor out front as look-out and Thoth and Horus at fore and aft of the Shrine.

One could well imagine the "work" done in the basements of such places as the Cairo Museum, British Museum, Metropolitan Museum of Art, Brooklyn Museum, Chicago Museum, Philadelphia Museum and museums in Australia, Britain, Germany, France, Austria, Turkey, Canada, Italy and so many more countries and cities as their teams of curators did the nose and other "jobs" and helped to omit and "correctly portray" Egypt or rather "incorrectly portray" the remains of these "Black Men of the Nile."

FREDERICK MONDERSON

After all, it is generally agreed, history has to be re-written and this work seeks to assist as far as possible, the avid reader, thinker, analyst and iconoclast in their ongoing work of African historiographic reconstruction. Consider that modern research, particularly in Europe and America, is gradually beginning to admit that the early Egyptologists and archaeologists made "some mistakes" in their "interpretation of the record." Yet, these are "opening the door" so slightly one could hardly see any light emanating there from. Hence, the need to present any evidence that aids modern knowledge, to allow the lay person as well as students and scholars to get a better picture of ancient Kemet/Egypt/Tawi for 21st Century interpretation of the role of people and culture in the Nile Valley experiment.

Where are the Kamite Kings Illustration. Nebpehtyra, Aahmes, Founder of the 18th Dynasty and New Kingdom.

WHERE ARE THE KAMITE KINGS?

This work is therefore dedicated to the black men and women, and right thinking European and American men and women of goodwill, scholars extraordinary, who labored during the last two centuries to challenge the distortions and include omissions of Nile Valley history and culture, systematically implanted by racist European and American historiography, having created and perpetuated the myth of a "white, European, Egypt" as enunciated by Hegel, Breasted and a whole host of others of like mind including Wortham. Of course, we must give credit to Martin Delaney and Dr. Yosef ben-Jochannan among the African stalwarts who for the longest wrestled with the question of the origins of the ancient Egyptians. However, in addition to "Doc Ben," there is also W.E.B. DuBois and Marcus Garvey, Drusilla Dunjee, Carter G. Woodson, John Huggins, J.A. Rogers, John H. Clarke, Jacob Carruthers, Ivan Van Sertima, Wade Nobles, Cheikh Anta Diop, Theophile Obenga, Molefi Asante, Maulana Karenga, Leonard James, John Jackson, Charles Finch, George Simmonds, and countless others, too numerous to mention. Lest we forget Counts Volney and Denon, and J.G. Higgins of *Anacalypsis* fame, Gerald Massey, Raymond Dart, etc. The labors of these stalwarts have been instrumental in challenging and correcting the ancient record and keeping alive the spirit and quintessence of black men and women whose efforts have influenced the ancient world by their daring actions and creative contributions, that have also helped advance the intellectual history of civilization and humanity in general.

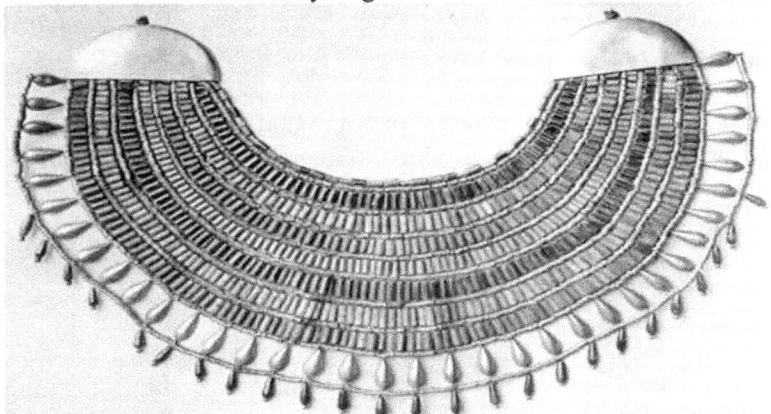

Where are the Kamite Kings Illustration. Another intricately beautiful necklace fitting to be worn on a royal neck.

FREDERICK MONDERSON

Where are the Kamite Kings Illustration. Khufu, builder of the Great Pyramid (left); and, Khafra, who built the second Great Pyramid that is fronted and guarded by the Great Sphinx on the Ghizeh Plateau.

Added to the above, the names of Kings and Gods sometimes vary according to the author and time period being referenced. Sometimes the New Kingdom principal deity name Amon is spelt Amun, Amon, Amen even Amon-Ra, Amun-Ra and Amen-Ra.

1. INTRODUCTION

During the later years of the New Kingdom, the Nineteenth Dynasty, Ramesside Period, a great African, King, Pharaoh, father, statesman, builder, artistic, scientific and intellectual patron, military hero and divinity, embarked on a campaign in southwest

WHERE ARE THE KAMITE KINGS?

Asia. This confrontation came to be known as the Battle of Kadesh. Embarking with four armies as Ra, Ptah, Amen and Sutekh, the King led in the frontal, with two flanks, and rear deployment of his regiments. In the vanguard, Rameses II "ran ahead" of his other regiments and found himself enveloped in a trap set by his adversaries, the princes of the Kadesh Confederacy.

Collecting himself in the middle of the night, as the attack on his camp began, this black, if you will brown, champion called upon his God, the God of his ancestors whom they had all worshiped. He beseeched Amon to never let so worthy a subject be overtaken by the forces of destruction and ignorance as these aliens. Immediately the King rallied his forces and with his charioteer, broke out of the orchestrated trap, linked with his main forces, "won the day," or night, as it was, and finally brokered the world's first peace treaty. He later immortalized this dramatic military engagement in depiction on temples illustrated at Abu Simbel, Abydos, Luxor, Karnak, Beit Wali, and the Ramesseum, his funerary temple. It is also recorded on papyrus.

These earliest of historical milestones are recorded in picturesque Kemet/Egyptian, African, art. However, the building of temples by pharaohs, on the other hand, came to express the highest admiration, glorification and gratitude to various Gods, but particularly the state God, who had brought military success and artistic and intellectual wealth to Kemet. During the New Kingdom, Amen (Amon, Amun, Amon-Ra, Amun-Ra, Amen-Ra) was the benefactor whose estates in return received extensive endowments from the victorious Kings. The moral example to be served from the conduct of these ancient and great Africans is there are inner strengths and beauty, fortitude, cultural appreciation and religious, spiritual and educational fortitude and growth to be experienced from praising African divinities and immersing in origins and roots.

This, notwithstanding, today the intellectual world is engaged in a serious re-evaluation of the historical record of ancient Egypt/Kemet. Such efforts come after the systematic exposure of Europe's falsification of the history of the Nile Valley, not giving credit to Egyptian Africans whom history has shown to be black, as Cheikh Anta Diop and the Afrocentrists have argued. These scholars have systematically challenged the falsity articulated by Hegel, Champollion the Younger (Cheronnet-Champollion), James Breasted and his "school" as well as a whole host of others who argued the ancient Egyptians were Indo-European or Asiatic in origin, essentially "white!"

Nevertheless, we now realize, building upon the pre-dynastic foundations of cultural and scientific accomplishments together with astute leadership, the "Archaic Period," or First and Second Dynasties, established the monarchy, system of central government, and religion and burial practices that endured throughout dynastic rule. Following right after, the creative, purposeful and opulent Old Kingdom, genius and bedrock of all that was created in the civilization of Kemet, has now come to be recognized; these accomplishments were the gifts of so called "Negroes." Other races who are later represented in the various attitudes of the culture are filtered small groups of foreigners who were of little consequence, in this early period of boldly creative and intellectual daring.

The first filtering of foreign influence occurred when the Kingdom of Upper Kemet (represented by the White Crown) and Lower Kemet (represented by the Red Crown) and their separate Crowns, were no longer united under the White resting on Red Double Crown at the end of the Old Kingdom. The trickle turned to a flood after the Middle Kingdom had reunited the land ushering in a period of great learning and cultural development, following the collapse of the Old Kingdom and the First Intermediate Period. With the collapse of the Middle Kingdom came the Hyksos invaders.

The Hyksos, whom Manetho described as "Shepherd Kings" or "Tent Dwellers," even were able to take advantage of Kemet's internecine strife and resultant weakness. These foreigners conquered and ruled the land for a century, forming the Fifteenth and Sixteenth Dynasties. This period is generally called the Second Intermediate Period. In fact, the Hyksos were able to seize the Kingdom of Lower Kemet/Egypt, destroy much of the culture, and still hold the North while the Kingdom of Upper Kemet/Egypt remained essentially intact. The South, however, paid a "tribute" to the foreigners in the North of whom, it was said, Hatshepsut uttered they "ruled in ignorance of Ra." This issue of tribute and some other irritations sparked a 50-year protracted war of liberation begun by Sekenenra I and his son Sekenenra II and his wife Tetisheri. It was

WHERE ARE THE KAMITE KINGS?

continued by their son Kamose and finally and completely won by Aahmose his brother, who married their sister, Aahmes-Nefertari, founder and ancestress of the Eighteenth Dynasty. An interesting historical fact can be added about this beautiful African queen. A painting in the British Museum depicts the lady as being "coal black Ethiopian" with her name in the royal Cartouche/Shennu. This, "the most venerated person in Egyptian history" is shown wearing the fashion of the times, heavily be-jeweled in a long flowing gown of White, Red and Blue, and wearing the queen mother crown or vulture headdress. This is the first time this tri-color concept is shown in history, 1500 years Before Christ, as part of the black queen's stately attire. Some scholars have equated the tricolor with the White Crown of Upper Egypt/Kemet, the Red Crown of Lower Egypt/Kemet and the wonderful blue of the Nile River. Today, nearly two-dozen nations have red, white and blue adorning their national flag color schemes. These include Britain, Canada, France, USA, all "western nations." Save Haiti and the Dominican Republic, no African nation has these colors exclusively in its flag. Do note, however, the concept is really "White, Red and Blue" not "red, white and blue!"

In the Eighteenth Dynasty triumph following the expulsion of the Hyksos and foundation of the New Kingdom, Kemet experienced unprecedented prosperity in this its third "golden age." Its success was accomplished under imperialist pharaohs who internationalized their relations and brought foreigners, gold and, tribute as animals, plants and slaves back to their land. This way, more whites became entrenched or settled in the Empire. Still, the dominance of Thebes reigned with its essentially black population in hegemony and its religious and political dominance in the society. This dynamic in the capital juxtaposed black social experience with whites who were visitors, emissaries, or had become domiciled through slavery, trade or as captives in war. However, Africans nevertheless set the tone, harmony, rhythm, and art, religious and philosophic and intellectual standards of the Kingdom of Ta-Merry/Tawi in the land of ancient Kemet. They built extensively such structures as temples, tombs, palaces; quarried and transported huge stone over great distances for state-sponsored projects; practiced medicine, surgery and dentistry; abounded in craftsmanship; practiced scientific surveying of the land after the Inundation for farming that was aided by irrigation canals; developed an educational system that taught morality, and love for family, as well as love of the knowledge of science as in astronomy, chemistry, mathematics, navigation, and religion, philosophy; equally, they excelled in mummification of the dead and burial practices.

Where are the Kamite Kings Photo. Erik Monderson "cools it" on the Ghizeh Plateau with camel and Khafre's Pyramid at his rear.

Where are the Kamite Kings Photo. Illustration. Shu, the Air God, separates the Goddess of the Heavens Tefnut, from the Earth-God Keb, who reposes in the prone position.

WHERE ARE THE KAMITE KINGS?

Where are the Kamite Kings Photo. Erik Monderson exploring at the "Tombs of the Nobles," Aswan, in 2018.

Where are the Kamite Kings Photo. View of statues south of the Eighth Pylon on the North/South Axis of Karnak Temple of God Amon-Ra. To the left are broken and decorated stones found on the premises and the south or First or Entrance Pylon further on.

FREDERICK MONDERSON

The effort of reconstruction in African historiography is under serious challenge by proponents of racism and improperly schooled individuals, who seek to deny black Africans a significant role in generating, practicing and continuously creating the ideas and conventions that became early engines of civilization. More importantly, denying African participation in Kemet/Egypt/Ta-Meri/Tawi, which has contributed so much to the character and culture of the modern western world especially, was well within the designs of falsifiers of history. This psycho-social rape and intellectual assault on Africa and Africans is unrelentingly being challenged by today's Afrocentric scholarship.

Where are the Kamite Kings Photo. **A**bu Simbel Temple of Rameses II. Rameses, wearing Double Crown, offers a bouquet and pours Libations from three vessels to Cataract God Khnum wearing the Khenemu Crown, as both the King and God stand on the same plane.

WHERE ARE THE KAMITE KINGS?

Even more, while foreigners called the state Egypt, the ancient Africans named it Kemet, Ta-meri, or Tawi, the "two lands." This country in North-East Africa, an area incorrectly called the "Middle East," was named by the ancient Africans for the blackness of the land and its people whose lives were regulated by well-established social norms, conventions, precepts, axioms and laws designed to cultivate Ma'at, meaning justice, order, truth, balance, harmony, even inner strength. Knowledge of this intellectual "rock" can become a decided buoy of inspiration to provide strength for young and old Africans as well as others who daily face life's challenges, mishaps, tragedies and notwithstanding can still boast of triumphs.

Right after the American Revolution, its Constitution, the challenges and triumphs of the young nation, Europe erupted in the French Revolution, Napoleonic wars and Metternich reaction. All, while Africans were held captive in a hostile "new world," their dehumanization enshrined through legal sanction in which a system of slavery was perpetuated by America and European nations and people. This enslavement, nevertheless, even with the blessings of the Church, incited the efforts and laid the foundations for English abolitionists Granville Sharpe, Clarkson, Buxton and a number of others, who from 1772 had begun the crusade to end the Slave Trade. They advocated, prayed and hoped to pass the mantle of abolition on to another generation whose task it was to end slavery. Much of their work influenced the American abolitionists. The early abolitionists Judge Samuel Sewell, the New Jersey Quaker John Woolman and Benjamin Franklin, Thomas Paine and James Otis were all sympathizers who attacked slavery and the dehumanization the institution perpetuated on its hapless victims. History has shown while ancient traders and writers visited Africa, they praised these blacks for their contributions to civilization. However, instead of praise, this current one is an age of debasement of the African and things black.

Significantly, the abolitionist movement in American got underway after the War of 1812. This was aided immensely by the emergence and growth of newspapers. Two Blacks, *Samuel Cornish* and *John B. Russwurm* founded *Freedom's Journal*. David Walker made his

FREDERICK MONDERSON

Appeal in 1826 and its radicalism found justification in the work of William Lloyd Garrison who published the *Liberator*. John Brown, a deeply religious white man, led a raid on Harper's Ferry, intent on getting arms to free enslaved Africans in America. Black abolitionists included William Wells Brown, Rev. Henry Highland Garnet, Charles Lennox Remond, Lunsford Lane and Prince Saunders as well as Sojourner Truth and Harriet Tubman. They lived in an age of Equiano, Gustavas Vasa, Gabriel Prosser and Nat Turner. Frederick Douglass founded the *North Star* in 1847 at Rochester, New York, and is today considered the "father of the protest movement." There were other abolitionists, whites as well as mixed couples including Abigail Goodwin, Thomas Garret, Daniel Gibbons, Lucretia Mott and William and Ellen Craft. Levi Coffin, "President" of the Underground Railroad, and John Fairfield, who aided numbers of blacks to escape slavery, are all social protesters whose influences extended into efforts of reform for women, the handicapped, prison and education.

Where are the Kamite Kings Illustration. One of the earliest pictures of boats on the Nile River, Archaic Period dating.

In that age at the end of the Eighteenth Century that saw Napoleon's invasion of Egypt, after his losses to the British, opened interest to an ancient African culture. The French Emperor took Savants or scholars to Egypt with him and through their researches found the ancient Nile Valley culture had centralized government and moral precepts guided by theological and theosophical systems and conventions, where praise, worship, and ritualizing of the Gods became driving forces of creative genius that impressed both ancient and modern minds.

From the time of Napoleon's soldiers' discovery of the Rosetta Stone, a tri-lingual inscription, in 1798, the keys to unlocking the ancient knowledge and culture were at hand. After an arduous and challenging struggle in 1822, Jean Jacques Champollion was able to

WHERE ARE THE KAMITE KINGS?

discover keys to unlock the long-lost language. Out of his untiring efforts at decipherment, aided by that of the scholars Sylvester DeSacy, Young and Akerblad, the discipline of Egyptology was born.

From Champollion's death in 1832 to 1884-85, the years the Berlin Congress partitioned Africa, gradual European interest in the continent escalated in full-scale and "enlightened imperialism." Just as the dynamics of 19th Century Europe led to nationalism, industrialism and imperialist clashes that culminated in World War I, concerted and systematic capture of African real estate and its administration; these actions opened new vistas for young European scientists whose careers were fueled by the challenge of discoveries and sensational press reporting about the ancient Egyptian phenomenon as well as rapid publication of their excavation reports.

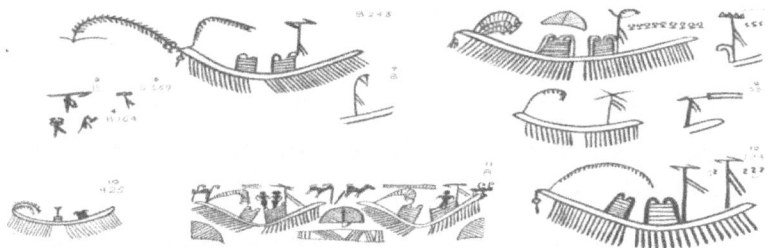

Where are the Kamite Kings Illustration. More evidence of early boats, Flinders Petrie's *Diospolis Parva* (1901).

In the age of imperialism and colonial administration, some say "intellectual imperialism," lucrative concessions were granted European economic, scientific and geographic consortiums that explored and exploited the land, conducted mineralogical surveys, and anthropological, botanic and zoological studies throughout Africa that essentially benefited European colonialism, science, intellectual development and industrialization. In Egypt, concurrently, from Napoleon's time onwards, the work of a number of Europeans scholars and others laid the foundations and molded the emerging discipline of Egyptology and essentially twisted the perception of who were the ancient Egyptians. This list included the "strongman" Belzoni, Jean-Baptiste Fourier, Robert Hay, Henry Salt, and Colonel Vyse, as well as Perring, Rosellini, Gardner

FREDERICK MONDERSON

Wilkinson, Joseph Bonomi, James Burton and Auguste Mariette, Lepsius etc., even adding Brugsch, Brugsch-Bey and Samuel Birch. In England, Prof. Owens, G. Eliot Smith, Flinders Petrie and still more, met at the **British Association for Advancement of Science** to discuss and mold ideas about the ancient evidence, naturally arguing from a Eurocentric, white supremacist, perspective. In the critical three decades, 1884-1914, especially after the "Berlin Congress," British, French, German, Swiss, Italian, Belgian, Turkish, American and Canadian interests were given lucrative excavation rights to unearth the evidence and study the ancient cultural remains with resulting shenanigans of allotting the pick of the "spoils" to museums and private collections in Europe, Australia and North America, especially. They did an excellent work unearthing the ancient culture but Egypt paid an enormous price in allotting artifacts.

Where are the Kamite Kings Photo. Erik Monderson in the "Ghizeh Pyramid perimeter" with the two great pyramids and Sphinx in the rear.

In an interesting work, Methods and Aims in Archaeology (1904), W.M. Flinders Petrie dedicated this effort to his friends: "L.L. Griffith, E. A. Gardner, F. J. Bliss, Lt. Carter, B. P. Grenfell, J. E. Quibell, J. Duncan, H. F. Petrie, N. de G. Davies, A. C. Mace, D. Randall-MacIver, R. Orme, A. E. P. Weigall, M. A. Murray, L.

WHERE ARE THE KAMITE KINGS?

Eckensten, H. Stannus, C. T. Currelly, E. R. Ayrton" who "have joined in various positions of the work here described, 1884-1903."

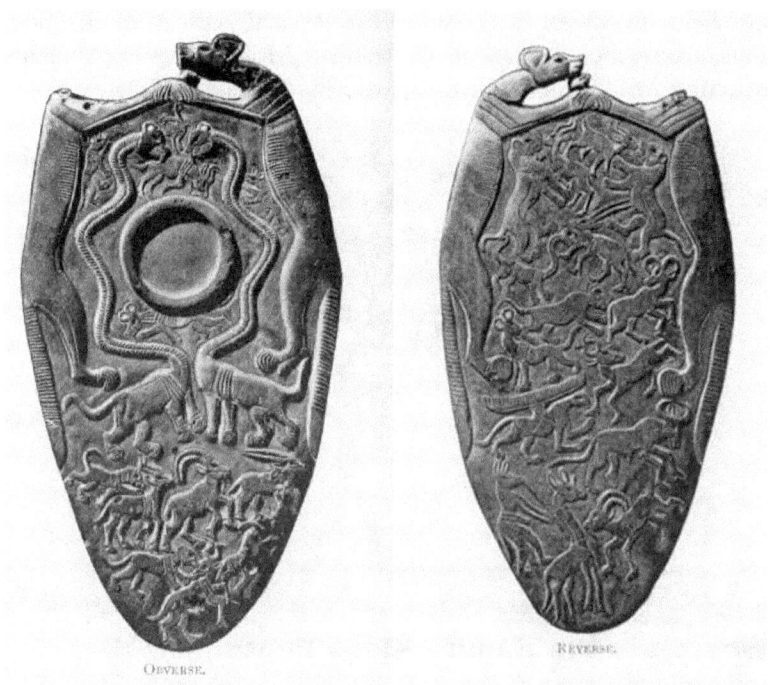

Where are the Kamite Kings Illustration. Dog Palette of slate. Obverse. Archaic representation of two very long necked animals encircling a circle and other animals (left); and, Reverse. An archaic representation of a lion attacking other animals (right).

To these could be added the Swiss Professor Edouard Naville and the Frenchman Gaston Maspero, later knighted by the British Monarchy. These scholars were contemporary with the Americans James Henry Breasted, Henri Winlock and Theodore Davis. Of particularly note, the Frenchman De Morgan, as Curator of Egyptian Antiquities, helped "rape" Egypt and by extension Africa, of its historical artifacts by giving away untold numbers of valuable pieces to museums worldwide. Later Hayes and J. A. Wilson, Kurt Sethe and Seele became part of the Chicago University "school of thought" founded by James H. Breasted. These individuals represent the architects of the foundations of modern European and

FREDERICK MONDERSON

American interpretation who have so influenced the discipline in the Twentieth Century. However, hot on their heels came many "old scrappers" including the more scholarly, Du Bois, Drusilla Dunjee, Carter G. Woodson, John Higgins, J.A. Rogers, G.M. James, Yosef ben-Jochannan, John H. Clarke, Ivan Van Sertima, etc., and those more directly involved in study of classical African civilization. This group included Jacob Carruthers, Molefi Asante, Maulana Karenga, Wade Nobles, Asa Hillard, Charles Finch, III, etc.

Where are the Kamite Kings Photo. Erik Monderson, still exploring at the "Tombs of the Nobles," Aswan, Egypt, 2018.

All this notwithstanding, by the end of the 19th Century, the blackness of the people of ancient Kemet was thoroughly substituted for a white European image. This distortion of history occurred for a number of reasons. Principally, from the enlightenment onwards, German, British, French, Italian and American scholars were fortunate to do the exploration and later the archaeological excavations, being involved in the plunder, theft, analysis, exhibit, publication, fund-raising, acquisition and collaboration in artifacts being smuggled away from the proper and rightful authorities. From these "keepers of ancient African antiquities" treasures found themselves on display in wonderfully laden museums that today radiate among the rich reservoirs of European and American national culture. Even private collections today can claim extensive holdings. Countries as the United Kingdom, Belgium, Canada, Denmark, Berlin, Moscow, Turin,

WHERE ARE THE KAMITE KINGS?

France and the United States have significant collections. Many countries number several institutions housing Egyptian artifacts in various cities, as for example in the United States, where the Brooklyn, Metropolitan, Boston, Detroit, Philadelphia and Chicago museums, among others, are examples. The movie "National Treasure" may be fiction or fact as an indication of appropriation, disbursement and acquisition of ancient Egyptian artifactual resources.

Where are the Kamite Kings Photo. Abu Simbel Temple of Rameses II. Eight colossal statues adorn the outer Hypostyle Hall with its decorated ceiling and looking deep into the Temple at the Sanctuary with its seated Gods.

FREDERICK MONDERSON

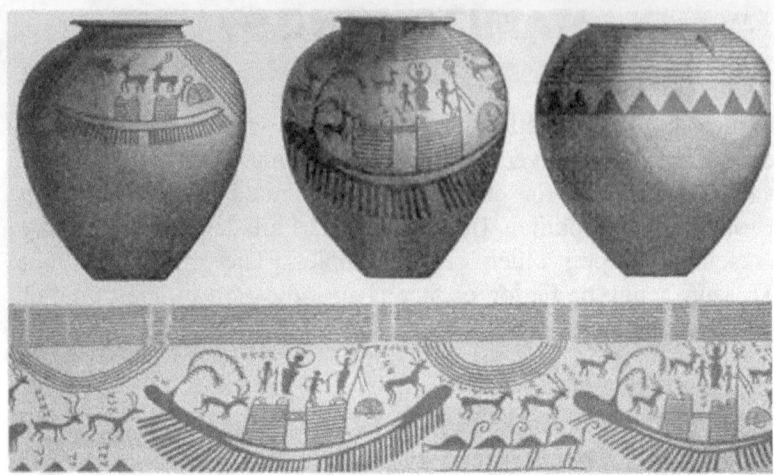

Where are the Kamite Kings Illustration. Even more evidence of boats and early pottery from James Henry Breasted's *A History of Egypt* (1905) 1923.

All this notwithstanding, by the end of the 19th Century, the blackness of the people of ancient Kemet was thoroughly substituted for a white European image. This distortion of history occurred for a number of reasons. Principally, from the enlightenment onwards, German, British, French, Italian and American scholars were fortunate to do the exploration and later the archaeological excavations, being involved in the plunder, theft, analysis, exhibit, publication, fund-raising, acquisition and collaboration in artifacts being smuggled away from the proper and rightful authorities. From these "keepers of ancient African antiquities" treasures found themselves on display in wonderfully laden museums that today radiate among the rich reservoirs of European and American national culture. Even private collections today can claim extensive holdings. Countries as the United Kingdom, Belgium, Canada, Denmark, Berlin, Moscow, Turin, France and the United States have significant collections. Many countries number several institutions housing Egyptian artifacts in various cities, as for example in the United States, where the Brooklyn, Metropolitan, Boston, Detroit, Philadelphia and Chicago museums, among others, are examples. The movie "National Treasure" may be fiction or fact as an indication of appropriation, disbursement and acquisition of ancient Egyptian artifactual resources.

WHERE ARE THE KAMITE KINGS?

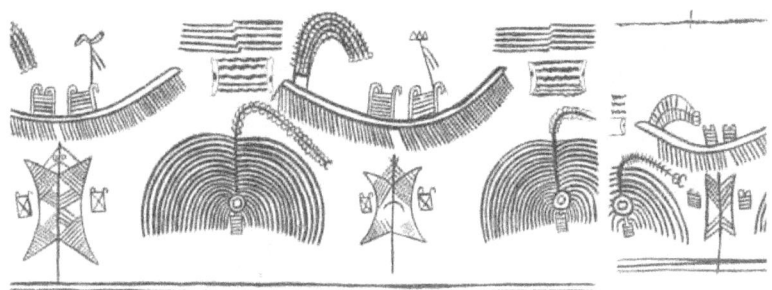

Where are the Kamite Kings Illustration. Further evidence of boats and other features from Sir Matthew Flinders Petrie's "prehistoric work" in Egypt.

Whereas, on the one hand, abolitionists were seeking the destruction of slavery and upliftment of the African in social, political and educational endeavors; on the other, there were others seeking to correct the just emerging distortion of the historical record. Historical truth, we are told, is immutable! A number of writers dared to face the scorn, enmity and sanction of western culture as they exposed the fraudulent manner in which historical and artifactual resources have been colonized and domesticated to the troubling climate, geography, intellect and mind-set of Europe and America. This "Eurocentric conspiracy" in turn distorted and misrepresented the role and nature of the ancient culture and country today called Egypt. Black Africans who were first maligned by being called Egyptians were later denied being Egyptians because they were black. As an example, the movie *Ten Commandments* is a significant distortion of the proper history of these Africans.

FREDERICK MONDERSON

Where are the Kamite Kings Illustration. Obverse side of the Four Dog Palette (left) and, Reverse side of the Four Dog Palette.

Where are the Kamite Kings Illustration. A group of Alabaster vases inscribed with royal names of the Vth and VIth Dynasties. These are Sahura, Teti, Neferkara Pepi II and Merira Pepi I.

WHERE ARE THE KAMITE KINGS?

Where are the Kamite Kings Illustration. Aahotep, mother of Aahmes.

In addition, those academic, media and publishing establishments, that maintain such a twisted view, are obviously misguided, perhaps purposefully. What is terribly significant about the movie *Ten Commandments* is the thousands of times the movie was shown, graphically implanting in the minds of so many, a distorted view of historical reality. This *modus operandi* was one aspect of strategy in the conspiracy against ancient Egypt/Kemet, and Africa and Africans in general!

Where are the Kamite Kings Photo. Erik Monderson in Al Fayal Garden at Aswan.

Where are the Kamite Kings Illustration. Pottery with designs dating to the Amratian Period, before **Unification**, from Breasted's *A History of Egypt* (1905) 1923.

WHERE ARE THE KAMITE KINGS?

Where are the Kamite Kings Illustration. King, wearing White Crown and with tool in hand, is shown in ceremonial scene "Opening the Agricultural Season," with fan-bearer in rear.

Among the modern European scholars who have defended the "African-ness" of the Egyptians, the people from the land of ancient Kemet, are included Count Volney who first commented on falsity of Egyptian reporting and Count Denon who drew the Great Sphinx at Gizeh as part of the Napoleonic contingent of savants. These were the first European scientists -to view the just awakened antique land. Denon claimed Napoleon's soldiers used canons on the sphinx as target practice and its nose fell off. He did draw the sphinx with its nose intact and this was probably before the gunplay. Part of the beard, which could have fallen off at this time, was housed in the British Museum. Concerning this piece and other similar artifacts elsewhere as "culture in captivity," battles are being waged for their return. Ivan Van Sertima, now deceased, bless his soul, affirmed in a lecture that after a lengthy fight with the British Museum, the beard of the Sphinx was returned to Egypt on "permanent loan." Seems this term "permanent loan" designation is designed to mute any attempts to make international law declare "all cultural artifacts removed from colonial areas must be returned." This would practically denude the great museums of the world filled with such artifacts.

FREDERICK MONDERSON

Where are the Kamite Kings Illustration. Menkaura, builder of the third Great Pyramid, Ghizeh Plateau (left); and, King User-En-Ra-An c. 3400 B.C., a statue dedicated by Usertsen I of the 12th Dynasty, honoring this Old Kingdom, predecessor King.

As the modern world woke to the significance of the ancient culture, Africans could not be given credit for Egyptian civilization because in many places worldwide they were prostrated as minions in the European and American practiced institutions of slavery and racism. In this, they helped transform the Americas in wake of European colonization following Columbus' misguided but fortunate voyage of discovery. Many were physically, psychologically and emotionally damaged en-route in the affective and effective dynamics of the horrible crossing called the "Middle Passage" of the "Triangular Trade." Here the psychological damages as inflicted against these Africans have created centuries-old implications in social, educational, economic and intellectual relations with others. Even more, others were still sharing the serene bliss of the protective bosom of mother Africa, on the verge of capture for service in the mindless, calculated, cold, cruel, and harsh new world reality of the Americas. The contradiction is that

WHERE ARE THE KAMITE KINGS?

in this land of America men were champions of life, liberty, and the pursuit of happiness. Some have argued you can't hold a man in the mud without getting mud on yourself. Hence, the denial of Africans' roles in Egypt.

The best examples of this, having infectious implications for revolutions worldwide were in Greece, France, Latin America, Haiti, and so on. Revolution aside, Europeans and Americans involved in the slave trade and slavery perpetuated one of the most vicious, racist and psychologically demeaning, depressive and destructive systems of "cultural genocide" on African people. DuBois, in his 1895 work *Suppression of the Slave Trade to America 1638-1870* (New York: Longman, Green and Co., 1904) estimated "Africa lost 100 million souls" in this "crime to humanity." Throughout it all, except for Haiti, and its example of black military, political and moral triumph against the might of western culture and the great military power of the French, much of Africa had been relegated to the periphery of influence in world affairs or confined in chains. Therefore, with the new discovery of the ancient African Nile Valley culture, notwithstanding the overwhelming archaeological, anthropological, historical, and physical evidence in art and literary sources attesting to Kemet's black African-ness, the fraud of Europe was systematic and thorough. Much of the literary and artifactual evidence of the ancient Africans that have survived and were not destroyed are held captive in faraway museums and private collections, oftentimes depicting or supporting some form of distortion, as a cultural attack on Africa. In coalitions of conspiracy between big business and wealthy individuals as patrons of art, the publishing industry, racist scholars, ignorant academics, and outlets for published works, a false version of this history has been fabricated, ossified and today reflects and represents the incorrect view. This is different to the view experienced and told by "European Afrocentrists" Counts Denon and Volney, and Godfrey Higgins, Gerald Massey, Kersey Graves, Raymond Dart and other European scholars. They have provided anthropological and historical connections with the ancient writers including Herodotus, Diodorus Siculus, Pliny, Strabo, Clement, Josephus, and Manetho. This ancient Egyptian priest Manetho, during Greek rule, and the other ancient scholars

FREDERICK MONDERSON

were more contemporary with the culture as early observers of the physical types of these ancient Africans.

Where are the Kamite Kings Illustration. Both sides of the Narmer Palette employ use of the Register, showing (left) the Goddess Hathor (above) and the King wearing the Red Crown with standards of various Nomes, decapitated prisoners, his sandal-bearer; attendants with fantastic beasts; and the King as a bull goring an enemy; and (right), he wears the White Crown in a larger size than previously, about to smite a kneeling captive, God Horus atop flowers, holds captive by the nostrils and below he tramples his foes.

Manetho, in the third century Before Christ, wrote a history of Kemet/Egypt based on evidence from the sacred archives held in the temples to which he had access. In this work, Manetho divided pharaonic rule into dynasties or rule by single families. In spite of some general inaccuracies, modern scholars have essentially retained his dynasties. However, Lepsius, a German Egyptologist of the 19th Century, divided the history into Ancient, Middle and New Empires. Even more, modern scholars gave names to the periods after the Old Kingdom, Middle Kingdom and New Kingdoms; respectively as the First Intermediate Period, Second Intermediate Period and Late Period.

WHERE ARE THE KAMITE KINGS?

Where are the Kamite Kings Illustration. A clearer image of the obverse side of the Narmer Palette found at the Hierakonpolis National Temple, Upper Egypt, by J.E. Quibell.

Where are the Kamite Kings Photo. Erik on the Plaza before the Mammisi with the Great Pylon in rear at Edfu Temple of Horus in 2018.

FREDERICK MONDERSON

Where are the Kamite Kings Illustration. Early dynastic pottery found in the temenos at Abydos, an early site of religious pilgrimage, showing different sizes and shapes.

After the New Empire came the Late Period in which foreign nations including Ethiopia, Assyria, Persia, Greece and Rome, all conquered this crossroad of the ancient world. In the cultural effervescence along the Nile, African nation-building bequeathed to humanity the arts, science, mathematics, building, navigation, and quarrying and extensive transportation of stone, as well as religion, burial practices and writing. Medicine, dentistry, poetry, record keeping, agriculture, astronomy and craftsmanship, viz., masonry, leatherwork, goldsmith, silversmith, and tinsmith are trades practiced by the Nile Valley peoples. These are some examples of ancient Africa's gifts. Other metalworking in gold, copper, bronze as well as precious stones used in jewelry, have all attested to a high level of cultural craft sophistication achieved by ancient Egyptians, Africans.

In ancient Kemet, there is significant history, religious and architectural remains from the time of the Greeks and Romans that

WHERE ARE THE KAMITE KINGS?

a Graeco-Roman Period is established. The significance of Graeco-Roman rule is represented in the Temples of Edfu, Kom Ombo, Esneh, Dendera, Kalabsha and Philae. The Greeks who conquered Kemet wished to emulate the illustrious pharaohs. They encouraged building and religious presentations designed to ritualize and worship the Egyptian Gods, in similar manner. They built their temples with Egyptian techniques, plans and conceptions tweaked by Greek innovation to contemplate and worship the African Gods on ancient sites already consecrated as being holy, because structures of the earlier religious houses of worship, were built there.

Where are the Kamite Kings Photo. Abu Simbel Temple of Rameses II. Queen Nefertari offers flowers to Hathor sailing through the marshes wearing horns, disk and plumes.

To say African Gods is essentially correct for these were African Gods in Egypt. This concept is just part of the continuing contradiction as European scholars seek to defend a "White Egypt" from the quicksand foundations of their falsity. The Gods were black and therefore African, and this presents an anomaly. If the Egyptians were non-Africans, how could they have conceived of their Gods being black and worship and ritualize black Gods! For example, in Western religion, God, the angels and even heaven reflects the color of Europeans. A second important part in the conspiracy against ancient Egypt is, though the Egyptians had their own names, and were conquered by Ethiopians, Assyrians, Persians, Greeks then Romans, the names these latter gave to various locations are names 19th Century scholars have used in their handling the ancient records. In this subtle maneuver, for example,

FREDERICK MONDERSON

Thutmosis replaced Thutmose; Amenophis replaced Amenhotep and geographical locations were subjected to the same treatment. Flinders Petrie's work is replete with Greek and Roman names. Consider then the Greco-Roman experience is the foundation of western civilization and culture, as a result, the tie-in becomes evident. Thus, today all history books on western civilization have a preliminary chapter on Egypt. Well, you do the math! Or analysis!

Nevertheless, migration, which has always been a significant catalyst for cultural diffusion and development of culture and history, has generally shown civilization emerged in river valleys, viz., Nile, Indus, then Hwango Ho, and Tigris-Euphrates. Evidence also shows how influence was created by the flow of the river. Prof. John H. Clarke in commentary on John Jackson's *Introduction to African Civilization* regarding the chapter on "Ethiopia's Eldest Daughter Egypt," believed civilization, like any stage-play or screen-script, needed a place of rehearsal. He argued, it was in the nations to the south of Egypt/Kemet where Civilization actually began, and the drama subsequently found fruition further down the river, where the climate and geography has preserved so much of their achievements.

Equally too, Bruce Williams of the University of Chicago has pointed to his discovery of pharaonic artifacts from Qustul, in Nubia, in "basement holdings," showing symbols of Pharaonic power and authority representing the "earliest monarchy." He identified the white crown, and Scepter, enthroned pharaoh, building façade, Nile boat, and an incense burner used in religious presentation, etc. evidenced at the "rehearsal site," 200 years before they appeared in Egypt at the inception of the First Dynasty (c. 3200 B.C.).

The earliest stone building was credited to the tomb of Khasekhemui, a Second/First Dynasty pharaoh. Even more, Imhotep's Step-Pyramid at Sakkara, dating to the Third Dynasty, was an equally significant accomplishment. Also, the "true Pyramids" at Giza built by the great rulers Khufu, Khafre, Menkaure of the Fourth Dynasty, represented tremendous advances and innovations in ancient Kamite/Egyptian/African stone building achievements.

WHERE ARE THE KAMITE KINGS?

Where are the Kamite Kings Photo. Erik Monderson poses with an employee (above); and, Map of the Kitchener Garden on the Island at Aswan.

Where are the Kamite Kings Photo. Erik Monderson stands before the Imhotep Museum at Sakkara, home of the Step Pyramid.

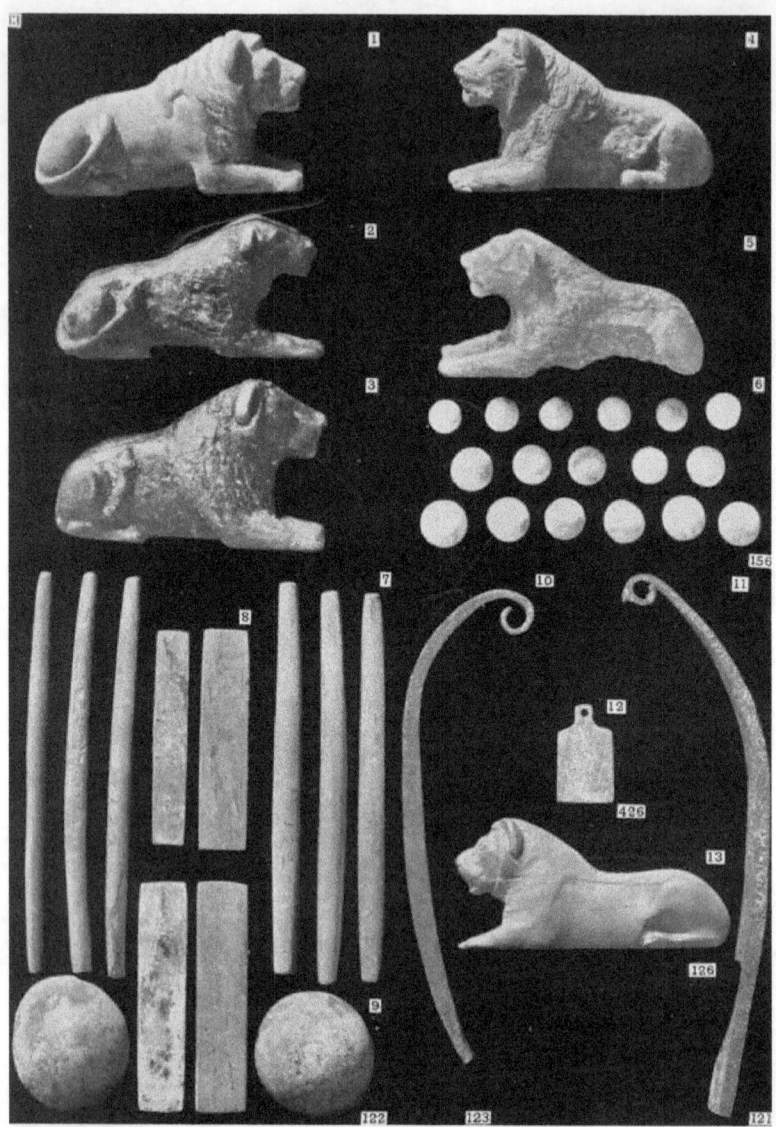

Where are the Kamite Kings Illustration. Gaming pieces of ivory, balls and copper bars of the First Dynasty in *Tombs of the Courtiers and Oxyrhynkhos* by Flinders Petrie with Chapters by Alan Gardiner, Hilda Petrie and M.A. Murray (1925).

WHERE ARE THE KAMITE KINGS?

Where are the Kamite Kings Photo. Abu Simbel Temple of Rameses II. Rameses in long flowing see-through attire holds two knives before a *Table of Offerings* dedicated to the ithyphallic Amen as Min with Ra Horakhty and Hathor at the God's rear. While Amon-Min stands on a pedestal, the King and the other deities are on the same, though a different, plane or level.

Another interesting fact came to light in discussion of the origins of agriculture and the role of Africans in this important development. Popular yet "ancient" and somewhat misguided belief held that agriculture was discovered in South-West Asia around 8000 B.C. and migrated to Egypt in c. 4500 B.C. Afterwards it spread in other areas of Africa. However, there is one source of evidence that shows an independent development of agriculture in West Africa about 4500 B.C. Even more, a *Science* magazine article in February 1982 dates the development of agriculture on the Nile to as early as 16,500 to 14,500, Before Present! This is actually 14,500 to 12,500 B.C. There is also evidence to show development of agricultural patterns at 11,000 B.C. in the Wadis or "catch basins" that sprang up along the Nile after rains or the inundation had deposited water. Much more significant, however, was a *New York Times* article of 1973 showing the discovery of an iron-ore mine in South Africa dated at 43,000 *Before Present*! That is, about 41,000 B.C! In commentary, Dr. John H. Clarke offered the view that "an iron mining community had to have been substantial and therefore necessitating the use of agriculture." As such, he argued further "agriculture must have been worked much earlier in Africa than generally thought." This is so important for young scholars who must challenge the dominance and distortion of western imperialist scholarship that developed more than a century ago fueled by notions of white supremacy and is so much alive and well today.

In defense of such relevant and somewhat new information, many people do not understand the roots and successes of African intellectual resistance in America and the Caribbean particularly when it establishes and reaffirms a sense of African-centeredness, especially since the rich Nile Valley culture added to the significance and legacy of Egypt. Serious intellectual research by black scholars has supported the blackness and cultural and intellectual proficiency of ancient peoples of Kemet, that *Black land*, along the Nile River. Slavery withstanding, emerging black African-American, Caribbean and African minds of the 19th Century examined and presented credible evidence that has continued to engage the cream of the African intelligentsia in America. This cultural and historical grounding and centeredness, is traceable through Martin Delaney, Henry Highland Garnett, Bishop Samuel Adjai Crowther, W.E.B. DuBois, Marcus Garvey, Carter G. Woodson, John Jackson, John Huggins, J.A. Rogers, Yosef ben-Jochannan, George Simmonds, George G.M. James, John H. Clarke, Ivan Van Sertima, Molefi Asante, Maulana Karenga, Jacob Carruthers, Wade Nobles, Leonard Jeffries, Leonard James, and especially Cheikh Anta Diop and Theophile Obenga. These great black minds have all wrestled with the question of "Who were the ancient Egyptians?" (People of Kemet) and all, after their lifelong and fulfilling quest involving the most extensive research, writings and teachings, are unanimously in agreement. They view the overthrowing of what Bernal called the "ancient model" and replacing it with a "modern model" as a deliberate falsification, distortion and misrepresentation of the ancient historical record. Such was to show the primacy of Europe and Europeans atop a prostrate Africa and Africans and this, sad to say, was the consequence of global white supremacy, the offspring of racism and prejudice!

WHERE ARE THE KAMITE KINGS?

Where are the Kamite Kings Photo. Temple of Isis at Philae Island. Northern columns of the Eastern Colonnade with its varied capitals stand before the decorated First Pylon of Nectanebo while image through the door is First Pylon proper of Isis' Temple.

Where are the Kamite Kings Photo. Erik Monderson in the Plaza at Horus Temple at Edfu in 2018.

FREDERICK MONDERSON

Where are the Kamite Kings Photo. Experienced Guide "Shawki" Abdel Rady, "the Black," who knows more than most about the ancient culture, with equipment. He stands in the Dromos past the stairway entrance with columns of the Western Colonnade in the background leading to the "First" Nectanebo Pylon.

All form of uncontrolled actions developed in this experience. The end result was what Brian Fagan called "The Rape of the Nile" where all types of behaviors manifested in the process of "Acquisition." This has shown evidence of captive Nile Valley cultural paraphernalia in the form of artifacts, viz., papyrus, gold,

WHERE ARE THE KAMITE KINGS?

mummies, stela, temples, textiles, wood, jewelry, sarcophagi, and equally publications that yet attest to the great gifts of early black African minds. Much of this stolen record is considered a veritable "culture in captivity." While Dr. Diop has also articulated this point, Prof. Carruthers has reiterated in-as-much-as Greece and Rome is the origin of Western Civilization, African scholars must ensure that the Nile Valley culture of Egypt and Nubia must be reckoned as part of African history and not of Europe.

Let us not forget, the several hundred thousand papyri in European academic institutions. This then is why the African American youth must remain interested in this important aspect of ancient African history. So crucial a bearing for our young scientists, both male and female, is the firm belief that our black intellectual champions have examined the phenomena of removing Egypt from Africa and removal of Africans from Egypt. The admonitions are clear. Therefore, challenge historical misconceptions and distortions, teach the young, old and indifferent, about the glorious history of Africa and her children, abroad and at home. Most importantly, teach them to defend Egypt/Kemet as African!

Where are the Kamite Kings Photo. J.H. Breasted's transition from **Barbarism to Civilization** from the Late Stone Age down to time of the Pyramids. Dr. Cheikh Anta Diop's work, on the other hand is entitled *Civilization or Barbarism* (1992) in which he questions the morality and ethical nature of European behavior that points to reverse of the transition stage, especially their actions in the modern world.

FREDERICK MONDERSON

Where are the Kamite Kings Photo. Aahmes and his mother, Aahotep. Notice his short beard.

WHERE ARE THE KAMITE KINGS?

2. PRE-DYNASTIC KEMET/EGYPT

Now, any attempt to discuss the pre-dynastic period of ancient Kemet's history must consider the innumerable years of "rehearsal" up the Nile before cultural migration down river; since man may have occupied the valley for many hundred thousand years. After all, science proves man originated in Central/East Africa and "Eve" was probably an African woman of East Africa, who lived 150,000 years ago, the mother of all people on earth. This fascinating view is based on DNA Reconstruction. However, Raymond Dart and even Albert Churchward mention esoteric, metaphysical and spiritual beginnings along the Nile dating back more 300,000 years.

Astronomy is significant as a solar phenomenon, in helping to determine the important questions of pre-dynastic Kemet, and in assisting the development of the calendar, that profound social register. Diop (1986: 78) quotes Neugebauer, that this Egyptian or Kamite: "calendar is indeed the only intelligent calendar which existed in human history." This profound Egyptian, African, system of continuous time measurement is generally thought to have been introduced around 4241/4240 B.C., the "first fixed date in history" as J.H. Breasted called it in 1915. The fixing is based on a "Sothic cycle" that some authorities believe should be extended another 1460 years earlier, making the potential date for introduction of the calendar as early as 5701/5700 B.C. or 1460 years *Before Nile Year 1*. In 139 A.D. (*Nile Year* 4379), a Roman astronomer Censorious observed the "helical rising of the star Sirius." We now know it is a phenomenon whose cycle evolves every 1460 years. The earlier ones when it may have been observed were probably dated at 1321 B.C., 2781 B.C. and 4241 B.C., and so on.

Moving from such examples of "dis-continuous time" in English "fortnight or 14-days," or native Americans' "snows" or "moons," the ancient Africans of Kemet introduced "continuous time" measurement. While these people of Kemet devised the first 360-day year, they soon discovered it was short. According to the Greek version of the myth, they added 5-epagomenal days, called the days of the birth of the Gods Osiris, Isis, Seth, Nephthys and Horus, thus extending the year to 365-days. However, sometimes in earlier more indigenous versions of the myth, the Gods are listed as Khnum, Osiris, Isis, Seth and Nephthys. That aside, Diop (1986: 78) has argued these early Africans knew of the existence of the leap year very early. However, it was not "our leap-year," actually first introduced in Europe by Julius Caesar after he had visited the Nile Valley around 45 B.C. Accordingly, the Kemetic Africans knew their 365-day year was short one-quarter day, so they waited 1460 years to add a single year to their calendar. This is the true "leap-year!" Therefore, evidence portends they knew of the adjustment of the calendar at least as early as 4241/4240 B.C. All this goes without saying further; Egyptian records indicate they have evidence of a recorded history called Precession, dated to 26,000 years.

In fact, it can be believed, in order to measure one precession may require the knowledge of another and possibly a third. That makes a recording of 26,000, 52,000 years and some scholars as Charles Finch mentions two precessions with certainly covering a period of 52,000 years. Possibly 78,000, maybe even 104,000 years of conscious African genius employed in stargazing. Now with Brophy and Bauval revelation in *Black Genesis* of early astronomy among Africans of Nabta Playa, these people may be the pioneer in this field. Imagine! Also, we ought not to forget Dr. Charsee McIntyre argued for evidence of "little Africans" in the Americas as early as 120,000 years; even though Professor Bettencourt has said "we only have evidence for about 70,000 years." That means Africans were roaming the "Old" and "New World" initiating the prototype of the intellectual, spiritual and social ideas that set humans on the road to ideas. In addition, on a lesser note, some scholars believe the Great Sphinx at Giza may be as old as 10,000 years. Additionally, evidence of agricultural practices at 16,500-14,500 B.C. can all argue against the theory of an alien 'superior race' invading and "bringing intellectual ideas and civilization to Africa." In fact, when Nile Valley Africans embarked on the path to civilization, Europeans and Asians nations were just hardly coming into vogue! Thus, and even more important, such theories a pre-eminence of whites are today viewed as cloaked in the mantle of white supremacist ideology.

WHERE ARE THE KAMITE KINGS?

Where are the Kamite Kings Photo. Temple of Isis at Philae Island. An Altar stands in the middle while sixteen of the seventeen columns of the first Eastern Colonnade (right) adorn the Dromos to the First Pylon of the Temple; and, the Western Colonnade (left) with 32 columns and the decorated First Pylon with its entrance openings to the rear.

Where are the Kamite Kings Photo. Erik Monderson on the Nile River at Aswan with the "New, New Cataract" in rear.

FREDERICK MONDERSON

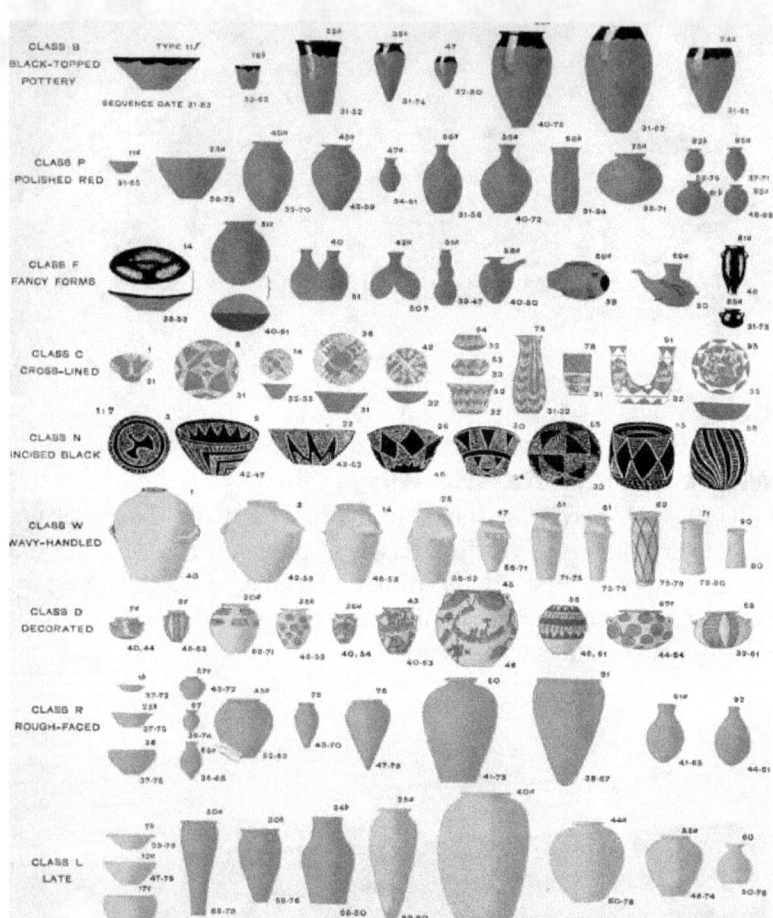

Where are the Kamite Kings Illustration. Commonest types of prehistoric pottery, *Diospolis Parva: The Cemeteries of Abadiyeh and Hu*, W.M. Flinders Petrie with a Chapter by A.C. Mace (1901).

Nevertheless, and in regard origins, during the late 19th Century, three theories were first promulgated as to the origin of the Egyptians. The first of these is the "Asiatic origin" that argues a migrating Caucasian race from South-West Asia, for some unknown reason brought a "superior mind and practices" that were imposed upon the lowly indigenous people and from this superior/inferior

WHERE ARE THE KAMITE KINGS?

interacting juxtaposition, the civilization of Kemet/Egypt was born. By the end of the Nineteenth Century, Vicomte J. de Rouge (1897: 393) discussed the question of the "Origin of the Egyptian Race" and articulated these three theories which he gives as follows:

(1) The entry of the population into Egypt was made by way of Asia, passing through the Isthmus of Suez;

(2) That Egypt became occupied by a colony, which came in part from Asia, but passed through Ethiopia;

(3) That the majority of the Egyptian population had its origin in Africa and passed into Egypt by the west and southwest. This last is a more recent theory which has been in a measure accepted by M. Maspero, and is supported by a large number of students of natural history and of ethnology, while the theory of the Asiatic origins is based on linguistic comparisons and a study of the monuments, especially the primitive monuments of Babylonia.

Even though the third theory from the west was accepted by Maspero, he considers these immigrants to have been Europeans not Africans who occupied this area. A more detailed explanation of this is given in Monderson's *Research Essays on Ancient Egypt* in the chapter entitled, "Who were the Egyptians?" Notwithstanding, Prof. Diop's *African Origins of Civilization*: *Myth or Reality* offers convincing proof, in chapters entitled: "Could Egyptian Civilization have originated in the Delta?" and "Could Egyptian Civilization be of Asian Origin?" as he demolished such arguments. In addition, his "Arguments Opposing a Negro Origin" and "Arguments Supporting a Negro Origin" are superbly presented on this issue.

Significantly, and because of the prominence of Judaism in western thought the terms Semitic and Hamitic have been imposed on the Nile Valley culture, by racists, giving such an undeserved place in this important history. In fact, the "Hamitic Hypothesis" as it relates to civilization in Africa has had a bizarre history. This view holds that "any evidence of civilization found in Africa was brought there by people of a white morphology," essentially Semitic/Hamitic.

FREDERICK MONDERSON

According to what Graves and Patti calls "Hebrew Myths," the white Hamites were part of Hamites, Semites and Japhites, children of Noah in the Bible. When the "flood" was over, Noah got drunk from drinking grape-wine, and cursed his son Ham making him "black." This myth has helped perpetuate untold sufferings on African people. Later, it was denied that the Hamites could be black because that concedes to them Kemet/Egypt, in the modern mindset. Interestingly enough, Felix Von Luschan (1911: 242) believed the Badawy people of East Africa, the "only real Semites."

One authority best explains this aspect of the Hamitic problem. Accordingly, Harris (1972: 14) quoting Gossett (1963: 5) notes during the Middle Ages this is how the *Babylonian Talmud* explained Noah's curse. In this respect, the quote runs: "It must be Canaan, your firstborn, whom they enslave .... Canaan's children shall be born ugly and black! Your grandchildren's hair shall be twisted into kinks.... [their lips] shall swell ...."

Where are the Kamite Kings Illustration. Head of Amon-Ra with features of Tutankhamon after **Restoration** following the young king's return to Thebes.

WHERE ARE THE KAMITE KINGS?

Where are the Kamite Kings Illustration. Profile view of Menkaure and his Queen.

Where are the Kamite Kings Photo. Dr. Fred Monderson giving his **Third Annual Dr. Ben-Jochannan Lecture** in Karnak Temple, Luxor Egypt, August 2018.

FREDERICK MONDERSON

Even further, Graves and Patai (1964: 121) have argued: "Men of this race are called Negroes; their forefather Canaan commanded them to love theft and fornication, to be banded together in hatred of their masters and never to tell the truth." Imagine! Even today, in an "age of correctness" such ridiculous thoughts are allowed to stand as history!

Where are the Kamite Kings Illustration. The earliest use of stone from Khasekhemui's Archaic Period tomb.

Where are the Kamite Kings Photo. Temple of Isis at Philae Island. From the northwest within the Temple, river entrance of the Mammisi partly visible (right), inner face of the First Pylon and northern columns of the Western Colonnade further on.

WHERE ARE THE KAMITE KINGS?

Von Luschan had further explained (1911: 244) the confusion in prevailing European intellectual circles that created, projected and perpetuated historical distortion. "Combination of philology with anthropology has in former times, especially through Friedrich Muller and his school, often led to serious mistakes. One spoke of Aryan races instead of people with Aryan languages, and one went so far as to speak of Aryan skulls and of Aryan eyes so that Max Muller formally protested against the intrusion of linguistics into ethnology, stating that one might just as well speak of a brachycephalic grammar as of an Aryan skull."

Today we know the Hamitic hypothesis was racist and sought to foster the pre-eminence of Europeans from South-West Asia and engrain Eurocentric hegemonic white supremacy as such related to African history, Egypt in particular. In his rather erudite scholarship, *African Origin of Civilization: Myth or Reality*, Cheikh Anta Diop demolished the position of an Asiatic origin and its influence in Kemet/Egypt. The third argument, put forward mainly by Maspero is called the "autochthonous" view that they were a European type occupying North Africa who migrated to the Nile Valley when that region began to dry up or desiccate. Even if such did, they would probably migrate to Northern Egypt not Southern Egypt where most blacks were found. The true and most valid theory is the "Central African" wherein, indigenous Africans often called "Negroes," as Diop and a host of African and even some European scholars have argued, experimented with the philosophic axioms and tenets of science, religions and artistic creativity, that molded mind and manner bequeathing to people of ancient Kemet allowing them to produce the most enduring of civilizations. That legacy is African and must be hotly contested and defended today. Now add this to findings at Nabta Playa and theories as Wortham and "Hamitic" lose their appeal.

This issue is particularly important since it has bearing on the chronology used in both the Pre-dynastic and Dynastic periods. Ever-since the birth of Egyptology scholars have alternated on the use of a "long" and "short" chronology, with some confusion. One scholar who provides an interesting pivotal contrast for modern scholarship best illustrates this alternation. Fleary (1899: 1) wrote regarding the beginnings of pharaonic rule in the First Dynasty:

FREDERICK MONDERSON

"From Wilkins on to Mariette dates have been attributed to Menes varying from 2479 B.C. to 5735 B.C., assigning (time) duration of two millennia at the lowest or more than five millennia at the highest to this ancient Empire. Each scheme differing from every other and satisfactory only to its author! At the present time the long chronology, which places Menes at somewhere about 5000 B.C. is fashionable; fifty years ago, the short system was in vogue, yet no discovery of the last half-century has been of such a nature as to require so radical a change in opinion." Today, the "short chronology" is in vogue and the standard is that provided by Murnane.

Where are the Kamite Kings Illustration. Golden Hawk of Hieraconpolis, now in the Cairo Museum.

Where are the Kamite Kings Photo. Erik Monderson, entering to discover, at "Tombs of the Nobles," Aswan, 2018.

WHERE ARE THE KAMITE KINGS?

Where are the Kamite Kings Illustration. Evidence of an early burial from Reqaqnah.

Another example of the German school at work is seen in the publication of Eduard Meyer's *Egyptian Grammar* in 1904 that posited the following results: "Introduction of the Egyptian calendar in Lower Egypt, July 19, 4241 B.C., Menes about 3315 B.C. Snefru about 2840 B.C., the fourth dynasty from 2840 to 2680 B.C., the fifth dynasty from 2680 to 2540 B.C.; the twelfth dynasty began between 2000 and 1997 B.C., the New Empire about 1580 B.C. The rule of the Hyksos was between 1680 and 1589 B.C. Dates assigned to individual Kings are: Amenophis I and Thothmes I, 1557-01;

FREDERICK MONDERSON

Amenophis III, 1415-1380; Rameses II, 1300-1234; Rameses III, 1200-1179. These dates are very different from those formerly accepted, and are important not only for Egyptian chronology, but also for that of the early civilizations of the Aegean, which is based upon Egyptian chronology."

Mahler (1905: 179) contested the conclusions of Meyer in his *Egyptian Chronology* holding: "... that the day of the Sothis festival fell always upon the 19th of July of the Julian year and shows that the Sirius year did not correspond with the Julian year and that the Helical rising of Sirius in the ninth year of King Ptolemy Euergetes recorded in the Decree of Canopus must not be identified with the 19th of July of the Julian year. He concludes that the older calculations of Oppolzer are more accurate than those of Meyer; and that the Sothis periods in their earlier occurrences fell several years earlier than Meyer assumes."

Where are the Kamite Kings Photo. Reverse of the **Gazelle Palette**. They are shown reaching to feed on the high grass.

WHERE ARE THE KAMITE KINGS?

While there were indeed differences in research findings, today, the "short" chronology is in vogue, and generally the dates vary from 3400 B.C. for the American Breasted to 3150 B.C. for Murnane. The dates for the First Dynasty have varied to as late as 3050 B.C. Therefore, depending on the chronology being used, the "pre-dynastic" period varies. Dr. ben-Jochannan gives 3200-2980 for the First Dynasty. Interestingly enough, Maulana Karenga at the Afrocentric Theory Conference at Temple University in 1993 stated, according to his studies, the First Dynasty should be dated to 6200 B.C. More, some scholars believe use of the "short" chronology is designed to give preference to or be contemporary with Babylonian/Mesopotamian civilization presented as earliest, owing to its proximity to "white origins" in the Caucasus Mountains.

Where are the Kamite Kings Illustration. Obverse side of the **Libya Palate** showing lions and hawks atop and within enclosures along with standards (left); and, fragment of the Libya Palette showing how the Register helped divide the decorated surface and allowed for orderly representation in the work (reverse).

Another argument that gives 3200 B.C. for the "short" chronology, compressing the pre-dynastic periods of the Badarian, Amratian or Naqada I and Gerzean or Naqada II into a "thousand-year" stretch from the calendar's introduction to the First Dynasty, is manageable. Still, there must indeed have been rapid cultural growth from the 4500 B.C. to 4241 (4240) B.C. Additionally, and diametrically, some scholars still believe all dates before 1750 are

FREDERICK MONDERSON

only "hypothetical" and therefore, dating becomes problematic for this early period.

Nevertheless, in ancient Kemet the period from 4500 B.C. to about 3200 B.C. is called the Pre-dynastic Period proper. During this time, three cultures developed before the dynasties began at about 3200 B.C., approximately. Murnane (1983: 351-54) dates the First Dynasty to 3150 B.C. In the *Nile Year* Calendar utilized in this work with 4240 B.C. as *Nile Year* 1, this date of Murnane, 3150 B.C., can then be considered *Nile Year* 1090. Dating aside, these cultures formed the foundations on which the dynasties were able to create the lasting Kemetic civilization in Ta Merry, North-east Africa. The first of these cultures, as stated, is called the Badarian. Gordon Childe (1969) described the Badarian as a "flourishing Neolithic culture older than any previously known." It was named after a group of cemeteries around Badari on the east bank of the Nile River, not far from Aswan in Upper Egypt/Kemet. The Badarians had a political system that was centralized.

Where are the Kamite Kings Photo. Temple of Isis at Philae Island. African-Americans on tour with Dr. ben-Jochannan within the Kiosk of Hathor include Keith Howe of Detroit, Dr. ben-Jochannan, Valerie Howell of Brooklyn, New York, Brother Al Norwood of Queens, New York, and Tom Quash of Brooklyn, New York, while the others are unidentified.

WHERE ARE THE KAMITE KINGS?

Childe, an archaeologist, further added there was "a fundamentally African character in the Tasian-Badarian and also in the Mermide-Omaria traditions." Even more, Childe (1969: 46) continued, "Brunton, Junker, Scraff, and Baumgartel have likewise insisted on the Nubian affinities of the Badarian and even the Merimdian cultures." Archaeologists are scientists who dig for remains of old cultures. These scientists then try to reconstruct and write a history of the people based on tools, pots or other artifacts left behind. Such objects tell us about levels of accomplishment of the ancient cultures. Much of the remains of the Badarians were found in graves. The graves also help us determine the physical size of the people as well as the level of cultural attainment they achieved.

These Africans buried their dead with many objects. Such "mortuary data," or "mortuary furniture" as shown in the Cairo Museum, according to ancient beliefs, were needed in the afterlife. Items buried were also called "goods of the grave."

Where are the Kamite Kings Photo. Erik Monderson's further explorations atop highlands of "Tombs of the Nobles."

FREDERICK MONDERSON

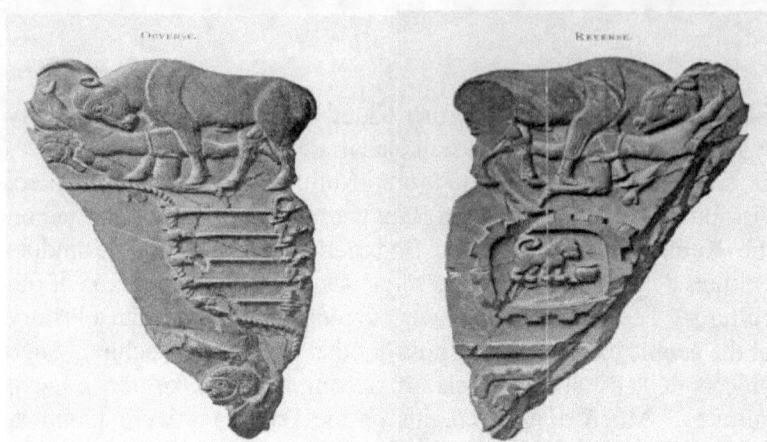

Where are the Kamite Kings Illustration. Obverse side of the **Bull Palette** showing the bull gorging a fleeing enemy with his hands raised upwards, hands holding a great rope with perhaps binding an individual with peppercorn hair (left); and, reverse side of the Bull Palette showing the bull gorging a fleeing enemy with his hands raised upwards and a lion in an enclosure.

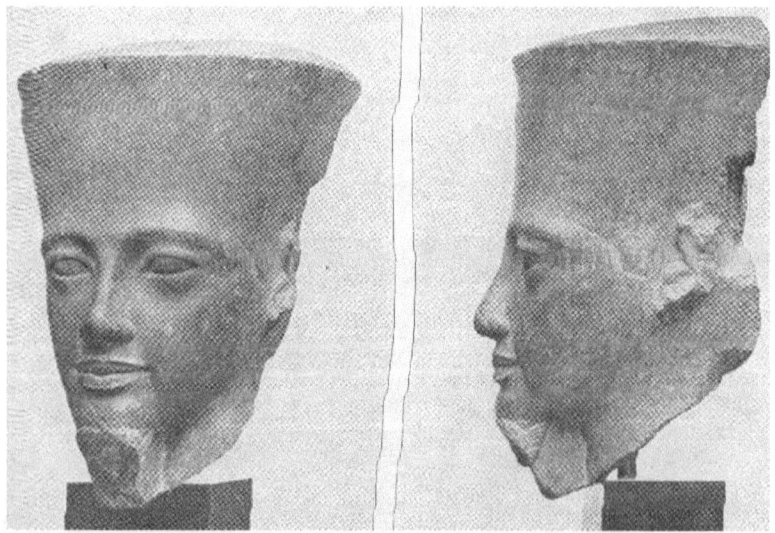

Where are the Kamite Kings Illustration. Another view of Amon with the face of Tutankhamon.

WHERE ARE THE KAMITE KINGS?

Where are the Kamite Kings Illustration. Amenhotep I, son of Aahmes and Nefertari, 18th Dynasty. Notice the vulture with outstretched wings in the center of the coffin.

FREDERICK MONDERSON

The Badarians believed they needed their utensils, viz., tools, pots, food, beverages and other objects to continue their lives in similar manner in the "next world." Their graves were rough circular pits about 1.5 meters across and one meter deep. In these early interments were found cooking pots, baskets, and some bone and flint tools. The body was covered with materials made from goat and gazelle skins. Their dresses were made from linen or skins, sewn with bone needles. They had studs for the nose and earrings made of beads and turquoise, a semi-precious stone. The Nile Valley inhabitants made stone and bead necklaces and girdles. Their ornamental decorations were also made from ostrich egg shells, segmented bone heads, and Red Sea shells.

The Badarians had bracelets of ivory, shell, bone and horn. Also, their combs and spoons were made of ivory and bone carved in animal or bird shapes. They painted or decorated their eyes with malachite. Dyes with green malachite and castor oil were used for cleaning and softening the skin. Other artifacts included ivory or shell fishhooks, and flint arrowheads. They also had vases made of ivory as well as hard stone palettes for grinding cosmetics.

The Badarians were very religious and this is shown by their preparation of the body and the care they took with the goods of the grave. They made ivory statues of women to accompany the deceased men in whose graves such were placed. These statues were buried at the side with the bodies in a pre-natal position. Also found in the graves were amulets of hippopotami and antelopes, that served as hunting charms.

Badarian economy was based on hunting, fishing, agriculture and domestication of animals. Domesticated animals included dogs, jackals, goats, donkeys, gazelles, cattle and oxen. The hunters used wooden boomerangs to kill game. They lived in mud-brick houses. Their pottery was of a high quality. Bowls were made with thin walls. They produced polished red ware and polished black and black-topped pottery. They also made polished red and brown pottery. They decorated the pottery with a ripple pattern representing water and stained them with red ochre dye. Animals and birds were some of their earliest decorated motifs. They also used the incised herringbone decorative pattern. The ancient

WHERE ARE THE KAMITE KINGS?

Badarians made cylindrical vases of basalt rock. Ladles were made of ivory and their handles had carved animals.

Where are the Kamite Kings Photo. Temple of Isis at Philae Island. Columns with varied capitals of the Western Colonnade showing the water level mark when the Temple was submerged during the Inundation Period.

In the remains of their graves were found small-scale copper implements. These were the very "first Egyptian metal artifacts." Such artifacts included: "a couple of beads and a rod, both of hammered copper." Most of this metal has not survived. However, the significance of having this metal means the culture was beginning to step out of the Stone Age. Stone tools had characterized man's existence in Africa for hundreds of thousands of years prior to the Badarians' experiments with copper.

The next phase of the pre-dynastic culture is called the Amratian or Naqada I Period. The name comes from the sites of El-Amrah and Naqada in Upper Egypt, North-East Africa. Randall-MacIver's excavations at El Amrah, six miles south of Abydos, as reported in *Man* April, 1901, mentioned prehistoric cemeteries, "containing six or seven types of graves, among the contents of which were model boats of various kinds and also pottery cattle, thus making it clear that the 'New Race' were pastoral people also. Among the objects illustrated are weapons of war and the chase, dolls representing the people themselves, who are figured with strongly curled hair, and specimens of basketwork. The most valuable find was an inscribed slate of a date considerably anterior to the first dynasty; this is by far the earliest known example of the use of hieroglyphs."

People of this ancient period built on earlier cultural gains of the Badarians. This formed a continuing development in Nile Valley evolution of civilization. Again, archaeologists were able to write about the Amratians due to information taken from their graves, mostly in well-preserved cemeteries. Pots were most often found. These included burnt red-ware with animals, birds, plant shapes and geometric patterns. Many forms and sizes of pottery were used including flasks, bowls, goblets, twin vases and tumblers.

Tools were made of stone and flint. This showed the birth of a professional class of toolmakers. Their tool repertoire included scrapers, razors, double-edged blades, fishtailed knives and lances with wood or bone handles. The cutting edge on some blades was saw-like with tiny teeth. Copper was being used for harpoons and pins. They also made use of gold, malachite, alabaster, basalt, ivory, bone and hard stone.

Weapons were mainly made of stone and flint. The throw-stick or boomerang was used. Ivory carvings represented animals such as giraffes, birds, elephants, sheep and hippopotami. Human figurines were made of ivory. Pottery figures of women had stumpy arms as

WHERE ARE THE KAMITE KINGS?

handles. There were early signs of tattoo marks on the bodies. Women wore jewelry of shells, carnelian and coral around the neck.

The houses of the Amratians were not much different from those of the Badarians. Their huts were made of mud brick and stood 1 or 2 meters in diameter. The walls were almost 30 centimeters thick. Villages were sometimes large.

During this time dogs, sheep, goats, oxen and pigs had become domesticated. There was plenty of game, fish, and fowl to be caught in the river and marshes or swamps. The cooking vessels were made of pottery. These included household utensils such as plates, cups, bowls, spoons, and stone, copper and later bronze knives. These were all of a high quality. Vases were still being made of stone and now of all sizes and very decorative.

Where are the Kamite Kings Illustration. The **Palermo Stone** fragment depicts annals of the earliest Kings from predynastic times to the middle of the Fifth Dynasty.

Agricultural grains were boiled for porridge and baked for bread. Grapes and barley were used to make beverages. Farmers planted flax and had looms for weaving. The burials were mainly in small graves with bodies in the pre-natal position. Enough space was left for the goods of the grave. These bodies faced south or Upper Egypt/Kemet. Figurines of women were placed in graves. The method of burial and things placed in their graves showed the continuation of their religious beliefs. Since the land received little rain, it's believed the early leaders of the Amratians were "rainmakers" who were killed as they grew older. They were probably drowned or cut up as their powers to bring rain failed.

With the development of fishing, the boat-building industry grew. Lashing or tying bundles of papyrus is the method used to made earliest boats. Some boats had sails and, in this period, boats appear in art motifs. Importantly, this form of transportation helped to develop trade for people who sought to exchange surplus goods resulting in diffusion of ideas about art, religion and similarly economics. Such activity marked the beginnings of commerce on the Nile that spread in Africa and elsewhere.

The Gerzean represents the third of three pre-dynastic cultures that set the stage for dynastic developments. It is named after el-Gerza in today's Middle Egypt. The culture sequence of Naqada II from Upper Egypt/Kemet also provides the basis for the Gerzean period. Developments of two earlier cultures brought the Gerzean Period to the threshold of civilization and dynastic rule. This period is dated between 3400-3100 B.C.

Metalworking became a big industry in this period. Copper was worked on a large scale. Other metals worked were gold, lead, silver, malachite, flint and ivory. Stone vases were widely used. Such crafts as ivory carvings and shipbuilding began to develop and spread throughout the country.

Kemet/Egypt, at this time finally entered the Metal Age. However, stone working continued well into the New Kingdom. Copper was mixed with tin to make a much harder metal, bronze. From the earliest times many weapons and domestic and farming implements were made of stone. Such usage continued, and the metal industry gradually replaced stone in these areas.

WHERE ARE THE KAMITE KINGS?

Where are the Kamite Kings Photo. Temple of Isis at Philae Island. King sporting plumes offers two "Eyes of Horus," to Horus enthroned, while Isis sits in rear of the God. Horus holds the Waz Scepter and Isis the Wadj Scepter.

The tougher metal, bronze, remained in use for weapons until the people of Kemet began using iron. This new metal, iron, was introduced on a large scale sometime in the Middle Kingdom. However, controversy still surrounds when in fact iron was first utilized in the Nile Valley and elsewhere in Africa. It should not be forgotten the "Followers of Hours," in the predynastic period, were ironworkers who "went north." In addition, Petrie, Colonel Vyse and Maspero, made several finds of iron dating to the Old Kingdom. Significantly, iron was stronger than all forms of metal previously used. Gold, a softer metal, could not be used for weapons. However, gold had a mystical, esoteric value and was used for religious purposes, decorative jewelry and also thought to aid procreation. So, gold first became prized and then later iron came into general use because of its durability.

FREDERICK MONDERSON

REFERENCES

Adams, B. *Pre-Dynastic Egypt*. Bucks: Shire Publications, Inc., 1988.

Aldred, C. *Egypt to the End of the Old Kingdom*. London: Thames and Hudson, 1965.

Childe, V.G. *New Light on the Most Ancient East*. New York: W. W. Norton and Company, Inc., (1928) 1969.

Diop, C.A. "Africa's Contribution to World Civilization: The Exact Sciences" in *Nile Valley Civilizations*. Edited by Ivan Van Sertima. New Brunswick, New Jersey: Transaction Publishers, (1985: 69-83).

"El Amrah." *American Journal of Archaeology* V (1901: 332).

Fleary, F.G. *Egyptian Chronology*. London: David Null, 1899.

Gosse, F. *Race: The History of an Idea in America*. Dallas: 1963.

Graves, R. and R. Patai. *Hebrew Myths*. New York:

Harris, J. E. *Africans and Their History*. New York: New American Library, 1972.

Hoffman, M. *Egypt Before the Pharaohs*. Austin, Texas: University of Texas Press, (1979) 1991.

Luschan, Von. F. "The Early Inhabitants of Western Asia." *Journal of Royal Anthropological Institute of Great Britain and Ireland*. XLI (NS XIV) (1911: 221-244).

Mahler, E. "Egyptian Chronology." *American Journal of Archaeology* X (1906: 170).

Meyer, Edouard. "Egyptian Chronology." *American Journal of Archaeology* IX (1905: 457).

Murnane, W.J. *The Penguin Guide to Ancient Egypt*. New York: Penguin Books, 1983.

Ruffle, J. *The Egyptians*. Ithaca, New York: Cornell University Press, 1977.

Sanders, E.R. "The Hamitic Hypothesis: Its Origin and Functions in Time Perspective." *Journal of African History* Vol. X, No 4 (1969: 521-33).

WHERE ARE THE KAMITE KINGS?

Where are the Kamite Kings Illustration. Sculptured scene on mace-head of Narmer in the Ashmolean Museum, Oxford.

Where are the Kamite Kings Illustration. Comparative lengths of the Year.

3. THE ARCHAIC PERIOD I

In the early development of Egyptology, scholars simply divided the history into the Old, Middle and New Empires. The First through Sixth Dynasties comprised the Old Empire. Now thanks to archaeological excavations and other work begun in the Nile Valley, starting more than a century ago by Petrie, Amelineau, Quibell, de Morgan, Garstang, Burckhardt, Edwards, Naville, Murray,

Baumgartel, Caton-Thompson, Davis, Winlock, etc., these experts have helped fine-tune the order of development and succession in that ancient cultural drama.

Now we recognize the first two dynasties are called the Archaic Period, that formative, cumbersome time when the new state had to contend with security considerations, social dynamics, emerging economic possibilities, division of labor and specialization of crafts, and political and religious syncretism. This section is an examination of some aspects of the history of this early period of the Nile experience.

Building upon cultural and economic developments of the pre-dynastic period, the state of ancient Kemet reached a pinnacle of unprecedented growth; technology advanced rapidly; and the arts, crafts and military grew equally in organized and regulated fashion. The evolution of building practices found full co-operation and support from the God-King whose father, the Sun God Ra, was glorified throughout the land by an emerging and very talented and ambitious priesthood. The King's titulary was established early and by the time of the Old Kingdom, his 5 names had evolved. Narmer, however, had only the *Horus, Two Ladies* and *Nesu-Bit* names at unification.

Seeking to imitate nature, builders used perishable, natural materials before beginning experimentation in stone. Quarrying and transportation of stone over long distances greatly aided the practices of navigation and boat building as well as encouraging architectural daring. The development of an administrative hierarchy, as needed, grew to organize, coordinate and execute those large-scale projects, characterized by large mastaba tombs and later pyramids of that Classical Age.

The *Archaic Period* comprised the first and second dynasties. It began at c. 3150 B.C., using Murnane's chronology; generally mentioned in most books today. On the other hand, ben-Jochannan (1981: 177) dated the First Dynasty from 3200-2980 B.C. and the Second Dynasty 2980-2680. However, an interesting interjection poses itself here. Diop, mentioned a view expressed in his book *Civilization or Barbarism: An Authentic Anthropology*, and he also wrote in another selection (1986: 79) that, "until today, with the Egyptian sidereal calendar which could very well be reactivated,

WHERE ARE THE KAMITE KINGS?

humanity or at least Africa has a scale of absolute chronology compared with which the Christian era, the Hegira and various landmarks, are completely relative." And even further, Diop (1986: 79) continued, "At the annual congress on Egyptology, held February 24-26, 1984, at Los Angeles Southwest College, Black Americans of the Diaspora reactivated this calendar using 4,236 (give or take 4 years) as the absolute chronological landmark." In this respect, and taking 4240 B.C., *Nile Year* I, as the point of departure, in this work, the First Dynasty and Narmer's ascension as Pharaoh dated at 3150 B.C. is, therefore, reactivated at *Nile Year* 1090 or N.Y. 1090. Thus, all subsequent references in this series will therefore utilize the above scheme of dating, wherein the year 2000 is represented as *Nile Year* 6240. That makes the year 2005, 6245 and 2006, 6246 and also the year 2008, 6248 and, again, 2010 is 6250.

Returning to the beginning of dynastic rule, Pharaoh Narmer, Mena or Menes, King of Upper Kemet, galvanized and moved military forces north from Thinis, and conquered Lower Kemet/Egypt. However, Diop does identify Narmer as Theban which means his military expedition began at a more significant social center. Nevertheless, we are assisted in the reconstruction of this early period's events by the archaeological discovery of the green slate *Narmer Palette* and the *Narmer Macehead*, now considered important "historical documents." Quibell found them both in 1898 at the Temple of Horus at Hierakonpolis, near Edfu, along with other artifactual pieces. As early dynastic documents, these treasures are a key to understanding the history of the time. On the *Obverse* side of the *Narmer Palette*, Budge (1902: 189-90) wrote, we see: "Two Hathor heads and the name Nar-Mer on the Horus standard. Below these we have the King, wearing the crown of Lower Egypt, followed by the sandal-bearer, and preceded by the personage Thet ... and by four men bearing standards; in front of these are two rows of decapitated prisoners, and near them is a boat, and the signs [denoting] 'great door.' In the largest division are two lions with greatly elongated and intertwined necks being lassoed by two attendants. In the lowest register is a bull, symbolizing the King, who has broken into a fortified village, and having thrown down a foe is about to gore him. On the *Reverse* we have at the top the two Hathor heads and the King's name as before. Below this, wearing the crown of the South, is a standing figure of the King, who is about to smite with his uplifted mace, an enemy whom he is grasping by the hair; he is, as usual, accompanied by his sandal-bearer. Above the King's enemy is a scene, which is not easy to explain. A hawk drags the head of a prisoner, of the same Asiatic type as that of the man whom the King is about to smite, by a rope attached to his nose; behind the head is a group of flowers, which has been read as 6000, and the whole scene has been interpreted to mean that the God Horus is bringing to the King 6000 prisoners."

Where are the Kamite Kings Photo. Temple of Isis at Philae Island. Composite capitals, a characteristic of the Graeco-Roman Period, each pattern different from the other.

As stated, the other significant piece of historical importance is the *Narmer Macehead* from Quibell's *Hierakonpolis* find. On this weapon, which now serves as a significant document, to further quote Budge (1902: 182-83) we see the: "King, in the character of Osiris, within a shrine which rests on a flight of steps, seated on a throne, wearing the crown of the North, and holding the flail in his hand. This flight of steps, which is also depicted upon a plaque of Sempti, is evidently intended for the staircase of the tomb of Osiris, which is mentioned in the *Book of the Dead*. By the side of the throne are two fan-bearers, and behind are a personage called Thet, the royal sandal-bearer, and three attendants bearing staves; in front are men bearing standards, cattle, goats, etc." Having accompanied the King, Hathor is thus obviously a southern Egyptian Goddess, thus establishing her connection to inner Africa. In this, Wallis Budge identified Hathor as Sudani.

WHERE ARE THE KAMITE KINGS?

Another Macehead, of this early period, thought to belong to the "Scorpion King" and identified with Narmer, shows the pharaoh wearing the White Crown, holding a plough in his hand, as if to inaugurate an agricultural project, and also followed by fan-bearers. Still another important piece of artifactual evidence that helps in the identification of Narmer is a lime vase with figures of hawks, scorpions, a bow, etc., found by Petrie at Abydos. Upon it in relief, Petrie, the "father of archaeology" found evidence of Narmer's name, which is considered a hammer and chisel. From all such information, we learn that Narmer's southern White Crown was victorious over the northern Red Crown. In a conciliatory manner, the King chose the White resting on Red Double Crown to represent a unified Kemet. The period he inaugurated lasted for some 500 years. It established social and political institutions of pharaonic rule that lasted the next three thousand years. In many respects these events establish Narmer as not just a conqueror but also a thinker and administrator.

Narmer or Menes, some think even Aha, established the city of Memphis as his administrative capital. He built the "white wall," a symbol of his supremacy and launched a number of civic projects. The wall is called "white" because it was painted such with limestone. In the Faiyum, he inaugurated the cult of the crocodile God Sobek, and established a temple and worship for the God Ptah at Memphis. He also began the cult of the Apis-bull in Memphis.

The new peace brought political stability and a monarchical type of government was set up with the pharaoh as head of state. The capital of Lower Kemet had been Buto and that of Upper Kemet/Egypt Hierakonpolis. Suddenly, from Memphis, in the name of the King, a centralized bureaucracy headed by the Grand Chancellor or Vizier administered the civil and religious relations of the state. The civil government was responsible for the treasury, judiciary, police and granaries. The religious government, comprising the priesthood, was responsible for worshiping and ritualizing the Gods, of whom the King was their earthly representative. This priesthood body also became the repository and perpetrators of the arts, sciences and history of the nation. They justified the person and role of the King as a representative of the

Gods. Burial customs of the Kings and nobles were elaborate in structure, decoration and endowment.

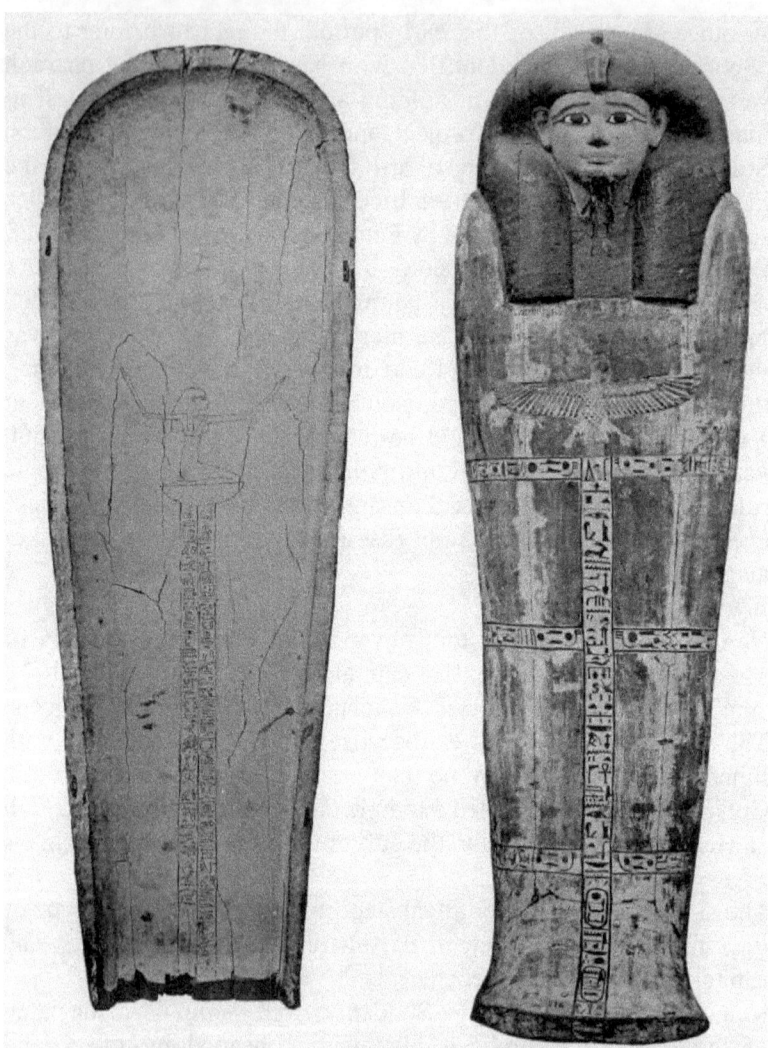

Where are the Kamite Kings Illustration. Coffin lids of the Lady Rai and Amenhotep I showing the interior of one and the exterior of the other, respectively.

Kamite/Egyptian theologians very early formulated the belief that, according to Woldering (1963: 41), the King of the united Kamite Kingdom, "not only derives his right to govern from the Gods but is himself the human incarnation of the falcon-God Horus." And more

WHERE ARE THE KAMITE KINGS?

profoundly, Woldering (1963: 41) continued: "The belief that the King is identical with the God Horus served to enhance the prestige and authority of the pharaoh among the subjugated tribes of Lower Egypt, for the divinity of the King is a guarantee of law and order. The lives and well-being of his subjects depend on him. He understands the language of the Gods; as a powerful figure, he can deal with the mighty on their own terms."

The sovereign emblem, the cone-shaped White Crown of Upper Egypt, the cap-like Red Crown of Lower Egypt, and the whisk and Scepter were all thought to be charged with magical force. Corollary of man's awakening consciousness in the Archaic Period was the desire to honor the divine powers, not only in the form of fetishes or animals, but also by creating an image of the deity. Herein was developed the concept of the Gods as beings who possessed mighty spirits incarnate in animal heads and human bodies. This way the divine manifested in nature.

These early beliefs also began to influence the preparation and practices of burials. As such, from this period, while the Kings ruled from Memphis in the North, most had two tombs, one at Memphis and the other at Abydos. Tombs of Kings of the first and second dynasties, discovered at Abydos, in the Thinite Nome of Upper Egypt/Kemet, were considered cenotaphs. On the other hand, some scholars argue that these were the real tombs and that those at Memphis were actually the cenotaphs or dummy tombs. If we understand Narmer only built one tomb at Abydos, then this site may hold the principal tomb and can thus be considered as opposed to Memphis. Notwithstanding, the Abydos tombs were robbed by the time of the Old Kingdom. Still, inscribed stelae, jar-sealings and wooden labels enable us to identify their Kings. Emery (1972: 91) listed the names of Kings found in these Abydos tombs as: "1. Narmer (B 10), 2. Hor-Aha (B 19), 3. Zer (0), 4. Meryet-Nit, 5. Zet, 6. Udimu, 7. Anezib, 8. Semerkhet, and 9. Qaya with names recorded on later lists of First Dynasty pharaohs, including the **Palermo Stone**, **Sakkara List**, **both Abydos Lists**, the **Karnak List**, and the **Turin List**, etc. With the exception of Semerkhet, all the Kings had both Abydos and Sakkara tombs. Only Semerkhet's Abydos tomb has been found."

FREDERICK MONDERSON

Petrie's *Royal Tombs* is an important source for all the Abydos tombs. While Emery's *Hor Aha* identified that King, his *Tomb of Hemaka* identified Udimu. For all the other first dynasty Kings, Emery's *Great Tombs* I, II, III, provide evidence for all Sakkara Tombs.

Where are the Kamite Kings Illustration. Graves 216 and 207, unopened and opened (left); and, Basket graves in *Tarkhan I and Memphis V* by W.M. Flinders Petrie with G.A Wainwright and A.H. Gardiner (1913) (right).

Where are the Kamite Kings Photo. Erik Monderson relaxes in Al Fayal Garden with the now closed Oberoi Hotel building across the Nile at Aswan.

WHERE ARE THE KAMITE KINGS?

Petrie gave an interesting account of his excavations at Abydos, a place of great reverence for all of dynastic Kemet and today still exudes that philosophic and esoteric mysticism. The jackal Khenti-Amenti was first worshiped at Abydos as guardian of the cemeteries. Later, by the time of the Old Kingdom he became fused with Osiris, the city's principal deity. The nature of Petrie's work allowed him to connect the prehistoric period with the historic, based on the excavated results. Hi effort was essentially successful, Petrie (1902: 64) for wrote: "We had explored the prehistoric age, and the system of sequence dates had enabled me to bring the various stages of undated remains into their consecutive order; and in the last two years the royal tombs of the earliest dynasties had yielded the material which placed the civilization of some eighteen reigns before us."

Historical.	Legendary.	Manethonian.
1st Dynasty		
Narmer [Uhamer?]	Mena	Menes
Aha	[Ateti (?)]	Athothis
Khent (?)	Teta [Ata?]	Kenkenes
Tja Ati (?)	Ateti	[Ouenephes]
	Ata [Teta?]	Ouenephes
		[Kenkenes]
Den Semti	Hsapti	Ousaphais
Antjab Merpeba	Merbap	Miebis
Semerkha Nekht (?)	?	Semempses
Ka Sen	Kebh	Bieneches
IInd Dynasty		
Hetepsekhemui	Betju	Boëthos
Raneb	Kakau	Kaiechos
Neneter	Baneneteru	Binothris
Sekhemab-Perenmaat } Perabsen	Uatjnes	Tlas
Send [Senedi]	Send!	Sethenes
		Chaires
—	Neferkara	Nephercheres
—	Neferkasokari	Sesochris
—	Hutjefa	Cheneres
IIIrd Dynasty		
Khasekhem [Khasekhemui] Besh Tjeser	Tjatjai [Bebi]	Necherophes
	Tjeser	Tosorthros'
Sa-nekht	Nebka	Tyreis
		Mesochris
		Soÿphis
—	Tjeser-teta	Tosertasis
	Setjes	Aches
Neferka	Neferkara	Sephouris
		[Kerpheres]
Senefru	Senefru	Kerpheres
		[Sephouris]

Where are the Kamite Kings Cartouche/Shennu.
Historical and Legendary Kings of the First Three Dynasties of Manetho.

FREDERICK MONDERSON

More particularly, Petrie (1902: 64) continued: "The ground which furnished these results is a town just outside the temple of Osiris, and within the great *temenos* of Osiris of later age. This town proves to have been started at about the time of the earliest Kings of Abydos, three centuries before Mena and the first dynasty; it continued to grow upward by successive strata of rubbish and weathered *debris* through all the history; but upper parts have been removed by the natives for earth, and so we had only the strata of about 5000-4000 B.C. to deal with. The town was founded on the clean sand edge of the desert; and we had only worked with those parts where we could still reach the basal sand, and so have a starting point for measurement."

Petrie's sequence dating placed the Town Level at "0" in SD 76 when it was founded, at approximately 5000 B.C. According to his chronological dating, Ka is at SD 78 at town level 20; Menes SD 79 at Town Level 40; Zet is SD 80 at Town Level 55; and Den at Town Level 70; Qa at Town Level 90; and Perabsen at Town Level 110.

The objects discovered in this excavation proved an informative collection of varied pottery and tools, with some peculiar types of flints. These included, Petrie (1902: 64) added, "knives without handles; knives with handles; hoes; scrapers, tailed, round, long, and various; flakes, plain, tipped, worked on edges, rounded and square; saws; crescent flints; animal figures; and combs .... The crescent flints seem from their associations to have been used as drills, at the end of a stick, for boring soft stones. The combs are hitherto unknown; the teeth are too slender to bear the strain of scraping, and the curvature is too varied for use in combing out materials, or for sawing; possibly they were used in preparing food, for shredding meat, etc. All of these belong to the earlier half of the first dynasty."

Continuing, he wrote: "an important group of eleven un-plundered tombs of the first dynasty was found in the town. They contain the bodies contracted and buried like those of the prehistoric people, and around the body a number of stone and pottery vases, varying up to 22 of stone and 50 of pottery."

WHERE ARE THE KAMITE KINGS?

Where are the Kamite Kings Illustration. The Sphinx covered in sand, with the second and third pyramids in its rear.

Where are the Kamite Kings Photo. Illustration.
45. Coffins sealed and unsealed *Tarkhan I and Memphis V* by W.M. Flinders Petrie, G.A Wainwright and A.H. Gardiner (1913).

Myers (1902: 52) offered the view, "later excavations at Abydos teach that the prehistoric passes by gradual stages into the dynastic period, and it is now possible to distinguish the culture of three periods - the early prehistoric, the late prehistoric and the proto-dynastic - from one another."

FREDERICK MONDERSON

Petrie also worked at Tarkhan near Kafr Ammar, about thirty-five miles south of Cairo, where 500 graves were excavated. The age of the cemetery, Petrie (1912: 73) has argued, ranged, "from Dynasty 0 to Dynasty I in full use, less frequently in II-V Dynasties, rarely on to the XI Dynasty. Then it was again used in the XXIII Dynasty and Ptolemaic times. From the absence of anything earlier than a few reigns before Mena, this does not seem to have belonged to a prehistoric site, but rather to have been the cemetery of the dynastic capital which preceded the founding of Memphis."

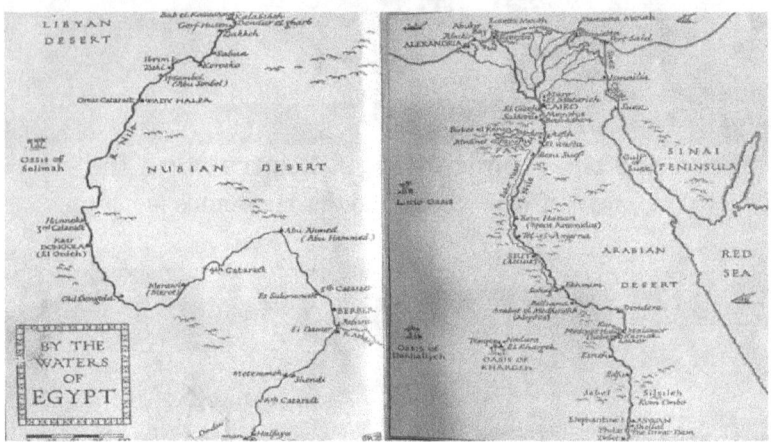

Where are the Kamite Kings Illustration. Map of Egypt and the Sudan from the work entitled *By the Waters of Egypt* by Norma Lorimer (1909).

Where are the Kamite Kings Photo. Temple of Isis at Philae Island. Close-up of composite capital showing intricate details.

WHERE ARE THE KAMITE KINGS?

The significance of this excavation is measured in the proliferation of woodwork reflected in the funerary find, and in addition, Petrie (1912: 73) indicated: "Large quantities of pottery and stone vases were found, and the complete record of the grave groups will enable us to place the produce of the earliest dynasties in exact historical order, by comparison with the dated objects from the royal tombs."

For more technical benefits he referred to the wood and other objects that reflected the level of craftsmanship accomplished on this threshold of the pharaonic period. Smith (1959: 46-47) added also: "Parts of two large wooden statues from Abydos in Oxford and the base and feet of two other standing figures found at Saqqara suggest that royal workmanship of Dynasty I may have been more advanced, at least in a softer material, that the few stone pieces which have survived would indicate, although expert treatment of harder materials is attested for this period by such pieces of a schist presentation vase or tray worked to simulate basketry."

Regarding his work, Petrie (1912: 73) continued: "The most important discovery was that of the system of portable wooden houses. From a study of the paneled pattern in stone and the wooden coffins modeled on the form of the house, it appeared that it was copied from timberwork. Now the actual house timbers have been found, re-used for making coffins or roofing over graves in this cemetery. One complete plank is 6 feet 7 inches high, and varies from 15 to 18 inches in width, of which 12 to 14 was the exposed surface, the rest being overlapped by the next plank .... Each of the different kinds of holes for lashing here represented has been found in different pieces of planking. The lashing was of palm-fiber cord, shown by some scraps left in the holes. On several planks the different surfaces can be seen where the overlapping protected them; and one plank is deeply weathered outside, and burnt inside by the conflagration of the house. We have thus recovered the timber prototype of the early stone decoration. The purpose of such moveable houses was doubtless to shift them up on to the desert at the inundation, and then to return to the green plain when the crops grew, so as to get coolness and absence of dust. Such a portable house of vertical planks is obviously the prototype of the Israelite Tabernacle."

FREDERICK MONDERSON

Where are the Kamite Kings Illustration. Roofing of graves in *Tarkhan I and Memphis V* by W.M. Flinders Petrie with G.A Wainwright and A.H. Gardiner (1913).

This work of excavation by the British School of Archaeology in Egypt was published in Petrie's *Tarkhan*. Even further, Petrie (1912: 73) commented on some rather unique forms of the burial, in baskets. In this he states: "The principal interest lay in the extraordinary preservation of the wood, basket-work, and clothing. The wooden coffins and domestic trays and bead-steads are often as sound and heavy as when new; the basket coffins are elastic and retain the leaf buds and details of twigs; the rather later cloth of the IV Dynasty is as clean and strong as when it was buried. Among the woodwork hitherto unknown are the trays for carrying sandals. The bed frames are of stout poles, usually with a swell in the middle to give stiffness, and a knob carved at the ends. The webbing was of rush-work or palm and turned over the poles in the commoner beds, like the modern Nubian *angareb*; in the better beds there were slots cut in the inner and lower sides of the poles, meeting in the axis, so that straps of leather could be stretched across without covering any visible part of the pole. Many head rests of various types were found, two of the less forms are shown on the plate, and with the basket coffin."

Elsewhere Petrie refers to the find at Tarkhan cemetery as significant for its "above-ground structure of tombs," a phenomenon rarely preserved, particularly from a time as remote as the time of King Zet, from the middle of the First Dynasty. He mentioned two large brick 100-feet mastaba tombs between which these peculiar tombs were sandwiched. Each contained: "two slight recesses in the form of a doorway, by which the soul was supposed to go out

WHERE ARE THE KAMITE KINGS?

and in." Again, Petrie (1912: 85) wrote: "On cutting these tombs open at the top (carefully leaving the sides perfect), it was found that the bricks had been laid over a pile of sand, which supported them when plastered. On digging down there were first three or four jars lying at the sides, about 3 feet down. Below these was a papyrus-sleeping mat, too long to go into the pit, and therefore turned up about 2 feet at one end. Under the mat was a lid of loose boards laid over a roughly made box coffin, in making which old house timber had been used up. The burials were contracted, head north, face east, on left side, accompanied by some small pottery and gazelle bones. In the middle view is a small mastaba. The four pots standing upright in the large square are those found in the anciently robbed grave, which is beneath them. The whole square was originally filled with sand, forming a mound banked round by a brick wall about a foot high. Such is the type of the Royal Tombs of the Ist Dynasty on the larger scale. The view is taken with the sand emptied out so far to show the depth of the wall. Nearer the spectator is the little court for offerings, only 2- or 3-feet square. The original whitewash covering may be seen still on parts of the wall. In the tomb wall are two slits, at which the offerings were presented, for their virtue to descend to the dead. Outside of the offering court are the rough pots in which offerings had been brought at the various festivals; the jars were then left derelict at the place .... Mastaba (No. 740) dates from sequence date 78-just before, or early in the reign of Mena, the beginning of the 1st Dynasty."

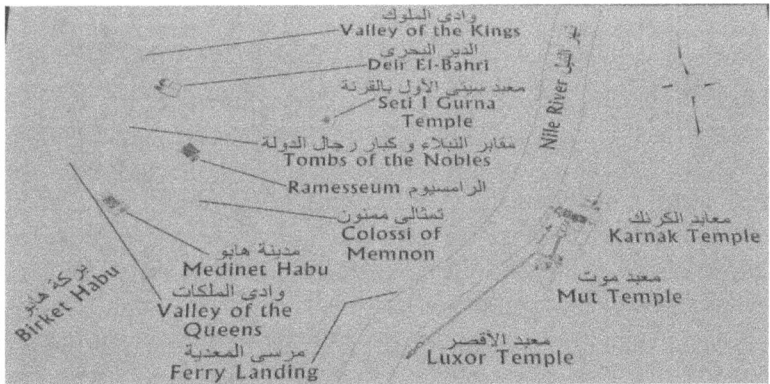

Where are the Kamite Kings Photo. Plan of monuments on the East and West Bank at Luxor, Thebes.

FREDERICK MONDERSON

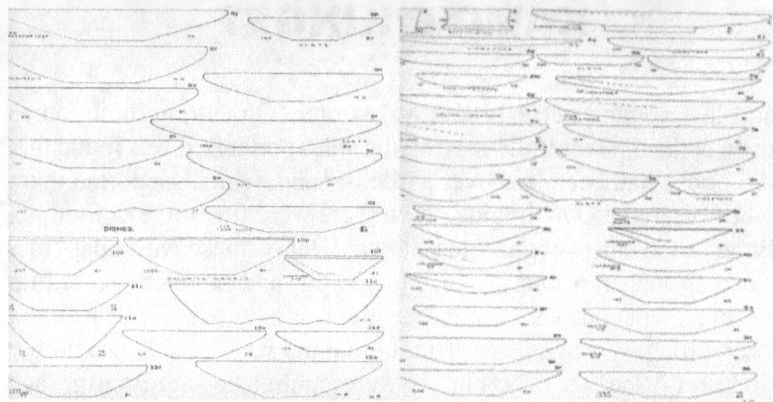

Where are the Kamite Kings Illustration. Alabaster platters and dishes (left); and, Alabaster, etc., platters in *Tarkhan I and Memphis V* by W.M. Flinders Petrie with G.A Wainwright and A.H. Gardiner (1913).

"The lower view shows a perfect burial (No. 1,845), slightly earlier, sequence date 77, rather before the Ist Dynasty. Here the whole of the sand filling has been removed, and the body is seen lying quite perfect, head south, and face west, contracted. The jars are around it, and beneath the knees and the arms is an alabaster bowl with a slate palette upon it. Outside of the mastaba wall, at the right, is seen at the back the offering court, with pans lying upside down in it; nearer is the stack of jars left from the offerings. Pottery of this type is seldom found in the graves; while the types found in graves are not found in stacks of offerings. From the contemporary pottery of this town at Abydos we see that the grave pottery was that in common use; the stack pottery, left subsequently, was apparently only made for such a transient purpose."

Modern scholars believe Narmer and Menes the same person. The classical historian, Herodotus, tells us Narmer built a great dam to divert the river so as to reclaim land on which he found Memphis at the juncture, or center, of the two lands. This "centralization" of rule and administration, was equally and politically a stroke of brilliance for it enabled the King to respond militarily in equal manner to problems in the north or south. Hor-Aha was related to Narmer and must have helped in completion of the unification process. According to Emery, "Hor-Aha's greatest achievement was the foundation of the new capital."

WHERE ARE THE KAMITE KINGS?

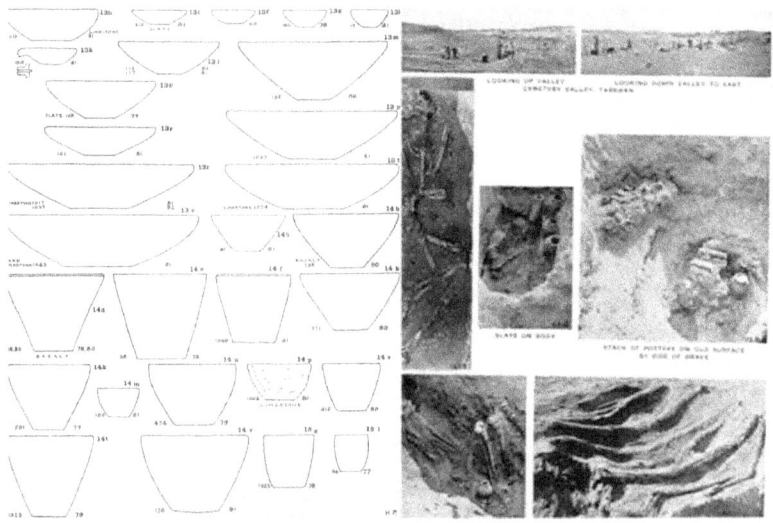

Where are the Kamite Kings Illustration. Alabaster dishes in *Tarkhan I and Memphis V* by W.M. Flinders Petrie with G.A Wainwright and A.H. Gardiner (1913) (left); and, evidence of the cemetery site and some examples of the burial in *Tarkhan* II by Flinders Petrie (1914).

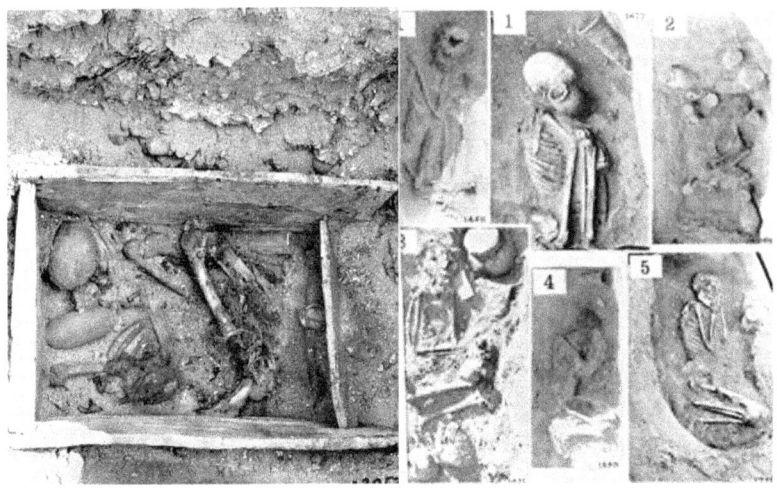

Where are the Kamite Kings Illustration. Close-up of a burial boxed (left); and various burials also showing "Goods of the Grave" in *Tarkhan II* by Flinders Petrie (1914).

FREDERICK MONDERSON

Nevertheless, as founder of the dynasty Narmer is credited with beginning centralized government and establishing written law. While Narmer's tomb at Abydos is numbered B-10, no second tomb of his has been discovered at Sakkara, a place where subsequent Kings built a second tomb signifying their relations with the two Kingdoms. It could be argued, if the northern tomb catered to the political and economic dynamics of the union, then the southern tomb at Abydos, should have more spiritual, cosmological and theosophic significance for the King as well as the society. Thus, it can be argued Abydos held the real tomb and Memphis the cenotaph or dummy tomb! Again, it can be further argued, since Narmer only built one tomb that is at Abydos then such is the real site and Sakkara housed the cenotaphs.

Where are the Kamite Kings Illustration. Another profile view of Amon, "King of the Gods."

WHERE ARE THE KAMITE KINGS?

Where are the Kamite Kings Illustration. Various views of burial at **Tarkhan** in *Tarkhan II* by Flinders Petrie (1914).

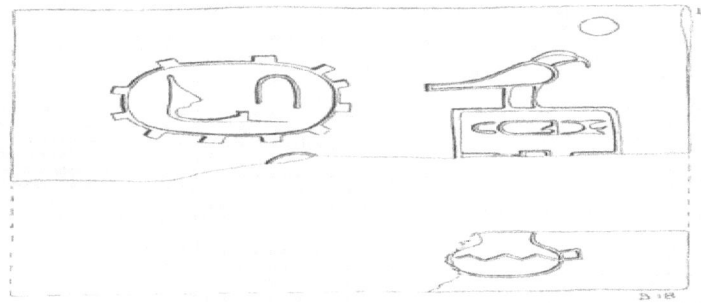

Where are the Kamite Kings Illustration. Tablet of King Narmer, showing the King's name, generally thought to be a fish and chisel, from *The Earliest Royal Tombs – Part I* by Flinders Petrie (1901).

FREDERICK MONDERSON

At this section of the exercise, two classics of ancient Kemetic literature are presented here as part of the **Blessing** in praise of this work. Wilson (1901: 35) has provided the first selection entitled "Abolishing the Slaughterings" that comes from the *Papyrus of Nebseni*, sheet 25.

The "Chapter of Driving Away the Slaughterings Which Are Performed in The Underworld." Nebseni, the scribe and designer in the Temples of Upper and Lower Egypt, he to whom fair veneration is paid, the son of the scribe and artist Thena, triumphant, saith: "'Hail, Tem, I have become glorious (or a *Khu*) in the presence of the double Lion-God, the great God, therefore open thou unto me the gate of the God Seb. I smell the earth (i.e., I bow down so that my nose toucheth the ground) of the great God who dwelleth in the underworld, and I advance into the presence of the company of the Gods who dwell with the beings who are in the underworld. Hail, thou guardian of the divine door of the city of Beta, thou [God] Neti (?) who dwellest in Amentet, I eat food, and I have life through the air, and the God Atch-ur leadeth me with [him] to the mighty boat of Khepera. I hold converse with the divine mariners at eventide, I enter in, I go forth, and I see the being who is there; I lift him up and I say that which I have to say unto him, whose throat stinketh [for lack of air]. I have life, and I am delivered, having laid down in death. Hail, thou that bringest offerings and oblations, bring forward thy mouth and make to draw nigh the writings (or lists) of offering and oblations. Set thou Right and Truth firmly upon their throne, make thou the writings to draw nigh, and set thou up the Goddesses in the presence of Osiris, the mighty God, the prince of everlastingness, who counteth his years, who hearkeneth unto those who are in the islands (or pools), who raiseth his right shoulder, who judgeth the divine princes, and who sendeth [Osiris] into the presence of the great sovereign princes who live in the underworld."

WHERE ARE THE KAMITE KINGS?

Where are the Kamite Kings Illustration. Ebony **Tablet of Mena**, also thought to be Narmer (top and bottom) from *The Earliest Royal Tombs Part I* by Flinders Petrie (1901).

FREDERICK MONDERSON

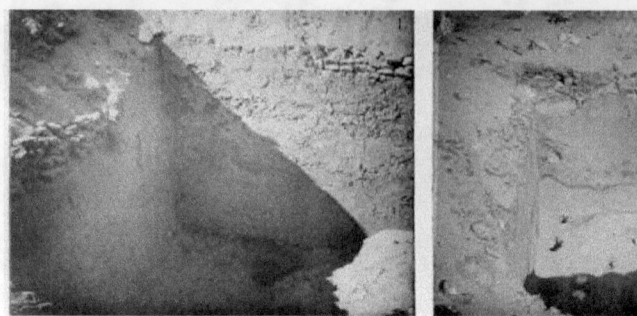

Where are the Kamite Kings Illustration. Tomb B-10 Period of Mena in *The Earliest Royal Tombs Part I* by Flinders Petrie (1901).

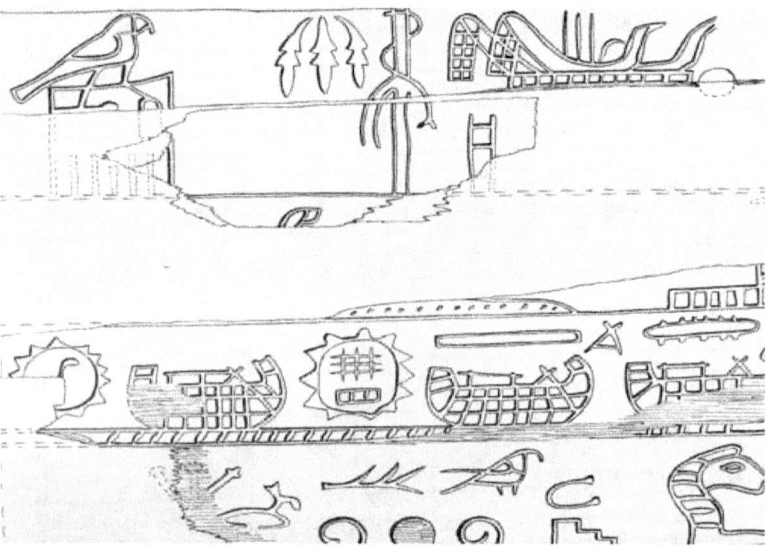

Where are the Kamite Kings Illustration. Hawks and boats, *The Earliest Royal Tombs – Part I* by Flinders Petrie (1901).

The other reading is also entitled "Abolishing the Slaughterings" and comes from *The Papyrus of Nu*, now in the British Museum No. 10,477, sheet 6. Wilson, again (1901: 36-38) adds: THE CHAPTER OF DRIVING BACK THE SLAUGHTERINGS WHICH ARE PERFORMED IN SUTEN-HENEN. Osiris Nu, triumphant, saith: "O thou land of the Scepter! (Literally, wood) O thou white crown of the divine form! O thou resting-place of the boat! I am the Child, I am the Child, I am the Child, I am the Child. Hail, Abu-ur, thou sayest day by day: 'The slaughter-block is made ready as thou knowest, and thou hast come to decay.' I am Ra, the stabilizer of

WHERE ARE THE KAMITE KINGS?

those who praise [him]. I am the knot of the God within the *Aser* tree, the doubly beautiful one, who is more splendid than yesterday (say four times). I am Ra, the stabilizer of those who praise [him]. I am the knot of the God within the *Aser* tree, and my going forth is the going forth [of Ra] on this day."

Where are the Kamite Kings Illustration. Gold hawk with a ram's head, inlaid with enamel, now in the Louvre (Erman 1894).

Where are the Kamite Kings Photo. Kalabsha Temple of Mendulese. With Isis at left, the King offers three feathers of Ma'at to deities wearing the Khnemu Crown, the Osiris Crown and the White Crown.

FREDERICK MONDERSON

Where are the Kamite Kings Illustration. Coffins of Thutmose I and Pinozem.

"My hair is the hair of Nu. My face is the face of the Disk. My eyes are the eyes of Hathor. My ears are the ears of Ap-uat. My nose is the nose of Khenti-khas. My lips are the lips of Anpu. My teeth are the teeth of Serqet. My neck is the neck of the divine Goddess Isis. My hands are the hands of Ba-neb-Tattu. My forearm is of Neith, the Lady of Sais. My backbone is the backbone of Suti. My phallus

WHERE ARE THE KAMITE KINGS?

is the phallus of Osiris. My reins are the reins of the Lords of Kheraba. My eye is the chest of the Mighty one of Terror. My belly and back are the belly and back of Sekhet. My buttocks are the buttocks of the Eye of Horus. My hips and legs are the hips and legs of Nut. My feet are the feet of Ptah. [My fingers] and my leg-bones are the [fingers and] leg-bones of the Living Gods. There is no member of my body, which is not the member of some God. The God Thoth shieldeth my body altogether, and I am Ra day-by-day. I shall not be dragged back by my arms, and none shall lay violent hold upon my hands. And shall do me hurt neither men, nor Gods, nor the sainted dead, nor those who have perished, nor any one of those of ancient times, nor any mortal, nor any human being. I am he who cometh forth, advancing, whose name is unknown, I am Yesterday, and Seer of millions of years is my name. I pass along. I pass along the paths of the divine celestial judges. I am the lord of eternity, and I decree and I judge like the God Khepera. I am the lord of the *Ureret* crown. I am he who dwelleth in the *Utchat* [in the Egg] and it is given unto me to live [with] them. I am he that dwelleth in the *Utchat* when it closeth, and I exist by the strength thereof. I come forth and I shine; I enter in and I come to life. I am in the [*Utchat*], my seat is upon my throne, and I sit in the abode of splendor (?) before it. I am Horus and (I) traverse millions of years. I have given the decree [for the stablishing of] my throne and I am the ruler thereof; and in very truth, my mouth keepeth an even balance both in speech and in silence. In every truth, my forms are inverted. I am Un-nefer, from one season even unto another, and what I have is within me; [I am] the only One, who proceedeth from an only One who goeth round about in his course. I am he who dwelleth in the *Utchat*, no evil thing of any form or kind shall spring up against me, and any baleful object, and harmful thing, and no disastrous thing shall happen to me. I open the door in heaven, I govern my throne, and I open up [the way] for the births [which take place] on this day. I am (?) the child who marcheth along the road of Yesterday. [I am] today for untold nations and peoples. I am he who protecteth you for millions of years, and whether ye be denizens of the heavens, or of the earth, or of the south, or of the north, or of the east, or of the west, the fear of me is in your bodies. I am he whose being has been molded in his eye, and I shall not die again. My moment is in your bodies, but my forms are in my place of habitation. I am he who cannot be known, but the Red Ones have their faces directed toward me. I am the unveiled one. The season wherein [the God] created the heavens for me and enlarged the bounds of the earth and made great the progeny thereof cannot be found out; but they fail and are not united [again]. My name setteth itself apart from all things [and from] the great evil [which is in] the mouths [of men] by reason of the speeches which I address unto you. I am he who riseth and shineth, the wall which cometh out of a wall, an only One who proceedeth from an only One. There is never a day that passeth without the things which appertain unto him being therein; passing, passing, passing, passing. Verily I say unto thee, I am the Sprout which cometh forth from Nu and my Mother is Nut. Hail, O my Creator, I am he who hath no power to walk, the great Knot is within yesterday. The might of my strength is within my hand. I myself am not known, but I am he who knoweth thee. I cannot be held with the hand, but I am he who can hold thee in his hand. Hail, O Egg! Hail, O Egg! I am Horus who liveth for millions of years, whose flame shineth upon you and bringeth your hearts to me. I have the command of my throne and I advance at this season, I have opened a path, and I have delivered myself from all evil things. I am the dog-headed ape of gold three palms and two fingers [high], which hath neither arms nor legs and dwelleth in Het-ka-Ptah (Memphis), and I go forth as goeth forth the dog-headed ape that dwelleth in Het-ka-Ptah."

Where are the Kamite Kings Photo. Kalabsha Temple of Mendulese. In the Open Court, three columns sporting different capitals, characteristic of the Graeco-Roman Period.

WHERE ARE THE KAMITE KINGS?

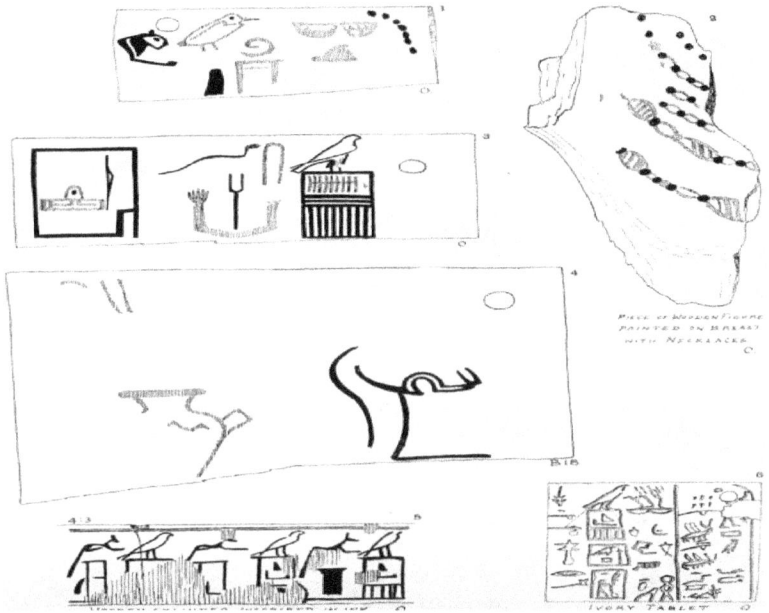

Where are the Kamite Kings Photo. Illustration.
60. Abydos - Painted inscription, Ivory Tablet, hawk atop a Serekh, etc. *The Earliest Royal Tombs – Part I* by Flinders Petrie (1901).

4. THE ARCHAIC PERIOD II

Besides his tomb at Abydos, Narmer's name has been found in votive offerings at the Temple of Osiris and in his wife Neith-Hotep's tomb at Neggadeh, excavated by de Morgan. This King sent trading expeditions to the Eastern Desert. His name has also been found, Emery (1972: 47) has shown, displayed in "rocks in the Wadi-el-Qash on the south side of the great trade route between Coptos and Quesir."

FREDERICK MONDERSON

Where are the Kamite Kings Illustration. Seal of Horus Aha, generally thought to be the son of Narmer or Menes.

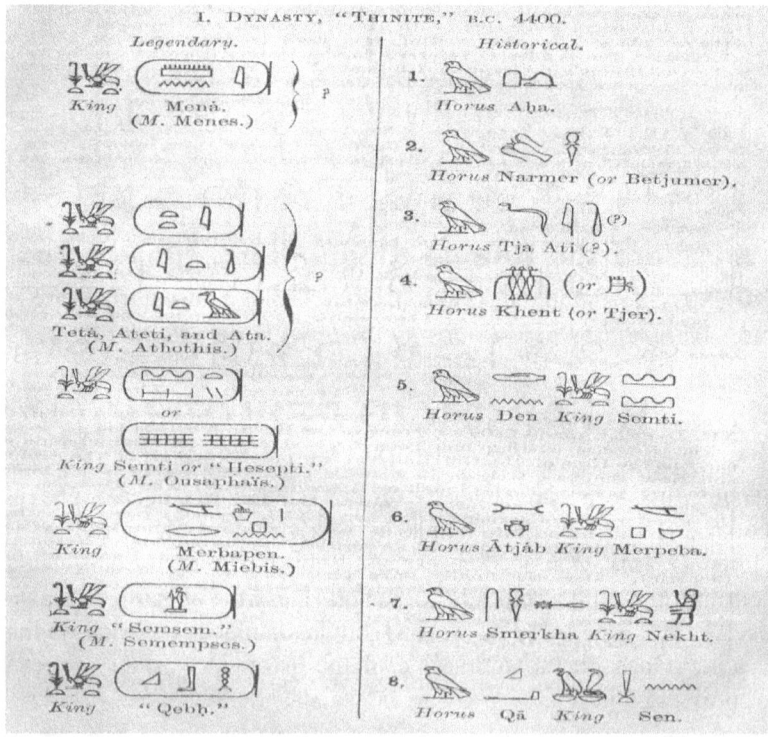

Where are the Kamite Kings Cartouche/Shennu. List of the Chief Royal Cartouches/Shennus of the First Dynasty, from H.R. Hall, *Handbook for Egypt and the Sudan* (1907).

Hor-Aha, whose name means "Fighting Hawk," was son of Narmer and Queen Neith-Hotep, and successor to the throne. He followed

WHERE ARE THE KAMITE KINGS?

a wise policy of conciliation with the north to mold a united nation, while he also fought the Nubians, extending the southern boundary to the First Cataract. At Sais, in Lower Kemet, he built a temple for the Goddess Neith, patron deity of the north as part of his reconciliation strategy. He was instrumental in creating the "white wall" described as "a great engineering feat," that facilitated the founding of Memphis as the administrative capital of the now united northern and southern Kingdoms. Ivory objects, wooden labels and clay jar-sealings indicate he had two names, the *Horus* (Hor) and *Nebti* (Men). Equally, one particular fragment shows evidence of a ceremony called "Receiving the South and the North." His mother's name, Neith-Hotep and several other queens with variants of the name, indicate worship of the Goddess Neith was well established at this time. Hor-Aha built a temple to Ptah, who remained patron deity of the city throughout dynastic history. His two tombs have been found at Abydos and Sakkara, supplying ivory objects and labels. The one at Abydos is the largest in this cemetery's northwest group. It is believed he built his mother Neith Hotep's tomb at Neggadeh.

Where are the Kamite Kings Illustration. Another seal of Horus Aha, son of Narmer or Menes.

The Abydos burials then the Sakkara tombs show a great departure from and advancement over earlier burials. The Abydos tomb is smaller than the one at Sakkara, probably indicating the former is the true burial and the latter the cenotaph. Afterall, why build a large tomb then go back and build a smaller one. As for example, Emery (1963: 54) writes: "The Abydos tomb B 19, which is the largest in the north-west group, has been identified as belonging to Hor-Aha from objects found during its excavations. As with all the archaic tombs the superstructure has entirely disappeared and only a great brick-lined subterranean chamber remains, in the floor of which are holes for wooden posts which must have supported its roof. The over-all measurement of the monument, including the heavy retaining walls, is 11.7 by 9.4 meters. In a smaller tomb adjacent to B 19 a small gold bar was found by Petrie. On it the name of Hor-Aha is incised but its purpose is not known."

Where are the Kamite Kings Illustration. Granite and alabaster vase inscriptions from Hierakonpolis showing a hawk atop a Serekh and the vulture with talon in *Hierakonpolis I* by J.E. Quibell and with notes by W.M.F. Petrie (1900).

WHERE ARE THE KAMITE KINGS?

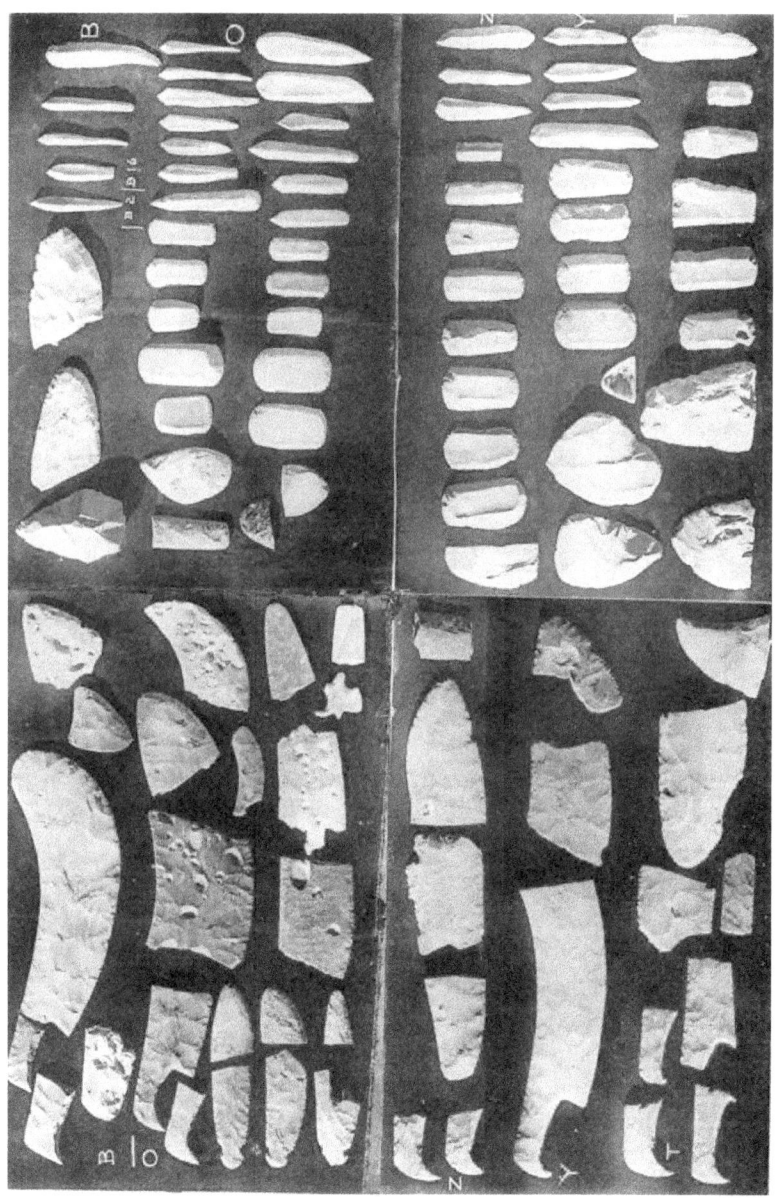

Where are the Kamite Kings Illustration. Worked flints of the Kings Mena (B), Zer (O), Zet (N), Merneith (Y), Den (T), from the Royal Tombs at Abydos in Flinders Petrie's *Abydos* I (1902).

FREDERICK MONDERSON

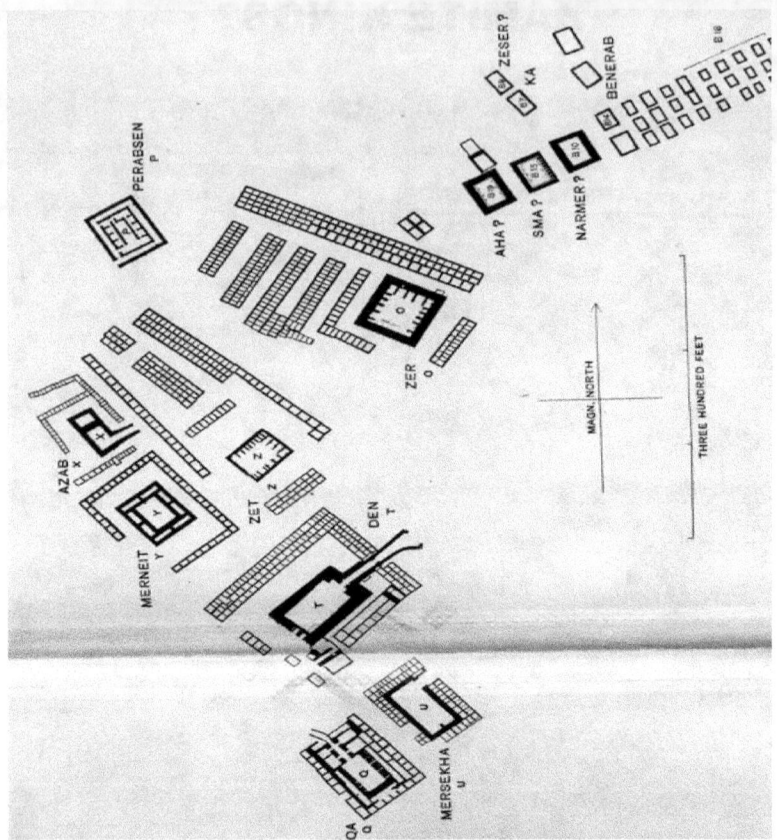

Where are the Kamite Kings Illustration. Plan of some of the Archaic Tombs at Abydos in *The Earliest Royal Tombs I* by Flinders Petrie (1901).

"The northern tomb at Sakkara, known as No. 3357, is a far larger and more pretentious structure, and although somewhat smaller than that of Queen Neithhotep and similar in general design it is more elaborate and shows a later development, principally in the subterranean burial chamber. This consists of a great rectangular pit cut in the gravel and rock which is divided by cross walls into five separate rooms. These subterranean rooms were roofed with timber and above, built on ground level, is a large rectangular superstructure of brick with a hollow interior divided into a series of twenty-seven magazines to contain extra funerary equipment. The superstructure, with its exterior decorated with recessed paneling and surrounded by two enclosure walls, has an overall

WHERE ARE THE KAMITE KINGS?

measurement of 48.2 by 22 meters. On the north side of the tomb were a series of small model-buildings and a large brick-built boat-grave. This had originally contained a wooden solar bark in which the spirit of the great King would travel with the celestial Gods in their journey across the heavens by day and through the underworld below the earth by night."

Pursuing an active foreign policy, he conquered Nubia and extended his reign as far as the first cataract, south of Aswan. To the north he kept the Libyans in check. Hor-Aha's queen was Berner-Ib, "sweet of heart" whose name was recovered from burials at Abydos and Neggadeh. Griffith's review of Petrie's *Diospolis Parva* (1902: 8) explains, the "style of Aha's inscriptions is important as a link between the style of his successors and that of other Kings who must have preceded him."

The next King in the succession was Zer or Djer to whom Manetho attributes a reign of fifty-seven years. Manetho's *Athothis* is credited with being a physician who wrote books on anatomy. Accordingly, Budge (1902: 191) connects him with a quote from the *Ebers Papyrus* that mentions a "pomatum, which was made from the claw of a dog, and the hoof of an ass, and some dates boiled together in oil in a saucepan, was made for Teta's mother, who was called Shesh." He built a palace at Memphis and his consort may have been Queen Meryet-nit. Some authorities hold she was his successor. This makes her the first "Queen" who ruled as "Pharaoh."

Where are the Kamite Kings Illustration. Sealing of King Zer, Ser (Djer) found at Abydos by Petrie.

FREDERICK MONDERSON

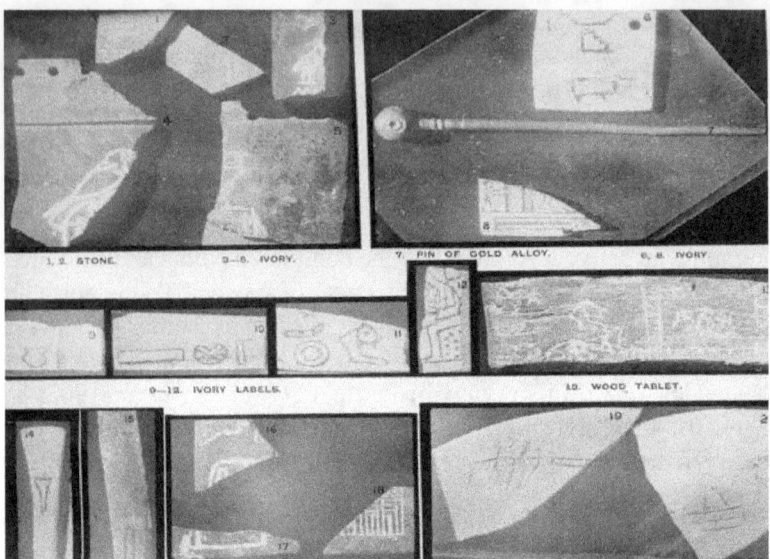

Where are the Kamite Kings Illustration. Stone, ivory, a pin of gold alloy and wood and ivory Tablets from the Tomb of King Zer-Ta in *The Earliest Royal Tombs I* by Flinders Petrie (1901).

Zer continued Hor-Aha's wars against Nubia and all enemies of the state. He established his power as far as the Second Cataract. His Horus name appears on an erected "sandstone slab found at Gebel el-Sheikh Suliman, about 11 kilometers south of Wadi Halfa on the west bank of the Nile." He had tombs at Abydos and Sakkara. Ivory and wood labels, rock inscriptions and inscribed palettes identify his name. An alabaster palette from his Sakkara tomb shows him striking a Libyan captive. In the Abydos tomb Petrie found four magnificent bracelets of gold, amethyst and turquoise, apparently abandoned by tomb robbers. Zer's consort may have been Queen Her-Nit. The tomb at Abydos was later identified as that of Osiris by Amelineau where hundreds of retainers were buried in satellite tombs nearby.

WHERE ARE THE KAMITE KINGS?

Where are the Kamite Kings Illustration. Ivory, charcoal, ebony, wood, agate, clay, wood, electrum, and marble implements from the Tomb of King Zer-Ta in *The Earliest Royal Tombs I* by Flinders Petrie (1901).

Where are the Kamite Kings Illustration. Tomb of Zer, stairs of the XVIIIth Dynasty and Chambers of North side of the Tomb of Zer in *The Earliest Royal Tombs I* by Flinders Petrie (1901).

FREDERICK MONDERSON

Of this, Emery (1961) (1963: 59) has written: "Of the two labels in question, that of Abydos seems to record a visit of the King to Buto and Sais, the sacred towns of Lower Egypt. The Sakkara label apparently records some important religious festival at which human sacrifice was performed. Zer continued the Nubian wars of his predecessor and his armies penetrated as far south as the Second Cataract. Near Wadi-Halfa, on the west bank of the Nile, there is a rock inscription that shows the Horus name of Zer, in front of which stands a human figure in the attitude of captivity holding the bow sign which represents Nubia. Another captive is tied to an Egyptian warship, below which are bodies of slain enemies. Whether this primitive monument records merely a punitive raid by Zer or an actual conquest it is impossible to say; but objects of undoubted Egyptian craftsmanship of this period have been found in Lower Nubia."

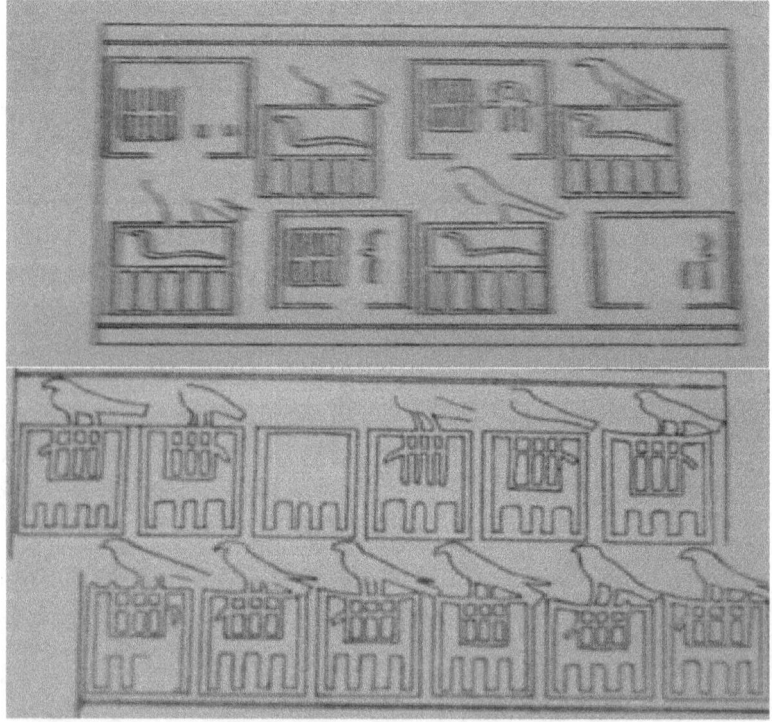

Where are the Kamite Kings Illustration. Sealing of Queen Den-Merneith, wife of Den (above); and Sealing of King Zet-Ta found at Abydos by Petrie.

WHERE ARE THE KAMITE KINGS?

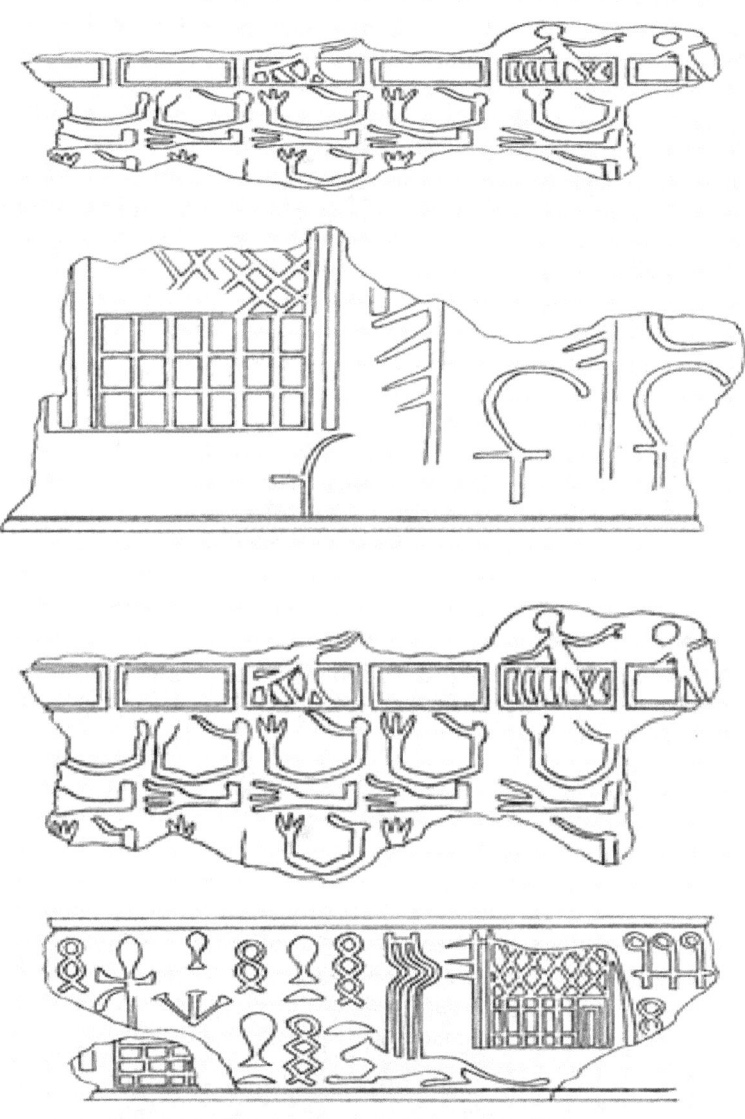

Where are the Kamite Kings Illustration. Sealing of King Zer found at Abydos from *The Earliest Royal Tombs I* by Flinders Petrie (1901).

FREDERICK MONDERSON

Where are the Kamite Kings Illustration. From the Tomb of King Zer-Ta, fragments of ivory carvings, labels, boxes, wooden labels, stone and pottery jar inscriptions, etc., (right); ivory lions, piece of a bracelet, crystal arrows and knife, flint arrows and flint in wood, *The Earliest Royal Tomb I* by Flinders Petrie (1901).

Continuing his consolidation efforts, Zer's (Djer) reign represented a time of great growth for, as Emery (1963: 61) writes: "there appears to have been a considerable step forward in prosperity, shown by expansion in the production of arts and crafts, outstanding examples of which may be seen in the jewelry recovered from the King's southern tomb at Abydos, the vast collection of copper vessels, tools, and weapons found in the northern tomb at Sakkara, and the magnificent gold-handled flint knife now in the Toronto Museum."

His tomb was surrounded by 338 subsidiary graves containing "bodies of retainers sacrificed at the royal burial. Most of these sacrificed persons were women and with many of them were crude stone stelae recording their names." Petrie, whose remarks concerned the work of the British School in Egypt, commented on this practice. A mile away from Abydos where courtiers were buried, archaeologists were seeing to understand this phenomenon. In explanation, Petrie (1922: 74) wrote accordingly: "Though many of these bodies appear to have been buried in a coffin, with vases of alabaster and pottery, and tools of copper and flint, yet there were several which seem to have been conscious when buried. Some with a knee raised, others with arms stretched out as if lifting the body. The clearest instance is illustrated here. The heels had evidently

WHERE ARE THE KAMITE KINGS?

been bound up to the hips, to prevent resistance; the body was thrown into the grave, upon a rising boulder, chest downward; the head was twisted round, at right angles to the spine both backwards and sideways. The forearm was raised in front of the face. That this appearance was not due to decapitation, was proved by lifting the skull, which was in articulation to the atlas vertebra, and tracing the vertebrae continuously down to the straight line of the back; then on replacing the skull in articulation it stood exactly as when found. There were no broken or wounded bones observed in any of the skeletons; it seems therefore as if the people, men and women, had been sandbagged, and then buried while stunned - a most painless kind of death. The frequent examples of property with Kings' names buried here shows that these people belonged to the royal household."

Where are the Kamite Kings Illustration. Coffin lid of Thutmose II and close-up.

Petrie (1922: 74) continued even further: "The custom of killing off the court at the King's death was a wholesome preservative of orderly government. Everyone around the King knew that he could not survive the King, and therefore might as well sacrifice his life to preserve that of the King from violence. It was the ancient custom in the Sudan, where the viceroy of the twelfth dynasty was buried with about three hundred Nubians, lying scattered about in the passages, which led to the tomb. In the first dynasty there are hundreds of burials to each King at the beginning and dwindling to dozens at the end of the dynasty. This custom was finally ended sometime at the start of the Old Kingdom."

Queen Meryet-nit may have been Zer's successor and third Pharaoh of the dynasty. She had two tombs, at Abydos and Sakkara, a status reserved only for monarchs. Petrie excavated the Abydos tomb. Budge (1902: 193) supplied dimensions showing: "The central chamber of the tomb is about twenty-one feet wide and thirty feet long, and around it are walls which vary in thickness from four feet to four feet four inches. It seems to have had a wooden floor, the remains of which show signs of having been burnt." Stone vases help to identify Meryet-nit, whose Sakkara tomb had subsidiary graves surrounding it. According to Emery (1972: 66-68) these graves: "were of great interest, for many of them were found undisturbed, containing the bodies of sacrificed servants buried with objects denoting their particular service to their royal mistress, such as model boats with her ship-master, paint pots with her artist, stone vessels and copper tools with her vase maker, pots of every type with her potter, etc."

This female pharaoh also had a solar bark interred in her burial. This boat was intended to ferry her across the sky to travel with the Sun God. Emery (1972: 68-69) noted further: "Apart from the two tombs at Abydos and Sakkara, a further group of seventy-five graves of Meryet-Nit's servants arranged in orderly rows round three sides of a rectangle was found at Abydos. Similar rectangles of servants' burials of the Kings Zer and Uadji are nearby. The meaning of these curious cemeteries has not yet been satisfactorily explained, but it has been suggested that the burials were arranged around great buildings which have totally disappeared."

Zet or Uadji (Djet) followed Meryet-nit and Djer. He had tombs at Sakkara and Abydos. Buried at Abydos, he too was militarily

WHERE ARE THE KAMITE KINGS?

engaged to pacify and unify the land. Budge (1902) described his Abydos tomb: "as a large chamber twenty feet wide and thirty feet long, with smaller chambers around it at its level, the whole bounded by a thick brick wall which rises seven-and-a-half feet to the roof, and then three-and-a-half feet more to the top of the retaining wall." This tomb contained a funerary stela with his Horus name that's now in the Louvre Museum. Zet's name was also found engraved on a rock in the desert east of Edfu." He celebrated one of the earliest Heb Sed Festivals. His chancellor, Hemaka, was buried at Sakkara.

Where are the Kamite Kings Illustration. King Zet or Uadji sealing was also discovered at Abydos by Sir Matthew Flinders Petrie.

FREDERICK MONDERSON

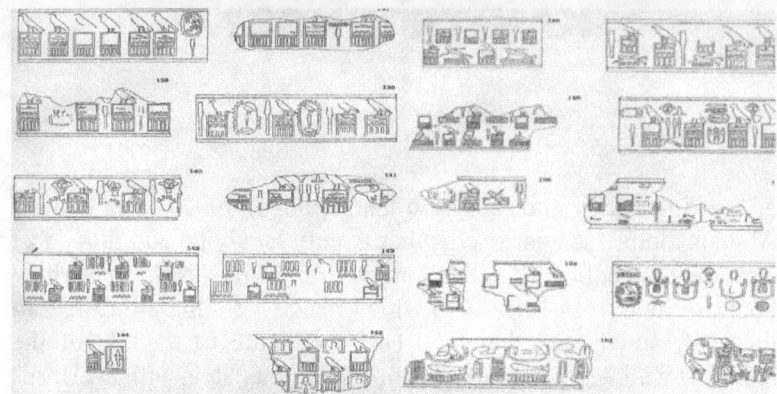

Where are the Kamite Kings Illustration. Sealings of King Den-Setui discovered at Abydos and included in *The Earliest Royal Tombs I* by Flinders Petrie (1901).

Den, Ten, Udimu or Sempti, was the fifth King of the First Dynasty and his reign was marked by much prosperity. Inscribed jar sealings and labels help us identify him. His name is on the Palermo Stone, by Manetho and on the Abydos King List.

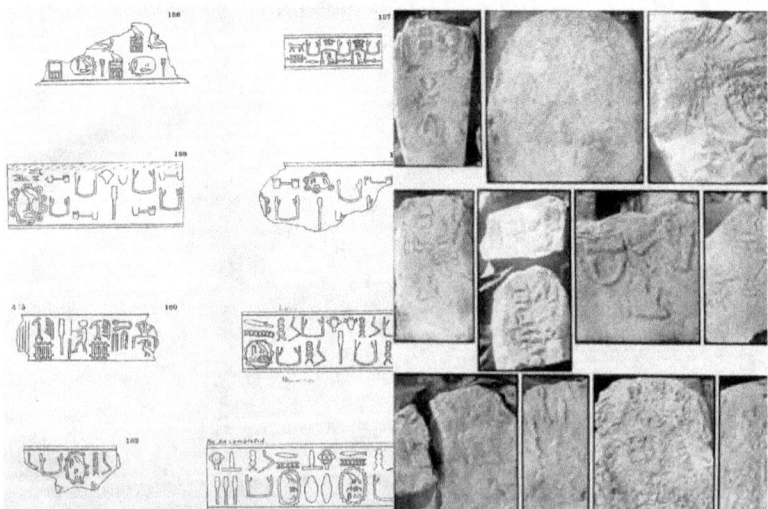

Where are the Kamite Kings Illustration. Jar sealings of King Den-Setui found at Abydos; and Steles from around the Tomb of Den-Setui in *The Earliest Royal Tombs I* by Flinders Petrie (1901).

WHERE ARE THE KAMITE KINGS?

He was the first to begin using the *Nebti* name and also first pictured wearing the White resting on Red Double Crown. He had two tombs. The tomb at Abydos was discovered by M. Amelineau who found, according to Budge (1902: 194-95) that the "massive walls of the large chamber in it had been covered with wooden panels, and that the pavement consisted of large slabs of red granite ...."

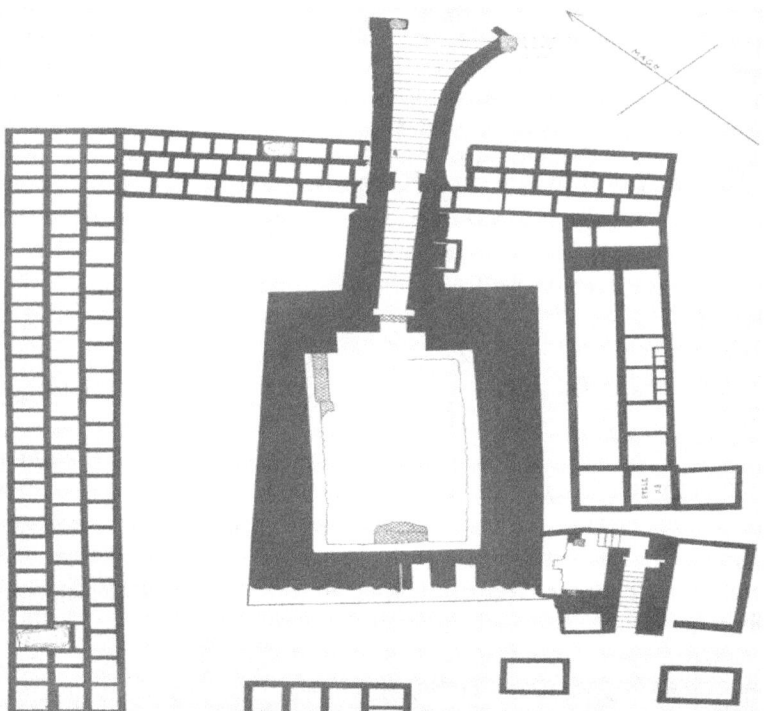

Where are the Kamite Kings Photo. Illustration.
86. Tomb of King Den-Setui in *The Earliest Royal Tombs I* by Flinders Petrie (1901).

FREDERICK MONDERSON

Where are the Kamite Kings Illustration. 87. Tomb of Den-Setui, *The Earliest Royal Tombs I* by Flinders Petrie (1901).

Of all objects recovered from this tomb, an ebony tablet now in the British Museum (No. 32,650) is considered the most important historically. Budge (1902: 196) has supplied a description of its inscriptions and scenes that "are divided into two groups by means of a vertical line; on the left we have the Horus name Ten side by side with the name of the 'royal chancellor' Hemaka and a number of hieroglyphic signs." Even further, Budge (1902: 196) added: "To the extreme right is the sign for 'year,' and in the uppermost register we see the figure of a God, who is, no doubt, Osiris, wearing the crown of the South, and holding a flail in his hands, seated upon a throne within a shrine which is set at the top of a staircase or flight of steps. Before the God is the figure of King Sempti, who wears the crowns of the South and North united, and who is dancing; his back is toward the God, and in his left hand he holds the paddle and in the right the flail .... In other words, King Sempti is performing an act of worship before his God by dancing before him."

WHERE ARE THE KAMITE KINGS?

Where are the Kamite Kings Illustration. Steles from around the Tomb of Den-Setui in *The Earliest Royal Tombs I*, Flinders Petrie (1901).

This ritual worship in the dance was no uncommon thing for Kings to so perform before the Gods. Budge (1902: 196-97) also supplied his views on this by mentioning other instances of this act being performed. Here he shows:

"Usertesen I, who danced before the God Amsu or Min, and Seti I, who danced before the Goddess Nekhebet, and a still earlier allusion to the custom will be found in the text of Pepi I, where it is said, 'He who (i.e., Pepi) is between the thighs of Nut is the pygmy who danceth for the God, and who maketh glad the heart before his great throne.'"

Additionally, Budge (1902: 198) continued: "To the left of the second register is what appears to be an early form of the Hennu boat, and it is difficult to see why it should occur on the tablet below the representation of a religious ceremony of dancing, if the King Sempti was not in some way connected with the ceremonies in which we know the Hennu boat played a most prominent part. Under the name Sempti and Hesepti the King is mentioned in various passages of the *Book of the Dead,* and in one place the occurrence of his name is of special significance."

Where are the Kamite Kings Photo. Kalabsha Temple of Mendulese. More columns with different capitals in the Open Court as well as a winged-disk with uraei on the architrave. Notice how the blocks of the architrave center upon the column, supporting and creating the "bridge across the void" to the next column.

Budge also commented (1902: 198) on the Rubric to a shorter version of the LXIVth Chapter, regarding a composition that was: "'found in the foundations of the shrine of Hennu by the chief mason during the reign of Hesepti' and though we have no exact idea of what the word 'found' here means, it is clear that in the reign of this King an important revision or discovery in connection with the literary history of the *Book of the Dead* took place. A parallel may perhaps be quoted in the narrative of II Kings, XXII. 8, where we are told that in the reign of good King Josiah the high priest Hilkiah said unto Shaphan Scribe, 'I have found the book of the law in the house of the lord.'"

The shorter version of Chapter LXIV is entitled "The Chapter of knowing the 'Chapters of Coming Forth by Day' in a single Chapter." This revision of the religious book became necessary at an early time in the history of the nation. It is Budge's (1902: 199)

WHERE ARE THE KAMITE KINGS?

view: "To meet this want the LXIVth Chapter in its shortened form was drawn up by priests, probably under royal command and supervision; in any case there must have been some good reason for mentioning Hesepti's name in connection with the chapter in the Rubric, and we may assume that certain important religious ceremonies were either first established or confirmed during his reign."

Reference to medicine contained in *Ebers Papyrus* gives a prescription that, according to Budge (1902: 199) came from "'a book which was found under the feet of the God Anubis in the city of Letopolis, and was brought to the King of the South and North Hesepti.'"

Commenting on prosperity and art during Udimu's reign, Emery (1972: 80) wrote, "One of the most notable objects recovered from the Abydos tomb is the lid of an ivory box which must have originally kept his gold seal of judgment, for it is so inscribed."

Anezib, described in the inscriptions as a Thinite King, had two tombs built for him at Abydos and Sakkara, though they were much smaller than earlier Kingly internments. His Abydos tomb was partly excavated by Amelineau and finally cleared by Petrie who found, "numbers of fragments of vases, jar-sealings, plaques of ivory for inlaying, etc., inscribed with his Horus and personal names."

Budge has noted (1902: 200) that in this internment: "the tomb is a plain chamber, with rather sloping sides, about twenty-two feet long and fourteen feet wide. The surrounding wall is nearly five feet thick; the entrance to the tomb was by a stairway descending from the east. The chamber was floored with planks of wood, and the roof was supported by wooden posts."

Much evidence of his reign has not survived though Semerkhet, his successor, erased Anezib's names and inserted his own.

Anezib is the first King mentioned in the *Sakkara King List*. Surrounding the tomb of Anezib at Abydos, Emery (1972:81) noted accordingly, were "sixty-four poorly built graves for the sacrificed retainers." With the introduction of new features, his northern tomb, according to Emery (1972: 84) contained an unusual feature: "double entrance stairways, one to the subterranean burial chambers and the other to a room above it, and a granary with built-in corn bins." He is also mentioned on the Palermo Stone and by Manetho.

Smerkhet, Manetho's *Semempses* ruled for eighteen years and is the only First Dynasty King whose Sakkara tomb has not been discovered, though a stela with his name has been found there. There were two stelae at the east side of his Abydos tomb. He is also the first King whose name is omitted from the *Sakkara King List*. An important ivory tablet belonging to this King also called Hen-Nekht was described by Budge (1902: 203) as follows: "To the right is the sign for year, and close by are figures of the Sektet and Atet boats, which call to mind the forms of them as given in the Pyramid Text of Unas between them is an ape of Thoth, and the legend .... To the left of the vertical line, we have names and titles of a King, followed by the sign which is evidently an archaic form of 'Hu' or 'Nekht.'"

Jar-sealings helped identify this King as Semerkha. Budge (1902: 204) provided a description of Semerkha's tomb at Abydos worked by Petrie, wherein the dimensions were: "about forty-four feet long and twenty-five feet wide, and is surrounded by a wall over five feet thick; it was floored with planks of wood, which M. Amelineau found to be charred, and he thought that the whole tomb had been burnt. Among the stelae found in this tomb were two of dwarfs, and the bones of dwarfs were found in two chambers; the copper bowl which was found in another chamber is the only large piece of metal-work that has been preserved. Prof. Petrie notes the space near the entrance to the tomb was filled to the depth of three feet with sand saturated with ointment, and that the scent of it was so strong that when cutting away the sand it could be smelt over the whole tomb."

Apparently, **Hen Nekht** had another tomb that was discovered near Girgeh, by John Garstang. He is considered as Myers (1901: 127) states "by far the earliest known King whose remains have been found" and this makes his bones extremely important.

WHERE ARE THE KAMITE KINGS?

Myers (1901: 127) describes this King as very big. "They proclaim him to have been a man of unusual height. His stature probably exceeded 1870 millimeters, while the average stature of later and prehistoric Egyptians was 1670 millimeters. The proportions of his long bones one to another were such as characterize Negroid skeletons, a condition frequently observed in the prehistoric period, and commonly in the later period of the early empire. The skull was very massive and capacious, and extraordinarily broad for an Egyptian, the cranial index coming almost within the bounds of brachycephaly. Its features agreed more closely with those of dynastic than with those of prehistoric skulls."

His Hawk name was also discovered on a great stela of black quartzose stone. Twenty-six subsidiary graves contained his retainers. He mined copper at Wadi Maghara in the Sinaitic Peninsula where he punished wild Bedouin tribes who attacked his expedition. His name is also in relief on rocks there.

Qaya's very large tomb was discovered by Emery in 1954 at Sakkara where jar sealings, labels and two stelae bear his Horus name. Iskander (1979: 34) adds that on the "north side of its paneled superstructure was found a funerary temple consisting of a series of rooms and corridors similar to those found in the mortuary temples of the pyramids and may be considered as their prototype." Few retainers were found near his tomb indicating the practice of sacrifices was probably coming to an end.

Qaya's reign ends the First Dynasty that ruled for over 200 years. Zaki Said, a native Egyptian archaeologist, discovered a middle-class cemetery at Helwan dated to the time of Qaya. He is shown on a stele wearing the White Crown.

Walter B. Emery's *Archaic Egypt* (Baltimore, Maryland: Penguin Books, 1931: 91) provided the following references to the tomb remains of First Dynasty Kings, who were principally buried at Abydos and Sakkara.

FREDERICK MONDERSON
KING'S NAME - MAJOR MONUMENTS

Hor-Aha	Tomb B 19 at Abydos. (Petrie, *Royal Tombs*)
	Tomb 3357 at Sakkara. (Emery, *Hor-aha*)
	Tomb of Neithotep at Nagadeh (de Morgan, *Recherches sur les origins de l'Egypt, Tombeau royal de Nagadeh*. Borchardt, 'Das Grab des Menes'. *Zeitschrift fur Agyptische Sprache* XXXVI)
Zer	Tomb O at Abydos. (Petrie, *Royal Tombs*)
	Tomb 3471 at Sakkara. (Emery, *Great Tombs*, 1)
	Tomb 2185 at Sakkara. Quibell, *Archaic Mastabas*)
Meryet-nit	Tomb Y at Abydos. (Petrie, *Royal Tombs*)
	Tomb 3503 at Sakkara. (Emery, *Great Tombs*, II)
	Enclosure of sacrifice burials. (Petrie, *Tombs of the Courtiers*)
Uadji	Tomb Z at Abydos. (Petrie, *Royal Tombs*)
	Tomb 3504, at Sakkara. (Emery, *Great Tombs*, II)
	Tomb at Gizeh. (Petrie, *Gizeh and Rifeh*)
Udimu	Tomb T at Abydos. (Petrie, *Royal Tombs*)
	Tomb 3035 at Sakkara. (Emery, *Tomb of Hemaka*)
	Tomb 3036 at Sakkara. (Emery, *Great Tombs*, II)
Enezib	Tomb X at Abydos. (Petrie, *Royal Tombs*)
	Tomb 3038 at Sakkara. (Emery, *Great Tombs*, I)
Semerkhet	Tomb U at Abydos. (Petrie, *Royal Tombs*)
Ka'a	Tomb Q at Abydos. (Petrie, *Royal Tombs*)
	Tomb 3505 at Sakkara. (Emery, *Great Tombs*, III)
	Tomb 3500 at Sakkara. (Emery, *Great Tombs*, III)

The Second Dynasty also came from *This*, the Thinite Nome, in the south, and was begun by King Hotepsekhemui. He was followed by Raneb, Neteren, Sekhemib-Perabsen, and Sendji. Also identified were Neterka, Neferkara, Khasekhem and Khasekhemwy who round out the list. A King of Dynasty 0, probably "Serpent" was also found at Abydos.

Hotepsekhemwy, Manetho's *Boethos* and Buzau of the King lists, is assigned a reign of thirty-eight, in a dynasty that lasted 302, years. During his reign a terrible earthquake struck Tell-Basta, killing many people.

WHERE ARE THE KAMITE KINGS?

His Sakkara tomb has not been found. However, a clay jar seal bearing his name was found in a subterranean gallery near the pyramid of Unas at Sakkara. This discovery has led to speculation that his tomb is in the vicinity.

The Abydos tomb was excavated in 1896-97 by M. Amelineau who discovered it. According to Budge (102: 207) the structure was: "about two hundred and sixty feet long, and to contain at least fifty-seven chambers; the tomb had neither been burnt nor plundered, and therefore many objects of great archaeological value were found in it. The earthenware vases in it contained wheat, figs, dried grapes, etc.; they were not closed by means of conical stoppers, but by pieces of clay of irregular shapes which were laid over their mouths and impressed with cylinder seals bearing the King's name upon them."

Quibell's work at Hierakonpolis, today's Kom-al-Akhmar, unearthed a number of "objects, vases, pottery, flints, etc.," that contained the King's names and titles. A granite vase of the King shows the earliest use of the symbol of the union of the two lands. In addition, mention is made of a granite doorjamb, inscribed with the King's Horus name, Hotepsekhemui. Two limestone and slate seated statues of the King are the earliest statues known.

Where are the Kamite Kings Photo. Rameses II Temple of Beit Wali. Two massive columns with 32 grooves characterize this small Temple with figures of Gods on its walls.

FREDERICK MONDERSON

Budge's commentary on these important artifacts (1902: 209) informs how "upon the bases of both statues, in front of the feet, is the Horus name, and around them we see a line of 'slain enemies in various distorted attitudes, and on the front are the register of northern enemies 47,209.'"

This pharaoh became, according to Budge (1902: 210), the "first King who caused his name to be enclosed in an oval or in a ring, and it is easy to see that the oval grew out of the ring, when the names became too long to be enclosed in it." Iskander (1977: 36) informs us further his Horus name signifies the "two powers" of Upper and Lower Kemet/Egypt "are at peace."

Emery (1972: 35) provided an interesting explanation of the early names of the Pharaoh, and respective manner of their use. "The Horus name is applied exclusively to the living King; it survives him only in the names of places or buildings. From the reign of Semerkhet, the seventh King of the First Dynasty, the dead King is defined by his *Nesu-bit* name in conjunction with his *Nebti* name. Then the *Nebti* was dropped and the *Nesu-bit* formed a distinct titulary by itself. The royal lists of Abydos, Sakkara and Turin cite the Kings by their *Nesu-bit* names because these lists deal with dead Kings. It can therefore be concluded that the *Nebti* name on the Neggadeh label is that of a dead King, while the Horus name is that of a living King."

And even further, Emery (1972: 35) adds some clarification to this issue. "The suggestion that in the Archaic Period the Horus name was only used in reference to the living King and the *Nebti* name to the King when dead is certainly wrong. With regard to the Horus name: it is difficult to reconcile this belief with the fact that it is the name which is used exclusively on the funeral stelae of the Kings found in the Abydos tombs. Furthermore, on the granite statue in the Cairo Museum the Horus names of the first three Kings of the Second Dynasty, Hotepsekhemui, Ra-neb, and Neteren, are engraved, in their order of succession. Presumably two at least of the three Kings must have been dead at the time of writing and should therefore have been indicated by their *Nebti* names. Again, we have the label of King Ka'ba with his Horus and *Nebti* names written together."

WHERE ARE THE KAMITE KINGS?

Raneb, Manetho's *Kaichos* and Kakau of the King list reigned thirty-nine years. His tomb has not been found, though clay jar-sealings helped to identify him, and also place him near Unas' tomb at Sakkara. Emery tells us (1972: 93) in the "vicinity of an ancient trade route to the western oasis behind Armant, Ra-neb's name has been found crudely inscribed on the rocks." During his reign, according to Manetho, the First Dynasty worship of the Apis Bull was continued. Budge, quoting Manetho in Cory's *Ancient Fragments* (1902: 211) indicated Ra-neb or Kaiechos "'reigned thirty-nine years, and under him the bulls Apis in Memphis, and Mnevis in Heliopolis, and the Mendesian goat, were appointed to be Gods.'" This author further quotes Manetho who referred to a statement of Aelian linking the worship of Apis to Menes and, Budge (1902: 212) continued, "it seems pretty certain from Manetho that some development of the worship of Apis, and perhaps of Mnevis also, must have taken place during the reign of Ka-kau. The Mendesian goat, or ram, is of course the Ram of Mendes, Bab-neb-Tattu, which was connected in very ancient times with the worship of Osiris."

Neteren, Manetho's *Binothris* and Banentiru of the King-lists, is assigned a lengthy reign of forty-nine years. Census and religious feasts during his sixth to twentieth years are mentioned on the *Palermo Stone*. Manetho relates during his time it was determined that: "'women might hold the imperial government.' His tomb has not been found, though indications on jar-sealings found at Giza, places his burial in the vicinity of Unas' Pyramid at Sakkara. Three large tombs of his reign have been discovered near Giza, and though a noble named Ruaben was found on stone jar fragments in one, it is thought it might also be Neter-ren's final internment. A small alabaster statue of the King in Heb Sed Festival attire, a celebration every thirty years, is shown wearing the White Crown and containing his Horus name. It is now in the Michalides collection in Cairo." Budge adds more to help identify him (1902: 212) in that, "the position of this King as the successor of Ka-kau is indicated by the statue at Cairo, and is confirmed by the fact that En-neter inscribed his name over that of Ra-neb (Ka-kau) on a stone bowl found at Abydos, a fragment of which is now in the British Museum (35,556)."

FREDERICK MONDERSON

Emery (1972: 93) also mentions in addition to building his palace, the important events of his reign, included "'construction of an important building called Hor-ren in year 7,' civil war in year 13, destruction of 'Shemra and Ha ('House of the North');' and 'running of Apis' in years 9 and 15."

Sekhemib, Perabsen, Manetho's *Has* and Uazmes of the King lists, witnessed revolution and weakening of centralized Thinite power. He changed his name from Sekhemib to Perabsen, and early adopted the God Set as his favorite. His tomb was discovered by Amelineau at Abydos, who credits Per-ab-sen's priest Sheri, for supplying the King's name on the door of his tomb.

Where are the Kamite Kings Illustration. Perabsen – Passage around tomb (left); and chamber looking north in the *Earliest Royal Tombs I* by flinders Petrie (1901) (right).

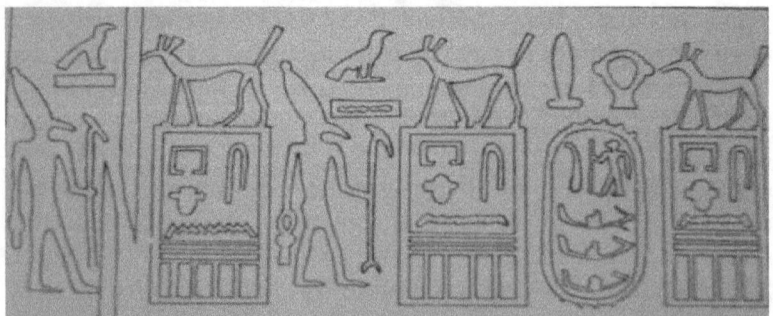

Where are the Kamite Kings Illustration. Hieroglyphic images of Sekhem-Ab-Perabsen, discovered at Abydos.

WHERE ARE THE KAMITE KINGS?

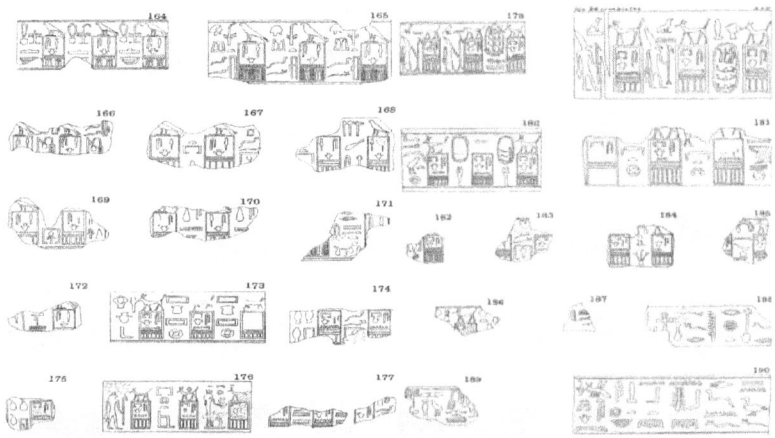

Where are the Kamite Kings Illustration. Sealings of King Sekhem-Ab-Perabsen in *The Earliest Royal Tombs I* by Flinders Petrie (1901).

Budge, commenting on an inscription (1902: 213) writes this King's "Horus name was Sekhem-Ab, and that Per-Ab-Sen, the name by which he is generally known, is his Set name." These names occur side by side. Further, Budge (1902: 213) adds, this "King is commonly known by his Set name, and it seems as if in later times the Set name of a King was made into his Prenomen. A massive sepulchral stele bearing his Set name is in the British Museum."

Where are the Kamite Kings Illustration. Sealings of Perabsen in *The Earliest Royal Tombs II* by Flinders Petrie (1901).

FREDERICK MONDERSON

Where are the Kamite Kings Illustration. Plan of the Tomb of Perabsen.

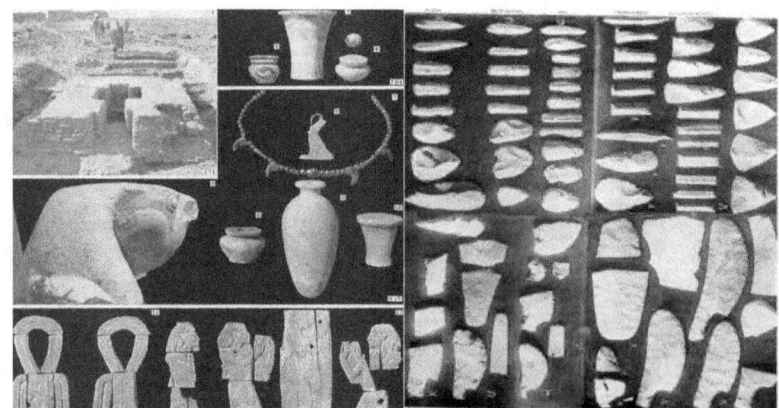

Where are the Kamite Kings Illustration. "Cats' Tomb," toilet vases and inlay of Unnefer from Abydos in *Tombs of the Courtiers and Oxyrhynkhos* by Flinders Petrie (1925); and, worked flints in Abydos' *Royal Tombs* featuring Azab (X), Mersekha (U), (Q), Perabsen (V), Khasekhemui (V), in Flinders Petrie's *Abydos* Part I (1902).

WHERE ARE THE KAMITE KINGS?

During his reign, political and religious rivalry is blamed for incendiary desecration of a number of tombs that belonged to this King's predecessors. This led Emery (1972: 97) to write: "Nearly all the royal monuments at Abydos, Neggadeh, and Sakkara have been found badly damaged by fire and it was at first thought that this was the work of the early plunderers who wished to obliterate all signs of their sacrilege. However, recent excavation at Sakkara has yielded evidence, which strongly suggests that this incendiarism was deliberately done with official sanction, and perhaps we have here the results of the warring factions seeking to destroy the afterlife of their dynastic opponents. The destruction by fire of these monuments certainly took place at an early date and we may not be in error in ascribing it to this period of obvious religious and political upheaval."

Despite these challenges that faced Sekhemib, Emery (1972: 97) has noted further, his "spirit was venerated and his cult was preserved at Memphis as well as that of his immediate successor Sendji, as late as the fourth Dynasty."

Sendji, Manetho's Sethenes, reigned forty-one years though not much is known of him. Emery (1972: 97) thinks it is "evident that apart from his long reign he was a monarch of importance and we know that his cult was preserved until a late period; indeed, a bronze statue bearing his name was made in the Twenty-Sixth Dynasty, more than 2000 years after his death." Budge notes even further that the priest Sheri (1902: 214) mentions the name of King Sent and of his successor on the door of his tomb, and slabs from it now preserved at Oxford and in the British Museum, also record his name.

Neterka, Manetho's *Chaires*, reigned 17 years and is mentioned on the Turin King List. A green steatite cylinder found at El-Kab also mentions his name.

FREDERICK MONDERSON

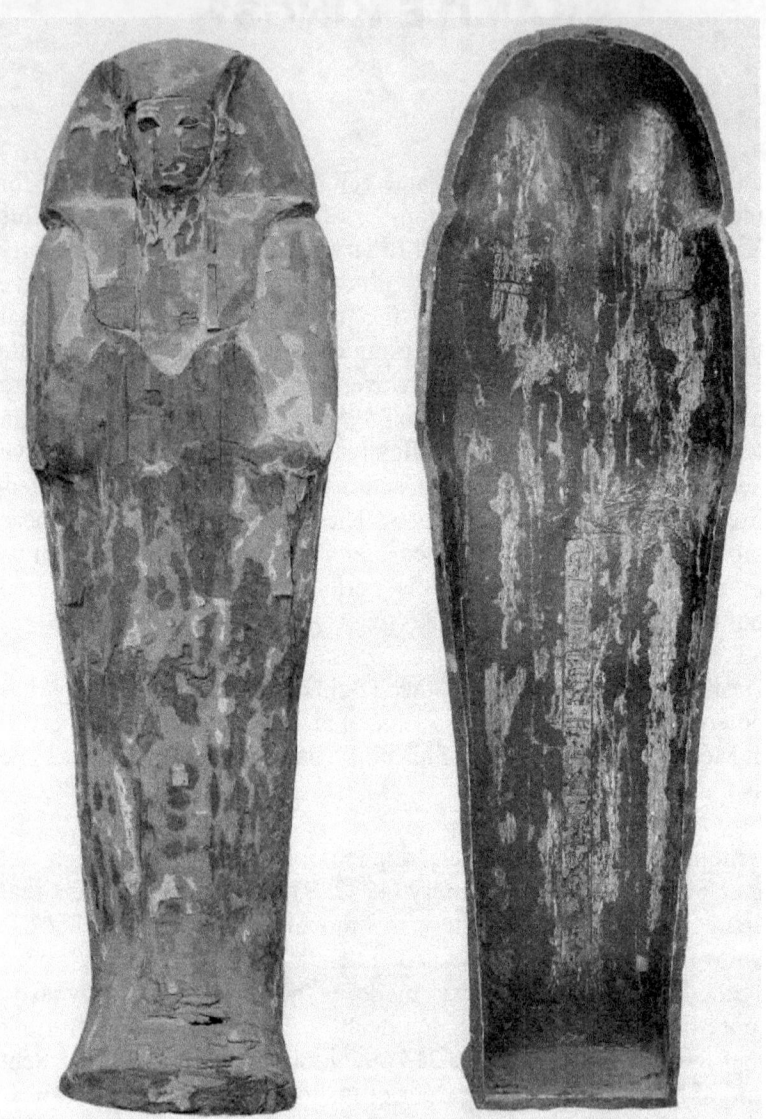

Where are the Kamite Kings Illustration. Coffin lid, in and out, of Thutmose III.

Neferkara, Manetho's *Nephercheres* reigned twenty-five years. No monuments of his reign are known. According to Emery (1972: 98) there is a legend that "during his reign the Nile flowed with honey for eleven days."

WHERE ARE THE KAMITE KINGS?

Where are the Kamite Kings Illustration. Sekhem, Perabsen sealing was found at Abydos.

Khasekhem, Manetho's *Sesochris* and Huxefa of the Sakkara and Turin King Lists was a giant at nearly 8 feet tall. His name 'Appearance of the Power' seems to imply efforts at unification. Many people believe he was also Khasekhmuwi, his successor, whose name means "Appearance of Powers." Baines and Malek (1980: 32) explains the use of these two names: "The name Kha'sekhem alludes to 'power' (*Sekhem*) which means Horus, while Kha'sekhemwy refers to two 'powers' - Horus and Seth - and is surmounted by figures of both Gods. It is accompanied by a sentence, 'the two lords are at rest in him.' The whole is therefore an announcement that the struggle is over." No tomb of his has been found at Sakkara or Abydos, though monuments have been found at Hierakonpolis, near Edfu, original capital of the "followers of Horus." Two statues, one of schist in Cairo and one of limestone in Oxford, and three stone vessels record war and conquest during his reign. Emery (172: 99) assesses these statues are of "exceptional artistic merit and they represent Kha-sekhem seated on a throne, wearing the crown of Upper Egypt and the robe usually associated with the Sed Festival."

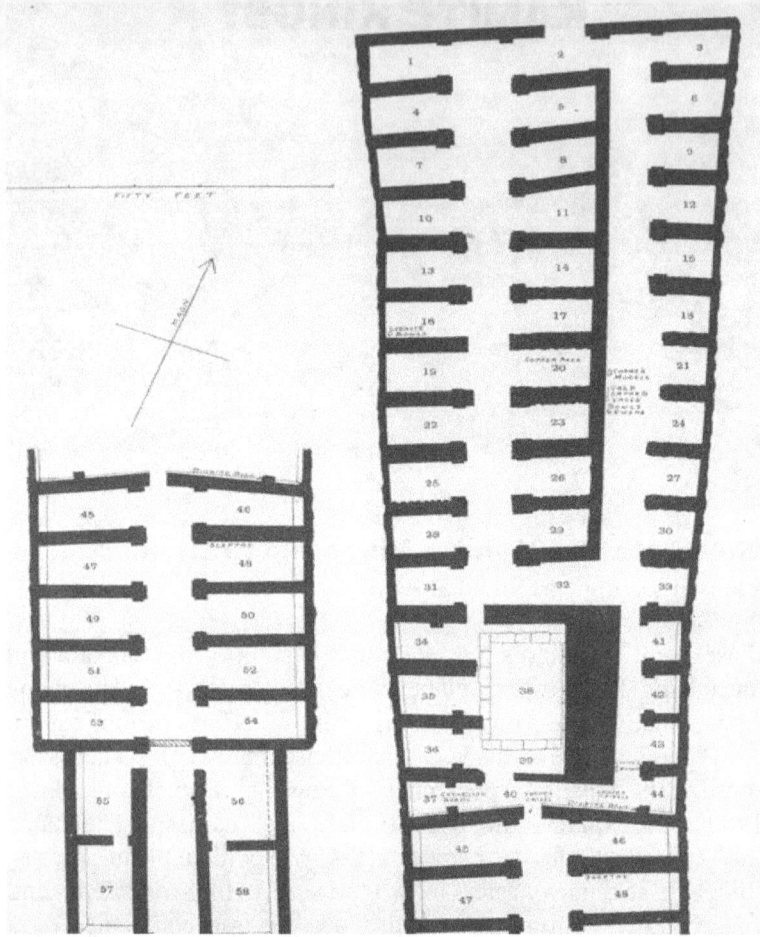

Where are the Kamite Kings Illustration. Tomb of King Khasekhemui in *The Earliest Royal Tombs I*, Flinders Petrie.

Even-more, Emery (1972: 100) indicated that on the statues: "the King is shown wearing only the White Crown of Upper Egypt and on the stone vases the hawk above his name also wears the White Crown. The impression gained from this admittedly limited evidence is that Kha-sekhem was a ruler of the Thinite family of Upper Egypt who restored the unity of the Nile valley after the religious wars between the followers of Horus and Set which had probably divided the country since the reign of Perabsen."

Inscriptions on the back, side and front base of these statues depict slain "Northern enemies" of the King. The belligerence is further

WHERE ARE THE KAMITE KINGS?

indicated by inscriptions on the three stone vessels that read, as Emery (1972: 99) notes, "'The year of fighting the northern enemy within the city of Nekheb.' The Goddess Nekhbet in vulture form holds a 'signet circle' within which is the word (rebels), while with the other claw she supports the emblem of the unity of Egypt."

Khasekhmuwi, Manetho's *Cheneres* and Zazai of the King lists, reigned for thirty years. His rule is significant in unifying the country and attests to his leadership abilities in consolidating foundations of Pharaonic rule that lasted for three thousand years.

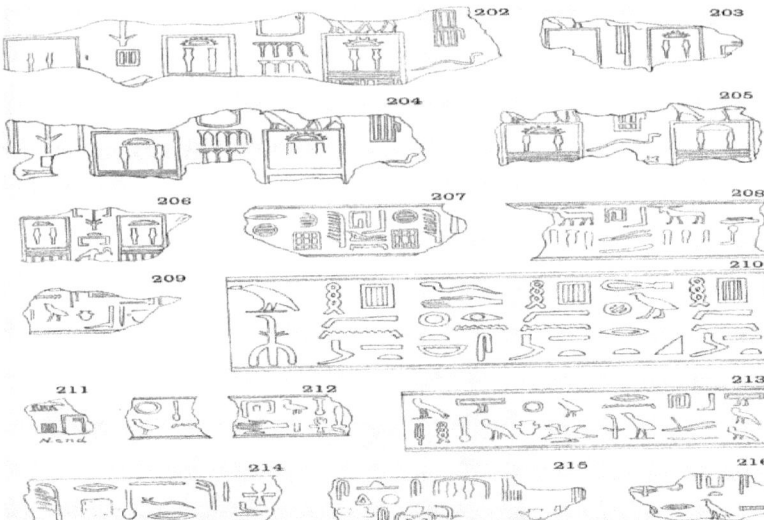

Where are the Kamite Kings Illustration. Sealings of King Khasekhemui, found at Abydos.

FREDERICK MONDERSON

Where are the Kamite Kings Photo. Beit Wali Temple of Rameses II. The King surrounded by two deities enthroned in the Sanctuary.

Where are the Kamite Kings Illustration. Sealing of King Khasekhemui, found at Abydos by Petrie.

He built a temple at Hierakonpolis that is considered transitional to Third Dynasty style of architecture. His name on jar-sealings contains both Seth and Horus emblems. Emery has argued (1972: 102) the "burial chamber" of this King, "was at one time believed to be the oldest example of stone masonry in existence, but excavation at Sakkara and Helwan has shown that building in stone

WHERE ARE THE KAMITE KINGS?

was known in the First Dynasty ...." This King's treasure trove of funerary artifacts included "stone and copper vessels, flint and copper tools, pottery, and basket-work, the King's Scepter of gold and sard was recovered from the tomb." Clay jar-sealings found at the Pyramid of Unas of the Fifth Dynasty at Sakkara, contain Hotepsekhemwy's name, a strong indication he was buried in the vicinity.

A definite expansion in the tomb's dimension is observed during the Archaic Period. The King's furniture became more elaborate in the graves. Quite probably a holdover from the pre-dynastic period, the need to provide companionship for the deceased, led to killing of persons to accompany the dead King. The reverence held for the Pharaoh led many people to choose this form of assured immortality. Meanwhile figurines or "ushabtis" were placed in the pre-dynastic burials. By this time, Emery (1972) added: "... human victims too - concubines, officials, servants, craftsmen - accompanied their royal master. At Narmer's funeral only 33 such persons are known to have been buried. But round Zer's tomb the accessory graves accommodated 275 harem ladies and 43 other members of the royal household, while a mile away 269 further familiars or courtiers were buried round a square that must have contained some monument to the same pharaoh."

Walter B. Emery's *Archaic Egypt* (Baltimore, Maryland: Penguin Books, 1931: 103-104) provided the following references to the tomb remains of Second Dynasty Kings, who were principally buried at Abydos and Sakkara.

KING'S NAME   MAJOR MONUMENTS

Hotepsekhemui	Tomb unknown, Jar-sealings from Sakkara (Barsanti, 'Fouilles autour de la Pyramidie d'Ounas', *Annales du Service des Antiquities*, vol. III, p. 182.
Ra-neb	Tomb unknown. *Tomb of Ruaben*, No. 2302 at Sakkara. (Quibell, *Archaic Mastabas*)

FREDERICK MONDERSON

Sekhem ib-Perabsen	Tomb P at Abydos. (Petrie, *Royal tombs*)
Senji	No contemporary monuments
Neterka	No contemporary monuments
Neferkara	No contemporary monuments
Kha-sekhem	Tomb unknown. Statues and stela from Hierakonpolis. (Quibell, *Hierakonpolis*)
Kha-sekhemui	Tomb V at Abydos. (Petrie, *Royal Tombs*) Temple Remains from Hieraconpolis (Quibell, *Hierakonpolis*)

The military organization that followed Narmer to conquer the north was founded on a feudal system.

With 42 Nomes in ancient Kemet/Egypt, the first was at Elephantine and the rest of 22 were in the south. The south extended to the apex of the Delta. The next 20 were in the north, from the Delta's apex to the Mediterranean. Each Nome had to supply soldiers for the national army and each had its own standard or banner to be identified in the military ranks. The symbol of each Nome was that of a plant or animal from each region.

The military was responsible for the protection of the state against internal and external threats. To this end, their equipment or weaponry included bows and arrows, spears, battle-axes and adzes. Kings carried mace or clubs and daggers. The river moved soldiers for distances before they traveled over-land on foot. The river was also significant for emerging trade patterns with distant areas to the north and south.

The art of dynastic Kemet developed from themes and conventions established in the Archaic Period that continued the pre-dynastic Badarian, Amratian and Gerzean (Naqada I and Naqada II) cultural build-up and traditions. This early explosion of cultural creativity influenced art and intellectual endeavor throughout dynastic times, and came to express social, political, economic, religious, funerary, botanical, zoological and geographic themes and dynamics. These ancient Africans pioneered sculpture in the round and sculpture in relief. Their artists were able to express ideas that depicted nature and they also created realistic human portraiture. Paintings, using Kemetic designs, decorated tombs, temples and palaces with

WHERE ARE THE KAMITE KINGS?

naturalistic serenity and showed the human or social side of man's existence. Intellectual ideas flourished in this early period.

The art of building emerged. Structures were created for civic, domestic and religious purposes. The earliest dwellings were reed huts and windbreaks. Three kinds of materials were available and pressed into service for building construction as the need and skills developed. First, reeds, rushes, papyrus and palm ribs as well as acacia and tamarisk trees were used. Second, wattle and daub gave way to mud and mud-brick. Then ancient Egyptian/African builders experimented with stone to build houses, domestic buildings, temples and tombs. This variety of materials and the daring and ingenuity of their craftsmanship set the stage for bold innovations in architecture that defied time as well as modern man, with the originality and significance of their creations.

Much controversy surrounds the origins of Kemetic script, called Hieroglyphic or sacred writing by Greeks, but whose learned priests called their writing *Medu Netcher*. Those scholars supporting Eurocentric supremacy argued the writings came from lands outside of Africa. However, both Cheikh Anta Diop (1974) and William S. Arnett (1982) see the writings beginning in Upper Kemet traceable to earlier developments in Central Africa. Yet, Winkler (1928) while recognizing these early beginnings subscribe to the view, it was foreigners from SWA who migrated to this area. Despite this, Diop's and Arnett's views are based primarily on the many ideas, words and concepts in the early language traceable to animals, plants and other nature symbols and themes found in that region of Africa.

The "painted tomb" discovered at the pre-dynastic site of Hierakonpolis, in Upper Kemet, gave the earliest clues and keys to the origins of early African writing, decorative painting and early travels on the Nile River. Evidence for early language was found scattered among inscriptions in the tombs and on early monuments, labels and jar sealings. Archaeologists also found inscriptions on stone, pottery and various objects, useful in historical reconstruction.

FREDERICK MONDERSON

Industry expanded rapidly based on the developments of crafts begun in the pre-dynastic period. The peace of the unification brought stability to the land. This in turn helped the nation to prosper in agriculture and craftsmanship. W. M. F. Petrie, "the father of modern archaeology," traced 9 types of pottery in pre-dynastic Kemet. These findings show a continuation and improvement of stone vessels in sizes, shapes and quality throughout the Archaic Period and into the Old Kingdom proper. Carpentry and boat building grew. Fish caught with nets and hooks became an important source of food but also bespeak of expanding craftsmanship. Weaving of textiles became important for clothing. The crafts that developed from these resulting industries also helped to fuel the expansion of trade.

Metalwork in gold, silver, tin, copper and bronze was improved. Gold, silver and several semi-precious stones such as turquoise, carnelian, jasper, amethyst, amber, agate and onyx were made into jewelry. Jewelry included scarabs, bracelets, pendants and girdles. Crowns, royal daggers and other paraphernalia, as well as religious objects were made of gold. Bone and ivory carvings represented animals and people.

Bone and ivory materials were used as household items. Sandals and arrow quivers were made of leather. A significant flint industry had developed. The papyrus plant in itself was also the basis of an industry. This plant helped to develop writing and assisted in methods of counting cows, sheep, goats, oxen, pots, pans, gold, grain, etc. Import and export trade flourished. Commerce involved goods, ideas and precious and semi-precious metals and stones including gold, silver, and so on. The significance of the Nile as a commercial highway underscored Kemet's rising prosperity.

Therefore, a summary of the Archaic Period or Dynasties One and Two shows a number of interesting developments among these ancient Nile Valley Africans of Kemet/Egypt. The Period lasted for nearly 500 years from about 3150 to about 2686 B.C, according to Murnane's chronology. That author has given nearly 100 years to "Dynasty 0," about 160 years for "Dynasty I" and another 304 years for "Dynasty II." Using 4240 B.C., *Nile Year* 1, as the beginning of Africa's absolute chronology, "Dynasty 0" ends at *Nile Year* 1190, "Dynasty I" at *Nile Year* 1350 and "Dynasty II" at *Nile Year* 1554.

WHERE ARE THE KAMITE KINGS?

At this time, thanks to new methods of classification of artifacts of industry, Walter Emery (1972: 206-35) has indicated pottery, stone vessels, woodwork, slate palettes, weaving, metalwork, bone and ivory carvings, stone and metal tools, jewelry, amulets, and beads, fine woodwork, carpentry, flint-work, papyrus, etc., have develop the clearest picture of the people and culture of ancient Kemet. Further, Fairservis (1962: 83) explained, "Cultures become suited to their environment and up to the limits of their individual technologies derive the maximum economic benefit from their local resources." Therefore, Africans on the Nile had already spun and weaved cloth and made cosmetics by the end of the period. They invented writing, paper, ink, and leather rolls. Their mathematics was well developed through teaching and practical uses. Standards of linear and capacity measurement were then in use. Their learned priests studied astronomy and computed time based on a twelve-month calendar. Lastly, the Archaic Period had begun to see the practice of medicine, surgery and dentistry.

REFERENCES

Arnett, W.S. *The Predynastic Origin of Egyptian Hieroglyphics.* Washington, D.C.: University Press of America, Inc., 1982.
Baines, John and J. Malek. *Atlas of Ancient Egypt.* New York: Facts on File, 1980.
ben-Jochannan, Y.A.A. *Black Man of the Nile and His Family.* New York: Alkebu-Lan Publishers, 1972.
Budge, E.A.W. *Egypt in the Neolithic and Archaic Periods.* New York: Henry Frowde, 1902.
Diop, C.A. "Africa's Contribution to World Civilization: The Exact Sciences" 69-83 in *Nile Valley Civilizations.* Edited by Ivan Van Sertima. New Jersey: *Journal of African Civilizations*, (1985) 1986.
Emery, W.A. *Archaic Egypt.* Baltimore, MD.: Penguin Books, (1961) 1972.
Fairservis, Walter A. Jr. *The Ancient Kingdoms of the Nile.* New York: New American Library, 1962.
Garstang, J. "Excavations at Reqaqnah in Upper Egypt." *Man* 1902, 50.
Griffith, F. LL. "Diospolis Parva." *Man* 1902, 8.

Iskander, Zaki. *Pharaonic Egypt.* Cairo: Arab World Printing Press, (1975) 1979.

Myers, C.S. "The Bones of Hen Nekht, an Egyptian King of the Third Dynasty." *Man* 1901, 127.

_____. "Note on the Early Dynastic Period in Egypt." *Man* 1902, 51.

Petrie, W.M.F. "Excavations at Abydos." *Man* 1902, 64.

_____. "A Cemetery of the Earliest Dynasties." *Man* 1912, 73.

_____. "The Earliest Perfect Tombs." *Man* 1913, 85.

_____. "Burials of the First Dynasty." *Man* 1922, 74.

Rogers, J.A. *World's Great Men of Color* Vol. I. New York: Macmillan Books, 1972.

Smith, W.S. *The Art and Architecture of Ancient Egypt.* New York: Penguin Books (1958) 1981.

Wilson, E. *Egyptian Literature.* New York: The Colonial Press, 1901.

Woldering, Irmgard. *The Art of Egypt: The Time of the Pharaohs.* New York: Greystone Press, (1962) 1965.

Where are the Kamite Kings Illustration. Vulture with outstretched arms holding **Ankh and Djed** pillars hovers above double **Cartouche/Shennu**, while King, above hawks smites kneeling captive.

WHERE ARE THE KAMITE KINGS?

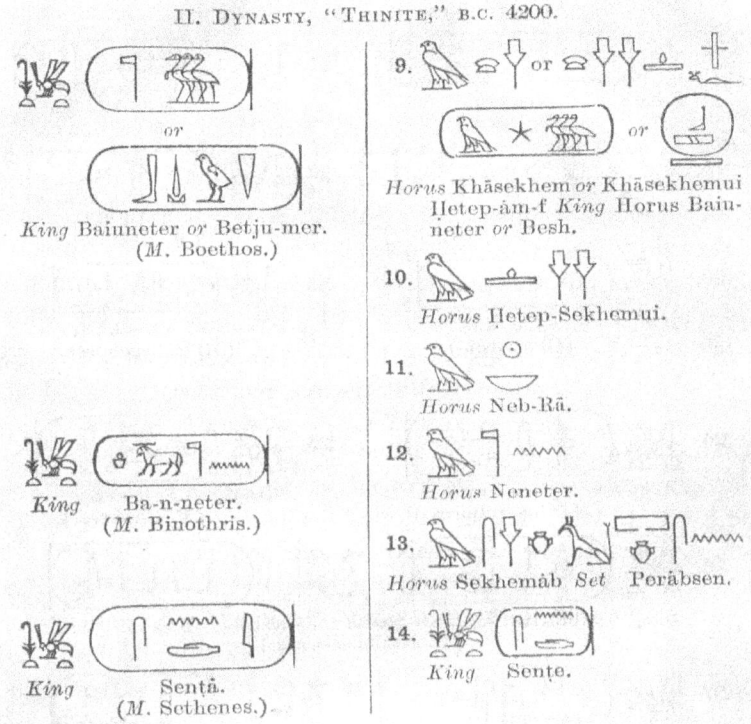

Kamite Kings Cartouche/Shennus. List of the Chief Cartouche/Shennu of the Second Dynasty from Thinis or Thinite Kings.

5. METHODOLOGY - I

The Criteria for Critical Reading is the method to help students gain more from the reading process. This problem-solving calculus was developed and taught us the scholar Dr. Leonard James, Professor, Emeritus, New York City Technical College's Department of African American Studies. Students read books, newspapers, magazines, or other sorts of literature. The Criteria helps them develop a critical methodology. They can then easily analyze what is being presented. In that case, the following elements comprise the Criteria for Critical Reading.

FREDERICK MONDERSON

Title - The title, table of contents, list of illustrations, graphs, diagrams and tables are very important. So too are the preface, pictures, bibliography, footnotes, glossary and index. They all help to give the clearest indication of what message the book contains. These provide the young scholar with much information to form a judgment about the source under study.

Author - There could be one or more authors. The biographical data can tell who the author is, and how many books he or she has written. It can also tell of his or her depth of knowledge and research of the subject and more. Further, it can also reveal to the reader a glimpse of the potential biases of the writer's position. For example, if a scholar from Mars came to write a story about earthmen, how accurate can he be? If he has not been an earthman, how objective can he be if he does not know how to be human?

Again, can a rich man write a true history of a poor man? Can a poor man write the true history of a rich man? None has experienced the other's gains, losses, glories, pains, pangs, failures and frustrations. Again, the Cowboys could not accurately write the history of the "Indians" or Native Americans, and vice versa. Again, no matter how benevolent the slave master, he cannot write the history of the slave. Neither can the slave write the history of the master. In this regard, with a few exceptions, only Africans and African-Americans can truly write the history of Africans and African-Americans.

Chronology - What is the date of the Publication? How current is the book? Does it contain new information? Is it outdated? These questions are answered by the date of the publication and the rate-rapid or slow-of providing new and accurate information.

Nature of the Source - Is the nature of the source of information primary or secondary? In ancient Egypt/ancient Kemet, the monuments - viz., temples, pyramids, tombs, civil structures, papyrus and other literary and mortuary evidence all provide primary sources of information. Books written about these monuments are secondary sources of information. Of course, reading directly from the monuments such as *Records of the Past* and Breasted's *Records of Ancient Egypt* as well as reports of archaeological excavations done within the last 150 years are primary sources considered "Ancient Records of the Ancient

WHERE ARE THE KAMITE KINGS?

Records," which should give the reader, researcher a fuller grasp of the history of Egypt. Importantly however, the primary source is always more accurate than the secondary source.

Major Thesis - What is the author's major position? Does it correct an old position? Does it support an old position? Does it support a new position? Is the old or new position right or wrong? Only through mastery of the Criteria for Critical Reading can the student 7locate and understand the author's major position and be able to critique its major and minor premises and the arguments that flow there from. In this regard, intellectual autonomy becomes an indispensable tool of analysis and synthesis.

Secondary Thesis - What positions flow from the author's major thesis? How do they support the major thesis? The secondary or minor thesis can provide additional details to support the author's major thesis.

 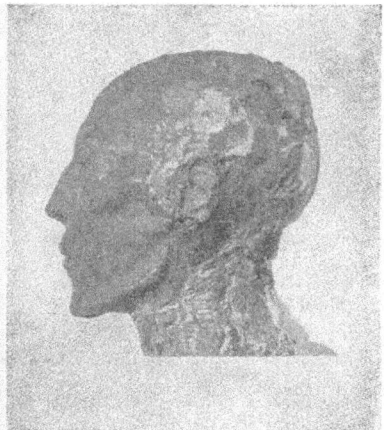

Where are the Kamite Kings Illustration. Seti I, father of Rameses II.

Catch Phrases -

FREDERICK MONDERSON

Reading Process - Every piece of material the student is asked to decode is a part of the Reading Process including newspapers, magazines, books, letters, reports, essays, instructions, brochures, diaries, wills, etc.

Where are the Kamite Kings Illustration. Coffin lid of Thutmose III, Amenhotep III and Siptah.

Develop a Critical Methodology - The critical scholar is not gullible, and, utilizing the Eight Major Social Sciences, he or she is able to weigh the evidence and make considered judgments regarding the information presented.

Table of Contents - This lists the sequential order of the book and indicates where particular segments are located, beginning on which pages.

WHERE ARE THE KAMITE KINGS?

List of Illustrations - These help the reader to further decode the message of the source, since graphic images convey even greater information.

Graphs, Diagrams and Tables - Such evidence provides additional information that enables young and aged readers to expand the ideas presented even further.

Message of the Book - Essentially, it is not simply the hard and fast factual information presented, but also the author's spoken and unspoken, or written and unwritten messages, tone and insinuation.

Biographical Data - This contains information about the author's schooling, experiences, research, writing, etc.

Depth of Knowledge of the Subject - We are able to ascertain how knowledgeable the author is about the subject, based on how many books he or she has written previously on the subject, what is the depth of research and how well the book stands up to criticism.

Potential Biases of the Writer's Position - The critical reader, having begun to read the source is pretty easily able to determine how neutral or biased the author is in presenting the information of his or her book.

FREDERICK MONDERSON

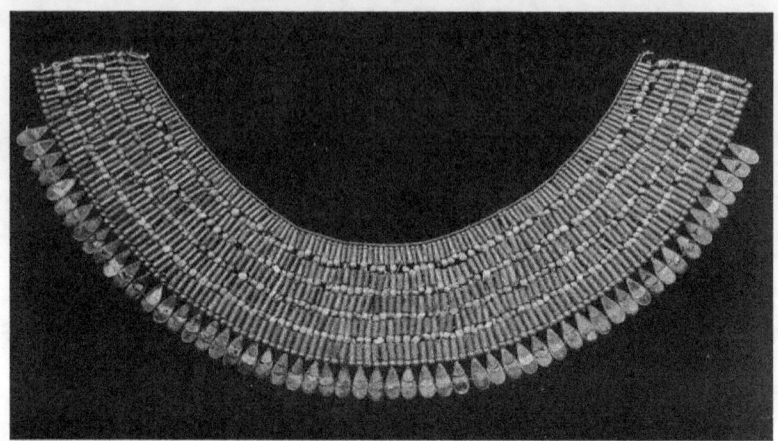

Where are the Kamite Kings Illustration. Another exquisite necklace.

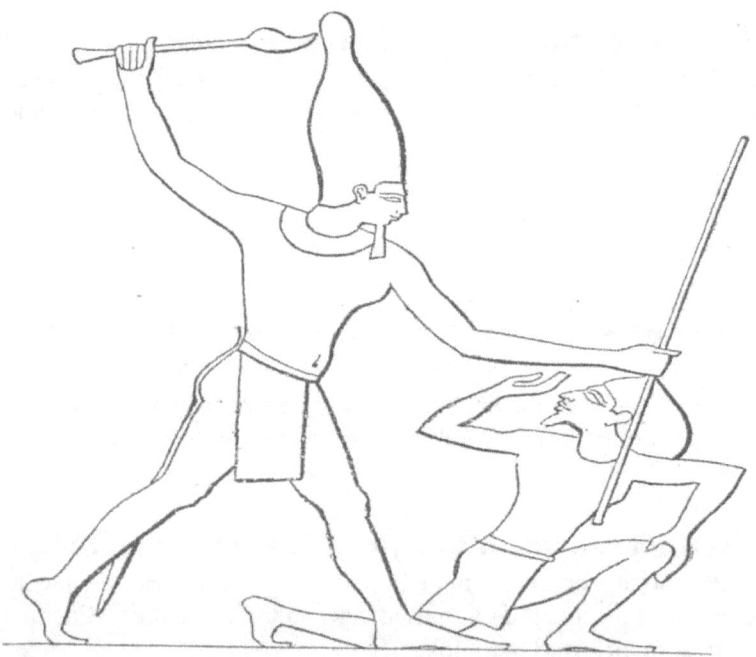

Where are the Kamite Kings Illustration. Sahure smiting a Bedouin in the Wady Maghara. Notice his belly button.

Supportive Arguments - What are the supporting arguments used by the author or authors? Does he or she use Geography, Anthropology, Archaeology, or History? How correct are his

WHERE ARE THE KAMITE KINGS?

sources? How complete are their analyses of the sources? Can their findings hold up against close examination?

School of Thought - What school of thought does the author subscribe to? Is he or she revisionist? Does he or she support the status quo? Is he iconoclastic? Is he shattering malicious and deadly stereotypic images and conceptions? Is the writer seeking to continue the old order of distortion and omission? Is he correcting the distortions and including what is omitted? These must all be understood by the young reader.

Audience - To whom is the source directed? Is it to the victim or the victimizer, or both? What is the price of the written material? What is the nature of its content? Is it too expensive? Is it too technical?

Motivation - What made the author write this piece? Is it written during some social or cultural developments? In 1857, the *Dred Scott Decision* was rendered during Slavery. In this constitutional landmark case, Chief Justice Roger Taney said essentially, "The Negro has no rights that a white man is bound to respect." In that same year, Samuel Cartwright's *Slavery and Ethnology* was published. He argued, "From time immemorial, the Nilotic monuments show the Negro as nothing but slaves in Egypt." In 1864, Dr Hunt published his *On the Negro*. "The Negro is a beast," he wrote. These works were all published during slavery and were justifying that odious system of exploitation and physical and psychological emasculation of African people in America.

FREDERICK MONDERSON

Where are the Kamite Kings Illustration. One of the earliest Egyptian paintings of the Old Kingdom, showing different kinds of geese feeding. The image is split so the two geese with their beaks to the ground should be facing each other.

On the other hand, Claude McKay's poem *If We Must Die* was written during the Harlem Renaissance, when the twentieth century lynchings and riots came at a low point for Black people in America. Yet, this author sought to socially, politically and culturally galvanize a people with his message. Also, Bobby Seale's *Seize the Time* on the Black Panthers was an outgrowth of the civil rights struggle. The motivating factors behind all these works were to influence social developments of their time.

Intent - Why did the author write this piece? Was it an attempt to continue the status quo? Was it an attack on the deadly myths, stereotypes and oppression of the time? What is hoped to be gained from the exercise?

Methodology - Does the author use *Cause and Effect* to examine and explain any social phenomenon. Does the author's explanation of any current state of affairs take into consideration the historical roots of the situation? What is the *Time-Order* frame of reference that the author uses? Does the author use yesterday's frame of reference to solve today's and tomorrow's problems? Is he consistent with the times? What form or type of *Comparison and Contrast* does the author employ in his position of analyzing the social situation? Does *Inferences* play a role in his conclusions?

Documentation - What is the nature of documentation that the author uses to support his position or positions? In 1857, when Dr.

WHERE ARE THE KAMITE KINGS?

Samuel Cartwright published his *Slavery and ethnology*, it stated, *inter alia*: "The Nilotic monuments have shown from time immemorial that Negroes were nothing but slaves in Egypt." The Quality or Quantity of his *Referents* was bare at best, non-existent at worst. Cartwright held a pseudo-scientific position without any substantive anthropological, archaeological, linguistic, historical or artistic references in support. His paper contained no primary sources. He had scant secondary sources. He was simply a defender of slavery bent on further denigrating or humiliating Africans and their descendants. His arguments, from the mantle of absolute wisdom, were fueled by arrogance and based on white supremacy.

Where are the Kamite Kings Photo. Wall mural of Nubian ladies with cones on their heads, playing musical instruments on a wall in the lobby of the now closed Oberoi Hotel at Aswan. This image no longer exists there, but it's here in this work!

On the other hand, Dr. Cheikh Anta Diop in *African Origin of Civilization: Myth or Reality?* and *Civilization or Barbarism: An Authentic Anthropology*; and Dr. Yosef ben-Jochannan in *Africa: Mother of Western Civilization, Black Man of the Nile and His Family, African Origins of the Major "Western" Religions*, and *Abu Simbel to Gizeh: A Guide Book and Manual*; as well as Dr. Ivan Van Sertima in his *Journal of African Civilization, Nile Valley Civilizations, Egypt Revisited*, and *Egypt: Child of Africa* have all demonstrated, without a doubt, that Egypt was a black culture. They have all used quantitative and qualitative primary and secondary sources. Their referents included philology, anthropology, archaeology, and relied on sophisticated dating methods and techniques, as well as other scientific disciplines in their studies. Thus, they vindicated their findings of the -black African cultural experience of the entire Nile Valley, including Egypt/Kemet.

Catch Phrases I.

Supporting Arguments - In addition to the central message of the book, what other ideas are deduced or stated to create the big picture of the message? These are considered supporting arguments.

Findings Hold Up Against Close Examination - Oftentimes statements and findings do not hold up against cross-reference or serious examination. Thus, the author must strive to remain credible in his presentation.

Supporting the Status Quo - Many times the writer's position is undertaken to justify or support some aspect of society, whether or not it may be improper.

Shattering Stereotypic Images and Distortions - The critical scholar has an obligation to attack and destroy social, religious and even educational inaccuracies and the negative fallout that flow from these.

Distortions and Omission - There is a perennial guilt of persons bent on supporting, particularly the negative status quo. As a result, they have a tendency to portray the wrong conclusions of their findings and to also leave out information they find threatening. As a result, the wrong conclusions hurt all concerned.

Price of the Written Material - If the book is too costly, then the audience to whom it is exposed is therefore restricted. This is one of the reasons why the "Paperback" edition became so crucial. That way more people were able to become familiar with the text.

Nature of its Contents - Does the written material include all the pertinent information regarding the subject matter?

WHERE ARE THE KAMITE KINGS?

Too Technical or Too Expensive - Again, not only can the book be too expensive, it can also be too technical and way above the head of the general readership. When the latter is the case, "higher scholars" are needed to interpret and then filter it to the general readership.

Social or Cultural Development - Society is replete with movements and dynamic changes and these generally create sometimes positive, sometimes negative reactions from its citizenry.

Where are the Kamite Kings Illustration. Large Old Kingdom vessel sailing on the Nile River. The size of the crew indicates size of the ship with high mast sails and oars.

Dred Scott Decision - The phenomenal 1857 Supreme Court case clearly defined the social and political status of the African-American in these United States. Though we have come a long way from this reality, there are individuals in this society whose thoughts and actions are still just as archaic and pernicious when it comes to the rights of Black people.

FREDERICK MONDERSON

Where are the Kamite Kings Illustration. The Mummy of Rameses II, and, the Mummy of Seti I, Rameses II's father. Note, the hands are crossed slightly different.

Nilotic Monuments - The evidence, primarily architectural, whether in the form of palaces, tombs, temples, and other social structures including "goods of the grave," helps us understand the Nile Valley culture of ancient Kemet. Of course, there is written documents, lots of it.

The Negro is a Beast - You could just smell the odious nature of an individual who holds to these views.

System Exploitation – This is when the grand structure of society exploits its people, as in the case of slavery in the antebellum south. Of course, in the Post-Civil War era, many of those

WHERE ARE THE KAMITE KINGS?

archaic ideas went underground and have consistently refused to die.

If We Must Die - Claude McKay felt "If We Must Die," we should also be dealing deathblows to the oppressor as this is the only way the victimizer will respect the victim.

Seize the Time - Oftentimes, groundswells of people's actions force the social order to make the necessary adjustments to level the playing field.

Black Panther - A group of revolutionary brothers and sisters, whose actions were greatly misconstrued because they had become too liberal and were easily infiltrated by those bent on their destruction. Many were killed and others thrown in prison. Their actions, however, forced the oppressor to take notice of the rising tide of disaffection across the wider spectrum of the nation.

Civil Rights Struggle - This movement became full blown in the 1950s resulting in government being forced to make significant social adjustments in the 1960s to redress problems in American society that had been festering for decades and centuries.

Deadly Myths, Stereotypes and Oppression - These help to keep the society divided and as a result, exploiters gain more ground in their nefarious actions.

Cause and Effect - One thing leading to or influencing another.

Social Phenomena - These are developments in society that have a significant impact on people, institutions and the times.

Current State of Affairs - The way things are today can constantly be compared with the past as a barometer for the future.

FREDERICK MONDERSON

To begin again, we must first define some terms to be able to understand clearly what we are about.

Culture - is anything a person can learn and teach or pass on to someone else. Here is a simple analogy. If my grandmother knew how to cook and knew a particular recipe, then taught my mother, who taught me, and I taught my daughter, and she taught her son, this is culture being transmitted. The concept can be applied across the board. The Units of Culture, therefore, are:

Language - Language is the means by which humans communicate. Language can be written or spoken. Language can also be expressed through signals and body rhythms, as well as cultural practice.

Music - Music is a universal language. It is a cultural form of expression. It is used on festive occasions - at celebrations, birthdays, parties, feasts, concerts, or in schools. Music is used at festive or sorrowful times, solemn times, death and burials. Music is also used in church and in the military. Even in the time of the Gods, music was pleasing to the spirit.

Where are the Kamite Kings Photo. View of the "Old," "New Cataract" Hotel from the Nile River at Aswan.

Art - Art in the form of painting, sculpture, ceramic, etching and sketching is man's attempt to express his aesthetic (aes-the-tic) nature. Art is also expressed in man's conception and construction

WHERE ARE THE KAMITE KINGS?

of shelter housing, architecture. Generally, in the Western World, art is hung on the wall at home, in galleries or in museums to be admired. In Africa, on the other hand, art serves a social purpose. For Africa, art is a cultural expression of the people. It is a tool. It is made to express social, religious, and political ideas and beliefs and is practiced in ceremonies. It is used at festivals, rites of passage, in the theater, and even during work. Art is generally made for a specific function or festival.

Religion - Religion is man's attempt to explain and prepare a place for himself in a believed afterlife. Religion teaches moral and spiritual values. In ancient Kemet, Ma'atian Principles, viz., order, balance, what is right, etc., undergirded religious beliefs and practices. In the African-American experience religion has been a fundamental part of the cultural dynamic. It has been a main element or cornerstone of the cultural expression. As such, the church has been and still is the strongest black institution in the African-American experience. It is attended by many and supported financially.

Taboos - Taboos are behaviors in the culture that members are prevented from performing. For example, you don't disrespect your mother, you don't marry a sister or brother, or you don't rob the church. Recently, and increasingly this latter has become a serious **problem.**

Conjugal Relationships - These have to do with the various types of marriages.

Polygamy - Poly means many; gamy means marriages. That is, two or more husbands with one wife or two or more wives with the same husband.

Polygyny - means one husband and more than one wife.

Polyandry - means one wife and more than one husband.

Monogamy - mono means one; gamy means marriage. Therefore, *Monogamy* means one husband and one wife.

Child Rearing - Child-rearing is the socialization of a young person by providing the basic necessities such as food, clothing, shelter, education, and moral values. It means providing positive role models for the child to identify with. Further it is incumbent on the guardian to know and teach the child about his or her roots or heritage; that is, his or her culture. This education is the most powerful gift the child could receive. It entails reinforcement of the most positive images for the child to identify with. These images can have life-long implications. Careful, concerned and constructive child rearing could mean the development of a positive self-image, creating self-love, and self-worth. It becomes the basis for self-achievement. Self-achievement, in turn, enables positive reinforcement so the child can grow strong, become a role model and teach his or her own children. This process needs to be repeated continuously. Grandparents can also play an important role in this process.

Catch Phrases II.

Learn, Teach and Pass On - Study more, teach those who need to know and encourage them, in turn, to share knowledge with others.

Universal Languages - Such as music, mathematics, astronomy, medicine, etc., can be taught and understood by all peoples.

Aesthetic Nature - The ability to appreciate, enjoy and help develop various aspects of culture, philosophy and other forms of secret or higher learning.

Construction of Shelter/Housing - Enabled early man in Africa to settle down from his nomadic ways, raise a family and develop his culture. After building housing early man constructed temples, palaces, tombs, settlements and fortresses.

WHERE ARE THE KAMITE KINGS?

Moral and Spiritual Values – These are the practices rooted in belief systems that help mankind become good and even better individuals? Parents play a significant role in the cultivation of these virtues along the philosophical path of Ma'atian principles and ethics.

Cultural Expression - When man's creativity enables him to make and fashion ideas and artifacts that are beautiful and lasting.

Don't Disrespect Your Mother - You could always get another wife, but there's only one mother; so, love, respect and take care of her as long as you are permitted.

Basic Necessities - Food, clothing, and shelter are so necessary for persons to move on to the more important things in life such as education, jobs, family, community service, etc.

Positive Images - Can help people improve themselves as they seek to identify with the positive examples those images portray.

Life-Long Implications - Sometimes what a person learns in a positive or even negative way can shape their life forever. That is why we must help to instill positive morals and values in the young who have so far to go.

Positive Self-Image, Self-Love, and Self-Worth - When you believe in yourself, carry yourself well, love yourself, feel you are unique and worth much, then you can feel good, do and be worth more, while becoming a shining example for others.

Role Model - One can become successful from work, learning, beliefs, actions, etc. Therefore, positive accomplishments can serve a good example that both young and old could copy and try to measure up to, while becoming examples in their own right.

Education - Education is the key to enlightenment. It is believed the philosopher Aristotle once said "The seeds of education are bitter, but the fruits are sweet." Therefore, the child must be prepared to spend his/her early years in long study to be ready for the important years ahead. Parents and guardians must try to keep the child focused. Don't leave all to the teacher! Parents must stay on top of what the child is doing and continue to encourage and praise good effort. Education is Knowledge. Knowledge is Power. Power is Freedom. Education is Freedom. To repeat, Education is not money. It is the Power and Freedom to make money!

Trade - Trade is the exchange of money or goods by one group of people for money or goods produced by another group. Trade is the surest way of bringing people together and exchanging and learning about ideas, beliefs, arts, crafts, industry, religion, medicine, and the philosophy of each other.

Government - Governments establish laws and work to uphold those same laws. Governments also protect the well-being of the people. They protect the state from the threats of external and internal enemies. Governments establish the methods and ways to set themselves up, and how to continue and change in a regulated manner. Governments should also have ways to regulate and control themselves.

Cuisine - Cuisine deals with the means to acquire food, whether by foraging, working, planting, fishing, etc. It also deals with the way people provide and prepare the foods they eat. Parties, weddings and even thanksgiving all have certain traditions of preparing and providing foods for the occasion. The ordinary person also has a way of preparing meals even if it is simple. It can mean much if one acquires and prepares it with love, thankfulness and contentment.

Apparel - Apparel is the type of clothing people wear based on the occasion, time and environment: You wear your "church clothes" to church. You don't wear a winter coat in the middle of August in 100+ degree heat. You wear and look your best to present and sell yourself.

Science - Science is the use of reason and experience to find truth. The Scientific Method involves an Aim, Hypothesis,

WHERE ARE THE KAMITE KINGS?

Observation, Experimentation, Data Collection, Evaluation, Generalization, and then a New Hypothesis. Thesis, anti-thesis, synthesis, is therefore a calculus or analytic tool of reason.

Where are the Kamite Kings Photo. Cherise Maloney of Brooklyn, New York, stands beside a sign at the Aswan Botanical Garden, sometimes called the "Kitchener Garden" housing plants from all over the world.

Technology - Technology is the making of tools and/or use of tools to build things that are useful to make life easier. Technology is nearly as old as man. After the making of tools, man secured shelter, sometimes in caves. Then he built huts, houses, and other forms of architectural structures including temples, tombs, pyramids, palaces, dwellings, fortifications and so on. He built towns and started urbanism where trade helped spawn art, learning and government administration.

Catch Phrases III.

Key to Enlightenment - The method or process by which one becomes more aware of the circumstances surrounding daily existence and preparation for the future.

FREDERICK MONDERSON

Seeds of Education - The basic preparation, social, familial, educational, moral, etc., by which one creates the foundational structures that dictate's one's path through life. This includes the early development of reading, writing and analytic skills and their consistent application in learning activities.

Fruits of Education – This is the end result of the numerous hours, years of study when one is able to apply one's self to whatever task with resultant rewards of money, prestige and power.

Long Study - Parents should take time to teach their children that "successful people are toiling through the night while their companions sleep."

Important Years Ahead - The best example is simply this. If you wish to drive from New York to California, then you must make sure your battery works well; there is a good spare in addition to good tires; there must be coolant in the engine, as well as oil; you must have gas and money to buy gas, and pay tolls, etc. Think about hotels and motels along the way, and obeying the traffic laws. Therefore, once you embark on that long journey, there should be no unscheduled stops. That's what life is all about.

Keep the Child Focused - Too many parents are allowing too many negative influences to impact on their children's early impressions. Instead, these individuals should pay more attention to their children's educational development, keep them focused, and keep them in the library.

Power and Freedom - Irrespective of what others say, Power and Freedom essentially emanate from the mind's conception. Of course, one has to develop the mind through education, study, discipline, respect for elders, respect for oneself and good judgment. Only then will our young people be able to free themselves from the morass of inadequacy, incompetence, insecurity, and an inability to dictate their path to Power and Freedom, which begins with self-respect, self-worth, and self-motivation.

Exchange of Money or Goods - Trade and barter are the most powerful of human endeavors for through this mechanism

WHERE ARE THE KAMITE KINGS?

individuals share or exchange ideas, beliefs, customs, traditions and mold their destinies.

Where are the Kamite Kings Illustration. Line drawing of Old Kingdom painting showing a river being crossed by men and cows. Interesting, the lead herdsman holds a calf of one of the cows; she shows an interest, the others do not; so, the concerned mother, follows the calf, and leads the others across the waters. Simple as this idea is, it is yet profound.

The Inter-disciplinary Approach in academic pursuit involves the use of 8 major social sciences to study man's interaction with the environment, society, institutions and other men. Utilizing these social sciences in critical study allows the scholar to grasp readily and well the fundamental tenets of sound research techniques of analysis. The hope is that these skills could be used to then teach the wonderful history of ancient Africans.

Geography - Geography is the science of the study of physical landmass and bodies of water. This includes oceans, rivers, mountains, deserts, savannahs, valleys, plains, etc. It involves any place on the earth that man sets foot on. The study can also apply to other planets particularly if their environment corresponds to earth's environment.

Archaeology - Archaeology is the science of digging up the remains of past societies. Mostly, tombs and graves provide mortuary data, which the Cairo Museum labels "Mortuary Furniture." Also, living sites provide clues to the culture. We can also add to the collection architectural remains. Together such sources supply the necessary information about the age of the society and its level of cultural attainment. This is what the archaeologist lays the groundwork for. However, archaeology, like so many other disciplines, can also overlook important parts of the culture under study. Human bias and the dynamics of the age of discovery came to inject false interpretations in evaluating the evidence about non-western culture.

Anthropology - Anthropology is the study of the physical and cultural heritage of man. For the most part this essay will be concerned about the cultural accomplishments of man. In addition, we must pay special attention to how people's cultures are interpreted by others. Therefore, unless carefully approached, this tends to result in distortion and omission about the culture under study. Africa, in general, and Kemet/Egypt in particular, has been the recipient of much study dictated by a predetermined bias.

History - History is a complete record of man. Everything that happens is history. However, only some things get told, and lots of information remains omitted. Then, it is up to scholars to do research and from a critical iconoclastic perspective, to shatter the false images that distort a people's cultural experiences and then rewrite history using a new approach that corrects distortions and includes omissions that help set the record straight.

Sociology - Sociology is the study of social relations between people and institutions that respect each other's beliefs and boundaries. It seeks to explore and understand class distinctions and social, economic and cultural exploitation. It also examines institutions, such as schools, churches, libraries, government agencies, business enterprises, etc., and what role they play in serving the interests of the society. It studies people of all ages to determine why their group acts in a set manner.

WHERE ARE THE KAMITE KINGS?

Where are the Kamite Kings Illustration. Coffin lid of Rameses I.

Political Science - Government is the science of making, interpreting, and executing the laws in support of a nation's social order. Study of government examines why some people are more equal before the law than others. How has government been used for or against its peoples' interests is another such concern. Consequently, the question then is asked whether it is money, social standing, education or connections, ideological orientation or hard work that determines a person's role and place in society.

FREDERICK MONDERSON

Economics - Economics is the science of money and wealth. It is also the ability to use what you have to get what you want. Further, it questions the origins of "seed money" or starting capital, and why some businesses succeed and others fail.

Psychology - Psychology is the science of the working of the human mind. You can't relate to or understand a person unless you know how that person's mind works. Understanding psychology gives one an edge in dealing with the complex human animal.

Distortion - Distortion is the systematic and deliberate attempt to change or twist information so that the wrong message is given and received about a people's culture. Generally, distortion may be due to a lack of sufficient information about the culture under study. Then again, cultural imperialists deliberately twist the evidence so as to incorrectly portray a particular people's history and culture.

Omission - Omission is a systematic and deliberate attempt to keep information hidden because it challenges accepted beliefs. Omission is encouraged because such missing information can redeem the downtrodden or challenge the position of the oppressor.

Together, distortion and omission about a people's culture, history, and achievements are designed to exploit those people by someone who stands to gain from such exploitation.

Cognitive Dissonance - Cognitive Dissonance is the inability to accept new information or data that threatens a person's accepted beliefs.

Iconoclastic - An iconoclast is one who shatters accepted false images, notions and beliefs about a people's culture, history and abilities.

Redemption - The redemptive or critical scholars are persons who see the need for and rewrite their history in their own images with more positive frames of reference and outlook about their culture. The redemptive or critical scholar takes an iconoclastic approach and perspective by correcting the distortions and including the omissions of African people's history and culture systematically implanted by racist Western, European and American

WHERE ARE THE KAMITE KINGS?

historiography. In so doing, the iconoclast, whether it's a he or she, does the "Lord's work," by correcting misinformation and setting the record straight.

Where are the Kamite Kings Photo. View of the Nile River and the new Movenpick hotel being built, as seen from the old Oberoi Hotel, a building that is no longer functional and so too are the mural from Oberoi's lobby and black images in the restaurant.

The redemptive scholar with an iconoclastic mandate helps free the minds of the people shackled by centuries of systematic denial of any history of a positive nature. In this respect, the following definitions may provide a better understanding of the issues.

The Interdisciplinary Approach - Utilizes the eight major social sciences to discover relevant facts for the study of African life and customs.

Man's Interaction with the Environment, Society, Institutions and other Men - Demonstrates his ability to adapt and live in different social settings showing respect and toleration for others.

Digging Up Past Societies - Allows archaeologists to dig for remains of past cultures to reconstruct the level of culture that the society had attained.

FREDERICK MONDERSON

Mortuary Data - Has to do with information provided by graves and tombs that includes mummification practices, paintings and other cultural artifacts, deposited in the sepulcher.

Levels of Cultural Accomplishment - This aspect asks 'How developed was the civilization up to that time?' The answer is found in assessing the level of civilization attained based on the cultural artifacts that have survived viz., architecture, pottery, tools, writings, etc.

Distortion and Omission - A twisting out of shape and deliberately excluding evidence of history, designed to undermine the culture of a people. So much so, people who write and control the distribution of information twisted or left out important facts.

Complete Record of Man - Includes everything known and unknown about man. History is more than what gets recorded and that is why modern research continues to unearth new facts.

Critical Iconoclastic Perspective - Allows scholars to never accept things without close examination and to intellectually attack old institutions and beliefs that are distorted, biased and incorrect. In similar manner, the thesis, antithesis, synthesis dynamic calculus is designed to continuously expand the limits of knowledge.

Beliefs and Boundaries - Include cultural practices and beliefs people have accepted, live by and cherish. They are guarded by traditions with built-in practices that give warnings and offer protection, when such beliefs and boundaries are threatened.

Class Distinction - When people's lifestyles, beliefs and practices are regulated by their education, jobs, contacts, wealth, etc. Oftentimes, this is used for negative purposes.

Threaten One's Accepted Beliefs - When new information is introduced that points out how wrong the past has been, this is called *Cognitive Dissonance*, because people generally reject any new approach that threatens their believed safe views.

WHERE ARE THE KAMITE KINGS?

Where are the Kamite Kings Photo. "Unfinished Obelisk" at Aswan. Evidence remains of how these "needles" were quarried before being separated from the "mother rock." This was Queen Hatshepsut's Obelisk that developed a crack and was abandoned. Her Cartouche/Shennu is there in this place.

Social, Economic and Cultural Exploitation - When the total of all a people's accomplishments is in turn stolen by others who often rape the exploited culture, this is the result.

More Equal Before the Law - Some people, because of their wealth, contributions, family connection, or social standing in society, receive better treatment by public servants and law enforcement personnel.

Redeem the Down Trodden - Work to help those at the bottom level of society to accomplish things to help them see their past and future in a more positive light.

Challenge the Position of the Oppressor - By being armed with facts based on research, and new approaches that

FREDERICK MONDERSON

question accepted beliefs, we are then able to challenge the oppressor.

Ability to Accept New Information - Can be difficult because people are generally set in the ways of their culture and past experiences.

Redemptive or Critical Scholars - Work to correct distortions and omissions of history, by setting the record straight, or by accepting and demonstrating an iconoclastic attitude and shattering false images in their work of interpreting history.

More Positive Frame of Reference and Outlook - Armed with facts, skills, and incentives that shape one's world view from a more positive perspective, the new scholar who has researched his subject can now teach and educate others and thereby create a better understanding of history.

Correcting the Distortion - Seeks to use new information to attack and change false beliefs and practices.

Including the Omissions - Realizing how distorted the past has been presented, when new information is introduced that has an impact on beliefs and practices, this creates a clearer view of historical developments.

Where are the Kamite Kings Photo. Erik Monderson stands on steps at Imhotep Museum, Sakkara, in 2018.

WHERE ARE THE KAMITE KINGS?

6. METHODOLOGY II

The soundest methodology or cognitive structure needed to aid African Historical/historiographic Reconstruction is comprised of a Criteria for Critical Reading, a Methodological Plan, a Systematic Conceptual Scheme or framework of analysis, as well as a Historical Perspective that is iconoclastic. As such, the proper study of history should include an Inter-disciplinary approach that utilizes 8 major social sciences, viz., Geography, Archaeology, Anthropology, History, Sociology, Political Science, Economics, and Psychology. Mastering this fundamental Social Science tool enables the reader to acquire a more complete grasp of human events, more easily, through critical reasoning in examination of the written, oral and artifactual evidence. Methodology thus becomes bedrock in sustaining the inquiry necessary to support the reconstruction of African history.

The use of the Syllogism, a logical tool of analysis, with its congruence in the major and minor premises and their inherent conclusion, is important in creating the methodological framework essential in acquiring intellectual autonomy.

The 8 major social sciences can thus be utilized in an interdisciplinary approach that examines the **Records** (Primary and Secondary Sources), to create **Critical Comparative Historical Analyses** into the **Cognitive or Effective Areas of Learning**. This approach forces **Critical Relearning** of any given phenomenon to generate a **New Hypothesis**. The second **Critical Comparative Historical Analysis** forces a **Reinterpretation and New Generalization**. So, we utilize **Inductive** rather than **Deductive** reasoning in the study of African history to arrive at irrefutable truth.

Now, the **Methodological Plan of Historical Evolution** lets critical scholars see contrary to racist western scholarship, viz., Hegel, Cartwright, Dr. Hunt, et. al., Africa has been an active participant in the undulative process of human experience, having both nadir and zenith, high and low points, in cultural evolution as opposed to being confined to the former, and remaining in Conrad's "darkness."

We can see the **Causes Stimuli** with their internal and external factors and antecedent and precipitate ingredients, acting positively and negatively as Africa boldly played its quintessential role in advancing the pageantry of human experience. These, *causes stimuli* then create the engines of human progress along the continuity of historical evolution.

Where are the Kamite Kings Illustration. Old photograph of the unexcavated Step-Pyramid at Sakkara, built by Imhotep for Pharaoh Zoser of the Third Dynasty.

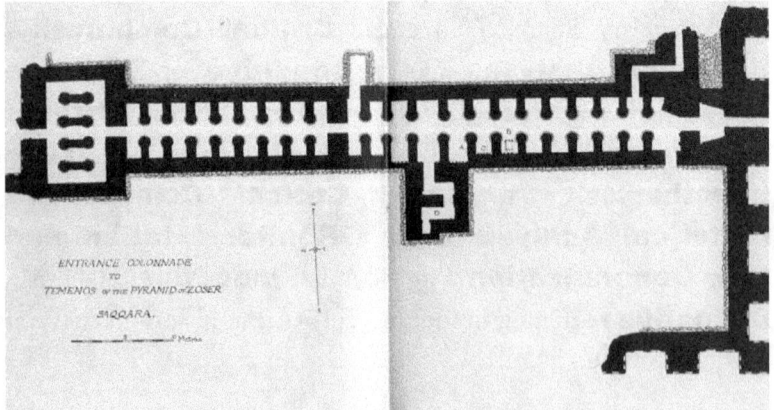

Where are the Kamite Kings Illustration. Plan of the Entrance Colonnade to the Temenos of Zoser's Pyramid at Sakkara.

WHERE ARE THE KAMITE KINGS?

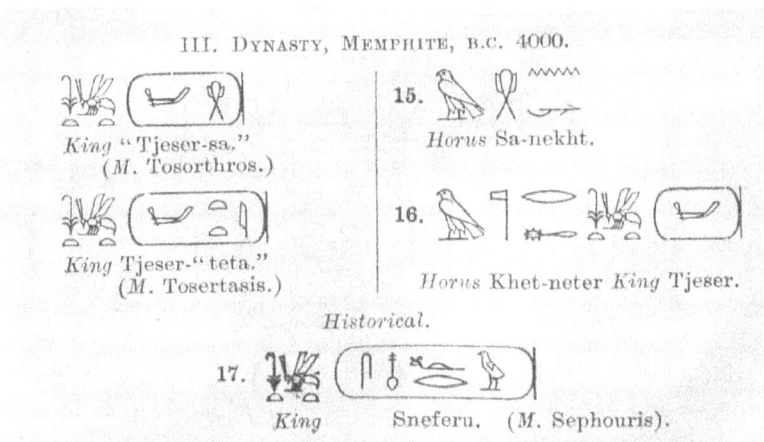

Kamite Kings Cartouche/Shennu. Kings of the Third Dynasty from Memphis.

7. THE OLD KINGDOM

The Old Kingdom is a period that has a particular relevance for the history of the Nile Valley and ancient Africa. It was a time of bold leadership as God-given bounty from the always predictable and most often favorable Nile River, that encouraged and contributed to the dynamics of human progress. The genius of ancient African man throughout this period is seen as he experimented and created fundamental systems of thought and institutions that have, for time immemorial, influenced how man-himself relates to elements, humanity and his or her God or Gods.

The Old Kingdom lasted from about *Nile Year* 1554-2067 (Murnane 2686-2181 B.C.) and included the Third thru Sixth Dynasties. This *Pyramid Age* was the result of the challenge of architectural innovation, religious syncretism, strong centralized government and systematic exploitation of the Nile for food, trade, transportation, recreation and military and funerary purposes. The pyramids that were built primarily of stone and the high technology, transportation of stone and coordination of such tremendous building efforts and bureaucratic organization attest to creativity and patience on the part of ancient Kamite/Egyptian/African Kings of Egypt and their architects and administrators, and all involved subjects. These builders of monumental structures had visions of unending permanence and resulting immortality that enabled their works of art to defy time and man.

King Narmer established the monarchy and feudal relationships at the time of Unification. The fundamental social norms and practices he initiated remained in effect throughout dynastic times. In the Old Kingdom, the institution of the Priesthood justified the divine nature of the Kingship. In return, as a result of the bounty of largesse showered upon them, this body's powers grew and ensuing conflicts pitted strong pharaohs against the various "noble houses" favoring the deities of their choice. Essentially, the principal deities were resident, as such, Ra at Heliopolis, Ptah at Memphis, Osiris at Abydos and later Amen (Amen-Ra) at Karnak and Luxor. In time and with support of particular Kings, the priesthood's theologians fused these deities to provide religious harmony in the state. Also, the role of the nobles and nomarchs, or rulers of the Nomes, in supporting the system of government, became further defined.

As social institutions and their functions expanded, a Grand Vizier was appointed administrative ruler of the country. At a later time, there would be Viziers of Upper and Lower Kemet/Egypt. Centralized government remained in effect until the end of the Sixth Dynasty. Social classes continued to grow from the time of Unification in the Archaic Period. Their power increased and peaked then exploded at the end of the Sixth Dynasty. Position in the social order was based on birth, education, employment, achievement and loyalty. O'Connor, *et al* (1989: 81) best characterized ancient Kemetic society as falling into "three groups." These were: "literate men wielding authority derived from the King, those subordinate to them (doorkeepers, soldiers, quarrymen, and so on), and the illiterate peasantry. Titles essentially put a man on the right side of society, the one of privilege and authority, something of which literary compositions (especially the Satire of the Trades) provides self-conscious expression."

Employment with the government was at central, regional and local levels. Agriculture employed a significant proportion of the population. O'Connor (1989: 82) again noted: "The agricultural

WHERE ARE THE KAMITE KINGS?

resources of Egypt seem to have been divided amongst three classes of estate: owned directly by the crown; belonging to pious foundations whose relationship to the crown was a subtle one; in the hands of private individuals and liable to taxation."

The **Palermo Stone** has provided accounts, according to O'Connor (1989: 82) of "regnal year" counts regarding taxation, "on the basis of 'canals, lakes, wells, water-bags and trees on an estate.'"

When Memphis ruled supreme, Ptah and that area received the greatest largesse from the state. Military service or a high position in this religious order became a prized social status position in the Old Kingdom. Pepi II is the final significant ruler of this period. He ruled for 94 years. This duration enabled competing and emboldened nobles to enhance their power at the state's expense. At his demise, with the absence of strong centralized leadership, the nation was plunged into anarchy and disorder. Suddenly, all that had endured for the millennia after Unification crumbled.

Architecture is the most predominant feature of the Old Kingdom. It involved a search for more permanent materials such as wood and mud brick that replaced lashed bundles of papyrus stalks, rush mat-wor, palm thatch and wattle and daub approaches. Bricks were made from Nile mud. In this evolution of ancient Kamite/Egyptian/African building practices, we can identify at least five types or social orders of architecture. These are royal structures in the form of palaces and pyramids; mastabas and private residences of the nobles; religious property as temples; civic structures and, domestic dwellings of other members of the society. Later, as the society became more militaristic and imperialist, there were added military fortifications.

Stone was introduced for parts of the house subjected to hard wear as lintels, thresholds and doorposts. Later houses and other dwellings were built entirely of stone. The pyramids, temples, palaces, and mastaba tombs were all built of stone and spawned a number of technical fields of craftsmanship. Equally too, some palaces and other buildings were also built of brick. These structures served as the first canvasses upon which artists reproduced nature in its many and brilliant manifestations. The pyramids were built 4500 years before the age of Cecil B. De Mills' *Ten Commandments* classic of distortion. After all, the movie was made in Hollywood and principally filmed in the Arizona desert, with some clips probably shot in Egypt.

The Third Dynasty ventured the state along the pathway of good government, witnessed the introduction of sun worship in the form of Re at Heliopolis, as well as architectural experimentation. Importantly, it is fitting that the dynasty furnished the names of Zoser and Imhotep, held in the highest esteem throughout dynastic times. Their visionary endeavors challenged and elicited exemplary pursuits of outstanding noble African men, whose women stood with them, as they raised their Nile Valley state to its first "golden age." Murray (1949: 14) believed Zoser, "a very remarkable man that his reputation for learning and his love for literature should have remained in the memory of his people for more than three thousand years." Imhotep's name has been and is a household word even today, having built the Step-Pyramid for his Pharaoh, Zoser, and later deified as the Kemetic/Egyptian God of medicine, during Persian and later Greek rule.

Crafts began to experiment with nature themes of Gods, seasons, flora and fauna. In addition, social and recreational motifs included fowling birds in the marshes, hunting birds in the orchards and fishing with harpoons.

Where are the Kamite Kings Illustration. Bedouins at the base of the Meidum Pyramid that is attributed to Snefru.

WHERE ARE THE KAMITE KINGS?

In the First Dynasty, we saw the *Register* as an art motif bring order into social and ethnographic representations. In the Third Dynasty, the *panel* became another important artistic innovation. We first see it on the walls of Zoser's Step-Pyramid, then later wooden panels such as the excellent work of Hesire, the scribe. Shallow and high raised, as well as sunken relief, were introduced in this Third Dynasty. Interestingly, sunken relief decorated architraves and exposed places where the sun shined and raised relief decorated those areas not exposed to the sun.

The first King of the Third Dynasty, **Sa-Nekht**, Manetho's *Necherophes*, Neb-ka-ra of the *Tablet of Abydos* is assigned 18 years, 1554-1527 *Nile Year* (2686-2668 B.C.). Not much is known of him. His name comes to us from Garstang's find at Bet Khallaf and also on a fragment No. 69 in the British Museum.

The next King and most famous of this dynasty is the Horus Neterkhet, whose name means "the powerful." He is Manetho's *Tosorthus*, son of Queen Ne-Maat-Hap, wife of Kha-Sekhemwi. This family connection is interesting, for the second dynasty King's lineage is continued here. However, because of the fame of Zoser, the dynasty's beginning is generally attributed to him. He reigned *Nile Year* 1572-1591 (2668-2649). The *Horus* name Neterkhet is given on a piece of the tomb preserved at the Berlin Museum and Budge tells us, M. Benedite copied Neterkhet's Horus name in the "Wady Maghara."

Zoser is the next King of this dynasty. His royal titles were as follows:

Horus	Neter-Kha
Two Ladies	Neter Kha
Golden Horus	Tcheser
Suten Bat	Tcheser
Son of Ra	Zoser

Zoser's *Suten Bat* name is given on the *Tablet of Abydos* as No. 16 and on the *Tablet of Sakkara*. In 1899, the now famous Wilbour, whose collection forms the basis of the library at the Brooklyn Museum, discovered the famous "Famine Stele" on the Island of Sahel at Aswan. This "document" contains the King's *Two Ladies* name that comes before his *Golden Horus* ahead of the Cartouche/Shennu *or Shennu* Tcheser. He is also known from his Pyramid at Sakkara and jar sealing at Bet Khallaf. The *Westcar Papyrus* mentions him and his name is on an ivory fragment from Abydos now in the British Museum.

Where are the Kamite Kings Photo. Yellow and ready to eat dates.

Where are the Kamite Kings Photo. Talk of "Low hanging fruit!"

WHERE ARE THE KAMITE KINGS?

Where are the Kamite Kings Illustration. Seated statue of King Zoser; Boundary Stela of the princesses Intkaes and Hetephernebti; and Imitation of wooden fence separating chapels.

Where are the Kamite Kings Illustration. Sealings from the Tomb of Neter-Khet, Zoser at Bet Khallaf in *Mahasna and Bet Khallaf* by John Garstang with a chapter by Kurt Sethe (1903).

FREDERICK MONDERSON

Zoser, a powerful black African was fortunate to have Imhotep, an equally great black, as his vizier, architect, friend and consultant. Mu'Min (*The Secret Waters of the Great Pyramid*, 1988: 72), in a powerful work, provides an interesting dialogue between these two great African Kings of Kemet/Egypt. The setting for their conversation, during the Third Dynasty, is the King's bedroom. Having just awakened from a dream, his eyes stared towards the ceiling.

Imhotep: "What have you seen, my Lord?"
Tcheser: "I don't like this one, my friend."
Imhotep: "Go on. Describe the scene to me."

Tcheser: "I see a ship. On this ship is a black pig being whipped by a white monkey. The ship is headed into the sunset. Next, Horus stands atop a flight of stairs with the Scales of Ma'at on his shoulder. He is facing the Osiris on the Judgment Seat."

Mu'Min's interpretation of this dream, as seen by Imhotep the world's first multi-genius and seer, is meant to say African people should begin unrelenting pursuit of intellectual efforts that would blaze a trail to advance progress and civilization. Dr. Leonard James characterized the skill as "Intellectual Autonomy."

Additionally, Mu'Min's dedication (1988: ii) is here offered to the great black constellations of moral and intellectual integrity, those 'keepers of the tradition' of the ancestors, the present and future. For, like Mu'Min has said, his and equally this work are both:

Dedicated to the Seeds of the New Era:

> May you Come Forth by Day
> From the darkness of Night,
>
> May you Reclaim your Heart
> And Regain your Sight,
>
> May you Strengthen your Limbs
> And Walk Upright;

WHERE ARE THE KAMITE KINGS?

May you Open your Mouth
And Uphold what is Right,

May you Remember your Name
And Learn how to Fight.

Where are the Kamite Kings Photo. Erik Monderson on the "Tombs of the Nobles" highland with the Nile and Kitchener Island at his rear.

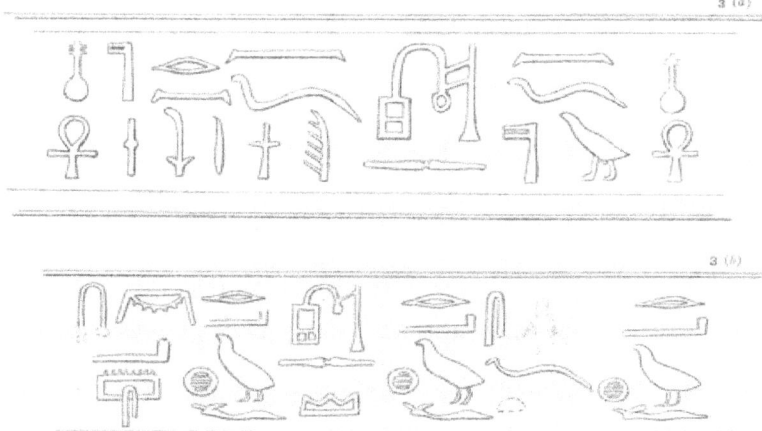

Where are the Kamite Kings Illustration. More sealings from Tomb of Neter-Khet, Zoser at Bet Khallaf in *Mahasna and Bet Khallaf*, John Garstang with a chapter by Kurt Sethe (1903).

FREDERICK MONDERSON

Where are the Kamite Kings Illustration. Tomb of Seker-Kha-Bau, IIIrd Dynasty from Sakkara.

Now, in the7 heyday of the second decade after the Napoleon expedition's discovery of the Rosetta Stone and Champollion's decipherment of Hieroglyphics in 1822, European men of diverse integrity and intent, converged on and began traversing the land of ancient Kemet, now Egypt, in North-East Africa. These individuals unleashed unrelenting efforts to collect ancient Kemetic artifacts "by any means necessary," as Malcolm X coined the phrase!

Circus Strongman Belzoni especially and Drovetti, Salt, and Burckhardt, figured significantly in plunder, acquisition, and exhibition, fueling curiosity and fascination in Europe with the ancient African culture newly discovered through architecture and linguistics. The modern western mind-set, heirs to a legacy of African enslavement, dehumanization, degradation and destruction, came to reflect a distorted view of this aspect of history. Or, as the Afrocentrists would say, in the European-African interaction following Columbus' discovery of the "new world," Africans were

WHERE ARE THE KAMITE KINGS?

victimized by a process of detachment, isolation, cultural de-centering and must now be located, reversed and "centered."

Where are the Kamite Kings Illustration. Limestone seated figures of Kha-em-Uast and his wife, 19th Dynasty.

Where are the Kamite Kings Photo. Erik Monderson strikes a pose among the ruins at **Sakkara**, **Home of the Step-Pyramid.**

FREDERICK MONDERSON

Where are the Kamite Kings Illustration. Coffin lids of Rameses I (left) and Seti I (right), 19th Dynasty.

In the post-Napoleonic age of supremacist Eurocentric hegemony, the Prussian General Minutoli conducted excavations at Zoser's Step-Pyramid at Sakkara beginning in 1819. As a reminder, this was the *Age of Metternich*, crafted by the Chief Minister of Austria

WHERE ARE THE KAMITE KINGS?

and representatives of Britain, Russia and Prussia. Their reaction followed Napoleon's demise. Autocratic governments of Europe under Metternich, Frederick William III and Czar Alexander I then orchestrated an attempt to turn back the clock of social progress in Europe that followed the French Revolution. Thus, it is easy to link the climate with the school of thought transforming the "ancient model" into the "modern model" where the systematic denial of a purposeful African role in ancient Kemet was hatched, nurtured and indiscriminately perpetuated. Hegel, a principal in this intellectual "crime against humanity," believed "Africa is not a part of history!" Some believe Hegel was confused and did not know African history! Later, another racist and biased but well-respected Emeritus Professor of History at Oxford University, G. Trevor-Roper also wrote "There is no history of Africa, only a history of Europeans in Africa." Now, here is a respected "Oxford Don" whose argument reinforced the Hamitic and Semitic syndrome as applied to ancient African/Kemetic history. It is the same statement and intent! Supremacist European academic racism that in most respects is now institutionalized. Buttressed by stolen intellectual knowledge. Hence, this mindset that blanketed Europe could not grant Africans a role in Egypt.

Indigenous Africans, at home and abroad, according to the racist boast, are incapable of initiating aspects of culture as was created along the Nile. In sports, the same line of argument was postulated by Morgan Worthy who mirrored the works of contemporary racists William Shockley and Christopher Jenks, when he presented his scientific paper on "The Eyes Have It." Claiming in the sport of football, there are self-paced and reactive tasks, Worthy used quarterback Joe Namath, as the initiator of self-paced tasks. He equates him with Pete Rose, the baseball legend, since both have blue eyes. The reactive tasks, he argued, were performed by blacks mainly who catch the pass initiated by the game's brain thrust, the quarterback. This way Worthy was able to affirm the inability of the black quarterback to win the super-bowl. Well, Williams put that myth to rest, and now we see more blacks at this important position, even black coaches winning the "big one." Nevertheless, it's the same wolf in different clothing. If you are black, it is always different. You have to do more and get less credit.

FREDERICK MONDERSON

To refocus! Seeking to immortalize and perpetuate the memory of his God-King Zoser, Imhotep innovated in architecture through conventions of stone, mastered in building practice using clay, brick and wood. This Step-Pyramid construction is a testimonial to ingenuity of early African building practice that created the world's first and still extant monumental structures.

Where are the Kamite Kings Illustration. Sphinx of Ghizeh covered in sand with the Stele of Thutmose IV between its paws. In rear, Pyramid of Khafre (right), that of Menkaure (left), and tip of a queen's pyramid to the far left. Bedouins are on the paws with camels indicating how high the desert had encroached on the monument.

On one of my early visits to Kemet, along with a companion, I actually crossed the barrier and touched the Step-Pyramid. We both offered silent prayers in appreciation and reverence for this great Kemetic/Egyptian/African monumental achievement, purely a bold innovation that created latitude for architectural experimentation and clearly has withstood the ravages of time and man.

Some interesting dimensions about the Step-Pyramid at Sakkara were supplied by Budge (1902: 219) who wrote: "The steps of the pyramid are six in number, and are about 38, 36, 34 1/2, 32, 31, and 29 1/2 feet in height; the width of each step is from six to seven feet. The lengths of the sides at the base are: north and south, 352 feet; east and west, 396 feet; and the actual height is about 197 feet. In shape this pyramid is oblong, and its sides do not exactly face the cardinal points. The arrangement of the chambers inside the pyramid is quite peculiar to itself, and the remains of the walls,

WHERE ARE THE KAMITE KINGS?

doors, of some of the chambers prove that they must have formed fine examples of the art and skill of the decorator of funerary buildings."

Where are the Kamite Kings Photo. Double Temple of Kom Ombo. Erik Monderson stands in the Peristyle Court before the twin temple's entrance. Notice the columns' varied capitals.

With all the theological, philosophical and technical implications of this structure, it turned out to be a "cenotaph" similar to those of the Thinite Period. This view is reinforced by the fact of Garstang's discovery of a tomb identified as Zoser's at Beit Khallaf. This discovery, reported in *American Journal of Archaeology* VI (1902: 58) states as follows: "A secret stairway revealed itself, and soon the name of Neter Kha, impressed upon the seal of a wine jar, made clear the importance of the discovery. This name was already known as that of the builder of the famous Step-Pyramid at Sakkara, the oldest of those great monuments of early Egypt. From an adjoining mastaba, built in imitation of the Step-Pyramid came a name new to history, Hen Khet, being the King apparently who succeeded the former. In the site around were large mastabas of the servants of these Kings; the plans of their tombs at once supplied the missing link with those of the earlier times. Meanwhile the excavation of the great tomb showed the stairway to descend under an arch - the earliest known - steeply into the sand, and to be protected at intervals, portcullis-wise, by massive doors of stone. Eventually at a depth of ninety feet from the surface of the mastaba, were found eighteen underground chambers, disturbed and plundered, yet filled with relics."

Their contents, wrote Budge (1902: 219) included "bowls and dishes of diorite, alabaster, porphyry, etc., copper implements, worked flints, alabaster tables for offerings, etc."

John Garstang conducted excavations at Reqaqnah in Upper Kemet, not far from Bet Khallaf, site of Zoser's tomb. At this location, according to John Garstang (1902: 50) an undisturbed portion of the site: "Provided a series and sequence in types of private burials belonging, seemingly, to the end of the Third and the beginning of the Fourth Dynasties. The date of the later tombs is fixed by two dated objects, a glazed cylinder seal of Khafra (*neteru mer*) and a stone bowl inscribed with the name of Snefru (*suten biti*)."

Where are the Kamite Kings Illustration. From the desert, Great Pyramid of Khufu with outer casing completely removed to provide stone for building construction after the Arab conquest of Egypt by 640 A.D. The "Boat Museum" is not yet built!

This archaeologist also found some tombs that were even earlier than those Kings. As a result, Garstang (1902: 50) noticed: "One feature is common to all the tombs: they are enclosed by a four-walled mastaba, in the east face of which were one or two recessed panels. In some cases, a rectangular enclosure was marked off with bricks, within which offering-vessels were found; in other cases, the recess was more probably architectural."

WHERE ARE THE KAMITE KINGS?

"In the Third Dynasty tombs the outer mastaba was an enclosing wall merely. Within a grave at no greater depth covered with a roof built like an untrimmed false arch. Similar dated tombs have been observed at El Amrah, at El Kab, and at Naga-ed-der; their range seems to have been the first three dynasties. In this site they were in all cases but one found surrounded by the wall with two paneled recesses on the east; in this exceptional case the burial was in the corner of a wide, square pit, two meters deep. The roof was supported partly on the principle of cantilever, with compensating weight of masonry superimposed; it was also supported by a horizontal friction, carried by the placing of each stretcher above the joint of the two below, the whole resting against a wall temporary or permanent at one end and so built upon a slope, a method of construction still familiar to the natives of Nubia and the vicinity of Assuan. The burial had only one permanent feature: its head was always to the north. But the face might be east or west, the position partly or fully contracted, or almost extended. In burial 72 the head rested upon a wooden headrest with fluted column. In some cases, a pit was found within - more commonly outside - the closed door."

Where are the Kamite Kings Illustration. Camel Riders before the Great Pyramids as seen from the desert with: Menkaure (left), Khafre (center) and Khufu (right). Smaller pyramid in the foreground is thought to be for pharaoh's female relatives.

FREDERICK MONDERSON

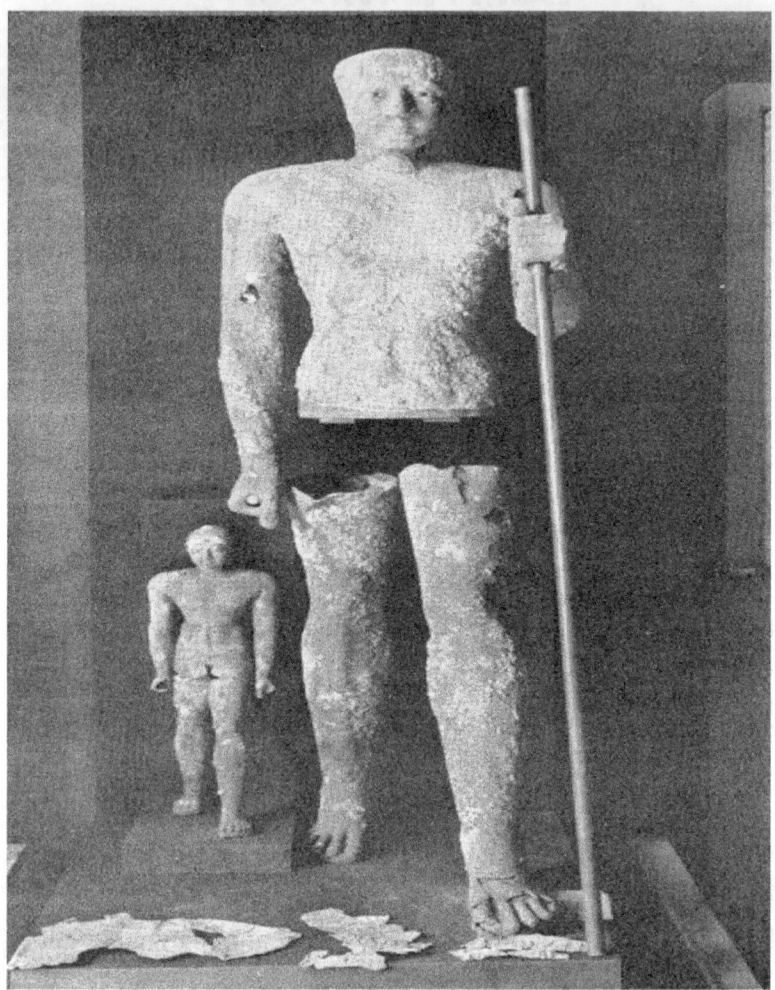

Where are the Kamite Kings Illustration. King Pepi I and his son Mentu-Em-Sa-F in beaten copper, discovered by Quibell at Hierakonpolis in *Hierakonpolis I* (1902).

"In the early tombs of the Fourth Dynasty the whole mastaba was solid, save for the shaft of a square pit descending in the center. This was found commonly three to five meters deep, with a small recess on the south side at the bottom. The burial was generally fully contracted, head north, face east, or head west and face north, and was accompanied by a few pots. In one case (63) a recess was in the north, and contained a deposit of stone vases and table; but in this instance the burial - partly contracted - lay in the pit itself."

WHERE ARE THE KAMITE KINGS?

"The slightly later series of the Fourth Dynasty also differed only slightly in detail; the retaining wall enclosed a larger area, and some space filled with rubbish intervened between it and the walls of the shaft. Some of the pits, tombs were, much deeper, reaching so far as seven, eight, and even nine meters. There is another class of burial of some interest; that which is covered by a large pottery bowl or *majur*. Some instances observed at El Kab by Quibell were attributable to the Fifth Dynasty .... The burial is always fully contracted with head generally north-east .... Two tombs (with paneled mastaba walls) were found built between tombs of the Third and early Fourth Dynasty; and another case was observed in the substratum of a large mastaba probably not later than the Fifth Dynasty. It thus seems that these *majur* burials may here be dated to the Fourth and Fifth Dynasties."

"This expedition was arranged for by Mr. F. Hilton Price, the funds being subscribed at his invitation by Mr. W. MacGregor, Mr. Martyn Kennard, Mr. R. Brocklebank, and Mr. Arthur J. Evans (for the Ashmolean Museum). Its object was to look for early tombs in the vicinity of the royal tombs of the Third Dynasty discovered last year at Bet Khallaf ...."

"In addition to the small private tombs - the character of which has been indicated - this same knoll contained some large mastabas of the Fourth Dynasty, with paneled walls (of the El Kab type), whilst in an adjoining mound were also excavated some large mastaba tombs characteristic of the Third Dynasty, in which a long stairway descends under a series of arches into the chambers deep below the surface. Some interesting stone monuments have been found, both vases and inscriptions. One further result may be mentioned, viz., that the "stairway tombs" of these early dynasties are now presented in a series, both architectural and chronological, linking the types found by MacIver at El Amrah, Petrie at Abydos, Quibell at El Kab, etc., not only with the large tombs of Bet Khallaf... but also with the well-known type of mastaba of the Old Kingdom, the development of which the present site illustrates is an interesting series." Let us not, reference to uniformity of culture throughout the country.

Commentary on this find was offered by the archaeologist, Randall-MacIver, who simply stated in *Man* 1904, 37: "Mr. Garstang maintains that the whole trend or recent archaeological discovery tends to prove the unbroken continuity of the archaic civilization. The great pyramid-builders, in his view, only inherited and developed a culture bequeathed to them by the first three dynasties, and these latter (the "proto-dynastic people") did nothing more than elaborate the details of a life, which was fixed in all essentials during the pre-dynastic period ...."

Where are the Kamite Kings Illustration. Copper bust close-up of statue of Pepi I's son, Mentu-Em-Sa-F; and, Copper bust of the statue of Pepi I also found at Hierakonpolis as seen in *Hierakonpolis Part II* by J.E. Quibell and F.W. Greene (1902).

Many of the types of pottery and objects characteristic of the first and second dynasties survive in the third with an admixture of precisely those which have hitherto been regarded as peculiar to the Old Kingdom, and a series of illustrations exemplifies the evolution of the complete mastaba from the early stairway tombs.

We need to be more conscious of the mis-placement of the King, Hen-Nekht in the Second Dynasty, Archaic Period selection. Hen-Nekht actually belongs, as determined by Garstang who discovered his tomb and attributed it, to the Third Dynasty, as successor to Zoser. Particular reference should be made to Hen-Nekht's "Negroid" features. As the only King from the dynasty whose bones has been recovered it supplied important evidence of the race of this and the previous dynasties. That of subsequent dynasties can also be rationalized or proved. Therefore, while the Third and Fourth Dynasties may be considered Memphite, the Third's unbroken tradition is related to the First and Second Thinite Dynasties.

WHERE ARE THE KAMITE KINGS?

Later, when we consider the Fifth Dynasty from Elephantine, the argument as made by Diop (1974) for the "Negro-ness" of the Old Kingdom, seems to rest on even more substantial foundations. Defense of this position, attacking falsification and distortion of the historical record of Classical African Civilizations, by modern racist European/American scholarship, is a substantial weapon in challenging the interpretation espoused from the mantle of the "absolute wisdom" of white supremacy and Eurocentric hegemony enshrined in its racist scholarship.

Now, let's return to the Step-Pyramid. This funerary complex had a tremendous enclosure wall of one-mile perimeter and a height of thirty-three feet. Enclosed buildings were dwarfed by the Step-Pyramid. One such structure was excavated by C. Firth in 1927. According to *American Journal of Archaeology* XXXII (1928: 71), as the report states: "After considerable and dangerous work a stairway was located leading to extraordinary funeral apartments. The rooms are lined with blue tiles broken by false doors, and beautiful low relief work of King Zoser. One room is tiled with panels representing mat-work. The ceiling is in an arched design. The artistic work in the reliefs is especially good; the anatomy of the figure is exquisite."

The stones used in these constructions were quarried from great distances. Decorations of architectural motifs included carvings and reliefs of plant forms such as lotus buds, papyrus stalks and palm fronds, we see so wonderfully displayed in capitals and on columns. Later this decoration of the stone sepulchers lent an air of freshness and great vitality to the buildings in the then evolving history of architecture. Such a natural setting was, however, a conflict with ideas of the dead that seemed to espouse conservatism.

Zoser was succeeded by **Sekhem-Kkhet**, Manethos *Tosertasis* who ruled from *Nile Year* 1591-1597 (2649-2643 B.C.). Not much is known about him except we have his bones that have become important not simply because of this one individual, but because from him can be postulated and defended the "Negro-ness" of ancient Kemet, particularly the Old Kingdom.

FREDERICK MONDERSON

"**The Bones of Hen Nekht, An Egyptian King of the Third Dynasty**" was written by C. S. Myers and published in *Man* 1901, 127. "From archaeological data, it appears that Hen Nekht ruled over Egypt in the Third Dynasty, about 4000 B.C. His tomb, with its contents of bones and pottery, was discovered last season near Girgeh, by Mr. John Garstang, to whom my thanks are due for permission to publish these remarks before they are included in the official report, which will appear later through the aid of the Egyptian Research Account."

"The bones of Hen Nekht are interesting, not only because he is by far the earliest known King whose remains have been found, but because they are the first which can with certainty be dated as belonging to the Third Dynasty. They proclaim him to have been a man of unusual height. His stature probably exceeded 1870 millimeters, while the average stature of later and prehistoric Egyptians was 1670 millimeters. The proportions of his long bones one to one another were such as characterize Negroid skeletons, a condition frequently observed in the prehistoric period, and commonly in the later period of the early empire. The skull was very massive and capacious, and extraordinarily broad for an Egyptian, the cranial index coming almost within the bounds of brachycephaly. Its features agreed more closely with those of dynastic than with those of prehistoric skulls."

"We turn now to history for the mention of an early Egyptian King of phenomenal stature. To such a King both Manetho and Eratosthenes allude. According to the former historian he was *Sesochris*, penultimate King of the Second (Thinite) Dynasty; according to the latter he was *Moncheiri*, first King of the Third (Memphite) Dynasty. It is in the highest degree probable that these are two names of one and the same King. The view I here offer seems to solve many difficulties."

"Mr. Randall-MacIver's measurements make it probable that from the late prehistoric times onward, a people distinguished by broader heads, longer noses, and other characters gradually made their way and became absorbed into the long-headed population of This and its neighborhood. These broader-headed people formed the ruling class of the earliest dynasties."

WHERE ARE THE KAMITE KINGS?

Where are the Kamite Kings Photo. Erik Monderson stands in the Court of the Step-Pyramid, built by the architect Imhotep for Pharaoh Zoser, Third Dynasty.

"According to history and tradition they founded Memphis, and doubtless multiplied there. By the Third Dynasty, according to Manetho, they began to build houses of hewn stone, and probably they constructed the earliest Egyptian pyramids. Up to the time of Hen Nekht, the broader-headed line of Kings styled themselves Thinite, and continued to be buried near *This*, in conformity with the ancient tradition of the people with whom they had come into contact. In the end, however, Memphis outlived *This*, and Kings who succeeded Hen Nekht began to forsake the simple Thinite burials for the pyramids of Saqqara, Gizeh, and Abusir. Thus, Hen Nekht may be considered in name and culture to be of the Third Memphite Dynasty; but, by his burial near *This*, came to be regarded as belonging to the previous Thinite Dynasty. The broader-headed race above mentioned is commonly thought to have arrived first in the Nile Valley at Koptos (Quft) from Punt, a land sacred to the later Egyptians, the situation of which is conjectured was near Somaliland and the opposite coast. There is, however, some geologic evidence to show that the Red Sea extended in historic times through the lakes near to Ismailia. Accordingly, the people of Punt, wandering northward from their home along the shores of the Red Sea, could conceivably have made their way with ease to the Nile Valley near Memphis. It is, however, but less probable that Asia rather than Punt was the home of this broader-headed race."

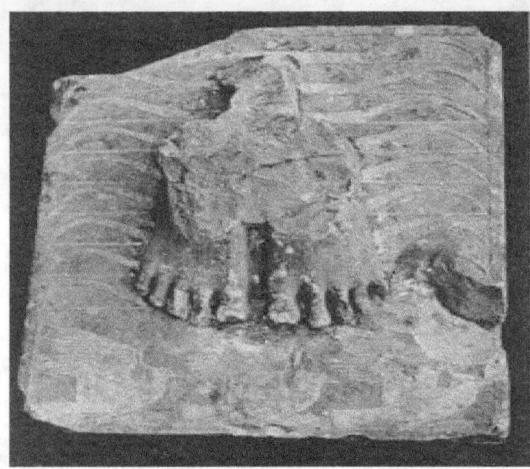

Where are the Kamite Kings Illustration. Base of a limestone statue of Zoser at Sakkara.

Where are the Kamite Kings Illustration. Front view of the base.

"The earliest dynastic Egyptians used the Babylonian seals and the Babylonian cubit. To Asia and Central Europe, we are wont to look for the broader-headed people. Moreover, according to the Greek legend, Memphis was founded by the marriage of Memphis, daughter of the Nile, with Epaphus, who born to the Grecian Io (Isis)

WHERE ARE THE KAMITE KINGS?

was carried off when a babe to Syria, and brought back by his mother to Egypt."

Because of the significance of the work of Randall-MacIver, two additional pieces of early archaeological literature are introduced here to add dimension to the discussion of the racial origins of the people of Kemet, the ancient Kamites.

Randall-MacIver's "A Prehistoric Cemetery at El Amrah in Egypt: Preliminary Report of Excavations" *Man* 1901, 40 states: "The village of El Amrah lies about six miles to the south of the famous site of Abydos, where Professor Flinders Petrie has for the past two seasons been engaged in unraveling the difficult history of Egypt's earliest Kings. It has been known for some years that valuable prehistoric cemeteries existed in the neighborhood, but their precise character could hardly be appreciated, inasmuch as nothing had been published which could be called a record of the excavations made there. It was with some anxiety that Mr. Anthony Wilkin and I, to whom Professor Petrie entrusted this part of the concession granted to him by the Department of Antiquities, commenced our season's work. A site, which had been already dug no less than four times, first by native plunderers, and then by professed archaeologists, might well have been supposed to be entirely exhausted. I am happy, however, to be able to state that our success has far surpassed our modest expectations, and propose in following pages to give a brief *resume*' of results which will soon be published in full in the official memoir of the Egypt Exploration Fund, at whose expense the work is being conducted."

"The cemeteries on which we have been engaged are situated close to the cultivation on the table-land, between two wide valleys which run down from that upper desert a short distance north of El Amrah. Here a tract of many acres of broken ground testify to the cupidity, if not to the knowledge of previous grave-hunters. At the southwest corner sherds of broken pottery showed that many at least of the graves were of prehistoric date, and it was at this point that we began to excavate on December 22nd. It soon became evident that a large number of graves had not been opened, while others had been insufficiently cleared. After a month's work three hundred graves had been fully registered from a piece of ground measuring only about 15,000 square yards. This proved to be the entire extent of a small but highly interesting prehistoric cemetery, which may have originally contained some 600 to 700 graves. In date it ranged from the very earliest 'New Race' times through the entire middle period down to the beginning of the 'Late Prehistoric.' The graves yielded not only a great quantity of the objects (familiar to all who have studied this period pottery, ivories, slate palettes, etc.,) but also a certain number which are wholly new in character. The most interesting are those, which bear directly upon the life of the people who lived in the country at that time. In the rubbish of a plundered grave was found a fragment, which evidently represented a house, the next day pieces were turned out which fit well together and almost complete the whole. The house is oblong in shape, sloping from the base and recurved at the top. From its form it may be supposed that it was built of wattle and mud; at one end is depicted a door (probably of wood), and at the other two small windows. No roof was found, but if it is permissible to judge from the construction of graves which occur in our second cemetery, it must have consisted of boughs on which was laid a wattle-work of twigs covered with mud."

"The 'New Race' had probably even more occasion to use boats than the modern Egyptians, for there is no doubt that the country was far swampier than that it is now. It is thought that some of these boats are represented on their well-known "decorated" pottery. In our first cemetery were found pottery models of two, if not three, difficult kinds, but they do not resemble those figured on the pottery. Again, that the 'New Race' was a hunting people has long been known from their carvings and drawings, as well as inferred from the objects, which occur in the graves. But it must now be added that they were of a pastoral people; for in no less than three graves were found pottery groups of kine. The grave from which the best group came was that of a man who held in his hand a model baton of clay, the stem of which was painted with a spiral red band like a leather thong, while the head of it was in the form of a mace and decorated with black lines; some fine pottery completed his tomb-furniture."

"Of weapons of war and the chase we find figs. 3-11 will give a fair idea. The breccia (fig. 3), the mace-heads (fig. 4.), and the forked hunting-lance of flint (figs. 7-11) all came from the same grave, which, indeed, contained five of these lances, a remarkable outfit at

WHERE ARE THE KAMITE KINGS?

a time when they must have been very rare and costly. The weapons and implements in these graves are generally of stone, copper is always rare, though occurring occasionally even in the earliest stage of the prehistoric. Fig. 12 shows a new type of copper dagger found in a plundered grave of the middle Prehistoric period."

"Flint implements of one class or another occur in almost every grave, though the fine specimens are, of course, uncommon. In several cases a small sheaf of flakes has been found lying between the hands and head; and one grave, from the number and variety of the flakes and implements found in it, would seem to have been that of a professional flint-knapper."

Where are the Kamite Kings Photo. Double Temple of Kom Ombo. From one of the columned halls, looking into the deep recesses of the Temple towards the Sanctuary.

"Other crafts are represented by the excellent cloth used to wrap round the body, by baskets such as those shown in figs. 13 and 14, and by clay vases which probably served in the manufacture of pottery. With regard to the pottery itself this cemetery yielded a considerable number of new varieties and one quite new class of ware."

"The dolls shown in figs. 15 and 16 may be taken to represent the inhabitants of the country, to such an extent at least as their artistic skill could interpret their own conceptions. It is worth remarking that the peculiar "sheath" which they wear, and the *strongly curled hair*, is the essential features of the figures carved on the splendid proto-dynastic slates (*Jour Anthr. Inst.* XXX, 0l. B., C., D.)."

"After this cemetery was finished, another was started some two or three hundred paces to the east of it. The ground between is full of 18th Dynasty burials, and it appears at the moment of writing as if the two prehistoric patches were quite separate and independent."

"The eastern cemetery is of very comprehensive character. It begins with burials of almost, if not quite, the earliest types, and continues down to the Ist or IInd Dynasty. In comparison with the other cemetery, it has not been much plundered. Up to the date on which this is written (February 17th) rather more than 100 new graves have been opened. One of these has produced the most valuable find of the season, namely, a slate palette which is conclusively dated, by the pottery and stone vases occurring with it, no less than by its own characteristic form, to the middle period of the Prehistoric (60 in Prof. Petrie's sequence dating). It bears in relief upon the face the brief inscription given in fig. 17, and is thus by far the earliest example yet found of the use of hieroglyphs. Hieroglyphic writing has been known to exist in a well-developed form as early as the Ist dynasty, but this slate belongs to a period considerably before Menes, the first King of the Ist dynasty. An especially interesting point in connection with the eastern cemetery is that the range and variety of the burials have made it possible to trace the evolution of all the types of early tomb-construction. The bodies are invariably buried in a contracted position, and the stages through which the tomb developed may be provisionally stated as follows: the first stage is the only one which has not yet been noted in this part of the ground, though it is of frequent occurrence in the western cemetery": -

WHERE ARE THE KAMITE KINGS?

Where are the Kamite Kings Photo. Cairo Museum of Egyptian Antiquities. Panoramic view of the Mariette Memorial with the Great Egyptologists represented by their busts.

"1. The earliest burials of all are in very shallow round graves. The body was generally wrapped in the skin of a sheep or goat.

"2. These are succeeded by graves several feet deep, and of a roughly oval or oblong shape. The body was commonly wrapped in cloth and laid on a reed mat, which was then folded round it. Sometimes the reed mat was further laid on a tray of twigs, and very rarely on a wooden dugout bier.

"3. Graves of the same depth as the last, in which the beginnings of a light recess occur, in which the body is laid; while the larger pots are outside the recess.

"4. Graves of the same depth, with a well-marked recess cut out for the body. The recess is sometimes fenced off by upright wooden baulks.

"5. A regular pit, about 6 feet deep and 2 to 3 feet in width, with a recess bricked off from it. The recess contains a clay, a wooden, or a pottery coffin, either oval or oblong, and one or two pots, which are almost the only tomb furniture found with this class. Such graves are very late in the prehistoric series, approaching closely to the period of the Ist dynasty, even entering into it.

FREDERICK MONDERSON

"From this point the solution branches off into two distinct lines. The pit with chamber became the regular well with chamber, a type which prevails from the IVth dynasty onwards all through Egyptian history. On the other hand, the bricked recess, considered in itself apart from the well or pit, becomes the brick tomb, which forms our sixth stage.

Where are the Kamite Kings Photo. Panoramic view of the three great Pyramids and current entranceway on the Ghizeh Plateau.

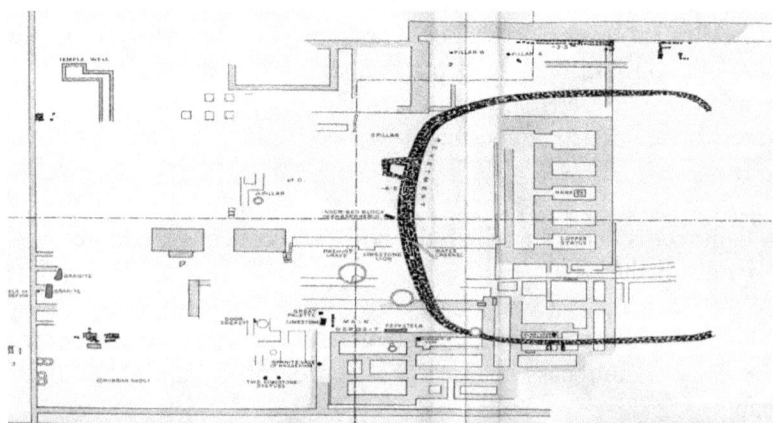

Where are the Kamite Kings Illustration. Plan of the temple area at Hierakonpolis in *Hierakonpolis Part II* by J.E. Quibell and F.W. Greene (1902).

"6. Four-sided tombs, consisting of brick walls sunk a few feet below the desert surface. At first these contain a coffin either of mud or of wood. Sometimes the coffin is replaced by a plank lining fastened against the walls; this feature has been found also in Prof.

WHERE ARE THE KAMITE KINGS?

Petrie's *Royal Tombs of the 1st Dynasty*. Sometimes, again, there is no coffin, but the body is wrapped in cloth and laid on a reed mat as in the early graves."

"N.B.-The burials under inverted pots which frequently occur in this cemetery do not fall naturally into any stage of the tomb development. They should perhaps be regarded as chief varieties of the pot coffin. The first stage in the history of this brick construction is a plain four-sided enclosure, larger or smaller according to the importance of the grave. The smaller graves are covered with mud bricks supported on more piles of bricks built up from the floor. For the larger a regular roof is made of unbarked boughs or trunks of trees of 2-4 inches diameter laid across the width of the grave. On these is then laid a wattle work of twigs and reeds, and the whole then covered with several inches of plastered mud.

"7. A natural development of such graves as those of the sixth class ensues when niches are walled off to receive the offerings put with the deceased person. First of all, a small dividing wall is built at one end or the other, thus barring off a small section of the whole length.

"Next, this section is itself divided by a small cross-partition, so as to form two niches. A greater elaboration still is reached when more niches are inserted in other parts of the tomb, and thus a natural progress is made to the complicated arrangement of the Royal Tombs of Abydos. The most detailed arrangement that has yet been found at El Amrah was that of a large brick tomb which has just been worked. It was a large room about 5 feet deep and 5 feet below the surface of the ground, with two chambers at the south end for offerings, and a third chamber at the north-east corner for the body of a cow. A staircase 24 feet long gave entrance to the tomb from the western side. From this tomb, which had been plundered very recently, we obtained fragments of fine stone vases, and half of a beautifully-inscribed steatite cylinder." David Randall-MacIver.

The clay model of a house is an interesting find that shows the significance of the "house" this early in the cultural development of these Nile dwellers. During the Old Kingdom, property transactions were conducted. *American Journal of Archaeology* XVI (1912: 561) tells of an article published by K. Sethe regarding an

FREDERICK MONDERSON

"inscription found near the valley temple of the pyramid of Chephren at Gizeh in 1910. The sale of a house in the time of the Old Kingdom (fifth or sixth dynasty) is recorded. A bed seems to be regarded as a permanent fixture in the house."

Where are the Kamite Kings Photo. Erik Monderson strolls in Al Fayal Garden, Aswan in 2018.

Where are the Kamite Kings Photo. Erik Monderson stands atop stairs with uraei on top of wall at his rear at the Step-Pyramid, Sakkara.

WHERE ARE THE KAMITE KINGS?

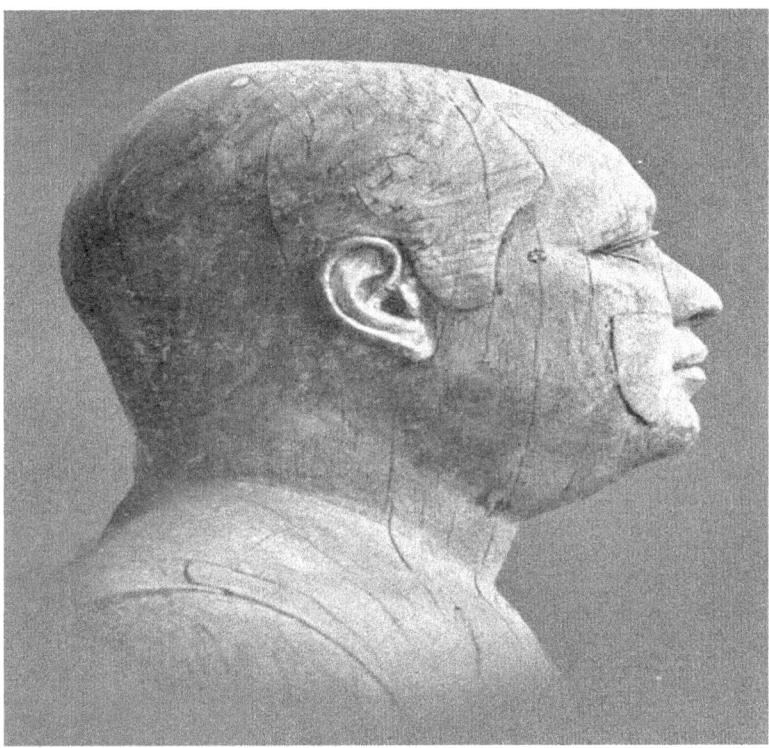

Where are the Kamite Kings Illustration. Old Kingdom bust of "Sheikh el Beled," upon discovery so named by workmen for likeness of the then Sheikh of their village.

Elsewhere, Mr. Randall-MacIver conducted additional research in an attempt to ascertain more about the ethnicity of the early people of Kemet. Anthony Wilkins complemented him in producing *Among the Berbers of Algeria*, a work published as part of his *Libyan Notes*, London: Macmillan, 1901, reviewed by C. L Myers. The following is his article published under *Algeria: Ethnology*.

"In these two volumes are contained the results of a brief visit paid in the spring of 1900 to some of the less-frequented parts of Algeria. The object of the expedition was to collect evidence among the purer-blooded survivors of the old Berber stock, as to the validity of certain current theories of the relations, racial and cultural, in which the stock stands to the ancient inhabitants of Egypt, and the authors are greatly to be congratulated, both on the success which attended their observations in the field, and on the manner in which they have worked up and presented their results."

"In the book which bears Mr. Wilkin's name only, the appeal is frankly to the man in the street, who knows nothing about the cephalic index, and cares less about the derivation of geometric ornament, but who may reasonably be expected to take an interest even in 'native races,' when they turn out, as in this case, to have so many points in common with his good-natured mongrel Philistine self. "Fully one-fifth of these [Chawia Berbers] we saw at El Arbaa were fair men - that is to say, men who would be counted fair in this country. Blue and grey eyes were even commoner than light (sometimes flaxen) hair .... Skins were white, or would have been if they had not been encrusted with the dirt of untold months .... We felt ourselves at home among so many rosy countenances; indeed, one youngster would have been taken anywhere but in his own village (where he would be without honor) for a freckled wee Scotchman" (pp. 77-79). Of these and kindred Kabyle folk, of their beautiful highlands, of the countless relics of bygone modes of life which strike the eye there at every turn, and of the quaint trivialities of cross-country travel, Mr. Wilkin has much to tell, and tells it in an easy animated fashion which makes his book seem at first reading less full of matter than it really is. We could wish, nevertheless, even so, that he had sometimes taken his public shade more seriously; word pictures like that of the Chawia potter and weaver (pp. 129-30) have a way of sticking in the memory which makes us wish there were more of them. The illustrations, from the author's own photographs, are admirable, and add greatly to the attractiveness of the book."

"The joint work entitled *Libyan Notes* contains a more detailed discussion of the problems which suggested the journey. Ever since Professor Flinders Petrie's announcement of a "New Race" in Egypt, the question of the race-relation of the Nile Valley to the rest of North Africa has entered a new phase, and the view has been widely held, with more or less modification in detail, first, that the course of the primitive civilization of Egypt was largely influenced, if not determined, by that of ancient Libya immediately to the westward; and, secondly, that to account for this cultural influence a strong 'Libyan' element must be presumed in the composition of the Egyptian people."

WHERE ARE THE KAMITE KINGS?

"In regard to this point, subsequent excavations in Egypt, in which Mr. Randall-MacIver himself has had some share, have resulted in the elaboration of an unrivaled sequence-series of prehistoric pottery, so typical of the character of the material civilization as a whole, that it is to the ceramic industries of Libya that one instinctively turns for the crucial counterpart; while by great good luck the Algerian journey resulted in the collection not only of a number of fine specimens of the commoner styles of the well-known "Kabyle pottery," but also of examples of several local fabrics which hardly go abroad at all; and, best of all, of precise observations of the localities and of the processes and materials which are employed. On this collection, which attracted much attention when it was exhibited at the Anthropological Institute last summer, and which is now to be seen in the Pitt-Rivers Museum of Oxford, the authors have founded a careful comparison of Berber and proto-Egyptian pottery, and come to the guarded conclusion that while some of the simpler fabrics are common to the two civilizations, and have persisted almost unchanged in Kabylia and the Aures mountains down to the present day, others are either peculiar to Egypt or can be shown to have been derived by Egypt from non-Libyan sources. On the non-Egyptian elements in the Kabyle and Chawia styles, on the other hand, some of the most distinctive are certainly of later introduction (probably from Cyprus, *via.* Carthage), leaving a small remainder to be attributed to a hypothetical Iberian origin; so that, on the whole, Egypt seems rather to have dominated Libya in early times than *vice versa*. These arguments, of which only the briefest outline is permissible here, are worked out with great detail and full illustration, and on the evidence, which is available at present, may be acceptable with confidence."

"Only three important points are very slightly dealt with: first, hardly anything is said of the native names of the processes or of the elements of the ornamentation, though a good many Berber terms are given in other sections of the book; second, no analysis is attempted of these same ornamental designs, nor is the very suggestive inference as to the importation of Cypriote motives in Graeco-Phoenician times marked out, as it deserves, in comparison with the Carthaginian and Cypriote *repertoires*; third, no mention is made of the remarkable series of parallels, both of form and ornament, which is supplied by the Early Bronze age pottery of Sicily. None of these omissions, however, affect the validity of the main inference as to the relation of the Libyan fabrics to the proto-Egyptian; the first would have confirmatory value only; the other two bear rather on the origin of the later and non-Egyptian elements in Kabyle art."

"Turning now to the question of community of race, the authors have a sufficiently decisive answer. Neither the skull measurements, nor the head measurements of living Kabyle and Chawia individuals, afford the smallest support to the theory of a Libyan element in the early population of Egypt. Taking the evidence of the cephalic index as typical of the rest, 'the difference between 742' [the lowest Berber figure] 'and 721 (rather, probably, 712)' [the figures of skulls from Abydos and Hou respectively] "is too great to be explained away .... The cephalic index, then, absolutely forbids any identification of the prehistoric Egyptians with the Berbers" (p. 206). Such language is precise and explicit, but it is based on a large introduction (as such series go), and is quite borne out by the evidence, which is discussed and tabulated in an original and effective fashion, and illustrated by a large number of photographs of individuals; special note being due to the ingenious and uncanny 'vault view' in Plate XXV."

"It must not be supposed, however, that the whole of these *Libyan Notes* is devoted to fabrics and anthropometry, or even to subsidiary arguments from history to archaeology on the Egypto-Libyan question. Besides an introductory note on the literary allusions to the old Libyans, and an excellent summary of recent French research on the language and social institutions of the modern Berbers, the book contains a valuable account of dolmen-sites at Bou Nouara, Bou Merzong, and Roknia, and of a new site at Msila, near Bordj-bou Areridj, with an analysis of the meager results of excavations up to date, with numerous photographs and useful facsimiles of the skulls from Roknia, described long ago by General Faidherbe. There are also a number of careful descriptions of Kabyle and Chawia architecture, of the primitive loom and oil-mill, and of other implements and processes of considerable ethnographical importance." J. L. Myers.

WHERE ARE THE KAMITE KINGS?

The structure at Zawiet el-Aryan contained inscribed vases bearing the name of the King, Hen Nekht, who followed Zoser. He in turn was followed by Kha-ba, Manetho's *Aches*, a name also given by Brugsch and Boriant, according to Budge, from the **Palermo Stone**. His reign is *Nile Year* 1597-1603 (2637-2613 B.C.). He is followed by a shadowy King Neb-Ka, *Sephairis* of Manetho.

The last King of the Third Dynasty was the **Horus Huni**, or **Nefer-Ka-Ra** of the **Tablet of Abydos** or Huni of the **Sakkara List**, is the ruler who preceded Snefru. He reigned *Nile Year* 1603-1627 (2637-2613 B.C.). Budge (1902: 222) informs, the *Prisse Papyrus* (pl. 2, II. 7, 8) mentions the two Kings' names and that when Huni died, "Snefru became the ruler of all the land; we may therefore assume that Huni and Nefer-Ka-Ra are one and the same person and it is in any case clear from Manetho's **King List** that Snefru was the first King of a new dynasty."

Snefru was first King of the Fourth Dynasty that scholars consider the start of the Old Kingdom. Manetho assigned him as Memphite though his roots go back to the Thinite Dynasties linked to the Archaic Period. He reigned *Nile Year* 1627-1651 (2613-2589 B.C.). Breasted I (1962: 75) has supplied reference to the King's mining exploits in Sinai. Wearing the *Atef Crown* with upraised war-club, he smites the Bedawi, and inscriptions tell of the names and titles accorded this Patron of the region of Sinai. Breasted I (1962: 75) has styled Snefru "King of Upper and Lower Egypt; Favorite of the Two Goddesses; Lord of Truth; Golden Horus; Snefru. Great God, who is Given Satisfaction, Stability, Life, Health, all Joy forever."

Snefru constructed two pyramids at Dashur, the Bent or Rhomboid ('The Southern Shining Pyramid') and the Northern Dashur Pyramid ('The Shining Pyramid' Modern name: 'The Red Pyramid'). Yoyotte (1959: 264) mentions textual reference to the "Double Town of the Two Pyramids of Snefru." Equally, Ruffle (1977: 35) has argued "Quarry-marks on both the monuments" served to "confirm that he was the builder of both the Northern and

FREDERICK MONDERSON

Bent Pyramid, in which the angle was reduced when the structure was half-finished. The Layer or Step-Pyramid at Meydum was begun by Huni and cased by Snefru who left his name on this structure." The Valley Temple of the Bent Pyramid was found by Ahmed Zakhry in 1951. He also discovered the Mortuary Temple of this structure.

Where are the Kamite Kings Illustration. Coffin lid of Seti I.

Snefru continued the foreign policy of his predecessors. Iskander (1979: 48) has shown that the **Palermo Stone** points out "Snefru sent a navy of 40 ships to Lebanon to fetch cedar wood. It is also recorded that he sent a military campaign against the Nubians whom he conquered and brought back 7,000 captives and 200,000

WHERE ARE THE KAMITE KINGS?

heads of cattle, and that he sent another successful campaign against the Libyans."

Thus, the size of his Nubian, human but particularly animal booty, is certainly basis for further discussion for this gives an indication of the cultural level and sophistication of a state which could afford such booty. Petrie's "New Race," which was not really "new," is thought to have been both hunters and boat people, possibly pastoral and agricultural, based on artifactual remains. Though, and nonetheless, contradicting Petrie, Steindorff as reported in *American Journal of Archaeology* VI (1902: 58) has argued to the contrary. "With the aid of the objects recently discovered we can now trace the progress of the indigenous Egyptian people from the pre-historic stage to the second dynasty. Nothing forces us to assume the immigration of a New Race." Therefore, we must give great credence to Brophy and Bauval's *Black Genesis* (2011) theory that people from the Western Desert of Upper Egypt were the precursor to the Pharaohs and laid the foundation for Egyptian civilization. Toby Wilkinson's *Genesis of the Pharaohs* (2003) found cultural motifs, petroglyphs later developed as pharaonic paraphernalia in the Eastern Desert, approximately opposite the area of the Western Desert.

Notwithstanding, the size of the Nubian cache of 200,000 heads of cattle posits a society of some means and structure. In comparison, at a later time during the Twenty-Fifth Kushitic Dynasty, when the capital was moved from Napata to Meroe after *Nile Year* 3710 (Murnane 530 B.C.), this "back country" boasted a prolific agricultural and pastoral reputation. Indications show Africans are some of the most resolute hunters. In early mastery of navigation practices, boats appeared in the Amratian Period and this art on the river fueled the engines of Kemetic civilization. It was the river and these expert African boatmen who brought Narmer, Mentuhotep II, Sekenenra, Kamose, Ahmose, Thutmose III, Amenhotep I, Amenhotep II, Amenhotep III, Rameses I, Seti I and Rameses II and III as well as Piankhy, Shabaka, Shabataka, Taharka and Tanutemon, along with untold military forces first to pacify, then to unify, glorify their God, and finally to extend the borders of the state. Such important links show the closeness of religiosity and cultures emanating from this southern region of the Nile civilization.

FREDERICK MONDERSON

Where are the Kamite Kings Photo. Illustration. 130. The "seated scribe" from a Fifth Dynasty tomb at Sakkara and now in the Louvre Museum, Paris. He has blue eyes; hence, the argument, "The Egyptians had blue eyes." However, we know the Egyptians used "inlaid eyes" in their sculptures. Thus, where does this leave the argument? Notice, blue eyes and all, but his nose is not broken and so he projects the false "European image of ancient Egypt" and he's not "painted black for the funerary ceremony"!

Snefru's wife was Queen Hetep-Heres, whose tomb, to the east of the Great Pyramid of her son Khufu, has yielded wonderful jewelry and household valuables, unearthed by its excavator, Reisner. The *American Journal of Archaeology* (XXXI 1927: 361) wrote accordingly: "The tomb, which was explored with minute care, contained a beautiful alabaster sarcophagus of the queen, which was surrounded by many precious objects. The grave lacked a superstructure and had thus escaped from plundering. Almost a year was spent on a careful clearing of the burial chamber before the sarcophagus itself could be reached."

Such a slow and tedious pace of clearing tombs is not surprising since such is indeed a time of precision. In the important queen's

WHERE ARE THE KAMITE KINGS?

tomb were found, "fragments of chairs, eight toilet vessels of fine alabaster, a bronze ewer, a basin, quantities of inlays and gold ... much wood, linen, a gold drinking cup, gold dishes, canopy, bed .... The contents of the tomb were the deposit of a reburial. The sarcophagus was recently opened and found quite empty."

A year later, in *American Journal of Archaeology* XXXII (1929: 72) mention was made of a "note giving a report from Dr. Reisner that upon finally clearing the tomb of Queen Hetep-Heres the alabaster sarcophagus was found empty; then on May 23 the recess in the west wall of the chamber blocked with masonry and sealed with plaster was opened and in it was found an alabaster Canopic box still containing the entrails of the Queen, but not the rest of her body. The discovery of this box shows that the body had been mummified."

Previously, Reisner had conducted excavations in the northeast corner of the pyramid of Khufu where in 1842-43 Lepsius had uncovered tombs numbered 26 and 27. The *American Journal of Archaeology* (1914: 91) also reported: "It was discovered that there was here a great complex of tombs belonging to one family that of Senezem-ib, built around a large offering court above older mastaba. Before the Roman period the tombs on the south and east sides were destroyed and some of the reliefs and paintings from them were found under the Roman pavement. The finest relief represented Nekhebuw, accompanied by his son Im-thepy, spearing fish. The tombs were those of three generations of architects and builders and date from about 2675 to 2600 B.C."

"One tomb, that of Im-thepy was intact. In it beside the wooden sarcophagus was a row of large jars with big plaster or mud stoppers, also jars and other vessels, model tables, dishes, model tools, and implements all of copper, and some objects of crystal and slate. These had once been confined in a box. There was also a stack of red polished pottery bowls and near the walls, bones showing where legs and ribs of beef, geese, ducks and other offerings had been placed. In the coffin, beside the head of the mummy, were a headrest and two jars of alabaster, and a copper mirror; a stick and some cakes of mud were by the left side; and a beautiful necklace of gold and faience beads on the breast. In the

FREDERICK MONDERSON

tomb of Yenty, besides the copper tools, etc., was a fine diorite cup inscribed with the name of Tety, probably a royal gift. In a chamber under the tomb of Mehy were five small wooden figures of kneeling prisoners, and, above, two wooden portrait statues one of which may have been the portrait of a son of Mehy. This is now in Boston, as are two of the prisoners, reliefs and paints of Nekhebuw, copper tools, tables, dishes, etc."

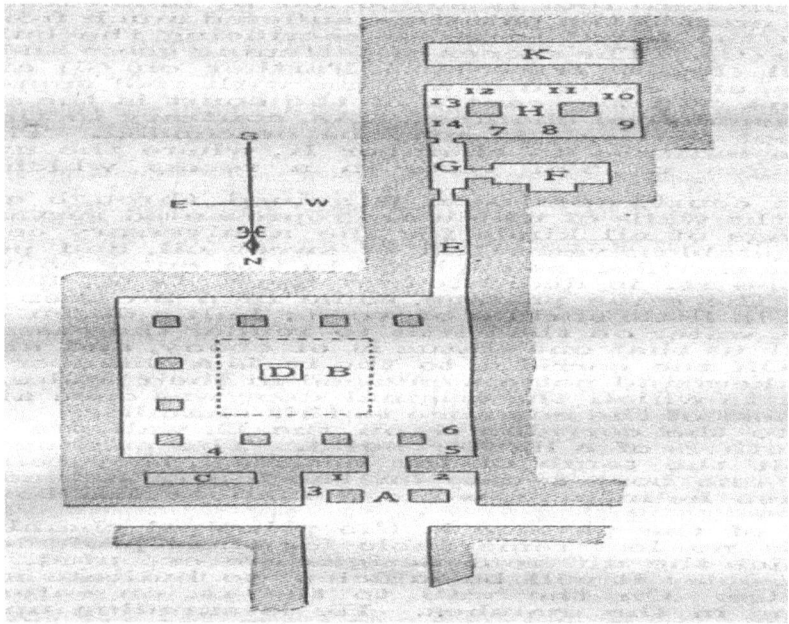

Where are the Kamite Kings Illustration. Plan of the Tomb of Ti (Thi).

THE FOURTH DYNASTY

The **Fourth Dynasty** is more appropriately, in the "Age of Pyramids," characterized by the resolute and determined nature of the architectural Pharaohs Khufu, Khafre and Menkaure, whose signature constructions adorn the Gizeh Plateau. It should be pointed out first, *American Journal of Archaeology* (1907: 343) tells of work at Gizeh. "The ground between the two cemeteries excavated in earlier years was cleared, and fifty-two mastabas opened. The most important discovery was a ramp leading to the roof of a mastaba, by means of which the body and the other contents of the grave were introduced." Statuary of the highest quality was produced in this reign. From the end of the dynasty

WHERE ARE THE KAMITE KINGS?

alabaster was used in making royal statuary. Of exceptional quality is the slate statue, now in Cairo, of Menkaure, flanked by the Goddess Hathor and Goddess of Diospolis Parva. In the development of art and other aspects of cultural growth, Murray (1949: 15) believed, "the IVth Dynasty is one of the most splendid periods of Egyptian history. There had been no wars since the civil war under Perabsen of the IInd Dynasty and the country had had time to develop the arts of peace and to amass wealth by trade." The baton was passed from the Third to Fourth Dynasty to continue trade, building and development of writing. Here we witness the first great flowering of African thought processes, moral precepts, and love and appreciation for learning and practice of principles of theology, religion, science, medicine, craftsmanship and government.

Khufu ruled for 23 years, *Nile Year* 1651-1674; Murnane gives (2589-2566 B.C.). The King's royal titles were:

Horus	Netercheri (?)
Two Ladies	Netercheri
Suten Bat	Khufu
Son of Ra	Khufu

His name is in the *Westcar Papyrus*, on the *Tablet of Sakkara*, and No. 21 on the *Abydos List*. Lepsius' *Denkmaler* lists his name as being in the Wadi Maghara, in Sinai, while Mariette included it in his *Mastabas*. Manetho's *Suphis* and Greek Cheops, his name is in the Great Pyramid on bricks and in the upper-most chamber. Even more, in 1915, C. S. Fisher, working under the auspices of the Boston Museum of Fine Arts opened several tombs at Ghizeh as reported in *American Journal of Archaeology* XX (1916: 97) that indicated: "The most interesting discovery was an offering-chamber of mud brick with a ribbed vault made of bricks with interlocking joints. This is not later than the sixth dynasty. Another discovery was an offering-table having a round of hieroglyphs in which appear the names of the Kings Khufu, Khafra and Dedefra."

The Great Pyramid, the "First Wonder of the World," according to Banks (1916: 30) was made of stone. "The material for the construction of the tomb was of red granite and limestone. The granite, which was used only for the lining of the walls of the inner chambers, was brought down the Nile from Syene (Aswan), in Upper Egypt, seven hundred miles away. The quarrymen worked in the ancient fashion, splitting the stones with wooden wedges, and cutting them into the desired shape with copper saws fed by emery powder ...."

Where are the Kamite Kings Illustration. Granite statue of King Sekhem-uatch-taui-Ra of the XIII or XIV Dynasty (left); and, granite statue of Usertesen III, XIIth Dynasty.

Kamite Kings Cartouche/Shennu. Memphite Kings of the Fourth Dynasty.

WHERE ARE THE KAMITE KINGS?

"A vast army of men was employed in the quarries. Another army, laboring upon the hill at Gizeh, where the pyramid was to stand, dug into the rock to the depth of eight inches that the foundation stones might remain securely in place, but a core of living rock was left to project upward in the center. A long-inclined passage was excavated far down into the solid rock, at the bottom of which a chamber was hollowed out ...."

Senusert III (Usertesen, Sesostris), whose pyramid of mud-brick was located at Dashur, penned the following poem in praise of divinity. While of the XIIth Dynasty, the sentiments were well apropos Old Kingdom beliefs regarding divinity.

Where are the Kamite Kings Illustration. Khufu, builder of the Great Pyramid at Ghizeh, 4th Dynasty.

"How the Gods rejoice; thou hast made their offerings to flourish.
How thy children rejoice; thou hast established their boundaries.
How thy fathers, who were aforetime, rejoice; thou hast increased their portions;
How the Egyptians rejoice in thy might; thou hast protected the old usages.
How the people rejoice in thy designs; thy might hast captured the
....

FREDERICK MONDERSON

How the Two River banks rejoice in thy strength; thou hast enlarged that which they need
How thy recruits rejoice in …. Thou hast caused them to grow.
How thine Honored One rejoices; thou hast renewed their youth.
How the Two Lands rejoice in thy strength; thou hast protected their walls.
O Horus, who extended thy boundaries, mayest thou continue in eternity."

Where are the Kamite Kings Photo. View of the entrance to the three great Pyramids on the Ghizeh Plateau with Khufu (right); Khafre (center); and Menkaure in the distance at left. The "white building" beside Khufu's Pyramid is the "Boat Museum."

"All the ingenuity of the Egyptian architect was employed to conceal the chambers within the pyramid. The entrance at the center of the north side was carefully concealed by the casing stone, and only when the stone was torn away was it discovered. Should you explore the interior of the pyramid, you climb to the eighteenth course of stones, or forty-seven feet from the base, to a small opening three and a half feet square leading within. With a guide and a torch, you enter."

"You must bend low, for the passage is but five feet high, and step carefully, for it slopes downward at an angle of twenty-three

WHERE ARE THE KAMITE KINGS?

degrees. It is a long descent down to the level of the foundation, and then down the shaft through the living rock 317 feet from the entrance. At last, beneath the very center of the pyramid, you enter a large chamber, by even the dim light of your torch you may see that the chamber was never completed. King Khufu was never buried there. The chamber was only a part of the plan of the wily old King to deceive the future grave robbers."

"You climb back up the passage to the level of the foundation, where the guide will take you to the entrance of another passage which was once carefully concealed. Still bending low, you climb up through twenty-five courses of stone, and then along the level to the center of the pyramid. There you reach the Queen's chamber, measuring 16 by 18 feet, and 14 feet in height. But the queen was not buried there; this chamber, too, was constructed to lead the grave robbers astray. From the Queen's chamber you go along the level passage to the point where your incline begins, and opening before you is a great gallery leading upwards. You enter, and here you may stand erect, for the gallery is 28 feet high. At the height of 138 feet above the foundation, or at the fiftieth course of stones, is a small antechamber, and beyond is the royal chamber. The chamber is 24 feet long, 17 feet wide and 19 feet high. The walls are of polished granite, and if you should climb above the ceiling, you would find several smaller chambers constructed to resist the pressure of the great weight of the stones above. The roofing slabs, weighing about fifty-four tons each, are the largest stones in the pyramid. From the ceiling small holes lead upward for ventilation. In a corner is a stone sarcophagus, which must have been built into the pyramid, for it, is too large to have been carried through the passageways. Perhaps there the King was buried, but we do not know. It has long been empty."

Of course, the pyramid as a paramount and early cardinal point in the emergence of civilization created a Greco-Roman-Western tradition and thus, the other "Six Wonders of the World," were non-African. Imagine, all that was accomplished elsewhere in the Old Kingdom; Mentuhotep's Middle Kingdom experiment at Deir el-Bahari; and, the New Kingdom building proliferation at Karnak, Luxor, Abu Simbel, Ramesseum, Deir el-Bahari, Medinet Habu,

FREDERICK MONDERSON

Seti I's tomb in the Valley of the Kings, Amenhotep III's temple of which only the Colossi of Memnon remain silent sentinels. All of these were outstanding pieces of architecture. We could mention the Temple of Soleb in Nubia, built by Amenhotep III, the "Magnificent." Yet still, none of these "other wonders of the world" are attributed here! Further, of all the original "Seven Wonders of the World" only the African created Pyramids have withstood the ravages of time and man. Even more, these other "non-wonders of the world" have outlasted the other six "Wonders of the World."

It is now a good time to interject the itinerary of my **Educational Tour** of the land of ancient Kemet. Of course, the scheduled Special Rate of $3995, pp based on double occupancy, includes air from JFK and Land Package.

My sojourn in the "Holy Land" will take me to Cairo and then on to Luxor by Air and bus to the hotel. Next day, we will have motor transportation to the West Bank Sites of the Colossi of Memnon, Ramesseum, Temple of Rameses II or Medinet Habu, Temple of Rameses III; Deir el Bahari, Temple of Queen Hatshepsut; the Valley of the Kings and an Alabaster Factory. The next day it's the Temple of Karnak and Temple of Luxor we visit. After that we visit the Temple of Dendera and Temple of Seti I at Abydos. Then we travel southward towards Aswan stopping at the Temple of Esna, Temple of Edfu, Temple of Kom Ombo, and into Aswan. Motor transportation takes us to Abu Simbel; twin Temple of Rameses II, and after the Philae Temple of Isis, High Dam, Lotus Memorial, Kalabsha Temple, Unfinished Obelisk and Granite Quarry. On the free day it's the optional Botanic Garden, Mausoleum of Aga Khan, all at Aswan. On the free day it's for a possible hike to the "Tombs of the Nobles", also optional. Then it's on to Cairo for the Pyramid of Giza, Khufu Boat Museum at Giza, Memphis Museum and Step-Pyramid of Zoser at Sakkara. The next day we visit the Cairo Museum of Egyptian Antiquities, possibly the Citadel and Two Mosques or the Faiyum and Pyramid at Lahun. Then we do a little shopping in the Khalili Bazaar before flying back to New York. The Price Package includes "Round trip air from JFK, 13 nights in 5-Star hotels, All domestic flights, Breakfast and Dinner daily at your hotel, and two Box Lunches, Deluxe Motor coaches, Luggage Handling (two bags per person); Entrance into all sites, English speaking Guides, all taxes and service charges. Quite frankly, no one gives this much even in a 14-day trip.

WHERE ARE THE KAMITE KINGS?

Where are the Kamite Kings Illustration. Head of a colossal seated statue of Amenemhat III, 12th Dynasty.

Nevertheless, he above should help under-score the relevance of this most contemporary reality of visiting Egypt, ancient *KMT* (Kemet). Clearly it relates to future direction of intent, designed to expose and educate people to the wonderful intellectual heritage of the Kamite ancestors along the Nile River in Northeast Africa. Much of this knowledge is today colonized by European academic and intellectual institutions, publishing and dissemination enterprises, within falsified and modern mind-sets. Nevertheless, this is an African culture and its reclamation and full integration into the respective order of African historical pageantry, as Diop pointed out, is a challenge that is worthy and must be met!

Khufu was a personality greater than life and classical commentators have left diverse accounts of him. Breasted I (1962: 85) tells of an inscription that reads: "Live the Horus: Mezer (*Md*[*r*]), King of Upper and Lower Egypt: Khufu, who is given life. He found the house of Isis, Mistress of the Pyramid, beside the house of the Sphinx [of Harmakhis] on the northwest of the house of Osiris, Lord of Rosta *(Rest's)*. He built his pyramid beside the temple of this Goddess, and he built a pyramid for the King's daughter Henutsen (*Hnwt s nt*) beside this temple." Manetho has also informed Khufu was "arrogant towards the Gods; but, repenting, he wrote the Sacred Book." Herodotus visited Kemet in 450 B.C. and wrote *The Histories*, devoting book II, *Euterpe* to that country. In explaining the history of the building of Khufu's masterpiece, the Great Pyramid, Herodotus wrote, according to Budge: "'Cheops [Khufu] succeeded to the throne, and at once plunged into all manner of wickedness. He closed all the temples, and forbade the Egyptians to perform sacrifices; after which he made them all work for him. Some were employed in the quarries of the Arabian hills, to cut stones, to drag them to the Libyan hills; and the 100,000 men thus occupied were relieved by an equal number every three months. 'Of the time,' he adds, 'passed in this arduous undertaking, 10 years were taken up with the construction of the causeway for the transport of stones, - a work scarcely less wonderful in my opinion than the pyramid itself; for it has 5 stades in length, 10 orgyes in breadth, and 8 in height in the highest part, and is constructed of polished stones, sculptured with the figures of animals. These 10 years were occupied exclusively in the causeway, independently of the time spent in leveling the hill on which the pyramids stand, and in making the subterranean chambers intended for his tomb in an island formed by the waters of the Nile, which he conducted thither by a canal."

WHERE ARE THE KAMITE KINGS?

Where are the Kamite Kings Illustration. Bust of a statue of Tutankhamon wearing the Nemes Headdress.

Where are the Kamite Kings Photo. The Author Dr. Fred Monderson and wife Carmen "mug" for this photo on the Ghizeh Plateau in 2017 depicting Khufu (right) and Khafre (left) in background. Notice the Sphinx just to the left of Carmen.

FREDERICK MONDERSON

Where are the Kamite Kings Illustration. The Nobleman Ti stands, while his beloved kneels at his feet. The stick or staff for support indicates he is an aged man.

"'The building of the pyramid itself occupied 20 years. It is square, each face measuring 8 plethra in length, and the same in height. The greater part is of polished stones, most carefully put together, no one of which is less than 30 feet long.'"

"This pyramid was built in steps, and, as the work proceeded, the stones were raised from the ground by means of machines made of short pieces of wood. When a block had been brought to the first tier, it was placed in a machine there, and so on from tier to tier by a succession of similar machines, there being as many machines as tiers of stone; or perhaps one served for the purpose, being moved from tier to tier as each stone was being taken up. I mention this

WHERE ARE THE KAMITE KINGS?

because I have heard both stated. When completed in this manner, they proceeded to make out (the form of) the pyramid, beginning from the top, and thence downwards to the lowest tier. On the exterior was engraved in Egyptian characters the sum expended in supplying the workmen with raphanus, onions, and garlic; and he who interpreted the inscription told me, as I remember well, that it amounted to 1600 talents. If that be true, how much must have been spent on the *iron* tools, food and clothing of the workmen, employing as they did, all the time above mentioned, without counting that occupied in cutting and transporting the stones and making subterraneous chambers, which must have been considerable!'"

Diodorus was the next authority who commented on personalities and culture of this classical African civilization on the Nile, during the time of Khufu. He wrote: "'Chembis (or Chemmis), a Memphite, who reigned 50 years, built the largest of the three pyramids, which are reckoned among the seven wonders of the world. They stand on the Libyan side (of the Nile), distant from Memphis 120 stadia, and 45 from the river. They strike every beholder with wonder, both from their size and the skill of their workmanship; for every side of the largest, at the base is 7 plethra in length, and more than 6 in height. Decreasing in size towards the summit, it there measures 6 cubits (9 feet). The whole is of solid stone, made with prodigious labor, having lasted to our time, a period no less than 1000 years, or as some say, upwards of 3400; the stones still preserving their original position, and the whole structure being uninjured. The stone is said to have been brought from Arabis, a considerable distance, and the building made by means of mounds (inclined planes), machines not having yet been invented. What is most surprising is that, though these structures are of such great antiquity, and all the surrounding ground is of so sandy a nature, there is no trace of a mound, nor vestige of the chippings of the stone: so that the whole seems as if placed on the surrounding sand by the aid of some deity, rather than by the sole and gradual operations of man. Some of the Egyptians try to make wonderful stories about them, saying that the mounds (inclined planes) were made of salt and nitre, which by directing the water of the river upon them, were afterwards dissolved without human aid when the work was completed. This cannot be true; but the same number of hands that raised the mounds removed the whole of the original place whence they were brought. For it is reported that 360,000 men were employed in this work, and the time occupied in finishing the whole was scarcely less than 20 years.'"

Again, Budge (1901) quotes Pliny regarding the monoliths of Giza, when he says: "The largest pyramid is built of stones from the Arabian quarries, 366,000 men are said to have been employed for 20 years in its construction; and the three were all made in 68 years and 4 months. Those who have written about them are Herodotus, Euphemerus, Darius of Samos, Aristagorus, Dionysius, Artemidorus, Alexander Polyhistor, Buroti Antisthenes, Demetrius, Demoteles, Apion; and yet no one of them shows satisfactorily by whom they were built; a proper reward to the authors of such vanity that their names should be buried in oblivion."

"'Some have affirmed that 1800 talents were spent in raphanus-roots, garlic, and onions. The largest covers a space of 8 acres (jugera), with 4 faces of equal size from corner to corner, and each measuring 883 feet; the breadth at the summit being 25 feet.'"

"'No vestiges of houses remain near them, but merely pure sand on every side, with something like lentils, common in the greater part of Africa. The principal question is, how the blocks were carried up to such a height? For some purpose that mounds, composed of nitre and salt, were gradually formed as the work advanced, and were afterwards dissolved by the water of the river as soon as it was finished; others, that bridges were made of mud-bricks, which, when the work was completed, were used to build private houses; since the Nile, being of a lower level, could not be brought to the spot."

One of the more probable modes of constructing the Great Pyramid was supplied by Flinders Petrie the "father of Egyptian archaeology" as he blazed a trail in the systematic and scientific excavation of this ancient land of Africa. He established the methodology, conventions and patterns that uncovered the corpus of historical evidence through archaeology and such became the basis for anthropological study of dynastic Kemet, along the Nile in Northeast Africa. Petrie's description of his work at the Great Pyramid of Giza is presented here, as recounted in Budge (1902) who states: "The site being chosen, it was carefully leveled, and the

WHERE ARE THE KAMITE KINGS?

lengths of the sides were set out with great exactitude. From several indications it seems that the masons planned the casing and some at least of the core masonry also, course by course on the ground. For on all the casing, and on the core in which the casing fitted, there are lines drawn on the horizontal surfaces, showing where each stone was to be placed on those below it. The means employed for raising such masses of stone is not shown to us in any representations. For the ordinary blocks of a few tons each, it would be very feasible to employ the method of resting them on two piles of wooden slabs, and rocking them up alternately to one side and the other by spar under the block, thus heightening the piles alternately and so raising the stone. This would also agree with the mysterious description of a machine made of short pieces of wood - a description which it is difficult otherwise to realize. This method would be also applicable to the largest masses we know of in the Pyramid, the fifty-six roofing beams of the King's chamber, and the spaces above it."

Where are the Kamite Kings Illustration. Granite Hall of the Great Pyramid of Khafre. Notice how the stones fit one upon the other.

"These average 700 cubic feet each; weighing therefore 54 tons, some larger, some less. That sheet iron was employed we know, from the fragment found by Colonel Howard Vyse in the masonry of the south air channel; and though some doubt has been thrown on the piece, merely from its rarity, yet the vouchers for it are very precise. No reasonable doubt can exist about its being really a genuine piece used by the Pyramid masons; and probably such pieces were required to prevent crowbars biting into the stones, and to ease the action of the rollers.'"

The question of Iron is an interesting one! While Herodotus mentions "iron tools," Diodorus and Pliny are silent; but Petrie speaks of "sheet iron" in reference to his specific discovery of iron. At the turn of the last century, H.R. Hall published two significant articles on the subject, entitled "Notes on the Early Use of Iron in Egypt" and "The Early Occurrence of Iron in Egypt." His views are generally considered foundational in the argument on iron, and as indicated, Hall (1903: 86) has written: "Now that Professor Petrie has discovered iron in deposits of VIth Dynasty date at Abydos, the contention of those Egyptologists who have always maintained that iron was known to the Egyptians from the earliest times must be acknowledged to be correct. The fact that iron was known to, and used by, the Egyptians over 2,000 years before it came into use in Europe is very remarkable, and is hard to square with current theories, but it is a fact. Professor Petrie's find is a lump of worked (?) iron, perhaps a wedge, which is rusted on to a bent piece of copper. The other objects of copper found with it are undoubtedly of VIth Dynasty date. They include a mirror, an axe-head, adze-blades, etc., of types intermediate between those of the IVth and those of the XIIth Dynasty (Petrie, *Abydos*, II., p. 33). They apparently belong to a building of Pepi I (*Ibid*.). Each had been carefully wrapped up in linen, the traces of which still remain. Those which have been presented to the British Museum, consisting of the fragment of iron, a mirror, axe-head, adze blade, and chisel ... are exhibited in the Prehistoric Gallery, Case J. The iron is in the lower right-hand corner of the illustration."

Where are the Kamite Kings Illustration. Bust of a statue of Amenemhat III, 12th Dynasty.

WHERE ARE THE KAMITE KINGS?

Where are the Kamite Kings Photo. Erik Monderson poses with young Egyptians just inside the Granite Hall of the Pyramid Complex on the Ghizeh Plateau in 2018.

FREDERICK MONDERSON

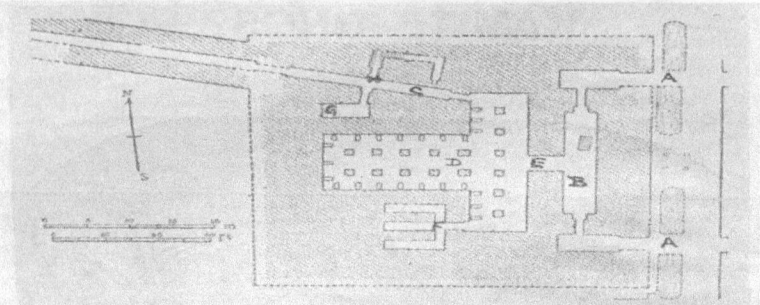

Where are the Kamite Kings Illustration. Plan of the Granite Temple of Khafre with the Causeway (top right) leading to his Pyramid.

Where are the Kamite Kings Illustration. Scarabs of Kings and Notables including Khafra, Menkaure, Unas, Amenemhat, Usertesen I, Usertesen III, Sobekhotep, etc., from the IVth to the XIIIth Dynasties.

"This is the third find of iron which can be attributed to the Old Kingdom. In 1837 a fragment of wrought iron was discovered in an inner joint of the stone blocks in one of the air-passages, which pass upwards from the interior of the Great Pyramid to the outer air. This is now in the British Museum, Egyptian Department, No. 2,433 (3rd

WHERE ARE THE KAMITE KINGS?

Egyptian Room, Case K, 29). In 1882, Professor Maspero found iron in the pyramid of a Vth Dynasty King at Abusir. Professor Petrie has now found iron in a VIth Dynasty deposit at Abydos."

"Until Professor Petrie's discovery it was, perhaps, allowable, in view of the certainty of the comparatively late appearance of iron in Europe, to doubt whether the finds at Giza and Abusir really dated back to the remote epoch of the Egyptian Old Kingdom. Accordingly, in 1888, Professor Montelius published in the Swedish anthropological publication *Ymer* (1888, p. 3), an article on the Bronze Age in Egypt, in which he rejected the evidence of the pyramid finds, and maintained "that the Egyptians during the whole period of the Old Kingdom and probably under the Middle Kingdom also - until about 1500 [more correctly 1700] B.C. - were unacquainted with the use of iron, and only used bronze for their weapons and tools." (p. 18). His doubts had been anticipated long previously (1862) by Rhind (*Theban Tombs and their Tenants*, p. 27)."

"These doubts were not, however, shared by those Egyptologists who have specially studied the inscriptions, one of whom, Professor Piehl, of Uppsala, at once replied to Montelius in an article entitled, "Brohsalder i Egypten?" (*Ymer*, 1888, p. 94 ff.), in which he traversed the latter's conclusions on the authority of the inscriptions, which, he maintained, actually mentioned iron as early as the time of the Vth Dynasty."

"This view remained, however, unconfirmed by unchallenged archaeological discovery until the present time. Now, Professor Petrie's find being incontrovertible, it is no longer open to us to say that the two earlier finds are doubtful. The presumption now is that the iron fragments from Abusir and from the Great Pyramid are of Vth and VIth date respectively. The Giza fragment will be about 150 years older than the piece from Abydos."

FREDERICK MONDERSON

Where are the Kamite Kings Photo. Temple of Horus at Edfu. Decorated entrance Pylon. Right-side illustration, dedicated to Ra-Horakhty and this is duplicated on the left dedicated to Amon-Ra; openings above are for flagstaves that fly the Temple's colors. Customary winged sun disk sits on cornice above entrance.

"That iron was known in the time of the Middle Kingdom seems to be shown by Maspero's discovery ... the date of this tomb will be XIIIth to XVIIth Dynasty, *circa* 2000-1700 B.C. Montelius' proposition is thus shown to be erroneous. Iron was known to the Egyptians as early as the VIth Dynasty (3700 B.C.) and continued to be known to them thenceforward. Its use was, however, probably by no means common until towards the end of the "New Empire." Professor Petrie (*Abydos*, II, p. 33; pl. ii, 10) notes an iron Halbert blade of Rameses III's time (exhibited in the British Museum, with the VIth Dynasty objects described above) as one of the oldest known specimens of an Egyptian iron weapon; its date is about 1200 B.C. Very probably it was during the XIXth Dynasty that its use became more or less general, though it in no way displaced or supplanted bronze. In the long tribute lists of the XVIIIth Dynasty it is never mentioned, but under the XIXth Dynasty it occurs in a religious text at Abu Simbel, in which the God Ptah is made to say that he has formed the limbs of King Rameses II of electrum, his bones of bronze, and his arm of iron."

WHERE ARE THE KAMITE KINGS?

Where are the Kamite Kings Illustration. Interior of the Coffin of Seti I.

"This is the oldest literary mention of iron with regard to which there never has been any doubt whatever. The word used for iron here is ba-n-pet, which means '*ba* of heaven,' i.e., originally aerolithic ba. Lepsius, however, took the word to mean 'metal' generally, rather than 'iron' specifically, thus differing from Brugsch, who preferred the restricted meaning. But, now that we know that iron was used under the Old Kingdom, it seems most probable that *ba* does mean 'iron' in the Pyramid Texts. Very possibly it originally meant only "metal" generally, but under the Old Kingdom was already used in a restricted sense to signify iron, 'the metal (of heaven),' the more general meaning being still occasionally used, as in such a phrase as *ba n nub*, 'mineral d'or.'" H.R. Hall.

Two years later, Hall's second article entitled "The Early Occurrence of Iron in Egypt," was published in *Man* 1905, 40, where he wrote: "In *Man*, 1905, 7, Professor Montelius has most courteously signaled his dissent from the view which I expressed in *Man*, 1903, 86, as to the sporadic early occurrence of *worked* iron in Egypt. Professor Montelius says that he "fully agrees" with me "that iron was rare as lately as the XVIII." "Certainly, I never maintained that iron was in *common* use before the time of the XIXth Dynasty, but I do still maintain that worked iron was known to the Egyptians as early as the days of the Old Empire. Professor Montelius does not believe this, and so says: "I cannot agree with Mr. Hall that my opinion about the first use of iron in Egypt is shown to be erroneous." May I be allowed to restate my view on the subject?

"The older archaeologists all believe that iron was known to the earliest Egyptians. We may leave out of account, for the moment, the arguments about the precise meaning of the word *ba*, which probably originally meant metal in general, though, as "metal of heaven," *ba-n-pet* was iron, and then *ba* alone was used, in a restricted sense, as iron only. One of the chief arguments for the occurrence of iron under the IV Dynasty was the piece from the Great Pyramid now in the British Museum (No. 2433) which I mentioned in *Man*, 1903, 86, but which Professor Montelius ignores in *Man*, 1905, 7, though when taken in conjunction with the Abydos fragment, which he discusses at considerable length, it is evidence of the first importance."

"I do not see how it is possible to ignore the evidence of the contemporaneity of the Great Pyramid fragment with the pyramid which was adduced by its discoverers, except on the supposition that it is a relic of the XXVI Dynasty rebuilding. The author of the rebuilding (*Umbau*) theory as applied to the pyramids, Dr. Burckhardt, does not, however, suppose that the Great pyramid was rebuilt from the top to bottom by the Saites, as would have to be supposed were it desired to show that the blocks between which the piece of iron was found were placed in position under the XXVI Dynasty, since they are down one of the air-shaft, and so well inside the mass of the pyramid. The complete rebuilding of the Great

WHERE ARE THE KAMITE KINGS?

Pyramid would certainly have been completely beyond the power and means of the Psammetici, nor does Dr. Burckhardt believe that anything very much was done by them to it. Professor Petrie has, perhaps, changed his view since then, but in 1883 (*Pyramids and Temples of Gizeh*, p. 85), when discussing the mechanical means used in the building of the pyramids, he wrote as follows: 'That sheet iron was employed, we know, from the fragment found by Howard Vyse in the masonry of the south air channel, and though some doubt has been thrown on the piece, merely from its rarity, yet the vouchers for it are very precise, and it has a cast of a nummulite on the rust of it, proving it to have been buried for ages beside a block of nummulite limestone, and therefore to be certainly ancient. No reasonable doubt can therefore exist about its being really a genuine piece used by the pyramid masons, and probably such pieces were required to prevent crowbars biting into the stones, and to ease the action of the rollers.' This was very emphatic testimony in favor of the early use of iron in Egypt."

In *Man*, 1903, 86, I have already mentioned the fragments of iron of Middle Kingdom date, described by Professor Maspero in the *Guide au Musee de Boulaq*, 1883, p. 296."

"In *Life in Ancient Egypt* (Eng. Trans. (1894, 461) Professor Erman accepted this evidence, and cited Maspero, as above, and Dr. Birch's edition of Wilkinson's *Ancient Egyptians*, II, 251 (describing the pyramid fragment) in support."

"So far, the Egyptologists. In 1888 Professor Montelius attempted to bring the Egyptian evidence as to the early use of metals into line with the European evidence in his article in *Ymer*, the organ of the Swedish Anthropological and Geographical Society, entitled *Bronsaldern i Egypten*. In this article he rejected the evidence for the use of iron in Egypt before 1500 B.C. (including the Pyramid fragment), thus more or less synchronizing the first appearance of iron in Egypt with its first appearance in Europe. To this article the late Professor Piehl replied in his article Bronsalder I Egypten? in the same periodical, 1888, p. 94 ff. The Egyptologists were evidently largely unconvinced, but the spokesman of European prehistoric science had decided against them, and his authority carried, justly, such weight that the question was shelved until further archaeological evidence should be forthcoming. [Note. As Professor Montelius quotes me (*Man*, 1903, 86) "In view of the certainty of the comparatively late appearance of iron in Europe, it was, perhaps, allowable to doubt whether they (the supposed fragments of iron) really dated back to the remote epoch of the Egyptian Old Kingdom."]

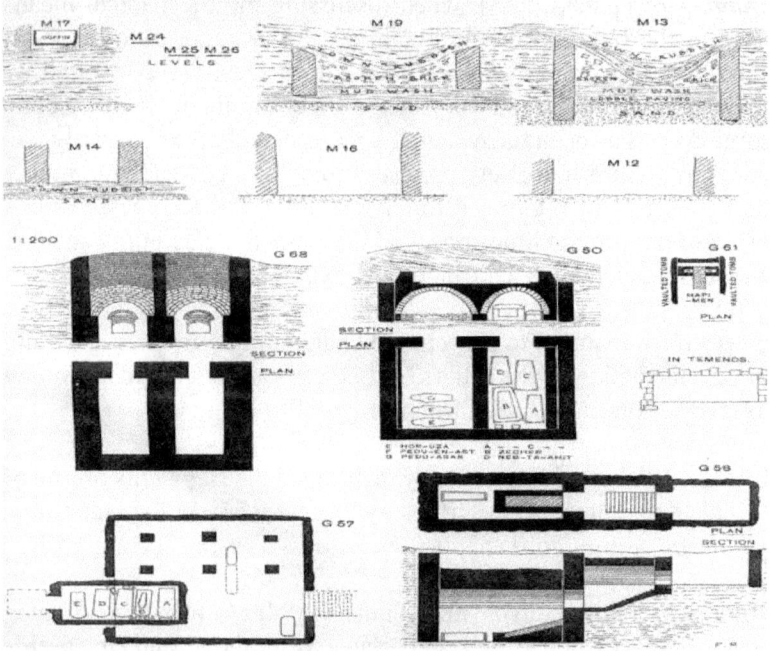

Where are the Kamite Kings Illustration. Sections and plans of early Tombs at Abydos.

"It came in 1902, when Professor Petrie discovered at Abydos the find (illustrated in MAN, 1903, 86, and described in the *British Museum Guide to the Antiquities of the Bronze Age in the Department and Mediaeval Antiquities*, p. 126) of copper objects (a mirror and tools) of the VI Dynasty found with 'a lung of hydrated oxide of iron (not metallic).' This iron is now chemically 'not metallic,' but it shows that an object of iron was buried with these copper objects. And, though the present lump of hydrated oxide or iron may now show no trace of being worked, what reason have we to doubt that the original iron object was not worked? Why should an unworked piece of iron be buried with these copper tools? Is it not more probable that it was a tool or other worked object like the rest, but of iron, not copper?"

WHERE ARE THE KAMITE KINGS?

"Evidently preferring to believe that it was not worked, Professor Montelius says (*Man*, 1905, 7) that 'it does not prove the *use* of iron, only the *existence* of that metal. And it is well known that iron-meteoric or telluric-existed at that time, as long before the first man.' Certainly, but the proof was hardly needed. I take it that what Professor Montelius meant to say was 'it does not prove the *use* of iron, only the *knowledge* of that metal.'"

"But if it was known, why should it not have been used? The VI Dynasty piece could be taken to prove that iron was known only, and not used, were it certain that the original iron object was not worked, and did stand-alone. It is not certain that it was not worked, and it does not stand alone."

"Professor Montelius omits to notice its relations to the other early finds of iron, the Pyramid fragment especially. Even were it demonstrably an unworked lump it would still (since its date is incontestable) go to support the real antiquity of the worked piece from the Great Pyramid. Here are the facts. We find in Egypt a piece of worked iron, to which a date of about 3500 B.C. is assigned on good *prima facie* grounds, but because iron did not come into general use in Egypt till about 1300 B.C., and in southern Europe till about 1100 B.C., and because we do not possess another piece of iron of the same date, we admit that this early date must be regarded as still *sub judice*. We need corroboration. We afterwards find in Egypt a piece of iron, worked or unworked does not matter to the argument, which is assigned on incontestable grounds to a date of about 3200 B.C. Does not the second find corroborate the first, and are we not justified in assuming that we have erred from excess of caution in denying that iron was not only known to, but occasionally worked by, the Egyptians in the fourth millennium B.C.? And as a matter of fact, as I have said, the probabilities are that the VI Dynasty fragment was originally worked, and not a mere meaningless lump. Why should a mere lump be buried with the tools?"

FREDERICK MONDERSON

Where are the Kamite Kings Photo. Temple of Horus at Edfu. The "Sphinx at Edfu" inside the entrance Pylon represents a Graeco-Roman Period introduction; recently oved to the Plaza.

"This was my point, and I content that I was justified in saying that Professor Montelius' view is now proved to be erroneous, and that iron was known and sometimes worked in Egypt as far back as the time of the Old Kingdom. We then see that it is quite possible that the word *ba*, originally 'metal' in general, was also used at an early period in the restricted sense of 'iron.' Piehl's argument from the color of weapons in early tomb-paintings is certainly open to discussion, but both these arguments about *ba* meaning specifically iron and the blue color of weapons are now superfluous in presence of the two-actual piece of iron from Abydos and Giza."

"Nor is it inherently improbable that iron was occasionally used in Egypt at an early period, far earlier than in Europe. It seems to be forgotten that Egypt is in Africa, not in Europe, and that arguments from European knowledge do not necessarily hold good for Egypt. I have it on the authority of my colleagues in the Ethnographical Department of the British Museum that many Negro tribes have worked iron from time immemorial, and have never passed through a copper age. May not the knowledge of worked iron have reached the Egyptians from inner Africa at a remote period, long before they began generally to abandon copper and bronze for iron (as far as weapons and tools were concerned) about the fourteenth century B.C.?" (H.R. Hall.)

The dimensions of the Great Pyramid have been variously stated by a number of ancient and modern writers. Budge says Herodotus gave the length: "8 plethra (800 feet) on each side at the base, and

WHERE ARE THE KAMITE KINGS?

the same in height; this last measured no doubt vertically, but along the sloping side. Diodorus makes it 7 plethra (700 feet) in length, and 6 (600 feet) in height. Pliny gives the length at 883 feet. Nine modern writers have equally varied in their calculations."

In 1880-82 Petrie conducted his own measurements giving the dimensions on the original platform as follows:

Great Pyramid	Feet	Ins.
North Side	755	9.4
East Side	755	7.7
South Side	755	9.5
West Side	755	8.6
Mean Length	765	8.8

The original height Petrie calculated to have been 481 feet, 4 ins. The actual present height is 451 feet. The area of the original base was 63,444 square yards, or rather more than 13 acres.

Khufu was followed by **Djedefre** who ruled *Nile Year* 1674-1682 (2566-2558 B.C.) though little is known about him.

Where are the Kamite Kings Illustration. Khafre, builder of the Second largest pyramid on the Ghizeh Plateau.

FREDERICK MONDERSON

Khafre

Khafre ruled 1682-1708 *Nile Year* (2558-2532 B.C.), and some believe he ruled for at least twenty-four years according to the *Turin Papyrus*. His royal titles were:

Horus	Usr-ab
Two Ladies	Usr-en
Golden Horus	Khafre
Suten Bat	Sekhen
Son of Ra	Rakhaf

His name is on the *Tablet of Sakkara* and the *Abydos List*, No. 23. It can also be found in Lepsius' *Denkmaler*. Khafre built the Second largest pyramid on the Giza plateau. Prince Nekure, son of King Khafre, has left the only surviving Old Kingdom will. This document has thrown important light on princely wealth and bequeathment. Breasted (1962: I, 89) tells: "The fortune which Prince Nekure bequeathed to his heirs consisted of fourteen towns and two estates in the pyramid-city of his father. The latter doubtless consisted of his 'town-house' and gardens. These he had left to a daughter, but she had evidently died, and on the reversion of the legacy to himself he left it to his wife. The fourteen towns he distributed among his five heirs, of whom one was his wife, and three his children, while the name of one is lost. Eleven of the fourteen towns are named after Khafre, and there is no reason to doubt that the other three were also so named, but they are now unreadable. Besides these fourteen towns, Prince Nekure had at least twelve towns in the mortuary endowment of his tomb, of which nine were named after Khafre."

The enormous construction projects of Khufu, Khafre and Menkaure, presented tremendous logistic and housing demands for the builders, to avoid the long commute every day to the work site. Surviving evidence on patterns of housing artisans and workers on these royal buildings come from the reign of Khafre. Such early "labor relationships" reflect the humaneness of the Pharaoh, dispelling myths of slave labor and foreigners toiling in building these structures. The best example of this distorted line of thought is illustrated by the Cecil B. De Mille's epic *Ten Commandments*,

WHERE ARE THE KAMITE KINGS?

where that artist, in panoramic splendor galvanized and indelibly implanted images in the minds of modern man, his version of the ancient phenomenon. De Mille's characterization is based on a distorted view of this aspect of ancient African history and experience, a thousand years after the building of these pyramids.
'

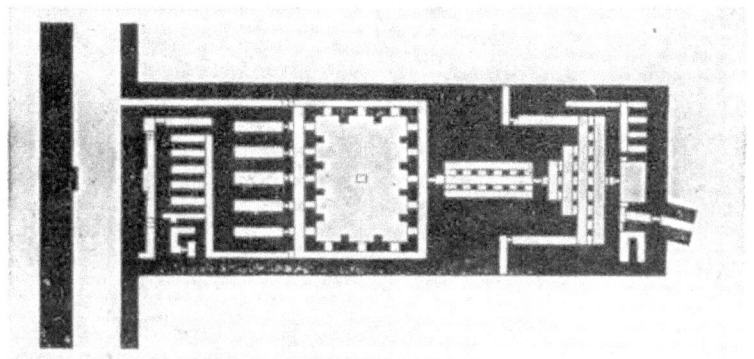

Where are the Kamite Kings Illustration. The Funeral Chapel of Khafra (Chephren).

Recently, Drs. Hawass and Lehner excavated an area; and accordingly, Hawass (1993: 9) wrote, its, "south-east of the Great Sphinx and south of the boundary wall along the base of the east-west ridge of the Giza Pyramids." Over an extensive area within the mega-complex comprising modern population centers Nazlet-el-Samman, Nazlet-es-Sissi, Nazlet-el-Batran and Kafr-el-Gebel, were found cities whose workers labored on the pyramids. Three major areas were revealed in the 1988-89 excavation. Hawass in *Horus* (1993: 9) mentions the "workmen's camp; the Institution area; the tombs of the workmen; and overseer." This find is therefore significant because it culminates over a century of observation, excavation and commentary dating to Flinders Petrie's work in 1880-1882. Hawass (1993: 8) noted Petrie's discovery of a number of rooms "located west of the outer enclosure wall of the pyramid of Khafra. He interpreted the groups of rooms discovered as being a city for the workers who labored on the pyramid. The structures consist of long narrow rooms, which back on to a large courtyard the walls of rough limestone blocks being cased with mud and plaster. It was estimated that the one hundred and eleven rooms could house approximately 5500 men."

Where are the Kamite Kings Photo. The Sphinx, "Guardian of Khafre's Pyramid," has its own tale to tell. However, while others such as Khufu's Pyramid was completely denuded of its casing stone to build structures in Cairo by Egypt's Arab conquerors, Khafra's still retained some casing stone at its zenith.

Following Petrie, the excavator Reisner investigated the third pyramid at Giza belonging to Menkaure, he used the Greek term Mycerinus, a later King of this dynasty. He found, Hawass (1993: 8) wrote, "remains of Old Kingdom mud-brick houses in the central open court just east of Menkaure's Lower Valley Temple." Further, and more recently, Saleh (1993: 8) investigated a "complex of stone rubble walls located about 73 meters south of the causeway of Menkaure."

WHERE ARE THE KAMITE KINGS?

Where are the Kamite Kings Illustration. Khafra (Chephren) builder of the second largest pyramid at Ghizeh (left); and, wooden statue of Prince Ewibre in Cairo Museum (right).

"He discovered long narrow foundations in association with an industrial complex of workshops which produced cult artifacts for the King. Fifteen buildings of rubble and mortar with different shapes and number of rooms were found in this area. Ovens for baking bread or firing ceramics as well as facilities for the preparation of clay were also uncovered."

Kromer' work between 1971-1975 on large mounds of settlement debris revealed excavated strata, continued Hawass (1993: 8) that consisted of, "pieces of bone, ashes, potsherds, flints, stone bowls, mud brick debris and mud seals of Khufu and Khafra. From these remains Kromer concluded that the mound represented a dump left by the specialized workmen who served under these rulers." And even Butzer's re-examination of the material concluded that they were the "remains of several settlements for specialized artisans."

FREDERICK MONDERSON

Where are the Kamite Kings Photo. The God Ptah and an unnamed King in the Cairo Museum.

Harvard University and the Boston Museum of Fine Arts sponsored Reisner's excavation in 1910 when he worked the northern part of the cemetery west of the Great Pyramid where tombs of the family of Khufu were located. The *American Journal of Archaeology* (1911: 407-08) noted he also located, "tombs belonging to priests and officials to whom were entrusted the performance of the offering rites to the dead. These cemeteries had fallen into decay, and were covered with sand by the sixth dynasty. In 1906-07, the pyramid temple of Mycerinus was excavated, and in it was found pieces of an alabaster statue of Mycerinus. South of this temple was the quarry for the pyramid of Mycerinus, with tombs of priests on its north and west terraces. The causeway running from the pyramid on to a valley temple was followed, and in 1908 the temple found. It was of mud-brick, but contained many valuable antiquities. In the portico were the bases of four life-size alabaster statues still in place, while the statues lay in fragments on the floor. Among them was the head of Shepseskaf, son of Mycerinus. In other rooms were unfinished statuettes, copper implements and weapons, magic wands of flint, and a great number of vessels of alabaster, porphyry, diorite, crystal, slate, and other stones. The excavations were

WHERE ARE THE KAMITE KINGS?

completed in 1910, when a beautiful pair of slate statues, now in the Museum of Fine Arts, was discovered. Remains of three temples were found on the site: 1. The foundation of a magnificent building of stone, laid by Mycerinus. 2. The mud-brick temple built by Shepseskaf, his successor. 3. A mud-brick reconstruction, built by Pepi II, of the sixth dynasty. The early death of Shepseskaf prevented him from finishing his father's temple in stone. Incidentally the foundations for a pyramid northwest of this temple were identified as those of Shepseskaf. The statues found make it possible to date the Sphinx and the diorite statue of Chephren in the time of Chephren. The Sphinx is the guardian of the sacred precincts of the Second Pyramid, and its head is a portrait of Chephren."

Menkaure succeeded Khafre. Actually, Chephren and Mycerinus were actually Khafre and Menkaure. He ruled *Nile Year* 1708-1736 or 1744 (2532-2504 B.C.). This King's names were as follows:

Horus	Ka-Kha
Two Ladies	Ka
Golden Horus	————
Suten Bat	Ka-men-Ra
Son of Ra	————

FREDERICK MONDERSON

Where are the Kamite Kings Photo. Erik Monderson stands at the rear of the Great Sphinx on the Ghizeh Plateau in 2018.

Where are the Kamite Kings Illustration. Menkaure (Mycerinus) (left) built the third largest pyramid at Ghizeh; and, Menkaure (Mycerinus) with Hathor and Diospolis Nome Goddess. Neither kings' nose is broken

His name is in his Pyramid at Giza, the third largest. It is also on a Stela of the King in Cairo and on a cylinder-seal found in Le Grain's

WHERE ARE THE KAMITE KINGS?

Annales and in Lepsius' *Denkmaler*. It is on the *Abydos List*, No. 24, the *Papyrus of Nu* (Sheet 5), on the *Second Abydos List*, No. 25 and on Men-Ka-Ra's coffin in the British Museum, No. 6,647.

Where are the Kamite Kings Photo. Temple of Horus at Edfu. In White resting on Red Double Crown, Pharaoh is embraced by two Goddesses in Red and White Crowns respectively.

FREDERICK MONDERSON

Where are the Kamite Kings Photo. Erik within the Perimeter of the Ghizeh Pyramids with the two great pyramid structures at his rear.

Shepsekaf, Menkaure's successor, ruled *Nile Year* 1744-1748 (2504-2500 B.C.) and his Queen was **Khenthawes**, daughter of **Djedefhor** who had two tombs at Giza and Abusir. His name on the *Abydos List* is No. 25. It is mentioned on the *Palermo Stone* and in Lepsius' *Denkmaler*, II, 41.

A few uncertain Kings including Sebek-ka-re from the *Tablet of Sakkara*, and a Queen end out this dynasty.

A final commentary can be added to this section regarding origins and inner Africa. It concerns discoveries made by Randall-MacIver and reported in summary in *American Journal of Archaeology* (1901: 332) that read: "The April number of *Man* contains an illustrated preliminary report of Mr. Randall-MacIver's excavations this winter at El Amrah, a village six miles south of Abydos. Two prehistoric cemeteries were explored, containing six or seven types of graves, among the contents of which were model boats of various kinds and also pottery cattle, thus making it clear that the 'New Race' were a pastoral people also. Among the objects illustrated are weapons of war and the chase, dolls representing the people themselves, who are figured with strongly curled hair, and specimens of basketwork. The most valuable find was an inscribed slate of a date considerably anterior to the first dynasty; this is by far the earliest known example of the use of hieroglyphs." (*Athen*,

WHERE ARE THE KAMITE KINGS?

March 16, 1901.) In addition, E. A. Gates published a "Description of Specimens exhibited at a Meeting of the Anthropological Institute," May 13, 1902, in *Man* that is of an ethnological nature, yet, underscoring the broad latitude of observation British citizens were asked to apply when traveling overseas. At the Bodlian Library of Oxford University, this researcher encountered a Questionnaire of 105 questions about music given to all English travelers to collect data about foreign cultures. It stands to reason other areas of scholarly interest were similarly accounted. All these fragments were then compiled about the ethnology of a country so as to acquire a wide understanding of the culture. *Man* (1903: 22) reads: "These Sudanese dolls were obtained in Khartoum. Although I have never seen Sudanese children actually playing with such dolls, yet I have no doubt that the dolls were made for their satisfaction and not the tourists; who, indeed, seldom, if ever, came across any specimens. The only other dolls, which I have seen, were some in the possession of a British officer at Khartoum, who had got them from the mother of one of his servants. The dolls shown in the photograph were obtained through a Greek merchant at Khartoum. Though made of Nile mud, native gum, and sticks, they are not in any ways an accurate copy of the women of the country, especially in the matter of their hair and its adornment. This hair is carefully plaited; the number of plaits corresponding to the wealth and social status of the woman, and each plait is fixed by a large lump of mud at the end, as the picture clearly shows. The decoration, however, is somewhat more profuse than is usually seen. The clothing, too, is not quite correct. The women, as a rule, wear a long piece of white calico round their bodies over a short apron of strips of leather, and a piece of colored silk round the lower part of the abdomen. No doubt the dolls' costume owes something to the European women, who, as wives of the Greek merchants, are living in Khartoum and Omdurman; but the difficulties of adapting the correct clothing to a piece of stick with a lump of mud upon it to represent the hips had something to do with their dress." E. A. Gates.

Whether modern imperial influences determined the nature of dress and appearance or not, it cannot similarly be argued in ancient times when this imitative motif applied. The ancient dolls truly represented the indigenous Kamite Africans of early Kemet and the clearest indication stems from the writer's probable bias; still, in the "strongly curled hair" syndrome we get a glimpse of who they are discussing. Equally, let us not forget the black Africans of Nabta Playa who migrated to the Nile Valley in Predynastic times and are thought to be the forerunners or precursors of the pharaohs.

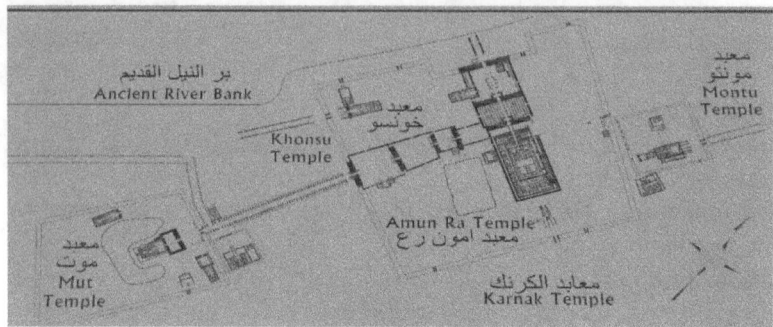

Where are the Kamite Kings Photo. Karnak Temple Complex showing Amon, Mut, Khonsu and Montu Temples.

Where are the Kamite Kings Photo. Temple of Horus at Edfu. Events of the war between Horus and Seth as depicted in the "Corridor of Victory."

The Fifth Dynasty was a period of continued growth, indicating a tremendous increase in travel and trade. Accounts tell not of wars but commerce and contacts, trade and travel, the import and export of ideas and crafts, cultural syncretism. This was a time of improvement of the lot of the common people. The society also experienced an increase in education. Murray (1949: 17) offers the

WHERE ARE THE KAMITE KINGS?

view: "There was a spread of luxury among the lesser people such as had not appeared in earlier times. There was also a spread of education; letters to and from the King are frequently mentioned, and papyrus began to be used for correspondence and accounts."

Maspero has supplied an appended list of the known Pharaohs of the Vth Dynasty, restored as far as can be, with the closest approximate dates of their reigns. While this list is somewhat outdated, as compared with Murnane and ben-Jochannan, it does come from references from the Turin Canon, the Monuments and from Manetho and can be used as a guide while it also supplies the most ancient names.

From the Turin Canon Manetho Monuments:

Userkaf (3990-3962?)	28	Ousirkheres	28
Sahure (3961-3957?)	4	Sepheres	13
Kakiu (3956-3954?)	2		
Nofiririkeri (3953-3946?)	7	Sen (3945-3933?)	12
Neferkhere 20 Shopsiskeri	? Sisires		7
Akauhoru (3121-3914?)		Kheres	20
....		?	
Usirnire Aznu (3900-3875?)	25	Rathoures	44
Menkauhoru (3874-3866?)	8	Menkheres	9
Dadkeri Assi (3865-3837?)	28	TAnkheres	44
Unas (3834-3804?)	30	Obnos	33

Where are the Kamite Kings Illustration. Kings of the Vth Dynasty read from the Turin Canon and the Monuments (left) and from Manetho (right).

This was also a period of descriptive biographies as evidenced by works of Weni and Ptahshepses then add to those that of Harkhuf, etc., of the Sixth Dynasty. Inscribed in their works in mines, quarries and recounting of various expeditions, these accounts are valuable as historical and ethnological depictions. This Fifth Dynasty was also a time in which distinction could be made between "real" and "purely honorary" titles of officials, a prerogative that peaked in the next dynasty.

FREDERICK MONDERSON

The Fifth Dynasty can also be considered a time of continuity and change. While the IVth and Vth Dynasty used more reliefs in their tomb constructions than the VIth Dynasty, the Fifth employed basalt and alabaster in pavements, while the Sixth Dynasty used limestone for floors.

THE FIFTH DYNASTY

The **Fifth Dynasty**, according to Manetho, is native to the Island of Elephantine at Aswan, and lasted *Nile Year* 1750-1903 (2498-2345 B.C.). The founder was **Userkaf** or **Weserkaf**, 1750-1757, Nile *Year* (2498-2491 B.C.). His official titles are as follows:

Horus	Ari-maat
Two Ladies	————
Golden Horus	————
Suten Bat	Userkaf
Son of Ra	————

Userkaf's name appears on the *Abydos List*, No. 26, on the *Tablet of Sakkara*, the *Palermo Stone*, on a cylinder seal (Mariette *Mon Divers*, Pl. 54) and on a stele in the British Museum, No. 1,143.

Where are the Kamite Kings Illustration. Fifth Dynasty Pyramid and Temple at Abusir in Murray's *Egyptian Temples* (1931).

Userkaf built a small pyramid near the Step-Pyramid at Sakkara. Ruffle (1977: 30) indicated its plan included the "funerary temple on the surface and only a small shrine against the east side." This funeral temple has furnished a remarkable limestone relief of "Birds

WHERE ARE THE KAMITE KINGS?

in a Papyrus Swamp" with paint traces, now in the Cairo Museum of Kemetic/Egyptian Antiquities. This is one of the early and enduring classics of Kemet art. Corteggiani's (1987: 51) commentary of the piece speaks of the "remarkable delicacy of the sculpture, the freedom of the composition and the breathtaking precision of the observation lead us to regret the loss of the remainder of the scene." In that author's description of the relief, Corteggiani (1987: 51) further attests to the high level of artistic depictions along the Nile at that time, indicative of other crafts as well. Given such, we are reminded of Dr. Diop's correction contention, "the ancient artist certainly knew and correctly depicted the people of time."

Of that relief he writes, "At the center is a black-and-white pied King-fisher (*Ceryle rudis*) caught in the moment of immobility in his flight which occurs just before he darts like an arrow on his prey. Elsewhere, from right to left, we identify the purple gallinule (*Horphyrio porphyrio*) with its strong feet and huge toes; the stripped hoopoe (*Upupa epops*) with its fan-shaped crest; the sacred ibis (*Threskiornis aethiopicus*) with beak long and bent; the bittern (*Botaurus stellaris*) which loves aquatic vegetation; the night heron (*Nycticorax nycticorx*) which fishes in the dark; and finally, the European Kingfisher (*Alcedo atthis ispida*) which waits on a perch for its prey to appear."

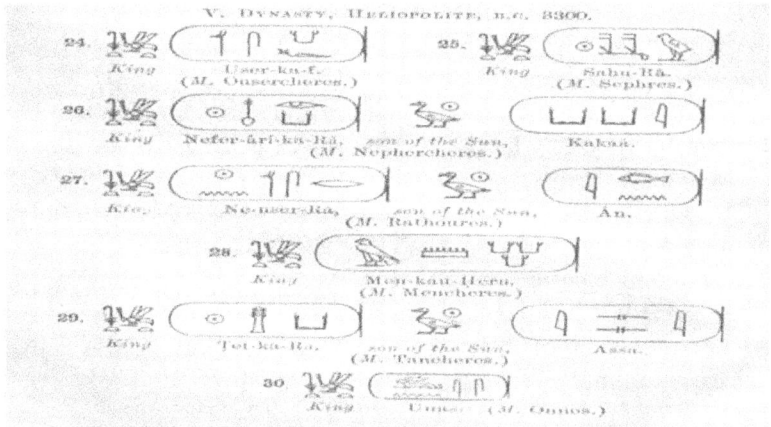

Kamite Kings Cartouche/Shennu. Memphite Kings of the Fifth Dynasty.

FREDERICK MONDERSON

Where are the Kamite Kings Illustration. Coffin lids of Rameses II and Rameses III.

During Userkaf's reign, Baines and Malek (1980: 83) mentions the existence of a "brick-built chapel at ancient Egyptian *Djerty* (Tuphium of the Greco-Roman Period), on the east bank of the Nile." On the road from Aswan to Luxor, *Djerty* or Modern Tod is midway between el-Mo-Alla and Gebelein and Armant. This King was also builder of the earliest preserved of the "Sun Temples" at Abusir. On a visit to Tod, an Inspector of Antiquities showed this writer a plaque of a 1st Dynasty King, indicating the site was active this early in time.

The name of Userkaf was discovered at the First Cataract, not far from Aswan, beginning a long list of individuals who have inscribed

WHERE ARE THE KAMITE KINGS?

their names at this most ancient of Nile cities, "Gateway to Africa." In actuality, the gateway to Africa is at the other end of the Nile, in the Delta. This is one of the enduring contradictions raised in the confrontation regarding ownership of the practical, artifactual and intellectual heritage of the culture of ancient Kemet, the gift of Africa.

Case in point. Archaeology is a useful science in historical reconstruction. It was born in Europe in attempts to locate "early man" in that environment. This was all part of the attempt to "prove" inherent superiority of Europe and Europeans, viz., or in cultural progress of "whites" over "non-whites." This endeavor found great motivation in the changes transforming the technical, cultural, political, social and intellectual environment in 19th Century Europe. Industrialism, nationalism and imperialism bred efforts to rationalize political and economic exploitation especially in Africa leading to the Berlin Congress' Partition of 1884-1885. In that climate racist intellectuals purposefully distorted the record. Equally, the terminology of archaeology and anthropology developed in systematic examination of Europe, were then applied to Africa to describe the same time periods and cultures. Oftentimes, the terms were inadequate and did not accurately describe the African experience. Even further, modern geographic orientation that was imprinted on the culture followed a pattern of European penetration. So much so, though the Nile River flows, even the culture, from south to north, it is the only major river in the world that does this as all others flow north to south, the First Cataract is in position where the Sixth Cataract should be, according to the modern mindset! Nevertheless, the numbers are in reverse recounting Europeans' ascent of the Nile.

A monumental granite head of Userkaf is in Cairo, No. 6,051. Additionally, J.H. Breasted (1962: 90) mentions a "will" from the reign of Userkaf-f made by Nekonekh concerning, the "disposal of two parcels of land of sixty stat each, given by King Menkaure: the one as endowment of the temple of the local Hathor of Royenet (Tehneh); the other as a wakf or endowment of the tomb of Khenuka, a nobleman of Menkaure's time. Both endowments were administered by one priesthood, who served at the same time as priest of Hathor and as mortuary priests of Khenuka.... Userkaf, as

FREDERICK MONDERSON

the first King of the Fifth Dynasty was plainly dispossessing some supporter of the old dynasty, and strengthening his own house by winning the allegiance of another noble family."

Sahure ruled *Nile Year* 1757-1771 (2491-2477 B.C.) and succeeded Userkaf. His official titles were as follows:

Horus	Neb-Khau
Two Ladies	————
Golden Horus	————
Suten Bat	Ra-Sahu
Son of Ra	————

Breasted I (1962: 108) provided his name, recorded in the Wady Maghara mining area in Sinai: "'Horus: Lord of Diadems; King of Upper and Lower Egypt: Sahure; who is given life forever. Smiter of all countries. The Great God smites the Asiatics of all countries.'"

On the *Abydos List*, his name is No. 27, and it is mentioned on the *Palermo Stone*, *Tablet of Sakkara*, and the *Tablet of Karnak*. It is also on a statue in Cairo, No. 42,004 and on a vase in the British Museum, No. 29,330.

His reign signaled turbulence when he moved from the Giza and Sakkara burial complex of the earlier period and built his pyramid at Abusir. 'The Pyramid where the *Ba*-spirit rises' is its ancient name. Accordingly, Baines and Malek (1980: 140) wrote: "Userkaf was followed there by successors Neferirkare and Niuserre. They built, respectively, 'The Pyramid of the *Ba*-spirit' and 'The Pyramid which is Established of Places.' The last King of the Fifth and the Sixth Dynasty Kings returned to Sakkara."

The six panels of Zoser at the Step-Pyramid supplies among other things, classic portrayals of several attires of the King. Fashion of the times was an interesting issue. In *Life in Ancient Egypt*, Adolf Erman (1894: 59) presents an illustration of a "Memorial of the Victories of Sa-hure in the Wadi Maghara." This piece is particularly interesting for the King's attire elicits the following Erman (1894: 59) comment: "In prehistoric ages, when the only garment was a girdle round the loins, with two or three ties hanging

WHERE ARE THE KAMITE KINGS?

down in front, it was considered a luxury that the ruler should replace these ties by a piece of matting or fur, and, as further decoration, should add the tail of a lion behind. In the rock steles of the quarries of Sinai the King Sahure is seen standing in this way, killing his enemies the Bedouins. This is only an ancient symbolical representation, and we must not imagine that the King really wore this costume of a savage chief." Today this is called roots, my good man!

Even further, Erman (1894: 59) continued: "In the time of the 5th dynasty the loin girdle had long become the dress of the lower orders, all the upper classes in Egypt wearing a short skirt. The King wore his skirt sometimes over, but more usually under his old official costume. Both corners of the piece of stuff were then rounded off, so that the front piece belonging to the girdle could be seen below. Sometimes the whole was made of pleated golden material, and must have formed quite a fine costume."

It is significant that the tail of the lion should also become a part of the High Priest repertoire. Much Later at the end of the Eighteenth Dynasty, Aye could be seen performing the "Opening of the Mouth Ceremony" on Tutankhamon, in the Valley of the Kings, while wearing the same lion garb and holding the magical adze.

A further commentary on dress is introduced for further understanding of the ethnological questions they raise relating to ancient Kemetic racial characteristics.

The following is a 1961 **Publisher's Note** that is appended to Hope (1962: xxi) who wrote nearly two centuries ago: "The ancient Egyptians were descended from the Ethiopians, and while their blood remained free from any mixture with that of European or Asiatic nations, their race seems to have retained obvious traces of the aboriginal Negro form and features. Not only all the human figures in their colored hieroglyphics display a deep swarthy complexion, but every Egyptian monument whether statue or bas-relief presents the splay feet, the spreading toes, the bow-bent shins, the high meager calves, the long swinging arms, the sharp shoulders, the square flat hands, the head, when seen in profile, placed not

FREDERICK MONDERSON

vertically but obliquely on the spine, the jaws and chin consequently very prominent, together with the skinny lips, depressed nose, high cheek bones, large un-hemmed ears raised far above the level of the nostrils, and all the other peculiarities characteristic of the Negro conformation. It is true that the practice prevalent among the Egyptians of shaving their heads and beards close to the skin (which they only deviated from when in mourning) seldom allows their statues to show that most undeniable symptom of Negro extraction, the woolly hair; the heads of their figures generally appearing covered with some sort of cap, or, when bare, closely shaven. In the few Egyptian sculptured personages, however, in which the hair is introduced, it uniformly offers the woolly texture, and the short crisp curls of that of the Negroes; nor do I know a single specimen of genuine Egyptian workmanship, in which are seen any indications of the long sleek hair or loose wavy ringlets of Europeans or Asiatics. The black streak, which, in the masks or faces carved and painted on the cases of the mummies, is carried from the outside corner of the eye-lids to the temple, seems to denote that anciently, as to this day, the natives of Egypt were in the habit of artificially deepening the hue and increasing the length of their eye lashes, by means of some species of pigment."

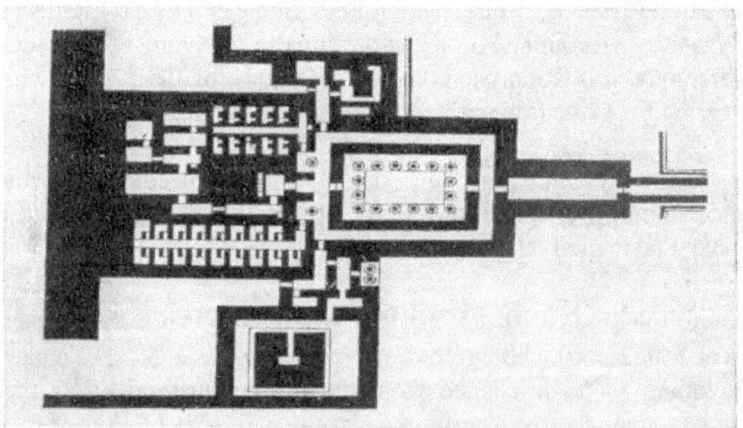

Where are the Kamite Kings Illustration. The Funerary Temple of Sahure.

While many "schools of thought" would find difficulty with this passage, still, the work first published in 1812 was republished in 1961 and being sold today. Nevertheless, the fundamental tenets and characteristics that influenced the author's contentions could

WHERE ARE THE KAMITE KINGS?

not have significantly changed much from then to now, despite the archaeological and anthropological evidence, whose interpretation may be subjects of bias. Dr. John H. Clarke, of Hunter College of the City University of New York, expressed the view: "People who preached racism colonized history" and "When Europe colonized the world, she colonized the world's knowledge." Nevertheless, such statements, characteristic of Hope and others as Denon, Volney, Higgins, Vail, Massey, Reade, Churchward, etc., offer critical commentary on the nature of western scholarship in the reactionary assault that distorted and perpetuated the acquisition, interpretation and colonization of African knowledge and culture. Much of what these moderns wrote was based on simple observation mainly with the naked eye. All commentators on ancient Kemet, whose credibility, elsewhere established, viz., Herodotus, Pliny, Diodorus, Strabo, Ptolemy, etc., based their writings on observations of the people. Adding fuel to the fire, Polybius, Julius Caesar, Livy, Josephus, Origen, Tacitus, Suetonius, Eusebius, Ammanus, Lucian, Assa, and in Philostratos' *Life of Appolonios*, Seneca's *Apocoloyntosis* Ch. 8, Porphyry, Solon, Euphantus, Hecataeus, Thucides, Scylax, Proclus, Aelian, Eudoxus, Homer-Odyssey IV, 477; XIV 257, all equally wrote on ancient Kemet. Many of these ancient commentators on Kemet were eyewitnesses or based their writings on "reliable" firsthand information from travelers. Theophile Obenga affirmed, "The ancient saw the Egyptians as living humans while the moderns saw t hem as mummies."

Much of today's visitors to Kemet see essentially the same things. The critical African-American sees the true nature of the ancient culture. They experience the warm hospitality of the indigenous "Nubians," understand the culture of the people and also observe modern visitors who continue to this day to desecrate and disrespect these ancient holy places, of the "ancestors," even as this note is penned.

Nonetheless, often times the King awarded personal favors to individuals who had distinguished themselves in some form or fashion. In one instance, Erman (1894: 319) has indicated: "King Menkere caused fifty of his workmen, under the direction of the high priest of Memphis, to erect a tomb for Debhen, an officer of his palace. He also had a double false door brought for him from the quarries of Tura, which was then carved for him by the royal architect." He further indicated, Erman (1894: 319) that is, "King Sahure also presented his chief Physician Sechmetna'e'onch with a costly false door, which was painted under the eyes of the Pharaoh by his own artists and painted in lapis lazuli."

Sahure's name is given by Breasted I (1962: 108) as "Horus: Lord of Diadems; King of Upper and Lower Egypt: Sahure who is given life forever." He was the first Pharaoh known to establish trade contacts with Punt, though First Dynasty pharaohs may have also made the voyage. This view is purported from the fact these early rulers were known to be using myrrh, a product of this part of Africa. Much later, in the Eighteenth Dynasty, Hatshepsut renewed this contact and re-established those important links with the "land of the Gods." This Punt expedition of Sahure, of which Breasted (1923: 127) wrote, was a voyage that "brought back 80,000 measures of myrrh, probably 6000 weight of electrum (gold-silver alloy) besides 2,600 staves of some costly wood, presumably ebony." However, while evidence is lacking regarding Punt, 6000 weight of the gold-silver alloy electrum is an indication of the level of mining and craftsmanship that may be attached to this early working.

Neferirkare-Kakai *Nile Year* 1771-1871 (2477-2467 B.C.) is one of those ephemeral Kings. His name appears on the *Tablet of Sakkara* and *Tablet of Karnak*. He is mentioned in the tomb's wall inscription of the Vizier, Chief Judge, and Chief Architect Weshptah, who stricken before the Pharaoh, had his tomb completed by his son, Mernuterseteni.

Ruffle (1977: 151) displays a hieratic script of the Old Kingdom with note indicating, it "is part of the records from the temple of the pyramid of Neferirkare at Abusir and was probably written in the reign of Niuserre or Isesi in the late Vth-dynasty: it is therefore one of the oldest papyrus documents known."

Neferefre *Nile Year* 1788-1795 (2460-2453 B.C.) is relatively unknown.

WHERE ARE THE KAMITE KINGS?

Niuserre, ruled *Nile Year* 1795-1826 (2453-2422 B.C.). We are informed by Breasted I (1962: 114) who places him at Sinai smiting the Beduin, where his name is given, that he was the: "'Great God, Lord of the Two Lands, King of Upper and Lower Egypt, Favorite of the Two Goddesses: Favorite; Golden Horus: Nuter; Niuserre ...; ... Smiter of all countries. Horus: Favorite of the Two Lands, Niuserre, who is given life forever, smiter of the Asiatics of every country.'"

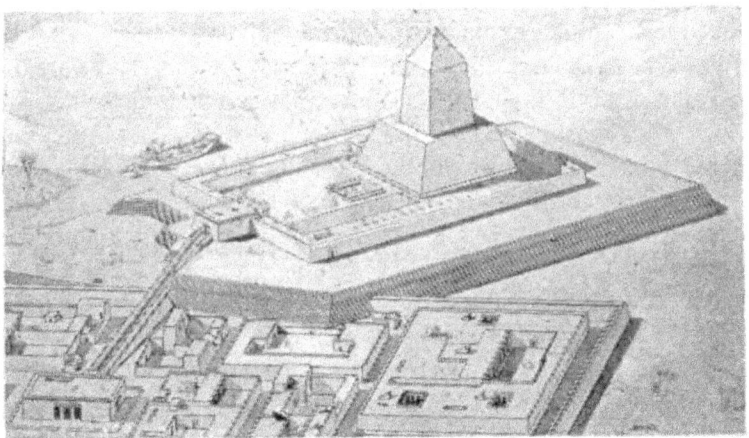

Where are the Kamite Kings Illustration. The Solar Temple of Niuserre at Abusir.

Niuserre's Pyramid at Abusir, near Sakkara, is notable in that, Liebovitch (1938: 23) tells of mortuary temple innovations, in which "for the first-time red granite columns with lotiform capitals were used which resemble in no way at all the pillars and fluted columns of the Zoser temple."

This King supplies one of the better-preserved stone buildings of this dynasty. Ruins of the Sun Temple of Niuserre, on the edge of the desert at Abu Gurab, were found with its calcite altar *in situ*. In this solar structure, Ruffle (1977: 38) comments: "There is an entrance porch, rather like a valley temple in conception, leading by a covered causeway, to a built-up platform, on which is a plain courtyard with a huge centrally placed altar and, on the north side, store-rooms and an area for preparing the sacrifice. Behind the altar is a tall-truncated pyramid, serving as a base for the squat obelisk that is the sun God's symbol. In a corridor on the east and south sides of the platform are reliefs showing the various seasons and in the small chapel are representations of the temple-founding ritual and the Sed festival. Just south of the temple a brick boat was built, a symbol of Re's daily journey across the sky."

The sun temple was designed to worship Re of Heliopolis. There was a special make-up to this temple that was different from the funerary or mortuary temple, a part of the pyramid complex. Baines and Malek (1980: 154) have pointed out, "the names of altogether six of these temples are known from Egyptian texts but remains of only two have so far been located by archaeologists." These are the Sun Temples of Niuserre and Sahure. These two temples contain some of the "most notable architectural innovations and outstanding artistic reliefs characteristic of the Old Kingdom. Particular mention is made of the Fifth Dynasty Temple of King Ne-user-re, at Abu Gurab, in the center of which was an immense obelisk." Baines and Malek (1980: 155) continued: "The temple, known to early travelers as the 'Pyramid of Reegah,' was uncovered by the German archaeologists Ludwig Burckhardt, Heinrich Schafer and F. W. Von Bissing in 1891-1901, and its relief fragments were scattered among museums and collections, mainly in Germany."

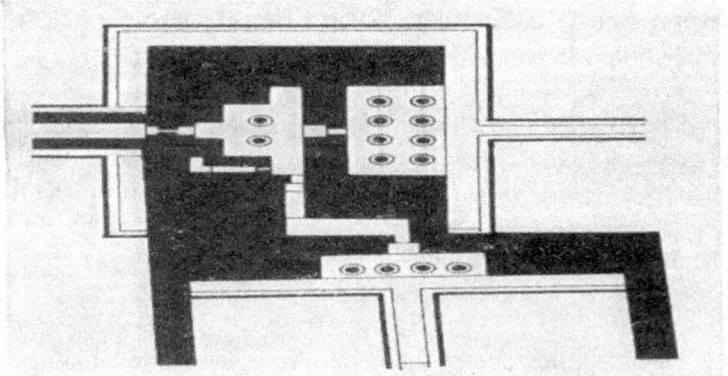

Where are the Kamite Kings Illustration. Plan of the Propylene of King Niuserre.

Excavations reported in *American Journal of Archaeology* IV (1900: 478) disclose: "Two rectangular chambers, ornamented with

WHERE ARE THE KAMITE KINGS?

bas-reliefs, were opened up. In one chamber were portrayed scenes of the royal jubilee, also the laying of the corner stone of the temple. The reliefs in the other chamber contain figures of animals and scenes of country life, also figures of men and women representing various provinces and districts which have the same names as in later times. How the animal figures, etc., hitherto found only in tombs, happen to be on the walls of a temple, is a mystery."

Further research, according to *American Journal of Archaeology* (1920: 374) tells, "reliefs represent the ceremonies of the foundation of the temple, and are the only such representations extant belonging to the Old Kingdom. Here the ceremony of cleansing the temple before it is handed over to the God is replaced by the Festival of Sed. The description and interpretation of this festival here given agree with the words of Rameses III in the Harris Papyrus, pls. 49 f."

Djedkare-Isesi ruled *Nile Year* 1834-1873 (c. 2414-2375 B.C.). His royal titles are as follows:

Horus	Tet-Khau
Two Ladies	Tet-Khau
Golden Horus	Tet
Suten Bat	Ra-Tet-Ka
Son of Ra	Assa or Issesi

His name appears on the *Abydos List*, No. 32, *Turin Papyrus*, *Tablet of Sakkara* and *Tablet of Karnak*. It is in the Wady Magharah according to Lepsius' *Denkmaler* II, 399, (15 l).

Unis or Unas, *Nile Year* 1873-1903 (2375-2345 B.C.), was the last King of the Fifth Dynasty. His royal titles are as follows:

Horus	Uatch-utaui
Two Ladies	Uatch-en
Golden Horus	Uatch
Suten Bat	Una
Son of Ra	Unal

FREDERICK MONDERSON

Kamite Kings 60. Carmen Monderson stands before a bust of Jean-Jacques Champollion and a copy of the Rosetta Stone he deciphered in cracking the Code Hieroglyph. The original Rosetta Stone is in the British Museum while the copy is in Cairo.

His name appears on the *Abydos List*, No. 33, the *Tablet of Sakkara*, the *Turin Papyrus*, and also in Lepsius *Denkmaler*, II, 75. It is on a vase in the British Museum, No. 4,603.

This King returned to build his pyramid at Sakkara, consisting of limestone and granite, where his name is recorded. Next to his pyramid mastaba-type tombs of the IInd Dynasty were discovered. One such structure that belonged to "Khnumhjotep and MiAnkhkhnum, was demolished, because it lay in the line of the causeway of the pyramid of Unas at Sakkara."

King Unis/Unas introduced the practice of decorating his tomb's interior with the "Pyramid texts." During the time of Zoser, decoration was introduced into the funerary practice. This custom was next extended to private tombs by the inspiration of one of the "Greatest Seers," Imhotep. However, while familiar royal themes show the King slaying his enemies and celebrating the Sed-Festival, thanks to Imhotep' ingenuity, private tombs began to portray social themes. According to Ruffle (1977: 47), in these we find, "scenes of hunting, fowling, driving cattle and boat-building were common, and liberally sprinkled with well observed minor incidents."

WHERE ARE THE KAMITE KINGS?

The **Sixth Dynasty** returned to Memphis and inherited a culture that had grown wealthy from trade, agriculture and economic proficiency, literary and artistic experimentation and a citizenry, noble and otherwise, who, with the deepest sense of loyalty and commitment, supported a system of government and social order rooted in divine justification. To this end, Murray (1949: 17) believed: "the VIth dynasty is remarkable for the records of trading expeditions with armed escorts, and for punitive campaigns against tribes who interfered with these expeditions. Chief among these early travelers was Harkhuf, the Sixth Dynasty explorer. He is now buried at Aswan atop the Island of Elephantine, among the "Tombs of the Nobles", where his Old Kingdom letter is sculptured on the entrance walls."

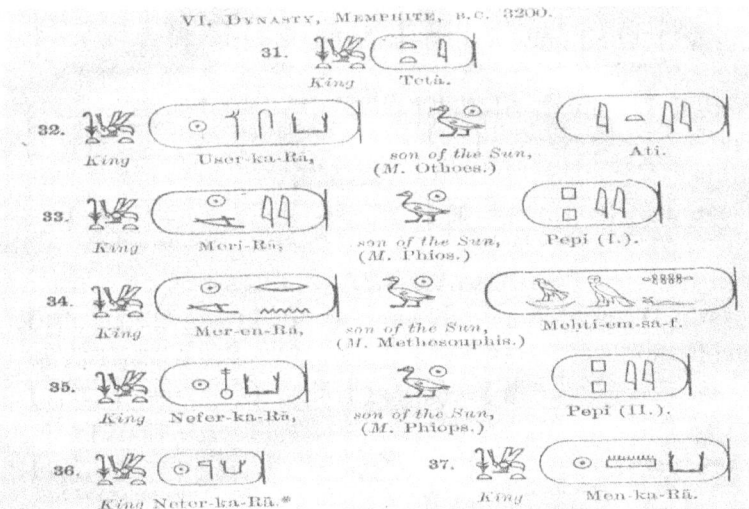

Kamite Kings Cartouche/Shennu. King of the Sixth Dynasty from Memphis.

The Sixth Dynasty was also a time of wonderful works of statuary, both private and royal. Craftsmen were attached to craft schools as that of Ptah at Memphis whose High Priest held the title "Chief of Craftsmen." Undoubtedly there were similar positions at the other centers of worship and learning. An existing statuary of slate shows Pepi I kneeling to offer libations. Another of alabaster shows the

FREDERICK MONDERSON

King in Sed Festival cloak. To complement such royal works, private statuary begun in the Fifth Dynasty and blossomed in the Sixth. Good examples of private statues from this dynasty are those of Rahotpe and his wife Norfret. From the Fifth Dynasty we see the beginning of group statuary of man, woman and child. Ruffle (1977: 47) tells of one such "group statue of the family Seneb of the time of Khufu and Radjedef."

The List of the VIth dynasty, with the approximate dates of the Kings, is as follows:

The Turin Canon   Manetho and the Monuments

Teti I, (3808-3798?) ?	
Othoes	30
Miriri Papi I (3797-3777?)	20
Phios	53
Mirinri I, Mihtimsauf I (3776-3762?)	14
Metesouphis	7
Nofirkeri Papi II (3761-3661)	90+
Phiops	100
Mirniri, Mehtimsauf II (3660-3659?) 1yr, 1 mo.	Mentesouphis 1
Nitauqrit (3658?) ?	Nitokris 12

Where are the Kamite Kings Illustration. Kings of the VIth Dynasty from the Turin Canon and the Monuments (left) and from Manetho (right).

Teti I founded the Sixth Dynasty, *Nile Year* 1903-1915 (2345-2333 B.C.) though, he is only credited with a reign of 12 years. His royal titles were as follows:

Horus	Sehetep-taui
Two Ladies	_____
Golden Horus	_____
Suten Bat	Teta
Son of Ra	Teta

His name appears on the *Abydos List*, No. 34, *Tablet of Sakkara* and *Tablet of Karnak*. It appears at the Temple at Mit Rahinah and on

WHERE ARE THE KAMITE KINGS?

inscriptions at Hat Nub quarries. They appear on a vase in the British Museum, No. 29,204, at El Kab in Lepsius' *Denkmaler*, II, 117, in Mariette' *Catalogue*, No. 1,464 and on a statue in the Chateau Borely.

The latest date of his reign with any certainty is the "sixth census" count that occurred once every two years. He married Iput, a daughter of Weni, whose son Pepi I succeeded to the throne. Grimal (1992: 80) explained some of the challenges facing this ruler. "The problem of growing provincial power was compounded at this time by the lack of a male heir. It seems that Teti's rise to the throne provided a solution to this double crisis. His adoption of the Horus name *Sehetep-tawy* ('He who pacifies the Two Lands') was an indication of the political program upon which he embarked. Indeed, this Horus name was to reappear in royal titulatures throughout subsequent Egyptian history, always in connection with such Kings as Ammenemes I, Apophis, Pedubastis II and Pi (Ankhy), who were attempting to re-establish the unity of the country after serious political troubles."

Where are the Kamite Kings Photo. Thutmose III kneels to present vases and receive Ankh from deity, presumably Amon-Ra. His **Suten Bat** Men-Kha-Ra and **Son of Ra** Thutmose III Cartouche/Shennus partially rests above.

FREDERICK MONDERSON

Where are the Kamite Kings Photo. Temple of Karnak. Hypostyle Hall. Close up of ceiling decoration with Cartouche/Shennu and clerestory opening.

The successes of his efforts are further recounted by Grimal (1992: 81) who maintained: "Clearly, Teti's policy of pacifying the nobles bore fruit. There is evidence at Abydos of his activity as a legislator, in the form of a decree exempting the temple from tax; he was also the first ruler to be particularly associated with the cult of Hathor at Dendera. The overall stability of his administration within Egypt itself is suggested by the fact that he was able to continue many of the links of the Fifth Dynasty: he maintained relations with Byblos and perhaps also with Punt and Nubia, at least as far as the site of tombs in northern Nubia."

WHERE ARE THE KAMITE KINGS?

Breasted I (1962: 131) tells of inscriptions left by a high official, Sabu, also called "Thety, at the courts of Unis," the last King of the Fifth, and Teti, the first King of the Sixth Dynasty. An inscription of his reads: "Today in the presence of the Son of Re: Teti, living forever, high priest of Ptah, most honored by the King than any servant, as master of secret things of every work which his majesty desired should be done; pleasing the heart of his lord every day, high priest of Ptah, Sabu. High Priest of Ptah, cup-bearer of the King, master of secret things of the King in his every place, honored by the King, high priest of Ptah, attached to the Double House, feast-day attendant, pleasing every artificer, honored by every sovereign, a member of his court, attached to the heart of his lord, the favorite of his lord's heart, beloved of his lord, revered of Ptah, doing that which the God desired of him every day in the King's presence."

User-Ka-Re, another ephemeral King is dated to *Nile Year* 1915-1916 (2333-2332 B.C.). His name appears on the *Abydos List* No. 35, and in the Wady Hammamat, as well as in Lepsius' *Denkmaler* II, 115.

Pepi I is assigned a lengthy reign by Manetho, *Nile Year* 1916-1965 (2332-2283 B.C.). His royal titles are as follows:

Horus	Meui-Taui
Two Ladies	Meri Khat, or Meri Taui
Golden Horus	
Suten Bat	Ra-Meri
Son of Ra	Pepi

His name appears on the *Abydos List*, No. 36, *Tablet of Sakkara* and *Tablet of Karnak*. It is in his pyramid at Sakkarah and the Wady Maghara. Lepsius' *Denkmaler* II, 115, places his name at Wady Hammamat. A vase in the British Museum, No. 22,559, also bears Pepi I's name. Breasted I (1962: 136) also found Pepi I at Wadi Hammamat, "with staff and war-club standing before the ithyphallic Min; above is his titulary, and in front: 'Beloved of the Lord of Coptos (Min).' Behind the King: 'First occurrence of the Sed Jubilee.'" The King's titulary occurs in Sinai inscriptions,

FREDERICK MONDERSON

according to Breasted I (1962: 138-39) as: "'King of Upper and Lower Egypt, Favorite of the Two Goddesses; Merikhet (*Mry ht*); Merire (*Mry-r'*), Pepi I, given all life forever.' His Horus-name Meri towe mrytwi 'Beloved of the Two Lands,' appears in a figure of him striding at a ceremonial proceeded by words 'First occurrence of the Sed Jubilee.' Establishment of the field ....'"

Where are the Kamite Kings Photo. Erik Monderson among the trees at Kitchener Garden, Aswan, Egypt in 2018.

WHERE ARE THE KAMITE KINGS?

Where are the Kamite Kings Photo. Erik Monderson stands before twin statues of Amon-Ra and Rameses II at the entrance to the Hypostyle Hall in Karnak Temple.

FREDERICK MONDERSON

We encounter other references to Min, God of the city of the thunderbolt, Coptos. *American Journal of Archaeology* (1912: 114) mentions the discovery of twenty-eight tombs from the City of Ekhmin. "They date from the sixth to the twelfth dynasty. One untouched burial of the Old Kingdom contained three painted wooden coffins...." Newberry (1910: 50) discusses cult objects that are identified with Min as being "double-headed darts," "arrow-like heads," and two have "rounded heads." Min was later fused with the attributes of Amen-Ra at Karnak. Even further, Newberry (1910: 50) noted: "Already at the time of the First Dynasty this deity had become anthropomorphous, and we see him as a standing ithyphallic figure wearing two plumes upon his head, with his right arm raised and balancing (not *holding*) in his right hand the so-called flagellum .... He is never, as far as I am aware, represented, as other Egyptian anthropomorphous deities are, wearing his cult-object upon his head. Now Min, as is beginning to be recognized, was the original form of Amon. Amon was Lord of Heaven and God of Thunder."

Where are the Kamite Kings Photo. The zenith of Hatshepsut's fallen Obelisk rests beside the Sacred Lake while her standing obelisk remains (right) beside that of her father Thutmose I (left) in the rear among the Hypostyle Hall and other ruins.

WHERE ARE THE KAMITE KINGS?

Where are the Kamite Kings Illustration. Coffin lid, interior and side of that of Hent-Taui, daughter of Rameses II.

Those early wooden coffins from the Old Kingdom, discovered at Ekhmin by Newberry were beginning to be decorated in a pattern to be amplified later, particularly in the Middle Kingdom. *American Journal of Archaeology* (1912: 255) tells of Wiedemann's analysis of early coffins, holding to the view, "the Egyptian monuments make it possible to follow the development of the decoration of the breast of the coffin. Originally it was reserved exclusively for the

FREDERICK MONDERSON

King, Antef for example, who had a right to the crowns of Upper and Lower Egypt. Later, the tutelary divinities were ascribed to the members of the royal family also, but this ascription sometimes led to the neglect of their primary signification. At last, the meaning of the picture was quite forgotten, the two heads, which represented the two countries, disappeared, only tutelary vulture remained, unless it had to give way to Nut. With the increasing importance of the Osirian conceptions was also connected the progressive substitution of the coffin in human form as it appears in the *rischi* coffins, for the old coffin in the form of a chest, or rather of the *magazine-tomb*. A compromise between the two conceptions is made when the deceased has two coffins, the inner one in the form of the mummy, the outer one in that of a chest."

Further, we know more about Pepi I from the autobiography of a very close and loyal official, Weni or Uni, who served this King and his successor. In the *Autobiography of Weni*, we are old of a conspiracy against the King by a wife of his harem. Weni, a faithful ally of the King had risen to prominence in service to the crown. Breasted (1923: 134) has sketched the rise of this important individual, in the following statement. "Under King Teti II he had begun his career at the bottom as an obscure under-custodian in the royal domains. Pepi I now appointed him as a judge, at the same time giving him rank at the royal court, and an income as a priest of the pyramid-temple. He was soon promoted to a superior custodianship of the royal domains, and in this capacity, he had so gained the royal favor that when a conspiracy against the King arose in the harem, he was nominated with one colleague to prosecute the case."

An extract from the "Autobiography of Weni" is supplied by Lichtheim (1975: 19) who notes: "When there was a secret charge in the royal harem against Queen Weret-yamtes, his majesty made me go in to hear (it) alone. No chief judge and vizier, no official was there, only I alone; because I was worthy, because I was rooted in his majesty' heart; because his majesty had filled his heart with me. Only I put (it) in writing together with one other senior warden of Nekhen, while my rank was (only) that of overseer of royal tenants. Never before had one like me heard a secret of the King's harem; but his majesty made me hear it, because I was worthy in his

WHERE ARE THE KAMITE KINGS?

majesty's heart beyond any official of his, beyond any noble of his, beyond any servant of his.'"

Where are the Kamite Kings Photo. Obelisks of Thutmose I (left) and Hatshepsut (right) stand on both sides of the Fourth Pylon. The Queen's Obelisk was erected in her father's Hypostyle Hall for which she removed some of his columns.

As a powerful noble in the Kingdom, Weni's activities increased. As a general, he led Nubian troops against Bedouins of the north on some four or five occasions. In the last and most vigorous of such campaigns, comprising Nubian, Kamite and Libyan troops, James Breasted (1923: 135) tells of his strategy: "Embarking his force, he carried them in troop ships along the coast of southern Palestine, and punished the Beduin as far north as the highlands of Palestine. This marks the northernmost advance of the Pharaohs of the Old Kingdom, and is in accordance with the discovery of a Sixth Dynasty scarab at Gezer below Jerusalem, in strata below those dated in the Middle Kingdom. Weni can be compared with an earlier nobleman whose lengthy life spans many reigns." As given by Breasted I (1962: 117), the individual was Ptahshepses, and the monarch was Menkaure at his birth, Shepseskaf during his youth and marriage, manhood spanning the reigns of Userkaf, Sahure,

FREDERICK MONDERSON

Neferirkere, and Neferefre with Niuserre in old age. This glorious career, under six monarchs, is traced through the titles he acquired.

Pepi I pursued a policy of unification by courting important families of nobles and building extensively throughout their Nomes. His monuments could be found at Hierakonpolis, Abydos, Dendera and Elephantine. At Hierakonpolis, in the old Temple of Horus, Quibell found the copper statues that now adorn the entrance gallery of the Cairo Museum. We generally credit Narmer with founding Memphis, the administrative capital of the United Kingdom and building the "white wall." However, though the city was called the "white wall" initially, it derives its name Memphis from the Pharaoh's pyramid complex named "Mennefer-Pepi."

The King, in a radical move, "changed his Coronation name from Neferdjahor to Merire ('The devotee of Ra'). He also issued, in the twenty-first year of his reign, a charter awarding tax immunity to the town that had grown up around Snofru's funerary domain at Dashur." The reign of Pepi I provides an important point of departure in throwing some light on the order of succession in the Old Kingdom. *American Journal of Archaeology* (1915: 458-59) mentions F. W. Read's attempts to "establish that there are no dates indicated on the Palermo Stone; what have been regarded as such are in all cases statements of periods of time, from which, of course, dates can be calculated."

Where are the Kamite Kings Photo. Titles of the King, "Suten Bat" Aakheperenra and "Son of Ra" of Thutmose II.

WHERE ARE THE KAMITE KINGS?

Where are the Kamite Kings Photo. Erik Monderson stands just before the Pool area at the Sonesta, St. George Hotel, in Luxor, Egypt, after returning by Motorboat from the West Bank.

FREDERICK MONDERSON

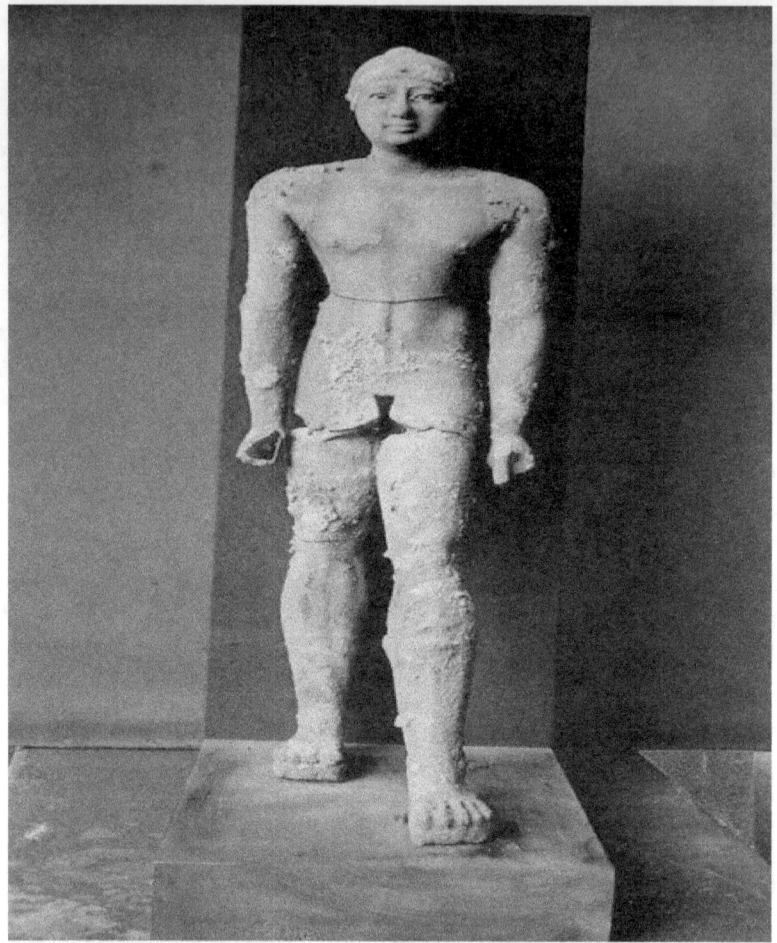

Where are the Kamite Kings Illustration. Copper statue of the son of Pepi I, Mentu-Em Sa-F, found at Hierakonpolis.

Accordingly, and in this regard, *American Journal of Archaeology* (1915: 459) stated further: "The year spaces on the stone denote regnal years assimilated to civil years; that is to say every space is equivalent to a civil year except at a change of reign. On such an occasion, the first set of figures in each pair denotes the portion of the civil year during which the predecessor ruled, and the second set the portion of the year in which the successor ruled; the sum of these two deducted from the full year gives the length of the interregnum. When a co-regent died leaving a surviving co-regent, the year in which the death occurred was denoted by one year-space, which was divided to indicate the end of the reign of the deceased, co-regent,

WHERE ARE THE KAMITE KINGS?

and in the first portion of which was inserted the length of time in that year reigned by the latter."

Where are the Kamite Kings Photo. Temple of Luxor. Ramessean Front. View from the south-west on the outside, the double row of Peristyle Columns of the "Ramessean Front" and inner face of the Pylon and the Mosque of Abu Haggag, "Patron Saint of Luxor," who came from Syria to preach Islam.

An even further elaboration of the *Palermo Stone's* function involves the work of Seymour de Ricci as recorded in *American Journal of Archaeology* (1918: 201-02) that the: "chief difficulty in determining the order of the years in the fragments of the 'Palermo Stone' consists in the fact that these years were named for festivals, incidents, etc., and not designated by numbers. For the fifth dynasty the order has been determined with considerable certainty. He argues that the second and third registers of the *verso* contained accounts of eight years each. The complete width of the stone was about 1.68 m. On the *recto* of the second, third, fourth, and fifth registers contained records of 74, 91, 110, and 87 years respectively, beginning with Menes. What is known of the chronology of the reigns of the early Kings from other sources confirms the positions given to the fragments by de Ricci."

Meren-ra *Nile Year* 1965-1970 (2283-2278 B.C.), succeeded Pepi I and ruled for a short time. Some authorities assign him five years, though inscriptions at the First Cataract seem later. His royal titles are as follows:

Horus	Ankh-Khau
Two Ladies	Ankh-Khau
Golden Horus	
Suten Bat	Ra-mer-en
Son of Ra	Mehti-en-sa-f

The *Tablet of Sakkara* and the *Tablet of Karnak* contain his name. It is in his pyramid at Sakkara and on a vase in the British Museum, No. 4,493. Lepsius' *Denkmaler*, II, 115 places Meren-Ra on the rocks at the Wady Hammamat. He continued expeditions against Syria-Palestine and exploited copper mines of Sinai. To construct his pyramid at Sakkara, that remained unfinished, the King secured granite from Aswan, alabaster from Hatnub and basalt from Nubia. Weni, now older, was a part of this campaign and also appointed to serve as "Governor of the South." **In the Old Kingdom, "Governor of the South" meant a domain of all lands above the Delta**. Weni tells us further of his final mission for King Merenre, where Grimal (1992: 113-14) writes: "'His majesty sent me to Ibhar to bring the sarcophagus 'chest of the living' together with its lid, and the costly august pyramidion for the pyramid 'Merenre appears in splendor,' my mistress. His majesty sent me to Yebu [Elephantine] to bring a granite false door and its libation stone and granite lintels, and to bring granite portals and libation stones for the upper chamber of the pyramid 'Merenre appears in splendor,' my mistress. I traveled north with them to the pyramid 'Merenre appears in splendor' in six barges and three tow-boats of eight ribs in a single expedition... His majesty sent me to Hatnub to bring a great altar of alabaster of Hatnub. I brought this altar down for him in seventeen days.'"

Even further, Grimal (1992: 114) wrote: "After it was quarried at Hatnub, I had it go downstream in this barge I had built for it, a barge of acacia wood of sixty cubits in length and thirty cubits in width. Assembled in seventeen days, in the third month of summer, when there was no water on the sandbanks, it landed at the pyramid 'Merenre appears in splendor - in safety.... His majesty sent me to dig five canals in Upper Egypt, and to build three barges and four tow-boats of acacia wood of Wawat. Then the foreign chiefs of

WHERE ARE THE KAMITE KINGS?

Irtjet, Wawat, Yam, and Medja cut the timber for them. I did it all in one year. Floated, they were loaded with very large granite blocks for the pyramid of 'Merenre appears in splendor.'"

In his fifth year and in a bold and diplomatic mission Merenre became the first pharaoh to visit the southern region of the country. At the cataract, fearing the power of the Pharaoh, the mentioned chiefs came to submit. Breasted (1923: 137) tells of an inscription and relief, left at Aswan showing the King with the chiefs, that read, "'the coming of the King himself, appearing behind the hill-country [of the cataract] that he might see that which is in the hill-country. While the chiefs of Mazoi, Irthet and Wawat did obeisance and gave great praise.'"

Erman (1894: 499) supplies an ethnological view of the relationship between Egyptians/Kamites and other indigenous Africans, neighbors to the south. "Even under King Pepy, the Negro countries of 'Ert'et, Med'a, 'Emam, Uauat, Kaau (?), and Tat'e'am were obliged to reinforce the Egyptian army with mercenaries. Under Merenre,' also the successor of Pepy, the princes of the countries of 'Ert'et, Uauam, 'Emam, and Med'a brought supplies of acacia wood to Elephantine for Egyptian shipbuilding .... Moreover, Elephantine itself was originally in the possession of Nubian princes, though even in early times they naturalized themselves as Egyptian officials and vassals of the Pharaoh; the most ancient of their tombs, belonging perhaps to the 6th dynasty; shows that the governor of that time was a dark brown Nubian, though his court seems to have been purely Egyptian." Today we call this Black!

Such individuals were the earliest entrepreneurs who encouraged early commerce with interior Africa through explorers as Harkhuf, who made three such journeys during the reign of Mernere and the last under Pepi II.

Pepi II was half-brother to Merenre and succeeded to the throne without much problems. Grimal (1992: 83) helped to simplify the lineage with the statement, "Ankhenesmerire I was the mother of Merenre and Princess Neith, who later married her half-brother Pepi II, the son of Snkhenesmerire II. These queens somehow seem to be connected with the conspiracy against Pepi I."

FREDERICK MONDERSON

Pepi II's royal titulary includes the following:

Horus	Neter Khau
Two Ladies	Neter Khau
Golden Horus	Sekhen
Suten Bat	Ra-nefer-ka
Son of Ra	Pepi

The King's name appears on the *Abydos List*, No. 38 and a *Second Abydos List*, No. 10. It is on the *Tablet of Karnak*, in the Pyramid at Sakkara, and on a vase in the British Museum, No. 4,492. They also appear on rocks at Wady Maghara, according to Lepsius' *Denkmaler* II, 116.

Pepi II was ascribed a lengthy reign, *Nile Year* 1970-2064 (2278-2184 B.C.). The Old Kingdom came to an end with this monarch because he was unable to check the increasing power of the nobles. Though he is popularly attributed this lengthy reign, Grimal (1992: 89) believed the "latest known regnal date is that of the thirty-third census, which would suggest a definite length of about fifty to seventy years."

The Tomb of Pepi II provides a unique opportunity to study the nature of *Table of Offerings* as was discussed by Gaston Maspero. In a similar title, the "Table of Offerings in the Egyptian Tombs," contained in the *American Journal of Archaeology* (1897: 396-97) Maspero explained: "Such tables are represented in all the Memphite tombs which are not irreparably mutilated. The deceased sits before a table surmounted by two palm branches supposed to be lying upon the objects with which the table is covered. Often there is under the table a short inscription stating that the offering placed upon or before it, - bread, cakes, game, meat, cloths, perfumes, - are counted by thousands, and when there is space enough all the substances mentioned are arranged in several registers in considerable quantities. A sort of rectangular tablet or schedule is fixed above the table, and contains a list of nearly all the objects represented. It is divided into registers, and these in turn into oblong compartments. Each compartment is divided into two or three divisions, one above the other; the uppermost contains the names of an object or the designation of a rite, the next a chamber or sign of

WHERE ARE THE KAMITE KINGS?

measure marking the required quantity of the object named or the number of times the rite is to be repeated; when there is a third division it contains the name of the person for whom the offering is intended. Often priests and slaves are represented offering prayers and bringing jars and food. Often the representation is abbreviated and reduced to the deceased seated before the table and the brief inscription accompanying it."

Where are the Kamite Kings Photo. Temple of Luxor. The Temple with "old front" (above); and now boasts a "new front" with all four standing statues replaced in their original position joining the two seated statues in 2019. Still, one obelisk is missing.

FREDERICK MONDERSON

Taking for this point of departure the Tomb of Ti, Maspero examines the schedule carefully, showing how the rites differed at different epochs, even though remaining essentially the same. The most complete extant version of the first part of the schedule is that of the Tomb of Pepi II. There we find: "(1) Two purifications, by water and incense; (2) A ceremony of *Opening of the Mouth*, with purifications and a summary meal; (3) The dressing of the deceased; (4) Two additional purifications by incense and water. The ordinary version, which of Orenas and Petemonophis, omits the dressing of the deceased. Other differences also exist. After these preliminaries the table is spread for the deceased, each offering being accompanied by its appropriate rite. Here, again, certain changes in formulas correspond with changes in rites, which are examined in detail in the article referred to."

The success of the earlier Step-Pyramid encouraged architects to attempt the Bent-Pyramid at Dashur. It had an approximate angle slope of 54 degrees at the base of the pyramid. Rather than continue upwards to the apex, there is a sudden change to an angle of 42 degrees. It was thought this change made the top collapse, or it was finished in a hurry. Pharaoh Snefru's second pyramid at Dashur had a rising slope of 43 degrees 36 inches instead of the earlier 53 degrees. The angle of 53 degrees became the normal angle of ascent of later pyramids. Thus, Snefru became the builder of the first true pyramid.

Some 80 pyramids were built by inhabitants of the Nile Valley. The three at Giza, however, characterized the concept, orientation and permanence of the pyramid idea and complex. There were also many pyramids in Nubia, to the south of Egypt. There were natural pyramids carved in the surrounding terrain, over the years, by sand and wind erosion and these conveyed the idea of the permanence of these structures. Dr. ben-Jochannan speaks of "silt pyramids" of a very early age in the Sudan predating the man-made ones made in stone. Nevertheless, in recap, essentially, the proper layout of the Pyramid Complex in Egypt encompassed a surrounding Enclosure Wall. At the river's edge there was a Valley Temple. From here a Causeway or walkway, led to the Sun Temple. A Mortuary Temple or temple of the dead, as well as a Sacrificial Altar was close-by.

WHERE ARE THE KAMITE KINGS?

The Main Pyramid was centrally located in the enclosure. In its rear was the Subsidiary or Smaller Pyramids. While earlier scholars believed these subsidiary pyramids were for queens, they may have been secondary burial sites for the pharaoh as well as his female relatives. The dead person's belongings were stored in Magazines. Other structures included a Sphinx, Obelisk and a Heb-Sed or Jubilee Festival Pavilion. There were buildings representing the 42 Nomes of the state. Lastly, the King had a Solar Boat, made of wood, buried nearby. Five such boats were discovered in Khufu's funerary complex. These vessels, symbolically used to sail across the sky to the next world, mirrored the voyages of the Sun God, in his solar boat. In addition, within the complex were mastaba tombs for nobles, officials and priests, who served the King and wanted to be with him in the afterlife. These individuals gained immortality in being buried next to or within the shadows of their God-King, so much so that we today discuss them. Such was the belief of the Cult of the God-King of the Old Kingdom.

While many smaller pyramids and mastaba tombs were decorated with frescoes of daily life and hunting and fishing scenes, in the Fifth Dynasty, King Teti I had the "Egyptian Bible" or "Pyramid Text" inscribed on his tomb walls. This, the earliest composed religious text, after that of Unas, began with "Rise of O Teti, thou shall not die!" These spells were intended to help the King survive in the afterlife. The motif was carried on into the Sixth Dynasty where Pharaohs continued to so decorate their tombs.

Throughout this period of splendid African creative genius, the frontiers of civilization became more clearly defined and beat back. By the end of the Old Kingdom, the treatment of medicine had expanded. This development was encouraged by two factors. First, ancient Kamites along the Nile cultivated a profound belief in the afterlife. This practice required special efforts be made to preserve the body until the deceased returned from the judgment to claim it. Such preservation required the process of mummification, an art that was astoundingly successful, judging from numerous mummies that have survived. Equally too, the notion of the "return" became a social barometer to guide the individual along the ethical principles as represented by the concept of Ma'at- viz., justice, truth, goodness, balance, order, honesty, etc., the 42 *Negative Confessions* or "42 Commandments," that made these people of Ancient Kemet want to stand proudly and confidently in front of their God to proclaim a good life based on reason, caring, concern and consideration of fellow man.

Physicians studied various diseases of the abdomen, bladder, rectum, eyes and skin. Rogers I (1972) mentioned methods of detecting illnesses based on observing visible parts of the body. Physicians looked at the skin, hair, nails and tongue of the patient to determine the nature of illness. We know oral surgery was practiced in the Old Kingdom. In *American Journal of Archaeology* XXII (1918: 441) E. A. Hooton's description of an: "Old Empire mandible which showed evidence of having been operated upon for the relief of an alveolar abscess. He says that the evidence establishes beyond a reasonable doubt the existence of a rudimentary knowledge of oral surgery in the Old Kingdom."

Where are the Kamite Kings Illustration. Vulture with outstretched wings holding weapons and Shen-rings in her talons.

Rogers I (1972) adds: "Physicians practiced medical surgery as well and listened to the heart. They knew of the blood's circulation. Medicine was generally specialized so that medical men treated different diseases including gallstones, gout and arthritis. Early African pharmacopoeia consisted of medicine extracted from plants and minerals."

The Gods were considered good to these ancient Africans of Kemet/Egypt. A profound religiosity perennially pervaded the land, particularly on festive days when all the temples of the land were lit and Pharaoh and his representatives made presentations to the Gods in their respective temples. Whether Heliopolis, Abydos, Memphis, or Karnak, as principal religious centers, and Abu Simbel, Soleb, etc., throughout the land, the Gods were constantly worshiped and

WHERE ARE THE KAMITE KINGS?

ritualized. Existing temples such as Kom Ombo, El Kab, Esna and especially Edfu were built much later during the Greco-Roman Period. They were, however, built on sacred ground of ancient temples making these areas very active in the earliest experiences of Kemetic religion and social culture on the Nile.

The "Pyramid Texts" of King Teti I of the Fifth Dynasty were theosophic, theological, and philosophic ideas of Kemetic religious belief systems and intellectual endeavors. Evidence indicates this "Kemetic Bible" represented the development of religious beliefs that were thousands of years old as oral practice and now put to writing. Its function and influence lasted for thousands more, thanks to a dedicated and functional Priesthood. Such an elite group of the respective centers of religious and intellectual activity became a powerful body whose employment included the study of sciences and the progress of the arts. They were also responsible for performing the various ceremonies on important occasions and presided over the administration of justice. They collected taxes, especially from the farmers and played a significant role in perpetuating the cult of the dead established through endowments.

During the Inundation or over-flowing of the Nile River, the boundary marks of landed property were washed away. Here the College of the Priesthood provided technicians as surveyors who measured the land to help determine the extent of property boundaries. Studies of the volume of the river helped predict the harvest yield. Taxes were based on the height of the Nile. Priestly teachers were also responsible for training all branches of civil administration. In addition, they collected tribute for the temples and taught mathematics, astronomy, geometry, philosophy and the arts.

On the walls of the Kamite/Egyptian tombs, paintings and drawings depicted daily life of the time. Sculpture in relief and in the round developed. Raised and sunk relief showed man, his culture and nature very realistically. This was an age of colossal human portraiture. Hieroglyphics or *medu netcher* and art portrayed drama in the afterlife.

FREDERICK MONDERSON

In politics, as the power of the nobles who administered the various Nomes increased, this threatened the central administration that kept the country united. The career of one such nomarch is commented upon by Moret and carried in *American Journal of Archaeology* (1919: 178-79) where inscriptions depict the career of a nomarch of Edfu in the Sixth Dynasty. The nomarch Kara, surnamed Pepinefer, lived under the first three Kings of the Sixth Dynasty.

Where are the Kamite Kings Photo. Two granite statues of Kings in the "living or traveling position," one wearing the White Crown, the other a headcloth; one has uraei on his kilt the other does not; one sports a beard the other does not, in the Cairo Museum.

WHERE ARE THE KAMITE KINGS?

Where are the Kamite Kings Photo. Temple of Luxor. "Ramessean Front." Statues with their White Crowns on the ground seem to emerge from between the columns of the Peristyle Court. An altar rests in this section of the Court.

"As a child he was included in the group of sons of nomarchs educated by the King. These boys had certain duties to perform at court, although they were really hostages. In the first year of Merenra he was made nomarch of Wtes-or at Edfu where his father had held the same office. The inscription throws considerable light upon certain Egyptian institutions."

This relationship that kept individuals in support of the monarchy broke down and resulted in anarchy and discontent. Importantly, Pharaoh Pepi II's lengthy reign helped to weaken the country. Reportedly, the longest reign in history, at his death the Old Kingdom came to an end. In fact, he was followed by a female ruler who was not able to provide strong leadership at the time. The nobles rebelled. Disorder and civil war ensued, leading to the First Intermediate Period or Dynasties Seven through Ten.

During the Old Kingdom, trade expanded by land, river and sea and particularly with the land of Nubia. Kemet exported food, crafts, technology, ideas, culture and religion. It imported wood, obsidian, gold, pottery and other items of commerce by retaining contact with the Levant and Nubia. In Nubia, the Pharaoh's administrative machinery secured gold, ivory and other exotic products. Industry bloomed with beautiful and delicate vessels, pottery, jars, pails and dishes. Materials used by various types of crafts included slate, rock crystal, faience, basalt, marble, alabaster and diorite.

Such trades products or items as flint-work, papyrus, jewelry, metalwork, weaving, woodwork, and bone and ivory carvings were common. Boat building and carpentry were expertly done by the early craftsmen.

Agriculture involved the swidden or shifting method of cultivation. Irrigation, plowing and hoeing helped tremendously. Farmers planted barley, corn, wheat, and cereals. These were harvested and placed in storage facilities. Domesticated animals included cows, oxen, sheep and goats.

Where are the Kamite Kings Illustration. Coffins of Sitamen and Senu.

Food meats included mutton, beef, goats and gazelle. Fruits and vegetables included lentils, beans, radishes, onions and garlic. Figs,

WHERE ARE THE KAMITE KINGS?

dates, grapes, raisins, pomegranates and melons are mentioned. Bakers made bread, cakes and pies. Animals provided milk, and from this cheese and butter. The fermented juices were wine from grapes, beer from barley, and arrack from dates.

To conclude, these were some of the accomplishments Africans of Kemet/Egypt made nearly 5,000 years ago. In this, the African-American youth and adult should recognize and speak proudly of their "ancestors" from the Nile Valley in North-East Africa, who built the wonderful civilization of ancient Kemet, the pyramids, and had such a profound impact on subsequent culture, on the Nile and elsewhere.

The following two selections are designed to appeal to the "spiritual side" as part of the **Blessing**. The first selection, Wilson (1901: 46-8) is entitled "Chapter of Knowledge" from the *Papyrus of Nu* in the British Museum No. 10,477, sheet 13.

"THE CHAPTER OF KNOWING THE 'CHAPTERS OF COMING FORTH BY DAY' IN A SINGLE CHAPTER." The overseer of the palace, the chancellor-In-chief, Osiris Nu, triumphant, begotten of the overseer of the palace, Amen-hetep, triumphant, saith: "I am Yesterday and To-morrow; and I have the power to be born a second time. [I am] the divine hidden Soul, who createth the Gods, and who giveth sepulchral meals to the divine hidden beings [in the Tuat (underworld)], in Amenti, and in heaven. [I am] the rudder of the east, the possessor of two divine faces wherein his beams are seen. I am the lord of those who are raised up, [the lord] who cometh forth from out of the darkness. [Hail,] ye two divine Hawks who are perched upon your resting-places, and who hearken unto the things, which are said by him, the thigh [of the sacrifice] is tied to the neck, and the buttocks [are laid] upon the head of Amentet. May the Ur-urti Goddesses (i.e., Isis and Nephys) grant such gifts unto me when my tears start from me as I look on. 'I know the abysses' is thy name. [I] work for [you], O ye *Khus*, who are in number [four] millions, [six] hundred, and 1,000, and 200, and they are [in height] twelve cubits. [Ye] travel on joining the hands, each to each, but the sixth [hour], which belongeth at the head of the Tuat (underworld), is the hour of the overthrow of the

FREDERICK MONDERSON

Fiend. [I] have come there in triumph, and [I am] he who is in the hall (or courtyard) of the Tuat; and the seven (?) come in his manifestations. The strength which protecteth me is that which hath my *Khu* under its protection, [that is] the blood, and the cool water, and the slaughterings, which abound (?). I open [a way among] the horns of all those who would do harm unto me, and those who are upon their bellies. The Eye shall not eat (or absorb) the tears of the Goddess Aukert. Hail, Goddess Aukert, open thou unto me the enclosed place, and grant thou unto me pleasant roads whereupon I may travel. Who art thou then, who consumest in the hidden places? I am the Chief in Re-stau, and [I] go in and come forth in my name of 'Hehi, the lord of millions of years [and of] the earth;' [I am] the maker of my name. The pregnant one hath deposited [upon the earth] her load. The door by the wall is shut fast, and the things of terror are overturned and thrown down upon the backbone (?) of the *Bennu* bird by the two *Samait* Goddesses. To the Mighty One hath his Eye been given, and his face emitteth light when [he] illumineth the earth, [my name is his name]. I shall not become corrupt, but I shall come into being in the form of the Lion-God; the blossoms of Shu shall be in me. I am he who is never overwhelmed in the waters. Happy, yea happy, is the funeral couch of the Still-heart; he maketh himself to alight upon the pool (?), and verily he cometh forth [there from]. I am the lord of my life. I have come to this [place], and I have come forth from Re-aa-urt the city of Osiris. Verily the things, which are thine, are with the *Sariu* deities. I have clasped the sycamore tree and I have divided (?) it; I have opened a way for myself [among] the *Sekhiu* Gods of the Tuat. I have come to see him that dwelleth in his divine uraeus, face to face and eye to eye, and [I] draw to myself the winds [which rise] when he cometh forth. My two eyes (?) are weak in my face, O lion [-God], Babe, who dwellest in Utent. Thou are in me and I am in thee; and thy attributes are my attributes. I am the God of the Inundation (*Bah*), and 'Qem-ur-she' is my name. My forms are the forms of the God Khepera, the hair of the earth of Tem. I have entered in as a man of no understanding, and I shall come forth in the form of a strong *Khu*, and I shall look upon my form which shall be that of men and women forever and forever."

[This section is added from the *Papyrus of Nebseni*.] [IF THIS CHAPTER BE KNOWN] BY A MAN HE SHALL COME FORTH BY DAY, AND HE SHALL NOT BE REPULSED AT ANY GATE OF THE TUAT (UNDERWORLD), EITHER IN GOING

WHERE ARE THE KAMITE KINGS?

IN OR IN COMING OUT. HE SHALL PERFORM [ALL] THE TRANSFORMATIONS WHICH HIS HEART SHALL DESIRE FOR HIM AND HE SHALL NOT DIE; BEHOLD, THE SOUL OF [THIS] MAN SHALL FLOURISH. AND MOREOVER, IF [HE] KNOW THIS CHAPTER HE SHALL BE VICTORIOUS UPON EARTH AND IN THE UNDERWORLD, AND HE SHALL PERFORM EVERY ACT OF A LIVING BEING. NOW IT IS A GREAT PROTECTION WHICH [HATH BEEN GIVEN] BY THE GOD. THIS CHAPTER WAS FOUND IN THE FOUNDATIONS OF THE SHRINE OF HENNU BY THE CHIEF MASON DURING THE REIGN OF HIS MAJESTY THE KING OF THE NORTH AND OF THE SOUTH, HESEPTI, TRIUMPHANT, WHO CARRIED [IT] AWAY AS A MYSTERIOUS OBJECT WHICH HAD NEVER [BEFORE] BEEN SEEN OR LOOKED UPON. THIS CHAPTER SHALL BE RECTIFIED BY A MAN WHO IS CEREMONIOUSLY CLEAN AND PURE, WHO HATH NOT EATEN THE FLESH OF ANIMALS OR FISH, AND WHO HATH NOT HAD INTERCOURSE WITH WOMEN.

IF THIS CHAPTER BE KNOWN [BY THE DECEASED] HE SHALL BE VICTORIOUS BOTH UPON EARTH AND IN THE UNDERWORLD, AND HE SHALL PERFORM EVERY ACT OF A LIVING HUMAN BEING. NOW IT IS A GREAT PROTECTION WHICH [HATH BEEN GIVEN] BY THE GOD.

THIS CHAPTER WAS FOUND IN THE CITY OF KHEMENNUM UPON A BLOCK OF IRON OF THE SOUTH, WHICH HAD BEEN INLAID [WITH LETTERS] OF REAL LAPIS-LAZULI, UNDER THE FEET OF THE GOD DURING THE REIGN OF HIS MAJESTY, THE KING OF THE NORTH AND OF THE SOUTH, MEN-KAU-RA (MYCERINUS) TRIUMPHANT, BY THE ROYAL SON HERU-TA-TA-F, TRIUMPHANT; HE FOUND IT WHEN HE WAS JOURNEYING ABOUT TO MAKE AN INSPECTION OF THE TEMPLES. ONE NEKHT (?) WAS WITH HIM WHO WAS DILIGENT IN MAKING HIM TO UNDERSTAND (?) IT, AND HE BROUGHT IT TO THE KING AS A WONDERFUL OBJECT WHEN HE SAYS THAT IT WAS A THING OF GREAT MYSTERY, WHICH HAD NEVER [BEFORE] BEEN SEEN OR LOOKED UPON.

FREDERICK MONDERSON

THIS CHAPTER SHALL BE RECITED BY A MAN WHO IS CEREMONIALLY CLEAN AND PURE, WHO HATH NOT EATEN FLESH OF ANIMALS OR FISH, AND WHO HATH NOT HAD INTERCOURSE WITH WOMEN. AND BEHOLD, THOU SHALL MAKE A SCARAB OF GREEN STONE, WITH A RIM PLATED (?) WITH GOLD, WHICH SHALL BE PLACED IN THE HEART OF A MAN, AND IT SHALL PERFORM FOR HIM THE 'OPENING OF THE MOUTH' AND THOU SHALL ANOINT IT WITH *ANTI* UNGUENT, AND THOU SHALL RECITE OVER IT [THESE] ENCHANTMENTS:

Wilson (1901) "PRESERVING THE HEART" from the *Papyrus of Ani* in the British Museum, No. 10,470, sheet 510.

THE CHAPTER OF NOT LETTING THE HEART OF OSIRIS, THE SCRIBE OF THE HOLY OFFERINGS OF ALL THE GODS, ANI, TRIUMPHANT, BE DRIVEN FROM HIM IN THE UNDERWORLD. He saith:

'My heart, my mother; my heart, my mother! My heart whereby I came into being! May naught stand up to oppose me at [my] judgment; may there be no opposition to me in the presence of the sovereign princes (Tchatcha); may there be no parting of thee from me in the presence of him that keepeth the balance! Thou art my *ka*, the dweller in my body; the God Khnemu who knitteth and strengtheneth my limbs. Mayest thou come forth into the place of happiness whither we go. May the *Shenti* (i.e., the divine officers of the court of Osiris), who form the conditions of the lives of men, not cause my name to stink.' ['Let it be satisfactory unto us, and let the listening be satisfactory unto us, and let there be joy of heart unto us at the weighing of words. Let not that which is false be uttered against me before the great God, the lord of Amentet. Verily how great shall thou be when thou risest in triumph!']"

The second selection, Wilson (1901: 49-50), "OF GAINING MASTERY OVER ENEMIES" comes from the *Papyrus of Nu* in the British Museum, No. 10,477, sheet 15.

WHERE ARE THE KAMITE KINGS?

THE CHAPTER OF COMING FORTH BY DAY AND OF GAINING THE MASTERY OVER ENEMIES. The chancellor-in-chief, Nu, saith:

Where are the Kamite Kings Photo. Temple of Luxor. From within the "photographer's paradise" of the Court of Amenhotep III. Looking west, the first row is intact, but the second is wanting. The "closed bud papyrus bundle columns" have two bands below the abacus supporting the overhead architrave, against a blue sky.

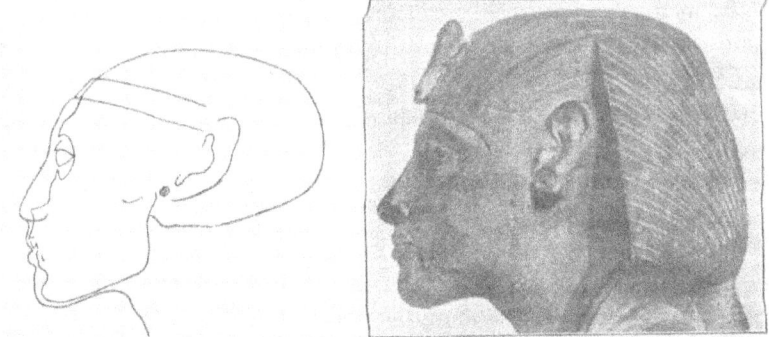

Where are the Kamite Kings Illustration. Two images of Amenhotep IV, Akhenaten.

FREDERICK MONDERSON

Where are the Kamite Kings Photo. Luxor Temple, Erik Monderson at a Hypostyle Hall doorway that faces west.

'Ra sitteth in his habitation of millions of years, and he hath gathered together his company of Gods, with those divine beings, whose faces are hidden, who dwell in the Temple of Khepera, who eat the God Bah, and who drink the Drink-offerings which are brought into the celestial regions of light; and conversely. Grant that I may take possession of the captives of Osiris, and never let me have my being among the fiends of Suti! Hail, let me sit upon his folds in the habitation of the God User-ba (i.e., he of the strong Soul)! Grant thou that I may sit upon the throne of Ra, and let me have possession of my body before the God Seb. Grant thou that Osiris may come forth triumphant over Suti [and over] the night-watchers of Suti, and over the night-watchers of the Crocodile, yea the night-dwellers of the Crocodile, whose faces are hidden and who dwell in the divine Temple of the King of the North in the apparel of the Gods on the sixth day of the festival, whose snares are like unto everlastingness and whose cords are like unto eternity. I have seen the God Abet-ka placing the cord; the child is laid in fetters, and the rope of the God Ab-ka is drawn tight (?) .... Behold me. I am born, and I come forth in the form of a living *Khu*, and the human beings who are upon the earth ascribe praise [unto me]. Hail, Mer,

WHERE ARE THE KAMITE KINGS?

who doest these things for me, and who art put an end to by the vigor of Ra, grant thou that I may see Ra; grant thou that I may be victorious over them in the presence of the sovereign princes of the great God who are in the presence of the great God. If, repulsing [me], thou dost not allow me to come forth against my Enemy and to be victorious over him before the sovereign princes, then may Hapi - who live upon law and order - not come forth into heaven - now he liveth by Maat - and may Ra - who feedeth upon fish - not descend into the waters! And then, verily shall Ra - who feedeth upon right and order - come forth into heaven, and then, verily, shall Hapi - who feedeth upon fish - descend into the waters; and then, verily, the great day upon the earth shall not be in its season. I have come against my Enemy, he hath been given unto me, he hath come to an end, and I have gotten possession [of him] before the sovereign princes.'"

Where are the Kamite Kings Photo. "Karnak men," Abdul, Shawki, and Handaka, Gate-keepers of the Temple of Amen at Karnak, Luxor, Egypt.

FREDERICK MONDERSON

Where are the Kamite Kings Illustration. Crowns, headdresses and beards worn by the Kings.

Wilson (1901: 50) in THE CHAPTER OF COMING FORTH BY DAY AND OF GAINING THE MASTERY OVER ENEMIES recounts: "'Hail, [thou] who shinest from the Moon and who sendest forth light there from thou comest forth among thy multitudes, and thou goest round about, let me rise,' or (as others say), 'let me be brought in among the *Khus*, and let the underworld be opened [unto me]. Behold, I have come forth on this day, and I have become a *Khu* (or a shining being); therefore, shall the *Khus* let me live, and they shall cause my enemies to be brought to me in a state of misery in the presence of the divine sovereign princes. The divine *ka* (double) of my mother shall rest in peace because of this, and I shall stand upon my feet and have a staff of gold,' or (as others say), 'a rod of gold in my hand, wherewith I shall inflict cuts on the limbs [of mine enemy] and shall live. The legs of Sothis are stablished, and I am born in their state of rest.'"

WHERE ARE THE KAMITE KINGS?

Where are the Kamite Kings Photo. Erik Monderson in the rear of Rameses III's Mortuary Temple at Medinet Habu.

REFERENCES

"Abu Gurab: Chambers with Reliefs." *American Journal of Archaeology* IV (1900: 478).
Baines, J. and J. Malek. *Atlas of Ancient Egypt.* New York: Facts on File, 1980.
Banks, Edgar J. "Seven Wonders of the Ancient World: I. The First Wonder. The Pyramid of Cheops." *Art and Archaeology* 3 (January, 1916: 30-33).
ben-Jochannan, Y.A. *Black Man of the Nile and His Family.* New York: Alkebu-Lan Books, 1981.
"Beit Khallaf: A Year's Excavation of Egypt." *American Journal of Archaeology* VI (1902: 57-59).
Brier, Bob. *Ancient Egyptian Magic.* New York: Quill, 1981.
Breasted, J.H. *A History of Egypt.* New York: Charles Scribner's Sons, (1905) 1923.
_____. *Ancient Records of Egypt* I. New York: Russell and Russell, (1905) 1962.
Budge, E.A.W. *Egypt in the Neolithic and Archaic Periods.* New York: Henry Froude, 1902.
Corteggiani, J. *The Egypt of the Pharaohs.* London: Scala Books, 1986.
"Egyptian Royal Accessions during the Old Kingdom." *American Journal of Archaeology* XIX (1915: 458-59).

"Ekhmim: Inscribed Tombs." *American Journal of Archaeology* XVI (1912: 114).

"El Amrah: Prehistoric Cemeteries." *American Journal of Archaeology* V (1901: 332).

Erman, A. *Life in Ancient Egypt*. London and New York: Macmillan and Co., 1894.

Fagan, B.M. *Rape of the Nile*. New York: Charles Scribner's Sons, 1975.

Gates, E.A. "Soudanese Dolls." *Man* 1903, 22.

"German Excavations in 1906." *American Journal of Archaeology* XI (1907: 343).

"Gizeh: The Egyptian Expedition of Harvard University and the Boston Museum of Fine Arts." *American Journal of Archaeology* XV (1911: 407-08).

"Gizeh: Excavations in 1913." *American Journal of Archaeology* XIX (1915: 343).

"Gizeh and Memphis in 1913-14: The Expedition of the University of Pennsylvania." *American Journal of Archaeology* XX (1916: 97).

Grimal, Nicolas. *A History of Ancient Egypt*. Cambridge: Blackwell, (1988) 1992.

Hawass, Zahi. "The Workmen's Community at Giza." *Horus* (July/September, 1993: 6-10).

"Hetep-Heres, Mother of Cheops." *American Journal of Archaeology* XXXI (1927: 361).

Hope, T. *Costumes of the Greeks and Romans*. New York: Dover Publications, Inc., (1812) 1962.

Iskander, Zaki. *Pharaonic Egypt*. Cairo: Arab World Printing House, (1975) 1979.

Kees, H. *Ancient Egypt: A Social History*. Chicago: University of Chicago Press, (1961) 1977.

Leibovitch, J. *Ancient Egypt*. Cairo: French Archaeological Institute, 1938.

Lichtheim, M. *Ancient Egyptian Literature*: Vol. I *The Old and Middle Kingdoms*. Los Angeles: University of California Press, (1973) 1975.

Mu'Min, R.A. *Amen: The Secret Waters of the Great Pyramid*. Greensboro, N.C.: A.M. Distributors, 1988.

Murnane, W.J. *The Penguin Guide to Ancient Egypt*. New York: Penguin Books, 1983.

Murray, M. *The Splendor That Was Egypt*. New York: Philosophical Library, (1949) 1957.

WHERE ARE THE KAMITE KINGS?

Myers, C.S. "The Bones of Hen Nekht, an Egyptian King of the Third Dynasty." *Man* 1901, 127.

Where are the Kamite Kings Photo. Temple of Luxor. From the southwest, view of the Processional Colonnade as the sun shines back upon it in late afternoon.

Newberry, P.E. "The Egyptian Cult-Object and the Thunderbolt." *Annals of Archaeology and Anthropology* 3 (1910: 50-52).
"A Nomarch of Edfou of the Sixth Dynasty." *American Journal of Archaeology* XXIII (1919: 178-79).
"Position of the Fragments of the Palermo Stone." *American Journal of Archaeology* XXII (1918: 201-02).
Randall-MacIver, D. and A. Wilkin. "Libyan Notes." *Man* 1901, 62.
Randall-MacIver, D. "A Prehistoric Cemetery at El Amrah in Egypt: Preliminary Report of Excavations." *Man* 1901, 40.
"Reliefs of the Sun-Temple of Rathures." *American Journal of Archaeology* XXIV (1920: 374).
Saber, M. *Pyramids and Mastabas*. Cairo: Lehnert and Landrock, [ND].
"Sakkara." *American Journal of Archaeology* XXXII (1928: 72).
"Sale of a House." *American Journal of Archaeology* XVI (1912: 561).
"The Table of Offerings." (Maspero) *American Journal of Archaeology* I (1897: 396-97).
White, J.E. *Ancient Egypt: Its Culture and History*. New York: Dover Publications, Inc., 1970.

FREDERICK MONDERSON

Wilson, E. *Egyptian Literature.* New York: The Colonial Press, 1901.

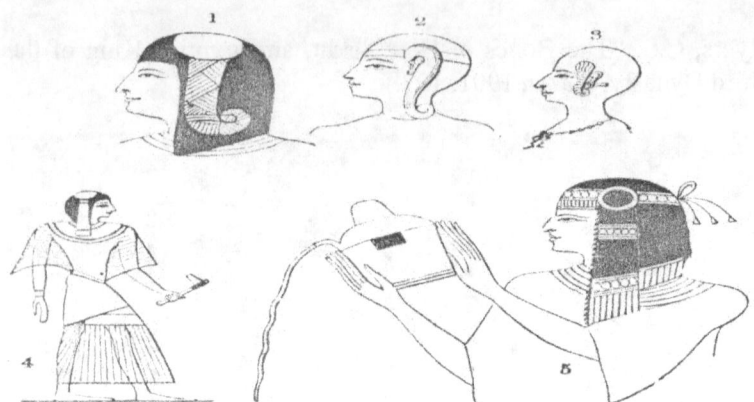

Where are the Kamite Kings Illustration. Hair styles. Especially the "side lock" worn by royalty.

8. FIRST INTERMEDIATE PERIOD

The First Intermediate Period began with the end of Pepi II's reign. The growing power of the nobles had weakened the central administration and competing centers of power in the north and south emerged. With this polarization, local rule was unable to maintain the standards of the Old Kingdom. The nation entered into a tremendous downward spiral where rule of law, administration of justice, collection of taxes and respect for individual rights and property were lost. This state of affairs was recounted in the writings of some sages of the period. Nevertheless, Baines and Malek (1980: 35) have provided some insights into this development: "At first the change to dual sovereignty probably made little difference to the running of the country, since the dynasties were too weak to exert much influence on local politics. Their power gradually increased, however, and there were frequent clashes at the border, which was mostly north of Abydos. The presence of considerable numbers of Nubian mercenaries in Upper Egypt is an indication of how violent the times were."

One example of the anarchy that ensued was wanton destruction of graves and monuments of the Old Kingdom. In this regard, James Breasted (1923: 147) wrote of desecration of symbolism in the holy

WHERE ARE THE KAMITE KINGS?

places. "The temples were not merely pillaged and violated, but their finest works of art were subjected to systematic and determined vandalism, which shattered the splendid granite and diorite statues of the Kings into bits, or hurled them into the well in the monumental gate of the pyramid-causeway. Thus, the old foes of the old regime wreaked vengeance upon those who had represented and upheld it. The nation was totally disorganized."

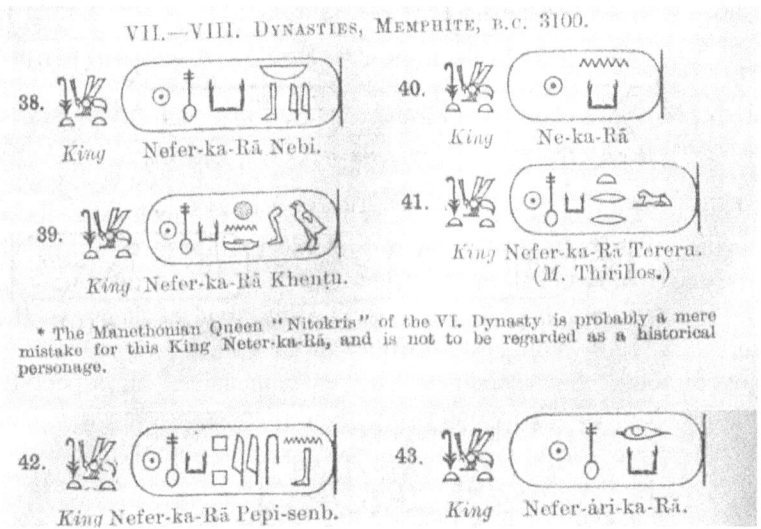

Kamite Kings Cartouche/Shennu. Kings of the Seventh and Eighth Dynasties.

The **Seventh and Eighth Dynasties** were weak and ineffective. They left little evidence of their rule. Breasted (1923: 147) best sums this up when he wrote, in the "mines and quarries of Sinai and Hammamat, where records of every prosperous line of Kings, proclaim their power, not a trace of these ephemeral pharaohs can be found." Hence and even further, James Breasted (1923: 148) continued, "a generation after the fall of the Sixth Dynasty a family of Heracleopolitan nomarchs wrested the crown from the weak Memphites of the Eighth Dynasty, who may have lingered on, claiming royal honors for nearly another century."

The princes of Assuit Nome typified the noble sense of loyalty, relationship with the crown, and ideal commitment to the pharaonic system. We saw this in the Thinites, and the Fifth Dynasty and nobles from Elephantine, at Aswan, who though removed from the actual center of government, they being at the southern frontier, de7fended the social order with great tenacity. The nobles of Assuit provide extant evidence of this magnanimity, as in a tomb that is now legendary. These nomarchs of Assuit, J.H. Breasted (1923: 149) wrote accordingly: "... enjoyed the most intimate relations with the royal house at Heracleopolis; we first find the King attending the burial of the head of this noble house; and while the daughter of the deceased prince ruled in Siut, her son, Kheti, then a lad, was placed with the children of the royal household to be educated."

This royal socialization served many purposes, for besides building friendships and loyalties with the young princes and princesses of the ruling family; the young nobles were "hostages" at court ensuring loyalty of their kinsmen. This keeping of potential young adversaries under scrutiny was well played out much later in the heyday of the medieval Western-Sudanic Empire of Ghana. The practice found full fruition in the drama of Sumanguru and Sundiata in the later state of Mali. Ostensibly, this royal tutelage was the surest way of facilitating loyalty to centralization and strong government. Such practices further emphasized an aspect of continuity of ceremony and symbolism, practiced over wide areas of Africa.

Concerning, the young prince Khety, whose mother shared a co-regency, also throws some light on the role of African women in this early day. Equally, the elaborate burial provisions made for women in Egypt speak to the respect and roles they held in ancient society here and elsewhere in Africa.

Breasted (1923: 149) judged Khety's administration of Assuit to have been effective and prosperous. To this end, he indicated, the Prince "dug canals, reduced taxation, reaped rich harvests, and maintained large herds; while he had always in readiness a body of troops and a fleet. Such was the wealth and power of these Siut nobles that they soon became a buffer state on the south of inestimable value to the house of Heracleopolis, and Kheti was made military 'commander of Middle Egypt.'"

Just as ephemeral as the Seventh and Eighth Dynasties, the Ninth and Tenth also left just as few remains. Providing some clues to

WHERE ARE THE KAMITE KINGS?

these dynasties, Flinders Petrie's "Excavations at Ehnasya" in *Man* 1904, 77 is included here as follows: "The site of the Arabic town, Ehnasya or Ahnas, is the Roman Heracleopolis Magna, the Egyptian Hennen Suten, a place well-known from the 1st dynasty onward, and even of mythological importance. It is now a great mass of mounds, of Roman and Arab age, about seventy miles south of Cairo, and ten miles from the Nile; the strip of four miles of cultivation between it and the desert is probably due to the rise of the Nile soil covering low desert between, so that the town may have been on the edge of the desert originally."

Where are the Kamite Kings Illustration. Costumes of the Kings.

"It was the home of the IX and X dynasties, of whom hardly anything is known, and there have been hopes that some trace of that period might be found there. Twelve years ago, Dr. Naville found the site of a temple; he uncovered the upper stones of the central hall, and the colonnade before that, and removed six columns of red granite, but no plan was made or any systematic historical research. This year-in default of better ground-I went to work the history of the site, and we found in course of work the two finest objects that have come to light in Egypt for some time past, the gold statuette ... and a colossal group of figures in granite. We uncovered not only the central hall to its lowest foundations, but also as large a space of the chambers behind it, and a still larger space of a great court with colossi in front of it. We have thus the history of another great Egyptian temple worked out as far as possible."

"The oldest temple on this ground was probably of the XII dynasty. But below this were ruins of older houses cut down and leveled for building of the temple. And against the foundations of these houses were burials, which must be older than the temple. These comprised scarabs of Antef V (Nub-Khepera-ra), a 'King of the Aamu (Syrians),' and other types, which have been supposed of recent years to be much later, and to belong to the XVI and XVII dynasties. Here, however, we have a clear succession of periods: -

I.   The Burials.

II.   A great temple.

III.   A great temple of Tahutmes III, XVIII Dynasty.

"As II cannot on any reasonable supposition be of the XVIII dynasty, and ruined before Tahutmes III, we must conclude that II was the temple of the XII dynasty, of which much sculpture remained on site. Hence the period I must be of the XI dynasty, agreeing with the date first credited for Antef V. This is one of the most important points yet in doubt in Egyptian history, and the evidence here is very strong, and must hold the field unless anything more decisive may come to light."

"The first temple was smaller than that of the XVIII dynasty and later times, according with the results of Abydos, where the early temples were of much less area than the later. It seems to have consisted of a small sanctuary, perhaps, 14 feet square inside, with chambers for treasuries on each side of it, and a great open court before it. In the foundations of this temple lay a block with figure of a King brought from some earlier site, probably of the VI dynasty by the style."

"Many pieces of the sculptures of the XII dynasty were found in the ruins, showing that Senusert (Usertesen) II and III and Amenemhat III all built here (about 2600 B.C.). The great architrave of the temple entrance can be restored from the size of the piece of jamb remaining; it must have been just the length of the later architrave

WHERE ARE THE KAMITE KINGS?

of the Ramesside temple, and the same as a great architrave reworked, now in the ruins of a Coptic church. Probably the same beam of stone has served every builder of temple or church for over 3,000 years. Two fine statues of quartzite sandstone were found in the ruins, also of the XII dynasty, but reworked by Ramessu II."

"After this early temple was destroyed a much larger one was built by Tahutmes III (1500 B.C.) of the XVIII dynasty, as is shown by a plan stretching much further back. The old sanctuary gave way to a much larger hypostyle hall of twenty-four columns, with a lesser hall of four columns behind it, and several treasuries by the sanctuary. At this period the lines of the building faces were all traced out by clear grooves upon the foundation blocks. It is dated by a scarab of the King, and other things of his age, found behind the stones."

Where are the Kamite Kings Photo. Raising hands in adoration, a pharaoh wearing the "Blue" or "War Crown" in Karnak Temple. Notice the Uraeus on his brow.

FREDERICK MONDERSON

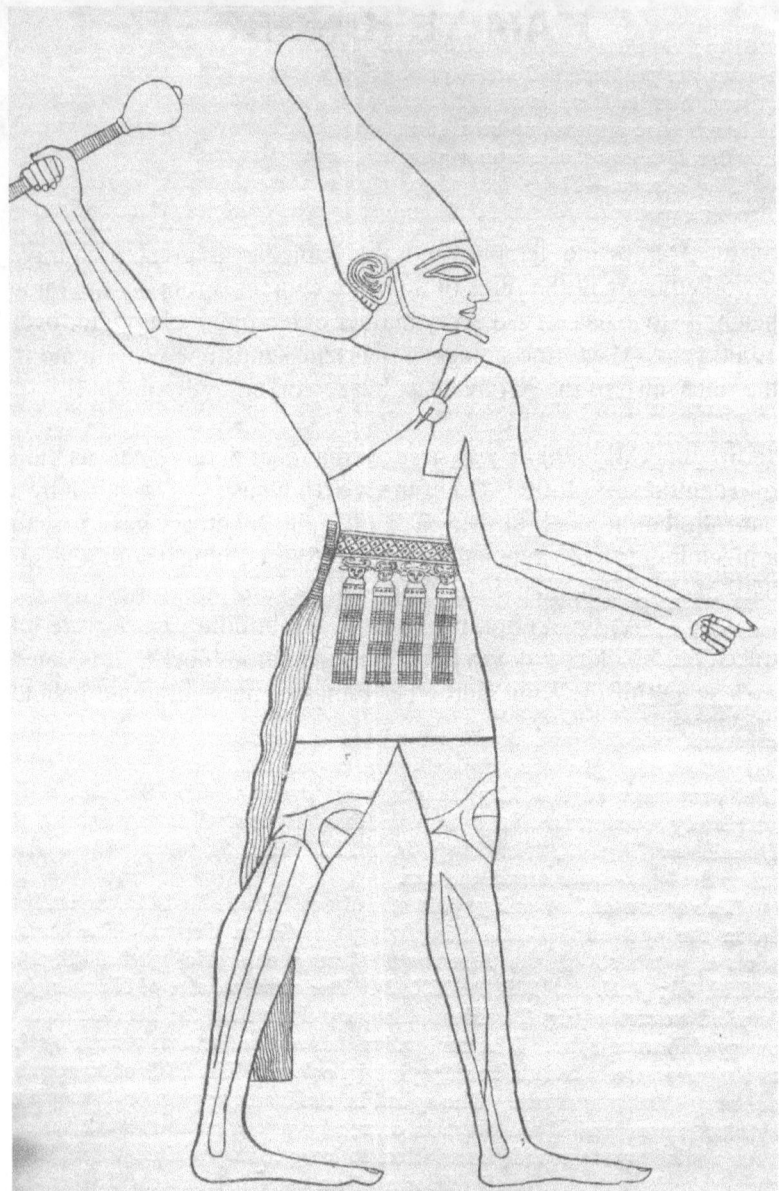

Where are the Kamite Kings Illustration. Wearing the White Crown and holding mace in his right hand, King Narmer sports a knot over his left shoulder. Notice his tail and short beard.

"This temple was more or less removed, and rebuilt by Ramessu II (1300 B.C.), at least as regards the facade. There still remains a line of large blocks of brown quartzite sandstone bearing an inscription

WHERE ARE THE KAMITE KINGS?

of Ramessu II, which formed the lower course of the whole front of the temple. The King also carved new architraves out of blocks of granite of the XII dynasty, and placed his figures and names upon the beautiful monolith columns of granite, also belonging to the first temple. In the forecourt he placed, up each side of the court, a row of colossi of limestone, 25 feet high, and two colossal groups of figures of himself between Ptah and Hershefi, the local God. One of these triads was seated, it is now broken; the other group was standing, 11 feet high, 8 feet wide, weighing about 20 tons. This is the finest such group known, and it is to be placed in the Cairo Museum."

"The building level was again raised for a later temple, and the plan slightly altered. This may have been in the XXII dynasty (900 B.C), as there was certainly a secure shrine in the XXIII dynasty when the gold statuette was dedicated. This figure is .... of the finest work in the anatomy of the muscular treatment and proportions, and is probably the largest gold figure, and perhaps the most artistic, that has been found in Egypt. The excellence of it is more surprising at so late a date as 700 B.C.; and it shows that artistry was by no means extinct in even a low period of general taste and ability. On the base is an inscription, which the engraver has bungled, in copying it probably, from some statue. It records the name and titles of the King under whom it was dedicated, Nefer-ka-ra Pef-di-bast-mer-bast. He was a vassal King of Piankhy the Ethiopian, and has hitherto only been known in an inscription of his suzerain, so that an original monument is very welcome, especially as it gives his throne name."

"At a later date the floor of the temple was again raised to a higher level, covering nearly all the inscriptions of the lower course. Rather than lift the great blocks of granite, which formed the basements of the colonnade, the builders inserted drums of quartzite sandstone beneath the columns, so as to raise them to the new level. This strange device has not been seen elsewhere. In this late temple stood a monolith shrine of red granite carved by Nekht-Hor-heb. The latest activity here seems to have been some rebuilding by Antoninus, of which several blocks were found reused in a later Roman house."

FREDERICK MONDERSON

Where are the Kamite Kings Illustration. Lid and sides of Sitkames' coffin.

WHERE ARE THE KAMITE KINGS?

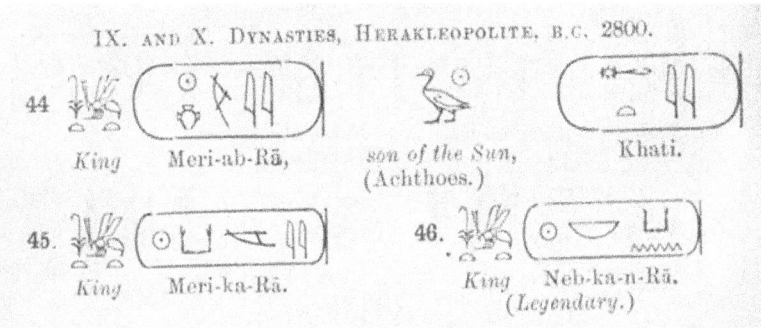

Kamite Kings Cartouche/Shennu. Kings of the Ninth and Tenth Dynasties.

"From the section of the earth over the temple it could be seen that after it had been removed for stone, several feet of earth had accumulated over the foundations, and then later digging had been made through this to extract the lower stones. This later digging was in the fourth century A.D., by the pottery in the hole; so, the first ruin of the temple was probably as early as the third century. Yet paganism flourished in Isis and Horus worship for two centuries longer, as we see by the figures in the houses. Thus, it seems the first effect of Christianity was to place animal worship in disfavor, and thereby to increase the Isis and Horus worship; and the latter was never overcome, but became incorporated in Christianity as the Madonna and Child. This view of the different status of parts of the earlier religion has not appeared so evident before."

"The gain in method this year has been in following the history of building by tracing the several sand-beds between the stones. No builder ever put some inches of sand between his courses. Hence when layers of sand are found between stones it proves that a complete re-foundation was made; the stones below the sand-bed having been left sunk in the ground and ignored, while a layer of sand was laid over them for founding a new temple. Thus, the view, which we exposed in the digging, of many courses of stones separated by three or four beds of sand can be read off as recording the founding of so many separate temples."

FREDERICK MONDERSON

"Though no whole dynasty of Kings has been brought to light, as in our work at Abydos, yet the fresh and strong evidence about the early date of some rulers and styles, and the recovery of two of the finest monuments known, and the plans of series of temples on a great site, makes this year another landmark in the clearing of Egyptian history."

"Besides the temple site we worked also in the town, entirely on burnt houses of Roman age. Thus, we have been able to date a long series of terra cotta figures, which are of much finer work than was expected in the third and fourth centuries A.D. And a tolerably complete *corpus* of Roman-Egyptian lamps was made, and the degradation of types traced throughout more than 1,000 varieties. This may, perhaps, be more fully described here in future." Flinders Petrie.

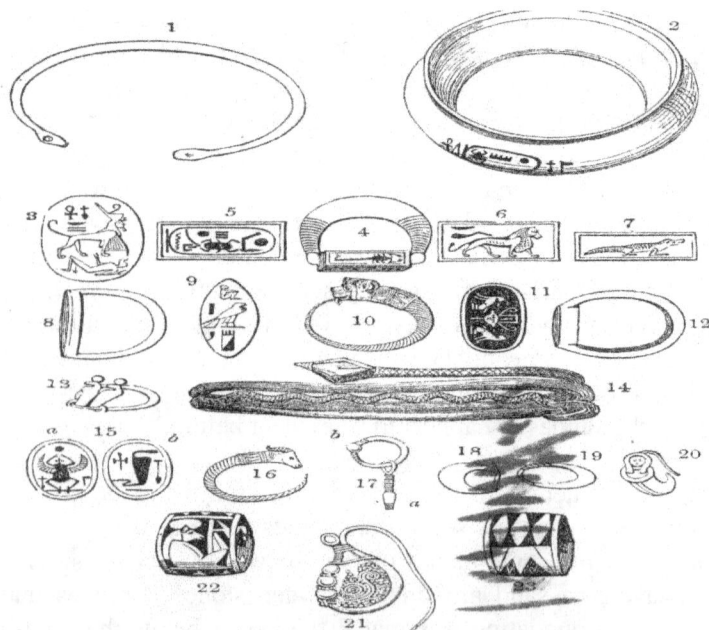

Where are the Kamite Kings Illustration. Rings, Bracelets and other Jewelry worn by the Kings.

While much of the above does not specifically refer to the period, it does provide some links with the ephemeral Ninth and Tenth

WHERE ARE THE KAMITE KINGS?

Dynasties, whose remains are scant, due to the turbulence of the age. However, we also need to be careful in the attribution of nomarchs as Antef V being "Syrian," for herein lie the bias of these early researchers. Then again, upon re-reading this may not be so/

Following the constant quest for supremacy, to begin the Eleventh Dynasty, the Houses of Intefs and Mentuhoteps gradually emerged to begin the final push for unification. Breasted (1923: 149-50) makes this known in that "an obscure provincial town and the neighboring Hermonthis was the seat of a family of nomarchs, the Intefs and Mentuhoteps."

"Towards the close of the Heracleopolitan supremacy, Thebes had gained the leading place in the South, and its nomarch, Intef, was 'Keeper of the Door of the South.' The South stood together and in time of scarcity we see the Nomes aiding each other with grain and provisions. Intef was soon able to organize the whole South in rebellion, mustering his forces from the cataract northward at least as far as Thebes .... This Intef was ever after recognized as the ancestor of the Theban line, and the nomarchs of the Middle Kingdom set up his statue in the temple at Thebes among those of their royal predecessors who were worshiped there."

Again, what is significant here, while James Breasted placed the Intef family in Upper Kemet, Petrie in the above, ascribed them to being Syrian. Here we have an aspect of perennial distortion, in attributing important aspects of Egyptian and African history to foreigners, particularly foreigners. Not just Petrie but other as A.E.P. Weigall attribute such personalities as Rameses II and the parents of Queen-Tiy, Yuya and Tuya, also as Syrian. This latter, despite Tiy being "so Nubian." It's all part of the distortion and the racist prejudice that drove Petrie's ideas.

Smith's (1981: 156-57) commentary is rather cogent as he supplied a chronological framework for the transition to the next period as the south mobilized for its triumph. He writes: "... around 2130 B.C. there were signs of a revival, with King Neferkara and his two strong successors, Wah-ka-ra Khety and Merikara, ruling in the north and Seher-tawy Intef I declaring himself King in Thebes. It was the house of the latter which was to triumph. Heracleopolis fell to Nebhepet-ra Mentuhotep about 2052 B.C., and it is with the uniting of the country under Thebes that the Middle Kingdom was really established."

Baines and Malek (1980: 35) tell further: "The most important King of the more stable Theban Dynasty was the fourth, Nebhepetre' Mentuhotep (called I or II by different writers, 2061-2010), who defeated the northern dynasty and reunited the country. Mentuhotep began with a programmatic Horus name, 'Who gives heart to the Two Lands,' which was replaced first by 'Divine of the White Crown' (the crown of Upper Egypt) and later by 'Uniter of the Two Lands.'"

Where are the Kamite Kings Photo. Temple of Hatshepsut at Deir el Bahari. Hathor Shrine. Behind the square pillar, a round column with Hathor Head capital depicts the Goddess with a female face, cow's ears and long flowing hair. It is interesting how everywhere one goes it seems the noses of features are attacked seemingly in a systematic way and perhaps, for a pernicious reason.

REFERENCES

Baines, J. and J. Malek. *Atlas of Ancient Egypt*. New York: Facts on File, 1980.
Breasted, J. H. *History of Egypt*. New York: Charles Scribers' Sons, (1905) 1923.
Petrie, W.M.F. "Excavations at Ehnasya." *Man* 1904: 77.

WHERE ARE THE KAMITE KINGS?

Smith, W.S. *A History of Art and Architecture of Ancient Egypt.* New York: Penguin Books, (1959) 1981.

Where are the Kamite Kings Illustration. Image of "Man from the land of Punt," thought to be on the East African coast around Somaliland.

Where are the Kamite Kings Photo. Temple of Dendera. Entrance of screen wall with elevated engaged column with Hathor Head Column and Abacus supporting the architrave and roof. Within, three rows of free-standing illustrated columns underscore the magnificence of this Goddess Temple.

FREDERICK MONDERSON

Where are the Kamite Kings Photo. Temple of Dendera. The roof, view of a Chapel to Goddess Hathor where her emblem was taken every morning to bathe in the rays of her father, the Sun God Ra.

Where are the Kamite Kings Photo. Temple of Dendera. Erik Monderson strolls on the roof before the Chapel to Goddess Hathor where she greets her father the Sun God Ra in the mornings as shown above.

WHERE ARE THE KAMITE KINGS?

9. THE MIDDLE KINGDOM

The Middle Kingdom, properly Dynasties XI and XII, *Nile Year* 2200-2458 (2040-1782 B.C.) but also XIII and XIV, was a significant period in ancient Kemetic history and civilization. It represented the apogee or zenith that achieved the second "golden age" of this ancient culture. Here the positive accomplishments of the Old Kingdom were experimented with, refined and transmitted to the later periods to be emulated and studied through copying and literary recitation. It was a famous period of vigorous Black African assertion setting patterns and standards of government, science, art and industry as well as humane and philosophic behaviors that influenced subsequent civilizations.

Some scholars consider the Middle Kingdom the period from the XI-XVII Dynasties. The XIIth Dynasty proper is also considered the Middle Kingdom. In a broader sense, the Middle Kingdom or Middle Empire can also be considered the period from the fall of the Old Kingdom to the assumption of the New Kingdom or XVIIIth Dynasty. Nevertheless, the XIth Dynasty truly ends the First Intermediate Period, Dynasties VII-X, with the unification of Upper and Lower Kemet/Egypt. The process of "southern supremacy" was gradual in wake of the uncertainties of the ephemeral and sometimes simultaneous VIIth-Xth Dynasties. First, Heracleopolis challenged Memphis for leadership of the nation. It was able to attract powerful nobles who supported the system, who in turn established themselves independent from the central government.

The loyalty of the princes of Assuit is an important example of support for an established order. This Nome, at mid-country, became a bastion of political and military support for the north, against the aspirations of Upper Kemet, beyond Abydos.

FREDERICK MONDERSON

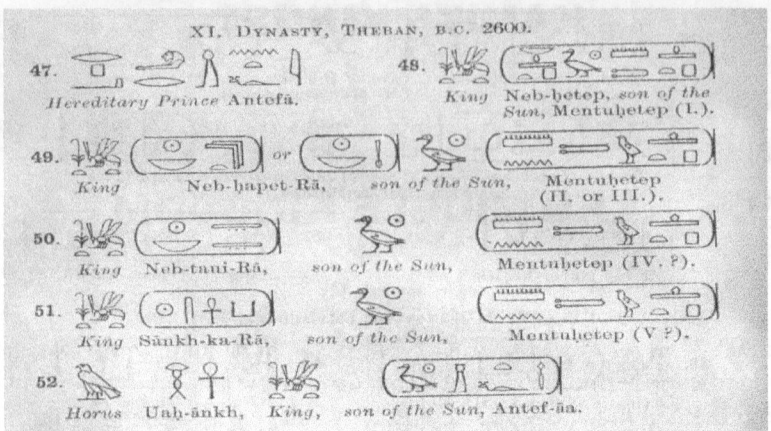

Kamite Kings Cartouche/Shennu 11. Kings of the Eleventh Dynasty of the Middle Kingdom, from Thebes, in Upper Egypt/Kemet.

In response, Thebes, home of the God Amon, and in the tradition of the Thinite Kings, Elephantine nobility and Lords of Hierakonpolis began to mobilize their powerful families. Intef emerged as the principal challenge to middle and northern supremacy. Having mobilized his forces, he began the systematic march northward after the conquest of *This*, or the Thinite state. Finally, Intef's successor, Mentuhotep I carried the battle and within two decades, emerged victorious and was able to claim Kingship over the entire land. The following is how Ruffle (1977: 53) explained it: "This new dynasty at first controlled only Upper Egypt: Wahankh Intef II captured the Thinite Nome and under his successors the Heracleopolitans came to accept the situation and a trading relationship emerged. When Mentuhotep II came to the throne in 2060 B.C.; however, his youthfulness encouraged them to try to recover the city of Thinis, but the new King carried the battle into their territory and Heracleopolis eventually fell in about 2040 B.C. A policy of restoration was put in hand at once. Some nomarch families changed allegiance and continued in office, and trusted Thebans were appointed to many state offices. Mediterranean trade was restored and contact with Nubia re-established."

Still, this is a period of some confusion. Breasted I (1962: 418) gives the reconstructed XIth Dynasty pharaohs as Intef I, Intef II, Mentuhotep I, Intef III, Mentuhotep II, Mentuhotep III, Mentuhotep IV. The confusion seems to rest with the particular Pharaoh

WHERE ARE THE KAMITE KINGS?

Mentuhotep who built the XIth Dynasty structure at *Deshret*, (Deir el-Bahari) and whose statue is in the Cairo Museum. His temple was chosen by the architect, Senmut, as the model for his Queen Hatshepsut's temple, 500 years later.

Where are the Kamite Kings Illustration. From Temple of Seti I at Abydos, the Barque of the Gods shows figure wearing the Double Crown (left), and wearing the White Crown (kneeling) to the right. Notice the uraei with Sun-Disks on top.

Throwing light on this question, Liebovitch (1938: 24) explained, "One of the Kings of the XIth Dynasty was buried in the side of the mountain at Deir el-Bahari, in front of which he had caused a funerary temple to be built." Murray (1949: 21) added to this, "Mentuhotep III built his mortuary temple and pyramid on the west side of the Nile at Deir el Bahari." Iskander (1979) further tells, Mentuhotep II "conquered the Heracleopolitans, the Asiatics, the Nubians, and the Libyans as represented on some blocks of stone remaining from a temple which he built at el-Gebelein (near Armant). He built for himself at Deir el-Bahari a small pyramid surrounded by colonnades and terraces and approached by a long causeway apparently from a lower temple."

FREDERICK MONDERSON

Where are the Kamite Kings Illustration. Statue of Mentuhotep II, 11th Dynasty, in *Heb Sed* Festival attire. Nebhepetra wears the Red Crown and he is of Smith's "black flesh."

Woldering (1963: 105) has argued: "After the fall of a family of Heracleopolitan nomarchs, who ruled over Lower Egypt, Mentuhotep II was able to unite the entire country under his domination. In the list of pharaohs his reign is given as the first of the XIth Dynasty, and thus the first in the history of the Middle Kingdom."

Even-more, Grimal (1992: 157) has written, the same monarch, Mentuhotep II: "while continuing the work of restoration undertaken by Inyotef III in the temple of Heqaib and Satis at Elephantine, also carried out further construction in Deir el-Ballas, Dendera, El Kab, the temple of Hathor at Gebelein (where his artists

WHERE ARE THE KAMITE KINGS?

depicted the submission of the North) and Abydos (where he made additions to the Osireion.) He added to the decoration of the sanctuaries of Monthu at el-Tod and Armant and in the cliffs of Deir el-Bahari, he built himself a funerary monument modeled on the pyramid complexes of the Old Kingdom."

Grimal (1992: 157) further indicated Mentuhotep II was followed by his son Mentuhotep III S'Ankhtawyef ('He who breathes new life into the Two Lands'), who inherited a prosperous nation.

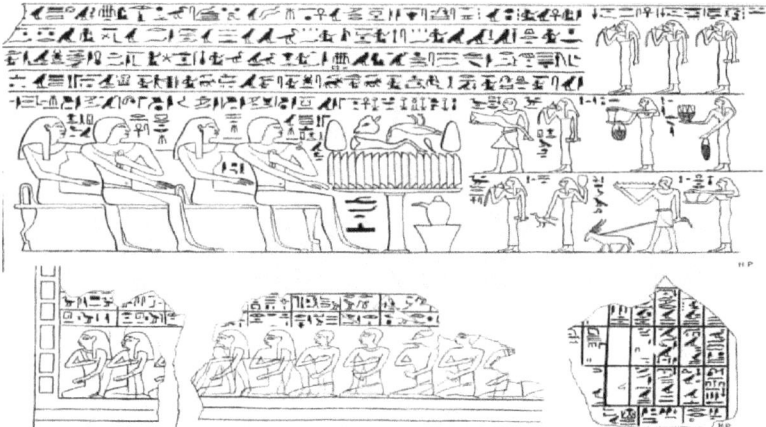

Where are the Kamite Kings Illustration. Stele of Mentuhotep and Sent, XIth Dynasty from *Tombs of the Courtiers and Oxyrhynkhos* by Flinders Petrie (1925).

Accordingly, "Since Mentuhotep III was already fairly advanced in years when he came to power, his reign was only to last for about twelve years. During this time, he continued to pursue the construction programs begun by his father at Abydos, El Kab, Armant, El-Tod, Elephantine and Western Thebes, where he built a chapel to Thoth. His own tomb, near Deir el-Bahari, was never completed."

Where are the Kamite Kings Illustration. Stele of Mentuhotep (top); and, an Altar with 43 names found at Abydos by Petrie (bottom).

Where are the Kamite Kings Photo. Column bases and stumps among the ruins in Mentuhotep II's Deir el Bahari Temple.

WHERE ARE THE KAMITE KINGS?

Where are the Kamite Kings Photo. Erik Monderson stands beside Mentuhotep II's seated statue in the Cairo Museum.

Significantly, Smith's (1981: 160) commentary on Mentuhotep's seated sandstone statue from Deir el-Bahari and now in the Cairo Museum, is an interesting one. In this "ground-breaking work,"

FREDERICK MONDERSON

published in 1959, he described a statue found (1903) more than half a century earlier, and now lying in the museum as "painted, and represented the King in Heb-Sed dress wearing the red crown of the north and with black flesh. Standing and seated sandstone statues, in similar dress and with the body treated in the same rude massive fashion, lined the way across the courtyard leading to the temple." This revelation, half a century after its discovery and lying in the Cairo Museum, was never mentioned in prior American print. Talk about omission and for so long!

Where are the Kamite Kings Photo. The author, Dr. Fred Monderson, equally stands beside Mentuhotep's statue in the Cairo Museum of Egyptian Antiquities.

WHERE ARE THE KAMITE KINGS?

Where are the Kamite Kings Illustration. Inscriptions of Mentuhotep III, Sankh-Ka-Ra, Usertesen I, etc., from *Abydos II* by Flinders Petrie (1902)

FREDERICK MONDERSON

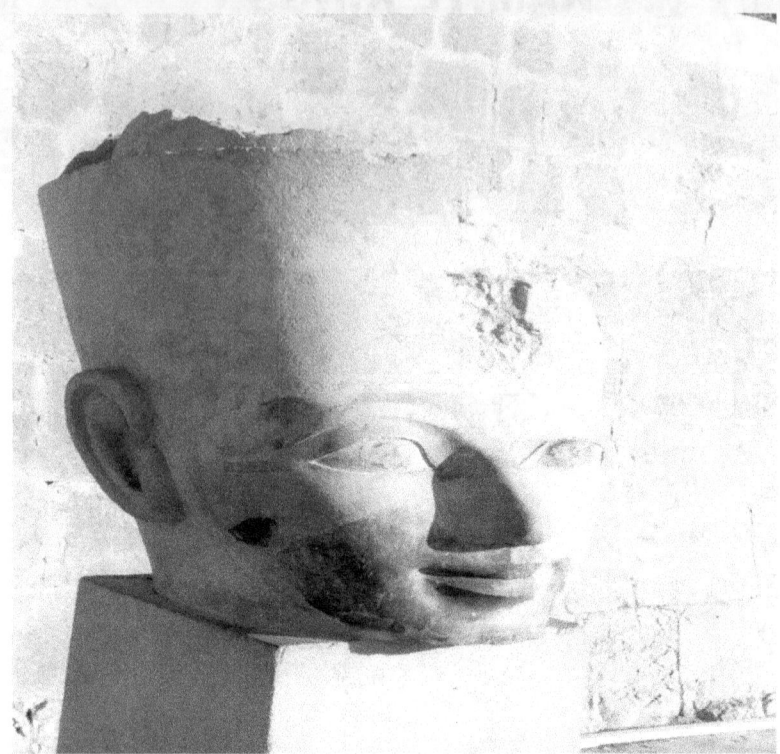

Where are the Kamite Kings Photo. Temple of Hatshepsut at Deir el Bahari. Face of broken Osiride Figure of the Queen on the Upper Terrace that supports the Upper Colonnade.

Muller (1987: 656) on the other hand, offered this view: "The royal tombs and the tombs of the retinue also required statues. The most significant sculpture in the round created during the XIth dynasty is the statue of Mentuhotep II enthroned, wearing the crown of Lower Egypt. This statue, which is made of sandstone and painted, substituted for the body of the King in the dummy burial under his pyramid. This representation has no predecessor in Memphite art but must be judged a new creation. Without prototype are the tense pose with arms crossed over the chest; the cubist treatment of the figure, which is emphasized by the block-like throne and square base; and the harsh color contrasts of the dark brown body, the white drapery, and the red crown. The abstract geometry of this statue betrays its development from a background of 'hieroglyphic' pictorial concepts. The major extant private statues of the XIth dynasty are made of limestone; none of these attains the

WHERE ARE THE KAMITE KINGS?

cohesiveness of the statue of Mentuhotep II." How interesting, "dark brown body" seems to hide his "black flesh."

Where are the Kamite Kings Illustration. Inner and outer coffin of Tausert.

FREDERICK MONDERSON

We have here two distinct color descriptions of the King's race. Still, importantly, in order to clarify the position of the Mentuhoteps, a note to the chapter in Smith (1981: 444) explained further: "Recent investigation favors the idea that the two Kings formerly called Mentuhotep II and III were the same man who assumed a different titulary after the conquest of Heracleopolis. It is also thought that his supposed predecessor, Mentuhotep I, may represent an earlier version of his name."

Reinforcing this view, Poesener (1962: 167) reiterated for clarity: "Mentuhotep I, who until recently was thought to have been three different Kings, brought the rival Kingdom of Herakleopolis to an end and re-established the unity of the country under his own rule. Thebes, which was until then a provincial town, became the capital of the whole country. The local hero, Mentuhotep I, was worshiped there nearly a thousand years after his death."

Where are the Kamite Kings Illustration. Temples of Mentuhotep III and Sankhkara, XIth Dynasty in *Abydos II* by Flinders Petrie (1902).

While some of these XIth Dynasty Kings left few records of their existence others have left extensive evidence. Mentuhotep I's name is found at the Temple of Gebelein (now in Glasgow Museum), on a rock tablet from Knossos and Private Stele No. 676 in the Louvre.

WHERE ARE THE KAMITE KINGS?

Antef II's name is on a coffin in the Louvre. Mentuhotep II is known from inscriptions at Wady Hammamat and Knossos as well as on scarabs. His mother was Queen Aam, according to Lepsius's *Denkmaler* II, 149 f. Antef IV's name is found on his pyramid at Thebes, on a stele in Glasgow Museum and on a rock Stele at Elephantine. His mother's name was Queen Achthoes. Antef V is known from his tomb and obelisk, at Thebes, a decree in the Temple at Koptos, on a statuette in the private Lee Collection and on scarabs.

We are told in *American Journal of Archaeology* XVIII (1914: 503), the German von Bissing described a relief found on rocks of Wadi es Soba Rigale. "It shows Mentuhotep IV, behind him stands his mother, is receiving submission and homage from Intef, behind whom stands Achthoes. Probably Intef came with his troops against Mentuhotep, but found, as he came out of the pass, that he was faced by overwhelming forces. Peace was made by the intervention of Chety (Achthoes) and Mentuhotep's mother."

Petrie I (1894: 138) mentions Mentuhotep III's name is found in his pyramid *Akhet-Asut* at Thebes. It is foremost in his Temple at Thebes, on Tablets at Shuter-Regal and Aswan. It is also on an altar in Cairo, a Scarab in the British Museum, a Gold Heart in Petrie Museum and a Menat of the XXVIth Dynasty, that's mentioned in the *Society of Biblical Archaeology* IX, 181. To repeat, though some of these sources are of considerable age, their recognition of names at various places are essentially correct. In addition, with subsequent research both in Egypt and abroad, the names are more widespread and thus this listing does not exhaust the location of these Kings' names. Mentuhotep's queens were Tumem and Aah.

Antef VI, Petrie I (1894: 141) states, is known from inscriptions at Wady Hammamat, Shuter Regal and a statue at Sakkarah. Also, we know of this King from alabaster blocks at Armant, an alabaster plaque, a gold ring with stone and a prayer to S-Ankh-Ka-Ra. Petrie I (1894: 143) further makes known scarabs first appear: "poor and small, under Mentuhotep II; under Antef V they improve; under Mentuhotep III the example we have is fine; and under his successor Sankhkara the work is beautifully delicate. In the sphere of power, we see some growth. Limited first to his Nome, Prince Antef is a humble servant of the suzerain in Herakleopolis; next, the King Mentuhotep I asserts his royalty on the southern frontier; next, Antef II and III appear with a fine royal tomb at Thebes and well-executed gilt mummy case. Then Mentuhotep II brings stone from Hammamat, and boasts of conquering thirteen tribes in the south. Antef V builds at Koptos, puts up obelisks at Thebes, and boasts of conquering both Asiatics and Negroes. Mentuhotep III builds a temple at Thebes, puts up many monuments, encourages art, and is reverenced to later ages; while Sankhkara sends out a foreign expedition, having apparently little to attract him at home."

An interesting insight is posed by the work of Petrie in connection with further discoveries relating to Antef VI, Sankh-Ka-Ra. At one time during the height of modern excavation of the ancient remains, scholars from Sweden, France, Germany, England, Italy, Turkey, and American Universities, museums, and other cultural institutions as the Smithsonian Institution, were simultaneously engaged in recovering antiquities on ancient Egypt and African science, building and social practice. We are told in *American Journal of Archaeology* XIII (1909: 349) regarding that year's archaeological excavations in the north: "Before Memphis was dry enough to work the past season, two months were spent by Professor Flinders Petrie at Thebes, where the ruins on top of the mountain were explored. They were found to be a chapel for the apotheosis of King Sankh-ka-ra, of the eleventh dynasty; it contained the pieces of the cenotaph and the Osiris statue of the King. Two of the desert valleys were exhaustively searched for concealed burials, and one untouched group was found. The coffin was covered only by about a foot of earth and stones. Around it was offerings of furniture, food, vases, and personal ornaments. On the mummy were a gold collar of four rows of rings, four gold bangles, earrings, and a girdle of electrum. This is one of the most complete burials known. Other interesting discoveries at Thebes were the clearing of a new temple site, two fine stone figures, and an untouched burial of the twenty-fifth dynasty."

It can be well imagined how the soldiers of intellectual imperialism swarmed over this region and so many other areas in quest of colonization of ancient African artifacts and knowledge.

WHERE ARE THE KAMITE KINGS?

Where are the Kamite Kings Photo. Temple of Hatshepsut at Deir el Bahari. The Sanctuary in the Upper Court. Notice to the left and right, different sized niches for statues, some destroyed, some beheaded or defaced.

Where are the Kamite Kings Illustration. Close-up of one of the statues of Usertesen I, 12th Dynasty (left); and, another view of some of the statues of Usertesen I, found in his tomb.

Nevertheless, and to refocus, whether the first Mentuhoteps may have been the same person or not, one thing needs attention. It regards the ethnology of this individual, his dynasty, the succeeding one and the population of Thebes and ancient Kemet in his time. This issue presents some interesting questions. When did these people like Mentuhotep and Antef, "come to Thebes" and when did they leave? Did all Thebans have "dark brown" color or "Black flesh?" If we accept Poesner's "local hero" theory, then how different was he from the local citizenry of this region. His statue and other representations in his temple, "The Holy Place," also throws into question the whole nature of artistic use of "color" in depiction of the ancient Kamites, in all facets of their existence.

Adams (1988: 21) mentioned mummification practices in the Middle Kingdom. She uses as example the princesses found associated with Mentuhotep's burial at Deir el Bahari, for "some of them are tattooed, the only instance of the practice found on ancient Egyptian bodies, although it is depicted on pre-dynastic figurines. This may be an Upper Egyptian, or even Nubian, custom; it seems that there was Nubian blood in the royal family."

Where are the Kamite Kings Photo. While wearing a Vulture headdress in Luxor Temple, Nefertari holds a Sistrum or rattle, symbol of Hathor.

WHERE ARE THE KAMITE KINGS?

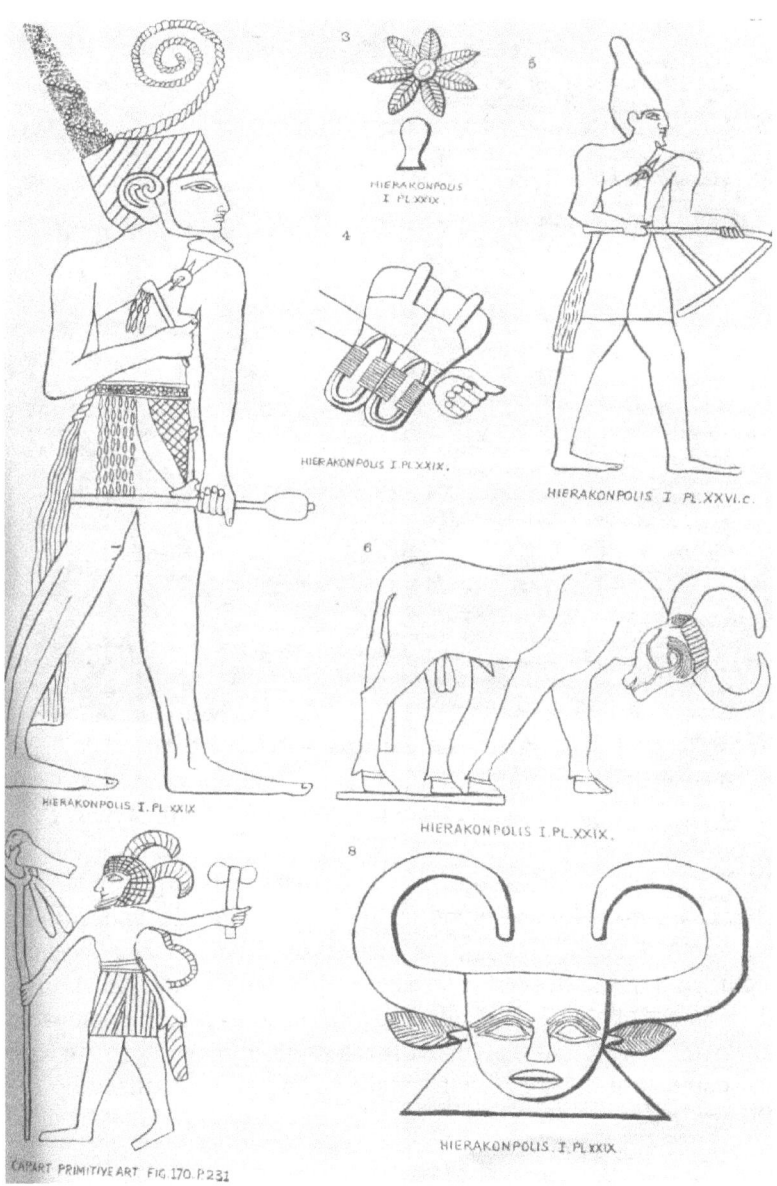

Where are the Kamite Kings Illustration. Costumes of various Kings, especially from Hierakonpolis.

FREDERICK MONDERSON

Where are the Kamite Kings Illustration. Clay seal of Shepsekaf, limestone base of Assa and granite head of a King, from the Temenos of Osiris from the IVth to the XIIth Dynasties

Whatever that meant! Diop, and the Afrocentrists, argue there was Black, Negro, Nubian blood in the formative Old and Middle Kingdom Pharaohs. The influence of whites never became significant until after the Hyksos conquest and the liberalization of the state following its imperial expansion, when subjugated northerners were brought generally as captives to amalgamate with the population, of the Upper Kamite Kingdom symbolized by the White Crown.

Mentuhotep began the unification, reorganization and consolidation of the nation. His temple at *Deshret*, (Deir el Bahari) is important architecturally, religiously, socially and ethnologically, in helping to unravel the dynamics of this pivotal period of African history, along the Nile River in North-east Africa. Location of the central

WHERE ARE THE KAMITE KINGS?

administration became significant for this dynasty having just triumphed over the north. While the XIth Dynasty emerged at Thebes under the Intefs and Mentuhoteps with Amen as principal deity, the XIIth Dynasty strengthened the legacy and moved their administrative capital to Lisht between Memphis and the Faiyum. Again, this move is somewhat reminiscent of Narmer's choice of Memphis, as being centrally located to control the Delta and the whole country. One thing is different from Narmer's time, however, that is, the support and challenges of the nobles, whose power had become hereditary, following the collapse of the Old Kingdom. The 12th Dynasty used a "carrot and stick" approach, "buy in to the new reality or lose what you have!"

Significantly, this supremacy of the south came to underscore the "Glory of the Ancestors." Narmer's unification, the founder of the Third Dynasty that initiated the Old Kingdom, was Ethiopian according to Petrie based on his Sinai researches, the Middle and New Kingdoms, the Ethiopian triumph of the XXVth Dynasty, all injected significant southern cultural, political, economic, religious, artistic and spiritual vitality into the Nile Valley civilization.

Where are the Kamite Kings Photo. One of two still standing Osiride Statues of the King at the south side entrance to *Akh Menu*, Festival Temple of Thutmose III.

FREDERICK MONDERSON

Where are the Kamite Kings Photo. Temple of Hatshepsut at Deir el Bahari. Beside the Hathor Shrine; the Goddess, as a cow wearing the White Crown, licks the hand of enthroned Queen Hatshepsut.

Petrie's argument for the Ethiopian who found the Third Dynasty is not based on firm evidence. When I asked this question of the scholar Dr. ben-Jochannan, he rightly remarked, 'Petrie did not supply a photograph of this monarch' he claimed he observed through a telescope. Dr. Ben-Jochannan reminded, "He did not produce a photograph." His description was based on mechanical observation as Petrie (1906: 43-44) indicated: "The next monument carved was that of King Sa-Nekht, the Founder of the IIIrd Dynasty about 4950 B.C. This is the first inscription directly connected with the mining industry, as it was placed over an early mine. Later mining had brought down the face of the rock, and destroyed part of this tablet ..., and also another tablet of Sa-nekht showing inferior work; a piece of the latter is now in the British Museum. By this mining the place was rendered quite inaccessible. On a ledge of rock, I could get a very clear view, which was rectified as far as possible by the swing-lens; but the face was so important that we examined it from about fifty feet distance with a powerful telescope. The drawing of the whole thus made will be given in the *Egyptians in Sinai*, and Mr. Currelly also made a large drawing of the head alone, which is here reproduced. It will be seen how strongly Ethiopian is the character of it, even more so than Shabaka, who was

WHERE ARE THE KAMITE KINGS?

the most marked of the Ethiopian dynasty, the XXVth. The type is one with which we are very familiar among the Sudanys of the Egyptian Army and police; it goes with a very dark brown skin and a very truculent character. This "very dark brown skin" seems moving the issue to the envelope's edge. From this sculpture, then, it may be inferred that the declining civilization of the IInd was overthrown by an Ethiopian invasion; and the great art of the IVth and Vth dynasties arose out of this mixture. This sculpture has never been copied or published before."

Characteristically, whatever may have been contributed by the north, delta and northern foreigners, pales in significance to the accomplishments of the southerners!

Poesener (1962: 170) expressed a view that achievements in art, literature, language, jewelry, peaceful relations and prosperity, followed the triumph, restoration and reorganization of the Twelfth Dynasty. However, the stark African features of their sculptures, with the dynasty's founder coming from Elephantine, after having been Vizier of the last ruler of the Eleventh Dynasty, juxtaposed them similarly to the displaced line. More so, the new dynasty's cultural and political dynamism is reflected by achievements in a number of areas that were never surpassed. Poesner's (1962: 170) description of some 12th Dynasty accomplishments are as follows: "Art at this period attained an exceptionally high level of perfection; its royal statues, for instance, possessed a vigor which was never again equaled. Its jewelry was finer than the more famous Tutankhamen treasures. Literature included, among other masterpieces, the story of Sinuhe. The language, Middle Egyptian, remained the classic model for scribes until Roman times."

FREDERICK MONDERSON

Where are the Kamite Kings Illustration. Head of Okheperkere, Usertesen or Senusert I, of the 12th Dynasty.

The **British Association for the Advancement of Science** in alternating cities highlighted the best intellectual establishment of that nation, by sponsoring debates and presentation of scientific papers. In a report to that institution, Petrie (1915: 670) provided an important description of the quality of precious metal craftsmanship attained during this time: "The XIIth Dynasty is recognized as the great period of jewelry in Egypt. This has been emphasized by the jewelry of a princess found by the British School at Lahun, which is in some respects finer than any yet known. The group belonged to different reigns; that of Senusert III, the father of the princess, and that of Amenemhat III under whom she lived. The most important objects were a pectoral of each reign, with hawks as supporters of the Cartouche/Shennu; a crown of gold, with rosettes around, and long plumes besides which were bracelets, necklaces, and vases of the known forms. All of the frames are of gold, and the inlays and beads are of turquoise, lazuli, carnelian, and amazonite. The workmanship and details are of the minutest and perfect quality."

WHERE ARE THE KAMITE KINGS?

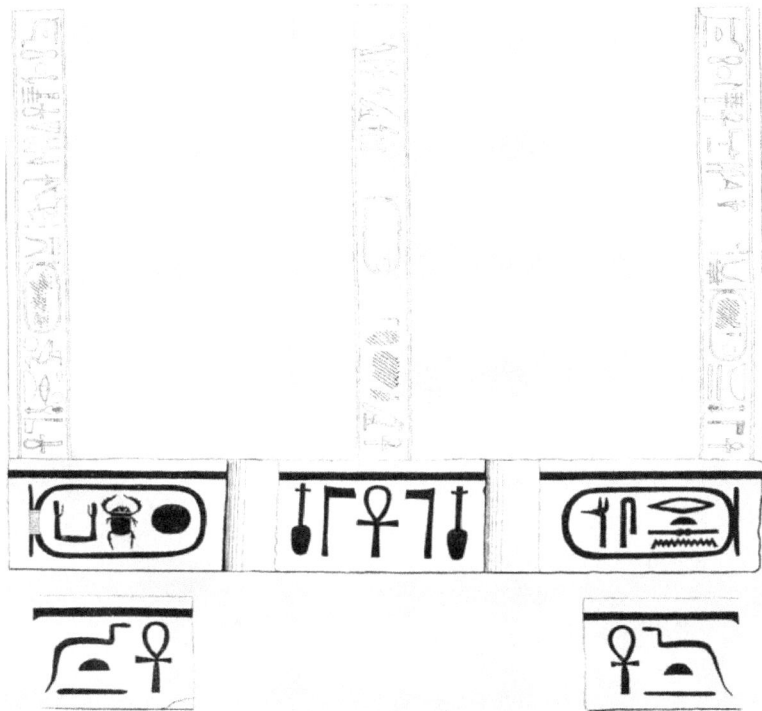

Where are the Kamite Kings Illustration. Inscriptions and Cartouche/Shennu of Okheperkere, Usertesen or Senusert I from his Temple at Abydos.

Ever more meaningful, an assessment of the period supplied by Poesner (1962: 170) asserts, "although we think of Cheops [Khufu] and Rameses as the epitome of Egyptian glory, the Egyptians themselves thought of the two centuries when the Kings Amenemes and Sesostris ruled as the classic period in their history."

Having to deal with the reality, we are thankful for the archaeological excavations at the turn of the Twentieth Century that helped in reconstruction of this critically important part of Egyptian and African history. The work of Petrie, Hall, Garstang, Naville, De Morgan, Davis, Currelly, Murray, Maspero, Lythgoe and Winlock, among innumerable others, are commendable in their efforts, though in such extensive undertakings, "skullduggery" is often suspect.

FREDERICK MONDERSON

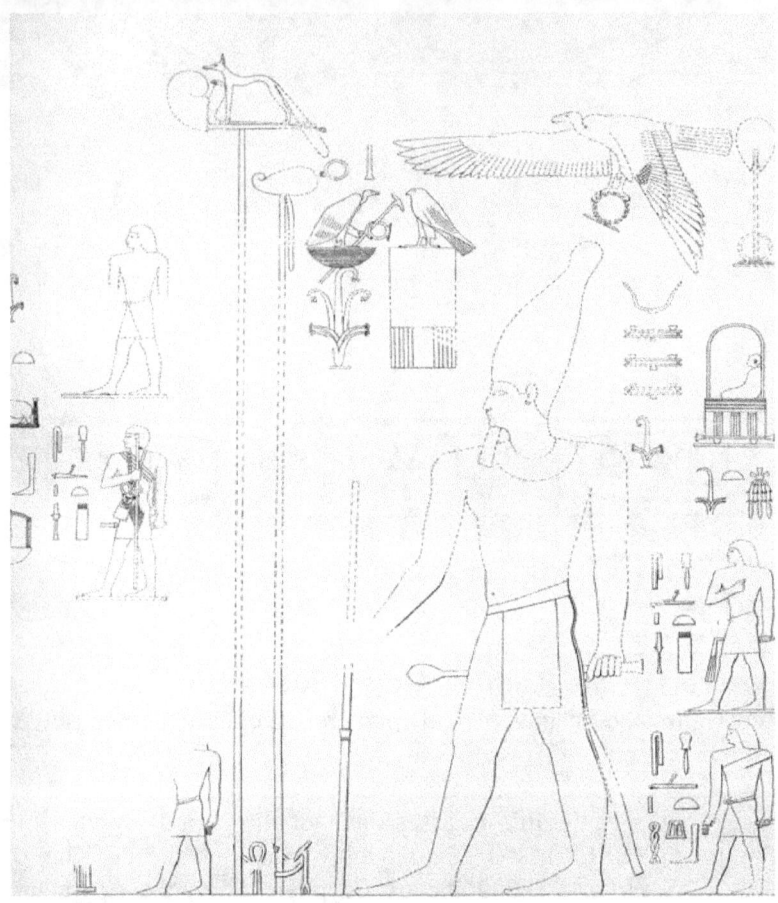

Where are the Kamite Kings Illustration. Palace pylon of Senusert I from Memphis showing the King in White Crown, loin-cloth and holding mace and staff as the vulture Goddess flies overhead holding a Shen Ring, *The Palace of Apries Memphis II* by W.M. Flinders Petrie with a Chapter by J.H. Walker (1909).

WHERE ARE THE KAMITE KINGS?

Where are the Kamite Kings Illustration. Palace pylon of Senusert I from Memphis showing the King wearing the White Crown and holding a whisk in a dancing mood as the Vulture Goddess hovers overhead holding Ankh, *The Palace of Apries Memphis II* by W.M. Flinders Petrie with a Chapter by J.H. Walker (1909).

FREDERICK MONDERSON

Where are the Kamite Kings Illustration. Palace pylon of Senusert I from Memphis showing the King wearing the Red Crown, holding a mace and with the Vulture Goddess hovering overhead holding an Ankh in *The Palace of Apries Memphis II* by W.M. Flinders Petrie with a Chapter by J.H. Walker (1909).

In 1904, Naville excavated Deir el-Bahari ("Convent of the North" in Arabic and *Deshret* indigenous), even though so many others had worked the site before him. Nevertheless, here he discovered the mortuary temple of Mentuhotep I. Ahead of him had been Pococke in 1737, and Jollois and Devilliers, two scholars from the French expedition who worked this area in 1798. Next were Champollion after his decipherment in 1822, and Wilkinson in 1827 who published his *Topography of Thebes* in 1835. In the second half of the Nineteenth Century, first came Lepsius, then Mariette, who worked the site in 1858, 1862, 1866. Later, after Naville's efforts of clearing Hatshepsut's temple there was unleashed a flurry of interest in this particular site and Mentuhotep's piece of

WHERE ARE THE KAMITE KINGS?

architecture. Its importance lies in establishing continuity between the Old and New Kingdoms, and being one of three surviving temples of the Middle Kingdom, the best preserved temple of this era and the oldest surviving temple at Thebes.

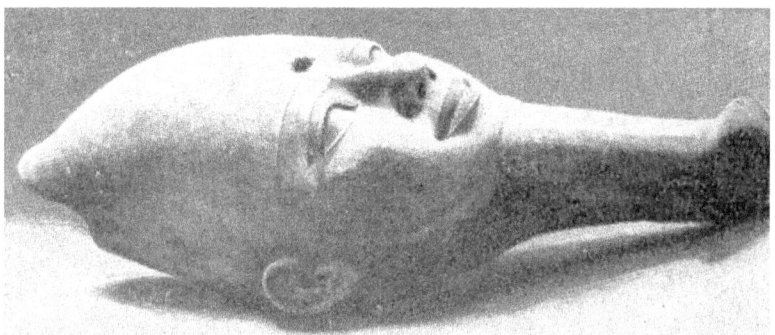

Where are the Kamite Kings Illustration. Head of Usertesen I, of the 12th Dynasty.

A significant development, particularly in England, then on the continent of Europe and finally in America, was annual exhibitions displaying Kamite antiquities in public and private collections. Institutions as the British Museum published catalogues, printed by Order of the Trustees, which gave detailed descriptions of antiquities found at selected archaeological sites by individuals and teams of scholars. Over a period of time and owing to the extensive exhibition, the growth of this aspect of a museum's tremendously extensive collection is easily traceable.

After nearly a century of systematic plunder, excavation, purchases and acquisition of antiquities, legally and illegally exported, from the ravaged modern Egypt, that government passed a law in 1911 regulating excavations and disposition of artifacts. As for America, Museums such as the Metropolitan of Art in New York, Boston's Fine Arts, Philadelphia, etc., inaugurated *Journals* and other periodicals that detailed their acquisitions and growth of the various representative periods in their collections. Private individuals also demonstrated the varieties in their holdings. Equally too, societies began using exhibitions to give notice of their involvement in archaeological excavations and other methods of acquiring antiquities and acquiring more artifacts and books for their libraries. More important, however, their efforts became mechanisms to gain contributions from their membership in order to sustain ongoing digs as well as to disseminate knowledge of recent publications.

Newspapers, magazines, scientific journals, publishing houses, authors, academic institutions, and even religious organizations used the power to publish as a means of educating their readership about ancient Kemet/Egypt. There were tremendous efforts expended to connect ancient Egypt with Bible history. Such efforts, however, without critical analysis figured significantly in the distortion of ancient Nile Valley history, particularly in this Age of the Penny Press,". More importantly, they all influenced the mind-set of their constituents. As such, they created a new vogue in relating to, appreciating and being informed about the historical archaeological, religious and anthropological dynamics of the ancient culture along the Nile. In the 19th Century imperialistic machinations of Europe, this region of Africa also fell victim to colonization. Professor John Henry Clarke, formerly of Hunter College of the City University of New York, has candidly identified the mechanisms of the "colonization of knowledge;" so much so, that today, European academic, cultural and business institutions are in control of millions of papyri, and untold numbers of Kamite artifacts as coffins, statues, vases, scarabs, mummies, sarcophagi, obelisks, temples, you name it!

Where are the Kamite Kings Photo. Ramesseum Temple of Rameses II. Kingly Osiride Figures of the King stand at the entrance while the head of a seated statue lies before them. Notice the ascent as one enters the Temple. Pillar and column contrast is continued in this Temple.

WHERE ARE THE KAMITE KINGS?

Institutions as the **British Association** equipped their members traveling abroad with questionnaires as to what aspects of visiting cultures to observe and report to the body. The reason for the ethnological campaigns to seize and control these sources of knowledge, are buried in what Bernal called the "ancient model" being overthrown by the "modern model." It is also because from the earliest times, this African culture of the Nile Valley has had profound influence in shaping modern foundations of science, art, architecture, medicine, knowledge and imperialism, even religious views.

An important observation is the role of both "ancient" and "modern" "debris" in helping to preserve, as an example, the Deir el Bahari site after it was "attacked" and became a quarry in the Ramesside Period.

Where are the Kamite Kings Photo. Front Elevation of the *Akh Menu*, Festival Temple of Thutmose III, built east of the Middle Kingdom Court and perpendicular to the Karnak Temple's principal east/west axis. This temple is east of or behind the Sanctuary. As such, from a particular vantage point, a seated Thutmose III could see through the open Sanctuary down to the western end of the temple of his day.

FREDERICK MONDERSON

Where are the Kamite Kings Illustration. Head of Khakaura, Usertesen III, of the 12th Dynasty.

One of the scholars of this age was Edouard Naville who excavated Queen Hatshepsut's Temple at Deir El Bahari (*Deshret*) during the 1890s. His report of Mentuhotep's temple after he had finished his work at t eh Queen's masterpiece, is presented here, and though over 100 years old, it is just as relevant today, in understanding the political and cultural geography of the ancient area. More so, the significance of King Mentuhotep rests in his unification of the land, construction of his temple and the color of his skin. These factors lend further credibility to the arguments of such critical scholars as Diop, ben-Jochannan, Van Sertima, among others, who claim the "blackness" of Kemet. The discovery of this temple was reported by Hall as an *Original Article* from Egypt: Deir el-Bahari. It is entitled *"Discovery of the XIth Dynasty Temple at Deir el-Bahari, Egypt."* H.R. Hall wrote and published the report in *Man* 1904, 43, (pp. 65-66).

WHERE ARE THE KAMITE KINGS?

Where are the Kamite Kings Illustration. Pectoral of Khakaura, Usertesen III, of the 12th Dynasty.

Where are the Kamite Kings Illustration. Rameses (right); and, Osiris (left), both holding the Heka Scepter or Crook and Flagellum or flail, but the hand arrangement is different.

FREDERICK MONDERSON

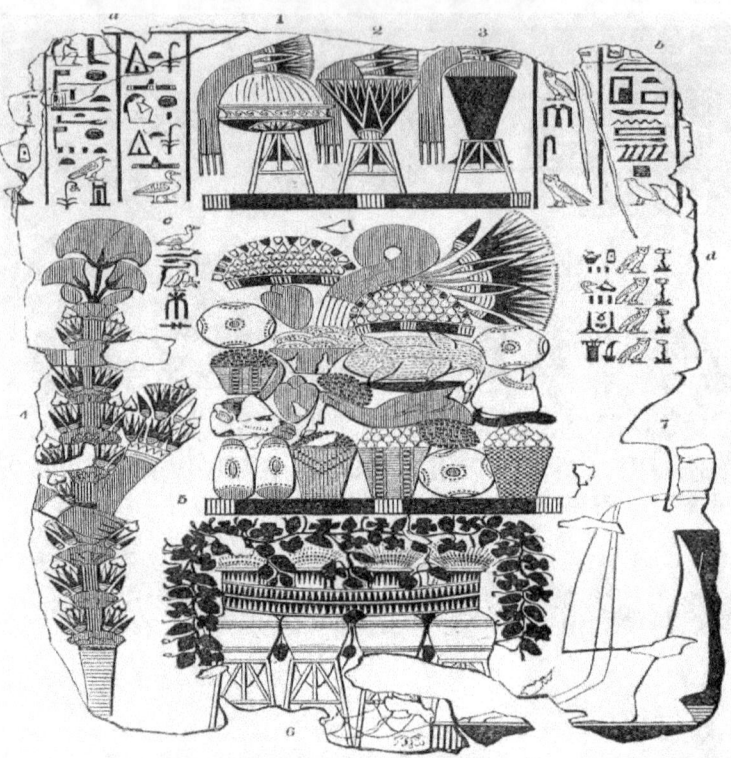

Where are the Kamite Kings Illustration. Wall painting from a tomb, now in the British Museum. 1, 2, 3 Vase of ointment, on stands crowned with Lotus Flowers. 4. Bouquets of lotus and other flowers presented by the son of the deceased. 5. "Table of Offerings;" the most remarkable of which are cakes, grapes, figs, hind leg and head of a victim, two hearts, a goose, lotus flowers, and the cucurbita. 6. Four vases on stands, with their mouths closed with ear of corn; over them is a wreath of leaves. 7. The person of the tomb seated. The inscription on the left is, "A royal offering to Ra, a royal offering to Seb, and the circle of the great Gods of the southern hemisphere. That on the right, which is imperfect, read, "in his house justified he receives …" Before the foot of the seated figure, at the right, is inscribed "thousands of bread and beer, of fish and fowl, of clothes and … of incense and wax," the usual sepulchral formula; and on the left the name of his son Aahmes whose hand offers the bunch of flowers.

WHERE ARE THE KAMITE KINGS?

Where are the Kamite Kings Illustration. Fragments of Senusert and Amenemhat III from the Temple at Ehnasya.

"The Excavations of the Egypt Exploration Fund at Deir el-Bahari, carried on during the past season under the direction of Professor Naville, assisted by myself, have resulted in the discovery of the oldest temple at Thebes and the best preserved of the oldest temples in Egypt. It is the funerary temple of the Pharaoh Mentuhotep Nebkherura, of the XIth dynasty, circa B.C. 2500. Most of the pillars of the excavated outer colonnade and several of those of the hypostyle hall are still in place and in one place some of the original XIth Dynasty colored reliefs are still *in situ*. A temple of the early Middle Empire, and one as well preserved as this, is a rarity."

"The building lay under the heaps of debris immediately to the south of the great Deir el-Bahari temple (XVIIIth Dynasty, B.C. 1500). These heaps of debris are not merely the 'tips' or rubbish heaps left by former explorers of the main temple; these are merely on the surface. Beneath them is ancient *debris*, which has certainly not been disturbed for a very long time, and beneath this, at depths varying from 5 to 20 feet, were found the pillars of the colonnade and hall. The pillars of the colonnade have not been seen possibly since the Ramesside period, when as seems probable at present, the XIth Dynasty temple was overthrown. Yet it had been known for many years before the actual discovery of the temple that some building of Mentuhotep had existed somewhere at Deir el-Bahari, because both M. Mariette and MM. Maspero and E. Brugsch-Bey had found slabs with the name of this King in the vicinity of the main temple; but the situation of this building and its character, were unknown till the excavations of this season. A great pillar-base and one of two fragments of octagonal columns of grey sandstone which lie away in the extreme southern corner of the cirque of Deir el-Bahari, at the mouth of the tomb excavated many years ago by Lord Dufferin, had been conjectured to belong to the unknown building of Mentuhotep, and the present excavations have proved this to be correct; they are pillars from the hypostyle hall."

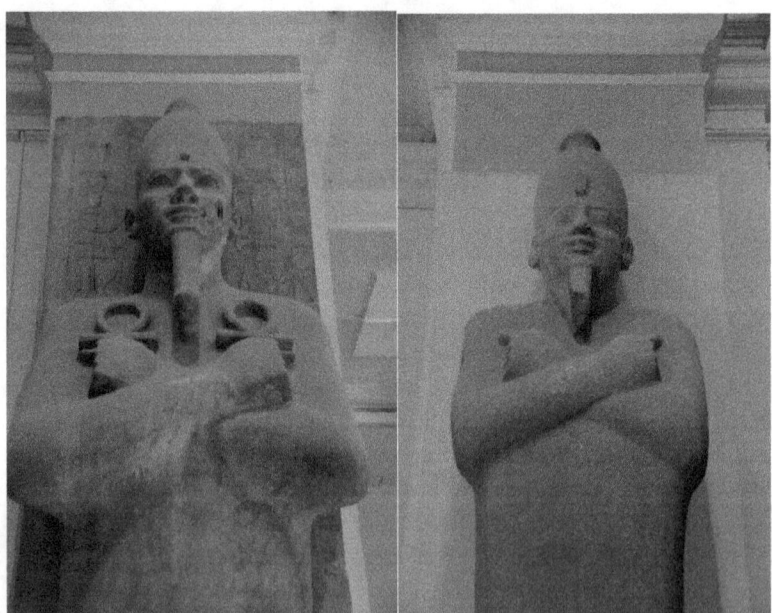

Where are the Kamite Kings Photo. Two Kings in the Cairo Museum wearing White Crowns. One holding Ankh and sporting an intact beard; and, the other, with arms folded in the royal position with a broken beard. Instruments he held are missing.

WHERE ARE THE KAMITE KINGS?

Where are the Kamite Kings Illustration. Stele of Usertesen III, of the 12th Dynasty.

"The main portion of the new temple is built upon an artificially squared platform of rock; separated from the wall of the Hathor-shrine of the main temple by an open court about 100 feet across. Two sides of the platform have been uncovered during this season's work, revealing a facing wall of the fine white limestone blocks, measuring sometimes 6 feet by nearly 4 feet, set in bonded courses, one large, one small, one large, one small, on a foundation of great sandstone blocks 5 feet across and 1 foot high. The joints are beautifully fine, and the stonework can be placed among the best in Egypt. It is typical Middle Kingdom work."

"In front of the western face of the platform (the temple is oriented in the same way as the great temple, the latter having been built parallel to it) is a colonnade, originally consisting of twenty-four square columns, each about 2 feet square and about 11 feet in height

FREDERICK MONDERSON

arranged in two rows of twelve each. One of these rows is perfect in number of columns, but all the columns are broken off at heights varying from 4 to 7 feet above the ground. Each bears the Cartouche/Shennu *Mentuhotep* and *Nebkherura* alternately, and the ka-name *Sam-Taui*. The pavement on which the colonnade stands is perfectly preserved ...."

Where are the Kamite Kings Illustration. Lid (left); outer coffin (center) and inner coffin of Tausert II.

"The facing wall of the colonnade was originally covered with reliefs, of which a fragment, representing a procession of boats, is still *in situ*. The rest of the facing wall has here been entirely

WHERE ARE THE KAMITE KINGS?

removed, probably by Ramesside spoilers. The pillars bear XIX Dynasty graffiti, which shows that at that time the building was falling into ruin; its destruction took place probably not long after."

"At the end of the colonnade is the ramp, leading up to the top of the platform 15 to 18 feet above the colonnade. The ramp is not yet uncovered. It goes up to a door-threshold of splendidly polished red granite, *in situ*, one of the finest things found. Of the remains of the gate itself, which was probably a red granite trilithon, like that, still existing, of the main temple, nothing has yet been found. This gate probably marks the center of the hypostyle hall of octagonal columns on to which it opens. These columns are small and thin, their circular bases measuring 4 feet across; the intercolumniations are very small, measuring only about 7 feet from center to center. The best preserved of those in position is 9 feet high. This bears the Cartouche/Shennu of Mentuhotep on the western face, as did all the rest originally. On one, the label of a Rameses has also been cut. These columns, like those of the colonnade, are of a dark, grey sandstone, with a white color-wash over them; the hieroglyphs are painted sometimes blue, sometimes yellow."

Where are the Kamite Kings Photo. Ramesseum Temple of Rameses II. View of the Temple from the bus depicting the Entrance Pylon, Osiride Figures at the ascent with similar figures behind, columns also, columns to the Portico and the Hypostyle Hall with its Clerestory windows and the other ruins of the structure.

FREDERICK MONDERSON

"On the walls of the hypostyle hall only the two lowest courses of fine limestone remain at any point. These walls were originally decorated with colored reliefs, on which many fragments were found. They are of two or three different styles, varying greatly in merit, some fulfilling our traditional idea of the rude work of the XIth Dynasty, while others are of very fine work, like the best XIIth Dynasty. The latter may well be the work of the famous sculptor Mertisen, who flourished in the reign of Nebkherura. The subjects are those appropriate to the funerary chapel of a King; scenes of boat-building and cattle-numbering, etc."

"From the smashed condition of these reliefs, none of which have as yet been found in *situ*, it is evident that the temple was at some period purposely overthrown and broken up, and the fact that a large number of wooden mallets, wedges, and levers, as well as a fine copper chisel with hardened edge, were found among the *debris*, confirms this conclusion. They are the last or thrown away tools of the Ramesside workmen who broke up the temple."

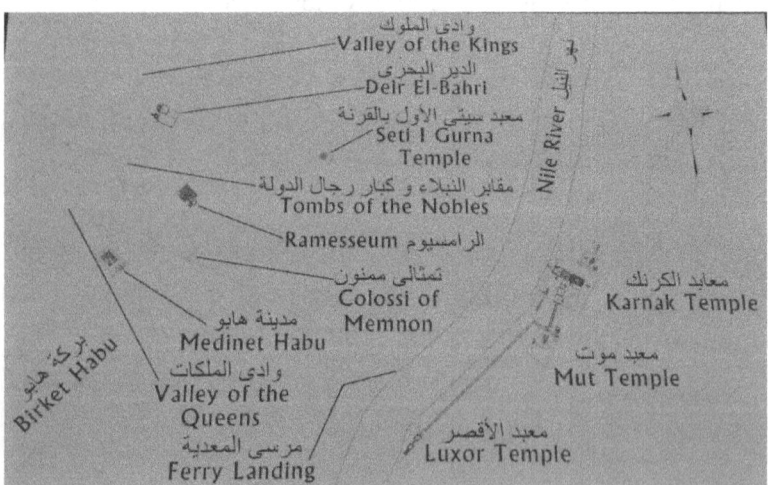

Where are the Kamite Kings Photo. Principal monuments on both banks of the Nile at Luxor, Egypt.

WHERE ARE THE KAMITE KINGS?

Where are the Kamite Kings Illustration. Head of Usertesen IV, 12th Dynasty.

"A number of fragments of statues and stelae were found, some of which show that the King Nebkherura was worshiped here as a tutelary deity of Deir el-Bahari in conjunction with Amen-Ra. On one battered figure, of the later Middle Kingdom, is an inscription containing adorations, to the Sun God and mentioning the land of Punt. I thought at first that it also contained a mention of the Hyksos King (?) Aapehti, to whose period it belongs, but further examination of it has convinced me that this is uncertain. In the court was found a rubbish deposit containing a great number of objects of blue faience, beads, scarabs, fragments of blue bowls and cups, and so on, some of which were obviously votive offerings from the Hathor-shrine in the main temple, thrown down into the court by the priests when the sanctuary became too full. They vary in date from the XII to the XXXth Dynasty, the major portion being of the XVIIIth."

"The excavation of the XIth Dynasty temple is now about half completed: when finished its ground plan will be of the highest interest to students of Egyptian architecture. One thing is already clear, that the main idea of the great temple of Deir el-Bahari, which Senmut built for Hatshepsut, with its terraces and colonnades, it taken not from the "terraced hills" of Punt or Somaliland, but simply from the older temple to the south, in which we have the prototype of the great temple, with its terrace, colonnade, and ramp, on a small scale. Only the arrangements on top of the platform are different in the two temples. Hatshepsut's temple was then in the time of the XVIIIth Dynasty a magnificent piece of archaism." H.R. Hall.

A lasting innovation of this temple was its use of space and column. The idea of the colonnade was first employed by Imhotep at Sakkara, and with the sun Kings of Abusir. It was boldly employed by Mentuhotep in his important funerary temple and tomb. Embodying Old Kingdom Mortuary Temple methods and motifs, his structure set the tradition of colonnade use in a New Kingdom style at Karnak, at Luxor, the Ramesseum and Medinet Habu. We see it again employed even further in Taharka's Peristyle of which one of ten, some say twelve, still stands in the First Court at Karnak. In the Greco-Roman Period, Edfu, Dendera, Philae, Esneh and Kalabsha were built

on earlier temple sites considered sacred from more ancient times. Therefore, an architectural continuity is traceable in the process supplied by Mentuhotep. However, if the temple site was sacralized from the earliest times, then the people who worshiped here were probably there until Graeco-Roman times.

In this glorious age of the Greeks and Romans in Kemet, they too used the colonnade in Peristyle and hypostyle halls, later to play so important a role in western religious and secular architecture. In

WHERE ARE THE KAMITE KINGS?

this regard, the colonnade found its finest expression in such medieval structures as Old St. Peter's, 4th century A.D., and Sta. Maria Maggiore, 4th-5th century, A.D., Rome, as part of early Christian art. We see it continued in Romanesque Art c. 1050-1150 A.D. at St. Sernin, Toulouse, 1080-1120, and St. Ambrogio, Milan, St. Etienne, Caen. Its fundamental elements have survived in American universities, courthouses, public buildings, certainly in Washington, D.C., and even in modern domestic and funerary displays.

Where are the Kamite Kings Photo. Ramesseum Temple of Rameses II. Osiride Statues of the King fronting the Vestibule to the Hypostyle Hall.

mortuary temple, the first of three significant temples in the Deir el-Bahari (*Desheru Deshret*) area. The others were built by Hatshepsut and Tuthmosis III. In an Original Article, published under Egyptian ARCHAEOLOGY, H. R. Hall did the write-up while his associate Naville principally conducted the excavation.

The Report was entitled: "The Excavation of the XI Dynasty Temple at Deir El-Bahari, Thebes" by H. R. Hall, M.A. and appeared in *Man* 1905, 66, (pp. 119-23), as indicated: "The discovery of the XI Dynasty Temple at Deir el-Bahari and the progress of the work of excavation by the Egypt Exploration Fund during the season 1903-04 were described in *Man* (May, 1904). Work has resumed at the end of October, and carried on without interruption to the middle of March of this year. It has not been found possible to complete the work of unearthing the whole building, but two-thirds or more of it have now been thoroughly excavated, leaving roughly a third to be done in another season's work. The progress of the work during the season may be described as follows-:

Where are the Kamite Kings Illustration. Nima'atra, Amenemhat III of the 12th Dynasty.

"It will be remembered that the court separating the XI Dynasty building from the XVIII Dynasty Temple of Hatshepsut, and the north-eastern corner of the platform on which the former stands, with a colonnade of square pillars below and eastward of it, were excavated last year. At the end of the season, we had a rough general idea of the nature of the temple and of the extent of the work that lay before us. It stood on a rectangular platform of rock, to which led a ramp flanked by colonnades, as in the Temple of Hatshepsu. Only the northern colonnade had been excavated, but there was no doubt that a southern one must exist beneath the *debris* beyond the ramp. The center of the platform was occupied by a remarkable construction of heavy nodules of flint, aligned symmetrically with the platform. The northeastern corner of this was discovered at the end of the first season's work, and there

WHERE ARE THE KAMITE KINGS?

seemed to me to be little doubt that it must be the pyramid of King Mentuhotep, which, as we knew from the texts, was situated at Deir el-Bahari. It was, however, advisable to say little or nothing about this until further excavations should prove the correctness of the idea."

Where are the Kamite Kings Illustration. Seated statue of Amenemhat III (left); and, more seated limestone statues of Amenemhat III, found at his Lisht Pyramid.

"This year's work had two primary objects in view - the uncovering of the pyramid and the southern lower colonnade. To get at the latter and free the ramp from the rubbish hiding it, it was necessary to drive a large trench up the further side of the ramp. One or two of the wooden beams with which the ramp was paved are still in position. The complete uncovering of the central erection, which had appeared to be the pyramid, has been effected. It is square with the platform, the center of the eastern side being in the axis of the ramp. Each side measures 60 feet. In only one place, the northwestern corner, has any of the outer facing been preserved. This is of fine white limestone-like the walls of the court discovered last year; it ... shows the back of the western side of the pyramid, with the octagonal pillars of the hall surrounding it, and the Temple of Hatshepsu beyond. It will be noticed that this facing-wall has not the gattor or slope of a pyramid. It is evident that the central erection was not a pyramid in the usual sense - it was a small pyramidal erection mounted on a pedestal or base, which was pyloniform, with the usual Egyptian cavetto cornice and the newel or angle-bead at each corner; of this base we have found the core of flint boulders and the remains of the limestone facing. Such erections were usual over tombs in the Theban necropolis."

Professor Naville investigated the interior of the pyramid after I left, but no trace of a tomb-pit was found, the only thing discovered being a remarkable pavement of what Dr. Schweinfurth pronounces to be a form of rock salt. I have in another place (*Proc. Soc. Bibl. Arch.* June 1905) given my reasons for believing that this pyramid erection does not really conceal the tomb of the King, but is a mere architectural survival in the temple, the real tomb being a rock-cut *bab* elsewhere, perhaps in the cliffs at the back of the building. (We may compare the pyramid of Queen Tetashera at Abydos (Excavated by Messrs. Mace and Currelly, which was a dummy, the queen having been really buried at Thebes). Although the form of pyramid mounted on a pyloniform base is quite usual, the combination of this with a roof hall or ambulatory of octagonal columns which ran round it and was enclosed by a wall sculptured with reliefs, outside which was an open Peristyle or colonnade looking out over a court at a lower level, is quite new in Egyptian architecture, and the effect of the whole must have been very peculiar."

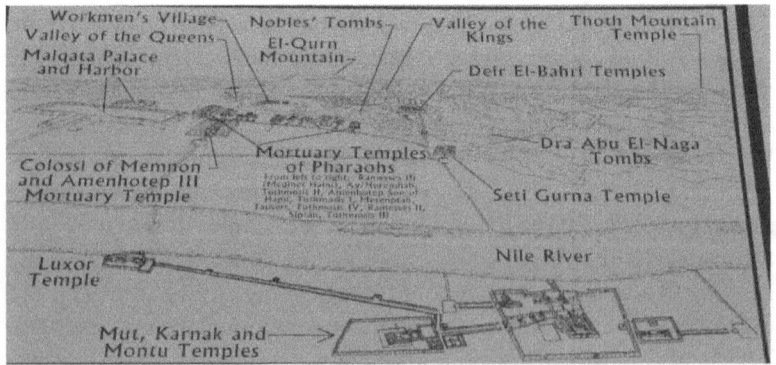

Where are the Kamite Kings Photo. Site of principal monuments on both sides of the Nile River at Luxor, Egypt.

WHERE ARE THE KAMITE KINGS?

Where are the Kamite Kings Illustration. Cairo Museum bust of Nima'atra, Amenemhat III, of the 12th Dynasty.

XVth Dynasty

The Shepherds of the Delta
 [Shalit], Salatis, Saites I.
? Bnon
? Apakhnan, Apakhnas
[Apopi I.] Apophis, Aphobis
? Staan, Iannas, Annas
? Asses, Asseth

The Thebans in the Said
Amentimaios

FREDERICK MONDERSON

XVIth Dynasty
The Shepherds over the whole of Egypt

Susirniri Khiani
Apopi II. Ausirri

XVIIth Dynasty

The Shepherds in the Delta	The Thebans in the Said
Apopi III. Aqnunri I.	Tiuaa I.
Saqnunri I	Tiuaa II.
Saqnunri II.	
Alisphragmuthosis?	Tethmosis?
Sakhontinibri?	Sanakhturi?
Hotpuri?	Manhotpuri?
Nubhotpuri	Tiuaqni Saqnunri III
	Uazkhopirri Kamosu
	Nebpehtiri Ahmosu I

Where are the Kamite Kings Illustration. Shepherd Kings or Hyksos XVth, XVIth and XVIIth Theban Dynasty that launched the War of Liberation.

"At the back of the pyramid was a row of shrines dedicated to certain priestesses of Hathor who were members of the King's *Harim* and were buried in rock-cut shaft-tombs on the platform behind the shrines. The colored high reliefs of these shrines are of very fine and remarkable work, and have given us a totally new idea of the art of the XI Dynasty. Other tombs of priestesses were found in the open Peristyle on the northern side of the platform. In each was buried a sacred Hathor-cow as well as the priestess herself. Some very interesting skulls of these cows have been found this year. The bodies of the priestesses were laid in sarcophagi of fine white limestone. The finest of these, the sarcophagus of the Princess Kauit, is a unique work of Egyptian art, and as the best object found during the excavations, has gone to the Cairo Museum. An interesting thing about them is that some of them were originally let down into the tomb in pieces, which were fitted together in the chamber. Kauit's was hoisted out again in its component pieces. One of these priestesses or princesses, Kemsit by name, was a

WHERE ARE THE KAMITE KINGS?

Negress; she is depicted as black on the fragments of her sarcophagus and on a band of fresco which runs round the interior of her tomb-chamber. Her mummy has been brought to England, and the skull appears to be of Negroid type. It will be remembered that tomb furniture, consisting of models of granaries and workmen, etc., were found in tombs of the same series excavated last year, and were shown at the annual exhibition of the Egypt Exploration Fund, Gower Street, in July last. The unique model of bakers and brewers at work, which was one of the chief features of that exposition, is now exhibited in the Fourth Egyptian Room of the British Museum, Case 188, No. 40,915. Remains of similar models were also found in the tombs excavated this year, but owing to the demands rightly made upon our transport facilities by the heavy statues and reliefs, of which we were able to bring back a much larger number than last year, it was thought best to leave these and the remains of the sacred cows for the exhibition and distribution of a succeeding year. In the tombs of Kemsit and Kauit were found small wooden model coffins with waxen figures representing the deceased, wrapped in mummy cloth, in them. These are probably an early form of *ushabti*. One is being exhibited this year." This Negress, Kemsit, is not described as "painted black for the funerary ceremony."

Where are the Kamite Kings Photo. Ramesseum Temple of Rameses II. Columns with Open Umbel Capitals of the Processional Colonnade and others, closed bud flanking columns of the Hypostyle Hall.

FREDERICK MONDERSON

Where are the Kamite Kings Illustration. Head of Amenemhat, from a Sphinx found at Tanis.

"The interesting, and from the anthropological point of view, important discovery of small votive offerings of the XVIII Dynasty, which was made last year (see MAN 1904, 43), has not been repeated, only a few stray votives have been found. Evidently the dust-heap of the Hathor shrine is nearly exhausted. A large number of these incense-burners, figures of cows, eye and ear amulets, bronze plaques, scarabs, and bead necklaces, which were dedicated by the fellahin of the XVIII Dynasty to the great Goddess Hathor of Deir el-Bahari, and when broken or repaired to make room for fresh additions were thrown by the sacristans over the wall into a dust-heap in the court of the XI Dynasty Temple below, are now temporarily exhibited in the North Gallery (Semitic Room) of the British Museum."

"But if we have not found so many anthropologically interesting small objects this year, we have on the other hand found large objects of art which are more important than any of the larger trophies of last year's work. Chief among these objects are six statues of black granite, over life size, representing King Usertesen or Senusret III, of the XII Dynasty. Four of these have the portrait perfectly preserved. And the interesting thing about these portraits is they represent the King at different periods of his life, from the

WHERE ARE THE KAMITE KINGS?

rounded features of his twenties to the haggard and lined face of an Egyptian past middle age. His face is, as is known from other portraits of him, of the type, which used to be called 'Hyksos;' the face of Amenemhat III of the same dynasty, is of the same type. It has usually been supposed that this strongly-marked type is non-Egyptian and of foreign origin, but there seems no particular reason for this theory, the type seems that of any Egyptian fellah. Three of these statues are now being exhibited."

Where are the Kamite Kings Illustration. Bust of a statue of Amenemhat III, Middle Kingdom Pharaoh, now in the St. Petersburg Museum; and, Brick pyramid of Sesostris II, at Illahun.

Where are the Kamite Kings Photo. From the Court of Rameses, the "Ramessean Front," statues between the columns two seated statues of the King and the entrance to the Processional Colonnade.

FREDERICK MONDERSON

Where are the Kamite Kings Illustration. A seated statue of one of the many Sobekhoteps of the 13th Dynasty; another of the Sobekhoteps of the 13th Dynasty.

"Other statues were found of Mentuhotep and of Amenhotep I, colossal, in Osiride form, and wearing the hieratic costume of the *sed-heb* festival. Both these monarchs were venerated as tutelary demons of the Western Necropolis of Thebes, and were invoked as protectors on the funerary stele of the Thebans; on one, found this year by us, we have a representation of these very Deir el-Bahari statues, to which invocations are addressed by the deceased."

"Of a later period two small statues of Paser, Governor of Thebes under Rameses II, were found, and a most beautiful alabaster head of a cow about half life-size, whose eyes were originally inlaid with lapis lazuli, while its horns were probably of silver with a golden disk between them. This was no doubt the head of one of the holy images of Hathor, preserved in the speos-shrine of the XVIII Dynasty Temple of Hatshepsu. It is a very fine specimen of the Egyptian sculptor's art."

WHERE ARE THE KAMITE KINGS?

"This sketch will be enough to show how interesting and important the excavations at Deir el-Bahari still continue to be. But excavations, be they as interesting and important as they may, cannot be conducted without money, and it is earnestly to be hoped that those who can will not only subscribe to the ordinary expenses of the Egypt Exploration Fund, but will provide Professor Naville with one or two special and direct gifts, in order to enable him to finish the work this year without fail. That such donations would be given to work which has already produced important scientific results, and will probably produce more, is evident from a simple recapitulation of the chief discoveries of the two seasons' work, which has been carried out at a total expenditure of only about 1,250 [British Pounds] from first to last. These are:-The oldest Theban temple, which is at the same time the best preserved of the older temples of Egypt, and is the only one of the Middle Kingdom of which we know anything as regards plan and construction; some of the finest specimens of ancient Egyptian masonry and wall-building known; sculpture in colored relief of the XI Dynasty, which has given us entirely new ideas concerning the art of that little-known period; new monuments of Kings of the same age; portrait-statues of the greatest King of the XII Dynasty; and anthropological material of great interest in the ex-votos of the Hathor shrine."

Where are the Kamite Kings Photo. Ramesseum Temple of Rameses II. Osiride Figures and columns at the Portico at rear of the ascent. Notice the comparative size of humans and Osiride Figures.

Where are the Kamite Kings Illustration. Scarabs from the Ramesseum, Mortuary Temple of Rameses II.

Where are the Kamite Kings Illustration. Inscriptions of Sebekhotep III, etc., from Abydos.

"The exhibition of the statues, reliefs, and other objects found this year was held in the rooms of the Society of Biblical Archaeology, 37, Great Russell March 17, W.C., during the month of July." H.R. Hall.

WHERE ARE THE KAMITE KINGS?

Where are the Kamite Kings Illustration. Obelisk of User-Tsen I which he placed before he re-built the temple to Horus-Ra at Heliopolis.

The Twelfth Dynasty

The period of the XIIth Dynasty, *Nile Year* 2249-2458 (1991- 1782 B.C.) was a time of vigorous African assertion that continued unification, reorganization, colonization in Nubia and increased prosperity and exploitation of mines and quarries. Not much of the architecture has survived though excellent statues have been found. The Kiosk of Sesostris I at Karnak is a fine testimony to the artistic creativity of the time. While two principal forms of temples from this time onwards were the worship temple and the mortuary temple, Sesostris' Kiosk was a third type, the processional temple, designed to accommodate the God's statue while in transition from one temple to another. Such delicacy of artistic achievement in no

FREDERICK MONDERSON

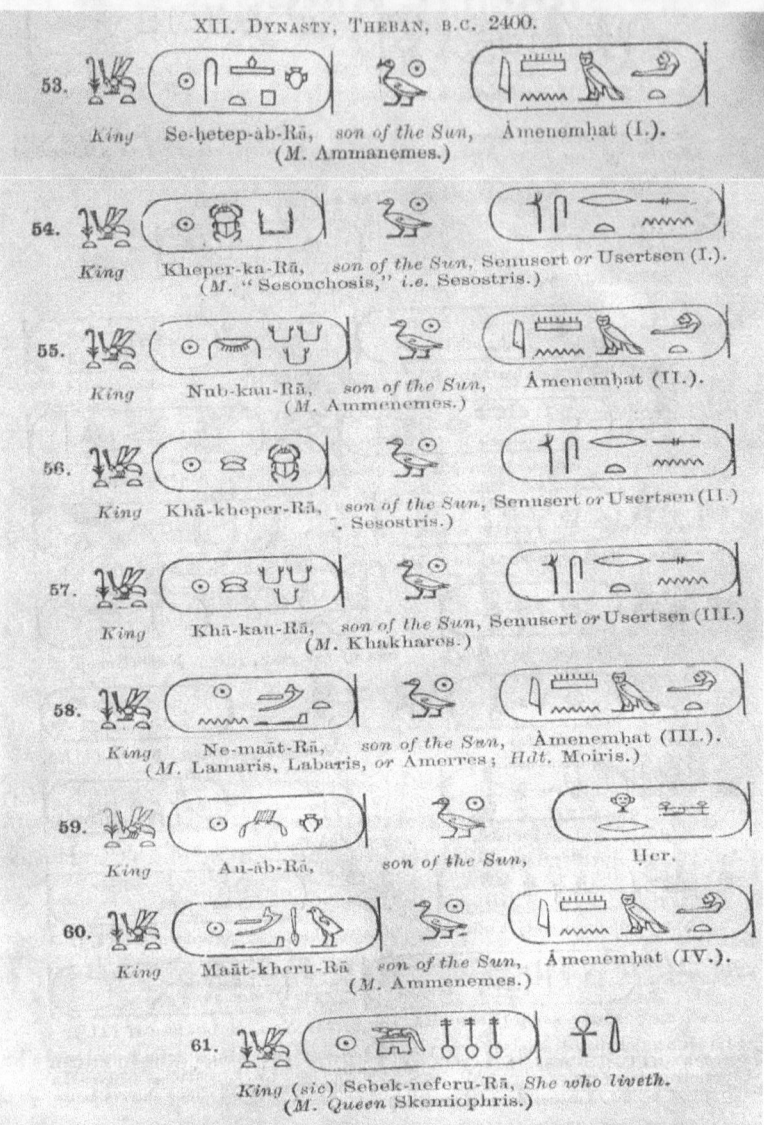

Kamite Kings Cartouche/Shennu. Kings of the Twelfth Dynasty of the Middle Kingdom.

way fully characterized the period. It was a time of tenuousness in that the monarchy was constantly challenged. To counter conspiracy and threats the Kings followed a policy of co-regency to ensure choice transition in the dynasty.

WHERE ARE THE KAMITE KINGS?

Where are the Kamite Kings Illustration.
Mentuhotep III of the XIth Dynasty wears the Double Crown and poses in a Chapel at Dendera.

The Kings of the Twelfth Dynasty undertook construction of extensive canals and other irrigation works, of which Lake Moeris is an excellent example. They also built pyramids on a smaller scale, though patterned after those of the Old Kingdom.

FREDERICK MONDERSON

Where are the Kamite Kings Photo. Erik Monderson and Native Egyptian Guide Shawki Abdel Rady share a humorous laugh as they leave Dendera Temple of Goddess Hathor.

Sehetepibra, Amenemhat or Ammenemes I, *Nile Year* 2249-2278 (1991-1962 B.C.), considered the founder of the dynasty, was a vizier of the last pharaoh of the previous dynasty. He was native to Elephantine, the first Nome in the south, and Gateway to Central Africa. This Nome had also supplied the Kings of the Fifth Dynasty. Therefore, there was precedence for constructive and vigorous rule. As such, this dynasty became one of the most outstanding in all Kemetic history. Ammenemes transferred the capital from Thebes to Lisht, and set the cultural, political and religious patterns for the next millennia. Their burial practices and choices are varied.

While Intefs began to be interred at el-Tarif, Mentuhotep built at Deir el-Bahari, while his successors and their courts choose Abu el-Qurna [Qurneh]. Even further, while the XIth dynasty built rock tombs, the XIIth Dynasty built pyramids at Lisht, not far from Memphis. We are informed of a number of expeditions by the Metropolitan Museum of New York to excavate this site. The first of these in reported in *American Journal of Archaeology* XI (1907: 344) on A.M. Lythgoe's work: "Undertaken by him for the Metropolitan Museum of New York at Lisht, were the pyramids of Amenemhat I and Usertesen I of the twelfth dynasty. The work has been concentrated on the east front of the former pyramid. After the

WHERE ARE THE KAMITE KINGS?

removal of a layer of remains of the Roman period, the remains of the pyramid temple have been particularly uncovered, and also the mastaba of Antef-aker, an important official of the period. Among single discoveries the most important is the 'false door' or offering-stele of the temple, which is the only royal stele yet found. The temple altar has also been recovered, and many architectural remains and inscriptions. The temple was evidently reconstructed at a later time, and part of the earlier material was used in the new foundations. The report on the excavations of a contemporary necropolis is to appear later."

A note on the Report of the 1907 season was presented in AJA XII (1908: 84) on the continued excavation of Lythgoe on work "in the cemetery, which contained tombs of the twelfth dynasty. Most of them had been plundered in ancient times. In the outer chamber were 108 pieces of pottery, mostly tiny models. In the outer coffin were several staves and a ceremonial whip; while in the innermost coffin were many ornaments of gold, silver, carnelian, beryl, and ivory. The body had been embalmed, and furnishes the first clear case of complete mummification before the eighteenth dynasty. The excavations threw much light on tomb-construction of this period, and also yielded many other examples of Egyptian art."

Where are the Kamite Kings Illustration. Details on a Pillar featuring the name of Senusert I of the 12th Dynasty, from his "White Chapel" at Karnak.

FREDERICK MONDERSON

In 1908, Lythgoe's work was mentioned in AJA XII (1908: 354) as follows: "The northern side of the pyramid was cleared and the entrance exposed. Work was also begun at the Oasis of Kharga, where the Museum has been granted a concession. It is believed that this site will prove very important for the Graeco-Roman and early Christian periods."

The second year's work was again commented on in AJA (1909: 71-72) in that: "The burial chamber in the pyramid of Amenemhat I could not be reached because

Where are the Kamite Kings Illustration. Angle of an architrave showing the Cartouche/Shennu of Senusert I from his "White Chapel" at Karnak.

of the water in the shaft leading down from the upper chamber. Next year a steam pump will be set up for the purpose of clearing this shaft. A beginning was made upon the excavation of the second pyramid, that of Usertesen I. Part of the causeway was cleared and the finely constructed wall which lines it on either side laid bare. Another Osiride statue of Usertesen, like those discovered by the French, was found in the course of this work. On the south side of

WHERE ARE THE KAMITE KINGS?

the pyramid the enclosure wall was uncovered. It is 2 m. thick and was originally about 5 m. high. The cemeteries adjoining the pyramid were also examined. Ibid. pp. 184-88 (6 figs.), further details are given of the work at the pyramid of Amenemhat. Along the north side were found remains of a large village of the twenty-second dynasty and later, built close up to the pyramid. Below this were many blocks from the pyramid which had belonged to earlier structures. The pyramid was, in fact, built out of stones from mastabas of the Old Kingdom. The entrance to the pyramid was laid bare. Two foundation deposits have been found so far. One of the most interesting discoveries was the portrait head of a twelfth dynasty King, probably Amenemhat III."

Where are the Kamite Kings Photo. Defaced Sphinx, at Deir el Bahari, presumably of Hatshepsut.

FREDERICK MONDERSON

Where are the Kamite Kings Illustration. Grand or outer coffin of Pinotem I.

Comment on a report for the 1909 season at Lisht appeared in AJA XIV (1910: 99) stating: "The twelfth dynasty cemetery west of the pyramid of Amenemhat I was further explored and about fifty tombs containing pottery, ornaments, etc., typical of that dynasty found. The greater part of the time was given to the excavation of the causeway and temple of the pyramid of Sesostris I. The former was

WHERE ARE THE KAMITE KINGS?

cleared for one hundred meters. It was of limestone, and consisted of a roofed passage 2.60 m. wide, the side walls painted a mottled red and black to imitate granite, and decorated above with colored reliefs representing fishing scenes, captives taken in foreign wars, etc. At intervals of ten meters on either side of the passage were niches in which stood originally Osiride statues of the King. Trenches at different points show that this causeway extended to the level of the Nile Valley. At the temple proper the work began on the south side of the entrance-hall and was gradually carried westward to the rear of the temple, which proves to be of the same general plan as the pyramid temples of the Old Empire. A large amount of relief sculpture from the temple walls, of excellent modeling and with the colors remarkably well preserved has been recovered. It is the most important material yet discovered for illustrating the sculpture in relief of the Middle Empire. At the Oasis of Kharga excavations were continued in the Christian necropolis and in the ancient city of Hibis. A number of the larger tomb chapels were cleared in the necropolis and several new streets with their houses at Hibis. Many small altars, plaster statuettes, stucco decorative figures, etc., were found, as well as a wall-painting with three deities on horseback. The skulls have been studied by A. Hrdlicka, who shows that those found in the tombs at Lisht belonged to Egyptians at the period of the highest development attained by the race. Only four broad, foreign skulls were found out of over two hundred. The graves at Kharga show Egyptians of small stature with considerable foreign admixture ...."

Manetho's **Amenemes**, the King list' S-hetep-ab-ra and Amenemhat from the monuments was the next King. His royal titulary included

Horus	Nem Mestu
Two Ladies	Nem Mestu
Golden Horus	Nem Mestu
Suten Ba	Ra-Sehetep-Ab
Son of Ra	Amenemhat

His name appears in Lepsius' *Denkmaler* II, 118 and his *Auswahl*, and the *Tablet of Karnak*. It is on the *Abydos List*, No. 59, the *Second*

FREDERICK MONDERSON

Abydos List, No. 33, the *Tablet of Sakkara* and Mariette's *Catalogue* No. 1338. Petrie (1894: 148) mentions Amenemhat I's name on his Pyramid Ka Nafer at Lisht, a Tanis statue, Khaha Nah lintel, Bubastis jamb, Memphis altar, Krokodopolis statue, Abydos altar and Wady Hammamat inscriptions. At Koptos we have sculpture of him, at Karnak an altar and sculpture, and Elephantine, Aswan and Korosko have inscriptions. In Berlin, an altar and cylinders and scarabs also carry his name. He is also mentioned in the papyrus Inscriptions of Amenemhat I and in Sa-Nehat's Adventures.

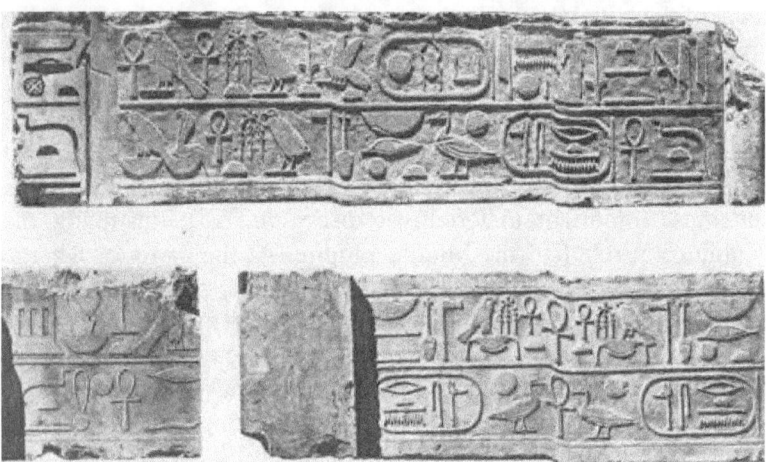

Where are the Kamite Kings Illustration. Architrave from Senusert I's "White Chapel" at Karnak, reassembled and now in the "Open Air Museum" requiring a separate ticket for entry.

He commissioned work in Wady Hammamat and Tura to secure stone for his pyramid at Lisht, about 30 miles south of Cairo. Amenemhat I, a vigorous pharaoh, traversed the country quelling pockets of resistance. He fortified the Delta against Bedouin of the north and instituted political reforms. Poesner (1962: 9) has said: "He endeavored to give the country a strong administration and to revise local boundaries. In order to bolster his doubtful title to the throne, the King proclaimed himself by means of an apocryphal prophesy as a Messiah. He was an adherent of Amun whose name he adopted, and who was an upstart like himself."

Yoyote (1962: 191) mentions his efforts to redraw the administrative map of the state, based on an ancient inscription.

WHERE ARE THE KAMITE KINGS?

"The King Ammenemes I restored what he found in disorder, separating each town from its neighbor; he made each town observe its boundaries and re-establish its confines which were as immovable as the heavens. He re-allocated their water-supplies according to what was written in the books, fixing their taxes according to the ancient records."

His reign was threatened by conspiracies with an end to assassinate. While he foiled one that is well recounted, he also fell victim to another after a meaningful rule. Budge (1902: 2) has given the events of one assassination attempt.

The King is made to narrate the story himself, and he tells how in the night-season, when darkness reigned, he seized the opportunity of taking an hour's rest, which is good for the heart, and how he had gone to lie down on his bed in his own chamber. He was tired, and had hardly begun to compose himself when he fell fast asleep, but almost immediately he was awakened by the noise of the weapons of a number of men who had conspired together to kill him, and who had burst into his room to carry their purpose into effect. The King leaped from his couch and attacked his attackers to such good purpose that, one after the other, he put them to flight, and so saved his own life.

After this incident vigorous actions suppressed resistance to his rule. He educated his son and successor to dangers of conspiracy and treachery. The *Sallier Papyrus* mentions a campaign he waged against Northern Nubia in the 29th year of his reign. It is generally though he instituted the co-regency with his son Senusert (Sesostris) I following the incident. We, however, know more of his reign from an official Khnemu-Hotep I, whose grandfather also bore the same name. This official, Khnumhotep I, J.H. Breasted (1962: No. 467) narrated, was "Hereditary Prince and Count, Wearer of the Royal [Seal], Sole Companion, Great Lord of the Oryx Nome, attached to Nekhen (judge)." His grandson, tells of the King in his tomb, according to Budge (1902: 3) that "Amenemhat I came to do away evil, and as appearing in splendor even as the God Temu himself; he restored that which had been overthrown, and what one city had stolen from another he gave back, and he marked out the frontiers of each principality, and arranged that each city should know its own boundaries, and he re-established the old laws in respect of the supply of water for irrigation purposes to the various districts, according to what he found written on the subject in the ancient registers. This he did because of the greatness of his love for justice."

Budge (1902: 5) tells of "Instructions" or "Precepts" he wrote for his son that became wisdom literature for later generations, particularly the scribes of the Eighteenth Dynasty.

The King begins his instructions by warning his son against making too many friends among his people, and against laxity of rule. He gave to the poor and the needy, he treated the poor with the same consideration as the rich, but it was the very folk to whom he had done good who stirred up strife, and those who put on his apparel and used his spices were the first to curse him. His works are known of and seen among men, but they are not sufficiently heeded by the people, who seem to be like an ox who hath forgotten yesterday.

The King narrated, Budge (1902: 6) continued, his tireless efforts to strengthen the country and ensure a peaceful succession. He says: "I advanced to Abu (Elephantine) and I returned to the Papyrus Swamps; I stood upon the ends of the earth and I saw it bend over, and I advanced to the confines by wonderful deeds of strength." He made corn to be plentiful, and no man went hungry or thirsty in his time, and all people were satisfied with his rule. He hunted lions and crocodiles ...." He built a palace ornamented with gold and lapis-lazuli, and furnished with bronze gates and bolts, and the walls thereof were built upon well laid foundations; and with some final remarks to Usertesen individually the "Instructions" came to an end.

WHERE ARE THE KAMITE KINGS?

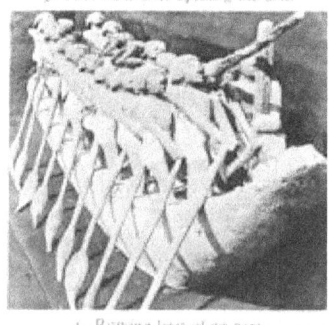

Where are the Kamite Kings Illustration. Excavation of the Tomb of Nefer-Y, the Physician, at Beni Hassan.

The Story of Sinhue became a classic story of an individual's longing for the sacred land of his birth. One day while the crown prince Senusert I was away with his army attacking the Libyans, his father fell victim to assassination at home. The news of his father's murder was overheard by Sinhue who thought he might be implicated in the conspiracy. He fled the country and after many years wished to return to his beloved country. The new pharaoh welcomed him home and made his last years comfortable."

Kheperkara, Senusert I or **Sesostris I**, Manetho's Sesouchosis, King lists S-hetep-ab-ra and Usertesen I from the monuments was son of Amenemhat I, with whom he shared a 10-year co-regency. He reigned *Nile Year* 2269-2303 (1971-1928 B.C.). On an expedition against the Libyans, when his father was felled by an assassin, he hurried home. Poesner (1962: 258) narrated "not for an instance did he hesitate. The Falcon sped onward with his companions without telling his army anything." Further we see

FREDERICK MONDERSON

him characterized by Posener (1962: 258) for "He is indeed a valiant knight who conquers with his strong right arm, a man of action without equal." He "subjugated the foreign lands" and expanded Kemet's borders southward. Posener (1962: 258) again asserted, the "pharaoh's armies were victorious far beyond the 2nd cataract. A factory operated beyond the 3rd cataract. Gold from Nubia and the produce of the Sudan flowed towards the capital. In Asia wide vigorous diplomatic activity widened Egypt's sphere of influence."

His royal titulary, according to Budge (1908) was as follows:

Horus	Ankh Metsy
Two Ladies	Ankh Metsy
Horus of Gold	Ankh Metsy
Suten Bat	Ra-Kheper-Ka
Son of Ra	Usertesen

His name is found on an obelisk in Lepsius' *Denkmaler* II, No. 118, his *Konigsberg*, No. 117, Mariette's *Abu* II, 23, the *Tablet of Sakkara*, the *Abydos List* No. 60, the *Second Abydos List* No. 34, *Tablet of Karnak*, *Turin Papyrus* and *Aswan in LD*. II, 118.

Petrie (1894: 156) shows evidence of the name of Usertesen I on Steles in Wady Maghara and Sarabut el-Khadem, Statues at Tanis, a Sphinx at Faqus, Obelisks at Heliopolis and Begig, Hat Nub Graffito and an Abydos statue. Inscriptions at Karnak and Wady Hammamat as well as Sculptures at Koptos, a Column at Hieraconpolis and Inscriptions at Aswan, all bear his name. The Brick Temple at Wady Halfa from which Steles are now at Florence and the Ashmolean museums contain evidence of this King's reign. A Statue of him is in the British Museum, a Statuette of carnelian, formerly in the Louvre, a Glazed Vase from Abydos, piece of a marble vase in the British Museum and Shells in the British Museum all carry his name. The Weight of Hor-mena, published in *Veinna Recueil* XII, 10 and Scarabs and Cylinders all identify him. The tradition of vigorous rule was continued. From the tomb of Amen-em-hat Ameni at Beni Hasan, we learn of an expedition to the south in the 43rd year of his reign. This same year began a co-regency with his son Amenemhat II. He reopened and exploited the turquoise mines at Wady Maghar. New quarries were opened at Serabut el Khadem in Sinai. He built extensively and erected the southernmost pyramid at Lisht, some thirty miles to the south of

WHERE ARE THE KAMITE KINGS?

Cairo. Great architectural works were built at Tanis in the Delta. He erected two obelisks at Heliopolis. Budge (1902: 14) narrated: "In the third year of his reign Usertesen re-built, or perhaps re-founded, the famous Temple of the Sun at Annu, the *On* of the Hebrews, and the Heliopolis of the Greeks. This shrine had been a very famous one for centuries, but is seems that during the prolonged struggle between the princes of Thebes and the Kings of Herakleopolis the whole place fell into decay, and the worship of the Sun-God declined greatly. Usertesen I, decided to restore the 'House of the Sun' to something like its former greatness, and he laid the foundation and set out with a cord the space for, apparently, a new edifice, which he dedicated to Horus-Ra, the rising sun, and to Temu, the God of the setting sun, who had become incarnate in the Mnevis bull."

He continued his father's work at Karnak. His name is the oldest surviving on any monument at this important site. At Abydos, that particularly venerated religious site, he did extensive work. Budge (1902: 15-16) informed about his efforts there: "The works at Abydos seem to have been under the direction of the high official Menthu-hetep, who, in his stele which was found at Abydos, tells us that he was royal architect and general surveyor of the district, that he succored the needy, and protected the poor, and that he was a man both of wisdom and peace. He crushed the enemies of the King in Egypt, he subdued the Aamu and the Heru-sha, he pacified those who dwelt in the Eastern Desert, and he made the people of the south to pay tax and tribute. At the end of the inscription, he says that he was the overseer of works in the Temple of Abydos, that he built the house of the God Osiris, and that he dug a well by the command of the majesty of the God Horus. In his account on the Memnonium, Brugsch expressed the view that this was the well Strabo mentioned. Further, and in perpetuation of his name, according to Budge (1902: 16) who wrote: "The buildings of the temple of Abydos, which were erected for the King by Menthu-hetep, were restored in the XIIIth Dynasty by a governor of the Temple of Abydos called Ameni-seneb, and in the stele of this official we are told that he cleaned the temple, both inside and outside, that he cleared the court-yards, and renewed the decorations of the buildings, and painted the inscriptions, and renewed everything which Usertesen I had built."

FREDERICK MONDERSON

Where are the Kamite Kings Photo. Erik Monderson in the Court of Rameses II, the "Ramessean Front," with statues coming out from between the columns and a seated statue at his right.

Usertsen's name has been found on numerous inscriptions from Thebes to the First Cataract. Champollion is reported to have found a stele with his name at Wadi Halfa in Nubia. In his forty-second year he associated his son Amenemhat II in a co-regency.

The 1913-14 work at Lisht is recounted in AJA XIX (1915: 88) which states: "It was found that the ancient town south of the north pyramid was much more extensive than had been imagined. The houses were of crude brick and mostly of one story with narrow passageways between them, Household objects of various kinds were found in great quantities. Beneath these houses were burial pits of the twelfth dynasty, about one hundred and thirty of which were cleared. Some objects of interest were found in them such as a magic wand of ivory, a standard gold weight of porphyry with the Cartouche/Shennus of Senusert I, a curious pottery head with close eyes which had apparently been used as a jar stopper, etc. On the east side of the pyramid a considerable space was cleared between the enclosure wall and the pyramid, and the pavement was found well preserved."

WHERE ARE THE KAMITE KINGS?

Nubkaura, Amenemhat II, Amenemenes II, *Nile Year* 2302-2336 (1929-2895 B.C.), grandson of Amenemhat I, served a two-year co-regency with his father Senusert I. Manetho's Ammenemes, Nub-kau-ra from the lists and Amenemhat from the monuments. He worked the turquoise mines at Wady Maghara and opened new mines at Serabut el-Khadem, where a temple of the Goddess Hathor was either built or rededicated. Wiedemann identified stelae and monuments of his twenty-eight year and Lepsius published inscriptions of his thirty-fifth year, the third year of his successor's co-regency.

His royal titulary included:

Horus	Heken-em-Maat
Two Ladies	Heken-em-Maat
Horus of Gold	Maat-Kheru
Suten Bat	Ra-nub Kau
Son of Ra	Amenemhat

Petrie I (1894: 164) identified his name in a number of places. They were on Rock Inscriptions at Aswan and on a Stele in Leyden published by Lepsius in *Auswahl*. He is No. 61 on the *Abydos List* and No. 35 on the *Second Abydos List*. The *Tablet of Sakkarah* and *Tablet of Karnak* mentions Amenemhat II. His pyramid at Lisht and a Temple at Sarabut el-Khadem as well as Granite Altars at Dehdamun and Nebesheh, all bear his name. At Beni Hasan, Khnemhotep's tomb and the colossus tomb at El Bersheh mentions him. At Abydos the Sahathor Stele, El Hosh Tablet, and Inscriptions at Wadys Gasus and Hammamat as well as cylinders and scarabs round out some instances of his name surviving for modern scholarship.

He continued his predecessors' policies in Nubia and worked its gold mines. Budge (1902: 20-21) tells of the Stele of Hathor-sa in the British Museum (no. 5696) wherein its owner states: "When I was a young man I made (or, worked) a mine, and I made the great ones to wash gold, and I brought back [to Egypt] loads thereof. I penetrated as far as Ta-kenset, the land of the Negroes, and I came there and reduced it to subjection by means of fear of the lord of the two lands. I journeyed, moreover, to the land of Ha, and I went round the lakes (?) thereof, and passed through the regions thereof."

This individual, a favorite of Amenemhat II, was appointed "Governor of the South" which assisted his efforts at exploiting the Nubian gold mines.

An inscription at Beni Hasan in the tomb of Prince Khnemu-hetep states, according to Budge (1902: 21-22) Amenemhat II in the nineteenth year of his reign made him Governor of the City of Menat-Khufu, and that "under the rule of this distinguished official the city prospered and waxed rich." Further, asserts Budge (1902: 22) the King "conferred great favors not only upon him, but also upon his eldest son Nekht and his second son Khnemu-hetep; the former he made govern of the Nome of the Jackal, and the latter was taken into high favor by his Majesty."

Where are the Kamite Kings Photo. Erik Monderson beside a surviving falcon of God Horus at his Edfu Temple in 2018.

Another high official was Djetu-nakht whose tomb at El-Bersheh, supplied the famous illustration of a colossal being transported. It also mentioned civil, military and religious titles Djetu-nakht attained during service in the reign of Amenemhat II. Budge (1902: 22-23) has declared: "The principal scene of interest in his tomb is that in which the hauling of a colossal statue from the quarries of

WHERE ARE THE KAMITE KINGS?

Hat-nub to the house of Tehuti-hetep is represented. The statue was a seated one, and was thirteen cubits high, and must have weighed about sixty tons; it was placed on a wooden sledge to which it was lashed by ropes that were made taut by means of short sticks twisted in them, and breakage of the sharp edges of the statue was prevented by the insertion of pieces of leather under the ropes. It was dragged over a road, specially prepared for this purpose, by about one hundred and sixty-eight men, who hauled at four ropes, forty-two men on each rope, and it seems as if it must have been transported some distance down the river by raft. This scene is of peculiar interest, because it explains the method by which such huge masses of stone were transported from the quarries, and proves that the mechanical means employed for the purpose were extremely simple."

In the King's twenty-eighth year an expedition, as indicated from the Stele of Prince Khent-khat-ur, Royal Chancellor and Overseer of the Palace, returned from a voyage to Punt. This contact with the land of Punt dates to the time of the Old Kingdom. It's believed that since no belligerence is mentioned in this expedition, it was a peaceful commercial relationship.

Amenemhat II was killed by his eunuchs.

Khakheperra, Senusert II, *Nile Year* 2334-2353 (1897-1878 B.C.), whose name "Guide of the Two Lands" is Manetho's Sesostris, Kha-Khepers-Ra of the lists and Senusert of the monuments. His queen's name was Nefert.

His royal titulary consisted of the following:

Horus	Semu-Taui
Two Ladies	Sekha-Maat
Horus of Gold	Neteru-hetep
Suten Bat	Ra-Kha-Kheper
Son of Ra	Usertesen

His name appears on a Stele at Alnwick Castle, published in Birch's *Catalogue*, p. 269, on inscriptions at Aswan and in De Morgan's

FREDERICK MONDERSON

Dashur, p. 60. It is also on the *Abydos List* No. 62, the *Second Abydos List*, No. 36, the *Tablet of Sakkarah* and in Legrain's *Annales* VII, 34. Petrie I (1894: 168) mentions his Pyramid "Hotep" and Temple at Illahun. He is also shown in connection with his wife Nefert at Tanis, on Inscriptions at Memphis, on Blocks at Ahnas, and in the Beni Hasan tomb of Khnum-hotep. A Stele of Khnum-Hotep is dated to the first year of his reign. Steles at Quseir and Aswan, Statues from Hierakonpolis, other Statues in Berlin and the Louvre, as well as scarabs and cylinders tell us of this pharaoh. His daughters with Queen Nefert were Atmu Nefera, Sat-Hathor and Sent-s-Senb found at Dashur.

Khakaura, Senusert III from the Monuments, Manetho's Lakhares and Kha-Kau-Ra from the lists, ruled *Nile Year* 2353-2390 (1878-1841 B.C.).

His royal titulary included:
Horus	Neter-Kheperu
Two Ladies	Neter-Mestu
Horus of Gold	Ankh Kheper
Suten Bat	Ra-Kha-Kau
Son of Ra	Usertesen

We know of him from De Morgan *Dashur*, p. 51, a Stele in Berlin, Lepsius' *Denkmaler* II, 136 h and Le Grain's *Annales*, VII, 34. *The Tablet of Karnak*, the *Abydos List* No. 63, *Second Abydos List* No. 37, and *Tablet of Sakkarah*, all contain his name.

Petrie II (1894: 176) mentions his brick-built Pyramid at Dashur. His name appears on an Architrave at Tanis, on Statues at Nebesheh, Mokdam, Abydos and Bigeh. They are also on inscriptions at Wady Hammamat, Sehel Island at Aswan, and on the base of a statue at Gebelin. An Elephantine Tablet and a tomb at Khataaneh, as well as the Forts and Temples at Semneh and Kummeh in Nubia, contain his name. Scarabs and Cylinders also provide valuable information about him. His Queens were Henat-Taui found at Dashur and Merskesr in LD III, 55a.

His name appears in a rock inscription at Aswan in the tenth year of his rule. It is also at the Wady Hammamat in his fourteenth year. His name also appears in connection with stone used in construction

WHERE ARE THE KAMITE KINGS?

of the Temple at Hierakleopolis, dedicated to the God of the city, Her-shef. Budge (1902: 34) identified his name on inscriptions on the Island of Sahel, at the First Cataract. Here, the "King is represented in the act of receiving life from the Goddess Anqet, who promises to give him 'life, stability, and health, like the Sun, forever.'"

Where are the Kamite Kings Illustration. Pinotem I's small coffin. Notice the winged beetle beneath his folded hands.

FREDERICK MONDERSON

Another of E.C. Wilbour's discoveries on the island mentions a canal dug in the eighth year of Usertesen/Senusert's reign. It was called, "Good are the paths of Usertesen [III living] forever." Budge (1902: 35) provided some important information regarding this engineering feat, when he wrote, "... this canal was 250 ft. 4 in. long, 34 ft. 7 in. wide, and 25 ft. 10 in. deep. When this had been done, the King sailed up the river to overthrow the abominable country of Kash (Nubia). Two other inscriptions close at hand tell us that Thothmes I., passed through this canal on the way to Nubia to punish the natives in the third year of his reign, and that Thothmes III., in the fiftieth year of his reign, caused this same canal to be reopened after it had become blocked; he gave it a new name, i.e., 'Open the good path of Thothmes (III) living forever,' and made a law to the effect that the boatmen of Elephantine were to clean this canal every year. It seems that this canal must have been in existence during the VIth Dynasty, and that it became stopped up from time to time, for it is undoubtedly of some work which he performed in connection with it that Una boasts in his inscription .... No trace of this canal has been found in recent days, nor of the works which the high official Ameni declares that he performed in connection with the quay of Elephantine, when Usertesen III was on his way into Nubia."

This expedition left a stele or boundary stone that read, "This is the frontier of the south which was fixed in the eighth year of Usertesen III, who liveth forever and ever." It prohibited Nubians "from passing that spot, whether by sailing down the river or marching along its banks, as well as the passage of all oxen, and sheep, and goats, and asses, except all such as were engaged in the traffic in cattle, and such as had need to come to Egypt for the purposes of barter and of business generally."

This famous boundary stele, set up near the fortresses of Semneh and Kumneh in Nubia, is described by Budge (1902: 36-37) who recounted: "Year 16, the third month of the season Pert. His Majesty fixed the boundary of the South at Heb. I made my boundary; I advanced [beyond] my fathers. I added much thereto, and I passed the decree. I am a King, and what is said [by me] is done. What my heart conceived my hand brought to pass. [I am] a crocodile to seize, and [I] beat down mercilessly, and [I] never relinquish [my prey]. The words which are in his heart are applauded by the impotent who

WHERE ARE THE KAMITE KINGS?

rely upon mercy [being shown to them] but he showeth none to the enemy. He attacketh him that cometh against him in attack; he is silent to him that is silent; and he returneth answer according to what hath happened in a matter. Now inaction (or, silence) after an attack giveth strength unto the heart of the enemy; vigorous must be the [counter] attack, for vile is he who turneth back and retreateth. The man who is beaten upon his own territory is a coward. Therefore, the Negro falleth down prostrate at the word which falleth from the mouth, and behold, a word in anger maketh him to turn back, and if he be attacked, he giveth back [to his attacker] even after he hath gone forth to attack. They are not men of boldness, but are poor and feeble, having nothing but buttocks for hearts. I the Majesty have looked upon them, and [what I say] is not a word [of falsehood]. I seized their women, I carried off their fold, I marched to their wells, I slew their cattle, and I destroyed their crops and burnt their corn. By my own life, and by that of my father, I swear that what I am saying is the truth, and what cometh forth from my mouth cannot be gainsaid. Whosoever among my sons shall preserve this boundary which he hath set; but he who relaxeth it, and does not battle for it, shall not be [called] my son, nor one begotten of me. And, behold, my Majesty hath caused a statue of my Majesty to be set up on this boundary, not only with the desire that ye should worship it, but that ye should do battle for it."

Where are the Kamite Kings Photo. Looking out beyond stumps of broken columns of the Hypostyle Hall from deep within Mentuhotep's 11th Dynasty Temple at Deir el Bahari.

FREDERICK MONDERSON

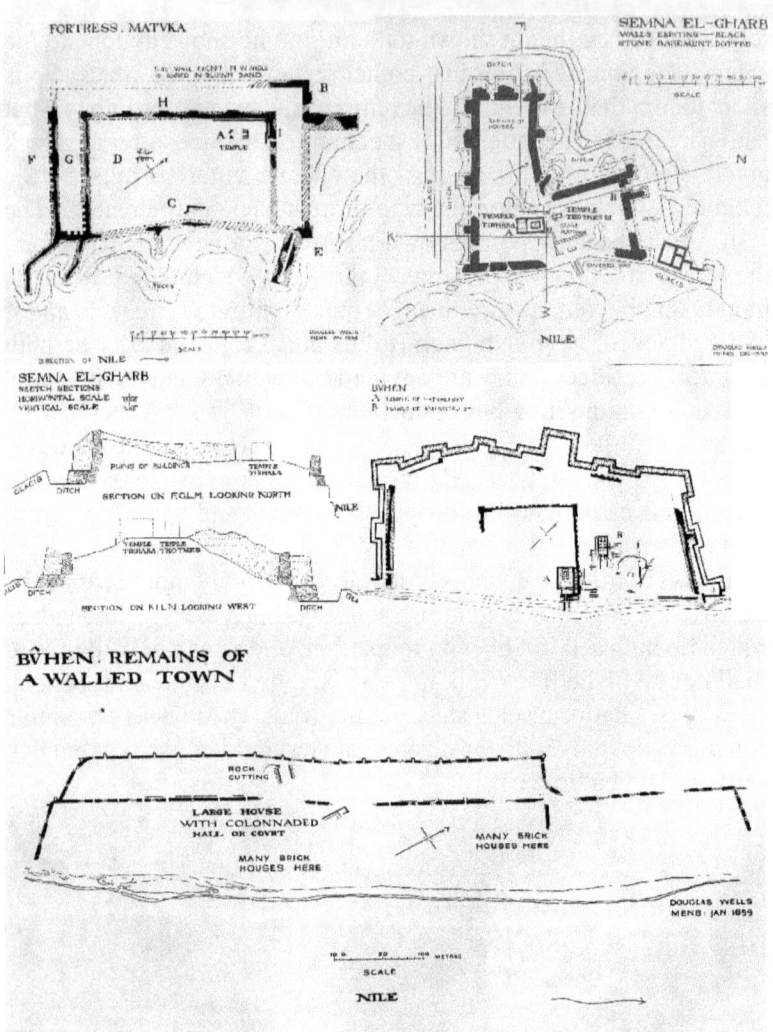

Where are the Kamite Kings Photo. Forts and other features of pharaonic construction in Nubia.

The forts in Nubia were set up between the Second Cataract and Wady Halfa. Those at Semneh and Kumneh were strategically important for defense and to insure the uninterrupted flow of commerce northward. At Semneh, Budge (1902: 40) informs, "Usertesen III built a temple which was restored by Thothmes III and Amenophis III; it consisted of a single chamber, which

WHERE ARE THE KAMITE KINGS?

measured about 30 feet by 12 feet. At Kumneh are the ruins of a larger temple which, however, dates from the XVIIIth Dynasty."

Usertesen was a vigorous builder who "repaired or rebuilt" parts of temples at Tanis, Bubastis, Abydos, and Elephantine. His name is found upon parts of buildings in many other cities.

He built his pyramid at Dashur which was excavated by De Morgan in 1894, and Budge (1902: 42) again mentioned, "the discovery of a number of tombs of royal ladies who were the wives and daughters of Usertesen, and it is only reasonable to assume that if these were buried round about the pyramid, the King himself was buried in it. If Usertesen II be identified with Sesostris, then his son Usertesen III., or Lachares, must be identified with the King Nencoreus, the son of Sesodes, or with Pheros, the son of Sesostris, each of whom is said to have dedicated obelisks one hundred cubits high at Heliopolis ....

Nima'atra, Amenemhat III, *Nile Year* 2389-2434 (1842-1797 B.C.) was the greatest of the XIIth Dynasty Kings of Kemet. His royal titulary was:

Horus (or Soul)	Aa-Baus (Horus Mighty of Will
Two Ladies	Thet-Auat-Taui
Horus of Gold	Uah-Ankh
Suten Bat	Ra-en-Maat
Son of Ra	Amenemhat

His wife was Phat-Neferu. His name can be found throughout the entire country. It is on black granite mortar in Cairo, in Daressy's *Recueil* X, 142 and in his *Catalogue* No. 9834, as well in Le Grain's *Annales* IV, 134 and Maspero's *Annales* III, 207 mentions Amenemhat III. Lepsius *Konigsberg*, No. 1836, D, Lepsius' *Denkmaler* II, 139, 1389 E, Dashur jewelry give his name. He is No. 164 on the *Abydos List* and No. 98 on the *Second Abydos List*. The *Tablet of Sakkarah* also mentions him.

FREDERICK MONDERSON

Petrie I (1894: 184) mentions his Pyramid and Temple at Hawara. His name is found on inscriptions at Wady Maghara, Hammamat, Aswan, Kuban, and Kumneh. At Sarabut el Khadem it's on the shrine, on Steles at Turrah and El Kab. It is on a pylon at Crocodopolis of the Greek, on colossi at Biahmu, a Vulture at Koptos and Statues at Hierakonpolis. At Semneh it is mentioned in connection with the Nile levels. Statues in Berlin, St. Petersburg, a Sphinx at Miramar Museum, a hawk in the Flinders Petrie Collection and scarabs and cylinders tell of this great African. The *Kahun Papyri* XIV also mentions him. His daughters were Phat-Neferu and Sebek-Neferu, who became a later Queen.

While the Wadi Hammamat provided stone for his building projects, a Stele at Serabut al-Khadem in the Sinaitic Peninsula mentions his forty-fourth year. Posener (1962: 9) has shown he erected the "Wall of the Prince" in the Wady Tumilat to repel the Asiatics. His reign was blessed with inordinate prosperity. He initiated extensive irrigation projects. Posener (1962: 9) again indicated, Amenemhat developed the Faiyum and there built his pyramid and his funerary temple, which was called the Labyrinth by Greek and Roman writers who greatly admired it. Ammenemes III was deified and was still worshipped in this area two thousand years after his death.

Even further, Posener (1962: 9) mentioned, "An extraordinary coincidence made him posthumously famous: his name Mares (from Nemaare his first name), by which he was later known, sounded like the name of the lake Karun, in the Faiyum – "the lake of (the town) Milwer." The two were confused in Lake Moeris and it was erroneously believed that Ammenemes dug the bed of the lake and named it after himself.

This purported mistake aside, Budge (1902: 48) explains the significance of Ta-she, "Land of the Lake" and how the area "... seems to have been reclaimed from the desert by the genius and energy of Amenemhat III., who made the lake. The last remaining portion of Lake Moeris is the Birket al-Karun with its water surface about 130 feet below sea level; its cubic contents are equal to 1,500,000,000 cubic meters. The largest circumference of Lake Moeris was about 150 miles; its area was about 750 square miles, and its average level was about 80 feet above the Mediterranean.

WHERE ARE THE KAMITE KINGS?

A number of classical authors have commented on the work of this King who built the lake. Budge tells, Herodotus is the first to remark in *Histories*, of which Book II *Euterpe* is devoted to Kemet and II, 149, contains his comments on the Lake: "Although this labyrinth is such as I have described, yet the lake named from Moeris, near which this labyrinth is built, occasions greater wonder: its circumference measures 3600 stades, or sixty schoines, equal to the sea-coast of Egypt. The lake stretches lengthways, north and south, being in depth in the deepest part fifty orgyae. That it is made by hand and dry, this circumstance proves, for about the middle of the lake stand two pyramids, each rising fifty orgyae above the surface of the water, and the part built under water extends to an equal depth; on each of these is placed a stone statue, seated on a throne. Thus, these pyramids are one hundred orgyae in height; and a hundred orgyae are equal to a stade of six plethra; the orga measuring six feet, or four cubits; the foot being four palms, and the cubit six palms. The water in this lake does not spring from the soil, for these parts are excessively dry, but it is conveyed through a channel from the Nile, and for six months it flows into the lake, and six months out again into the Nile. And during the six months that it flows out it yields a talent of silver every day to the King's treasury from the fish; but when the water is flowing into it, twenty minae. The people of the country told me that this lake discharges itself under the ground into the Syrtis of Libya, running westward towards the interior by the mountain above Memphis."

Strabo (XVII, 37) a classical writer, according to Budge (1902) commented on the volume of water in the lake. He wrote: "The Lake Moeris, by its magnitude and depth, is able to sustain the superabundance of water, which flows into it at the time of the rise of the river, without overflowing the inhabited and cultivated parts of the country. On the decrease of the water of the river, it distributes the excess by the same canal at each of the mouths; and both the lake and canal preserve a remainder, which is used for irrigation. These are the natural and independent properties of the lake, but, in addition, on both mouths of the canal are placed locks, by which the engineers store up and distribute the water which enters or issues from the canal."

FREDERICK MONDERSON

Following, Pliny (V, 9) was the next visitor who left us his thoughts on this body of water, in the statement, which Budge (1902) quotes: "Between Arsinoites and Memphites, a lake, 250 miles, or, according to what Mucianus says, 450 miles in circumference and fifty paces deep, has been formed by artificial means: after the King by whose orders it was made, it is called by the name of Moeris. The distance from thence to Memphis is nearly sixty-two miles."

Pliny, added further, in regards the "place where Lake Moeris was excavated" (XXXVI, 16) "an immense artificial piece of water, cited by the Egyptians among their wondrous and memorable works."

After came Diodorus Siculus (I, 4) who stated, as Budge (1902) notes: "After the death of this King [Uchoreus], and twelve descendants, Meris came to the crown of Egypt, and built a portico in Memphis towards the north, statelier and more magnificent than any of the rest. And, a little above the city, he cut a dyke for a pond, bringing it down in length from the city three hundred and twenty-five furlongs, whose use was admirable, and the greatness of the work incredible. They say it was in circuit three thousand and six hundred furlongs; and in many places three hundred feet in depth. For being that the Nile never kept to a certain and constant height in its inundation, and the fruitfulness of the country ever depended upon its just proportion, he dug this lake to receive such water as was superfluous, that it might neither immoderately overflow the land, and so cause fens and standing ponds, nor by flowing too little, prejudice the fruits of the earth for want of water. To this end he cut a trench along from the river into the lake, fourscore furlongs in length, and three hundred feet broad; into this he let the water of the river sometimes run, and at other times diverted it, and turned it over the fields of the husbandmen, at seasonable times, by means of sluices which he sometimes opened, and at other times shut up, not without great labor and cost; for these sluices could not be opened or shut at a less charge than fifty talents. This lake continues to the benefit of the Egyptians for these purposes to our very days, and is called the lake of Myris or Meris to this day. The King left a place in the lake, where he built a sepulcher and two pyramids, one for himself, and another for his queen, a furlong in height; upon the top of which he placed two marble statues seated in a throne, designing, by these monuments, to perpetuate the fame and glory of his name to all succeeding generations. The revenue arising from the fish

WHERE ARE THE KAMITE KINGS?

taken in this lake, he gave to his wife to buy her dresses, which amounted to a talent of silver every day. For there were in it two-and-twenty sorts of fish, and so vast a number were taken, that those who were employed continually to salt them up (though they were multitudes of people), could hardly perform it."

The other great achievement of Amenemhat III was the famous Labyrinth. A number of classical scholars have equally commented on this wonderful architectural structure. Herodotus was again one of the first of the early travelling scholars. According to Budge (1902) Herodotus wrote: "Now, they [i.e., the twelve Kings] determined to leave in common a memorial of themselves; and having so determined, they built a LABYRINTH, a little above the Lake of Moeris, situated near that called the city of Crocodiles; this I have myself seen, and found it greater than can be described. For if anyone should reckon up the buildings and public works of the Grecians, they would be found to have cost less labor and expense than this Labyrinth; though the temple of Ephesus is deserving of mention, and also that in Samos. The pyramids likewise were beyond description and each of them comparable to many of the great Grecian structures. Yet the labyrinth surpasses even the pyramids. For it has twelve courts enclosed with walls, with doors opposite each other, six facing the north, and six the south, contiguous to one another, and the same exterior wall encloses them. It contains two kinds of rooms, some underground and some above ground over them, to the number of three thousand, fifteen hundreds of each. Two rooms above ground I myself went through and saw, and relate from personal inspection. But the underground rooms I only know from report; for the Egyptians who have charge of the building would, on no account, show me them, saying, that there were the sepulchers of the Kings who originally built this labyrinth, and of the sacred crocodiles. I can therefore only relate what I have learnt by hearsay concerning lower rooms; but the upper ones, which surpass all human works, I myself saw; for the passages through the corridors, and the windings through the courts, from their great variety, presented a thousand occasions of wonder, as I passed from a court to the rooms, and from the rooms to halls, and to other corridors from the halls, and to other courts from the rooms. The roofs of all these are of stone, as are also the walls; but the walls are full of sculptured figures. Each court is surrounded with a colonnade of white stone, closely fitted. And adjoining the extremity of the Labyrinth is a pyramid, forty orgyac in height, on which large figures are carved, and a way to it has been made ground."

Strabo, XVII, 37, is also another important classic commentary of this structure. He wrote: "There is still in Egypt, in the Nome of Hierakleopolites, a Labyrinth, which was the first constructed, three thousand six hundred years ago, they say, by King Petesuchis or Tithoes: although, according to Herodotus, the entire work was the production of no less than twelve Kings, the last of whom was Psammetichus. As to the purpose for which it was built, there are various opinions: Demoteles says that it was the palace of King Moteris, and Lyceas that it was the tomb of Moeris, while many others assert that it was a building consecrated to the Sun, an opinion which mostly prevails. They [i.e., the Labyrinthos of Egypt, Crete, Lemnos, and Italy] are all of them covered with arched roofs of polished stone; at the entrance, too, of the Egyptian Labyrinth, a thing that surprises me, the building is constructed of Parian marble, while throughout the other parts of it the columns are of syenites. With such solidity is this huge mass constructed ...."

Maakherura, Amenemhat IV, *Nile Year* 2433-2445 (1798-1786 B.C.) was the last King of the XIIth Dynasty. This short reign did not allow for any major accomplishment. His royal titulary is as follows:

Horus	Khepera Kheper Kheperu
Two Ladies	_____
Horus of Gold	_____
Suten Bat	Ra-maa-kheru
Son of Ra	Amen-em-hat.

His name is in Lepsius' *Denkmaler* II, 140, 152. On the *Abydos List* it is No. 65 and on the *Second Abydos List* No. 39. The *Tablet of Sakkara* and *Tablet of Karnak* mentions his name. A plaque in the British Museum, No. 22,879 also bears his name.

His name has been found on rocks at Serabut el Khadem and at Wady Maghara in the Sinai Peninsula. An inscription in his sixth year shows exploitation of the mines in Sinai.

WHERE ARE THE KAMITE KINGS?

An ephemeral Usertesen IV is mentioned by Legrain *Annales* II, 272. His Titulary included:

Horus	_____
Two Ladies	Sankh-taui
Horus of Gold	Nefer-Khau
Suten Bat	Ra-Sennefer-ab
Son of Ra	Usertesen

Queen Sebek-Neferi-Ra, *Nile Year* 2446-2449 (1785-1782 B.C.), a queen, is also mentioned in connection with this dynasty.

Garstang's excavations at Beni Hasan in 1902-03 have supplied important information about the Middle Kingdom. The reports are included here to lend clarity and further knowledge about this middle age of pharaonic Kemet. Here too, the role of ancient debris has been significant in preserving a site long visited by tourists and plunderers. The first is "Excavations at Beni-Hasan" 1902-03, by John Garstang in *Man* 1903, 54 (pp. 97-98).

"Excavations have been made during the past season, beginning with December and ending in March, in the vicinity of Beni- Hasan, in Upper Egypt. A necropolis of the Middle Empire (circa. 2000 B.C.) was found lying half way up the face of the cliff, over which looks the famous gallery of rock-hewn tombs. The presence of this site was already indicated by the numerous open mouths of square shafts sunk in the limestone; betokening pit-tombs anciently plundered. There was little sign of recent disturbance, so that it could not be determined without excavation whether other tombs remained under the surrounding debris, or whether, indeed, in a place so conspicuous and so much visited, the plundering of ancient times had left anything to reward investigation. It soon proved that the greed of plunderers to secure the treasures of the large upper tombs had preserved to the expedition a number of tombs undisturbed in the lower range by covering them with debris. The limestone itself, and the white dust powered from it had helped also to preserve the remains entire, by resisting the inroad of the "white ant" and small wood worms, which, in tombs dug, as was more common, in the sand, would have totally destroyed the wooden inscribed coffins and models with which these burials were found to be chiefly furnished."

"In all, 492 tombs have been examined. Some have been robbed or destroyed in various ways, from some others though disturbed it was possible to extract information either by analogy or by the finding of some objects lying neglected in the rubbish .... the doors of these tombs at the foot of their shafts were found still closed as they had been left in the third millennium B.C. It was thus possible to record by photograph the appearance of each burial chamber with its tomb furniture complete and in its original position, as well as the disposition of each object step by step as the clearing of the tomb proceeded. Although some 450 photographs have been taken, of which probably about a hundred are interior views obtained by reflected light ...."

"These tombs proved to be largely those of the officials and retinue of the princes buried in the rock tombs of the upper gallery, as may be gleaned by comparing the names and titles recovered with those upon the inscribed walls. It is thus representative of the middle classes of an important town in Egypt during the Middle Empire, chiefly the XI and XII dynasties. The history of the necropolis itself, however, is taken back to the very beginning of the Middle Empire, in the VI dynasty, by the discovery of a lower gallery of rock-hewn tombs, eight or nine in number, in one of which, curiously, the original burials were found intact at the bottom of its tomb-shaft, though the same had been re-used during the XII dynasty for burials which had themselves been plundered. This tomb, No. 481, which was apparently that of a prince, Apa (described as an official of the temple, confidential friend of the King, &c.) and his wife Teta, is decorated in low relief and in color, which is in parts well preserved, with agricultural and other scenes in the style of art characteristic of the period."

"One class of burial deserves special notice. It pertains seemingly to the XI or early XII dynasty. The body is generally enclosed in a coffin of thin wood, inscribed with names, titles, and formulae, which is then placed again inside a stout coffin inscribed with texts and possibly painted with various representations. Upon the coffin, or by its side also if numerous, are wooden models, which generally include: (a) A sailing boat with men punting; (b) rowing boat; (c) granary; (d) scene representing the sacrifice of an ox; (e) scene

WHERE ARE THE KAMITE KINGS?

representing the making of beer (from fermented bread); (f) girl carrying birds in hand and basket on head....the sailing-boat and rowing - boat from the tomb of Antef (No.1) have one unusual feature, in the double-steering oars, controlled by a steersman, who controls the turn of these rudders by a thin pole, the weight of the large oars being supported by posts. The usual method was a single steering oar on the same principle, as seen in the case of the large rowing boat, 116. (A similar method is now in use on Lake Como). In the sailing boats the essential figures are seemingly three men to hoist the sail, two men using punt poles over the side, a look-out (or reis) and a helmsman. The boat from tomb 186 combines rowing with sailing; it has also other curious features. In the forepart of the ship stands a Negro with bow in left hand and two arrows (or spears), and under the shadow of it two men play a game with moveable pawns on a chess-board table."

"From tomb 366 is a unique representation of the sacrifice of the black spotted bull; while tomb 275 supplies, also additional to the usual deposit, a number of small models of laborers and artisans, two of which are shown."

"The tomb 116 (of a chief physician, Nefery) was furnished with some remarkable models, three of which are pictured. The whole process of brewing, by fermentation of bread (the kneading, straining, &c.), is shown, while another smaller group, not shown depicts the making of bread. The model of the granary is very perfect: it consists of a courtyard with three sealed chambers on either side. The floor is filled with grain (barley), which men are gathering into sacks and small tubs. Other models, and the walls of the painted tombs, show the laborers ascending the stairway and filling the chambers from above by means of holes provided from which he overlooks the work. (This method still survives in principle in the granaries of the rich in Egypt, and is employed freely; it seems, in parts of India.)"

"Other objects in wood of some interest are figures of foreigners, a Libyan woman with child on back, and men with the beard and appearance of the Aamu sheik. A wooden capital in form of a lily seems to be the earliest of its kind. There are some ancient musical instruments, flutes, lutes, a drum (of wood and skin); while several pieces of basket and wicker work are in good preservation."

"These excavations were made partly under the auspices of the patrons who supported the excavations at Bet Khallaf and Reqaqnah last year. The names are now as follows: Mr. Martyn Kennard, Mr. William MacGregor, and Mr. Hilton Price (Dir. S.A) (privately), Lady O'Hagan (for a museum at Towneley, Lancs.), Mr. A. J. Evans (for the Ashmolean Museum), Dr. M.R. James (for the FitzWilliam Museum), and Mr. J. Rankin (on behalf of the Museum of University College, Liverpool)." John Garstang.

The excavation was continued later that year with even more success in completing the picture of Middle Kingdom culture. This second Original Article on Beni Hasan, with Plate I-J was entitled "Excavations at Beni-Hasan," 1902-03 (11), by John Garstang in *Man* 1903, 74 (pp. 129-30).

"The pages of MAN for July of this year, in Article No. 54, contain a preliminary account of excavations made at Beni-Hasan during last winter season, with a general review of the nature of the discoveries. It was seen that a chief feature of the tomb furniture of the Middle Empire (before 2000 B.C.), in that locality, was a number of wooden models illustrating in themselves the industrial methods of the country as well as the burial customs of the period. The illustrations of that article presented a selection of the more characteristic objects that had been found, including four varieties of boats, a model of a granary with compartments, a brewing scene, a sacrifice, and some artisans at work. By request of the editor a photograph is now reproduced showing the disposition of some of the objects in one of the tombs exactly as found, before removal or disturbance. It was the good luck of last winter expedition to find a number of these instructive burial places entire, exactly as the original users had left them, so that it was possible to obtain a unique series of photographic views, illustrating the Egyptian ideal of furnishing the tomb of an official or courtier, as that time, in the district known as the Oryx Nome."

"The picture accompanying this note is one of these. It is a first view of the interior of the tomb of Antef, a courtier, which was the first tomb opened in the early days of December last. It shows clearly the remarkable preservation of the various objects, which are all of

WHERE ARE THE KAMITE KINGS?

wood, and the freshness of the colors upon them. On the right hand is the rowing boat, with spreading prow and stern, rowed by eight oarsmen in pairs, and steered by a man who controls a tiller with each hand. To the left is a model representing the making of bread, and behind are sandals and a man leading an ox. In this photograph the objects are seen on the coffin-lid, and the granary, which has been removed, stood in the foreground L. The other various objects, the girl with geese, a sailing boat, and man brewing, which completed the group, stood by the side. The chamber was small and the objects necessarily crowded."

"A comparison of the furniture from six different tombs shows that each contained almost exclusively models of the following: - (a) A rowing boat; (b) a sailing boat; (c) a granary; (d) a bread-baking group; (e) a beer-making group; (f) a girl carrying basket and birds. In two cases there was an ox-sacrifice represented, and in one an ox was being led. One tomb group included also two additional boats, but these were of special character, containing armed men and spears. In three cases the remains of a real leg of ox were distinguished .... there was a definite custom in the matter of funeral provision, and while there are many smaller points to be explained, the general suggestion of elaborate provision for a journey seems to be the underlying motive ...."

"In one boat, the sailing boat from the tomb of Antef, an open space beneath a canopy was left vacant. In another, two white figures, presumably Isis and Nephthys, were mourning at the head and foot of a bier, upon which rested the small model of a mummy (as familiar from wall-paintings). A third instance, equally of symbolic significance, was of rarer character. In a panel, between the eyes on the east side of a painted coffin of one Neteru-hetep, was a small carved wooden figure, in a seated position, with a somewhat special dress of hair. It seemed to be emblematic of the escaping Ka."

"The other photographs of the plate illustrate objects of special character. In the center are two dolls, made entirely of string and beads. The ink or paint upon them shows that they are intended to represent females. The larger one is adorned with beads arranged as a collar of several strings and colors, while an anklet encircles the left leg, and the end of each hair is adorned with a cluster of small

FREDERICK MONDERSON

blue beads. The smaller doll has short hair, decorated with blue beads, which resemble a cluster over the head. These objects were found in positions which did not give any evidence of their use."

1. Head of a King, represented as offering fish, from a dark grey granite dyad. Tanis.
2. Head of Khentekhtayemsafsonb, a noble of the Middle Kingdom. Quartzite. Abusir.
3. Amenemhēt III. Limestone. Hawára.
4. Profile of Amenemhēt III. Dark grey granite. Karnak.

Where are the Kamite Kings Illustration. Images of important individuals from the 12th Dynasty.

"The wooden figure shown in front and in profile is the model of a woman, with long skirt, carrying a child upon her back, apparently under a shawl. (Actually, the head of the babe is fitted by a short peg to the rounded back of the woman.) The custom and dress are not recognizably Egyptian. In the survey of the famous rock tombs of Beni Hasan, made some twelve years ago, Mr. Percy E. Newberry discovered a scene which had up to that time eluded the attention of all visitors. It is published by him in Beni-Hasan 1, Plate XLV11., and two-colored figures in Plate XLV. The scene shows an Egyptian

WHERE ARE THE KAMITE KINGS?

officer introducing a group of seven foreigners. Three of them, his report tell, are warriors with yellow skin, blue eyes, and thick matted hair, in which are stuck five or six ostrich feathers. They are clothed in red garments fringed at the bottom; in the right hand they carry ostrich feathers, in the left a curved club. The remaining four figures of the group represent women. They also are fair-skinned and blue-eyed, and have light brown or red hair. They are clad in simple long skirts of red color. Two of them carry children in a basket slung over their shoulders, and two carry a red-colored monkey on their backs. These peculiarities point to their being Libyans. This object represents in model what the artists of the time painted upon the walls of Khnemhotep's tomb (No. 14). The chief features of the statuette, which is about 8 inches in height, are the character of the skirt, the wealth of hair arranged around the face, rolled back from the brow, and the prominent nose with rounding end. On top of the head a small hole is pierced, suggesting that the woman carried also on her head something which is now lost, the tomb having been previously disturbed."

Where are the Kamite Kings Photo. View of 16-sided columns from within Hathor's Chapel at Deir el Bahari.

FREDERICK MONDERSON

Where are the Kamite Kings Illustration. Various heads and styles. Call it a wig on the first but it certainly looks like a well-groomed Afro. The last one is of Mentuhotep II, found at Gebelein.

"A selection of objects discovered in this excavation was exhibited during July in the rooms of the Society of Antiquaries, and the committee had in view the possibility of meeting a request for another exhibition next year. Meanwhile the collection has been distributed to museums practically interested in the results. The Ashmolean Museum at Oxford has received the boat with armored men and canopy, and the barque with model mummy. The whole tomb deposit of Khety (366), including the sacrifice, is to be shown in actual position upon its coffin at the Fitzwilliam Museum, Cambridge. The University of Liverpool, by the generosity of Mr.

WHERE ARE THE KAMITE KINGS?

J. Rankin, the donor, will be provided with a series of objects useful to students, including the model of a granary, and the painted coffin of User-het, a warrior, inscribed with long funeral text."

The report of these excavations will probably take the form of a volume on the Burial Customs of the Egyptians in the Middle Empire, to be published next year. The report for the previous season's work at Reqaqnah is being issued to the public by Messrs. Constable under the title of The Third Egyptian Dynasty." John Garstang.

References

Adams, B. *Egyptian Mummies*. Bucks: Shire Publications, Ltd. (1984: 1992).
Budge, E.A.W. *History of Egypt Under the Amenemhats and Hyksos*. New York: Henry Frowde, 1902.
Breasted, J.H. *A History of Egypt*. New York: Charles Scribner's Sons, (1905) 1923.
Dodson, A. *Egyptian Rock-Cut Tombs*. Bucks: Shire Publications, 1991.
Grimal, N. (Trans by Ian Shaw). *A History of Ancient Egypt*. Cambridge: Blackwell, (1988) 1992.
Hope, C. *Egyptian Pottery*. Bucks: Shire Publications, 1987.
Leibovitch, J. *Ancient Egypt*. Cairo: French Institute, 1938.
Murnane, W.J. *The Penguin Guide to Ancient Egypt*. New York: Penguin Books, 1983.
Murray, M. *The Splendor That Was Egypt*. New York: Philosophical Library, 1949.
Posener, G. With S. Sauneron and J. Yoyotte. *A Dictionary of Egyptian Civilization*. London: Methuen and Co., Ltd. (1959) 1962.
"The Relief at Wadi es Saba Rigale near Gebel Silsila." *American Journal of Archaeology* XVIII (1914: 503).
Ruffle, J. *The Egyptians*. Ithaca, New York: Cornell University Press, 1977.
Shaw, I. *Egyptian Warfare and Weapons*. Bucks: Shire Publications, Ltd., 1991.
Smith, W.S. *The Art and Architecture of Ancient Egypt*. New York: Penguin Books, (1958) 1981,

FREDERICK MONDERSON

Taylor, J.H. *Egyptian Coffins*. Bucks: Shire Publications, Ltd., 1989.

Thomas, A.P. *Egyptian Gods and Myths*. Bucks: Shire Publications, Ltd., 1986.

Watson, P. *Egyptian Pyramids and Mastaba Tombs*. Bucks: Shire Publications, 1987.

Wilson, E. *Egyptian Literature*. New York: The Colonial Press, 1901.

Woldering, I. *Art of Egypt: In the Time of the Pharaohs*. New York: Greystone Press, (1962) 1963.

"The Sinai Expedition, 1904-05" by W.M. Flinders Petrie, D.C.L., F.R.S., F.B.A., Edwards Professor, University College, London appeared in *Man* 1905, 64 (Pp. 113-16).

Where are the Kamite Kings Illustration. Amenhotep III, "the magnificent," 18th Dynasty.

WHERE ARE THE KAMITE KINGS?

Where are the Kamite Kings Illustration. Outer and inner coffin of Pinotem II.

The scantiness and incompleteness of our knowledge of the Egyptian remains in Sinai induced me to devote a season to exploring those settlements. Of the 250 inscriptions, which we copied in full size facsimile, few had been completed before, and many were entirely new to us. The temple of Serabit el Khadem was only known by small plans of those walls which happened to stand up amid the ruins, and no intelligible view of it could be had until we had recovered the larger part of the structure which was yet unknown. The very purpose of the mines was uncertain and misstated. Our party consisted of four to six Europeans and twenty eight Egyptian workmen, most of who were brought from Upper Egypt by Mr. Currelly across the desert and the Red Sea. The first center was at Wady Magharah, at a distance of five days camel journey from Suez. Half of the inscriptions there had been destroyed by recent mining; the remainder we copied, and-at the request of Sir W. Garstin-all but one of these inscriptions were cut out by Mr. Currelly and removed to the Cairo Museum for safety. The main anthropological results were the re-discovery of the large scene of the King Semerkhet of the I Dynasty, which is the oldest known figure group on a large scale, and the discovery of a scene of King Sa-nekht, the founder of the III Dynasty. He had Ethiopian features, even more strongly marked than those of the Ethiopian Kings of Egypt of later age. The rapid declension of sculpture by the reign of his successor bears out the view of an Ethiopian conquest of Egypt overthrowing the II Dynasty and beginning a new era. The mine heaps were also examined. Great numbers of flints worn by working in the sandstone were found, but scarcely any were from the heaps from Egyptian mines with inscriptions, and hence the flints were probably tools of Bedawin workers of various dates. All of the mines here were for turquoise, fragments of which abound in the mine heaps. No copper ore was found here.

We then moved some miles northward to Serabit el Khadem, where the temple ruins cap the plateau of sandstone. This site of worship is certainly very early, as a limestone figure of a hawk with the name Snefru in contemporary hieroglyphs takes it back to the end of the III Dynasty. This King is often named in later monuments here, and also Mentuhotep of the XI Dynasty. The XII Dynasty has left a continuous series of remains of every King. The principal work was under Amenemhat III, who executed the sacred cave, and his successor, faced the front with sculptures. It had been supposed that this cave was originally a tomb for an official who is named on the wall, but as we found it in an altar of the Goddess Hathor, dedicated by Amenemhat III., with the name of this same official, it is clear that there is no ground for this being other than a rock shrine. The officials who were sent here placed their names far more freely on all monuments than was the custom in Egypt.

The cave and courtyard before it was all that was arranged in the XII Dynasty. A thousand years later, in the XVIII Dynasty, Amenhotep I reconstructed the cave front; and then Hatshepsut and

WHERE ARE THE KAMITE KINGS?

Tahutmes III built several chambers and courts extending far before the cave, and also cut a second and smaller cave for the God of the east, Sopd.

In front of this temple proper, four other Kings added a series of pilgrim cubicles, down to Sety I; and later Kings put up tablets or made alterations until Ramessu VI, after whom the place fell to decay. The whole purpose of the worship here was to propitiate the Goddess of turquoise in the interest of the miners who came here.

The main interest of the temple is as giving an insight into early Semitic worship. One excavation showed, what had never been suspected, the prominence of ceremonies of ablution. A tank was placed at the door of the temple; the largest covered court had a circular basin in the middle of it surrounded by four pillars, and another tank in the corner next to the exit door; while the next largest court had a long tank in the midst with four pillars around it. These show for certain how important the ceremonial of ablution was in the worship here; and they are the direct counterpart of the laver of the Jewish Tabernacle and the Brazen Sea of the Temple, while the hunafiyeh court of the Muhammedan mosque shows how essential such a system still is in Semitic worship.

Another great feature was the immense quantity of burnt offering on the hill ridge before the cave. For more than a hundred feet in length stretches a bed of wood-ashes, often as much as half a yard thick. The sacrifices on the high places are familiar in the worship of Palestine.

A third characteristic of the Bethel system, of oracular dreams and memorial stones, was in the story of Jacob. The custom of placing upright stones is very common throughout Sinai, as a token of a pilgrimage or passing visit, as it is in India, and they often show along a hill crest like the teeth of a saw. Over the mines and near the temple they are associated with rude shelters of stones, which are generally placed singly, and have no grouping like the more permanent huts of miners at Maghara. These are evidently the shelters for pilgrims who came to sleep at the shrine, and who probably slept in the cave itself until it was built up by the Egyptians. This system of incubation for oracular purposes was common in Syria, and extended to other countries. The later Kings met it by providing cubicles in front of the temple, banked over with sand and stones so as to be substitutes for the sacred cave. The total length of the temple was about 250 feet.

The whole of the mines here were entirely for turquoise, as shown by the mine heaps and the geological level.

We have then three characteristics of Semitic worship, the ablutions, the burnt sacrifices on the high place, and the bethels and incubation system, all of which are familiar in Syria, and none of which belong to Egyptian worship.

Seldom has an expedition produced so much from a very small expenditure on excavation .... excavating has settled the purpose of the mines and shown for the first time the antiquity of these customs of Semitic worship, which the Egyptians adopted, just as Romans worshipped the local Gods of the countries to which they went.

Where are the Kamite Kings Illustration. Image of the official Montuhotopou.

The name is not "Serabit el-Khadem," but Serabit el Khadem. The small plans hitherto published were only of such portions of the building as happened to be visible, and omitted large parts of

WHERE ARE THE KAMITE KINGS?

construction now exposed. The steles in the shrine court are not "much older than the rest," the earliest steles being the long series in the XII Dynasty approach to the temple. The temple was not "merely a little provincial Egyptian shrine," but a structure over 200 feet long, for the building of which many architects and masons were specially sent from Egypt at various times, as stated on the steles. The numerous Bethel stones in the neighborhood are some of them inscribed by Egyptians, who adopted the local worship. No such system of stone records of visits is known in Egypt, no one familiar with Egyptian works could write that they "are ordinary Egyptian monumental tablets of Egyptian type." That is even incorrect of the mining records in the temple. The Egyptian language does not make monuments to be of Egyptian type any more than a Latin inscription makes a gravestone to be of Roman type. The frequency of the memorial stones without inscriptions seems to have been unnoticed by this traveler.

More strange is to read of the Babylonian temples, which were founded by Sumerians, as being Semitic .... Certainly, none of the strongly Semitic worship that I have described is obvious in Babylonia. The statement that it is "probable that the ashes are the remains of the fires of the XII Dynasty copper smelters who left their mounds of slag lying round the site" is indeed strange .... There is no copper slag within six miles of the site, so far as I could find, and there was no copper ore at the level of the temple .... W.M. Flinders Petrie."

An Original Article with Plate K entitled "Note Upon Excavations Made 1904-5" by John Garstang, M.A., B. Litt., F.S.A. University of Liverpool appeared in *Man* 1905, 79 (Pp. 145-46).

"Hierakonpolis (Kom-el-Ahmar) was the place selected for first excavation. The palace site is well known from the researches of former explorers, and consequently the present excavations were made rather in the outlying township, which proved to be almost wholly of proto-dynastic age. Immediately below the rubbish of more recent times, strata representing the third and earlier dynasties were come upon; it was even possible in some instances to trace the walls of houses and the disposition of rooms and passages of that remote date, about 3,000 B.C. Vases of alabaster and granite, as well as flint knives of conspicuously delicate workmanship, and other small objects, served to illustrate the archaeology of the time and locality ....

Meanwhile within the great fortress which stands immediately opposite upon the edge of the western desert, and seems to have been built in a contemporary age for the protection of this palace, it was found by experiment that previous excavators had not penetrated deeply enough to reach its lowest historical strata. At a depth which varied according to the accumulation of sand from two to three meters below the existing surface, a whole necropolis of the prehistoric age was discovered and excavated; 188 graves were registered and photographed in detail. They seem to range in date from about the middle portion of the pre-dynastic sequence until the beginning of the first dynasty .... the walls of the fortress, associated with the tomb structures of later date upon the outside, have furnished reliable evidence that the fortress itself belongs to a date lying between the first and third dynasties. A photograph in the plate illustrates the approximate relation between the stratum of the necropolis and the walls of the fort.

After the completion of the excavation, after nearly two months of work, explorations were made throughout the whole region lying southward as far as Hissayeh. Tentative excavations were made at several points. At Edfu the remains seem to be of Ptolemaic times, while at Hissayeh some interesting funeral furniture and hieroglyphic papyri of pre-Ptolemaic date were discovered in the debris of a former excavation. Plundering during very recent times had rendered these sites unsuitable for the continuous work of an organized expedition; consequently, after the third month, camp was fixed at Esna on the northern limit of the concession.

As is often the case, rumors that the place had been plundered had in some measure saved it for the excavators. The smaller tombs of the great necropolis at once gave evidence of their origin during the Hyksos period; it seems probable (though the results of further excavation must be awaited before a definite conclusion can be established) that the site came into being during the pressure from the north in those troubled times upon the capital at Thebes. During the XVIII and XIX Dynasties the site at Esna seems to have fallen into neglect; but from the XX Dynasty, which heralded the period

WHERE ARE THE KAMITE KINGS?

of decline of the Egyptian power, about 1000 B.C., Esna again came into prominence.

Two great mounds, conspicuous in the desert from afar, proved to be tomb structures of this later date. These, cleared of their accumulated sand, disclosed great structures of brick in good preservation, which comprised a series of eight or ten chambers upon the ground-floor with a stairway leading up to a similar series above. The arches and vaults were pointed in nearly every case. In a stone-lined chamber within the largest structure there was found the head of an Apis carved in stone of the time of Rameses VI, and numerous remains of animals sacrificed at that shrine were found within the chamber. These structures were in reality great tombs, built it would seem, for the permanent use of some family. Unfortunately, a conflagration within the chamber, which seemed to have been deliberately brought about, had destroyed much archaeological evidence, but the architecture illustrated is of a new interest. The largest of these tombs stood upon a base 14.8 meters (nearly 50 feet) square, and its height was half its length, measured from its lowest course deep in the sand to the existing summit, which seems to be original .... John Garstang

An Original Article with Plate G, entitled "Excavations at Beni-Hasan in Upper Egypt (Second Season)" by John Garstang appeared in *Man* 1904, 67 (pp. 97-98).

".... It was a burying place for the officials and upper classes of that part of Egypt during the Feudal period, beginning with the VI Dynasty, but more generally representative of the XI and XII Dynasties; and dispute the existence, for the Oryx Nome at any rate, of any independent VII, VIII, IX, and X dynasties as tradition have brought these down. From archaeological and historical considerations, it must appear probable that these four dynasties represent four independent centers of feudal power, contemporaneous, or nearly so, with one another one with portions of the VI and XI dynasties of the royal houses of Memphis and Thebes respectively. The whole range of Egyptian history becomes by such consideration much less than tradition believes in.

FREDERICK MONDERSON

Locally it was found the custom that interment in rock-hewn tombs is at least as early as the close of the archaic period and the rise of the Pyramid age, about the III Dynasty. A whole range of small tombs was examined in the cliffs far back in the desert above the cluster of houses known as Nuerat, some three or four miles north of Beni-Hasan .... In this was the coffin, which in two cases observed was of pottery, similar to that pictured on Plate G, No. 925, and in another case was of wood, with paneled east face. In each case the coffin was so small that the burial was perforce contracted in the archaic fashion, as the picture shows. The body does not seem to have been preserved in any way, but it was covered by, or wrapped in, a linen cloth.

The next epoch, the Pyramid age, or Old Empire, or Memphite period, as it is variously called, is represented by a row of tombs similarly hewn in the rock, but in this case about two miles to the south of the better known necropolis, and just to the south of the Speos Artemidos .... In one tomb, which had escaped robbery, the recess was bricked up, and within, on the west side, was a plain thick wood coffin. ....

Where are the Kamite Kings Illustration. Red granite lintel of Sesostris III.

WHERE ARE THE KAMITE KINGS?

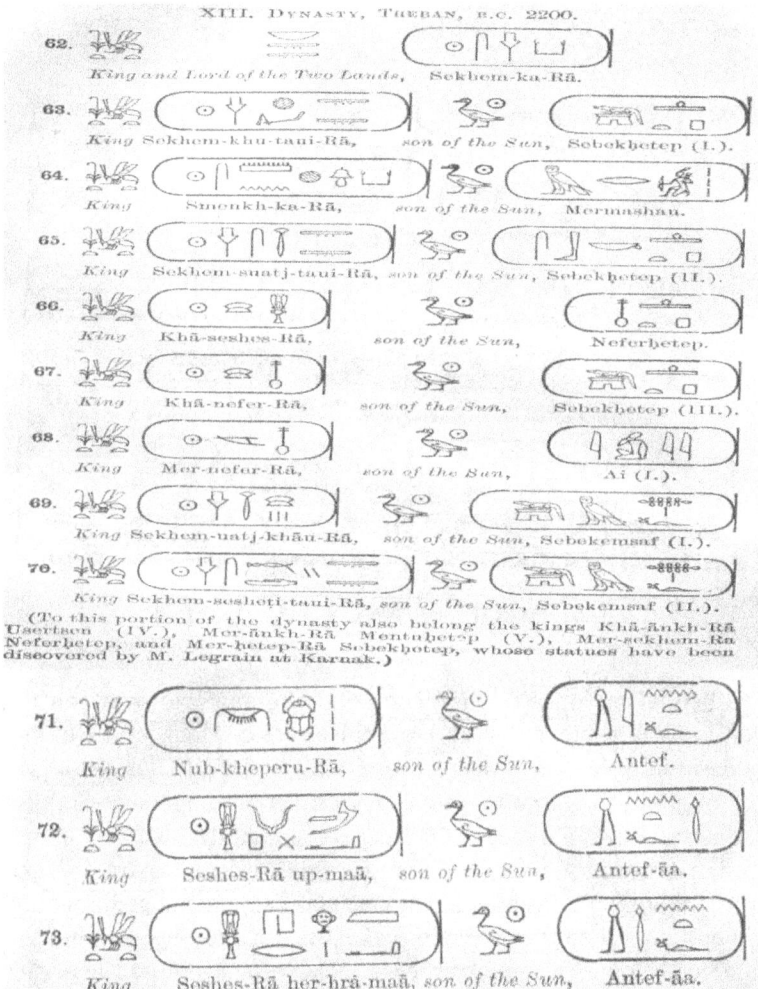

Kamite Kings Cartouche/Shennu. Kings of the Thirteenth Dynasty from Thebes. There's that "quintessential face" in Antef's Cartouche. Burckhardt defines it as "Prince of his city."

FREDERICK MONDERSON

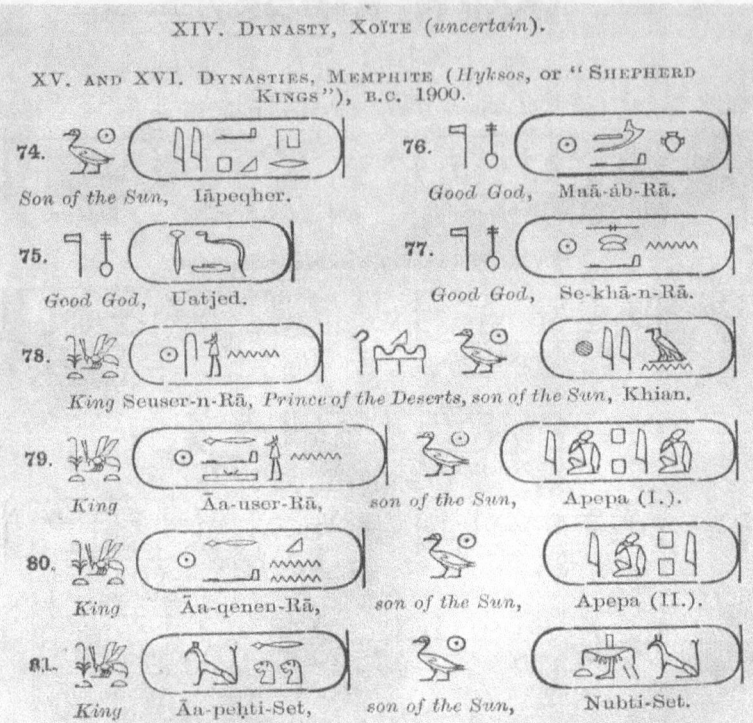

Kamite Kings Cartouche/Shennu. Kings of the Fifteenth and Sixteenth Dynasties, the "Hyksos Kings," or "rulers of foreign lands."

The Feudal period sees the necropolis beginning to grow on the well-known white cliffs of Beni-Hasan, two miles north of the modern village. Its first stage, seemingly, in the VI Dynasty, was a row of small rock tombs similar in form and arrangement to those last described, at the foot of the steeper slope of the cliff, about one-third up the ascent. Some eight or ten of these were constructed, and two of them were inscribed. The one showed a name compounded of Pepy, and the other the name of APA, an Erpa-ha. Within the latter was found an undisturbed deposit of the pointed alabaster vases characteristic of the period. The great Feudal chieftains of this and neighboring provinces next began to build their massive tombs in the rock higher up the slope, while their courtiers and officials dug their tomb-shafts on the slope of the cliff before them. The character of these great tombs was an elaboration of the earlier ones. Architectural features, particularly the column and portico, were now introduced in the rock tombs. The conventional agricultural or

WHERE ARE THE KAMITE KINGS?

religious incident which had formed the subject for mural decoration led on to the representation of scenes full of detail and incident of daily life, which are, indeed, a chief source of knowledge of the life and culture of the age. The tomb-shaft now has deepened, for security of the burial; and in all probability the funeral customs of the time were those which the funeral necropolis has so full illustrated, as described in the numbers of MAN already quoted.

The conspicuous feature of these Middle Empire burials was the deposit of wooden models within the funeral chamber. A further series of undisturbed tombs has confirmed the first impression that the customary objects were a rowing boat, a sailing boat, a granary, a baking and a brewing scene, and sometimes a sacrifice. These types were varied either by some detail, as the addition of a soldier with a battle-axe and shield in tomb 585 (Plate G), or by some different or additional object, such as the wooden portrait statue numbered 720. This exquisite object is only some 7 or 8 in. high, but the skill of the sculptor has created a work as impressive for the sense of fidelity in portrait as it is remarkable for minuteness of detail. It was, unfortunately, in several pieces when taken from a disturbed tomb.

Sometimes the models were replaced by real objects, as in the battle-axe (No. 511), the arrows (723), and the metal bowls (845), illustrated in the Plate and in Fig. 1 ....

Another object of interest, not figured in the Plate, is a reed used for separating the warp in weaving. It works in the sley behind the heads. Two such were found, similar in every respect, except the exact length, to one which was seen in use in the modern village of Abu-kirkas across the river and secured for purposes of comparison ....

The history of Beni-Hasan from the end of the Feudal period is almost a blank up to the close of the Theban rule. The Hyksos period and the great Imperial period are hardly represented. The Speos Artemidos is almost alone for an interval of nearly 1,000 years; and it is significant that it is not until the general decentralization of power in the XXII Dynasty that a sign of local activity re-shows itself. This age of Ethiopian, Libyan, and

FREDERICK MONDERSON

Assyrian, is represented by a considerable necropolis near to the Speos Artemidos, from which some characteristic funeral objects were recovered.

The concluding item of the season's work was the re-examination of the royal tomb of Neggadeh of the Ist Dynasty. Its chief result was the discovery of the missing portion of the ivory tablet of Mena, a duplicate of the same, and three other small tablets of Abui, Narmer (? Bezau) and Neithhotep respectively, as well as carved objects in crystal, obsidian, diorite, ivory and other materials with numerous seal-impressions. John Garstang.

An Original Article, with Plate C, entitled "Paleolithic Implements from the Thebaid" by H.R. Hall, M.A., appeared in *Man*.

In the year 1882 Major-General Pitt-Rivers, then President of the Anthropological Institute, published in the Journal (XI., 382) an article "On the Discovery of Chert Implements in Stratified Gravel in the Nile Valley near Thebes," in which he described his discovery, in the deposit of diluvial detritus which lies between the cultivation and the mountains on the west bank of the Nile opposite Luxor, of Paleolithic flint flakes, and noted the occurrence of implements of Paleolithic type on the surface of the desert nearby.

Attention was once more drawn to the subject of the Egyptian Paleolithic implements by the extensive collection of worked flints from the desert surface made by Mr. H. Seton-Karr in various parts of the Nile Valley, notably in the Wadi esh-Sheikh, opposite Maghagha. There was no doubt that a great number of the flints discovered by him were of late neolithic (predynastic) and even of historical age, but among them were also what appeared to be Palaeoliths resembling those noted by Pitt-Rivers, and after him by Legrain, at Thebes. To Dr. H.O. Forbes, of Liverpool, however, it seemed very doubtful that these supposed Palaeoliths were in reality Paleolithic at all, and he dated all the Wadi esh-Sheikh implements of the twelfth dynasty or later, or possibly as far back as the fourth, and supposed that the patination or brown oxidization found on them was no proof of immemorial age (*Bulletin Liverpool Museums*, 11., Nos. 3 and 4 (January, 1900), pp. 77- 115). His conclusions have, however, been criticized by Mr. H.J.L. Beadnell, of the *Geological Survey of Egypt*, in an article on "Neolithic Flint Implements from the Northern Desert of the Fayum" (*Geological*

WHERE ARE THE KAMITE KINGS?

Magazine, New Series, V., X. (1903), p. 53 ff.), who points (p. 57) that the weathered and patinated flints (which are the supposed Palaeoliths as it happens) must be of great age: that Dr. Forbes's assumption that as both the "Palaeoliths" and the later flints were found together it is probable that they are of the same age is unsound, because, "if a superior quality of flint occurs in the Wadi el-Sheikh, I do not see why it should not have been discovered and worked even in Paleolithic times, or why subsequent races should have rediscovered and worked the same beds, and their products have mixed on the surface."

Mr. Beadnell also thinks unsound the assumption on which rests Dr. Forbes's argument that "it is impossible to believe that these-the Paleolithic flints - could remain (even in a single instance) undisturbed from the Paleolithic days of Europe to the present time, when the forest under which they were made and the forest soil on which they reposed have been entirely carried away." As Mr. Beadnell says: "Is it certain that the high plateau was then clothed with forests?"

What evidence is there to show that it differed in any important respect from its present aspect? And if, as I suggest, desert conditions obtained then as now, and man merely worked his flints along the edges of the plateau overlooking the Nile Valley, I see no reason why flint implements, dating even from Paleolithic times, should not in favorable cases be still found in the spots whey they were left, surrounded by the flakes struck off in manufacture. On the flat plateau the occasional rains which fall - once in three or four years - can affect but little transport of material, and merely lower the general level by dissolving the underlying limestone, so that the plateau surface is left with a coating of nodules and blocks of insoluble flint and chert. Flint implements might thus be expected in many localities to remain for indefinite periods, but they would certainly become more or less 'patinated,' pitted on the surface and rounded at the angles after long exposure to heat, cold, and blown sand. Finds that retain their original clearness and sharpness of angles cannot be of high antiquity unless they have been protected by superficial deposits."

FREDERICK MONDERSON

Mr. Bednell's conclusions .... are entirely in favor of the Egyptian surface flints of Paleolithic type being in reality Paleolithic, yet he does not pronounce either for or against the existence of Paleolithic man in Egypt (p. 58). German investigators have no fear of accepting it; they have no doubt whatever that the Pitt-Rivers flints from Thebes and those of Paleolithic type from the Wadi esh-Sheikh and elsewhere in Egypt are in reality Paleolithic. Three articles have recently appeared, one by Dr. Blankenhorn in the *Zeitschrift der Gesellschaft fur Erdkunde zu Berlin*, 1902, pp. 694, 753 (Die Geschichte des Nilstroms in der Tertiar und Quartarperiode, sowie des palaolitischen Menschen in Agypten), the others by the veteran Dr. Schweinfurth in the Verhandlungen der Berliner Anthrop. Ges., 1902, p. 293 (Kiesel-Artefacte in der diluvialen Schotter-Terasse und auf fen Plateau-Hohen von Theben), and 1903, p. 798 (Steinxzeitliche Forsenhungen in Oberagypten). These relate to the same set of investigations carried on by Dr. Schweinfurth and Dr. Blanckenhorn of the terrain described by General Pitt-Rivers.

Dr. Schweinfurth gives photographs of some of the flints found, and contributes to Dr. Blanckenhorn's paper a map of the terrain, marking the places of General Pitt-Rivers and his own discoveries of flints, both exposed on the high desert surface and from the sides of the grave pits in the diluvial "Schotter-Terasse." Dr. Allen Sturge accompanied Professor Schweinfurth on one occasion, and identified typical flints as belonging to the epoch of Le Moustier. Messrs. Schweinfurth and Blanckenhorn examined the terrace of diluvial debris in which General Pitt-Rivers had found worked flints. Schweinfurth dates its formation to the Second Glacial Period ....

The debris-bed is formed of the stuff washed down by the ancient streams of the Wadiyen, the great valley running into the western hills from the village of Kurna, which bifurcates into the Valley of the Tombs of the Kings, the Biban el-Muluk properly speaking, on the western valley. On the tops of the ridges separating the various branches of the wadi from one another, and on the semi-circular plateau at its end which forms the watershed between it and the valley which debouches into the Nile valley towards Erment, are the remains of ancient manufactories of flints, and innumerable specimens of the handiwork of the ancient knappers lying about on the surface ....

WHERE ARE THE KAMITE KINGS?

Dr. Blanckenhorn further thinks, following the generally accepted theory, that the Paleolithic men who worked the flints found lying on the high desert surface at Thebes, and embedded in the debris brought down from that surface by the ancient streams of the Wadiyen to Kurna, lived on the plateau, not in the Nile valley itself, which was still marshy and uninhabitable, the area of the Libyan desert being in the Pre-Glacial or First Interglacial Period relatively well fitted for the inhabitance of man. This is the view taken by Professor Petrie (*Naqada and Ballas*, p. 49), who speaks of the high plateau as having been "the home of man in Paleolithic times, ... the rainfall, as shown by the valley erosion and waterfalls, must have caused an abundant vegetation on the plateau where man could live and hunt his game."

This view Mr. Beadnell considers faulty (*loc cit.*, p. 58); he minimizes the effects of erosion in forming the lateral Nile - Wadis, and as has been seen, disbelieves in the whole theory of the Paleolithic Egyptians, if they ever existed, having lived where they found and knapped their flints. For him the desert-plateau were as dry and uninhabited in Paleolithic days as now .... impossible that we should find, as we do, Paleolithic implements lying in situ on the desert surface, around the actual manufactories where they were made. Dr. Blanckenhorn does not resolve this difficulty. Yet if the constant rainfall and the vegetation of the Libyan desert area in Paleolithic days is all a myth (as according to Mr. Beadnell it is), and erosion played little or no part in the formation of the Theban Wadiyen, for instance, how came the embedded Palaeoliths of Kurna into the conglomerate-bed which Blanckenhorn and others declare to be debris from the plateau brought down by the ancient streams of the wadi? This view seems to be reasonable.

Erosion has surely taken place since the working of the Paleolithic flints. The surface of the plateau and the ridges between the valleys shows greatly varied weathering, ranging from the orange color of excavations made on the ledges of the cliffs under the XVIIIth Dynasty to the almost black surface of some parts, which must have remained undisturbed for ages .... We may reasonably suppose the imbedded flints of Kurna originally came from these denuded tracts. This fact speaks for Blanckenhorn's and against Beadnell's view.

FREDERICK MONDERSON

Yet this water erosion may possibly not have been that which would result from perennial streams flowing down from wooded heights (the idea of Petrie and Blanckenhorn), it may simply have been the result of water-torrents like the sels of to-day which fill the Wadis once in three years or so after heavy rain, but repeated at much closer intervals .... In his second article (pp. 801, 812) Dr. Schweinfurth hold that the climate of Egypt in the period corresponding to the Glacial Ages of Europe cannot have been very different from that of to-day.

Where are the Kamite Kings Illustration. Outer and inner coffin of Ma-Ka-Re of the 22nd Dynasty discovered in the 1881 Deir el Bahari "Cache." Notice the detail on both coffins.

WHERE ARE THE KAMITE KINGS?

However, this may be, it would seem that the possibility of the Paleolithic-seeming implements from the Egyptian desert-surface being in reality Paleolithic has been sufficiently vindicated.

.... The implement in the left-hand lower corner is broken off short. That on the right is an interesting specimen of a conveniently shaped pebble artificially modified and sharpened into a pear-shaped implement. The flint of this is naturally dark in color, whereas the material of the majority of the Theban implements is a very light-colored chert. The tool at the top of Fig. 1 on the left is a scraper, with fine bulb of percussion, paralleled by an English scraper of similar type. The two next parallel specimens are alike trihedral in shape. The next two are more or less similarly asymmetric. The lowest couple are leaf-shaped specimens, the Egyptian (on the left) being strongly patinated.

The third illustration (Fig. 2) shows some interesting smaller specimens, the larger leaf-shaped one above has little weathering or patina. In the center is a worked ring made from a "morpholith" or round nodule of flint of a type common in the Theban Hills, figured by General Pitt-Rivers (Fig. 9, 13). It has been split in two, and the lower side (shown) has its inner edge carefully smoothed or beveled .... On the assumption (which is probably to be rejected) that the Paleolithic inhabitants lived on the high plateau, and gradually migrated downhill as the climatic conditions approximated to those of the present day, the level of the river fell, and the swamps dried up, one ought to find the most primitive and most weathered implements on the highest plateau, and the more modern ones progressively lower down on its slopes and the small subsidiary plateau between the branch Wadis. This does not appear to be the case. The work scraper of Fig. 2 came from the high plateau, the equally worn and primitive-looking adze and triangular implement of Plate C. from a subsidiary plateau, whence came also the two fine St. Acheul types also on the plate, both of which are finely patinated, while the upper one (broken) is worn and weathered, the lower one not.

.... Dr. Blanckenhorn's investigations of the surface- implements were apparently confined to the summit of the ridge between Deir el-Bahari and the Tombs of the Kings, and the path thence to Deir el-Medina, i.e., the lowest subsidiary plateau. Dr. Schweinfurth has also investigated the neighborhood of the caravan-route from Kurna to Farshut (following Legrain), which runs up on to the high plateau by the side of western valley and the great kopje which he calls "Luciana-Hugel," and the surface of the plateau southwards, as well as the district generally speaking .... It is, therefore, beyond the Kurn or high southern peak of the Theban mountain-complex, and may be identified as being below the smaller peak marked in the upper left-hand corner of Schweinfurth's map, and looking across the great Erment wadi, already referred to above. Here our best implements were found, including those of Plate C. The desert surface was evidently very ancient and undisturbed, everything, limestone as well as flints, being black with weathering."

The Blessing

Wilson (1901: 100-02) mentions "THE INTRODUCTION TO MAATI" from the *Papyrus of Ani* in the British Museum No. 10,470, sheet 30.

THE CHAPTER OF ENTERING INTO THE HALL OF DOUBLE MAATI; A HYMN OF PRAISE TO OSIRIS, THE GOVERNOR OF AMENTET. Osiris, the scribe Ani, triumphant, saith:

"I have come, and [I] have drawn nigh to see the beauties; my hands [are raised] in adoration of thy name 'Right and Truth.' I came and I drew nigh unto [the place where] the acacia-tree growth not, where the tree thick with leaves exist not, and where the ground yields neither herb nor grass. Then I entered in to the hidden place, and I spake with the God Set, and my protector (?) advanceth to me, and his face was clothed (or covered), and [he] fell upon thee hidden. He entered into the Temple of Osiris, and he looked upon the hidden things which were therein; and the sovereign chiefs of the pylons [were] in the form of khus."

WHERE ARE THE KAMITE KINGS?

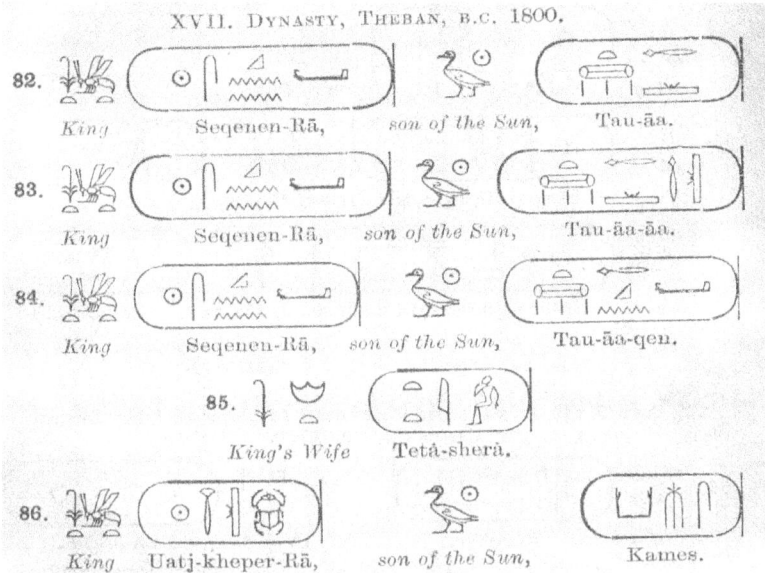

Kamite Kings Cartouche/Shennu. Kings of the Seventeenth Dynasty from Thebes.

10. New Kingdom: Politics, Priesthood, Culture, Architecture

The New Kingdom or New Empire can be considered the greatest "Golden Age" in ancient Nile Valley history. It comprised the XVIIIth thru XXth Dynasties and lasted for 500 years, from *Nile Year* 2668 to 3168, Murnane's (c. 1570-1070 B.C.), and ben-Jochannan's (c. 1580 to 1085 B.C.). The period boasted colorful, strong, visionary, and warlike Pharaohs, who ushered in peace and prosperity at home. Concomitantly, they expanded the nation's borders by conquest and arranged political marriages that all brought wealth and fame to Kemet. This African nation's glorious rulers supported beautiful innovations in art, encouraged the practice of medicine, language and literary compositions. They also built monumental works of architecture reflecting the genius of these black rulers who called their ancient land, Kemet, and whose

FREDERICK MONDERSON

minds were so powerful, way back then, because they were guided by the principles of Ma'at!

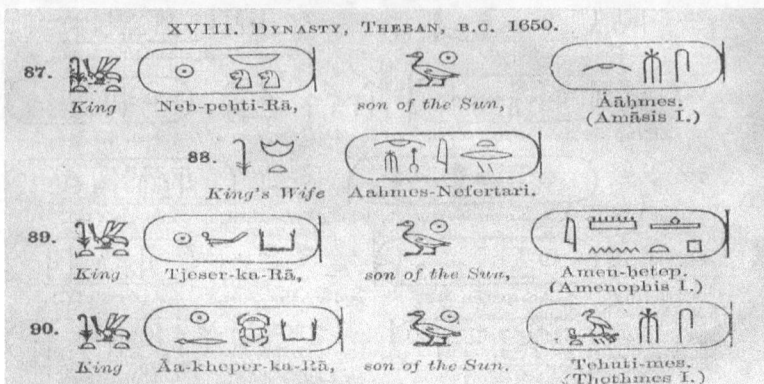

Kamite Kings Cartouche/Shennu (1). Kings of the Eighteenth Dynasty, New Kingdom from Thebes.

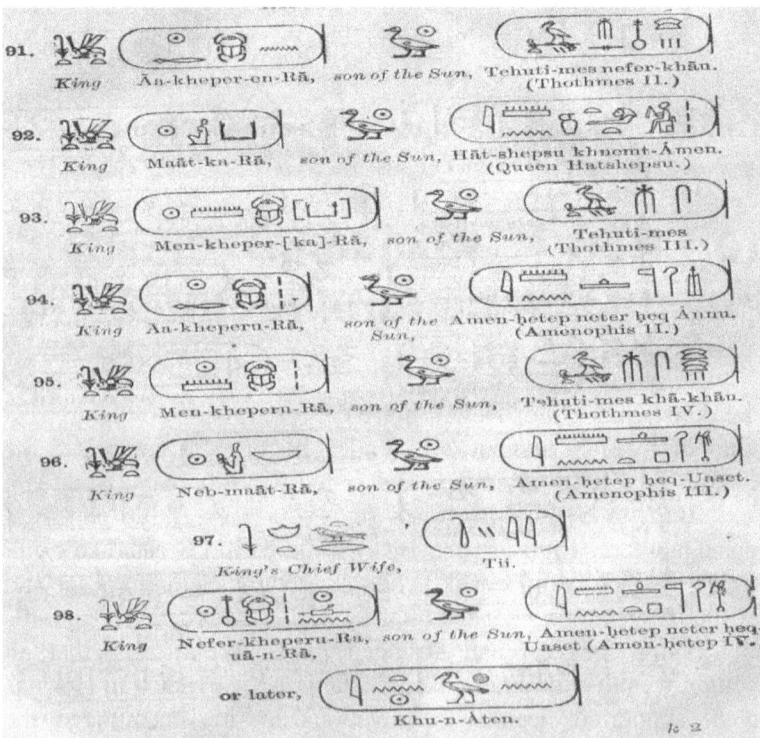

Kamite Kings Cartouche/Shennu (2). Kings of the Eighteenth Dynasty from Thebes.

WHERE ARE THE KAMITE KINGS?

To recall, the Pyramid Age or Old Kingdom (IIIrd to VIth Dynasties) came to an end when noblemen expanded their power at the expense of the aging monarch, Pepi II, whose reign lasted some 94 years. The result was anarchy, internecine warfare, and breakdown of centralized administration created in the VIIth-Xth Dynasties, the First Intermediate Period. Then, Intefs and Mentuhoteps, black princes of Thebes, united the South or Upper Kemet and consolidated their power. Expanding northward, they conquered the rebellious princes of the North and finally reunited Upper (Lotus) and Lower (Papyrus) Kemet. Founding the Middle Kingdom, Dynasties XIth-XIIIth, they reasserted centralized control, reorganized the state, and began an expansionist policy.

Similar problems as at the end of the Old Kingdom - inability to field strong leaders to continue the tradition - reemerged, and ushered in the Second Intermediate Period. Now the first significant influx of foreign people entered Africa from the north. They were called Hyksos or "Shepherd Kings," who were "a lowly people," according to Manetho, a second century B.C. Egyptian/Kamite chronicler, during the Greek period. These foreigners or "rulers of foreign land" were successful because the Africans had again become disunited and weakened. The Hyksos controlled the country from the north or Lower Kemet and founded the XVth and XVIth Dynasties. These were still contemporaneous with Theban control of the South.

Queen Teti-Sheri was a powerful personality. When her husband Sekenenra was away leading the war of liberation, a palace coup broke out, led by "Tety the handsome." She rallied the faithful and put down the rebellion. A strong woman, she lived to see the victory and her sons begin the new era. Her son, Ahmose married his sister Ahmes-Nefertari.

The XVIIIth Dynasty According to the Monuments and to Manetho

Ahmosi I. Nibpahitiri	1	Amosis
Ahenhotpu I. Zosirkheri	2.	Khebros

FREDERICK MONDERSON

Tuthmosi I. Akhpirkeri
Thutmosi I. Akhpirkeri
Thutmosi III. Akhpirniri
Amenhotpu II. Akhpiruri
Thutmosi IV. Manakhpiruri
Amenhotpu III. Nibmauri
Amenhotpu IV. – Nafirkhopiru Khuniaton. Ri-Uaniri Sakeri Sozirkhopiru Ankhkhopiruri
3.   Amenophthis
4.   Amensis
5.   Misaphris
6.   Misphragnouthosis
7.   Thoutmoisis
8.   Amenophis
9.   Horus

10.   Akherres I   Tutankhamonu – Haq-On-Risit
11.   Rathos Nibkhopiruri   Iotnutir Ai Nutir-Hiq-Oisist Khopirkhopiruri Iri-Mait
12.   Khebres   13.   Akherres II.

The Theban Princes of the Upper Kingdom comprising the XVIIth Dynasty ended the Hyksos occupation. They launched a war of liberation that lasted some 50 years. It began with Sekenenra I, followed by Sekenenra II and several others. Finally, Sekenenra II continued the fight and was killed by an axe blow to the head, and whose mummy is now in the Cairo Museum. Then Kamose his son continued the fight. Finally, Kamose's brother Ahmose expelled the invaders. Ahmose founded the XVIIIth Dynasty and began the New Kingdom, or New Empire.

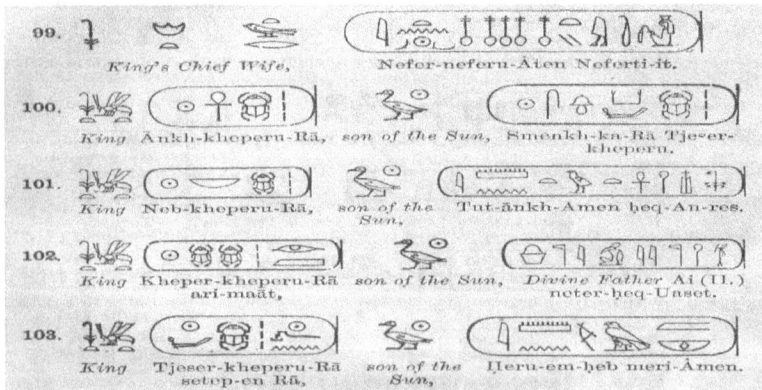

Kamite Kings Cartouche/Shennu (3). Kings of the later Eighteenth Dynasty, also from Thebes.

The new Queen, Aahmes-Nefertari, dubbed the ancestress of the XVIIIth Dynasty, is also significant for modern reconstruction in an

WHERE ARE THE KAMITE KINGS?

age of political correction. Her portrait, now in the British Museum depicts a "coal-black Ethiopian" with attendant racial and cultural implications. In addition, her attire is even more significant. She is shown, in the fashion of the times, wearing a long flowing gown fit for a Queen. The color of the materials of her dress is also important. The Queen is shown wearing the colors red, white and blue, renowned tri-color, 1500 years before the Christian era. This "Coal Black Queen" of the Nile Valley in ancient Africa, is shown wearing the colors symbolic of some 20 modern nations including America, Britain, Canada, France, Haiti, etc.

	Manethonian Equivalents.	Order in Manetho.	Approximate Date B.C.
1. Nebpehtira Aahmes I	Amosis	1	1580–1559
2. Tjeserkara Amenhetep I	Amenōphis	3	1559–1539
3. Aakheperkara Thothmes I	Tethmōsis	(1)	1539–1514
4. Aakhepernera Thothmes II	Khebron	2	1514–1501
5. Maatkara Hatshepsut	Amensis	4	1501–1479
6. Menkheperra Thothmes III [Manakhpirriya]	Mephres (Misaphris) Misphragmouthosis	5, 6	1501–1447
7. Aakheperura Amenhetep II	Amenōphis	8	1447–1421
8. Menkheperura Thothmes IV	Touthmōsis	7	1421–1412
9. Nebmaatra Amenhetep III [Nimmuriya]	Horos	9	1412–1376
10. Neferkheperura Amenhetep IV Akhenaten [Napkhururiya]	*Eusebius*		1380–1362
11. Smenkhkara	Akenkheres (daughter) (*Eusebius*) (*Josephus*)		1362–1360
12. Nebkheperura Tutankhamen	Khebres (Akherres) (*Africanus*) (*Eusebius*)		1360–1350
13. Kheperkhepruarimaatra Ai	Akherres (Kherres) (*Africanus*) (*Eusebius*)		1350–1345
14. Tjeserkheprura Harmahabi [Horemheb]	Harmaïs		1345–1321

Where are the Kamite Kings Illustration. Another list of XVIIIth Dynasty Kings with potential dates.

To refocus, Aahmose I was a military dictator. He made his country warlike with a large and reorganized army using horses and chariots. Horses increased the military's mobility and striking speed, making them a force to be reckoned with. This new warfare terrified Egypt's enemies in Palestine, Syria and Nubia. Ahmose was followed by Amenhotep I and Thutmose I. These last two Pharaohs reigned 21 and 12 years respectively. It was Thutmose I who overran Palestine and extended the borders of Imperial Kemet to Syria.

FREDERICK MONDERSON

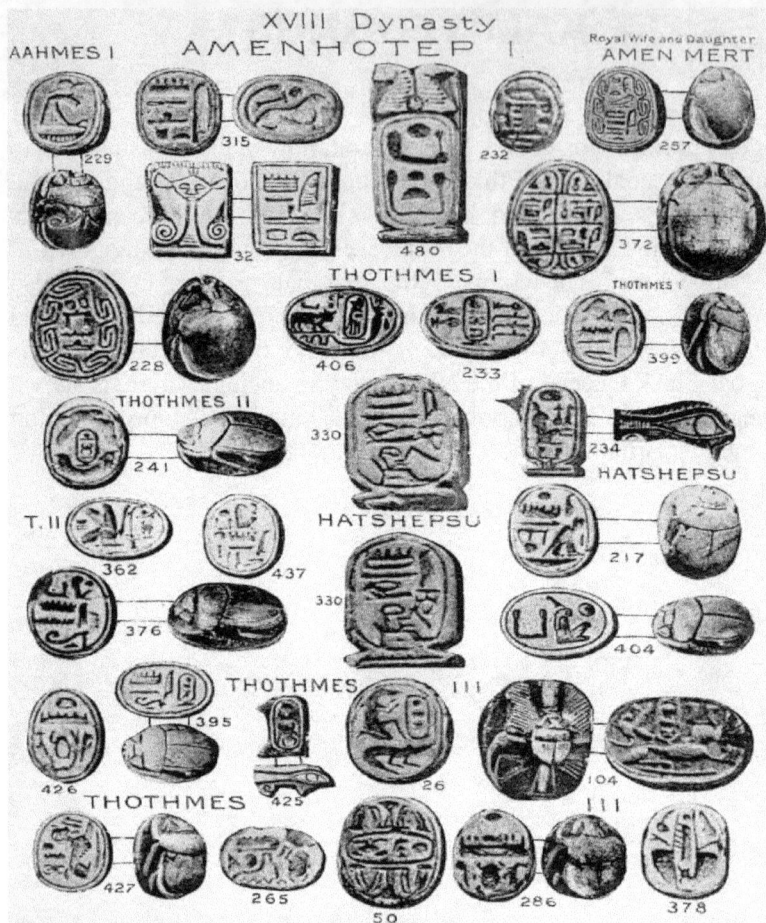

Where are the Kamite Kings Illustration. Early New Kingdom Scarabs of Aahmes, Amenhotep I, Thutmose I, Thutmose II, Thutmose III, Hatshepsut and Amen-Mert.

Hatshepsut was the daughter of Thutmose I and great granddaughter of Queen Ahmose-Nefertari. In time, when her legitimacy was questioned, she relished in, and boasted of, this great black ancestral heritage. In her own right, she was a powerful Egyptian, and thus African, Queen who surrounded herself with a number of loyal and favorite men. Devoted to her father Thutmose I, she was first married to Thutmose II. At his death, she seized the throne from her half-brother and Co-Regent, Thutmose III. She ruled as Pharaoh, proclaimed herself "Son of Ra," the Sun God, wore a beard and dressed in male attire. This revolutionary act, unheard of previously, challenged male dominance, and she later paid for such daring.

WHERE ARE THE KAMITE KINGS?

The female Pharaoh was an able administrator who improved industry and agriculture. The nation prospered during her reign. Her architect Senmut built the famous *Deshret* (Deir el-Bahari) funerary temple at Thebes, a remarkable work of architecture, and favorite of modern visitors to that ancient land. In seven months, Senmut quarried two obelisks at Aswan, transported and erected them at the renown Temple of Karnak. This was the home of the Theban Triad - deities Amen, the Sun God, his wife Mut, the earth Goddess, and their son Khonsu, the Moon God.

Queen Hatshepsut also had a tomb built in the Valley of the Kings. She intended a half-mile long tunnel linking her mortuary temple with this tomb. This other "revolutionary" act also won her disfavor with subsequent Kings. Later deposed by Thutmose III, he desecrated her tomb, destroyed her statues and defaced her images and inscriptions.

Thutmose III was a splendid warrior Pharaoh who reigned for a total of 54 years, including the span of Hatshepsut's reign. At Megiddo, he crushed an uprising of Syrian Kings called the Kadesh Confederacy. During his many campaigns in Palestine and Syria, Egyptian power was permanently established there. Libya and Nubia were also subdued and gold tribute poured in from these and many quarters. Amenhotep II was the next powerful Pharaoh. He reigned for 26 years. During the reign of Amenhotep III, Son of Thutmose IV and great-grandson of Thutmose III, Kemet reached the pinnacle of its "golden age." His reign lasted for 38 years.

These imperial Pharaohs were followed by Amenhotep IV, whom some called a pacifist and heretic. This son of Amenhotep III and Queen Tiy, changed his name to Akhenaten and ushered in a religious revolution. He abolished the state God Amen and religious beliefs, adopted the Sun or "Aten" as the new religious symbol and composed beautiful and naturalistic hymns to his deity. Some moderns have hailed him as the first naturalist, for recognizing and praising the science of nature manifested in the sun's bounty.

FREDERICK MONDERSON

The XIXth Dynasty
From Monuments   From Manetho

Sosirkhopiruri-Sotpuniri Harmhabi
     Usirkhopiruri Miamon Siti II   Miamon Minephtah
Manpanhitiri Ramisu I   Manmiri-Sotpuniri
                                         Amendesisu Haq Osit
Manmaitri Siti I. Miamon   Khuniri-sotpuniri Siptah
Usirmaitri Ramisu II. Miamon   Minephtah
Baniri Miamon Minephtah   Hotpuhimait Minephah

Akhenaton or Ikhnaton moved the capital from Thebes to a newly created city, Akhenaten, today's Tell el-Amarna. This followed in wake of flagrant attacks on the Theban or Amen Priesthood and was not accepted lightly. After 18 years they deposed him. Next, Tut-Ankh-Aton, whose name was later changed to Tut-Ankh-Amon, the boy King, reigned for 10 years. In *Nile Year* 6162, or 1922 of our era, Howard Carter and Lord Carnarvon discovered Tutankhamon's tomb in the Valley of the Kings. Two life-size statues of the young Pharaoh were found in his internment. On display in the Cairo Museum, both these replicas show him as a black Pharaoh. Aye succeeded him and the dynasty ended with Horemheb, a military general who seized power and ruled for 28 years. King Tut's statues again reinforced a crucial anthropological and ethnological fact of history. In this regard, surviving documents, in graphic and colorful depiction lend evidence to the debate on 'Who were the Egyptians?' This important dynasty is shown similarly as "coal Black Ethiopians." However, Chancellor Williams, in his book, *Destruction of Black Civilization*: *Great Issues of a Race 4500 B.C. to 2000 A.D.*, has argued that though the dynasty began as black, military alliances and political marriages with Asiatic princesses and importation of their women to be concubines, caused the dynasty to be "whitened." Nevertheless, by Tutankhamon's time, well, his skin color is evident. Interestingly, to the millions who visit the Cairo Museum, and pass these statues as they visit the hall with the young King's treasures, these visitors only see the gold and jewelry, nothing else. Yet still, we can at least see technology or craftsmanship in the art of working in precious resources.

WHERE ARE THE KAMITE KINGS?

The XIXth Dynasty was begun by Ramses I, who reigned for 2 years and followed by Seti I, who reigned for 14 years. Seti I's successor was his son Rameses II, one of the most colorful Pharaohs, who reigned for 67 years. On one of his campaigns in Syria he was ambushed at Kadesh. Invoking his ancestral Gods, he rallied his forces, escaped, triumphed and emerged victorious. The sequence of events became an important propaganda display adorning many of his wonderful architectural works at the Temples of Abu Simbel, the Ramesseum and at Karnak. This great Egyptian and African military genius, architect, administrator, statesman, father and husband, was followed by Merneptah, his 13th son, who reigned for 20 years. In the XXth Dynasty, the important Kings were Rameses III, 31 years; Ramses IX, 18 years; and Rameses XI, 31 years.

Throughout the New Kingdom, the King headed the civil and religious bureaucracy. According to David O'Connor (1989), he administered the conquered territories through Governors of the Southern and Northern Lands. He also presided over the Army, Royal Domain, and had to be concerned about dynastic continuity. His lineage included the Crown Prince and relatives.

The Civil Government was administered by the Northern and Southern Viziers or Prime Ministers. They were Overseers of Treasury, Granaries of Upper and Lower Kemet and of Cattle. There were also a Civil Bureaucracy, Judiciary, and Police. Village Chiefs, Town Mayors and Councils that handled local affairs. The army had a Commander, Two Deputies, and General Officers. The Religious Government had an Overseer of the Prophets, High Priest, and a Priesthood Bureaucracy. The Royal Domain had Chancellor or Chief Steward, Chamberlain and its Bureaucracy.

The Priesthood was the most powerful institution in all Kemet during the New Kingdom. From the earliest times, the King was in theory, man and God. However, unable to be in more than one place, he relied on the Priesthood to conduct the regular religious worship and rituals. Over time their power expanded and that body's functions and influence steadily increased. The Priesthood was responsible for training the administrative bureaucracy for the civil government. This body also controlled education and had a monopoly on teaching astronomy, medicine, mathematics, astrology, architecture and the arts. They were in themselves a bureaucracy, a social institution, as the wealth of the priesthood throughout the land became enormous.

Where are the Kamite Kings Photo. Top portion of a statue of Hatshepsut on the Upper Terrace of her Deir el Bahari Temple.

The main sites of religious or priestly concentration with their temples and other wealth were Annou, On (Hebrew) or (Greek) Heliopolis, Memphis, Abydos and Thebes. The respective deities worshiped at these religious centers were Ra at Heliopolis, Ptah at Memphis, Osiris at Abydos and Amen at Karnak, Thebes. Religious syncretism found Ra being fused with Amen, as Amen-Ra, during the heyday of the New Kingdom. Some scholars believe it was the Middle Kingdom. We also see Amon being fused with Min as Amon-Min. In all this, the wealth of the various priesthoods, whose adherents were in the ascendancy, was enormous. Petrie's (1923) commentary is that, "Each great God owned estates and lands, flocks and herds, vineyards, vegetable gardens, boats and ships, slaves, soldiers and sailors, and the value of the offerings made to Amon of Thebes and Osiris of Abydos was well-nigh incalculable." To further underscore this wealth, examples are given here of two pharaohs who made gifts to the Amen Priesthood.

WHERE ARE THE KAMITE KINGS?

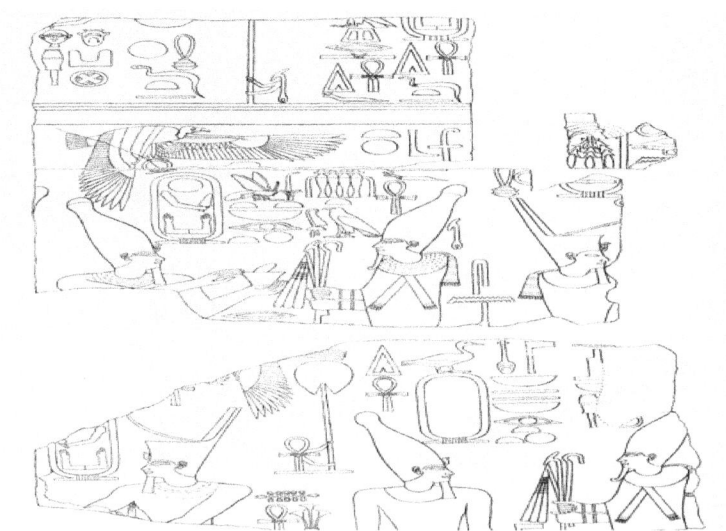

Where are the Kamite Kings Illustration.
Illustrations from the Temple of Amenhotep I at Abydos in *Abydos* Part I by W.M. Flinders Petrie with a Chapter by A.E. Weigall.

Where are the Kamite Kings Photo. Diminutive statue of God Bes, the Court at Hathor's Temple at Dendera. Notice his necklace, some say comprises 100 penises.

FREDERICK MONDERSON

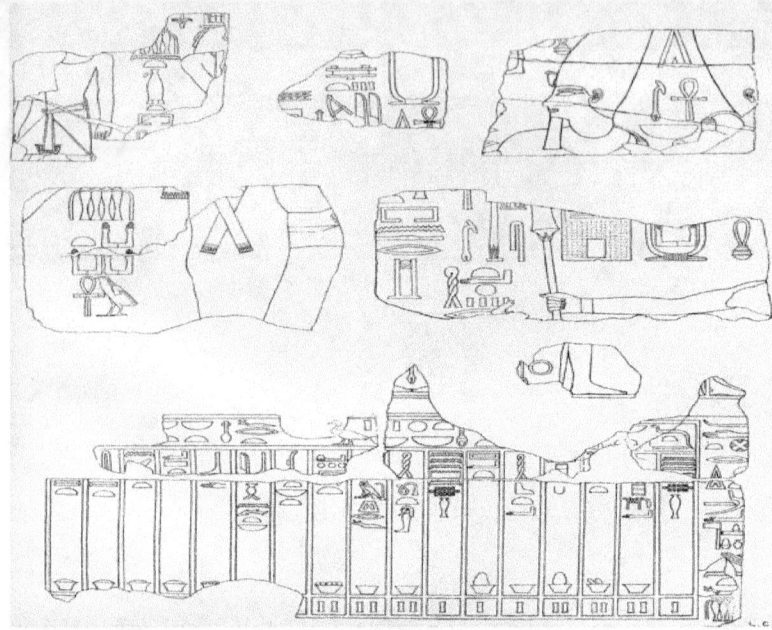

Where are the Kamite Kings Illustration. More illustrations from the Temple of Amenhotep I at Abydos in *Abydos* Part I by W.M. Flinders Petrie with a Chapter by A.E. Weigall (1902).

First, Thutmose III, records in his *Annals* that he gave, by way of the Priesthood, to: "Amon 1,578 slaves, male and female from Syria, four cows of a special breed, three cities in Syria and all the annual taxes taken from them, masses of gold, silver, lapis-lazuli, copper, bronze, lead, ochres, etc., for use in the temple buildings, 1,000 geese for offerings, fields, gardens, corn lands, bulls, poultry, incense, wine, fruit, bread, honey, etc., and increased existing endowments and established new festivals to provide the necessary offerings." This may very well be one annual offering.

Today's Black Church, a mainstay of African-American culture, similarly elicits support from its members, even if not on such a stupendous scale. These institutions also need to parlay this significance into the areas of political, intellectual and nationalist parlance activism.

WHERE ARE THE KAMITE KINGS?

Where are the Kamite Kings Illustration. Osiride statues of Thutmose I in Karnak.

Second, the *Harris Papyrus* I, now in the British Museum, lists offerings the XXth Dynasty Pharaoh, Rameses III, made to the Temple of Amon at Thebes. These offerings included: "2,844,347 loaves of fine bread, 42,030 jars of wine, 304,093 measures of incense, 110,000 jars of oil, 310 jars of honey, 3,100 measures of wax, 559,000 loaves of fruit, 15,500 bundles of figs, 15,110 papyrus sandals, 75,400 bricks of salt, 449,500 measures of dum palm, 3,029 head of cattle, 126,250 geese, pigeons, etc., 441,000 fishes, 770,200 bundles of vegetables, 1,975,800 bunches of flowers, 18,252 *teben* of fine gold and silver, 112,132 *teben* of copper, lead, and tin, and 18,214 *teben* of precious stones."

FREDERICK MONDERSON

The employees of the Temple of Amon in the reign of Rameses III numbered 62,626, which show that the cult of this God operated very much as nigh a "social system." When one considers the other religious sites throughout the country, no more needs to be said. Every Pharaoh regularly made offerings of some sort. The priests were deputized to act in his name since he could not visit all the temples.

Where are the Kamite Kings Illustration. The proper behavior to approach the King.

This therefore underscores religiosity as being sort of natural to ancient Egyptian and African expression.

The functions of the priest were to worship and ritualize the Gods. They also had to help in training the administrators of the state. They collected temple taxes and tribute, mummified the dead and officiated at funerals and festivals.

WHERE ARE THE KAMITE KINGS?

Where are the Kamite Kings Illustration. Temples of Amenhotep I and Thutmose III at Abydos in *Abydos* Part I by W.M. Flinders Petrie with a Chapter by A.E. Weigall (1902).

The grades of priests begin with the Pharaoh who was High Priest. Next was the Kheri-Heb or "Possessor of the Book." He was very knowledgeable, wore the leopard skin, and performed the "Opening of the Mouth Ceremony" on the deceased. Others poured libation and still others recited texts for the rites. They buried the dead of their order, provided coffins, ushabti figures, scarabs, and other miscellaneous objects. They also painted and decorated the coffins and tombs.

FREDERICK MONDERSON

Funerary practices and religious observances formed the psychological profile of the human personality. Accordingly, there were three entities to the personality, the *Ka*, or *Double*, the *Ba* and *Khu* or *Luminous*. Maspero (1926: 128) was very instrumental in delineating the nature of these psychological features of the human personality. He notes that the *Ka* or *Double* was attached to the visible part of the body during life. Further that: "The *ka* was a replica of the body, of a substance less dense, a colored but ethereal projection of the individual; the ka of a child would reproduce the child, that of a woman the woman, that of a man the man, each of them feature for feature. Then there was the *ba,* the soul represented in the form of a bird, sometimes with a human head. There was also the *khu* or *luminous* and one or more other entities perhaps of less importance ...."

Even more, Maspero (1926: 128) continued: "The existence of the *ka* depended on the body, and to save that from destruction was the object of the survivors. By the process of drying and embalming, the body then could prolong its existence for ages, while by means of prayers and offerings they saved the *double*, the *soul*, and the *luminous* from the second death, and procured for them all that was necessary for prolonged existence. The *double* scarcely quitted the place where the mummy dwelt; and the *soul* and the *luminous* left it to follow the Gods, but they always returned to it as a traveler returns home .... The tomb's decoration thus addressed the needs of each. The first lived in the *Fields of Reeds* in the netherworld. Another remained in the tomb and was dependent for its survival on offerings from the world of the living, mainly the Priests. The third was able to leave the tomb by day and enjoy the light. Thus, the arrangements the Egyptian made on earth for his afterlife were not extra precautionary measures in case he failed to gain access to the plentiful Fields of Reeds in the netherworld, but were absolutely necessary for the survival of the different entities of his personality."

In their roles, the Priests had become expert at mummification of the body. Importantly, during the XVIII Dynasty, in this process, the: "brain was removed through the nose, and the viscera were packed with linen smeared with resin and resinous material was applied to the surface of the corpse to preserve it and wads of linen were placed under the eyelids."

WHERE ARE THE KAMITE KINGS?

After two thousand years of cultural growth, the New Kingdom stood ready to take ancient Kamite culture one step further. In this process the most important unifying factor was the religious beliefs of the people. This was carried to greater heights on the eastern bank of the Nile River at Thebes. From the earliest times this area was called *Waset*. Here the glory of Kemet dwelt!

The Nile regulated the lives of the inhabitants of this land, along the river, by its annual and continuous, yet unchanging pattern. It also shaped the religious beliefs that explained the Egyptian/Kamite cosmos and worldview. Accordingly, their world was created by supernatural beings that were in the heavenly bodies. "Atum, who created himself out of himself on the top of a hill that emerged from the eternal ocean, brought forth four children, Shu and Tefnut, Keb and Nut."

Of these children of Atum: "Keb was the God of earth and Nut the Goddess of sky. They made four children Osiris, Isis, Seth and Nephthys. Osiris and Isis had a son named Horus. The sun also had a profound impact on the inhabitants of Egypt. At different sites the cult had many forms."

The City of *On* (Heliopolis) was an early center of religion and learning. Here the Sun God was known as Ra (the Solar Orb) or Atum (the Setting Sun). Under one priesthood he was Khepra (the Beetle) and under another Horus (the Brilliant Plumed Hawk). During the Middle Kingdom and the New Kingdom, Thebes triumphed as the center of political, religious and cultural dominance. The Theban Priesthood became wealthy and the local God Amen or Amon or Amun was merged with the Sun God Ra. Amen became the Solar God, the King of the Gods, the Great God, Amen-Ra.

The *Harris Papyrus*, written during the reign of Rameses III, lists the wealth of this Priesthood. They possessed, Petrie (1923) wrote, "over 5,000 divine statues, more than 81,000 slaves, vassals and servants, well over 421,000 head of cattle, 433 garden orchards, 691,334 acres of land, 83 ships, 46 building yards and 65 cities and towns." Thus, it is clear how influential the Priesthood became in the lives of these ancient Africans in Egypt. Religion and the priests were thus considered King makers.

Where are the Kamite Kings Illustration. Decorated limestone sepulchral stele of Sebek-hotep, a scribe of the wine cellar and his sister Tchauf, priestess of Hathor. XVIIIth Dynasty, now in the British Museum from E.A.W. Budge's *The Mummy* (1925).

The art of the New Kingdom is reflected in its reliefs, paintings and sculptures. The art is considered a final development of the Classical Kamite/Egyptian style, begun in the Old Kingdom and grown up in the Middle Kingdom. There were many original themes, much vitality, energy and mature art. They show rural life, fishing, fowling, hunting and funeral scenes. Also, farming and reaping of the harvest are represented. Much of this art decorated tombs of Kings and nobles where the crafts and craftsmen plying their trades were depicted on the interior walls.

WHERE ARE THE KAMITE KINGS?

Carpentry as an industry produced beds, chairs, headrests and chests. Craftsmen made draughts-boards, scribes' palettes, statues and even staffs. Other professions are shown. These include leather workers making sandals, shields for the military, and quivers for arrows. Brick-makers used molds to mix earth with straw and water to form bricks. Also, persons are shown weaving and making baskets.

Rope making and bee-keeping were also shown. Children's games are included. The subjects were depicted jumping, spinning around in a circle and balancing. Adults are shown in mock battles, throwing darts at a target, as well as wrestling. Banquets were well attended with much food, gaiety and music. The musical instruments included harps, lyres, single or double-pipe flutes and tambourines. Dancers are shown clapping and these themes help to round out the good times.

The funerary scenes depict sailing and transport ships with mourners. Other scenes show the plucking and grilling of geese and other birds. Also shown are workers baking bread and making beer, agricultural scenes and animal husbandry, as well as offering bearers and offering lists.

The cultural developments of the New Kingdom include full development of the writing system. There were 22 alphabetic signs. There were generally no C, Q, X, or Z as in our alphabet, though other signs doubled for some of these. In all, there were more than 600 signs in the language, which the ancients called (*Mwd Ntr*) *Medu Netcher*, but the Greeks, Hieroglyphics. The other systems of writing were Hieratic (script) and Demotic, used by the commoners.

The priests taught writing, geography, astronomy, music, law, medicine, mathematics and agriculture. Their scholars also wrote many books on these subjects. The earliest science book on surgery was known. It mentions the brain controls the limbs. They knew that an injury to this organ paralyzes the limbs. Rules of arithmetic based on the decimal system were known. So too were the beginnings of algebra, and both plane and solid geometry, were taught and utilized in building construction.

Trade with Syria, Palestine, Crete, Punt, and especially Nubia was extensive. Wheat, gold, wares, ideas, and linen were exported. Ivory, cedar wood, tapestries and linen were also imported. Copper mining, stone quarrying, and bronze making were important industries. The religious drama of Osiris' life, death, burial and resurrection was centered at Abydos and remained fruitful, yet independent of all other religious practices. And so, African culture through Kemet enlightened the world!

The enduring art of Kemet is reflected in its architecture. Not only was the subject of architecture taught in schools, but Kamite craftsmen, architects and engineers built tombs, palaces, temples and raised obelisks. They also erected military as well as civil and domestic structures. In the Old and Middle Kingdoms, the Pharaoh built pyramids to be interred. Their officials and other nobles built mastaba tombs close to the rulers' resting places. These, however, were vulnerable to tomb robbers. Such vulnerability led the Pharaohs of the New Kingdom to build tombs tunneled into the hills of the Valley of the Kings and also for their ladies in the Valley of the Queens. Equally too, there was a Valley of the Nobles and also a Valley of the Artisans, or those who built and decorated tombs and other social, civil and national projects. These final resting places, during the New Kingdom, were generally at Thebes in Upper Kemet/Egypt. Thutmose I was the first pharaoh to build his tomb in the Valley of the Kings.

The tombs of officials of the New Kingdom provide important sources of knowledge. They supply the most detailed look at daily life, religious and social beliefs and practices of these ancient Africans. The tombs of the cemeteries at Thebes were scattered among a number of sites. At Sheikh Abd-el-Qurna, the higher slopes were reserved for the important officials, while the lower slopes were for lesser officials. Minor officials were also buried at Dira Abu-el-Naga. The sites of el-Khokha and el-Assasif had quality stone and they replaced the other crowded and more popular sites. In the Ramesside Period of the XIXth and XXth Dynasties, the poorer tombs were also located at Deir el-Medina.

These tombs all shared the same general characteristics of layout. The tomb's public area had a court, two halls, and a shrine or cult

WHERE ARE THE KAMITE KINGS?

room. The court was either totally cut into the face of the mountain, or was partially cut into the rock. It was partly constructed of mud brick, and often its walls were cased with stone or mud-brick.

The owner and his family were represented at an offering table or in adoration before the Gods. There were rock cut statues of the owner and his family. The tomb's ceilings were flat and decorated. Those of Senmut (tomb No. 71) and Amenemhat (tomb No. 82) were decorated with scenes of the underworld or afterlife.

Some tombs had pillars in the public area, additional rooms and niches in the walls. Tomb decorations showed the owner's accomplishments and his efforts to acquire justice and his hopes to survive in the next world. The deceased hoped people would continually give offerings at the tomb.

The most far-reaching architectural accomplishments, however, were the temples constructed at the holy sites of Thebes, Abydos, and Abu Simbel. Present temples at Kom Ombo, Edfu, Dendera, and Philae were built during the later Greco-Roman Period, though they replaced earlier temples on these sites considered sacred from the beginning of Kamite history. Obelisks erected at Karnak and at Luxor were splendid quarrying, transportation and architectural feats. The Great Temple of Amon at Karnak and the Temple of Amon at Luxor are masterpieces. The Great Temple of Amon at Karnak is a huge complex of buildings, built over a two-thousand-year period, and considered a museum of ancient Kemetic art and architecture.

FREDERICK MONDERSON

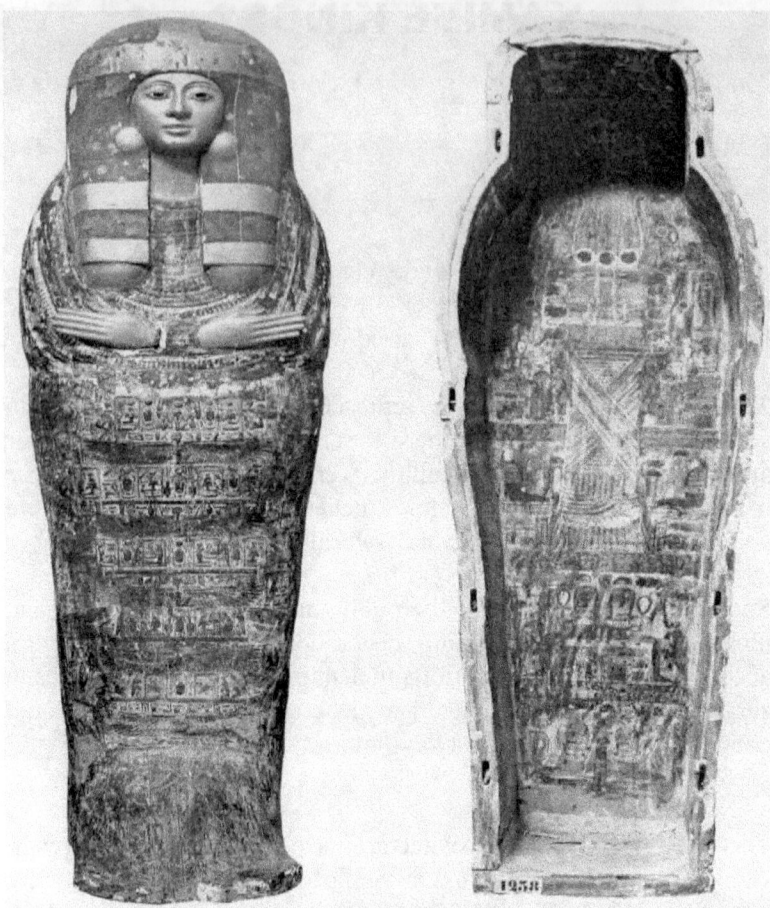

Where are the Kamite Kings Illustration. Top and bottom coffin of D'Ast-m-Kheb with its illustrated interior.

The Karnak site was begun with a Pavilion of Sesostris I, of the XIIth Dynasty. Its walls were made of fine limestone. They contained beautiful reliefs minutely and precisely done. There is, however, the belief that this religious site goes back to the beginning of dynastic rule.

The modern approach to the Karnak religious complex is from the west along an *Avenue of Sphinxes* thru the *First Pylon* built by the XXVth Nubian Dynasty pharaohs. The pylon is a huge stone tower sloping inward from the base. It entrances into a *Great Court* or *Court of the Bubastites*, built by XXII Dynasty pharaohs, that covers a massive area of 8,919 square meters. In this *Court* is a *Shrine of*

WHERE ARE THE KAMITE KINGS?

Seti II dedicated to Amen, Mut and Khonsu, the Theban Triad, and opposite is a *Temple of Rameses* III.

The *Second Pylon*, built by Rameses II gives entrance into the massive *Hypostyle Hall* with its 134 columns. The 12 center columns were erected by Amenhotep III, of the Eighteenth Dynasty, while the other columns were begun by Seti I and completed and decorated by his son Rameses II, of the Nineteenth Dynasty.

The *Hypostyle Hall* is the fruit of Kemetic power and wealth, art and architectural creativity, as well as one of the most massive of human constructions. It covers an area of 4,983 square meters and the roof is supported by the 134 columns arranged in 16 rows.

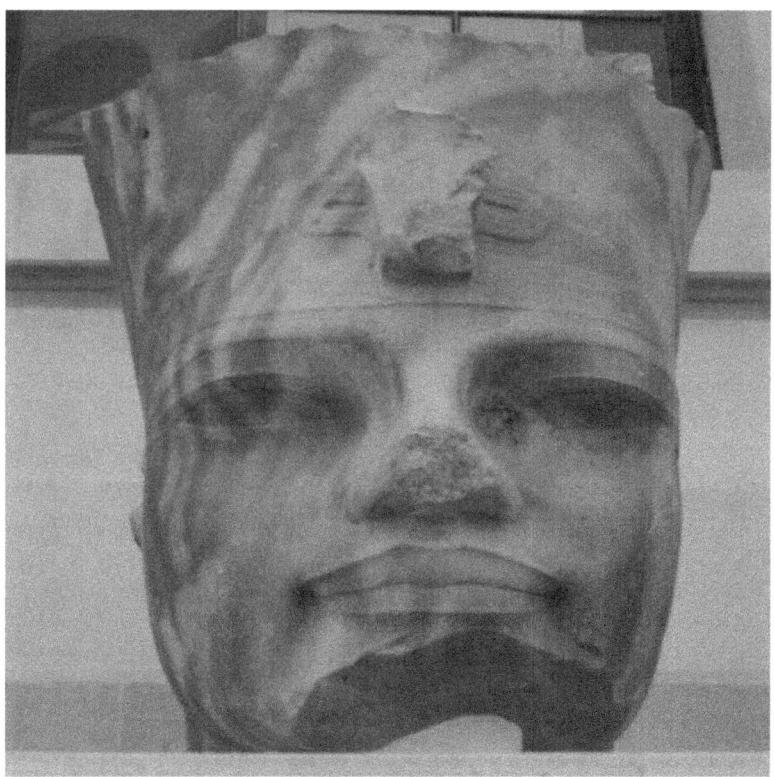

Where are the Kamite Kings Photo. Monumental image of Amenhotep III in the British Museum.

FREDERICK MONDERSON

The *Third Pylon* was built by Amenhotep III. The *Fourth Pylon* was built by Thutmose I and his daughter Queen Hatshepsut. The King erected four obelisks and his daughter erected two pairs of these "needles." The *Fifth Pylon* was also erected by Thutmose I. Thutmose III built the Sixth Pylon and the Hall of Records. The most important feature of the *Hall of Records* are the two granite pillars, one bearing the Lotus of Upper Kemet and the other the Papyrus of Lower Kemet, signifying a united country. Behind is the *Sanctuary*. As the visitor enters the temple. this is the reverse of how the temple was built. Anciently, pylons were constructed as follows - 4, 5, 8, 6, 7 9, 10, 2 and 1.

The *Annals of Thutmose* III are before the outer walls of the *Sanctuary*. They record his 18 military campaigns against the Syrians mostly. This King also built the *Festival Hall of Thutmose III*, which is 44 meters wide and 16 meters deep, and lies beyond the Sanctuary. This rectangular *Akh Menu* is supported by 20 columns in two rows in the inside, and 32 square pillars on the outside of this structure, enclosed by a surrounding wall. There is a Sacred Lake and Seventh, Eighth, Ninth and Tenth Pylons, on a north-south axis as leading to the Temple of Luxor to the South. In addition, there were some 20 other temples and buildings at Karnak including the temples of Mut, Khonsu and the war God Montu.

The Temple of Luxor was built by Pharaoh Amenhotep III. It has a picture of his beautiful black Queen Tiy (Tiye). While not as large, its majestic architecturally as Karnak and sometimes called the "grand lodge" of esoteric and metaphysical teachings. It serves as a lasting testimony to ancient Kamite science, art and architecture.

This then, represents the Nile Valley African antecedents that all people of African ancestry are heirs to. Reflecting upon such a majestic past can buoy any intellectual quest of urban as well as rural youth, in efforts to gain strength in the struggle of upliftment. The Greeks and Romans served a similar purpose for the west. So, whether medicine, mathematics, architecture, warfare, political adroitness, navigation, art or religion, Africans globally can claim this heritage and its powerful legacy to uplift the human spirit seeing refuge in the panorama of history. Let us not forget Dr. Diop' admonition to connect the Nile Valley culture Egypt and the Sudan with the history of continental Africa.

WHERE ARE THE KAMITE KINGS?

XXth Dynasty

Nakhutusi-Miamon, Usirmari-miamon
Ramses III. Haq-Notir-Onu-Usirmari-Sot punri
Ramses IV. Mairi-Miamon, Usirmari-sotpuniri
Ramses V. Amonhikhopshuf-Miamon, Usirmari-Sakupirniri
Ramses VI. Amonhikhopshuf-Haq-nutir-onu, Nibmari-miamon
Ramses VII. Atamon-Haq-Nutir-onu, Usirmari-mia-mon-Sotpuniri
Ramses VIII. Sithikhopshuf-miamon, Usirmari-khunia-mon Maritumu-miamon
Ramses IX. Siphtah, Sakha-nini-miamon
Ramses X. Miamon, Nofir-keuri-sopuniri
Ramses XI. Amenhikhopshuf, Khopirmari-sotpuniri
Ramses XII. Khamosit-Haq-Nutir-onu-miamon, Man Mari-sotpuniphtar

Where are the Kamite Kings Illustration. The above is the order of the Kings of the XXth Dynasty, as Maspero proposed in his *History of Egypt and Assyria* (1904).

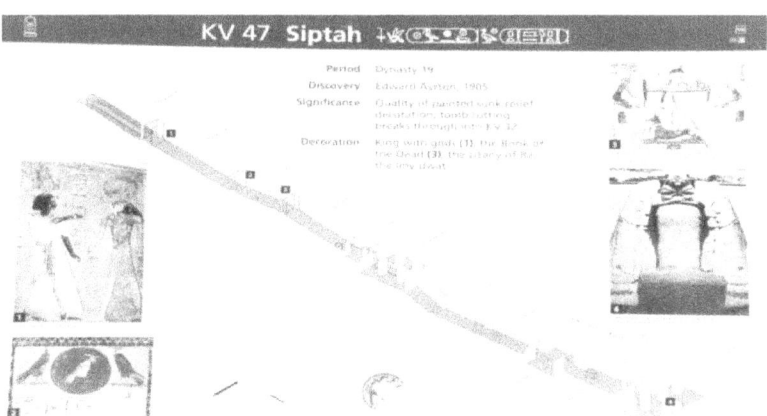

Where are the Kamite Kings Photo. Valley of the Kings. Tomb of Siptah. Illustration depicts the layout and location of the various features of the interior. Significance: Quality of painted sunk relief decoration and tomb cutting breaks through into KV 32. Decoration showing *King with Gods*, the *Book of the Dead*, the *Litany of Ra* and the *Imw-dwat*.

FREDERICK MONDERSON

In looking back at the significant finds of mummies at Deir el Bahari and in the tomb of Amenhotep II, we are fortunate that the art of mummification had developed to such a high level in the New Kingdom. Further and indicated previously, the *British Association for the Advancement of Science* emerged as an institution where much information of an important historical nature was presented, debated, and afterwards generally disseminated. Their historical studies were particularly relevant to much of the cultural records of Egypt and elsewhere on the African continent. Therefore, in an age of political correction, that institution can seem a vanguard agent in the age of cultural and intellectual imperialism, vigorously accumulating records of the ancient artifactual remains.

One such subject of significant relevance was the art of mummification as sketched by G. Elliot Smith, the famed anatomist, essentially based at the University of Manchester. In a *Report to the British Association* at Dublin (1908: 847) Elliot Smith presented the following paper on "The History of Mummification in Egypt."

"In pre-dynastic times in Egypt it was the custom to bury the bodies of the dead in the sand, roughly wrapped in skins, linen, or matting. As the result of the dryness of the soil, and the exclusion of the air by the close adaptation of the sand to the body, desiccation often occurred before any putrefactive changes set in, and the corpse thus became preserved in a permanent form."

"This phenomenon must have been perfectly familiar to the prehistoric Egyptians themselves, for we have abundant evidence of the fact that plundering of graves was common even at this early period. Moreover, the people of later times must have learnt for themselves how excellently nature preserved the corpses of their predecessors, when they came to make tombs for themselves in long-forgotten pre-dynastic graveyards."

"Thus, the idea must have naturally presented itself to the Egyptian people, perhaps in early dynastic times, to attempt to secure by art the preservation of their dead, which was no longer attained naturally, once it became the custom to put the body into a coffin or a rock-cut chamber, because the air thus buried with the corpse favored putrefaction. The Egyptians would be encouraged in these attempts, to which they no doubt were prompted by their religious

WHERE ARE THE KAMITE KINGS?

beliefs no less than by the natural inclination of all mankind to preserve the remains of those dear to them, by the help which the properties of their soil and climate afforded them, as well as by their knowledge of the properties of the preservative salts, found ready at hand in such abundance in Egypt, and of the resins obtained from neighboring lands, with the properties of which they had been familiar even in pre-dynastic times. In this way the origin of the idea, the reason for attempting to put it into practice, and the means for doing so become intelligible to us, and render it more than ever improbable that the custom of embalming could have been imported into Egypt from some foreign land, where none of these reasons for the initiation of the practice holds good. We have no exact data to permit us to say exactly when embalming was first attempted in Egypt. Although the earliest bodies certainly known to have been embalmed are of the period of the tenth dynasty (found at Sakkara by Mr. Quibell), there is some slight evidence to suggest that some form of mummification was attempted in the times of the earliest pyramid-builders."

"By the time of the Middle Empire the general technique of the operation had attained the stage, which in its main features was the conventional procedure for the succeeding two thousand years. But it was in the time of the New Empire that the process of mummification reached its highest development. Then for the first time the embalmers learnt how to remove the brain and pack the cranium, and put into practice the elaborate and difficult measures for restoring to the dead body a greater semblance to the form it had had in life; so that the statue of the deceased, which had been an essential part of the furniture of the tomb in earlier times, when the body either underwent corruption or was imperfectly preserved, became superfluous, and was no longer put into the tomb."

"Further stages in the evolution of the art of embalming were followed by a rapid decline."

The **Blessings** are introduced in order to supply words of encouragement to complete this difficult and challenging project.

FREDERICK MONDERSON

Wilson (1901: 107-111) supplies an "ADDRESS TO THE GODS OF THE UNDERWORLD" from the *Papyrus of Nu* in the British Museum No. 10,477, sheet 24. [THEN SHALL THE HEART WHICH IS RIGHTEOUS AND SINLESS SAY:]

"The overseer of the palace, the chancellor-in-chief, Nu, triumphant, saith: 'Homage to you, O ye Gods who dwell in the Hall of double Maati, I, even I, know you, and I know your names. Let me not fall under your knives of slaughter, and bring ye not forward my wickedness unto the God in whose train ye are; and let not evil Hapi come upon me by your means. Oh, declare ye me right and true in the presence of Neb-er-tcher, because I have done that which is right and true in Ta-mera (Egypt) [Kemet]. I have not cursed God, and let not evil Hapi come upon me through the King who dwelleth in my day. Homage to you, O ye Gods, who dwell in the Hall of double Maati, who are without evil in your bodies, and who live upon right and truth, and who feed yourselves upon right and truth in the presence of the God Horus, who dwelleth in his divine Disk: deliver ye me from the God Baba who feedeth upon the entrails of the mighty ones upon the day of the great judgment. Oh, grant ye that I may come to you, for I have not committed faults, I have not sinned, I have not done evil, I have not borne false witness; therefore, let nothing [evil] be done unto me. I live upon right and truth, and I feed upon right and truth. I have performed the commandments of men [as well as] the things whereat are gratified the Gods; I have made the God to be at peace [with me by doing] that which is his will. I have given bread to the hungry man, and water to the thirsty man, and apparel to the naked man, and a boat to the [shipwrecked] mariner. I have made holy offerings to the Gods, and sepulchral meals to the Khus. Be ye then my delivers, be ye then my protectors, and make ye not accusation against me in the presence of [the great God]. I am clean of mouth and clean of hands; therefore, let it be said unto me by those who shall behold me, 'Come in peace; come in peace,' for I have heard that mighty word which the spiritual bodies (*Sahu*) spake unto the Cat in the House of Hapt-re. I have been made to give evidence before the God Hra-f-ha-f (*i.e.*, he whose face is behind him), and he hath given a decision [concerning me]. I have seen the things over which the Persea tree spreadeth [its branches] within Re-stau. I am he who hath offered up prayers to the Gods and who knoweth their persons. I have come and I have advanced to make the declaration of right and truth, and to set the balance upon what supports it within the region of Aukert.

WHERE ARE THE KAMITE KINGS?

Hail, thou who are exalted upon thy standard, thou lord of the *Atefu* crown, whose name is proclaimed as 'Lord of the winds,' deliver thou me from thy divine messengers who cause dire deeds to happen, and who cause calamities to come into being, and who are without coverings for their faces, for I have done that which is right and true for the Lord of right and truth. I have purified myself and my breast with libations, and my hinder parts with the things, which make clean, and my inner parts have been in the Pool of Right and Truth. There is no single member of mine, which lacketh right and truth. I have been purified in the Pool of the South, and I have rested in the northern city, which is in the Field of the Grasshoppers, wherein the divine sailors of Ra bathe at the second hour of the night and at the third hour of the day. And the hearts of the Gods are gratified (?) after they have passed through it, whether it be by night, or whether it be by day, and they say unto me, 'Let thyself come forward.' And they say unto me, 'Who, then, art thou?' And they say unto me, 'What is thy name?' 'I am he who is equipped under the flowers [and I am] the dweller in his olive tree' is my name. And they say unto me straightway, 'Pass thou on;' and I passed on by thy city to the north of the olive tree. What, then, didst thou see there? I see the leg and the thigh. What, then, didst thou say unto them? Let me see rejoicings in those lands of the Tenkhu. And what did they give unto thee? A flame of fire and a tablet (or Scepter) of crystal. What, then, didst thou do therewith? I buried them by the furrow of Manaat as 'things for the night.' What, then, didst thou find by the furrow of Manaat? Scepter of flint, the name of which is 'Giver of winds.' What, then, didst thou do to the flame of fire and the tablet (or Scepter) of crystal after thou hast buried them? I uttered words over them in the furrow, [and I dug them there from]; I extinguished the fire, and I broke the tablet (or Scepter), and I created a pool of water. 'Come, then,' [they say,] 'and enter in through the door of this Hall of double Maati, for thou knowest us.'

FREDERICK MONDERSON

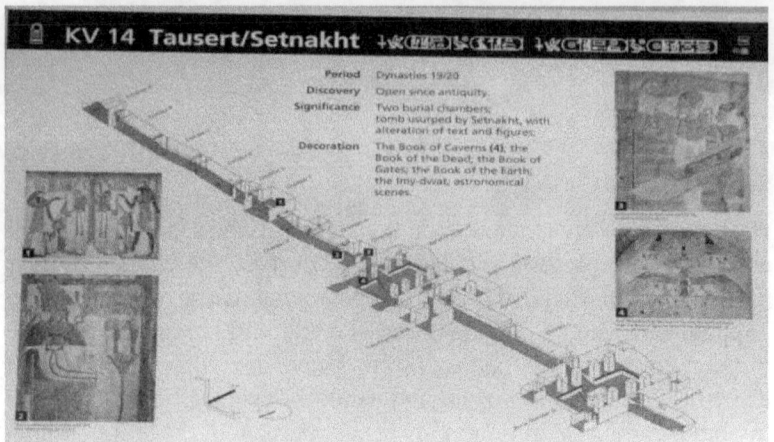

Where are the Kamite Kings Photo. Valley of the Kings. Tomb of Tausert and Setnakht. Significance: Two burial chambers, tomb usurped by Setnakht, with alteration of text and figures. Decoration includes: The *Book of Caverns*, the *Book of the Dead*, the *Book of Gates*, the *Book of the Earth*, the *Imy-dwat* and astronomical scenes.

'We will not let thee enter in through us,' say the bolts of the door, 'unless thou tellest [us] our names.' 'Tongue [of the Balance] of the place of right and truth' is your name. 'I will not let thee enter in by me,' saith the [right] lintel of the door, 'unless thou tellest [me] my name.' 'Balance of the support of right and truth' is thy name. 'I will not let thee enter in by me,' saith the [left] lintel of the door, 'unless thou tellest [me] my name.' ['Balance of wine'] is thy name. 'I will not let thee pass over me,' saith the threshold of this door, unless thou tellest [me] my name.' 'Ox of the God Seb' is thy name. 'I will not open unto thee,' saith the fastening of this door, 'unless thou tellest [me] my name.' 'Flesh of his mother' is thy name. 'I will not open unto thee,' saith the socket of the fastening of the door, 'unless thou tellest me my name.' 'Living eye of the God Sebek, the Lord of Bakhau,' is thy name. 'I will not open unto thee [and] I will not let thee enter in by me,' saith the guardian of the leaf of this door, 'unless thou tellest [me] my name.' 'Elbow of the God Shu when he placeth himself to protect Osiris' is thy name. 'We will not let thee enter in by us,' say the posts of this door, 'unless thou tellest us our names.' 'Children of the uraei-Goddesses' is your name. 'Thou knowest us,' [they say] 'pass on, therefore, by us.' 'I will not let thee tread upon me,' saith the floor of the Hall of double Maati,

WHERE ARE THE KAMITE KINGS?

'because I am silent and I am holy, and because I do not know the name[s] of thy two feet wherewith thou wouldst walk upon me; therefore, tell them to me.' 'Traveler (?) of the God Khas' is the name of my right foot, and 'Staff of the Goddess Hathor' is the name of my left foot. 'Thou knowest me,' [it saith,] 'pass on therefore over me.'"

"'I will not make mention of thee,' saith the guardian of the door of this Hall of double Maati, unless thou tellest [me] my name. 'Discerner of hearts and searcher of the reins' is thy name. 'Now will I make mention of thee [to the God]. But who is the God that dwelleth in his hour? Speak thou it' (*i.e.*, his name). Maau-Taui (*i.e.*, he who keepeth the record of the two lands) [is his name]. 'Who then is Maau-Taui?' He is Thoth. 'Come,' saith Thoth. 'But why has thou come?' 'I have come, and I press forward that I may be mentioned.' 'What now is they condition?' 'I, even I, am purified from evil things, and I am protected from the baleful deeds of those who live in their days; and I am not among them. Nor will I make mention of thee [to the God].' '[Tell me now,] who is he whose heaven is of fire, whose walls [are surmounted by] living uraei, and the floor of whose house is a stream of water? Who is he? I say.' It is Osiris. 'Come forward, then: verily thou shall be mentioned [to him]. Thy cakes [shall come] from the Eye of Ra, and thine ale [shall come] from the Eye of Ra, and the sepulchral meals [which shall be brought to thee] upon earth [shall come] from the Eye of Ra. This hath been decreed for the Osiris, the overseer of the palace, the chancellor-in-chief, Nu, triumphant.'"

FREDERICK MONDERSON

Where are the Kamite Kings Illustration. Queen Aahmes-Nefertari, from a wooden statuette.

(THE MAKING OF THE REPRESENTATION OF WHAT SHALL HAPPEN IN THIS HALL OF DOUBLE MAATI.) THIS CHAPTER SHALL BE SAID [BY THE DECEASED] AFTER HE HATH BEEN CLEANSED AND PURIFIED, AND WHEN HE IS ARRAYED IN APPAREL, AND IS SHOD WITH WHITE LEATHER SANDALS, AND HIS EYES HAVE BEEN PAINTED WITH ANTIMONY, AND [HIS BODY] HATH BEEN ANOINTED WITH UNGUENT OF *ANTI*, AND WHEN HE OFFERETH OXEN, AND FEATHERED FOWL, AND INCENSE, AND CAKES, AND ALE, AND GARDEN HERBS. AND, BEHOLD, THOU SHALT DRAW A REPRESENTATION

WHERE ARE THE KAMITE KINGS?

OF THIS IN COLOR UPON A NEW TILE MOLDED FROM EARTH UPON WHICH NEITHER A PIG NOR OTHER ANIMALS HAVE TRODDEN. AND IF [THOU] DOEST THIS BOOK UPON IT [IN WRITING, THE DECEASED] SHALL FLOURISH, AND HIS CHILDREN SHALL FLOURISH, AND [HIS NAME] SHALL NEVER FALL INTO OBLIVION, AND HE SHALL BE AS ONE WHO FILLETH (*i.e.,* SATISFIETH) THE HEART OF THE KING AND OF HIS PRINCES, AND BREAD, AND CAKES, AND SWEETMEATS, AND WINE, AND PIECES OF FLESH SHALL BE GIVEN UNTO HIM UPON THE ALTAR OF THE GREAT GOD; AND HE SHALL NOT BE TURNED BACK AT ANY DOOR IN AMENTET, AND HE SHALL BE BROUGHT IN ALONG WITH THE KING OF UPPER AND LOWER EGYPT, AND HE SHALL BE IN THE TRAIN OF OSIRIS CONTINUALLY AND REGULARLY FOREVER.

Wilson (1901: 111-12) offers "OF THE FOUR APES" from the *Papyrus of Nu* in the British Museum No. 10,477, sheet 24.

"The overseer of the palace, the chancellor-in-chief, Nu, triumphant, the son of the overseer of the palace, the chancellor-in-chief, Amen-hetep, triumphant, saith: 'Hail, ye four apes who sit in the bows of the boat of Ra, who convey right and truth to Neb-er-tcher, who sit in judgment on my misery and on my strength, who make the Gods to rest contented by means of the flame of your mouths, who offer holy offerings to the Gods and sepulchral meals to the Khus, who live upon right and truth, and who feed upon right and truth of heart, who are without deceit and fraud, and to whom wickedness is an abomination, do ye away with my evil deeds, and put ye away my sin [which deserved stripes upon earth, and destroy ye any evil whatsoever that belongeth unto me], and let there be no obstacle whatsoever that belongeth unto me], and let there be no obstacle whatsoever on my part toward you. Oh, grant ye that I may make my way through the underworld (Amentet), let me enter into Re-stau, let me pass through the hidden pylons of Amentet. Oh, grant that there may be given to me cakes, and ale, and sweetmeats (?), even as [they are given] to the living *khus*, and grant that I may enter in and come forth from Re-stau.'"

FREDERICK MONDERSON

Where are the Kamite Kings Photo. Kings Valley. Sandbags to break sliding earth or debris from wind or when it rains.

"[The four apes make answer, saying], 'Come, then, for we have done away with thy wickedness, and we have put away thy sin, along with the [sin deserving of] stripes which thou [didst commit] upon earth, and we have destroyed [all] the evil which belonged to thee upon the earth. Enter, therefore, into Re-stau, and pass thou through the hidden pylons of Amentet, and there shall be given unto thee cakes, and ale, and sweetmeats (?), and thou shall come forth and thou shall enter in at thou desire, even as do those *khus* who are favored [of the God], and thou shall be proclaimed (or called) each day in the horizon.'"

Wilson (1901: 112-13) "OF THE PRAISE OF THE GODS" from the Tomb of Rameses IV, see Naville, op cit. Bd. I. Bl. 141; Lefebvre, *Tombeau de Rameses* IV, Plate 13.

THE BOOK OF THE PRAISE OF THE GODS OF THE QERTI WHICH A MAN SHALL RECITE WHEN HE COMETH FORTH BEFORE THEM TO ENTER IN TO SEE THE GOD IN THE GREAT TEMPLE OF THE UNDERWORLD.

"And he shall say: 'Homage to you, O ye Gods of the *Qerti*, ye divine dwellers in Amentet! Homage to you, O ye guardians of the doors of the underworld, who keep ward over the God, who bear and proclaim [the names of those who come] into the presence of the God Osiris, and who hold yourselves ready, and who praise

WHERE ARE THE KAMITE KINGS?

[him], and who destroy the Enemies of Ra. Oh, send ye forth your light and scatter ye the darkness [which is about] you, and behold ye the holy and divine Mighty One, O ye who live even as he liveth, and call ye upon him that dwelleth within his divine Disk. Lead ye the King of the North and of the South, (Usr-Maat-Ra-setep-en-Amen), the son of the Sun, Ra-meses-meri-Amen-Ra-heq-Maat), through the doors, may his divine soul enter into your hidden places, [for] he is one beyond you, and he hath shot forth calamities upon the serpent fiend Apep, and he hath beaten down the obstacles [which Apep set up] in Amentet. Thy word hath prevailed mightily over thine enemies, O Great God, who livest in thy divine Disk; thy word hath prevailed mightily over thine enemies, O Osiris, governor of Amentet; thy word hath prevailed mightily over thine enemies in heaven and in earth, O thou King of the North and of the South, (Usr-Maat-Ra-setep-en-Amen), the son of the Sun, (Ra-meses-meri-Amen-Ra-heq-Maat), and over the sovereign princes of every God and of every Goddess, O Osiris, Governor of Amentet; he hath uttered words in the presence [of the God in] the valley of the dead, and he hath gained the mastery over the mighty sovereign princes. Hail, ye doorkeepers (?), hail, ye doorkeepers, who guard your gates, who punish souls, who devour the bodies of the dead, who advance over them at their examination in the places of destruction, who give right and truth to the soul and to the divine *khu*, the beneficent one, the mighty one, whose throne is holy in Akert, who is endowed with soul like Ra and who is praised like Osiris, lead ye along the King of the North and of the South, (Usr-Maat-Ra-setep-en-Amen), the son of the Sun, (Ra-meses-meri-Amen-Ra-heq-maat), unbolt ye for him the doors, and open [ye] the place of his *Qerti* for him. Behold, make ye his word to triumph over his enemies, and indeed let meat-offerings and drink-offerings be made unto him by the God of the double door, and let him put on the *nemes* crown of him that dwelleth in the great and hidden shrine. Behold the image of Heru-khuti (Harmachis), who is doubly true, and who is the divine Soul and the divine and perfect Khu; he hath prevailed with his hands. The two great and mighty Gods cry out to the King of the North and South (Usr-Maat-Ra-setep-en-Maat), they rejoice with him, they sing praises to him [and clap] their hands, they accord him their protection, and he liveth. The King of the North and South (Usr-Maat-Ra-setep-en-Amen), the son of the Sun, (Ra-meses-meri-Amen-Ra-Heq-Maat), saith, 'Open unto me

the gate[s] of heaven, and of earth, and of the underworld, for I am the divine soul of Osiris and I rest in him, and let me pass through their halls. Let [the Gods] sing praises unto me [when] they see me; let me enter and let favor be shown unto me; let me come forth and let me be beloved; and let me go forward, for no defect or failure hath been found clinging unto me.'"

Where are the Kamite Kings Photo. Remains of destroyed or disfigured double statue holding hands.

Where are the Kamite Kings Photo. From the Sphinx Avenue, Luxor Temple before 2019 restoration of standing statues.

WHERE ARE THE KAMITE KINGS?

Where are the Kamite Kings Illustration. Queen Aahmes-Nefertari in her long flowing dress of white, red and blue, as she wears the Queen Mother Crown of Vulture headdress, surmounted by a mortar supporting Uraei wearing Double Crown.

Wilson (1901: 114-15) The "ADORATION OF THE GODS OF THE QERTI" from the *Papyrus of Ptah-mes* (Naville, op. cit., Bd. I, Bl. 142).

FREDERICK MONDERSON

A CHAPTER TO BE RECITED ON COMING BEFORE THE DIVINE SOVEREIGN CHIEFS OF OSIRIS TO OFFER PRAISE UNTO THE GODS WHO ARE THE GUIDES OF THE UNDERWORLD.

"Osiris, the chief scribe and draughtsman, Ptah-mes, triumphant, saith: 'Homage to you, O ye Gods who dwell in the Qerti, ye Gods who dwell in Amentet, who keep ward over the gates of the underworld and are the guardians [thereof], who bear and proclaim [the names of those who come] into the presence of Osiris, who praise him and who destroy the enemies of Ra. Oh, send forth your light and scatter ye the darkness [which is about] you, and look upon the face of Osiris, O ye who live even as he liveth, and praise [ye] him that dwelleth in his Disk, and lead [ye] me away from your calamities. Let me come forth and let me enter in through your secret places, for I am a mighty prince among you, for I have done away with evil there, and I have beaten down the obstacles (?) [which have been set up] in Amentet. Thou hast been victorious over thine enemies, O thou that dwellest in thy Disk; thou hast been victorious over thine enemies, O Thoth, who producest (?) statutes; thou hast been victorious over thine enemies, O Osiris, thou Governor of Amentet, in heaven and upon earth in the presence of the divine sovereign chiefs of every God and of every Goddess; and the food (?) of Osiris, the Governor of Amentet, is in the presence of the God whose name is hidden before the great divine sovereign chiefs. Hail ye guardians of the doors, ye [Gods] who keep ward over their habitations (?), who keep the reckoning and who commit [souls] to destruction, who grant right and truth to the divine soul which is stablished, who are without evil in the abode of Akert, who are endowed with soul even as is Ra, and who are ... as is Osiris, guide ye Osiris the chief scribe, the draughtsman, Ptah-mes, triumphant, open ye unto him the gates of the underworld, and the uppermost part of his estate and his *Qert*. Behold, make [ye him] to be victorious over his enemies, provide [ye him] with the offerings of the God of the underworld, make noble the divine being who dwelleth in the *nemes* crown, the lord of the knowledge of Akert. Behold, stablish ... this soul in right and truth, [and let it become] a perfect soul that hath gained the mastery with its two hands. The great and mighty Gods cry out, 'He hath gotten the victory,' and they rejoice in him, and they ascribe praise unto him with their hands, and they turn unto him their faces. The living one is

WHERE ARE THE KAMITE KINGS?

triumphant, and is even like a living soul dwelling in heaven, and he hath been ordered to perform [his] transformations. Osiris triumphed over his enemies, and Osiris, the chief scribe and draughtsman, Ptah-mes, triumphant, hath gained the victory over his enemies in the presence of the great divine sovereign chiefs who dwell in heaven, and in the presence of the great divine sovereign chiefs who dwell upon the earth.'"

Where are the Kamite Kings Photo. Temple of Dendera. Great Court. The Goddess Hathor, divinity of merriment depicted with broad nose, cow's ears, lips and wearing a necklace.

References

"Abu Simbel: Excavations at the Great Temple." *American Journal of Archaeology* XVI (1913: 113-14).
"Abydos: The Recent Excavations." *American Journal of Archaeology* XVII (1913: 98-99).
"Behen: The Temple of Amenhotep II." *American Journal of Archaeology* XV (1911: 82-83).
ben-Jochannan, Y. *Abu Simbel to Ghizeh: A Guide Book and Manual*. Baltimore, MD: Black Classics Press, 1987.
Breasted, J.H. "The Temple of Soleb: A New Form of Architecture." *American Journal of Archaeology* XIII (1909: 53-54).

FREDERICK MONDERSON

Clarke, Sommers and R. Engelbach. *Ancient Egyptian Construction and Architecture*. New York: Dover Publications, (1930) 1990.

"The Cow of Deir El-Bahari." *American Journal of Archaeology* XII (1908: 214).

"An Entrance into the Lower World at Thebes." *American Journal of Archaeology* XIV (1910: 488).

Erman, Adolf. *Life in Ancient Egypt*. Trans. H. M. Tirard. With a New Introduction by Jon Manchip White. New York: Dover, (1894) 1971.

"Excavations of the Metropolitan Museum." *American Journal of Archaeology* XVII (1913: 97-98).

Iskander, Z. *Pharaonic Egypt*. Cairo: Arab World Printing House, (1975) 1977.

Maspero, Gaston. *Manual of Egyptian Archaeology*. New York: G. Putnam's Sons, 1926.

"Medinet Habu: Excavations in 1913." *American Journal of Archaeology* XX (1916: 359-60).

"Memphis: The Palace of Merenptah." *American Journal of Archaeology* XVII (1918: 75-77).

Petrie, W.M.F. *Religious Life in Ancient Egypt*. London: Constable and Co., 1923.

"The Reign of Amenhotep II." *American Journal of Archaeology* XVI (1912: 561).

"The Scarabs of Amenhotep III." *American Journal of Archaeology* XVIII (1914: 503).

Smith, G.E. "The History of Mummification in Egypt." *Report of the British Association for the Advancement of Science* 1908: 847.

"Tell es-Shibab: An Egyptian Monument." *American Journal of Archaeology* V (1901: 334).

"The Temple of Wady Halfa." *American Journal of Archaeology* XIV (1910: 487).

"Thebes: The Tomb of Queen Thyi." *American Journal of Archaeology* XI (1907: 344-45).

"Thebes: Tomb of Thutmose IV." *American Journal of Archaeology* VII (1903: 362-63).

"Thebes: The Tomb of Thyi." *American Journal of Archaeology* XII (1908: 355).

"Tomb of Amenhotep II." *American Journal of Archaeology* III (1899: 59).

"Tomb of Thutmose." *American Journal of Archaeology* IV (1900: 479).

WHERE ARE THE KAMITE KINGS?

Trigger, B.G., B.J. Kemp, D. O'Connor, and A.B. Lloyd. *Ancient Egypt: A Social History*. New York: Cambridge University Press, (1983) 1989.

Wilson, E. *Egyptian Literature*. New York: The Colonial Press, 1901.

Where are the Kamite Kings Photo. Temple of Dendera. On the roof. The Chapel of Hathor. A frieze depicting the King wearing the Red Crown making adoration to the enthroned Hathor in her shrine. Notice the winged disk overhead and the uraei with their orbs chipped. There are smaller figures wearing the Double Crown offering Sistrums or rattles to both the King and Goddess.

Where are the Kamite Kings Illustration. Ant, wearing the "Bundle Amulet."

FREDERICK MONDERSON

Where are the Kamite Kings Illustration. Top and bottom of coffin of D'Ast-m-Kheb II with excellently picturesque decoration.

11. THE NEW KINGDOM

The XVIIIth Dynasty, *Nile Year* 2668-2945 (c. 1570-1293 B.C.) is somewhat reminiscent of the XIIth Dynasty of the Middle Kingdom, in that bold, vigorous, warlike, creative, colorful and devoutly religious Kings dominated the ancient world-state for nearly three centuries. A significant contribution of this dynasty is the extensive architectural constructions built to propitiate a

WHERE ARE THE KAMITE KINGS?

religious system deeply rooted in Egyptian and other African beliefs and practices. The numerous civic and religious structures that have survived to this age, attest to the great ingenuity of these ancient African Kings and queens. This was indeed a "glorious age" in African history.

Ahmose I, founder of the 18th Dynasty who finally expelled the Hyksos. Founder of the dynasty, his *Suten Bat* and *Son of Ra* Cartouches/Shennus of Aahmose, follows below.

Nebpehtyra, Ahmose I, *Nile Year* 2668-2692 (C. 1570-1546 B.C.) is considered the founder of the new dynasty. He continued the work of his brother Kamose, by expelling the Hyksos and extending the borders of ancient Kemet into Asia.

Where are the Kamite Kings Illustration. Image of Aahmose, found at Abydos by Petrie. Notice his straight beard while he wears the White Crown. A viper is straddled by symbols of Health, Waz Scepter, Ankh or "life," etc.

FREDERICK MONDERSON

Where are the Kamite Kings Illustration. Seated limestone statue of Queen Teta-Shera, ancestress of Aahmes I, founder of the XVIIIth Dynasty, listed No. 22,558 in the British Museum collection and in E.A.W. Budge's *The Mummy* (1925).

Where are the Kamite Kings Photo. Temple of Luxor. "Ramessean Front." In the Procession of "Ascent of the Princes," a Nubian lady emerges from one of the lead cows' head.

WHERE ARE THE KAMITE KINGS?

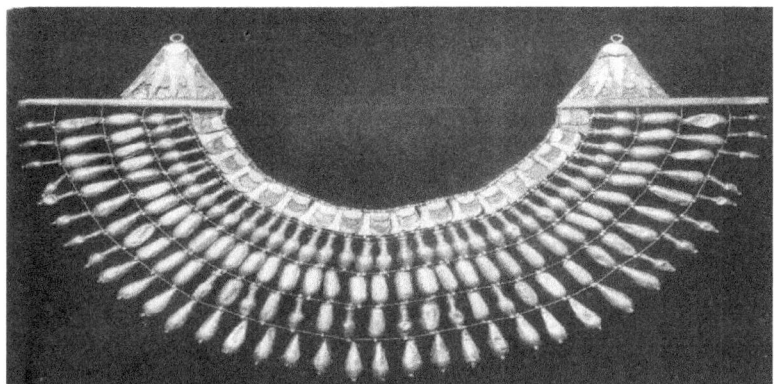

Where are the Kamite Kings Illustration. Gold necklace of Queen Tiye.

Where are the Kamite Kings Illustration. Stele of Tetisheri (Teta-Shera), Aahmes placed in Karnak praising her for saving rulership of the throne in face of the Coup d'état by "Tety the Handsome," while the Thebans were away fighting the Hyksos.

FREDERICK MONDERSON

The royal titulary of this important pharaoh is as follows:

Horus	Uatch-Kheperu
Two Ladies	Tut-Mestu
Horus of Gold	Thes-Taui
Suten Bat	Ra-Neb-Pehti
Son of Ra	Aahmes

Budge identified his name on an axe and jewelry in Cairo. Prisse *Monuments* Pl. 3, Ushabti No. 32,191 in the British Museum, and a coffin in Cairo all have his name. His name is on the *Tablet of Sakkara*, the *Abydos List* No. 66 and the *Second Abydos List* No. 40. Petrie II (1894: 34-35) has supplied more extensive insights into the places of this Pharaoh's identity. His name is found on inscriptions at the Turrah quarries, a brick building at Thebes and at Semneh, where it is also mentioned by Thutmose II. On private monuments, the tomb of Sa-ast at Abydos, and at Thebes, as well as many steles that are now in the Turin Museum bears his name. At El Kab the tombs of Ahmes and Pen-Nekheb mention Aahmose (Aahmes).

An alabaster vase, a blue glaze hawk, another vase and ring bearing his name, are all housed at Glasgow Museum, in England.

His Queen, **Aahmes-Nefertari**, is known from a coffin in Cairo. There is another coffin at Glasgow Museum, with her name. The mummy of the Queen, now destroyed, is also at this Museum. She is known from inscriptions at El Boska, a statue at Karnak and model adze in Turin. Her portrait is also in the British Museum. This particular piece throws significant light on the personality of the famous Queen, ancestress of the XVIIIth Dynasty. Nefertari is considered, "The most venerated person in Egyptian history." As indicated in the portrait, the Queen is pictured "Ethiopian" or "coal black," or with Smith's "black flesh." She is also shown bejeweled and wearing the fashion of the times, the first instance of the Red, White, and Blue historic Tricolor, a theme so significant in flags of modern nations.

If she is known to have been black, and to have married her brother, then he too must have been black. So too must have been Kamose their other brother. Their mother, Teti Sheri and father Seqenenra all reinforce the continuity of the blackness of the Theban

WHERE ARE THE KAMITE KINGS?

population as evidenced in the portrait sculpture of Mentuhotep of the Eleventh Dynasty. Since population shifts in early Africa were not that significant, these "coal black" Africans are easily traceable to the earliest dynastic and pre-dynastic inhabitants of early Kemet.

Where are the Kamite Kings Illustration. Enthroned Pharaoh Amenhotep III in Blue or "War" Crown receives a briefing from a subordinate. Notice uraei above and bound prisoners below.

Nefertari had several children, mostly females for her husband. Meryt-Amen, Sat-Amen Infat, Sat-Kames, and Aah-Hotep who later became a Queen of this dynasty. Their son was Amenhotep I. Aahmes also had other Queens, including Anhapi whose daughter was Hent-Ta-Meh; Teni-Hapi's daughter was Hent-Tamehu; and Kasmat's daughter was Tair.

FREDERICK MONDERSON

Djeserkara, Amenhotep I. *Nile Year* 2687-2714 (C. 1551-1524 B.C.) followed his father Aahmose and continued the work of unification, reorganization and expansion.

Where are the Kamite Kings Illustration. Amenhotep I on a broken slab.

His royal titulary is as follows:

Horus	Ka-Uaf
Two Ladies	_____
Horus of Gold	_____
Suten Bat	Ra-Tcheser-Ka
Son of Ra	Amen-hetep

His name is on a limestone statue in the British Museum, No. 683. On the *Abydos List*, it is No. 67, on the *Second Abydos List* No. 41. It is on the *Tablet of Sakkara* and *Tablet of Karnak*. His coffin is in Cairo, Prisse *Monuments* Pl. 3, a brick in Lepsius' *Denkmaler* III, 4B and a stele LD III, 4 E.

WHERE ARE THE KAMITE KINGS?

Where are the Kamite Kings Illustration. Wearing the White Crown, Amenhotep I stands before Osiris with Aahmes to the right, while his *Suten Bat* Cartouche/Shennu is above.

Where are the Kamite Kings Illustration. Image from the Temple of Amenhotep at Abydos.

Petrie II (1894: 45) mentions his coffin and mummy found at Deir El-Bahari. The *Abbott Papyrus* mentions an inspection of his tomb. At Karnak, his name is found on a granite jamb, seated limestone statue and was named by Taharka of the Twenty-Fifth Ethiopian Dynasty. At Thebes he constructed a temple. There are sketches on limestone in the Glasgow Museum and also in the Turin

Museum. One of his statues is in the Turin Museum that identifies him. His name is also found on bricks at Deir el-Bahari and at Medinet Habu.

Where are the Kamite Kings Illustration. From the Temple of Amenhotep I and Thutmose III at Abydos.

Where are the Kamite Kings Illustration. Seated statue of Queen Isis, mother of Thutmose III.

WHERE ARE THE KAMITE KINGS?

Where are the Kamite Kings Illustration. Foundation deposits of green glaze, including a slab of Thutmose III, lintels of Thutmose II and III, model tools, vase, etc., of Thutmose III and limestone of Amenhotep III from Abydos in *Abydos* Part I by Flinders Petrie with a Chapter by A.E. Weigall (1902).

At Shut er Regal he is mentioned in the inscriptions of Penaati. At Silsileh, the *Tablet of Paynamen* mentions his name. His name is on a doorjamb at Kom Ombo. At Ibrin the King is under a canopy. At Meroe were found wooden tablets now in the Turin Museum. That Museum also has a statuette of him. Part of a stele with his head is in the Glasgow Museum. A naos fragment is in the Ghizeh Museum. A black granite altar No. 2,292 and vase No. 16,376 are at Berlin. A vase at the Louvre and a brick stamp in the British Museum No. 5,993 are his. Various wooden tablets, as well as cylinder seals, plaques and scarabs carry his name.

FREDERICK MONDERSON

Aakheperkara, Thutmose I, *Nile Year* 2714-2720 (C. 1524-1518 B.C.) was the next pharaoh in this line. We are told by Budge II (1908: 113-16) this pharaoh had seven Horus names in his royal titulary.

Horus	Ka-Nekht-Meri-Maat
	Ka Nekht-En-Ra
	Ka-Nekht-Ra-En-Ouet
	Ka-Nekht-Ankh-Em-Maat
	Ka-Nekht-Peuti-Ma-Auie
	Ka-Nekht-Ur-Baui
	Ra-Meri-Kha-Em-Hetchet
Two Ladies	Kha-Em-Nesert-Peuti
	Kha-Em-Nesert-Aa-Peuti
	Khet-Taiu-Neb
	Tem-Tau-Kha-Khau
Golden Horus	Nefer-Renput-Sankh-Abu Hu Peti
	Aa-Peuti-Usr-Khepesh
	Uatch-Renput-Em-Het-Aa-Maat
Suten Bat	Ra-Aa-Kheper-Ka; and with the additions:
	Setep-En-Ra, Ari-En-Ra, Taa-Amen-Mer-En-Ra
Son of Ra additions:	Tehuti-Mes: and with the
	Kha-Ma-Ra,
	Kha-Neferu,
	Ari-En-Amen,
	Setep-En-Amen,
	Meri-Amen

His name on the *Abydos List* is No. 68 and on the *Second Abydos List*, it is No. 47. It is on Tombos inscriptions and on the Obelisk at Karnak.

WHERE ARE THE KAMITE KINGS?

Where are the Kamite Kings Illustration. Queen Aahmes, wife of King Thutmose I.

Petrie II (1894: 59-60) mentions Thutmose I's name on his coffin and mummy at Deir el Bahari. His mother's name was Senseneb.

Petrie again states the King began the Deir El Bahari Temple, later made famous by Hatshepsut, his daughter. His name is on the Temple at Nubt and on bricks at Deir Medineh. At Medinet Habu he offers to Amen and his name is on a door. At Karnak, his name is on pylons IV, V and VIII. At this most holy site, it is also on Osiride figures, pillars, obelisks, portions of a statue and other scenes and inscriptions.

FREDERICK MONDERSON

A canal inscription bears his name at Aswan. Further to the south of Kemet, at Ibrim in a shrine, at Semneh a list of gifts, and in the temple at Kurneh, the King is represented. At Tanguy (21 D 15 'N) a Tablet, Tomboys (19 D 40 'N) steles, and Argo (19 D 27 'N) a stele; all identify him. There are portraits in Lepsius *Denkmaler* III, 292. A seated diorite statue is in the Turin Museum. A glazed steatite vase is in the British Museum, No. 4,762. A glazed pottery vase is in the Paris Museum, No. 502. A blue glaze Menat belongs to the Wiedemann collection. In addition, there are scarabs, etc.

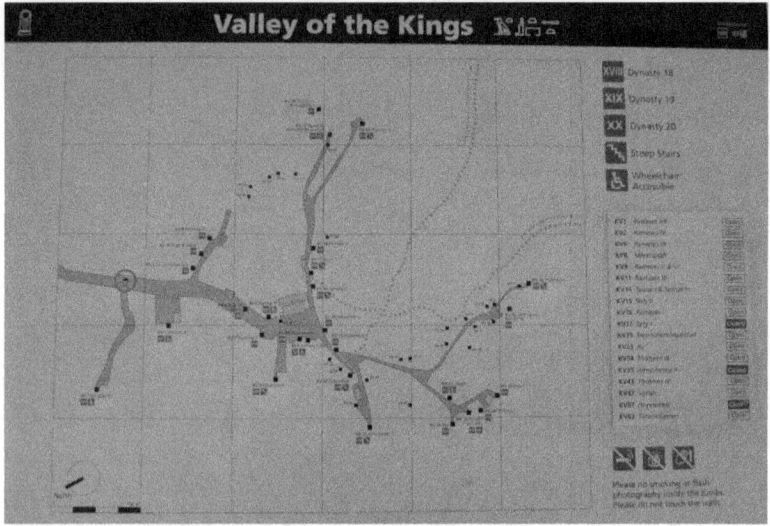

Where are the Kamite Kings Photo. Valley of the Kings. Image depicting tombs that are open and closed. Such openings vary slightly by today's standards.

Thutmose I's Queens were firstly Aahmes, mentioned in the Deir el Bahari Temple, on an ivory wand at Turin Museum and on scarabs in the British Museum. Another wife, Mut-Nefert, is known from the statue of Tii, at Karnak and another statue at Qurneh now in the Ghizeh Museum.

Thutmose I's children by Aahmes, according to Lepsius *Denkmaler* III, 8 B, are Khent-Neferu and Hatshepsut, both from Deir el Bahari. Mut-Nefert was the mother of Thutmose II, from a statue now in Cairo. Isis was the mother of Thutmose III.

Some officials of his reign, according to Petrie II, were Penaati, Director of Works; Pu, Great Builder; Tehuti, Director of Hewers;

WHERE ARE THE KAMITE KINGS?

Aa-Kheper-Ka, Keeper of Equipment; Sebekhotep, Guardian of the Palace; and Pet-Em-Ra, Tutor of the Princes.

According to *American Journal of Archaeology* IV (1900: 243- 44) in May, 1899: "Loret discovered the tomb of Thutmose I, the first of the Pharaohs to make his tomb in the rock of the valley instead of building it in the plain. The tomb is a small one, of only two chambers. It had been rifled and the mummy unwrapped. But the robbers had wrapped it up again and restored it to its mummy case. In the tomb were a papyrus containing texts from the *Book of the Dead*, with colored pictures finely executed; a draught-board, with a full set of draught-men; some garlands; thirteen large earthen beer jars, and a large number of other vessels; weapons; two beautiful armchairs; and remains of food. The most remarkable piece of all is a large and beautiful piece of a large and beautifully preserved couch, consisting of a quadrangular wooden frame, overspread with a thick rush mat, over which were stretched three layers of linen with a life-size figure of the God of death, Osiris, drawn upon the outer layer. The figure itself was smeared with some material intended to make the under-layer waterproof. Over this, mingled with some adhesive substance, soil had been spread, in which barley was planted. The grains had sprouted, and had grown to the height ...."

Aakheperenra, Thutmose II *Nile Year* 2720-2734 (C. 1518-1504 B.C.) followed his father on the throne. Budge II (1908: 117-18) gives his royal titulary as follows:

Horus	Ka-Nekht-Usr-Peuti
Two Ladies	Neter-Sutenit
Horus of Gold	Sekhem-Kheperu
Suten Bat	Ra-Aa-Kheper-En
Son of Ra	Tehuti-mes

On the *Abydos List* he is No. 69, and on the *Second Abydos List* he is No. 43. His name is at Deir el-Bahari and Karnak. It is also at the Temple of Medinet Habu, as well as on the coffin and mummy in Cairo. Lepsius *Denkmaler* III 16 mentions a pylon at Karnak and inscriptions at Aswan.

FREDERICK MONDERSON

Kamite King Photo 107. Queen Aahmes, wife of Thutmose I, the mother of Queen Hatshepsut (left); and, Queen Hatshepsut (right).

Petrie II (1894) identified Thutmose II's name in different parts at Deir El Bahari and Medinet Habu. At Karnak it is on the IX Pylon begun by this Pharaoh. There are 2 statues by Pylon VIII in chambers X, Y, Z. At Esneh it is on red granite pillars and inscriptions at Semneh. At Kumneh, it is on an alteration done to the name of Thutmose I. A stele at El Ayun Oasis bears his name.

A stele in the Turin Museum, depicts Pak Hen making an offering to Thutmose II. In the Lee Collection, statuettes of Isis and Horus also bear his name. In addition, scarabs, etc., also tell of this King.

His Queens were Hatshepsut and Aset, mentioned in mummy wrappings of Thutmose III. His children by Hatshepsut were Neferura and Meryt-Ra Hatshepsut. Queen Aset bore him Thutmose III.

Menkheperra, Thutmose III, *Nile Year* 2734-2784 (C. 1504-1450 B.C.) was one of the most colorful and flamboyant rulers of the ancient world. Budge II (1908: 122-29) supplies his royal titulary.

WHERE ARE THE KAMITE KINGS?

Where are the Kamite Kings Photo. Bust of Thutmose III now in the British Museum.

Horus	Ka-Nekht-Kha-Em-Uast
	Ka-Nekht-Kha-Em-Maat
	Ka-Nekht-Kha-Em-Maat-Neb-
	Ari-Khet-Ra-Men- Kheper
	Ka-Nekht-ha-Em-Maat
	Ka-Nekht-Ra-Meri
	Hetch-Qa-Ra-Meri
Two Ladies	Uah--Sutenit, or Uah Sutenit-

FREDERICK MONDERSON

	Ma-Ra-Em-Pet Sekha-Maat-Meri-Taui Aa-Shefit-Em-Taui-Neb
Golden Horus	Tcheser-Khau-Sekhem-Pehti Aa-Khepesh-Hu-Pet-Paut Her-Her, Nekht-Hu-Hequ-Semti
Suten Bat	Ra-Men-Kheper, with additions Ari-Em-Ra, Setep-En-Ra, Mer-En-Ra, Heq-Maat, Heq-Maat-Taa-Ra, Taa-Amen-Ra-Saa-En, Nekht-Khepesh, Neb-Nekht-Ka, Heq-Uast, Neter-Nefer-Ka
Son of Ra	Tehuti-Mes with additions Nefer-Kheper, Nefer-Kheperu, Sma-Kheper, Nefer-Khau, Heq-Maat, Heq-Uast, Heq-Annu, Neter-Heq, Sekha-Nefer.

Where are the Kamite Kings Photo. From the northwest, Front Elevation of the *Akh Menou*, Festival Temple of Thutmose III (left); and, Luis Casado of Brooklyn, New York, just left of the north-face of the *Akh Menou* with the Obelisk of Queen Hatshepsut at his rear. A keen eye could just notice the tip of the Queen's father Thutmose I's Obelisk further on.

WHERE ARE THE KAMITE KINGS?

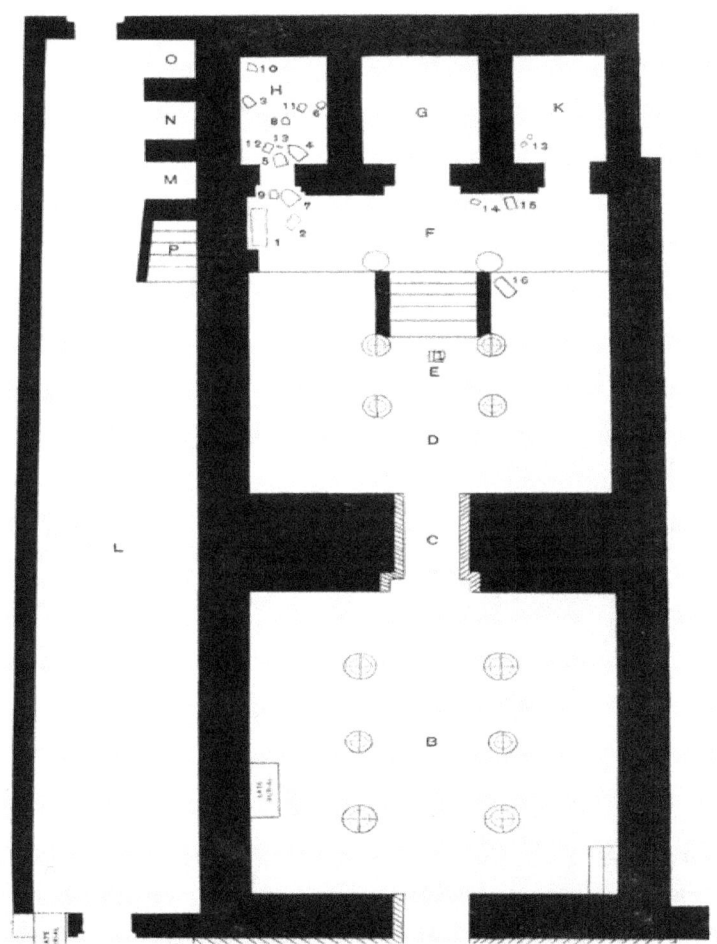

Where are the Kamite Kings Illustration. Temple at Gurob for worship of Thutmose III during the XIXth Dynasty.

On the *Abydos List* Thutmose III is No. 70 and on the *Second Abydos List* he is No. 44. Meryt-Ra Hatshepsut was the daughter of Hatshepsut and wife of Thutmose III. Maspero's *Mommies* indicates, Ast was the mother of this King. The *Annales* III indicates Aah-Sat, was a wife of Thutmose III. Another of his wives was Nebtu, as indicated in the tomb of Neb-men, recorded by Bouriat in *Recueil* IX, 97. Lepsius *Denkmaler* III, 55a, line 12, informs, that according to the Temple of Semneh, Mersekr was another of Thutmose III's wives.

Where are the Kamite Kings Illustration. Bust of Thutmose III, of the XVIIIth Dynasty, one of the greatest conquerors who ever lived.

He had a number of children. Birch's *Two Papyri*, XII, I, mentions Nebau, daughter of Princess Sa-Tem. Other princesses were Taui, Tha-Kheta (?), Pet-Ka-Aa, Petpu, surnamed Ta ... Ani and Ptah-Memt, Sat-Herna, Nefer-Amen, Uaai, Henut-Annu and Nehi, a Prince, Governor of Nubia.

WHERE ARE THE KAMITE KINGS?

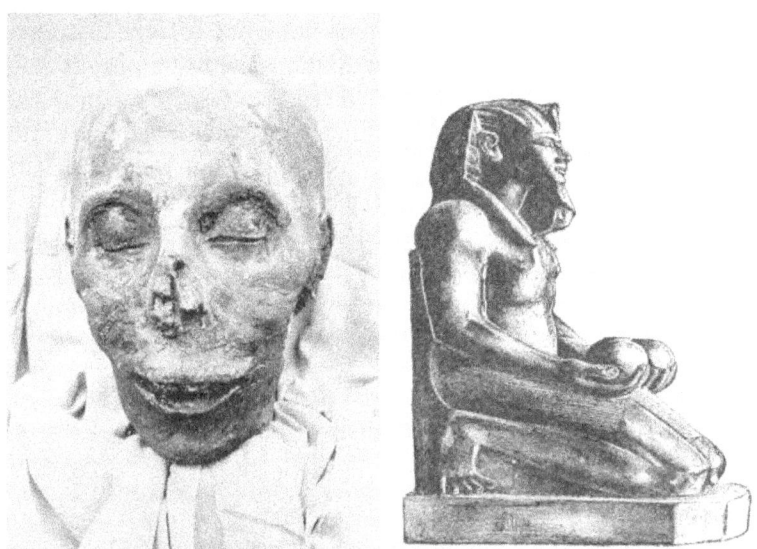

Where are the Kamite Kings Illustration. Head of Thutmose III's mummy (left); and, kneeling statue of Thutmose III.

Petrie II (1894: 97-100) is just as informative in terms of the occurrence of the name of this most important King of the XVIIIth Dynasty. The name of Thutmose III is found on his coffin and mummy. At Serabut el Khadem, steles of his 23rd and 27th year exist. Here also, the jamb of a doorway and glaze vase bits record his name. It is in foundation deposits at Kom el Kisn. Heliopolis boasts a gate jamb, one of which is in Cairo, as is a stele of his 45th year. The famous Lateran obelisk, one at Constantinople, and others in New York and London are important monoliths, erected by this Pharaoh.

Inscriptions at Abusir, on the work of Amenemhat of the Twelfth Dynasty, probably a graffiti as well as at Ekhmin, Wady Hammamat, Aswan, Kuban and Dakkeh all identify Thutmose III. Evidently very religious, we find him connected with the Temple of Ptah at Memphis, Gurob Temple, one at Koptos, and another at Elephantine, that is now destroyed. He probably founded the Temple of Dendera, a rock shrine at Speos Artemidos, two temple fragments at El Kab and the town and temple at Nubt.

FREDERICK MONDERSON

At Karnak, his name is on the East Hall of Pillars, South of Pylon VII, Temple of Ptah, possibly he helped to begin the Temple of Mut, though Hatshepsut's architect Senmut did work on this structure. Also, at Karnak, the *Akh Menu*, the hinder sanctuary, surrounding courts of the temple and other structures here bear his name. He was connected to the temple of Medinet Habu, another temple north of the Ramesseum, and he built a small temple at Deir el Bahari between those of Mentuhotep and Hatshepsut. Here he also erected an obelisk. Another one was raised at Elephantine (Sion Ho) and there is a block at the station with his name on it.

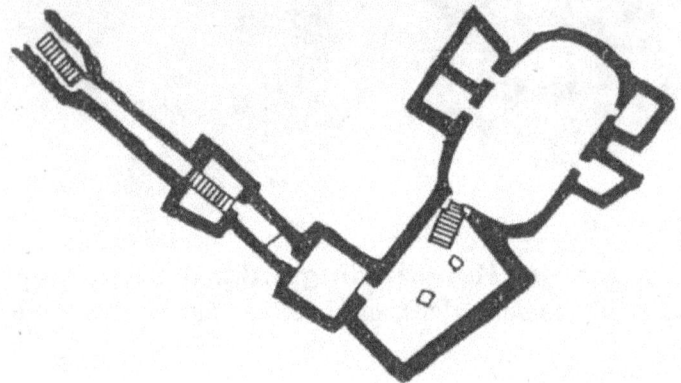

TOMB OF TUTHMOSIS III

Where are the Kamite Kings Illustration. Valley of the Kings. Tomb of Thutmose III.

At Kom Ombo a pylon, now lost, and lintel bears his name. In addition to the steles at Sarabut el Khadem, and Heliopolis, there were others at El Bersheh, Esneh, and Ekmin. At Abydos there were two statues of the King and an Osiris statue. At Kalabsha, a granite statue and block bear his name. Korti, stone and foundation, Amadah a scene, the gate and lintel tell of him.

Ellesiyeh contains scenes and a stele of his 42nd year. In Nubia, a number of temples were begun or added to by him, including Wady Halfa, a southern brick temple, and temples at Semneh, Kummeh, Sai (20 d 42' N), a rock shrine at Do Sheh (20 D 30' N) and he began the temple of Soleb. Also, a stele was erected by him at Bahriyeh Oasis. The Temple of Wady Halfa is extremely important

WHERE ARE THE KAMITE KINGS?

for inaccuracies reported in the original reports, yet indicate the lengths to which the monarchs of Kemet went to erect structures and propitiate the ancestral deities.

Where are the Kamite Kings Illustration. Pharaoh holding Aba Scepter and incenser prepares to make a Presentation while his wife holds two Sistrums or rattles at his rear.

The *American Journal of Archaeology* XIV (1910: 487) reports: J. H. Breasted attacks the article of P. Scott-Moncrieff in *S. Bibl. Arch.* 1907, pp. 39-46: "in which he claims that there is no evidence of an erasure of the name of Queen Hatshepsut and of feminine pronouns and endings referring to her, and the substitution of the name of Thutmose II, in the temple at Wady Halfa. He shows by photographs that Scott-Moncrieff has failed to observe all the evidence, and has copied the inscriptions inaccurately; and exhibits in detail the evidence that the temple was erected originally by Thutmose III and Hatshepsut jointly, and that the name of Thutmose II has been repeatedly inserted in the place of Hatshepsut, and that feminine pronouns and endings referring to her have been changed to the masculine. Ibid. pp. 333-338, P. Scott-Moncrieff replies to Professor Breasted, by saying that the inaccuracy in his article was due to the fact that he was not intending to make a complete scientific report of his investigations."

Where are the Kamite Kings Illustration. Seated statue of one of the ladies of Thutmose III. How European she looks with "broad nose and thick lips!" Ha! Ha! Ha!

Statues and portraits of Thutmose III abound. The head of a granite colossus is now in the British Museum, a seated limestone colossus at Karnak and inscriptions at the base of a throne in that temple, are his. A standing red granite statue at Karnak, seated black granite here, and a seated black and white diorite statue now in the Turin

WHERE ARE THE KAMITE KINGS?

Museum, are also his. A seated grey granite from Nubia is now in the Florence Museum. His torso and throne were found at Abydos. A seated black granite from Alexandria, a torso behind the temple at Karnak, a torso in a small temple of Opet at Karnak, and a red granite bust at this site all carry his name. A bronze statue in Marseilles, and statues mentioned by Thutmose IV and Neb-Ua-Iu are some of the many representations of this great Egyptian African. Also, a trial piece in the Turin Museum bears his name as well as red fragments of sphinxes found at Karnak, and a figure on wooden canon board now in the British Museum.

The Turin Museum contains a stele of him with Min, the fertility God, and another stele in the temple of Uazmes is now in the Ghizeh Museum. A high red granite altar of his is in the British Museum, another is still at Karnak, one is in the Vatican. One altar of alabaster, another of red granite, and still a further one is dedicated to Amen Salinka.

Where are the Kamite Kings Photo. Valley of the Nobles. Tomb of Sennufer. Sennufer to the left, with Thoth as a phoenix in Khnemu Crown, Ra Horakhty wearing solar orb and grasping Waz Scepter while other Gods sail in the Solar Barque.

FREDERICK MONDERSON

Where are the Kamite Kings Illustration. Gurob. Steles and Shabti jars of the XVIIIth and XIXth Dynasties.

Alabaster vases abound. In the Turin Museum there are 9, the British Museum has 21, there are 2 in the Ghizeh Museum and 3 are in Berlin. The Petrie Museum and Leyden also have alabaster vases. The British Museum has a glass vase, there are ivory tablets at Marseilles, and a feather of Amen is in the Turin Museum. A fish-shaped cup of green glaze is in the Ghizeh Museum. A scribe's palette at Bolonga, Papyrus at Turin, Berlin and Munich as well as rings and scarabs with his name are innumerable. A gold ring is at Ashburnham.

A queen of Thutmose III was Merytra-Hatshepsut whose sphinx is in the Baracco Collection. Her name is in the Temple of Medinet

WHERE ARE THE KAMITE KINGS?

Habu, in her tomb and on scarabs in the Petrie Museum and Turin Museum. Queen Nebtu bore him a son, Amenhotep II.

Thutmose III had many daughters including Taui, Ta-Kheta, Pet-Ahu-Ha, Pet-Pui-Ta-Khet-Aui, Meryt-Ptah, Sat-Hora, Nefer-Amen, Ua-Ay and Henut-Anu.

Where are the Kamite Kings Illustration. Bust of Queen Hatshepsut wearing Nemes headdress and sporting a beard.

Ma'at-Ka-Ra, Hatshepsut, *Nile Year* 2740-2755 (c. 1498-1483 B.C.) was a female Pharaoh, whose reign is often counted as part of the greater reign of Thutmose III. What Breasted entitled the "Feud of the Thutmosids," pitted this ruler against male dominance of the times and the struggle led to her demise and name erasure from history, only to be resurrected later.

Budge II (1908) provided her royal titulary.

Horus	Usert-Kau
Two Ladies	Uatchet-Renput Thet Taui-Nebu

FREDERICK MONDERSON

Horus of Gold
Suten Bat
Son of Ra

Netert-Khau Sankh-Abu
Ra Maat Ka
Hatshepsut

Where are the Kamite Kings Illustration. From the "Red Chapel" of Hatshepsut, (above), the Queen kneels as enthroned Amun in plumes and Mut in Red Crown lay hands on her person; and below, to the left, Mut in Red Crown embraces Hatshepsut with her Cartouche/Shennu *Ma'at-Ka-Ra* above; and right, the Queen offers enthroned Amon (Amun) two ointment jars.

Conspicuously absent from the *Abydos List* (Seti I) and *Second Abydos List* (Rameses II), Lepsius' *Denkmaler* III, 22, 23, 24 mentions her obelisk at Karnak. Naville's *Deir el-Bahari* is an important source on her life and work. A statue at Kurna and alabaster vases from Abydos, now in Cairo, as well as Lepsius' *Konigsburch* No. 347, all tell us of her.

WHERE ARE THE KAMITE KINGS?

Where are the Kamite Kings Illustration. Outer and inner coffin of Mashira.

Petrie II (1894) provided more information of her life. At Karnak, two obelisks, sandstone blocks and chamber sculptures are evidence of her work. The Temple of Mut was begun in her reign. The Deir el-Bahari temple was her mortuary masterpiece. This site was also important for the spiritual and psychological salvation of the

FREDERICK MONDERSON

"ancestors" who started it all. The entrance to the underworld lay at Thebes, near Hatshepsut's temple at Deir el Bahari.

Where are the Kamite Kings Photo. From the mountain, "Bird's Eye View" of Queen Hatshepsut's temple at Deir el Bahari. Notice First and Second Ramps, First and Second Courts, Middle and Upper Colonnades before Upper Court that entrances the Sanctuary, while Mentuhotep's 11th Dynasty is further on.

The *American Journal of Archaeology* XIV (1910: 488) mentioned G. Foucart's discussion of "the Egyptian representation of that moment of the second life when the ghost of the deceased, about to cross the boundary of the world of the living, finds itself at the foot of the Mountain of the West. The divine cow, or the edifice in pyramidal form, or better still the cow and the edifice combined, form the principal subject of the scene. These represent a group of ceremonies and buildings, which had a real existence. Their site was at the bottom of the amphitheater of Deir el-Bahari, and the subterranean chambers and temple pyramid found by Naville on this spot are the remains of the buildings so often figured by the Egyptians in their funerary monuments."

We are told in *American Journal of Archaeology* XII (1908: 214) of Naville' description of the statue of this Hathor cow, that: "If the accessories which characterize the Goddess are removed, there remains a striking piece of animal sculpture, of great delicacy of

WHERE ARE THE KAMITE KINGS?

modeling and as full of life as to recall the praise of the cow of Myrow. In the words of Maspero, 'Neither Greece nor Rome has left us anything comparable with it.'"

Where are the Kamite Kings Photo. A sacrificial altar with the groove for the blood to drain.

Where are the Kamite Kings Illustration. Queen Hatshepsut in male attire.

FREDERICK MONDERSON

Hatshepsut can certainly take credit for this outstanding piece of work, which she continued. At Buto, her name is on the seal of the Temple of Amen. Sculptures are in the Speos Artemidos. At Kom Ombo, she is on the gateway. Stone bearing her name was found at Edfu Temple in the walkway of the Great Court. This was removed to the Cairo Museum, for its rarity is greater than the Edfu pieces. At Medinet Habu, her name is erased on existing bricks. A glazed bowl comes from Serabut el Khadem. Inscriptions are known from El Kab and bricks at Qurneh. A stele of her 16th year is known at Wady Maghara and at Aswan, the stele of Senmut informs of this female pharaoh. She dedicated a stele to Thutmose I and another stele is in the Vatican. Still, another stele is in the Grant Collection. Statues are scattered throughout the world, in New York at the Metropolitan Museum, a headless statue is in Berlin and the head of another statue is also in Berlin. Two statues and heads of others are also at Leyden. Ushabti are at the Hague. A wooden box comes from Deir el Bahari. Her throne was found at Biban el Moluk.

Where are the Kamite Kings Photo. Valley of the Nobles. Tomb of Sennefer. Classic picture of Osiris painted Green in his Shrine watched over by two "Eyes of Horus" as the deceased presents a sumptuous feast at the God's "Table of Offerings."

Draughtsmen, a draughtboard and part of a Cartouche/Shennus are in the British Museum. A lion's head draughtsman is in the Ghizeh

WHERE ARE THE KAMITE KINGS?

Museum. A draughtboard and plaque are in the Petrie Museum. Alabaster vases were found at Abydos. Models of tools, beads, glass or obsidian, scarabs and plaques tell of her.

She prepared a tomb in the Valley of the Queens and after she became pharaoh, she had another dug in the Valley of the Kings. The wooden box contained a tooth scientist recently used in matching a missing molar on an obscure female mummy. Turns out, the tooth helped identify the mummy as that of Hatshepsut. This process of identifying the Queen was shown in a Discovery Channel documentary. Hatshepsut is the only other pharaoh beside Tutankhamon whose identify has been "water tight" confirmed.

Where are the Kamite Kings Illustration. From the "Red Chapel" of Queen Hatshepsut, (above) dancers perform their routine; while (below), as dancers and musicians perform, to the right, priests hoist high and "carry out" the barque of the God Amon.

FREDERICK MONDERSON

Where are the Kamite Kings Illustration. From the "Red Chapel" of Queen Hatshepsut, (above) Hatshepsut and Thutmose make offerings to the Barque of Amon; while (below), priests hoist high and "bring in" the Barque while Hatshepsut and Thutmose follow.

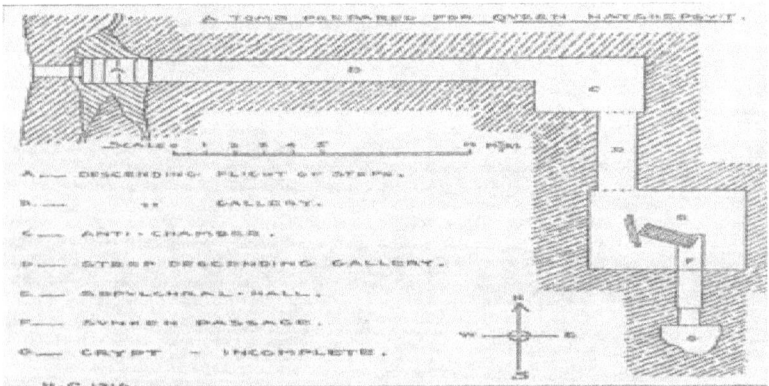

Where are the Kamite Kings Illustration. A tomb prepared for Queen Hatshepsut.

WHERE ARE THE KAMITE KINGS?

Where are the Kamite Kings Photo. A defaced Queen Hatshepsut presents two wine jars and a Table of Offerings to enthroned Amon-Ra, from the "Red Chapel" in Karnak's Open Air Museum, that requires a separate ticket to enter.

Where are the Kamite Kings Illustration. Block statue of Senmut, Hatshepsut's architect, with his charge, the Queen's daughter, Neferu-Ra.

Where are the Kamite Kings Illustration. Queen Mut-Emuea, mother of Amenhotep III and wife of Thutmose IV.

Where are the Kamite Kings Illustration. Façade and entrance to the Temple of Amenhotep II at Karnak before clearance.

WHERE ARE THE KAMITE KINGS?

Where are the Kamite Kings Photo. The Temple of Amenhotep II on the North/South Axis, between Pylons 9 and 10.

Aakheperura, Amenhotep II, *Nile Year* 2781-2815 (c. 1453-1419 B.C.) followed Thutmose III, after the latter had deposed Hatshepsut. *American Journal of Archaeology* XVI (1912: 561-62) mentions H.R. Hall's attack "on the theory that the reign of Amenhotep II was mainly contemporaneous with that of his father and that he died after three years of sole reign in 1447 B.C. He shows there is no trace of any such co-regency in the inscriptions and that the inscription of Amenemheb distinctly speaks of Amenhetep succeeding his father as a new King on the throne."

Where are the Kamite Kings Illustration. Workers sit and stand in the Sanctuary (left) and Hypostyle Hall (right) in the Temple of Amenhotep II near the 9th Pylon on the North/South Axis at Karnak Temple.

The new King's titulary, according to Budge I (1908: 129-32) is as follows:
Horus   Ka-Nekht-Ur-Pehti

FREDERICK MONDERSON

Two Ladies   Usr-F-Au-Sekha-Em-East
Golden Horus   Thet-Sekhen-F-Em-Taiu-Neby
Suten Bat   Ra-Aa-Kheperu
Son of Ra   Amen-Hetep with additions:
                          Heq-Annu,
                          Heq-Uast

On the *Abydos List* he is No. 71 and on the *Second Abydos List*, No. 45. Petrie II (1894: 152-53) supplied extensive data on the whereabouts of this Pharaoh. At Karnak, his name appears on walls and halls between the southern pylon Nos. IX and X. There is a scene with the King in front of Pylon IX. Here also is a red granite stele and before the sanctuary, were reused blocks. In addition, there were re-erected columns near the obelisk.

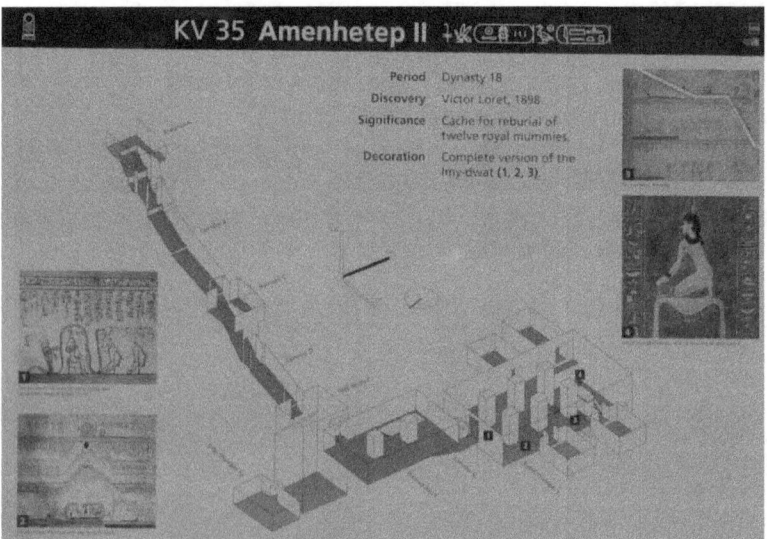

Where are the Kamite Kings Photo. Valley of the Kings. Tomb of Amenhotep II. Cache for reburial of twelve royal mummies and complete version of the *Book of Imy-dwat*.

From Tell el-Hesy, we have a jar stamp. At Bubastis there are scenes of offerings. Nubt has provided a blue glazed Uas. Medamot pillars and lintel carry his name. At Qurneh, he built a temple north of the Ramesseum. Blocks from Erment are now in the Ghizeh Museum. This site also supplied his stele of conquest. His name is at Silsileh. At Elephantine, blocks and an obelisk, now destroyed

WHERE ARE THE KAMITE KINGS?

were erected by him. Graffiti found at Aswan, and those belonging to Pa-Nehy-Amen at Sehel, bear evidence of Amenhotep II.

Where are the Kamite Kings Illustration. View from the northwest angle of the Temple of Amenhotep II (left) taken in 1924 and defaced pillar of the King taken in 1923.

A statue of his was found at Bigeh. At Kalabshah, a pronaos and Ibrin painted rock shrine, belong to him. Amadeh has temple finishings. At Wady Halfa a sandstone brick temple was built by him. At Kumneh, columns and temple scenes show the King. He is on the remains of the Temple at Sai and the Napata Temple mentions him. The Temple at Semneh was an important work of his.

The University of Pennsylvania's *Museum Journal* of 1910 carried a brief description by David Randall MacIver of the Temple of Amenhotep II. This was reported in the *American Journal of Archaeology* XV (1911: 82-83) after it had been cleared down to its foundation.

FREDERICK MONDERSON

Where are the Kamite Kings Illustration. Stele of Amenhotep II near the 8th Pylon in Karnak.

"It continued in use during the nineteenth and twentieth dynasties; but it was preceded by an earlier temple, as is proved by a doorway inscribed with the name of Aahmes, the first King of the eighteenth dynasty, and by walls at a different angle lying underneath the eighteenth dynasty temple. Three statuettes of scribes, several stelae, and some painted stone jars, all of the eighteenth dynasty, were discovered. The priests' dwellings were interesting for the light they throw on the domestic life of the time. The hearths, granaries, grinding-stones, ovens, pots, etc., were found as the owners had left them."

WHERE ARE THE KAMITE KINGS?

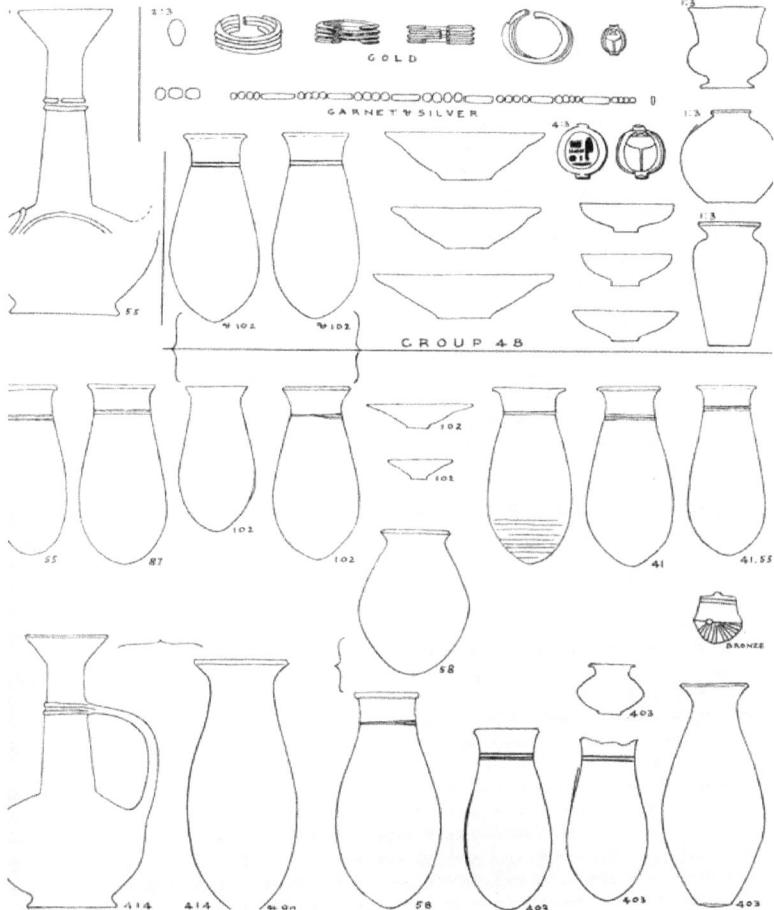

Where are the Kamite Kings Illustration. Pottery from the age of Amenhotep II found at Tell el Yehudiyeh.

A number of statues have been recovered. At Karnak, a statue was found before Pylon IX. A kneeling statue at Beni Naga and also one of granite at Bigeh belongs to him. A large kneeling statue of his is in the Turin Museum. A headless, kneeling statue is in the Paris Museum. The body of a seated statue at Karnak and a headless seated statue was found at Qurneh Temple, with his name.

This name is also found in the foundation deposits at Qurneh Temple. Ushabtis were purchased from dealers at Qurneh. A stele of the King adoring Amen was found at Luxor. A vase in the foundation of the Temple of Qurneh is extant. A papyrus of his fifth year is in Paris. Also, mummy wrappings of Thutmose III, mentions Amenhotep II. A toilet box is in the Rhind Collection in Edinburgh. There are also rings and scarabs with his mother's name. His Queen was Ta-Aa and sons were Thutmose IV and 5 or 7 others.

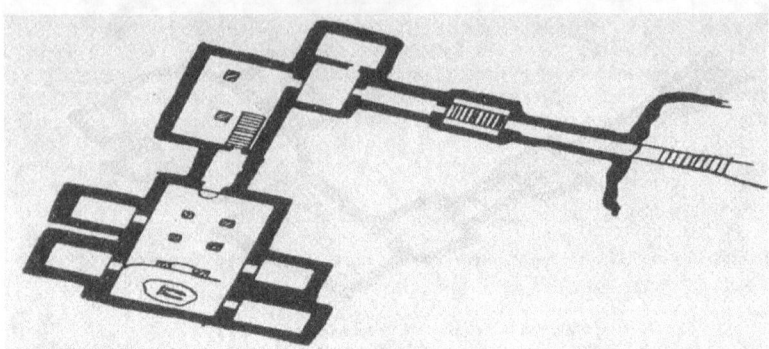

Where are the Kamite Kings Illustration. The Tomb of Amenhotep II, where Loret discovered the significant "second cache of Royal Mummies."

Another important function of this King in the modern mind-set is the significance of his tomb as discovered by Loret in 1899. *American Journal of Archaeology* III (1899: 59) mentions Professor A. Wiedemann's account of the discovery of the Tomb of Amenhotep II in the Valley of the Kings.

Where are the Kamite Kings Illustration. Haremhab among the divinities as seen in his tomb.

WHERE ARE THE KAMITE KINGS?

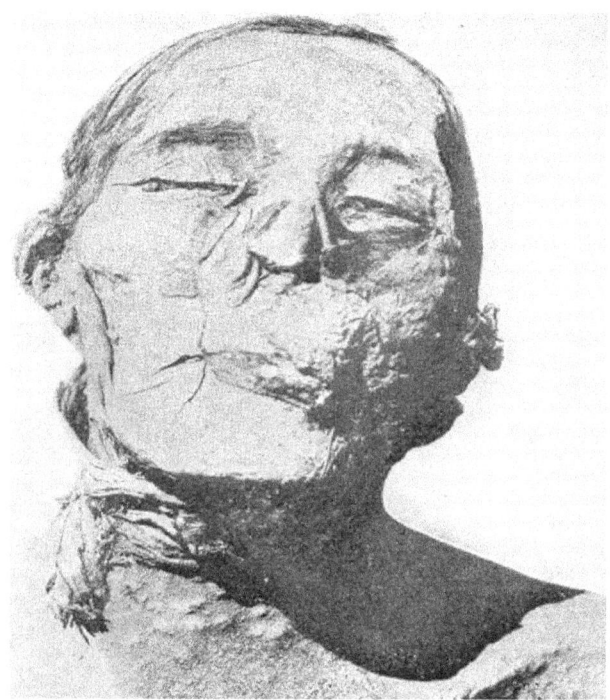

Where are the Kamite Kings Illustration. Mummy head of Amenhotep II, son of Thutmose III.

"The tomb itself has the ordinary shape of the royal King-tombs of the eighteenth and nineteenth dynasties. A passage leads downwards into the mountain; then follows a staircase, and then some rooms. The principal of these has a roof supported by quadrangular pillars and painted blue with golden stars, in imitation of the night heaven into whose realm the King has now entered. The walls were covered with appropriate representations. The sarcophagus, made of sandstone, was standing in a niche on a block of alabaster. Besides that of Amenophis II; nine other mummies were found in a small chamber to the right, two without names, but the others are proved by their inscriptions to be those of Thutmose IV, Amenhotep III, Seti II, Setnakht and Rameses IV, VI, and VIII. These mummies had evidently been removed from their original tombs in ancient times, probably to be deposited in a safer place. The floor of the newly found tomb was covered with gifts offered to the dead Pharaoh. In the tomb were also found four human corpses not embalmed, but merely dried. All the bodies bore marks proving that they had been killed. This seems to point to human sacrifice."

This find was similar to one made in 1881 by Antiquities Director Mariette at Deir el Bahari, where mummies of several equally famous pharaohs were discovered. These are in the Cairo Museum.

Where are the Kamite Kings Photo. Thutmose IV among the Gods – Osiris, Anubis, Isis and Hathor.

Menkheperura, Thutmose IV, *Nile Year* 2813-2844 (c. 1419-1386 B.C.) followed Amenhotep II.

WHERE ARE THE KAMITE KINGS?

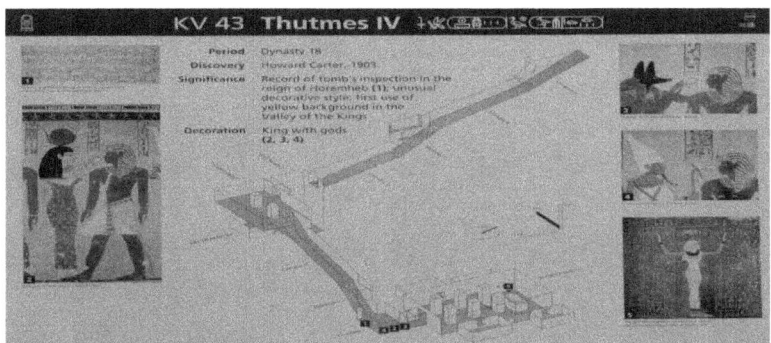

Where are the Kamite Kings Photo. Valley of the Kings. Tomb of Thutmose IV. Contains a record of its inspection in the reign of Horemhab of the 18th Dynasty, an unusual decorative style; first use of yellow background in Valley and King with Gods.

Where are the Kamite Kings Illustration. Thutmose IV and his mother, Queen Ta-Aa.

FREDERICK MONDERSON

Where are the Kamite Kings Photo. Thutmose IV receiving Ankh or Life from Osiris. Notice the African lips of both God and King!

His royal titulary, according to Budge I (1908: 132-35) are as follows.

Horus	Ka-Nekht-Tut-Khau
Two Ladies	Tettet-Sutenit-Ma-Tem
Golden Horus	User-Khepeh-Ter-Pet-Paut
Suten Bat	Ra-Men-Kheperu with additions: Heq-Maat-Ka-Mer-En-Ra-Ari-En-Ra-Setep-En-Ra
Son of Ra	Tehuti-Mes

The *Tablet or Stele of the Sphinx* tells an interesting story of the young prince, who, while out riding, rested under the sphinx nearly covered with sand. He fell asleep, and dreamed the colossal implored him to clear away the sand and that he would become Pharaoh. He complied, became King and erected the stele which still stands. On the *Abydos List* he is No. 72 and the *Second Abydos List* No. 46.

WHERE ARE THE KAMITE KINGS?

Where are the Kamite Kings Photo. Valley of the Nobles. Tomb of Sennufer. Sennufer and spouse before the Gods.

Petrie II (1894: 165-66) has found his name at Sarabut El Khadem and on columns at Alexandria. A statue at Abydos and fragment at Dendera identify him. The religious site at Karnak contains his name in a list on a wall around the obelisk, colossal before the pylon and scene of Pylon IV. At Qurneh, his name is on a temple south of the Ramesseum. At Luxor he is in a scene in the birth-hall. At El Kab, a building of the small temple bears his name. Fragments at Elephantine, steles at Sehel and Konosso, in the temple at Amadeh as well as scarabs, rings, uaz eyes etc., all tell of this King.

FREDERICK MONDERSON

Where are the Kamite Kings Illustration. Enthroned king and standing coffin-statues in a museum display.

Where are the Kamite Kings Illustration. Lintel from the Sanctuary of Thutmose IV at Karnak.

WHERE ARE THE KAMITE KINGS?

Where are the Kamite Kings Photo. Thutmose IV receiving Ankh or Life from Anubis.

American Journal of Archaeology VII (1903: 362-63) mentions a letter of Maspero to *Le Temps* April 10, 1903, giving an account of the opening of the tomb of Thutmose IV, in the Valley of the Kings at Thebes.

Where are the Kamite Kings Photo. Thutmose IV receiving Ankh or Life from Goddesses Isis, Hathor and another.

FREDERICK MONDERSON

"The excavations were conducted by Mr. Carter, the chief inspector, at the expense of Mr. Theodore Davis. Work began in January, 1902, but it was February 3, 1903, before the tomb was finally opened. It had been pillaged of its valuables in gold, silver, and jewels long ago. Indeed, inscriptions showed that under Armais, less than a century after the burial of the King, restorations had been needed. The rock chambers, however, contained a large quantity of the funeral furniture, which had been broken and cast aside by the plunderers. The King had evidently died before the chamber was finished, as the walls were still rough and undecorated. Among the objects is the body of a chariot of leather and wood decorated with fine reliefs. The fragments are to be removed to the museum at Cairo, where they can be put together, ..."

His Queen was Ta-Aa, found at Luxor. A bark in the British Museum and scarabs have his name. His son was Amenhotep III.

Nebma'atra, Amenhotep III, *Nile Year* 2844-2881 (c. 1386-1349 B.C.) was one of the greatest of all the Kamite Kings. He was dubbed "the magnificent." His royal titulary, according to Budge I (1908: 135-44) provides an extensive array of names.

Horus	Ka-Nekht-Kha-Em-Maat
	Sma-Hetchet-Mer-Annu
	Uah-Renput-Asht-Heby
	Ka-Nekht-Sekhem-F-Au
	Ka-Nekht-Qeq-Hequ
	Ka-Nekht-tut-Kuau
	Khenti-Kau-En-Khibu-Nest
Two Ladies	Smen-Hepu-Sekerh-Taui
	Smen-Hepu-thes-taui
	Ur-Mer-Er-Tchat-Peht,
	F-Shen-Em-Annu-Meut,
	Er-Annu-Resu
	Khenti-Kau-Ankhiu-Nebu
Golden Horus	Aa-Khepesh-Hu-Satia
	Hu-Mentiu-ter-Thehennu
	Petpet-Antiu-Thet-Ta-Sen
	Ka-Nekht-Suten-Suteniu-Ter-pet-
Paut	

WHERE ARE THE KAMITE KINGS?

	Thehen-Kheperu-Ra-Bait
	Hefenu-Nebu-Mati-Ra
	Netch-Neteru-Mes-Henu-Sen
	Khentiu-Kau-Ankhiu
Suten Bat	Ra Neb Maat with additions:
	Mer-En-Ra,
	Ari-En-Ra,
	Taat-Ra,
	Setep-En-Ra,
	Asu-Ra,
	Thehen-Ra,
	Mer-Amen,
	Setep-En-Tem, etc.
Son of Ra	Amen-Hetep with additions:
	Heq-Uast,
	Sa-Ra and Neter-eq-Uast

Amenhotep III is No. 73 on the *Abydos List* and No. 47 on the *Second Abydos List*. Lepsius' *Denkmaler* mentions bricks, rock inscriptions at Silsileh, Philae, Aswan and a granite column in the British Museum, No. 64.

Where are the Kamite Kings Photo. Valley of the Nobles. Tomb of Sennufer. Sennufer and spouse are fed libations and other goodies by the "Tree Goddess."

FREDERICK MONDERSON

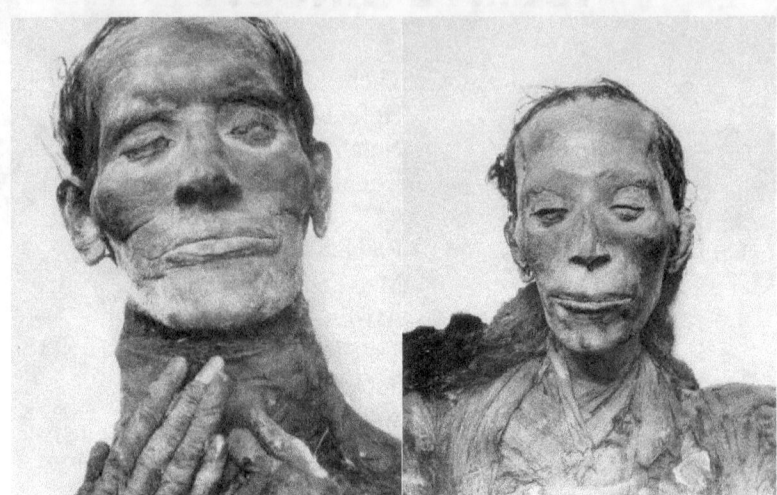

Where are the Kamite Kings Illustration. Yuya (left); and, Tuya (right) parents of Queen Tiye, wife of Amenhotep III.

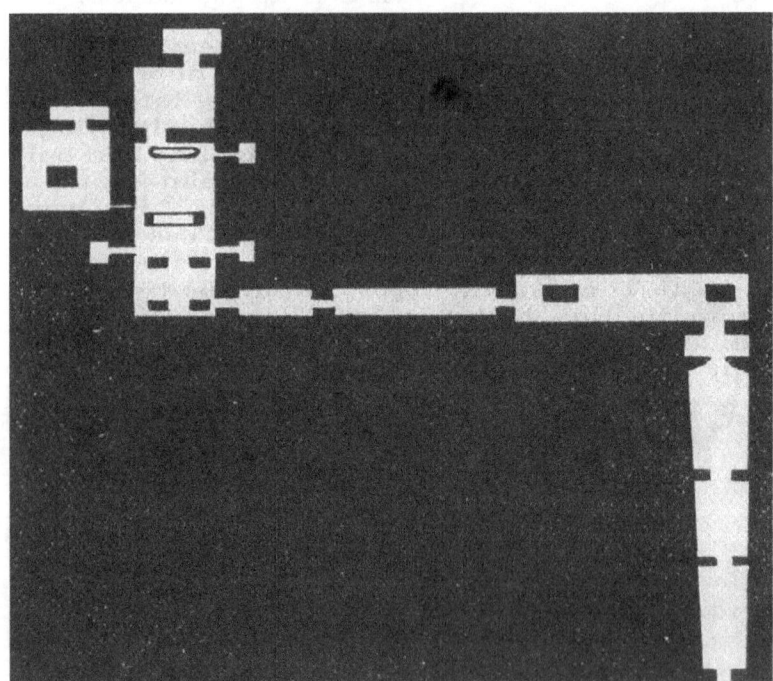

Where are the Kamite Kings Illustration. Tomb of Amenhotep III in the Western Valley.

WHERE ARE THE KAMITE KINGS?

Where are the Kamite Kings Illustration. Canopic Jar covers of Queen Tiye, wife of Amenhotep III, 18th Dynasty.

Petrie II (1894: 174-77) supplies an equally extensive listing of the occurrence of Amenhotep III's name. Some scholars like to view the Karnak religious complex as a museum, and as such, significant Kings are mentioned here. Amenhotep III's name is found to the north of Monthu's Temple and in a small temple east of it. He built the 128 sphinx-avenue linking Karnak with Luxor. His name is on Pylon III. Inscriptions of his are here. Amenhotep built the Processional Colonnade at Karnak. A colossal stand before Pylon IX. His name is on Pylon VIII and on a building to the south as well as in the Temple of Mut. He built the original Temple of Luxor, including the Processional Colonnade. Other temples were erected at Meshaikh, Kom el Hettan, Deir el Medineh, the Elephantine Temple, now destroyed, and the Temple at Soleb. The Sedinga Temple was dedicated to his wife, Queen Tiy.

FREDERICK MONDERSON

Where are the Kamite Kings Illustration. Bust of Amenhotep, Son of Hapu, architect of Amenhotep III, 18th Dynasty.

At Memphis, a slab was found that's now in the Ghizeh Museum and also the Apis Tomb found there. At Gurob were found, an altar to Tiy, a box lid and a kohl tube. At Rayaneh a fort and adoration scene at Dendera, name this King. From Napata at the Temple of Soleb, were removed two rams, the base of a hawk and lions that are now in the British Museum.

American Journal of Archaeology XIII (1909: 53-54) carried an article by Professor James H. Breasted, of the University of Chicago, entitled, "The Temple of Soleb: A New Form of Egyptian Architecture." This work throws light on the role of architectural experimentation in Nubia, and its full fruition elsewhere.

WHERE ARE THE KAMITE KINGS?

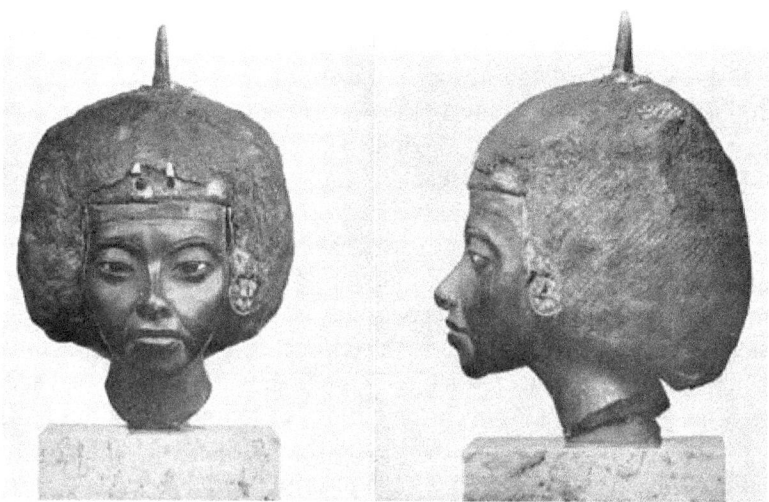

Where are the Kamite Kings Illustration. Bust of Queen Tiye, wife of Amenhotep III.

"The colonnade as an architectural form emerges in Egypt as early as 2750 B.C., although it is not found in Babylonian architecture at all. In the earliest Egyptian colonnades, the columns are all of one size and the roof is on the same level throughout each hall. This continued till about 1400 B.C. By 1350 B.C. we find in the famous hypostyle hall at Karnak a double row of taller columns in the middle, with smaller columns on each side, and the roof correspondingly higher in the middle over the taller columns, producing a clear-story, and presenting the fundamental elements of basilica architecture."

"None of the introductory or transitional stages which must have gradually led up from the old halls (with roof all on one level) to the basilica type first found complete at Karnak, has hitherto been discernible. The huge double row of columns at Luxor, standing in the axis of the temple, but lacking any side aisles, is evidently an unfinished basilica hall like that at Karnak. This carries the basilica type back to the early fourteenth century B.C."

"During the work of the University of Chicago Expedition at Soleb in Upper Nubia, I noticed what had already been observed by

FREDERICK MONDERSON

Lepsius's architects that just as at Luxor, there is at Soleb a similar double row of vast columns in the axis of the temple, in front of the first court and in front of the pylon. The question at once arose: 'Is this also an unfinished basilica hall, left without its lower colonnades, just as at Luxor?' In lieu of the lacking side colonnades, just as at Luxor, a wall has been erected on each side, parallel with and close to the double row of columns, producing a long narrow hall in the extended axis of the temple. Are these sidewalls a makeshift to enclose the unfinished basilica as at Luxor? Unfortunately, the superstructure of the Soleb hall has perished and only the ground plan is now discernible. The pylon back of this hall, upon which its side walls abut, is the work of Amenhotep III, the builder of the entire temple, as the inscriptions upon it show. An examination of the masonry showed that these sidewalls from bottom to top engage in the masonry of the pylon, and do not merely impinge upon the pylon. This proves that the builder of the pylon had planned these sidewalls from the beginning, erecting them as he did along with pylon course by course. He therefore planned a nave without side colonnades, and without side aisles. Such a nave must have been for a time, then, a recognized form of temple architecture. It was not a pleasing form, nor one which the Egyptian long retained, but as the development continued, it is for us an interesting transitional stage, through which the architecture of Egypt passed, on its way toward the noble basilica form, which was to furnish later Europe with the greatest fundamental elements of cathedral architecture."

At Kom el Hattan were found colossi of Amenhotep III before pylon XI. A colossal base is in the Paris Museum. A number of statues bearing the King's name were found, including white limestone from Qurneh, some material from Medinet Habu, black granite from Thebes, the base of a statue now at Avignon and another of white limestone at the Ghizeh Museum.

WHERE ARE THE KAMITE KINGS?

Where are the Kamite Kings Illustration. Another image of the face of Queen Tiye, wife of Amenhotep III and mother of Amenhotep IV, Akhenaten, the Religious Reformer.

To the south of the Medinet Habu Temple, the King built his palace and the Metropolitan Museum of Art in New York conducted excavations there in 1912, where *American Journal of Archaeology* XVII (1913: 97-98) indicated: "This building was under construction from about 1400 to 1375 B.C., and consisted of a series of rambling one-story structures erected from time to time. There were dwellings for the use of officials and houses and shops for workmen. The whole aggregate of buildings was enclosed by a brick wall, with a gateway to the west and probably others to the north and east. The harem was separated from the rest of the palace by a wall in which was a single door. One passed through a vestibule, which opened, into a pillared hall. Passages led to the sides, and a stairway to the roof. A royal dining room with apartments for the King was in this part of the palace, and eight suites for the ladies of the harem. The sun-dried bricks of which the palace was built bear the name of the King, in one place the name of the palace, Neb-maat-re, "house of rejoicing," and in the latest part the names of the King and his queen, Tiy. The floors were of brick; the roof was supported by palm logs. Floors, walls, and ceilings were covered with plaster made of mud and chopped straw, which, in the principal rooms, was covered with frescoes. In one room the ceiling design consisted of spirals surrounding cows' heads, which have rosettes between the horns; in another, pigeons and ducks. Many small objects were unearthed, some of them in the process of manufacture."

Where are the Kamite Kings Photo. Valley of the Nobles. Tomb of Vizier Rekhmire. Artisans at work. One individual seems to be fashioning a Kingly figure painted black.

WHERE ARE THE KAMITE KINGS?

Where are the Kamite Kings Illustration. Relief representing Queen Tiy, from the Tomb of Userhai at Thebes and now in the Brussels Museum, seen in *The Treasury of Ancient Egypt* by Arthur Weigall (1911).

A portrait of the King was found in his tomb in the Valley of the Kings, at Thebes. Ushabti figures are in Paris. A group of Amenhotep and Tiy are in the Swarma Collection. A sphinx was found at Karnak while another is now at the Academy in St. Petersburg.

Sekhet statues were found in the Temple of Mut. One each of standing and seated diorite statues of Ptah are in the Turin Museum.

FREDERICK MONDERSON

A seated basalt Anpu statue is in the Sabatier Collection. A wooden tablet with Haremakhti is in the British Museum. A wooden label with tiles is in the Turin Museum. A wooden stamp not yet engraved is also at Turin. Ostraka of Amenhotep's coronation day is in the British Museum. Papyrus copied from a roll is also at the British Museum. That institution also has a medical papyrus of his reign. A stick is in Leyden. A box handle and an inscribed strip of ivory inlay are both in the British Museum. Inlay from boxes found in the King's tomb is now at the Ghizeh Museum.

A number of kohl tubes of wood were found. One is in Paris. Another with Tiy is also in Paris while another is at Ghizeh. Still another is in Turin. Another glazed kohl tube with Hent-Ta-Neb is in Cairo. Glazed tubes were found at the Temple of Amenhotep III. A glazed polychrome jar of the King with Tiy is at Ghizeh. A blue double cylinder vase is in the British Museum. A vase of alabaster is in Leyden. Another of pottery is in Paris. Still another glazed vase with Tiy is at Paris Museum. A dish is at Ghizeh.

Where are the Kamite Kings Photo. Valley of the Nobles. Tomb of Vizier Rekhmire. A pool and workmen engaged in all forms of enterprise. Why are these not painted black for the funerary ceremony?

Scarabs of the King's marriage to Tiy are in the Edinburgh Collection. Another scarab of the King slaying 102 lions is in the same Collection. The King is shown making a great tank. A scarab of the arrival of Kirgipa or Gilukhipa is in Cairo. The princess of Thadukhippa came to Kemet for a political marriage with the old

WHERE ARE THE KAMITE KINGS?

King but ended up marrying his son. The Kamites changed her name to Nefertiti "the fair one cometh."

It is interesting that in the mind games played on young women of African descent, particularly African Americans, "Nefertiti Earrings" were pushed as an African fashion item. Though the queen adapted very well in the powerful family she entered, the earrings should have been styled after the more indigenous and blacker, Queen Nefertari. Therefore, young black designers ought to bring out a line of earrings styled the "Ahmes-Nefertari" to replace the "Nefertiti" line.

Rings, beads, and scarabs with titles, all bear the name of this famous ancient Egyptian, and by extension African, pharaoh, Amenhotep III. *American Journal of Archaeology* XVIII (1914: 503) mentions Wiedemann's article in *Society for Biblical Archaeology* showing: "that there is a long series of scarabs of the time of Amenhotep III. The use of scarabs as a means of making known his religious feelings, his personal characteristics, and his famous deeds, to his subjects and to posterity, was quite in accordance with the usual practice of Amenhotep III. The most popular fact recorded on the King's scarabs was his marriage with Tiy. Among the titles given to Amenhotep III the most interesting is that which connects with Aten; it is evidence that the Aten-cult did not arise after the accession of Amenhotep IV, but had already been planned in the time of Amenhotep III. Some Egyptologists have of late been inclined to overestimate the personal influence of Amenhotep IV over the religious movement of his time."

His great Queen was Tiy, daughter of Yuaa and Thuaa. A Cartouche/Shennu of the Queen is in the quarry at Tell el-Amarna. An alabaster ushabti mentions Queen Tiy. Her toilet case is in Turin. A figure of her son, Amenhotep IV was found at Tell el-Amarna. A trial piece, found at Amarna is in the Flinders Petrie Collection. She is shown as an Osiris, frequently with Amenhotep III on statues, scenes, scarabs, rings, etc.

FREDERICK MONDERSON

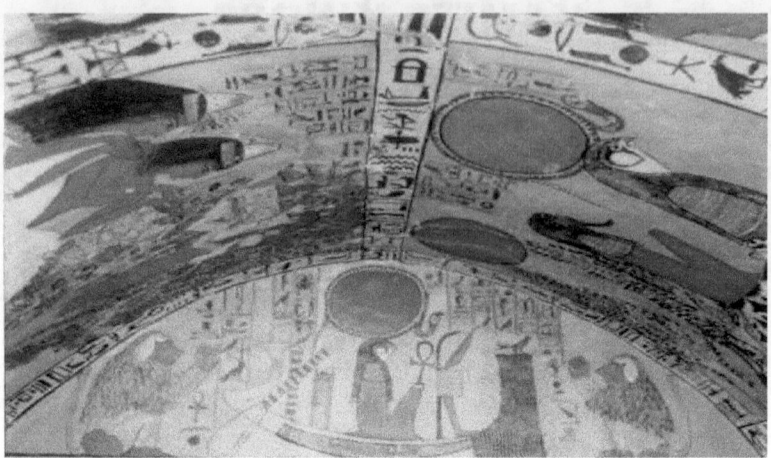

Where are the Kamite Kings Photo. Valley of the Nobles. Tomb of Sennufer. With Sennufer and spouse seated and being nourished by the "Tree Goddess," and with Ra Horakhty and another God at rest, baboons greet the Solar Barque with Ra aboard.

American Journal of Archaeology XI (1907: 344-45) discuss an account of the work of E. R. Ayrton and Theodore Davis, who discovered Queen Thyi's tomb in the Valley of the Kings rather than in the customary Valley of the Queens. They state its location: "in the same hill as the tomb of Rameses IX. A flight of steps leads to a corridor, which opens, into a large room with a small side chamber. This room was originally covered with white stucco and left unpainted. Fragments of a large wooden coffin lay on the floor, while on one side was the royal mummy in a case of exquisite workmanship, inlaid with precious stones set in gold. The whole of the woodwork is so fragile that it was impossible to move it, but the contents of the tomb were photographed before any attempt was made to handle them. The doors of the room were covered with gold leaf and decorated like the coffin with scenes of Aten worship. Accounts in the *Nation*, February 14, 1907, add that buried with the queen were solid gold plates and jewelry. On her head was the royal gold crown, representing a vulture with a signet ring in each talon. Of special beauty and interest are several portrait busts of the queen in alabaster set with obsidian and lapis lazuli. The mummy had been damaged by water, and fell to pieces when uncovered. The name of her son, the heretic King, Khuenaten, had been everywhere erased from the inscriptions but otherwise the tomb was not damaged."

WHERE ARE THE KAMITE KINGS?

Where are the Kamite Kings Illustration. The head of a Canopic Jar belonging to King Harmhab.

A further report in *American Journal of Archaeology* XII (1908: 355) states: "The tomb-chamber contained an immense wooden shrine originally covered with gold-leaf, on which had been worked a scene of sun-worship as introduced by King Amenhotep IV. Against the west wall stood a four-legged couch bearing the coffin of the Queen. The legs of this couch had given way, allowing the coffin to fall to the floor below. The lid had fallen in, breaking into two pieces and forcing the mummy out to one side. The lid had been a beautiful piece of work, covered with gold leaf and inlaid with carnelian. The mummy had been wrapped in plates of gold. On the head lay a crown of gold in the form of a vulture, grasping an emblem of eternity in either claw. Around the neck of the mummy had been a necklace of plaques of gold inlaid with stone, and below these four rows of hollow gold drops. The four canopic jars were discovered with the lids carved as portraits of the Queen."

The sons of Queen Tiy and Amenhotep III were a Thutmose and Amenhotep IV. A daughter of Tiy was Bakt-Aten. Other daughters found at Soleb were Ast and Hent-Mer-Heb. Hent-Ta-Neh was found at Gurob. Sat-Amen's box is in the British Museum. A stele of this princess is in the Ghizeh Museum.

Neferkheperura-Waenra, Amenhotep IV, Akhenaten *Nile Year* 2880-2896 (c. 1350-1334 B.C.) followed his father, and created one of the most controversial reigns in all of dynastic Egypt/Kemet/Ta-meri. Budge I (1908: 145-150) supplied the royal titulary of this important, yet highly maligned monarch. Amen-Hetep IV had two sets of names. In the first set he adored Amen and in the second, the Aton.

Where are the Kamite Kings Illustration. Standing "Taharka Column" in the Great Court with Second Pylon's entrance into Karnak Temple's Processional Colonnade, centerpiece of the Hypostyle Hall of Rameses I, Seti I and Rameses II.

WHERE ARE THE KAMITE KINGS?

A.

Horus	Ka-Nekht-Aa-Shuti
Two Ladies	Ur-Sutenit-Em-Semt-Aten
Golden Horus	Thes-Khau-em-Annu-Qena
Suten Bat	Ra-Nefer-Kheperu-Ua-En-Ra

"High-Priest of Heru-Khuti, exalted one in the Horizon in his name Shu-in-the Disk"

Son of Ra   Amen-Hetep with additions:

                                Neter-Heq-Uast (or Annu) Aa-em-Aha-F

On a stele at Gebel Silsileh

                                Amen-Hetep IV (Khu-En-Aten)

B.

Horus	Ka-Nekht-Aten- Meri
Two Ladies	Ur-Sutenit-Em-Khut-Aten
Golden Horus	Thes-Ren-F-En-Aten
Suten Bat	Ra-Nefer-Kheperu-U-En-Ra-Aten-Meri
Son of Ra	Aten-Khu-En with additions: Aa-Em-Aha found at Tell El Amarna.

FREDERICK MONDERSON

Where are the Kamite Kings Illustration. Artistic rendering of the face of Amenhotep IV, Akhenaten.

Petrie II (1894: 205-07) supplies some instances where the King's name has been recovered and the places where his artifacts have been dispersed to.

Where are the Kamite Kings Photo. Valley of the Nobles. Tomb of Sennufer. Sennufer stands before various Gods above and below the Nobleman and guests.

WHERE ARE THE KAMITE KINGS?

At Heliopolis was found fragments of granite. At Memphis, tablets with Cartouche/Shennu, fragments in Cairo, re-used blocks now at the Sydney Museum, and a stele of Huy. Gurob provided fragments of a scene with the King. Kahun produced a papyrus of his 5thyear. At Eshmunen was found a granite pedestal.

Where are the Kamite Kings Illustration. Another portrait of Amenhotep IV, Ikhnaton, Akhenaton.

While he built a temple off to the east of Karnak, the most significant finds of this King come from Tell el-Amarna. His palace and temple were located here. He erected three rock steles on the western bank of the Nile and eleven rock steles on the eastern bank. The King's death mask is at Ghizeh Museum, Cairo. Statues of the King are in the British Museum and Amherst. Colossi were found at Amarna. Ushabtis are in the Ghizeh Museum. Ushabtis and a tiara with the King are in the Flinders Petrie Collection. A sculpture and trial piece are known. Steles are in the Edinburgh Collection and the Ghizeh Museum. Cairo has fragments of steles, part of the pavement of a house, sculptures, vases, etc. Jar-sealings and rings are at Amherst Museum.

Where are the Kamite Kings Illustration. Nefertiti seems to be offering Amenhotep IV flowers. Some believe he used the crutch because of a disability.

Where are the Kamite Kings Illustration. Akhnaton with his wife and daughter in their chariot as the Aten rains down "helping hands."

WHERE ARE THE KAMITE KINGS?

Where are the Kamite Kings Illustration. Bust of Ikhnaton, religious reformer and revolutionary, world's first monotheist. (The Louvre.) He wears the Blue or War Crown!

Where are the Kamite Kings Illustration. Amenhotep IV, Ikhnaton, makes an offering to the sun disk, while his wife Nefertiti assists as six daughters stand in the rear. The sun offers rays of hands with Ankh signs to the royal couple who have a prepared "Table of Offerings."

FREDERICK MONDERSON

Wady Hammamat has rock cuttings and Qus supplied blocks. At Thebes were found fragments used by Horemheb, stone on the Quay at Luxor, and stones at Karnak bear his name. Erment has a block. Silsileh has a stele about building. East Silsileh has a stele of Amen-Ra. The Aswan stele of Bati has his name. At Soleb, a statue of the King is shown worshiping his father.

A statuette is in the Paris Museum, while the shoulder of a limestone statue is at Ghizeh. Fragments of statues are in the Amherst Collection. A body of quartzite is in the Flinders Petrie Collection. The limestone head of a statuette is in Turin.

Where are the Kamite Kings Illustration. Statues of Amenhotep IV, Akhenaten (Akhnaton) found at Karnak.

Portraits of the King, the best of which was found at Karnak, shows him as a young man while an older one is in Paris. Steles of quartzite are at Ghizeh, Paris, alabaster in the Edinburgh Collection and in Berlin. One of stone is in Berlin. A door jamb fragment is in Berlin.

Cartouche/Shennu on blocks of limestone are in Turin. One of red granite is in the Sabatier Collection while limestone and blue glaze are at Amherst. Part of a granite altar is in the Ghizeh Museum. Part of red granite mortar is in the Fitzwilliam Museum and in the Flinders Petrie Collection. An alabaster vase is in Leyden. Rings

WHERE ARE THE KAMITE KINGS?

of gold and copper, scarabs, plaques, etc., and a gold-plated heart scarab are known.

Where are the Kamite Kings Illustration. Bust of Nefertiti, wife of Akhenaton, Amenhotep IV.

His Queen was Nefertiti. Fragments of 5 statues are in the Amherst Collection. Her portrait is in Berlin. Another portrait is at Tell el-Amarna. Vase fragments, rings, etc., are known. His daughters were Mert-Aten who married Ra-Smenkh-Ka; Makt-Aten, died before the King; Ankh-S-En-Pa-Aten became Ankhsenamen and married Tutankhamen; Nefernefruaten married the son of Burna Buryas; and Nefer-Nefre-ra-Sotep-En-Ra.

FREDERICK MONDERSON

Where are the Kamite Kings Illustration. Statue of Amenhotep IV (Akhenaten, Akhnaton) shown with hands crossed in a royal position holding crook and whisk, symbols of authority; and, Lid of the supposed coffin of Amenhotep IV, Akhnaton.

Ankhkheperura, Smenkhkare, *Nile Year* 2894-2896 (c. 1336-1334 B.C.) is known from a ring at Gurob, and at Tell el-Amarna his name is in tomb No. 2. This site also supplied piece of a vase and knob as well as rings. His Queen was *Mert-Aten,* also in Tomb No. 2, where was found a ring.

Nebkheperura, Tut-Ankh-Amen, *Nile Year* 2896-2905 (c. 1334-1325 B.C.) was the next King during this turbulent period. His royal titulary, supplied by Budge I (1908: 150-151) is as follows:

WHERE ARE THE KAMITE KINGS?

Horus
Two Ladies
Golden Horus
Suten Bat
Son of Ra

Ka-Nekht-Tet-Mes
Nefer-Taui
Renp-Khau-Sehetep-Neteru
Ra-Kheperu-Neb
Tut-Ankh-Amen

Where are the Kamite Kings Illustration. Bust of King Tutankhamon of the XVIIIth Dynasty.

Le Grain's *Annales* and *Recueil*, and Prisse *Monuments* all mention this King.

Petrie II (1894: 235) provides additional insights into the King's identity. At Memphis, in addition to pottery and rings, his name is found in the Serapeum burial of Apis II. An alabaster vase was found at Gurob along with a wooden cubit and rings and pendants. Tell el-Amarna has provided rings and pendants. A tomb that mentions him is located at Ekhmin. At Abydos, his name is on a stele of Khonsu. Karnak has 6 blocks in a pylon and blocks reused by Horemheb. A block and statue exist, and he is also represented

FREDERICK MONDERSON

in the Temple of Mut. Luxor Temple has a seated alabaster statue of the King and his queen, where she embraces him. He is also found on the restored temple of Thutmose IV and inscriptions on wood are in the Hilda Petrie Collection. The tomb of Hui has his name. A scribe's palette with Cartouche/Shennu identifies him. Knob handles are at Leyden Museum, in the Glasgow and Flinders Petrie Collections. Kohl tubes are in the Leyden Museum and in the British Museum.

His Queen, Ankh-S-En-Aten, later Ankh-S-En-Amen, is on an alabaster vase and wooden cubit in the Flinders Petrie Collection. It is also on a kohl tube and scarabs and rings contain his name.

Where are the Kamite Kings Photo. Goddess Mut as Hathor in Horns and Disk represented in Karnak Temple.

WHERE ARE THE KAMITE KINGS?

Where are the Kamite Kings Illustration. Enthroned Tutankhamon giving audience to one of his officials, Huy, Governor of Ethiopia (Erman 1894), while his *Son of Ra* Cartouche/Shennu is above left and his *Suten Bat* is at right.

Where are the Kamite Kings Photo. Tutankhamon's burial mask with its many splendid gold and precious jewelry inlay.

FREDERICK MONDERSON

In November 1922, Howard Carter discovered the Tomb of Tut-Ankh-Amen. Carter had been working for nearly two decades in the Valley of the Kings, before he made the important discovery for his patron Lord Carnarvon.

An article according to *American Journal of Archaeology* XXVII (1923: 76-78) is entitled "The Tomb of Tutankhamon," and it's considered: "the most important royal tomb excavated in recent years, and contains objects of unique interest and value. Its situation is just below the tomb of Rameses VI. From the outer door found by Mr. Carter a flight of sixteen steps and a sloping passage led to a door in the east wall of a chamber of twenty-five feet long, twelve feet wide, and about nine feet high. The longer axis of the chamber is north and south, at right angles to the passage. The north wall is a partition wall, and contained a blocked-up door, indicating that beyond it was the actual burial chamber. On either side of this door were found wooden statues of the King. The body and limbs of each of these were painted black, while the headdress, skirt, and sandals were covered with gold leaf. In the west wall an irregular opening, made by ancient robbers, allows a glimpse of a confused mass of tomb-furniture in an inner chamber. The outer room itself had been robbed of objects of precious metals, probably not long after the death of the King but the other furnishings were not much disturbed, and include an elaborately carved and ornamented royal chair or throne; three great state couches of gilded wood, three chariots, musical instruments, pottery and alabaster vases, boxes of clothing, boxes of preserved venison, mutton, duck, etc. Folded sheets, which were at first thought to be papyri, proved to be napkins. Among objects of special artistic interest is a wooden box covered with fine miniature paintings of hunting scenes: the pursuit of gazelles, wild asses, ostriches and hares is represented. A footstool is significantly inlaid with a row of figures of captives and prisoners. The largest chariot, which is semicircular in form and opens at the back, is of wood covered with gold leaf with delicately embossed decorations and exquisite inlaid designs in carnelian, malachite, lapis-lazuli, blue glaze and alabaster. At each corner is a small inlaid circle enclosing the sacred eye of Horus. These eyes are inlaid in blue, black and white. The inner surface of the chariot is of plain gold with large embossed Cartouche/Shennus of the King and his queen under the royal vulture which has wide, up-spreading wings."

WHERE ARE THE KAMITE KINGS?

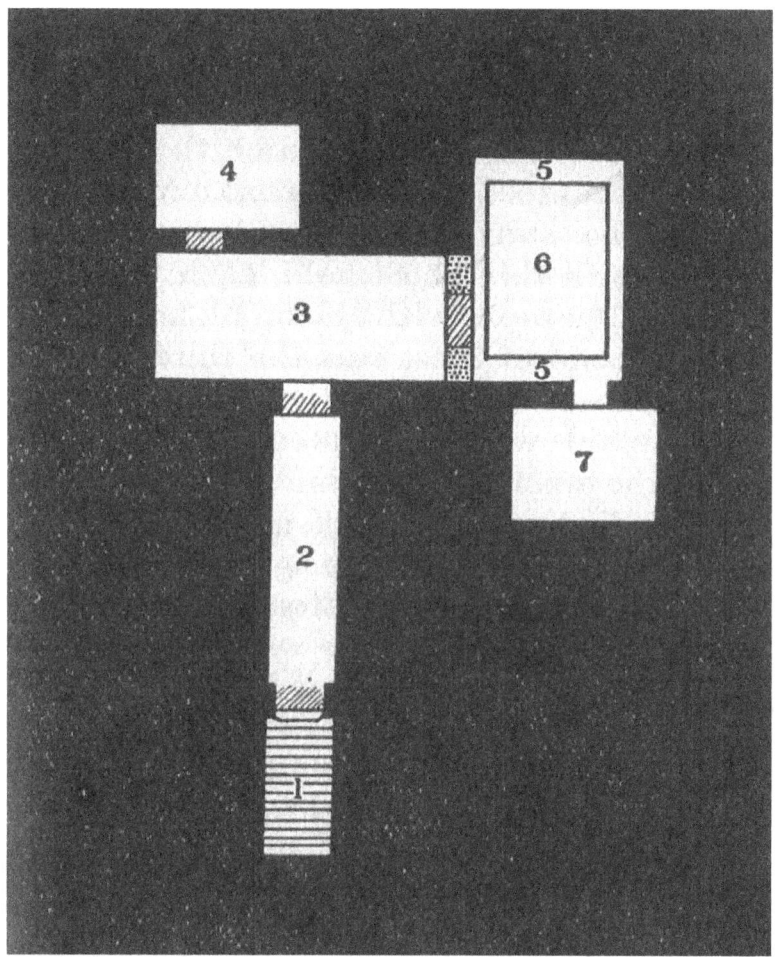

Where are the Kamite Kings Illustration. Tomb of Tutankhamon showing, 1) Entrance staircase; 2) passage; 3) Antechamber; 4) Annex to 3; 5) Burial Chamber; 6) Funerary shrines (now removed); 7) Store-chamber.

"The edges of the chariot and the hand-rail around the top are covered with red leather, but the bottom, which was also of leather, has fallen away. Between the rail and the body in front are small-carved figures of Semitic captives. This is the largest Egyptian chariot known, and was doubtless used by the King and queen on state occasions. A yoke, which went across the necks of the horses, was found with it. Still more important than the chariot is a bust, perhaps representing the young queen, exquisitely carved in wood and covered with a thin coating of plaster. The figure has on its head a crown similar to that designed by Akhnaton for his queen. This is painted yellow to represent gold."

"It has the *uraeus* over the forehead. The face and neck are brownish yellow and the eyes and eyebrows black. The arms of the figure were intentionally cut off at the shoulders, but the body, which is draped in a white robe, extends far as the waist. The features show the soft expression characteristic of the artists of Akhnaton, whose daughter the figure may represent. The nostrils are finely carved, the lips are clear-cut and full, and the cheeks and chin round and youthful. The figure is an important work of art. On February 16 the burial chamber was opened and found to contain a gilded canopy almost filling the room. Within this was a second canopy enclosing the sarcophagus. Adjoining the burial chamber was another room full of chests, works of art, etc. The tomb lies so low that it is not free from damp, and some of the objects, which have been found in it, will need special care to prevent disintegration. In the work of clearing the tomb the discoverers are assisted by Dr. A.M. Lythgoe of the Metropolitan Museum and other Egyptologists. (A.E.P. Weigall, Philadelphia *Evening Bulletin*, Jan. 20-Feb 12, 1923.")

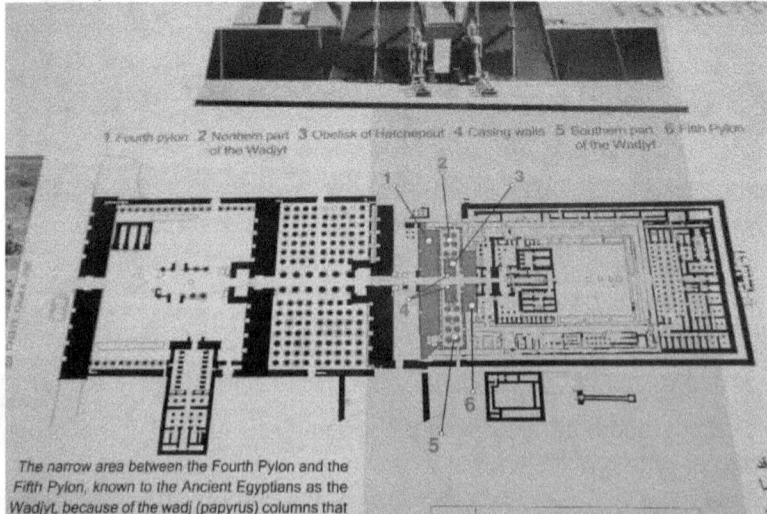

The narrow area between the Fourth Pylon and the Fifth Pylon, known to the Ancient Egyptians as the Wadjyt, because of the wadj (papyrus) columns that

Where are the Kamite Kings Photo. Plan of the Temple of Karnak between Pylons four and five – Obelisks Court.

WHERE ARE THE KAMITE KINGS?

Where are the Kamite Kings Photo. Erik Monderson stands beside the Great Sphinx on the Ghizeh Plateau.

Where are the Kamite Kings Photo. On the Ghizeh Plateau, Carmen Monderson stands in the shadow with Khufu's Great Pyramid and Khafra's Sphinx in rear.

FREDERICK MONDERSON

American Journal of Archaeology XXVIII (1924: 84) continued its commentary on the Tomb of Tutankhamon, discovered by Howard Carter in 1922. Following all the excitement at the tomb's first opening, it was closed and later reopened with Howard Carter beginning a systematic cataloguing of the precious contents.

Accordingly: "The two large wooden statues of the King, which stood on either side of the door which leads from the antechamber to the burial chamber, have been carefully packed and removed. To facilitate the removal of the elaborately constructed series of shrines, which enclose the sarcophagus of the King, it has been necessary to take down the wall between the antechamber and the shrine. The fresco on the inner face of the wall, though not of special interest, has been preserved. From the narrow space between the wall of the sepulchral chamber and the outermost shrine a considerable number of interesting objects have been recovered: wine jars; eleven black paddles; an inlaid royal staff; gilt emblems of Anubis. The great outer shrine, which is of wood, elaborately ornamented with designs in gold and in blue faience, has been dismantled. Within this shrine was a linen pall, supported on a wooden frame, and ornamented with gold rosettes. This originally concealed the next inner shrine, but was in a state of partial disintegration, and had to be removed with great care."

Such antiques with historical and cultural relevance had to be preserved with great care and it became a significant task of the discoverers and those concerned to protect these valuables for posterity. Not only would these artifacts serve historical, cultural, and artistic purposes, it allowed those in the field of preservation to also be a part of preserving such evidence for posterity.

WHERE ARE THE KAMITE KINGS?

Where are the Kamite Kings Illustration. Bust of Khonsu, of the Theban Triad.

The *American Journal of Archaeology* XXVIII (1924) continued that: "Some valuable objects were removed from the space between the first and second shrines, including a gold staff and a silver staff, each surmounted by a statuette of the King. The second shrine is of wood covered with gold; and the doors are ornamented with representations of the King in acts of adoration. Within this, a third and a fourth shrine have successively been revealed. The decorations of the inner shrine are said to be more sumptuous and of finer quality than those of the outer shrine. The problem of removing without injury the parts of these structures has presented grave mechanical difficulties; but these have been so far overcome that in January the stone sarcophagus of the King was disclosed within the fourth shrine: and in February the granite cover was raised. Beneath a pall was found the gold case, which contains the mummy of the King, resting on a couch of a form, which resembles that of the couches discovered in the outer chamber. Adjoining the sepulchral chamber to the east is another room, containing an elaborate shrine in which it is expected that the canopic jars of the King will be found. Much funeral furniture is heaped up in front of and at the side of this shrine. At the present writing the investigation of the tomb has been halted by a disagreement between the excavators and the archaeological service of the Egyptian government."

Where are the Kamite Kings Photo. Ghizeh Plateau. Classic image of the Great Pyramid of Khafra.

Kheperkheperura-Irma'at, Aye, who reigned *Nile Year* 2905-2909 (c. 1325-1321 B.C.), followed Tutankhamon and tried to clear up the mess of the Amarna heresy. His royal titulary is as follows:

Horus	Ka-Nekht-Thethe-Khau (or Kheperu)
Golden Horus	Heq-Maat-Sekheper-Taui
Suten Bat	Ra-Kheper-Kheperu-Ari-Maat
Son of Ra	Ai with additions: Neter-Heq-Uast

Aye is known from the rock temple at Ekhmin and his tomb in the Valley of the Kings.

WHERE ARE THE KAMITE KINGS?

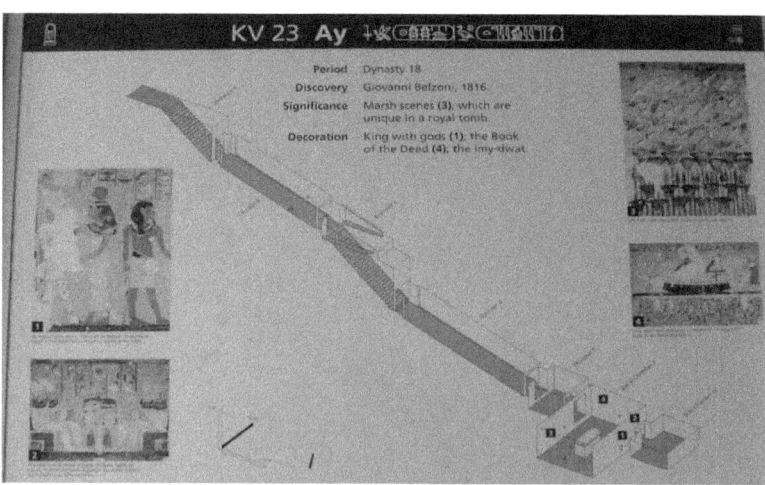

Where are the Kamite Kings Photo. Valley of the Kings. Tomb of Ay, late 18th Dynasty. This tomb's significance is that it contains marsh scenes that are unique in a royal tomb; the King and Gods; it contains the *Book of the Dead* and the *Imy dwat*.

Petrie I (1894: 238-39) identified his name at Memphis and Gurob by rings now in the Flinders Petrie Collection. At Karnak his name is on reused blocks. Shatawi (22 D 17' N) contains a shrine of Pasar. The King's portrait is in his tomb. Steles of Min-Nekht of the King's 4thyear exist. One is in Berlin and another in the Louvre. The stele of Tutu is in the British Museum No. 130. Gold rings are in the Leyden Museum. Pottery and various scarabs also carry his name. His Queen was Ty, whose head is at the Ekhmin shrine and a figure in the King's tomb. The important Abydos List, begun by Seti I and finished by his son Rameses II, supplies the names of Kings dating from Menes to Seti. Conspicuously, there are 5 blank Cartouche/Shennus where the names of Hatshepsut, Amenhotep IV, Tutankhamon, Smenkhare and Aye or Ai are missing. That of Hatshepsut is missing because she was bold enough to rule as Pharaoh, proclaimed herself "Son of Ra," wore a beard, dressed like a man, built a temple greater than her ancestor Mentuhotep II, built a tomb in the Valley of the Kings and planned to link her mortuary Deir el Bahari temple with her final resting place, via a tunnel. Those associated with the Amarna heresy, Rameses II, also refused to recognize.

FREDERICK MONDERSON

Where are the Kamite Kings Illustration. Bust of Amon, "King of the Gods" and Presider of Karnak Temple.

Where are the Kamite Kings Illustration. Group statue of Amon, King of the Gods and wife Mut, the Earth Goddess.

WHERE ARE THE KAMITE KINGS?

Where are the Kamite Kings Illustration. Bust of Horemhab (Horemheb), last King of the 18th Dynasty.

Where are the Kamite Kings Photo. Amenemhat III 12th Dynasty, Cairo Museum.

FREDERICK MONDERSON

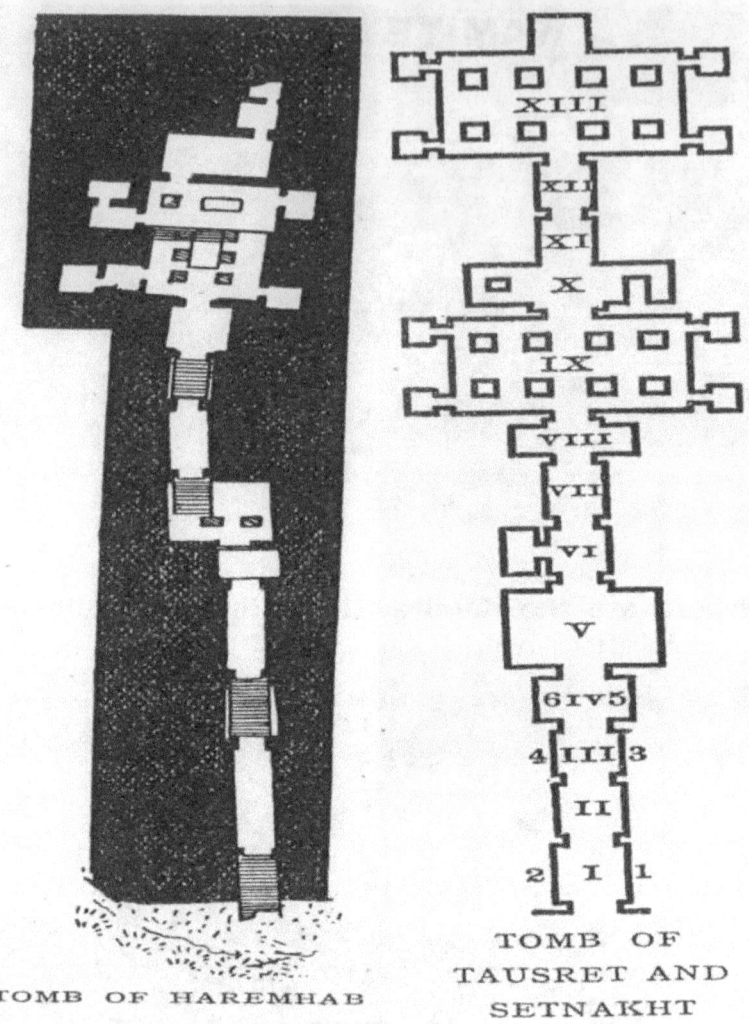

TOMB OF HAREMHAB

TOMB OF TAUSRET AND SETNAKHT

Where are the Kamite Kings Illustration. Valley of the Kings. Tombs of Horemhab, last King of the 18th Dynasty and Tausert and Setnakht of the later 19th Dynasty.

Djeserkheperura-Setepenra, Horemhab, Horemheb, *Nile Year* 2909-2937 (c. 1321-1293 B.C.) was a general dating to the time of Amenhotep III and the subsequent Kings. He seized the throne during the unsettling times that produced the religious controversy.

Budge I (1908: 154-55) supplied his royal titulary.

WHERE ARE THE KAMITE KINGS?

Horus	Ka-Nekht-Sept-Sek-Heru
Two Ladies	Ur-Bait-Em-Apt
Golden Horus	Heri-Her-Maat-Sekheper-Taui (1)
	Aa-Khepesh (2)
Suten Bat	Ra-Tcheser-Kheperu with
additions:	
	Setep-En-Ra Heq-Maat-Setep-En-Ra,
	Heq-Uast-Setep-En-Ra,
	Heq-Annu-Setep-En-Ra
Son of Ra	Heru-Em-Heb with addition:
	Mer-En-Amen

This King is No. 74 on the *Abydos List* and No. 48 on the *Second Abydos List*.

Petrie I (1894: 242-44), again has provided extensive information regarding the location of Horemheb's (Haremhab's) name. His tomb before ascension has been located at Memphis. At that site his name has been located at the Apis burial at the Serapeum. A ring, piece of a stele, and a capital are in Cairo. At Tell el-Amarna, a temple fragment was located. Abydos produced a frog with his Queen's name.

At Karnak his name is on Pylon IX and X and a connecting wall of that pylon. It is on the Avenue of 128 sphinxes. On a stele and wall between Pylon V and the sanctuary, the King's name is depicted. There are inscriptions in the Temple of Ptah. It is on blocks in the Pylon of Khonsu Temple. At Luxor it is on a usurped colonnade. At Deir el Bahari and Medinet Habu, it is on restoration inscriptions. At the Silsileh rock temple it is in scenes of the Gods. This rock temple recounts the Sudan war. Kom Ombo blocks were reused by the Ptolemies. Kuban produced a lion with his name.

FREDERICK MONDERSON

Where are the Kamite Kings Photo. Photo. 128. Ghizeh Plateau. The Great Pyramid of Khufu and the White Building to the left, Khufu's "Boathouse Museum."

Three Steles of Horemhab as a general are in the Paris Museum. Another stele is also in the Louvre. A fragment from his tomb is in the Zizinia collection. Another fragment is in Vienna.

Colossal statues from Medinet Habu are in Berlin. A seated colossal statue is in the Luxor Hotel. A statue with his Queen and another with Amen is in the Turin Museum. Another statue with Horus is in the Castle Cattajo. A bust of a kneeling statue is in the Florence Museum. Also in this Museum is a Hathor Cow suckling the King. The Metropolitan Museum of Art has a grey granite statue, 3 feet, 10 inches, of Horemheb as a General that was given by Mr. and Mrs. V. Everit Macy. The *Bulletin of the Metropolitan Museum of Art* MCMXXIII (1923: October: 3) says, "The statue, of gray granite at a scale fully life sized, is of a man seated cross-legged, wearing the dress of a well-to-do person of the late Eighteenth Dynasty."

WHERE ARE THE KAMITE KINGS?

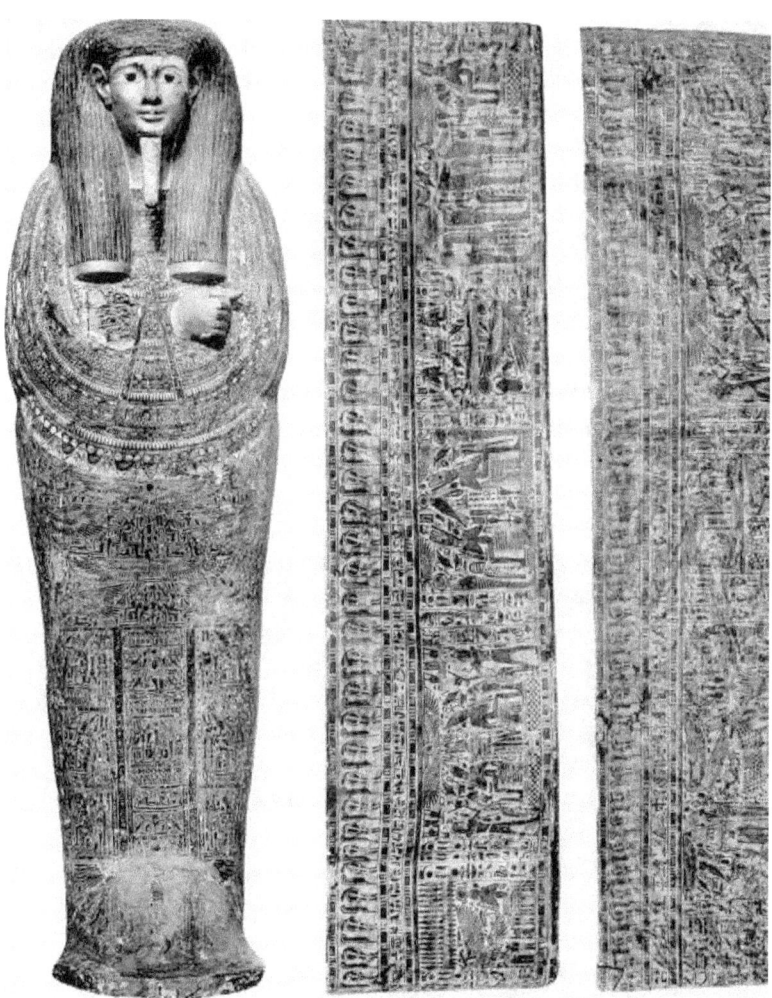

Where are the Kamite Kings Illustration. Lid and side views of Zod-ptah-auf-Ankh-Grand coffin.

The best portrait of Horemheb comes from a statue and a pylon at Karnak. Ostracon from his 21st year is in the British Museum. Six lines from a broken papyrus is in Cairo. A bronze plaque is in Paris. Finally, a wooden vase, rings, amulets and scarabs, all identify Horemheb. A statue with his Queen Nexem-Mut is in Turin. Rings in the Flinders Petrie Collection and a scarab in Berlin, belong to this King.

FREDERICK MONDERSON

Where are the Kamite Kings Photo. Ghizeh Plateau. Earliest. Old Kingdom, form of columnar support with lintel, shaft and abacus supporting the architrave that in turn supports the roof.

Where are the Kamite Kings Illustration. In the barque of the Gods, the King is baptized with "laying on of hands" or "steadying."

WHERE ARE THE KAMITE KINGS?

12. NINETEENTH AND TWENTIETH RAMESSIDE DYNASTIES

THE NINETEENTH DYNASTY

Menpehtyra, Rameses I, *Nile Year* 2937-2939 (c. 1293-1291 B.C.) was the founder of the XIX Dynasty after the confusion of the Amarna Revolution and following Horemhab's reign. The Ramesside Kings of this era were successful in adding luster to the golden age. They restored the primacy of Amen of Thebes, continued the imperialist policies of the past and relished in prosperity. Extensive and meaningful building projects were undertaken. After this time, however, the world began to change significantly. Whereas in the past, Pharaonic troops carried the sword to the world, the legacy could not be continued by their successors. The later Ramesside Kings could not hold back the inevitable hordes that had scores to settle with Kemet/Ta-meri (Egypt). The weak Kings of this era could not stem this tide and the nation entered into a relative, though not inevitable, decline that lasted for another thousand years.

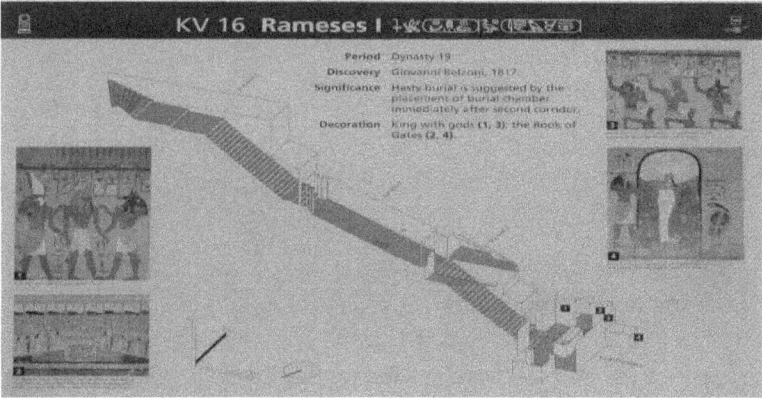

Where are the Kamite Kings Photo. Valley of the Kings. Tomb of Rameses I, 19th Dynasty. A hasty burial is suggested by the placement of the burial chamber immediately after the second corridor and the King with Gods and the *Book of Gates*.

FREDERICK MONDERSON

For the first of the Ramesside Kings, Rameses I, Budge supplied the royal titulary as follows.

Horus	Ka-Nekht-Uatch-Suteniu
Two Ladies	Kha-Em-Suten-Ma
Golden Horus	Em-Khet-Taui
Suten Bat	Ra-Men-Pehti
Son of Ra	Ra-Messu, or Ra-Meses

His name is on the *Tablet of Sakkara*, the *Abydos List* No. 75 and *Second Abydos List* No. 49. While his tomb is No. 16 in the Valley of the Kings, his mummy and coffin lid are in Cairo.

Where are the Kamite Kings Photo. Tomb of Rameses I. *The Book of Gates*, 3rd Division, with goddesses personifying hours flanking the serpent who creates and consumes them. Above, the gods who follow Osiris lie in their Sarcophagi.

WHERE ARE THE KAMITE KINGS?

Petrie III (1905: 4) has identified occurrences of his name where at Serabit el Khadem two steles, at Qantara the base of a hawk and el Merg has inscriptions concerning Rameses I. From Memphis, the base of a statue of his is in the Louvre. Rameses' Ka name is at Abydos. At Karnak, his name is on the pylon before the Hypostyle Hall and again on the west side of that magnificent structure.

A stele of his second year from Wady Halfa is in the Louvre. Scarabs of his reign are somewhat rare. In a number of instances, he is shown being worshiped as at the Temple of Qurneh by Seti I and again by Rameses II. At Abydos, he is pictured by the barque of the ancestors of Seti I, and in the list of ancestors he is featured. Also, at the Ramesseum, he is among the statues of the ancestors. This distinguished position is again repeated at Medinet Habu. In the tomb of Anhurkhaui and that of Penuby, Rameses I, is represented. On a stele of Hora from Abydos now in Cairo, he is mentioned.

Where are the Kamite Kings Photo. Tomb of Rameses I. Osiris in a shrine attended by ram-headed Anubis and a cobra; from the Book of Gates, 3rd Division.

FREDERICK MONDERSON

His Queen, Sistra, is in a tomb in Bab el Harim, or, the Valley of the Queens. She is also in the tomb of Sety I, and with a barque of Seti I.

Men-Ma'at-Ra, Seti I, *Nile Year* 2939-2952 (c. 1291-1278 B.C.) is the next King in this line. A marked distinction of this King and subsequent ones of this dynasty is the proliferation of names in the royal titulary as supplied by Budge I (1908: 158-65):

Horus Taui	Ka-Nekht-Kha-Em-Uast-Sankh-
	Ka-Nekht-Nem-Mestu
	Ka-Nekht-Sekhem-Khepesh
	Ka-ekht-Ter-Pet-Paut
	Ka-Nekht-Nem-Khau
	Ka-Nekht-Matet-Mentu
	Ka-Nekht-Sa-Tem
	Ka-En-Ra-Meri-Maat
	Ka-Nekht-User-Pet
	Ka-Nekht-User-Pet
	Ka-Nekht-Pet-Pehti
	Ka-Nekht-Sekhem-Pehti
	Ka-Nekht-Sekhem-Pehti
	Ka-Nekht-Aa-Khepesh
	Ka-Nekht-Kha-Khau
Two Ladies	Sekhem-Pehti-Ter-Pet-Paut
	Uafu-Semti-Ter-Mentiu
	Mentiu-En-Meri-Mak-Qemt
	Mak-Qemt-Uafu-Semti
	Nem-Mestu-Sekhem-Khepesh-Ter-Pet-Paut Nem-Mestu-Sekhem-Ter-Pet-Paut
	Nem-Mestu-User-Peti
Golden Horus	Nem-Khau-User-Peti-Em-Taui-Nebu User-Peti-Em-Taui-Nebu
	Mer-En-Ra-Saa-Ka-F
	Sehetep-Em-Ra-Mert-F
	Sekhem-Neter-En-Khepera

WHERE ARE THE KAMITE KINGS?

Suten Bat

Ra-Maat-Men with additions:
Heq-Taui Asu-Ra Taa-Ra Ptah-Meri Heq-Uast
Setep [en] Ra

Ari-En-Ra

Ari-En-Ra-Meri-Amen
Heq-Annu
Taa-ra-Meri-Amen

Son of Ra

Seti with additions:
Meri-Ptah, or Mer-En-Ptah
Mer-En-Ptah-Mer-amen
Meri-Ptah-Ra
Meri-En-Amen

Seti I is No. 76 on the *Abydos List* and No. 50 on the *Second Abydos List*. Petrie III (1905) has supplied extensive evidence of the occurrence of the name of this King.

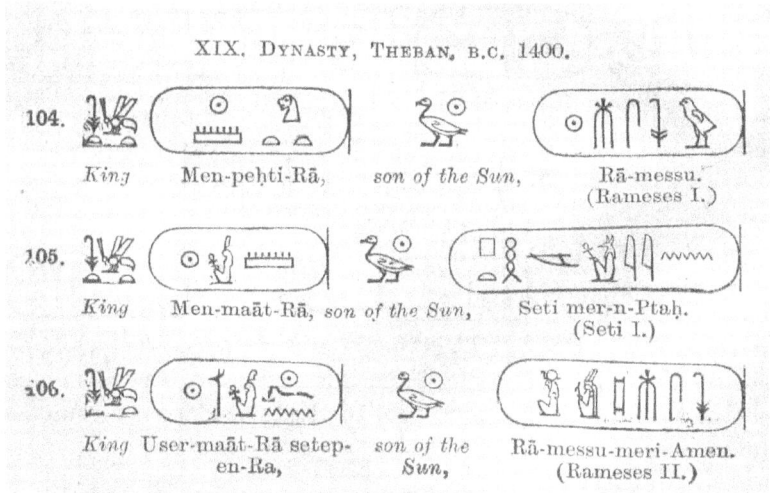

Kamite Kings Cartouche/Shennu. Kings of the Nineteenth, Ramesside Dynasty.

FREDERICK MONDERSON

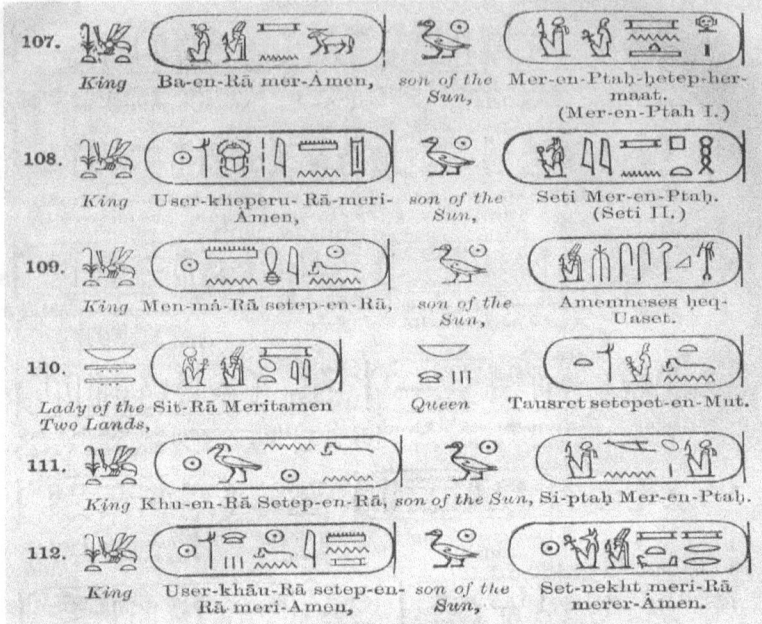

Kamite Kings Cartouche/Shennu. Kings of the Ramesside Dynasty, from Thebes.

A Tell Esh-Shibab stele and vase fragments as well as inscriptions and vases from Serabit el Khadem contain his name. At Alexandria, a door jamb, inscriptions and figures identify Seti I. Qantara has provided the base of a hawk. An altar from Tanis is in Vienna. Cartouche/Shennus come from Khataanah and a model of the Temple of Heliopolis was found at Tell el-Yehudiyeh.

From Heliopolis an eight-sided pillar is in Berlin. Slabs with Gods and Kings are in Brussels. A granite altar is in Cairo. The Flaminian obelisk in Rome also comes from this same site. The Flaminian obelisk was copied on Sallustian. The King's palace is mentioned at Heliopolis.

WHERE ARE THE KAMITE KINGS?

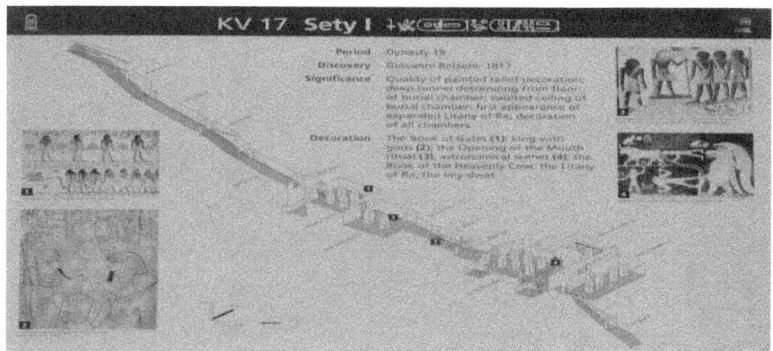

Where are the Kamite Kings Photo. Valley of the Kings. Tomb of Seti I. The significance of this tomb is in its quality of painted relief decoration; deep tunnel descending from the floor of the burial chamber, vaulted ceiling of the burial chamber, first appearance of an expanded *Litany of Ra* and decoration of all chambers. It contains the *Book of Gates*; the King with Gods; *Opening of the Mouth Ceremony*; astronomical scenes; the *Book of the Heavenly Cow*; and the *Imy-dwat*.

From Memphis a sanctuary is named. His name is on blocks from this site and on deposits of the Temple of Ptah. Sakkara has supplied the Apis Chapel and a granite weight now in the Cairo Museum. From the Fayum, a stele of his second year was recovered. Seti is mentioned in inscriptions at Speos Artemidos. Here also inscriptions of Thutmose III mention Seti. He evidently must have made some restorations to the work of this earlier pharaoh.

Where are the Kamite Kings Photo. While the Gods are on parade above, they sail their boat below, in the Tomb of Seti I.

FREDERICK MONDERSON

Where are the Kamite Kings Photo. Sethi as part of the heavenly drama.

The Temple of Osiris at Abydos was begun by Seti I and completed by his son Rameses II. The *American Journal of Archaeology* XVII (1913: 98-99) mention excavations by the Egypt Exploration Fund on the Osireion, behind the main temple. This work centered around "a sloping passage lying in an axis passing through the subterranean chamber in the temenos of Seti's temple, the temple itself, and so out to the desert. The past season had brought to light the buried remains of a colony of pre-dynastic Egyptians. Beneath the wind-swept sand, a few inches deep, is a thick, dark stratum-sand, mingled with burned potsherds, animal bones, and decaying vegetable matter. This rubbish, accumulated until decency or circumstances compelled a removal, yielded objects of interest. Two hearths, each about 20 feet in diameter, were buried in ashes, from which came arrow-heads, borers, scrapers, knives, and saws. A cylindrical seal shows four animal forms, one of them possibly an elephant. A small copper chisel was found. Grain was ground on flat slabs of stone. The abundance of bones attests a meat diet, with the bones cracked to extract the marrow. Traces of buildings have disappeared; it was a colony of the common people. In one corner was a primitive furnace, 23 jars, arranged 12 and 11, packed close together and bolstered up by vertical fire-bricks. Masses of charred logs suggest a slow-heat furnace for keeping things warm a long time."

WHERE ARE THE KAMITE KINGS?

Where are the Kamite Kings Photo. Ra-Horakhty embraces Seti I in his tomb in the Valley of the Kings.

FREDERICK MONDERSON

At Wady Hammamat, Seti I is shown on a stele offering to Amon. Similarly, at Tell Esh-Shibab, *American Journal of Archaeology* V (1901: 334) mentions inscriptions discovered there, of which, one of the "Cartouche/Shennus is that of Seti I, and that King is represented presenting libations to the God Amen, behind whom stands the Goddess Mut." Elsewhere, Koptos supplied a sandstone sphinx and Medamot contains blocks of this King.

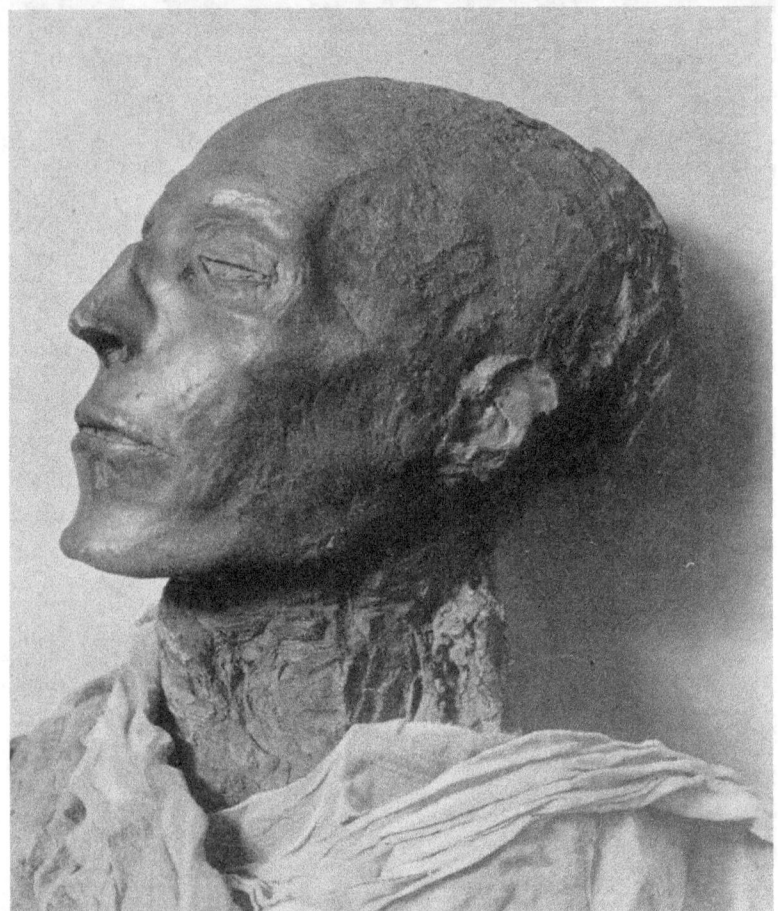

Where are the Kamite Kings Illustration. Head of the Mummy of Seti I, now in the Cairo Museum. The nose is not broken. Hence, the argument that "we break the statue's nose" so as "to remove the brain," does not hold-up and is simply spurious.

At Karnak the King's name is on northern pillars and the east face of the Hypostyle Hall. Also, on the North and South sides as well

WHERE ARE THE KAMITE KINGS?

as the western face of the Hypostyle Hall the name of Seti I can be found. An alabaster stele and edited inscriptions are also at Karnak. At Luxor, his name is on pillars of the colonnade.

Where are the Kamite Kings Photo. All assistants to divinity line up and pull the "Boat of the Gods."

Qurneh and Redesieh Temples contain his name. Redesieh has rock steles. At Medinet Habu, on the back of a statue of Amenhotep I the name of Seti I is found. Gebelein contains inscriptions of Huy and a building with the King's name. A rock chapel, stele and quarry inscriptions at Silsileh bear evidence of the King. At Elephantine a stele of the Temple of Khonsu bears his name. A well at Qobban, inscriptions at Dakkeh, Aswan inscriptions of Amenemapt and at Kalabshah Temple the King is shown with Horus and Set.

At Dosheh a stele offering to a triad, Ibrin stele of Amenemapt, another stele of the first year at Wady Halfa and a Temple at Sesebi, all provide evidence of the King's name.

Statues and portraits of Seti I are many. A statue is in the Vatican. A portion of a statue from Abydos is in Cairo. A wooden statue from his tomb is in the British Museum. A statue fragment is in

Florence. Ushabtis are common. Group statues with Amen and Mut from Karnak are in Cairo. Another group statue of the King with Amen comes from Luxor.

A number of works of restoration were carried out by this King, particularly after the erasures of Amenhotep IV. At Karnak, Pylon IX, Pylon X, a stele at Thutmose III's Temple, a stele of Amenhotep II, and an obelisk of Hatshepsut bear his name. At Qurneh, a stele of Amenhotep III mentions Seti I. He did restoration work at Deir el Bahari. The Temple of Thutmose III at Medinet Habu, Amenhotep III's Temple at El Kab, and at Amada, Thutmose III's Temple, were all restored by Seti I.

Small objects bearing his name are many. A papyrus contains a plan of gold mines. Another papyrus of his 2nd and 3rd years is known. A grey granite weight from Sakkara is in the Cairo Museum. Stone and wood clamps are at Cairo and the British Museum. The handle of a stick is in the Paris Museum. An Asa-Amulet of wood is in Cairo. So too, is a heart amulet of green glaze. A granite altar is in Carlsberg. Another altar is in Miramar. The base of an altar is in Cairo. A stele of Seti I offering to Amenhotep I is in the Turin Museum. Scarabs, cylinders and vases round out this lot.

His Queen was Tuaa, mother of Rameses II. A statue of her is in the Vatican and another at Medinet Habu. Her name is on colossus at Abu Simbel and a portrait is also in the temple. A head is at Abu Simbel. Her name is at the Ramesseum and also at Tanis. Twelve statues of her were reworked. Another statue was re-appropriated. She is with Rameses II on a stele at Miramar. Also, a granite paint palette of hers is in the British Museum.

Seti I's sons were Amen-Nefer-Neb-F and Rameses II. A statue of his daughter Hent-mara is in the Vatican. She is also in a group with Rameses II at Abukir.

WHERE ARE THE KAMITE KINGS?

Where are the Kamite Kings Photo. Sakkara Home of the Step-Pyramid. The Step-Pyramid was built by Vizier Imhotep for Pharaoh Zoser of the 3rd Dynasty, c. 2600 B.C., and it still stands.

Seti I is worshiped by Rameses II at Qurneh, in the Hypostyle Hall at Karnak and in a chapel at Abydos. He is worshiped by Siptah at Qurneh and in a procession of Kings' statues at Abydos.

The names of a number of officials of his reign have survived. These include Any, Prince of Kush and Amenemapt, Prince of Kush, found at Aswan. The slate palette of the scribe Amenemes is in the British Museum. Pasar was a Vizier. A scene of Hormin is in the Louvre. From Gebelein, we know of Huy, who was a scribe of quarrymen. The stele of Huy-Shera, a scribe of gold is in Stockholm, No. 25. Ruru, stud-keeper is in Paris Museum. Ruma, scribe of guard is in Cairo. The Stele of Baka, the foreman, is in Turin. Nianuy was an official of the Temple of Seti I, and Dudua, was a scribe of the Temple of Amen. Hunefer was a chief priest of Seti. The *Papyrus of Hunefer* is important regarding the origins of the Egyptians. It states, purportedly, "We came from the foothills of the Mountains of the Moon where the God Hapi dwells." This has been determined to be the plains of East Africa beneath Mounts Ruenzori, Kenya and Kilimanjaro. A pedestal of Ned, the royal fan-bearer, from the Temple of Sobek, is in the Cairo Museum.

FREDERICK MONDERSON

Where are the Kamite Kings Photo. Isis embraces Seti I in his tomb. Notice the Goddess' Crown or symbol, "A Throne!"

Rameses II, *Nile Year* 2951-3018 (c. 1279-1212 B.C.) became one of the most colorful and interesting Pharaohs of all ancient Kemet/Ta-meri/Egypt, because of his daring, lengthy reign and proliferation of monuments that adorned the artistic landscape of ancient Kemet/Egypt.

Budge supplies his royal titulary that was the most extensive of all Kings of this state. His names included:

Horus	Ka-Nekh-Meri-Maat
	Ka-Nekht-Mak-Qemt
	Ka-Nekht-Kha-Em-Maat-Sankh-Taui
	Ka-Nekht-Uafu-Semti
	Ka-Nekht-Ra-Meri
	Ka-Nekht-Sa-Seb
	Ka-Nekht-Sa-Seb

WHERE ARE THE KAMITE KINGS?

Ka-Nekht-Sa-Asar
Ka-Nekht-Sa-Tem
Ka-Nekht-Sa-Tenen
Ka-Nekht-Sa-Khepera
Ka-Nekht-Sa-Amen
Ka-Nekht-Ur-Peuti
Ka-Nekht-Ur-Nekht-Her-Aha-
Khepesh-F
Ka-Nekht-Ur-Hebu-Meri-Taui
Ka-Nekht-Aha-Her-Meri-Taui
Ka-Nekht-Usr-Pehti
Ka-Nekht-Usr-Maat-Khepesh
Ka-Nekht-Usr-Renput
Ka-Nekht-Usr-Renput-Hefennu
Ka-Nekht-Thes-Maat
Ka-Nekht-Men-Ab-Sekhem-
Pehti-En-Ra-Set-Sati
Ka-Nekht-Merui-Maat
Ka-Nekht-Seqa-Uast
Ka-Nekht-Meri-Maat-Neb
Ka-Nekht-Hebu-Ma-Tef-Ptah-Tu-
Nen
KaNekht-Meri-Maat-Menthu-En-
Suteniu-Ka-En-Sequi-Ur-Pehti-
Ma-Atef-Set-Em-Nubti
Ka-Nekht-Meri-Maat-Heb-Her-
Qen-I-Ner-Nekht

Two Ladies   Mak-Qemt-Uafu-Semti
Mak-Qemt-Uaf-Semti-Ra-Mer-
Ne-Teru-Ker-Taui
Mak-Qemt-Uafu-Semti-Ari-Uru-
Sen-Em-Antiu-Sma-Em-Ast-Set
Mak-Qemt-Uafu-Semti-An-Uru-
Sen-em-Antiu-Sma-en-Ast-Sen
Mak-Qemt-Uafu-Semti-An-Uru-
Erta-Mera-Sen-Em
Mak-Qemt-Uafu-Semti-Neb-
Sent-Shefit-Em-Taui-Nebu-Ari-

FREDERICK MONDERSON

	Ta-En-Kerhi-Em-Tem-Un-Ta-En-Ta
	En-Kheta-Ab-Re-f-Smenku-Mennu-Em-Apt-Rest-En-Tef-Amen-Ta-Su-Her-Nest-Aha-En-Heh-En-renput-Mau-Se-Khem-Ab
	Seshep-Neb-Neter-En-Khepera
	Sekher-Peh-Su-En-An-Pehui-Ta
	Ur-Shefit-Mak-Qemt
Golden Horus	Usr-Renput-Aa-Nekhtut
	Usr-Renput-Aa-Nekhtut-Ra-Mes-Neteru-Ker-Taui
	Usr-Renput-Aa-Nekhtut-An-Tcheru-Pe-Huui-Ta-Ei-Heh-Aha-Seheng-Nef-Re-Useth-En-Semtiesh-Meri-Ta-Heh-Khu-En-Meses
	Shuti-Ma-Ra-Am-Uast-Suten-Bat-Aat-Meri-En-Heru
	Ur-F-Uatu-Sekhem-Pehti
	Ur-Nekhtu-Her-Semti-Nebt
Suten Bat	Ra-User-Maat-Setep-En-Ra
	Ra-User-Maat-En-Ra-Meri-Amen
	Ra-User-Maat
	Ra-User-Maat-S
	Ra-User-Maat-Taa-ra
	Ra-User-Maat-Taa-En-Ra
	Ra-User-Maat-Heq-Uast
	Ra-User-Maat-Asu-Ra
	Ra-User-Maat-Ra-Men
	Ra-User-Maat-Setep-En-Ra?
	Ra-User-Maat-Ra-Meses-Meri-Ptah-Ra-Amen
	Ra-User-Maat-Ra-Messu-Meri-Amen
	Ra-User-Maat-Setep-En-Ra-Meri-Amen
Son of Ra	Ra-Messu

WHERE ARE THE KAMITE KINGS?

Ra-Messu-Neter-Heq-An-Meri-Amen
Ra-Meses-Meri-Amen
Ra-Meses-Meri-amen-Neter-Heq-Annu
Ra-Meses-Meri-Amen
Ra-Meses-Pa-Neter-Aa
Ra-Meses-Neter-Heq-An-Meri-Set
Ra-Meses-Meri-Amen-Neter-Aa-Neb-Pet

Where are the Kamite Kings Illustration. Ehnasya Temple. Throne of Rameses II with his *Suten Bat Usr-Ma'at-Ra* and *Son of Ra* Rameses names in Cartouche/Shennu.

Petrie III (1905: 28-39) provides an extensive listing of the occurrence of the name of this King whose architectural constructions, repairs and expropriations stagger the imagination. The tomb of User-Maat-Ra, Rameses II, is No. 7 in the Valley of the Kings. His coffin and mummy are in Cairo.

FREDERICK MONDERSON

Where are the Kamite Kings Photo. Sakkara. Home of the Step-Pyramid. The entrance colonnade, c. 2600 B.C. that started it all and revolutionized architecture in stone.

Where are the Kamite Kings Illustration. Ptah enthroned on a XIX-XXII Dynasty stela from Ehnasya.

WHERE ARE THE KAMITE KINGS?

Where are the Kamite Kings Photo. Erik Monderson within the Sakkara Colonnade in 2018.

At Nahr el Kelb and Saadiyeh (Bashai) steles were erected. Serabit el Khadem had steles and a doorway. From this site vases and Menats are in the British Museum. A granite triad of sphinxes was found at Abukir. A group statue of Rameses II and Hentmara exists. Alexandria boasted a sandstone pyramid and Schedia blocks of stone. At Kom el Abqain block, and Kom el Hisn groups and block statues have survived. At Kom Zimran, a block has his name. Qantara produced a base of a hawk with the King's name.

FREDERICK MONDERSON

Tanis revealed obelisks, and several statues, of which 4 are in Cairo. A fragment is in Berlin. There were also shrines from this site. In the Delta a palace Ankhuast was revealed. Nebesheh had two statues and a statue of Uati. At Qantir were blocks with his name. At Thmuis-Mendes, inscriptions and at Semenud columns with his name have survived. Tell Mokdam had statues. Tell el Maskhuta had a granite triad and sphinxes. Inscriptions from Tell Rotab and a statue from Saft el Henna are known. At Bubastis were statues and steles, some of which were usurpations. Here was also a granite column. From Belbeis a block and Benha a granite lion is now in the British Museum. Here also were blocks and a quartzite base that's now in the British Museum. A block from Terraneh and a statue from Tell el Yehudiyeh were known.

At Heliopolis a great well and obelisk are mentioned in connection with this monarch. A stele of his, C. 94 is in the Paris Museum. Near the site of Heliopolis were found blocks. At Ghizeh were blocks and a stele. Two steles were found near the Sphinx and are in the Paris Museum. At Memphis is housed the largest statue of Rameses. Another granite statue exists and a granite fist is now in the British Museum. The Temple of Memphis has his name and so too do statues of Ptah there.
At the Serapeum eight Apis burials, as well as the base of a granite statue there, all have his name. Stones with his name were used in the Mosque at Atfih. While Illahun revealed graffiti with his name, a group of objects were found at Gurob. Rameses' name is also in the Temple of Herakleopolis. Inscriptions at Esneh by the Wady Maghara and the Temple at Antinoe bear his name. A granite statue was found at Eshmunin and the King's name is in the quarry at Tell el Amarna. A column at Ekhmin and stele and statue at El Birbeh all belong to him.

The Mesheikh Temple, a stele and statues bear the name of Rameses II. Abydos, a holy site from the earliest times, had a Temple of Osiris, the Temple of Sety I and Temple of Rameses II, all bearing the name of this King. At Dendera was found blocks and a bronze vase. The Temple of Set at Nubt and a triad, steles and baboon, were unearthed at Koptos. Medamot had reused blocks.

WHERE ARE THE KAMITE KINGS?

Where are the Kamite Kings Photo. Sakkara. Home of the Step-Pyramid. Courtyard wall with engaged columns entrancing a Mastaba structure.

Where are the Kamite Kings Photo. Erik Monderson in the Great Court before the Step-Pyramid of Zoser in 2018.

FREDERICK MONDERSON

Where are the Kamite Kings Photo. Sakkara. Home of the Step-Pyramid. Portrait of Nobleman wearing necklace, kilt and holding staff and an object in the other hand. Miniature female figure stands before him.

At Karnak, Rameses' work enclosed an earlier temple. It is in the Great Hall, and a building East of the *Akh Menu*, Festival Temple of Thutmose III. There are statues before the North Temple. A bust of the young King is here also. His name is in the Temple of Mut. It is on a building south of the Lake. The *Poem of Pentaur* is at Karnak and so too is the Treaty with the Hittites. A pillar of his is in the Cairo Museum. His name is also on a colossus in the Temple of Rameses III, as well as other colossi and statues throughout Karnak. Parts of the Ramesseum, his mortuary temple, were expropriated for Medinet Habu temple.

WHERE ARE THE KAMITE KINGS?

Where are the Kamite Kings Photo. As evidenced, work being done at the Step-Pyramid, that is today complete.

At Luxor, the First Court by Rameses II is an addition to the Temple of Amenhotep III. One of two obelisks remains standing in front of the entrance pylon, placed there by Rameses. Besides the obelisk are seated statues of the King with the Nile Gods uniting the two lands. The statue bases have cynocephali and in this temple is also the *Poem of Pentaur*, recounting the *Battle of Kadesh*.

Rameses finished the Qurneh Temple of his father Seti I. His mortuary temple, the Ramesseum, contains historical and religious reliefs, a horoscope, and a list of his sons and as well, a plan of the structure. At the Ramesseum were found ostraka and a bust that's now in the British Museum.

Where are the Kamite Kings Photo. A crumbled Pyramid at Sakkara.

FREDERICK MONDERSON

He restored the Temple of Deir el Bahari. At Medinet Habu were found reused blocks. At El Kab his name is in a chapel and on the now destroyed Temple of Sobek. Here is also a stele as well as inscriptions on the Temple of Amenhotep III in the desert at El Kab. Here too are inscriptions of Taa in the 29th year of the King.

Silsileh revealed a stele and rock shrines. Ombos contained stones, and a bust from Elephantine is in the British Museum. The King's name is on the quay and on a statue. An Aswan stele was made in his second year. There is a family stele and other steles of his 33rd and 40th years. Temples at Beit el Wally and Gerf Hussein (Hirsheh) and stele and blocks at Qubban, all tell of him.

Where are the Kamite Kings Illustration. The Temple of Rameses III in the enclosure of the Temple of Goddess Mut at Karnak, March 31, 1925.

The Wady Sebua Temple, stones and the Derr Temple as well as the rock shrine at Ibrin all bear Rameses II's name. He built the rock-hewn great Abu Simbel Temple and the smaller Temple for his beloved wife, Nefertari. At this important site in Nubia a number of different steles were erected including one of his 35th year.

American Journal of Archaeology XVI (1912: 113-14) mentioned the work of excavation begun at Abu Simbel in 1909, where: "A wide terrace was uncovered; here was a small chapel in which stood an altar with two obelisks before it and a shrine beside it. In the shrine were a large scarab-beetle and an ape, and upon the altar four apes. A row of statues - figures of the Pharaoh and of the sacred hawk of the sun alternating – extends across the whole breadth of

WHERE ARE THE KAMITE KINGS?

the terrace. These statues heighten the effect of the enormous rock-cut colossi of the facade. The colossi themselves have been repaired."

A more extensive and detailed description of Abu Simbel is supplied by Murray's *Handbook for Egypt* (1888), from almost a century ago. Though the temples have been removed to the higher elevation, as they are today, the essential features and locations are the same. However, the entrance today is from the south, or the right, as you enter the exterior of the Great Temple.

Where are the Kamite Kings Illustration. Clearance of the Sanctuary area of the Temple of Rameses III in the enclosure, Temple of Mut at Karnak.

"It also is excavated in the rock the surface of which has been cut away so as to form a gigantic facade, more than 100 feet high, and nearly 100 wide. It does not directly face the river, but looks across it in an oblique direction northward. The cornice formed by 22 seated cynocephali is surmounted by a frieze, on which is the dedicatory inscription, and in a niche over the entrance is a large statue of the sun God Ra, the divinity of the temple and the protector of the place, to whom Rameses II, the founder of the temple, is offering a figure of Truth."

FREDERICK MONDERSON

Where are the Kamite Kings Illustration. Outer coffin lid and bottom and inner coffin of Sod-ptah-auf-Ankh.

"But the wonder and marvel of this stupendous facade are the four gigantic statues which adorn it, the most beautiful of all Egyptian colossi. They represent Rameses II. They are seated on thrones attached to the rock, and the faces of some of them, which are fortunately well preserved, evince a beauty of expression, the more striking as it is looked for in statues of such dimensions. Their total height is about 66 ft. without the pedestal, the proportion being low, on only six heads. The ear measures 3 ft. 5 in.: forefinger (*i.e.*, to the fork of the middle finger), 3 ft.; from inner side of elbow-joint to end of middle finger, 15 ft., etc. The head of one of the statues is completely broken off, but the others are tolerably intact. On the

WHERE ARE THE KAMITE KINGS?

leg of the first, to the left as you approach the door of the temple is the curious Greek inscription of the Ionian and Carian soldiers of Psammetichus, first discovered by Mr. Bankes and Mr. Salt, as well as some interesting hieroglyphic tablets. This is one of a series of most interesting inscriptions, of which some are in Greek, some in Phoenician, and others in an alphabet supposed to be Carian."

"The Greek inscription is of very great interest upon several accounts. It appears to have been written by the troops sent by the Egyptian King after the deserters, who, to the number of 240,000, are said by Herodotus to have left the service of Psammetichus because they had been stationed in garrison at Syene for three years without being relieved, and to have settled in Ethiopia. It is an early style of Greek, with a rude indication of the long vowels, the more remarkable as it dates more than 100 years before Simonides. These Greek inscriptions are probably the oldest existing to which a date can be given, and have been of the greatest use in the study of the history of the Greek alphabet. They were written in the 7th century B.C. The letters most resemble Ionian form of the alphabet. Taylor, in his work on 'The Alphabet,' gives a facsimile of one of the inscriptions."

"Besides this inscription are others, written by Greeks who probably visited the place at a later time as 'Theopompus, the son of Plato;' 'Ptolemy, the son of Timostratus;' Ktesibius, Telephus, and others. There are also some Phoenician inscriptions on the same colossus."

"Interior - The interior was formerly closed by the sand that pours down from the hills above. Burckhardt was the first to notice the existence of this wonderful temple; and it was afterwards in 1817 visited by Belzoni, Captains Irby and Mangles, and Mr. Beechey, who resolved to clear the entrance, and succeeded in doing so after a hard fortnight's work. The sand quickly closed in, but their efforts enabled others to penetrate without much difficulty. In 1869 the facade and the interior were completely cleared of sand."

"We pass through the entrance (A) into a large Hall (B) supported by 8 Osiride columns. Each of the figures attached to these columns is, without the cap and pedestal, nearly 18 ft. high; their other dimensions are, from the shoulder to the elbow, 4 ft. 6 in.; from the elbow to the wrist, 4 ft. 3 in.; from the nose to the chin, 8 in.; the ear, 13 3/4 in.; the nose, about 10 in.; the face, nearly 2 ft.; and the total height, without the cap and pedestal, 17 ft. 8 in."

Where are the Kamite Kings Photo. Two broken statues sandwich Ptah (center) in the Heb Sed Court at Sakkara.

Where are the Kamite Kings Photo. Sakkara. Tomb of Ptahhotep. The Nobleman seated and smells the Lotus Flower Cup.

"The sculptures on the walls are chiefly historical subjects relating to the conquests of Rameses II. A large tablet, containing the date of his first year, extends over a great part of the North wall: and

WHERE ARE THE KAMITE KINGS?

another, between the two last pillars on the opposite side of this hall, of his 35th year, has been added long after the temple was completed. The battle-scenes are very interesting. Among the various subjects are the arks of the Egyptians, which they carried with them in their foreign expeditions. The subjects on the South wall are particularly spirited. A charioteer, just bending his bow, with the reins tied around his waist, is full of life."

"From this hall we pass into another (C) supported by 4 square columns, on which and on the walls are depicted religious subjects, among them the procession of the sacred bark. Three doors lead from this hall into a third (d) covered with similar scenes, out of which open three rooms. The center is the sanctuary (E), with an altar in the middle, and at the end four seated figures, the first of which to the right is Horus [Ra-Horakhty], and then comes Rameses himself, Amen, and last Ptah. Eight other rooms open out of the large Hall, but they are very irregularly excavated; some of them have lofty benches projecting from the walls."

"The total depth of this excavation, from the door, is about 200 ft., without the colossi and slope of the facade. A short distance to the South of the large temple is some hieroglyphic tablets on the rock, bearing the date of the 38th year of the same Rameses."

"In 1874, a party, which included Miss A.B. Edwards, the authoress, and Mr. A. Macallum, the artist, discovered to the South of the Great Temple a rock-cut chamber, 21 ft. by 14 ft. in width, elaborately sculptured and painted, with inscriptions by Rameses II. This chamber is preceded by the ruins of a vaulted atrium, in sun-dried brickwork, and adjoins the remains of what would appear to be a massive wall or pylon, which contains a staircase terminating in an arched doorway leading to the vaulted atrium before mentioned. The bones of a woman and child, evidently a Nubian internment, were found in it. The sculptures and inscriptions relate chiefly to the worship of Amen-ra by Rameses II, and are in excellent preservation, with much of the inscriptions quite fresh. Some of the inscriptions are devoted to Thoth, the God of letters, and it has been conjectured that the grotto was the library of the adjoining temple."

FREDERICK MONDERSON

"The small Temple of Hathor was dedicated to his wife Nefertari and is to the north of the Great Temple."

"The facade is adorned with several statues in prominent relief of the King and the deities. The interior is divided into a hall of six square pillars bearing the head of Hathor, a transverse corridor, with a small chamber at each extremity, and an adytum, in which the Goddess Hathor is represented under the form of the sacred cow, her emblem, which also occurs in the pictures on the wall. Her title here is 'Lady of Aboshek' (Abocicis), the ancient name of Aboo Simbel which, being in the country of the Ethiopians, is followed in the hieroglyphics by the sign signifying 'foreign land.' Among the cotemplar deities are Ra, Amen-Ra, Isis and Ptah; and Kneph, Sate, and Anouke, the triad of the Cataracts. The monarch is frequently accompanied by his queen Nefertari. The total depth of this excavation is about 90 ft. from the door."

Where are the Kamite Kings Photo. Sakkara. Tomb of Mereruka. This image shows the Nobleman with his staff of office and coming out of the "false door" in his Tomb to partake of offerings left for him.

At Faras (-Makhakit) a rock shrine, Aksheh (-Serreh) Temple and the Napata Temple all contain his name. A number of statues not listed above are scattered in diverse places, particularly in Europe. A seated black granite statue and a standing syenite one is in the Turin Museum. Two standing and two seated statues are in Cairo. A kneeling black granite statue and a seated granite one is in

WHERE ARE THE KAMITE KINGS?

Alexandria. The head of a black granite head and another head of syenite are in the Cairo Museum. A grey granite head is in the British Museum. A seated statue is in the Vatican. A wooden figure and bronze kneeling figure are in the British Museum. The Paris Museum has a seated diorite statue that has been usurped. A seated diorite is in Alexandria. The Paris Museum has a bronze ushabti.

Events at the *Battle of Kadesh*, in which the King was ambushed, are depicted at several temples. In this conflict, Rameses called upon his God and the God of his ancestors, to aid his efforts. Now Petrie III (1905: 55-61) has provided the entire poem of the King, calling upon the God Amen and the reply he received, as indicated in the *Papyrus Sallier* I, 5. Here then is the full account of the King's side of the events surrounding the *Battle of Kadesh* that is recounted as part of the Pharaoh's exploits at the temples of Ramesseum, Abydos, Abu Simbel, Karnak, Beit Wally (Wali), and at Luxor.

As indicated in the Introduction, as the ambush unfolded:

The Peril of Ramessu

>Then his Majesty arose like Mentu,
>he seized his panoply of war,
>he clad him in his habergeon,
>himself like Baal in his hour.
>The great horses that were with his Majesty,
>named "Victories in Thebes,"
>were from the stable of Usermara,
>chosen of Ra, beloved of Amen

>Then did his majesty dash on;
>then he entered into the midst of the foes, of the vile Kheta;
>he alone by himself, no other with him.
>When his Majesty turned to look behind him

FREDERICK MONDERSON

he found around him 2500 chariots, in his outward
way;   all the light troops of the vile Kheta,
with the multitudes who were with them;
from Arvad, from Mausum, from Pidasa,
from Keshkesh, from Arwena, from Kataua-dana,
from Khilbu, from Okran, Qedesh, and Lycia,
they were three men on each chariot,
they were united.

"But there was never a chief with me,
there was never a charioteer,
there was never an officer of the troops,
never a horseman;
being abandoned by the infantry,
the chariots fleeing away before them,
there remained not one of them for fighting along with me."

The Invocation of Amen

Then said his Majesty,
"What is in thy heart, my father Amen,
Does a father ignore the face of a son?
I have made petitions, and hast thou forgotten me?
Even in my going stood I not on thy word?
I never broke the decrees thou ordained.
Very great is the great Lord of Egypt,
to make to flee the people who are in his path:
What is thy will concerning these Amu?
Amen shall bring to naught the ignorers of God.
Made I never for thee great multitudes of monuments?
I filled thy house with my prisoners,
I built for thee a temple of millions of years,
I have given all my goods to thee by decree,
I give thee the whole of every land for offerings to thy holy altar,
I have slain for thee myriads of oxen
With all perfumes sweet to smell.

WHERE ARE THE KAMITE KINGS?

I have not put behind my hand (neglected) any good thing
which has not been done for thy courts,
Building for thee the pylons of stone unto completion,
setting up for thee their masts myself:
Bringing for thee obelisks of Elephantine,
I have caused eternal stones to be brought.
Moreover, I bring to thee transports on the great sea, to
ship to thee tributes of the countries.
Let thou order an evil fate to befall him who attacks thy Excellent decrees, and a good fate to him whom thou accountest just.

Amen! Behold this has been done to thee out of love, I call on thee, my father Amen,
for I am in the midst of many nations whom I know not, the whole of every land is against me,
I alone am my guard, no other is with me,
being abandoned by these many troops;
my chariots never look once for me, though I cry to them; there is not one amongst them that listens when I call.
I find that Amen is worth more than millions of troops, more than myriads of brethren or children,
if they were together in one place.
Never the deeds of an abundance of people,
but the excellence of Amen exceeds them!
I end this waiting on the decrees of thy mouth, Amen!
Never overstepping thy decrees,
even making to thee invocations from the ends of the earth.

The Coming of Amen

The voice was repeated in Anu of the south (Hermonthis) -

FREDERICK MONDERSON

Amen came because I cried to him,
He gave me his hand, and I rejoiced:
He cried out to me, "My protection is with thee,
my face is with thee, Ramessu, loved of Amen,
I am with thee, I am thy Father,
my hand is with thee,
I am more excellent for thee than hundreds of thousands
united in one.
I am Lord of might,
Those who love valor shall find me a firm heart, a rejoicing heart,
All that I have done has come to pass;
For I am like Mentu,
I strike on the right hand;
In seizing in the left hand,
I am like Ball in wrath upon them."

The Deliverance

"I found 2500 chariots,
I being in the midst of them,
They became in dread before my mares.
Never found even one among them his hand to fight,
Their hearts rotted in their bodies for fear,
Their arms were all powerless,
They were unable to shoot an arrow.
Never found they their hearts to carry their lances;
I caused them to plunge them in the water,
even as plunge the crocodiles;
they were fallen on their faces one over the other;
I was slaying among them,
I loved that never one among them should look behind him,
never another should turn his face,
Every fallen one among them did not lift 'himself up."

WHERE ARE THE KAMITE KINGS?

Behold the vile chief, the smitten one, of the Kheta,
stood among his troops and his chariots,
for gazing on the fight of his Majesty,
for that his Majesty was alone by himself,
there being never a soldier with him, never a chariot.
He was standing and turning about for fear of his Majesty,
Then ordered he many chiefs to come,
every one among them being with chariots,
and they were arrayed with all weapons for fight;
The chief of Arvad, and this of Masa,
the chief of Arwena, and this of Luka,
the chief of Dardeny, and this of Keshkesh,
the chief of Darkemish, the chief of Kirkash, and this of Khilbu
the brethren of this Kheta, to the bounds of the whole of them,
being all together 2500 chariots.

"I came up to them quicker than fire,
I was carried among them,
I was like Mentu;
gave I to them the taste of my hand,
in the passing of an instant.
I was upon consuming among them,
upon slaying in their places (as they stood)."

The Terror of the Foe

One was crying out among them to another, and saying,
"Never a mortal this, which is among us,
It is Sutekh great of might; it is Baal in the flesh.
Never did a man like the deeds of him
The one alone terrifies the multitudes,
and there is never a chief with him, never a soldier.
Come; hasten, save ourselves from before him,

FREDERICK MONDERSON

seek we for us the life, to breathe the breath.
Behold thou! All who meet with him fall powerless,
His hand is on all their limbs;
They never know how to grasp the bow,
or the spear likewise."

When he saw them come to the union of the roads,
Then his Majesty was behind them like a gryphon.
He was on slaying among them, they escaped him not,
He shouted to the soldiers and the charioteers, to say,
"'Steady yourselves! steady your hearts!
My soldiers and my chariots;
Behold ye these my mighty acts,
I am alone, and it is Amen who sustains me,
His hand is toward me.
When Menna my charioteer beheld that,
namely multitudes of chariots completely around me,
he became weak, his heart failed,
a very great terror went through his limbs;
behold he said to his Majesty -
"'My good lord! my brave prince!
Oh, mighty strength of Egypt in the day of battle!
We are standing alone in the midst of the enemy,
Behold they abandon us, the soldiers and the chariots,
make a stand to save the breath of our lips.
Oh, save us! Ramessu, loved of Amen, my good lord.'"
Then said his Majesty to his charioteer,

"'Steady! steady thy heart! my charioteer,
I am going in among them like the striking of a hawk,
I shall slay in smiting, and throw in the dust.

WHERE ARE THE KAMITE KINGS?

What is in thy heart about these Asiatics?

Where are the Kamite Kings Illustration. Seti I offers Ma'at, an image of truth, to enthroned Osiris, in the Abydos Temple of the God. In Blue or "War Crown," with necklace, he wears a long-flowing gown with apron sporting uraei. Notice the intricacies of the bouquet of flowers as well as his kilt.

By Amen! They are extremely vile in ignoring God, Who never shall shine his face on millions of them.'"

FREDERICK MONDERSON

His Majesty then led rapidly,
He arose and penetrated the enemy,
To whom six times he penetrated in among them.
He was like Baal behind them in the time (of his power),
He was slaying among them, none escaping him.

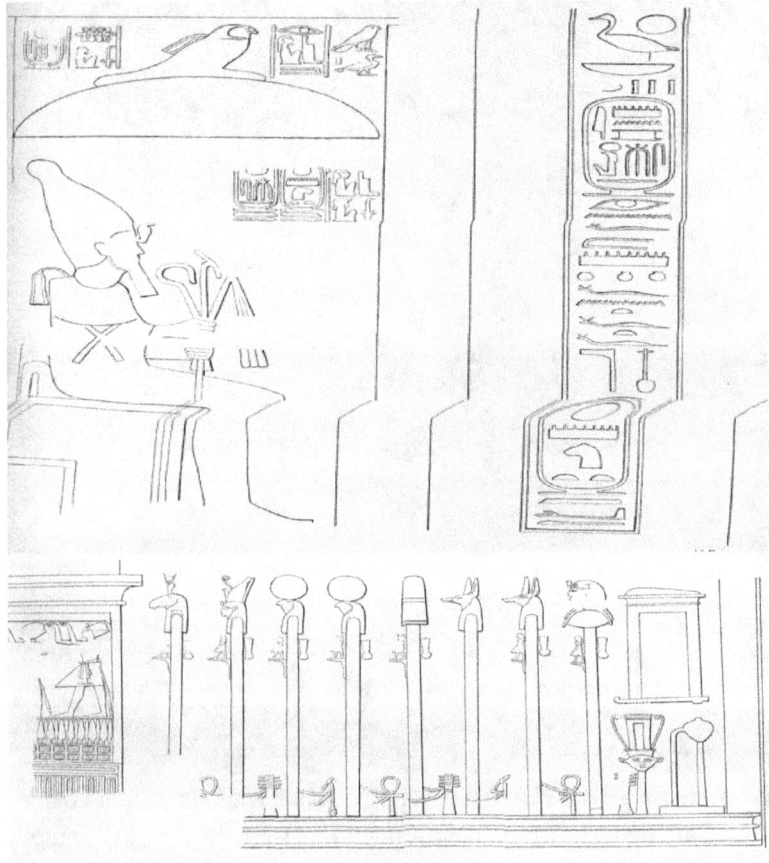

Where are the Kamite Kings Illustration. Qurneh Temple of Seti I, showing a chamber of his father Rameses I (top); and showing standards in the XIXth Dynasty Qurneh Temple of Seti I, in *Qurneh* by W.M. Flinders Petrie (1909).

WHERE ARE THE KAMITE KINGS?

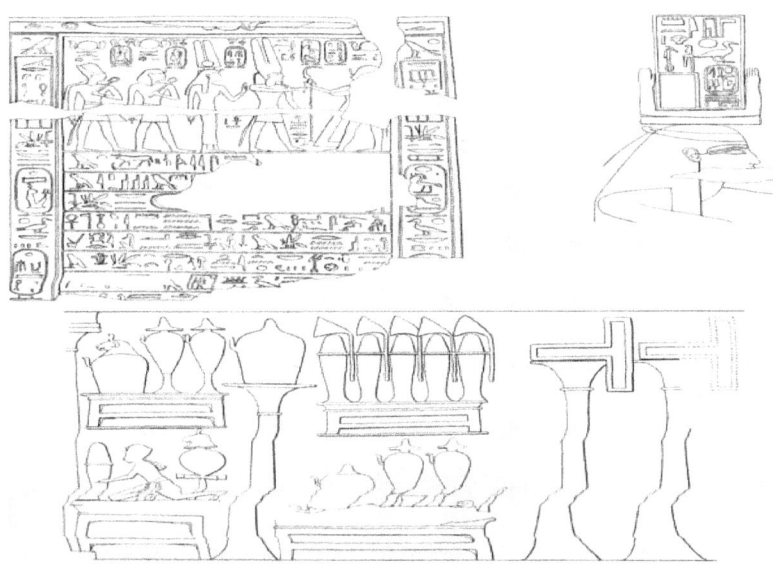

Where are the Kamite Kings Illustration. XIXth Dynasty Qurneh Temple of Seti I, showing a Siptah Stele, Temple Ka and offerings in *Qurneh* by W.M. Flinders Petrie (1909).

Where are the Kamite Kings Illustration. XIXth Dynasty Qurneh Temple of Seti I, showing sealings from Storehouses of Seti I in *Qurneh* by W.M. Flinders Petrie (1909).

FREDERICK MONDERSON

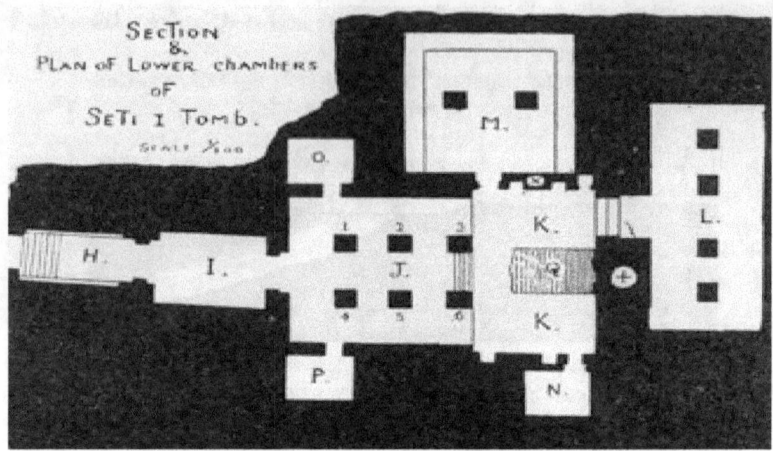

Where are the Kamite Kings Illustration. Plan of the Lower Chambers of the Tomb of Seti I.

Reproaches of the King

Then called his Majesty to his soldiers and his chariots,
likewise, to his chiefs who ignored the fight,
His Majesty said to them,
"'It is evil in your hearts, oh my charioteers,
It is unworthiness that fills your hearts amongst you,
There is not one among you but what I have given him good fortune in my land;
Had I never risen as lord, ye were in poor estate.
I give to make you chiefs in positions every day,
I give to the son to succeed to the goods of his father;
If any pest comes in the land of Egypt,
I remit to you your tribute:
Never give I to you the things plundered?
Whoever asks requests (of the Gods),
Behold I make petitions for him myself daily (as High Priest),

WHERE ARE THE KAMITE KINGS?

Where are the Kamite Kings Illustration. A XIXth Dynasty image of a cobra or uraeus on the brow of King Rameses II wearing the White Crown while his Cartouche/Shennu rests nearby, scene at the Temple of Ehnasya in *Ehnasya* by Sir Flinders Petrie 1904 (1905).

> Never a lord did for his soldiers what his Majesty did for your hearts.
> I gave you to rest in your houses and in your towns,
> There were no orders given by the captains,
> Nor likewise by my charioteers.
> I gave them a way to their many towns,
> For that I sought likewise for them the day and hour of rising up for war.
> Now behold ye have made a miserable return, the whole of you together,
> Never stood any among you to give his hand to me;
> I was fighting, I swear by the *ka* of my father Amen,
> Behold me over Egypt as were my fathers,
> Who had never beheld the Syrians.'"

In Year 1, Epiphi 10, a *Hymn to the Nile* was erected at Silsileh. Abu Simbel is generally believed begun on Paophi 25. During Athyr, Rameses visited Thebes and left on the 23rd day of that month. Wine jars were left at the Ramesseum this year and in various other years of his reign. The Stele from the Sphinx, now in the British Museum, No. 440, was also placed in this year.

FREDERICK MONDERSON

Where are the Kamite Kings Photo. Temple of Rameses II at Abydos. Notice the steps that elevate the temple inwards.

Where are the Kamite Kings Photo. Temple of Rameses II at Abydos. Priests in a procession (left); and, within the Court, again, the steps upward!

In Year 2, a Stele at Nahr el Kelb and another at Aswan were placed.
Year 3, Tybi 4, Kuban Stele.
Year 4, Khoiak 2, another Stele at Nahr el Kelb.
Year 5, the Great war with the Kheta is recorded on the Left at Zalu on Pauni 9. On Epiphi 8, a report of war is at Luxor, and on Epiphi 9, work was done at Abu Simbel.
Year 7, the Pauni copy of the **Poem of Pentaur** is recorded.
Year 8, there was War in Palestine. On Mesori 25, a list of officials is in the *Turin Papyrus*.

WHERE ARE THE KAMITE KINGS?

Year 10, the Statue of Khay, Vizier, is in the Cairo Museum.
Year 12, On Khoiak 13, the *Papyrus Turin* records revenue collection.
Year 13, the King erected an Apis Stele.
Year 16, Apis II burial took place in the Serapeum.
Year 21, the Treaty with the Kheta was placed on the south of the Hypostyle Hall at Karnak on Tybi 21.
Year 23, the King is mentioned on an Apis stele.
Year 26, Apis III, burial is recorded at the Serapeum.
Year 30, Apis IV, another burial at the Serapeum. At Silsileh, the King recorded his Heb Sed Festival.
Year 31, was erected the Stele of Baknaa, now in the British Museum, No. 164.
Year 33, the Karnak Stele, now in the Bibliotheque Nationale in Paris, records a later romance of Rameses. His Heb Sed is recorded at Bigeh and again at Sehel.
Year 34, a Stele at Abu Simbel records a political marriage with a Princess of Kheta. Also, at Silsileh, his Heb Sed is recorded.
Year 35, a Decree of Ptah is recorded at Abu Simbel, on Tybi 13.
Year 36, at Silsileh, his Heb Sed is recorded.
Year 37, at Silsileh, his Heb Sed is again recorded.
Year 38, a Stele by Setau was erected at Abu Simbel.
Year 40, a Heb Sed is recorded at Silsileh. The Stele of Khaemuas is recorded at Sehel. Also, the Khay Stele was erected at Silsileh.
Year 41, a Stele was placed at the temple of Amenhotep III, at El Kab.
Year 42, the Stele of Unnefer was placed at Abydos. Ostrakon from this year is at the Paris Museum.
Year 46, the Stele of Khay at Silsileh, records the King's Heb Sed. The *Berlin Papyrus* is dated to Paophi 14, of this year.
Year 52, the *Leyden Papyrus* I, 350 mentions Pauni 27-9 and Epiphi 1-4.
Year 53, Ostrakon is now in the Paris Museum.
Year 62, the Stele of Neferher, now in the British Museum No. 163, is dated to Pachons 29.
Year 66, the Stele of Bakur is dated to this year. Ostrakon is dated to Athyr 5 of this year.
Year 67, was the end of his reign as indicated by a Stele of Rameses.

FREDERICK MONDERSON

Userkheperura, Setepenra, Merenptah, *Nile Year* 3018-3028 (c. 1212-1202 B.C.), the 13th son, followed his father, Rameses II, as Pharaoh. He is thought to be the "Pharaoh of the Exodus," though some scholars doubt this. For that matter, many scholars doubt there was any exodus from Egypt, particularly on the scale of Cecil B. De Mille's epic, the *Ten Commandments*.

Petrie III (1905: 104-07) provided instances in which Merneptah's name is mentioned throughout the land.

At Serabit el Khadem, a door jamb and vases bear the King's name. Tanis provided evidence of blocks and two granite statues were made by this King. At Nebesheh were found a column with a hawk over the King and blocks of limestone. Mendes had blocks and Tell Mokdam, a usurped statue.

Tell el Yehudiyeh provided an alabaster vase and lotus column and group. Bubastis revealed fragments of a statue, scenes of the King as a young prince and a statue of red limestone. His name is mentioned in a building at Heliopolis, while Memphis revealed a granite column and a headless sphinx from the Serapeum, now in the Paris Museum.

At Memphis the King built his palace. *American Journal of Archaeology* XXII (1918: 75-77) contains an account of a report by C. S. Fisher, on the University of Pennsylvania's excavations at the Palace of Merenptah.

WHERE ARE THE KAMITE KINGS?

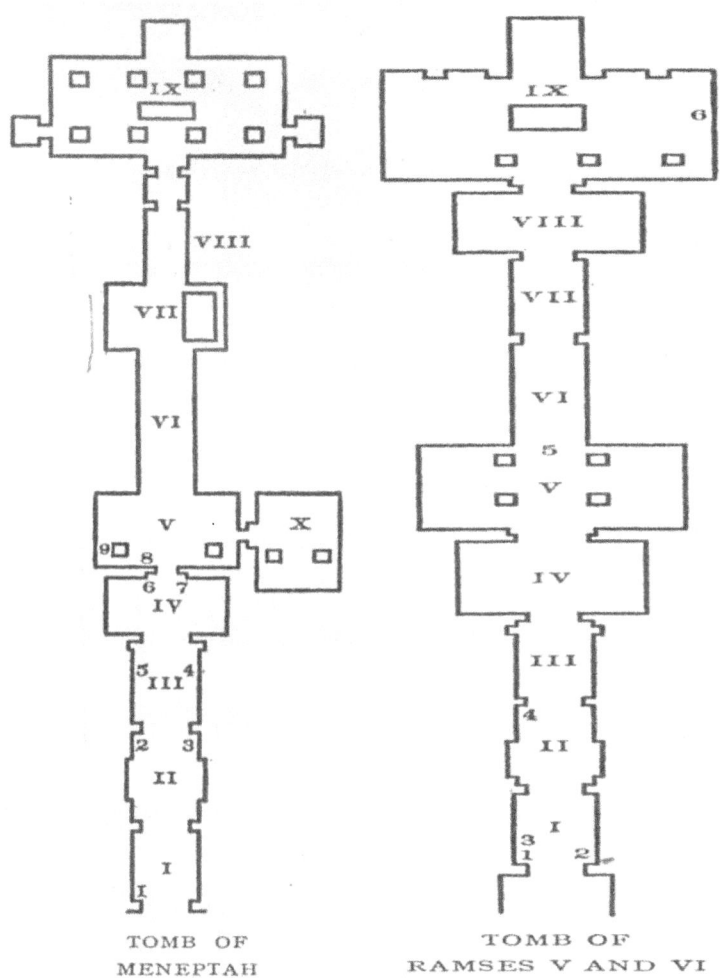

Where are the Kamite Kings Illustration. Valley of the Kings. Tombs of Meneptah, XIXth Dynasty and Rameses V and VI of the XXth Dynasty.

"The building was constructed with massive walls of sun-dried bricks and columns and door-facings of limestone. The ancient level is from 16 to 18 feet below the modern so that, although much digging had been done by natives on the site, the remains of the palace were not disturbed. So far, a portion of the eastern wing only has been excavated. There was a court 175 feet long and 80 feet wide paved with irregular limestone blocks and surrounded by a colonnade of thirty-two columns with papyrus capitals. The floor under this colonnade was a little higher than that of the court. The columns, which were built up of separate drums, stand upon bases inscribed with attributes of the King, no two inscriptions being exactly alike. The shafts of the columns were also inscribed, and carved with reliefs usually representing Merenptah performing rites before Ptah. The background was yellow and the inscriptions were filled in with blue. The walls of the court were coated with mortar over which was a hard white stucco painted with regular panels and patterns in red, yellow, and blue. In the middle of the south side of the court was a doorway 10 feet wide and 23 feet high. The doorframings were of limestone with inscriptions inlaid with faience. On the lintel were gilded figures in relief of the King before the Gods. In front of this doorway was a vestibule the roof of which was supported by twelve columns similar to those of the court, but larger."

"The inscriptions on them were inlaid in faience, and the figures in the bands of relief overlaid with thick gold leaf. The floor was of sun-dried brick covered with a painted stucco pavement. Three doors led from this vestibule, the middle one opening upon the throne-room which was 60 feet long and 41 feet wide. Six columns of the same design as the other supported the roof. The dais on which the throne rested was 13 feet long and 16 feet wide and raised twenty inches from the floor. It was approached from in [the] front by a ramp, but there were steps on the sides for the use of the King."

"The entire surface of both ramp and dais was covered with colored reliefs representing the ten nations subdued by the King. The walls of this room were adorned with painted stucco with some details picked out in gold. In the narrow passages to the east and the west of the throne-room were limestone windows. Near the throne-room were apartments evidently used by the King on state occasions. At the north end of the great court there was another doorway similar to that at the southern end and remains of a balcony which had been above it. This is the first instance of such a structure actually found, though they are known from reliefs. A flight of steps still partly preserved at the west of the vestibule within this doorway led up to it. This vestibule was considerably smaller than the one in front of the throne-room. Only four small columns supported the roof, but

WHERE ARE THE KAMITE KINGS?

these were richly decorated. East of the southern apartments is a long narrow passageway bordered by a wall twelve feet thick and outside of this another passage shut in by the boundary wall of the palace twenty-one feet thick. West of the great court is an outer court with pavement of colored stucco as yet only partly excavated. The palace also seems to extend a considerable distance to the north. After the death of Merenptah the building was used for different purposes and some of its doors blocked up, and shortly afterwards it was destroyed by fire. Five distinct towns were later built upon the site. Few small objects were brought to light by the excavators; the most interesting was a fine portrait-head, a little less than life size, perhaps of Akhenaton. In the strata of Ahmose II, the last King before the Persian occupation in 525 B.C., a cache of gold and silver jewelry of very fine workmanship was found. The palace has so far been cleared for about three quarters of an acre. It was probably about 400 feet long from north to south."

Where are the Kamite Kings Photo. Memphis Museum. The author and photographer pose with a native Egyptian Guide and sign depicts sites and times of operation of the location.

Merenptah's name is mentioned in the Temple of Herakleopolis. He is in a rock shrine at Surarieh, on a pylon at Eshmunin, and is named in the Tell el-Amarna quarry. At Meshekh, he repaired the temple of Rameses II. At Nubt, there are inscriptions of him on the temple gate and a block at Koptos. He is at the Osireion at Abydos, where three statues of him were probably usurped.

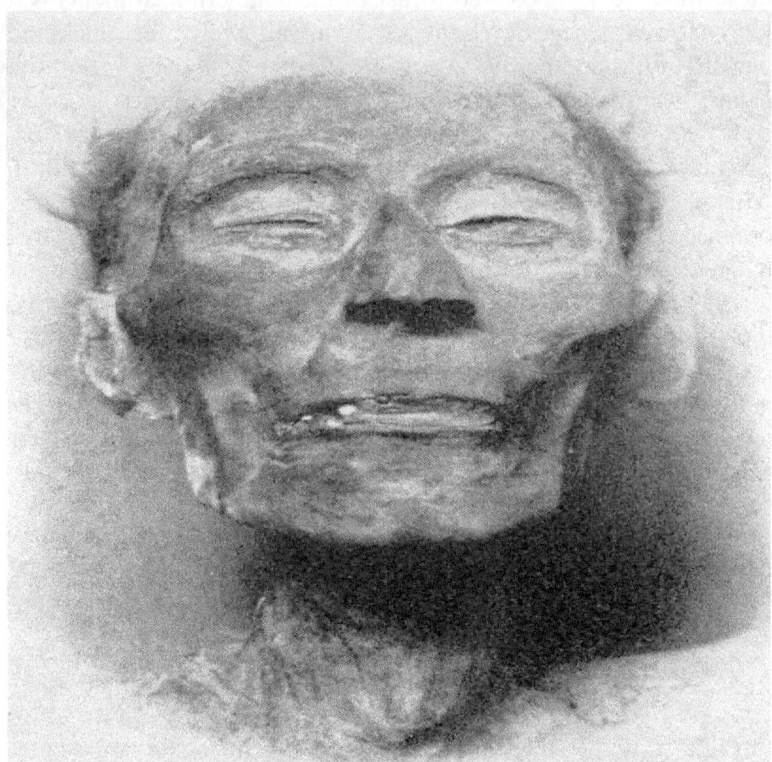

Where are the Kamite Kings Illustration. Image of the head of the mummy of Rameses II, taken from his mummy in the Cairo Museum. Note. The nose is not broken!

Professor Wallace N. Stearns, of the University of North Dakota, reported in *AJA* XVI (1912: 108) on excavations at Deir el Bahari and Abydos in which Merenptah is mentioned. Accordingly: "The finds at Abydos cover a long period. A temple of Osiris stood here as early as the sixth dynasty, possibly before the first. Inscriptions cover with intervals a period from the sixth to the thirtieth dynasty. Back of Menes is a line of Kings whose tombs have been recovered at Abydos. Earlier than these are the square or oval pits, pre-dynastic tombs, with their contracted burials - the bodies not mummified, but protected above and below by a layer of skins, which is in turn protected by a layer of matting. 'These tombs belong to a people that had attained to the neolithic stage of culture.'

WHERE ARE THE KAMITE KINGS?

Of Paleolithic folk there remain great numbers of crude flint implements scattered about on the surface of the desert and now exposed by denudation. Present interest centers at the temple of Seti I, dedicated to Osiris. A trial working made in 1901-02 unearthed a long passage within the temenos back of the temple. The work of 1902-03, conducted by Miss Murray, reached a maximum depth of forty-one feet down to the desert level, and brought to light a sloping

Where are the Kamite Kings Illustration. Head and inscriptions of Rameses II from the Temple of Ehnasya in *Ehnasya* by Flinders Petrie 1904 (1905).

Subterranean passage 200 feet long, the sandstone pavement of a great hall (34 X 15 ft. and 17 ft. high). From this led out three doorways, - south, north, and east, - the last leading to a sloping passageway. The roof and east wall have been defaced or destroyed. The west wall shows in three panels: 1, a colossal scene of the revivication of Osiris; 2, the chapter (119) on 'Knowing the Names of Osiris;' and 3, Merenptah standing before a table heaped with offerings and offering incense. The walls of an adjoining chamber show the 148th chapter of the Book of the Dead, a chapter otherwise known only from three papyri. A line following the axis of Seti's temple also follows the line of a sloping passage (worked in 1902-03), the center of the great hall, through the desert pylon to the royal tombs. 'That this hypogeum should be a part of the temple dedicated to the worship of the dead, with special apartments for the celebration of the Osireion rites seems natural and fitting.' Here once more at Abydos the Egypt Exploration Fund is at work, 1911-12, under the direction of Professor Naville."

At Karnak a statue of his was found along with Libyan war inscriptions. He also usurped the work of others at this important religious site. At Qurneh, the Temple of Seti I has his name. He also built the Temple of Merenptah at this site, where can be found the Great stele of war, in addition to statues.

Where are the Kamite Kings Illustration. Rameses II receiving offerings at the Temple of Ehnasya in *Ehnasya* by Flinders Petrie 1904 (1905).

At the Ramesseum were inscriptions on a pillar. At Deir el Bahari were inscriptions on a granite door. Inscriptions were also found at Medinet Habu, all mentioning Merenptah. At West Silsileh were

WHERE ARE THE KAMITE KINGS?

found rock steles where the King is shown offering to Amen with the official Roy. He is also shown with Nehesi

Where are the Kamite Kings Photo. Memphis Museum. Alabaster Sphinx at Memphis. Notice neither the nose nor uraeus is damaged though he sports a curved beard. Some have argued, the Sphinx may represent Rameses II as a God.

offering to Amen. He is shown offering to Osiris, Isis and Horus. He is further shown offering to Osiris, Isis and Rameses II. He offers to Astnefert, Nehesi, Amen, and Mut. Here he is also shown offering to nine Gods, to Amen, Horus and Isis. Along with his son, Merenptah is shown with Astnefert offering a *Hymn to the Nile*.

FREDERICK MONDERSON

At Elephantine was found a statue. At Aswan the Stele of Messuy bears the name of Merenptah. There were inscriptions on the temple at Dakkeh. A triumphal inscription is at Amada while at Wady Halfa, to the south of the temple, he is shown in adoration by Nehesi.

Where are the Kamite Kings Photo. Erik Monderson stands beside the Alabaster Sphinx at Memphis Museum.

A number of statues of Merenptah are known. In the Cairo Museum, he is shown kneeling and holding an Osiris statue. Two pieces of a bust are at Alexandria. The head of a lost bust is in the Ceuricoffre Collection. At Turin there is the base of a statue, while a fragment of a statue is in Copenhagen. Many usurped statues are at Tanis and other sites. Portraits of the King exist. A stele offering a captive to Ptah is in Florence. A red granite sphinx is in the Paris Museum. Many scarabs are shown with Thutmose III and Rameses II.

WHERE ARE THE KAMITE KINGS?

Where are the Kamite Kings Illustration. Coffins of anonymous.

A papyrus is dated Khoiak 4 to Athyr 29 in his third year. The *Papyrus of Kakenamen* is in Bologna while a papyrus of his 8th year is in the same city.

His Queen was Astnefert, probably 9th daughter of Rameses II. Sety Merenptah II was his son. A daughter was Arit-Nefert who is mentioned in a papyrus account. Merenptah is worshiped on a stele from the Serapeum, that's now in the Paris Museum.

FREDERICK MONDERSON

Where are the Kamite Kings Illustration. Shrine of Ramessu II at the Temple of Ehnasya in *Ehnasya* by Flinders Petrie 1904 (1905).

A number of dated documents are known from his reign.

Year 1, the Stele of Rameses-Heru that is now in the Paris Museum. The Stele of Pentaur is in the Cairo Museum. A stele at Silsileh is dated to Paophi 5.
Year 2, work was done at Medinet Habu on Thoth 29. A stele at Silsileh is dated to Mesore 5.
Year 3, an inscription at Deir el Bahari is dated in the month of Hathor. That year, a Frontier diary is dated between Pakhons 15 and 25. The King is mentioned in the *Papyrus Bakenamen* on Pauni 10.
Year 5, News of Libyan advance is dated to Pauni 5. The Libyan battle and the Israel stele is dated to Epiphi 3. Another stele in Cairo is also dated to Epiphi 3. He is mentioned in connection with the Temple of Nubt in the same year.
Year 8, the *Papyrus Bologna* is dated to Hathor 29.

WHERE ARE THE KAMITE KINGS?

Where are the Kamite Kings Illustration. A relief in the tomb of Merenptah, son and successor of Rameses II, showing the King in Osiris Crown sporting horns, Sun-disk, feathers encompassing the White Crown with uraei sporting sun disks, all before Ra-Horakhty who holds the Waz Scepter and Ankh.

A number of officials are known from his reign. A limestone statue of the scribe Amenemheb is in Liverpool. The tomb of the high priest of Anhur, Anhurmes is at Mesheykh. A stele of Banazana of Zarbasana is known. A statue of Hora in charge of scribes of the royal table is in Paris. Kha-em-tir's tomb is at Qurneh. A limestone statue of Khera-uti is in Bologna. The stele of Mes, Prince of Kush is at Aswan. Another stele of Messuy, Prince of Kush is also at Aswan. The Vizier Nehesi erected 4 steles at Silsileh and is mentioned in the Temple of Wady Halfa. A stele of Pentaur, the washer of the King's hands, is at Abydos. A stele of the priest Rameses is in the British Museum. Another stele of Rameses-em-per-Ra, called Meranu, the chief washer of the King's hands is in the Cairo Museum. His father was Yupa-Aa. At Silsileh is a stele of Roy a high priest of Amen. Also, a statue of Roy is at Karnak and another in Cairo. A statue of the scribe of the granary and palace keeper, Sa-ast, is in Vienna. A stele of the scribe Yuy is on Sehel Island.

Where are the Kamite Kings Illustration. Heb-Sed Festival images of Rameses II at the Temple of Ehnasya in *Ehnasya* by Flinders Petrie 1904 (1905).

Sety II, *Nile Year* 3031-3037 (c. 1199-1193 B.C.) was a son of Merenptah. His Mummy and coffin were found in the tomb of Amenhotep II and is now in the Cairo Museum. His tomb is No. 15 in the Valley of the Kings.

Sety II, according to the *Papyrus Anastasi* V, is mentioned at a fortification in Palestine. At Serabit el Khadem his name is on vases and on a usurped pylon. At Tanis it is on a block and a usurped sphinx at Nebesheh. At Bubastis, a statue of him as a prince is

WHERE ARE THE KAMITE KINGS?

known. A limestone figure of him kneeling was found at Tell el Yehudiyeh. A block of red granite was found at Heliopolis. He is mentioned in a rock shrine of Merenptah at Surarieh. He is on a large pylon at the temple at Eshmunen. The scribe Saamen mentions him in the quarry at Isbayda.

The Karnak complex contains much evidence of him. He has a granite stele between the sphinxes. Two small obelisks were erected before pylon I. He built a small temple or kiosk in the northwest area of the large forecourt, at the temple's entrance, that was dedicated to the Theban Triad, Amen, Mut and Khonsu. His inscribed name is on the jamb of a door of pylon IV. His name is also on the gallery of Thutmose III. His name is on pylon VI and he did repairs in the court east of pylon VI. He also repaired Hall G (of Mariette). His name is on the west wall between pylons III and VIII. On pylon IX he is a part of the Hymn to Amen. He appropriated a sphinx next to pylon IX. He is in a frieze by the Temple of Khonsu and on the gate of the Temple of Mut.

At Luxor, his name is on the colonnade of Amenhotep III. At the Ramesseum, tiles bear his name. His name is behind the Temple of Medinet Habu and a rock stele was usurped by Setnakht. At Silsileh, his stele of offering was defaced in Horemheb's shrine. At this site, he is mentioned in inscriptions of the quarry master Yaa. Officials of his are on a rock stele at Sehel Island. At Abu Simbel his name is on the second colossus and he is mentioned on a stele of Mery. His name is on rocks at Wady Hammamat.

FREDERICK MONDERSON

Where are the Kamite Kings Photo. Pygmy statue of God Ptah in the Memphis Museum.

A number of portraits of Sety II exist. A statue of his queen is in the Cairo Museum. Another statue with a standard is in the Paris Museum. A statue is in Turin, a bust in Florence and the head of a statue is in the Paris Museum.

The *Papyrus d'Orbiney* belonged to Prince Sety. *Papyrus Anastasi* IV is dated to his first year and *Papyrus Anastasi* VI is dated to his reign.

WHERE ARE THE KAMITE KINGS?

His name is on the back of a statue of Rameses II now in Cairo. It is on a pillar of Thutmose IV in Vienna. The British Museum has a wooden tablet of him adoring Amen and Ptah. From Gurob comes a steatite tray that is now in the Ashmolean Museum. The base of a statue of his was usurped by Amenemenes and is now in Liverpool Museum. Incised plaques are in Turin and Leyden G. 571. Glazed inlaid tile Cartouche/Shennus of his are common. So too are scarabs. Dated monuments of his are few.

Where are the Kamite Kings Illustration. Seated statue of Rameses II, "the great," 19th Dynasty.

FREDERICK MONDERSON

Where are the Kamite Kings Photo. Erik Monderson stands beside a prone, colossal statue of Rameses II at the Memphis Museum.

Where are the Kamite Kings Illustration. Throne of Quartzite statue of Rameses II at the temple of Ehnasya in *Ehnasya* by Flinders Petrie 1904 (1905).

WHERE ARE THE KAMITE KINGS?

Year 1, *Papyrus Anastasi* IV is dated to Mesore 15.
Year 2, a shrine at Silsileh is dated to the month of Pharmuthi.
Year 3, wine jars of his were found in the Temple of Siptah in this and
Year 4, a statue, of his Queen, Ta-Khat is in the Cairo Museum. His sons were Amenemeses, Siptah and Setnakht. His daughter was Tausert (Sitra-Mery-Amun).

Where are the Kamite Kings Photo. Memphis Museum. Prone frontal view of a colossal alabaster statue of Rameses II, dragged to this location, abandoned, and finally covered in the structure that became the Memphis Museum.

Where are the Kamite Kings Illustration. Scarabs of the New Kingdom bearing the names of Seti I, Rameses II, Nefertari, 19th Dynasty Queen of Rameses II and Sety II and Tausert.

FREDERICK MONDERSON
THE TWENTIETH DYNASTY

The Twentieth Dynasty - *Nile Year* 3045-3160 (c. 1185-1070 B.C.), continued the Ramesside tradition of architectural constructions, and maintaining and defending the empire, though they faced a changing geo-political reality in the ancient world. Having dominated the world stage and been the principal imperialist nation, Ta-meri/Kemet, today's Egypt, now faced the combined wrath of a confederation of her traditional enemies. Struggled as the nation did to hold back the inevitable historical changes, it was only a matter of time before the Nile River state was overcome by external foes as she grew weaker internally.

The first Pharaoh of this dynasty was **Userkhaura-Setepenra, Setnakht** *Nile Year* 3045-3048 (1185-1182 B.C.). The *Harris Papyrus* mentioned the length of his reign and his efforts to re-establish law and order after the short period of anarchy at the end of the Nineteenth Dynasty. He was succeeded by his son, one of the last great Egyptian Africans of the New Kingdom, Rameses III.

Userma'atra-Mery-Amun, Rameses III, *Nile Year* 3048-3079 (c. 1182-1151 B.C.) continued the reorganization begun by his father. He faced the hordes of Kemet's enemies and surprisingly, won a number of wars. Iskander (1977: 131) tells of some of his exploits. "In the fifth year of his reign, the Libyans made an alliance with the Aegeans and invaded the Western Delta, but Rameses defeated them. In the eleventh year of his reign, they again attacked Egypt and Rameses defeated them and killed their leader. His victories were decisive for they did not attack Egypt at all after this reign."

This daring pharaoh severely defeated several Asian tribes and re-established Ta-meri's power in Asia. He built extensively, and his magnificent Medinet Habu structure was the last great architectural construction of the New Kingdom. His mummy and coffin were found at Deir el Bahari and are now in the Cairo Museum. He had two tombs in the Valley of the Kings. Tomb No. 3 was his earlier sepulcher and Tomb No. 11 his later and final resting place, before he was removed and interred with the other pharaohs, due to

WHERE ARE THE KAMITE KINGS?

security considerations, in the Twenty-Second Dynasty. His sarcophagus, of red granite, is in the Paris Museum, while the lid is in Cambridge.

Petrie III (1905: 142-47) supplies much of the data about the whereabouts of this King's name.

At Serabit el Khadem, a stele and lintel bear his name. From this site also, vase pieces are now in the British Museum, No. 4,803c. At Tanis, a kneeling sandstone figure of the King and a kneeling grey granite figure are known. At Kantara by Faqus was found a stele.

Where are the Kamite Kings Illustration. Head of fallen 1000-ton statue of Rameses II at his mortuary temple, the Ramesseum.

At Tell el Yehudiyeh, he constructed a palace, from which tiles are in the British Museum, Cairo Museum, Sevres, etc. Here was found a statue. An alabaster vase in the British Museum, No. 32,071, comes from this site. At Heliopolis, he is associated with the Chapel of Mnevis, that's now in the Cairo Museum. From this ancient holy site, were found blocks with his name. An inscribed block was also found at Khasus.

FREDERICK MONDERSON

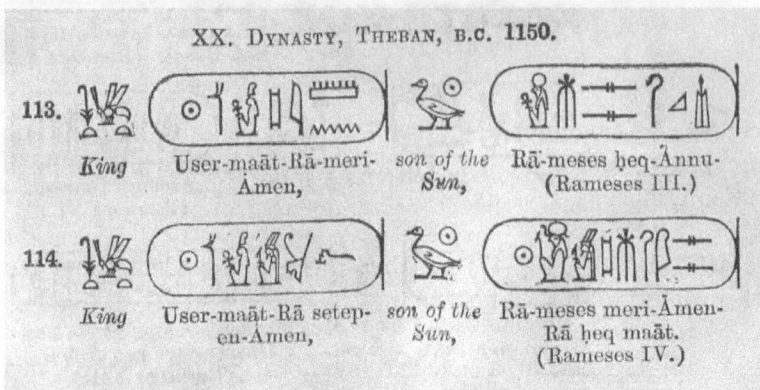

Kamite Kings Cartouche/Shennu. Kings of the Ramesside Twentieth Dynasty from Thebes.

Kamite Kings Cartouche/Shennu. Kings of the Ramesside Twentieth Dynasty from Thebes.

At Memphis a pillar bears his *Ka* name, while a block was usurped by Rameses VI. Also, at Memphis, a Serapeum Apis is known. At Surarieh a shrine and at Tehneh a stele with Sebek and Amen bear his name. In the Tomb of Helleh, a charioteer, we find his name. He had a statue at Abydos, while his name is on the doorway of the Temple of Seti I. Here also, a slab with Thiy-merenast and a Triad

WHERE ARE THE KAMITE KINGS?

by Se-ast identifies Rameses III. A block at Denderah and a lintel at Nubt are his. A Koptos Stele is in the Cairo Museum. Koptos also supplied a Baboon of sandstone that is now in Manchester. A Kus Stele of black granite records his XVIth year.

At the Great Temple of Karnak, he built his temple in the First Court, on a north to south axis, perpendicular to the temple's principal axis, which is east to west. He restored the north gate at the Temple of Ptah. He built the southern Temple of Khonsu. Today, this temple is considered the most complete surviving temple of the New Kingdom, with all of its essential parts intact. He was associated with a Temple within the enclosure west of the Temple of Mut. An altar of his is in the court of the same temple. There are inscriptions of his on Pylon IX at Karnak. There are also inscriptions in the great hall. His name is on columns in this Hypostyle Hall. In addition, inscriptions on a chamber in the east end of the temple mention his name.

At Luxor, in the Temple of Amenhotep III, his name is on a block and wall. Also, a quartzite stele bears his name. There is an inscription on a pylon at Qurneh and a block of his was found to the north of this site. At the Ramesseum, a lintel and inscribed pillars bear his name.

Where are the Kamite Kings Photo. Erik Monderson at the Ramesseum with the ruins at his rear.

FREDERICK MONDERSON

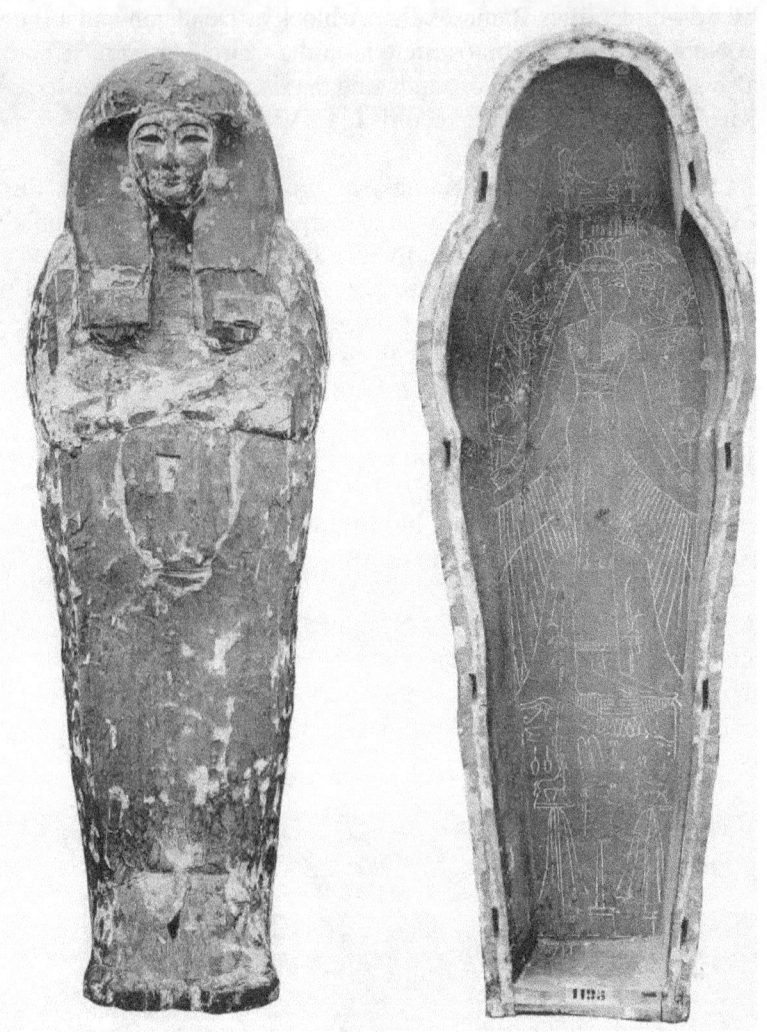

Where are the Kamite Kings Illustration. Lid and bottom of the coffin of Nozemat. Notice the illustrated Goddess within has wings.

WHERE ARE THE KAMITE KINGS?

Where are the Kamite Kings Illustration. Pharaoh Seti makes a presentation to enthroned Osiris, while Isis and Horus back up the God.

Rameses III built the Medinet Habu Temple, where his name survives on a window opening. The temple had its own bathroom, which is still visible today. In fact, there were four bathrooms altogether at Medinet Habu. A molding from this site is in the Berlin Museum. In this famous structure, the King is in a group with Horus and Set. He is on a stele with Setnakht and another stele behind the temple belongs to him. His name is on the Temple of Thutmose III within the Medinet Habu complex or outer enclosure, Maspero called "a Migdol.". His mortuary temple, thought to be the last significant New Kingdom construction, mirrors the efforts of the King to preserve the integrity of his great, yet declining nation.

AJA XX (1916: 359-60) comments on H. Burton's description of Theodore M. Davis's 1913 excavations at the palace of Rameses III beside the Temple of Medinet Habu. "Among the interesting discoveries was a bathroom 5 ft. 7 in. by 4 ft. The bath consists of a stone slab hollowed out in the middle to a depth of four inches and to a length and breadth of 3 ft. 6 in. and 3 ft. 4 in. respectively. At one end is a hole for the water to run through from which it passed into a stone receptacle. To the east of this room was found a small limestone base for a throne, with two steps leading up to it; and fifteen feet to the north a throne dais of limestone, measuring 6 ft. 7

in. by 5 ft. 3 in. with three flights of steps, one in front of four steps and one on either side of three steps. On either side of the front steps is the lower part of a sandstone column upon a base of black basalt, upon which are carved the King's names. Behind were two square pillars with portraits of the King. Further north were several pieces of sandstone which proved to be parts of three windows. One of these is now in New York and the others in Cairo. Further north a larger bathroom was found, and to the west of this a third bathroom. North of the principal bath, a throne base smaller than either of the others was uncovered, and immediately behind it a fourth bathroom."

In the Tomb of Setan at El Kab, an inscription of the King's Heb Sed festival is recorded. His name is on the Ra Temple and on blocks in the Temenos. At the Silsileh quarries, the King erected steles with the Theban Triad of Amon (Amen, Amun), Mut and their son, Khonsu. He is also shown with Amen and Sebek on 9 columns. The King is pictured with the divinities Ptah and Selket and Sebek and Hathor.

At West Silsileh, graffiti of Rameses III is dated to the month Pachons of Year V. Here too, a stele of Year VI of the King is dedicated to Amen, Hor and Hapi.

His name is on re-used blocks at Kom Ombo. Two inscriptions at Elephantine and Aswan boast of depictions of two officials adoring Cartouche/Shennus or Shennus of the King. His name is here and he is shown with other Gods. At Semneh, an official adores his Cartouche/Shennus in that temple.

WHERE ARE THE KAMITE KINGS?

Where are the Kamite Kings Photo. Hatshepsut as a Sphinx (left); and, in a kneeling posture (right) in the Cairo Museum of Antiquities.

Where are the Kamite Kings Illustration. Rameses II sits enthroned and surrounded by Amon-Ra (left) in Double Crown, Seshat (center) with star headdress, and Thoth (right) with moon headdress, as they write his name in the Persea "Tree of Life," signaling his years of rulership. The King holds Ankh and Flail.

FREDERICK MONDERSON

The head of a sandstone statue is in the Florence Museum, while both the Paris and British Museums have ushabtis of his. The Paris Museum has a bronze ushabti of Rameses III, and a portrait is in the British Museum.

A pillar in the Paris Museum, D 63; an alabaster vase in the Alexandria Museum; a stele of the King adoring Horus, now in the Paris Museum, c. 217; a Stele of Osiris, Isis and Horus in Cairo and ushabti of limestone in Cairo, all bear the King's name. A wooden ushabti in Paris, a gilt bronze inlaid pectoral belonging to the H. Collection and mortar of red granite in Cairo, were all attributed to Rameses III. Scarabs of his reign are common.

Papyri seem to abound from his reign. The *Great Harris Papyrus* in the British Museum is extremely important, for it tells of the exploits of the King and his father. Turin seems to be a significant repository for papyri including a Sorcery case; works at the Ramesseum; works at the Temple of Hathor; the war in Syria; and the name of Rameses III, are all in that Museum. His name is also in Vienna and on a list of papyri documents. A papyrus on Rameses' Heb Sed Festival is in the Paris Museum and Ostraka from his tomb are in Cairo.

His Queen was Ast-amasereth whose name is on a statue of the King. She is mentioned on a Stele of Amenemapt and in Tomb No. X in the Valley of the Queens. Another Queen, Humazery, is also mentioned at *Deshret* (Deir el-Bahari).

Rameses III, had a number of sons, the first was Pa'ra-her-amif who is mentioned in the queen's tomb at Thebes. A portrait of another son Mentu-her-khep-shef exists and he has a heart scarab in Berlin. Other sons of Rameses III, mentioned in Lepsius' *Denkmaler* include another Rameses, Ra-maat-neb, Mer Amen; Rameses, At-Amen; Rameses, Set-her-khopshef; Rameses Mery-Atmu; Rameses Amen-her-khepshef; Rameses Mery-Amen.

Dated remains of Rameses III abound, and as such, Petrie III (1905: 146) believed, "the temple of Medinet Habu is the main authority for the history of this reign, it is needful to refer to it constantly and systematically."

WHERE ARE THE KAMITE KINGS?

Year 1, Pachons 26, Accession of Medinet Habu.
Year 3, graffiti at Silsilch.
Year 4, Mekhir, at the Southern part of Medinet Habu.
Year 5, historic text and quarrying graffiti at Silsileh during the month of Pakhons.
Year 6, during the month of Phamenoth, a hymn to the Nile was left at Silsileh. That is the same year of a *Turin Papyrus*.
Year 8, an historic text was recorded at Medinet Habu.
Year 10, another *Turin Papyrus* was written.
Year 11, on Mesore 10, a *Triumphal text* was registered at the Medinet Habu temple. during Mekhir 9, another *Triumphal text* was again registered at the temple.
Year 12, the *Revenue Text* at Medinet Habu was engraved. That same year, the Speech of Ptah was made at the temple. A stele was also recorded at that time.
Year 16, during the month of Pauni, offerings were made to Amen at Karnak. On the first of that same month, a stele was erected at Kus.
Year 17, Pharmuthi to Pharmenoth 15 mention is made of this King.
Year 18, another *Turin Papyrus* is recorded.
Year 22, endowments were made for Amen.
Year 24, another *Turin Papyrus* is known.
Year 26, an Apis burial occurred.
Year 29, Mesore 25 to Pakhons 15, another *Turin Papyrus* is dated.
Year 31, *Papyrus Massallet* is known from this date.
Year 32, Epiphi 6, the *Harris Papyrus* was recorded and the building of the tower at the temple was completed.

For much of the years of this King he was concerned with mobilizing his army, and engaging and expelling the foreigners who had forcefully settled in the Delta region. Iskander (1979: 132) further informs, the King paid "attention to trade, sending expeditions to punt to bring myrrh and other precious products. Copper was extracted from Sinai and gold from Lower Nubia."

Succeeding Kings Rameses IV to XI struggled with the changing state of affairs and a number of royal tombs were robbed during this time. The *Abbott Papyrus* and the *Amherst Papyrus,* now in the British Museum record the inquiries into these ancient tomb desecrations. Conflict soon ended the dynasty and thereafter the Priesthood of Amen at Thebes rose to prominence and challenged the rulers for control of the state.

Where are the Kamite Kings Photo. Memphis Museum. Gallery in the Open Court Garden with the towering statue of Rameses II wearing the White Crown.

13. Great Temple of Karnak

Murray's *Handbook for Egypt* (1888) provides the following description of the Theban temple that had such a meaningful role in the New Kingdom, even from the Middle Kingdom down to the Greek and Roman Period.

"The principal entrance to the Great Temple of Karnak is about 5 minutes to the North of the Temple of Rameses III. This entrance lies on the North-West side, facing the river, and about 1/2 a mile distant from it."

Plan of the Temple

"From a raised platform commences an avenue of Croi-sphinxes, in some of which has been found the name of Rameses II, about 200

WHERE ARE THE KAMITE KINGS?

feet in length, leading to the *First Pylon* (A), before which stood two granite statues now mutilated and buried in the soil. One of the two pro-pylon towers retains a great part of its original height, but has lost its summit and cornice. In the upper part their solid walls have been perforated through their whole breadth, for the purpose of fastening the timbers that secured the flagstaffs usually placed in front of these propyla; but no sculptures have ever been added to either face, nor was the surface yet leveled to receive them. The total breadth of this enormous pro-pylon is about 370 feet, and its depth 50 feet; the height of the standing tower is 140 feet. A narrow staircase leads up to the top, whence is obtained an excellent bird's eye view of the ruins."

"Passing through the gateway of this pro-pylon, you arrive at a large open area, the *First Court* (B), 275 feet by 329 feet, with a covered corridor on either side, and a double line of [Taharka] columns down the center, of which only one remains standing. The corridors are 50 feet high: that on the North presents an even front of 18 columns, the one on the South is broken by a small Temple of *Rameses* III, (L) the entrance to which abuts on the great area."

"This court was added by Shishak of the XXII Dynasty. Mr. Maspero considers that he intended to roof over the columns but never completed the work. Between it and the second pylon in the South East angle of the court is a space, which has been called the Hall of the Bubastites, from the sculptures on the walls containing the names of the Kings of that dynasty. In the Northeast corner of this court are the remains of a small Temple of Sethi II (M). A flight of seven steps, on either side of which was a granite statue of Rameses II, only one of which now remains, much mutilated, led up to the entrance, through the *Second Propylon* (C), of:

FREDERICK MONDERSON

Where are the Kamite Kings Photo. Illustration. 292. As a vulture hovers over his head, Rameses II in *Nemes* Headdress offers two plants to Nephthys, holding the Wadj Scepter and Ankh.

"The GREAT HALL (D), the largest and most magnificent of the old Egyptian monuments. The lintel stones of its doorway were 40 feet 10 inches in length. It measures 170 feet by 329 feet and is supported by a central avenue of 12 massive columns, 62 feet high (without the plinth and abacus) and 11 feet 6 inches diameter; besides 122 of smaller or (rather) less gigantic dimensions, 42 feet 5 inches in height, and 28 feet in circumference, distributed in nine lines of seven each wanting four: 134 columns in all. Originally the mass was roofed over, and the light only penetrated into it through a sort of clerestory, remains of which may still be seen on the South side. The oldest King's name found in this hall is that of Sethi I, and he is generally credited with its construction, but there is some reason for supposing that it was projected by Rameses I. Attached to the doorway are two large towers, closing the inner extremity of the hall."

"At the East end of the Great Hall is a *Third Pylon* (E), much ruined which served as the entrance to the temple up to the reign of Rameses. Through it we pass into a narrow-uncovered court,

WHERE ARE THE KAMITE KINGS?

extending along the whole width of the building in which stood *Two Obelisks* of red granite (d) about 75 feet in height. One is thrown down and broken, the other still stands. They bear on one side the name of Thothmes I, of the XVIIIth Dynasty, and added at either side of the original inscription, another by Rameses II of the XIXth, showing a difference of age of the sculptures of 250 years."

"To this court succeeds a *Fourth Pylon* (F) of smaller size, passing through the vestibule of which - about 40 feet long - we reach the *Hall of Osiride Figures* (G), surrounded by a Peristyle of the pillars so-called. In it are *Two Obelisks* of red granite (e) like the others, but of larger dimensions, the one now standing being 97 feet 6 inches high. This is the second tallest obelisk in the world, being surpassed in height by that of St. John Lateran at Rome. The latter obelisk was erected by Thothmes III at Heliopolis. It is 105 feet 7 inches high. This part of the building bears the name of Thothmes I; the obelisk, that of his daughter Hatshepsut. From a part of the inscription on one of these obelisks we learn that only seven months were employed in its erection, including the time spent in transporting it from the quarries of Aswan. From this hall we pass through the portal of a small-dilapidated pylon into a small area, at either end of which a door led into two chambers each with two rows of columns, and communicating with the passages. A very small pylon, on the West face of which are some of the celebrated *Geographical Lists*, containing the names of 1200 towns, of which 628 remain, leads into a small vestibule in front of the granite gateway of the towers which form the facade of the court before the "*Sanctuary* (H). This is of red granite, divided into two apartments, and surrounded by numerous chambers of small dimensions, varying from 29 feet by 16 feet, to 16 feet by 8 feet."

"The actual sanctuary itself is one mass of ruins, but some of the chambers are still standing, and are covered with sculptures of the XVIIIth Dynasty. The date of the sanctuary itself is much earlier, though the blocks now *in situ* bear the name of Philip Aridaeus, who restored it; in the large *Open Court* (I) immediately are some polygonal columns (f), with the Cartouche/Shennu of Osirtasen I, of the XIIth Dynasty, in the midst of fallen architraves of the same era; showing that the original construction of the sanctuary dated from that era. Further on in this open space are two pedestals of red granite. They may have supported obelisks; but they are not square, like the basements of those monuments, and rather resemble, for this reason, the pedestals of statues. Their sub-structures are of limestone."

"At the end of this open court is the Columnar Edifice of Thothmes III (K). Its exterior wall is entirely destroyed except on the North side. Parallel to the four outer walls is a row of square pillars, going all round, within the edifice, 32 in number; and in the center are 20 columns, disposed in two lines, parallel to the back and front row of pillars. But the position of the latter does not accord with the columns of the center. An unusual caprice has changed the established order of the architectural details, the capitals and cornices being reversed, without adding to the beauty or increasing the strength of the building. The latter, however, had the effect of admitting more light to the interior. Observe on some of the columns traces of the walls of a Christian church, built here after the abolition of idolatry. Several columns still bear pictures of saints, among which a figure resembling the conventional representations of St. Peter may be made out. Adjoining the South-West angle of its front is a small room, commonly called the *Hall of Ancestors* (g), from its having contained on its walls a bas-relief representing King Thothmes III making offerings to 56 of his predecessors. This valuable monument is now at Paris. A series of small halls and rooms occupy the extremity of the temple."

"In the southern side adytum are the vestiges of a colossal hawk, seated on a raised pedestal; the sculptures within and without containing the name of Alexander, by whose order it was repaired and sculptured."

WHERE ARE THE KAMITE KINGS?

Where are the Kamite Kings Illustration. In his palace attached to the Temple at Medinet Habu, Rameses III plays with ladies of his harem.

"The total dimensions of this part of the temple, behind the inner propylon of the grand hall, are 600 feet, by about half that in breadth, making the total length, from the front propylon to the extremity of the wall of circuit, inclusive, 1180 feet. And from this it will appear that Diodorus is fully justified in the following statement, that: 'the circuit of the most ancient of the four temples at Thebes measured 13 stadia,' or about 1½ mile English. The thickness of the walls, 'of 25 feet,' owing to the great variety in their dimensions, is too vague to be noticed; but the height he gives to the building of 45 cubits (67 feet), is far too little for the pavement to the summit of the roof inclusive, is not less than 80 feet."

Comparative Antiquity of Buildings of the Great Temple.

No part, probably remains of the earliest foundation of the temple; but the name of Osirtasen I suffices to support its claim to great antiquity; and if no monument remains at Thebes of the earliest dynasties, this may be explained by the fact of its not having been founded when the Kings of the Pyramid period ruled at Memphis.

FREDERICK MONDERSON

The original sanctuary, which was probably of sandstone, doubtless existed in the reign of that monarch, and stood on the site of the present one, an opinion confirmed by our finding the oldest remains in that direction, as well as by the proportions of the courts and propyla, whose dimensions were necessarily made to accord with those of the previous parts, to which they were united. All is here on a limited scale, and the polygonal columns of Osirtasen evince the chaste style of architecture in vogue at that early era. It was added to by Amenemhat II and III, but remained little changed until the XVIIIth Dynasty."

"Then Thothmes I built the court of Osiride columns, and put up the two obelisks in the open space outside it. The great obelisks inside the Osiride court were erected to his memory by his daughter Hatshepsut, whose name also appears on the walls of some of the chambers near the sanctuary." Thothmes I also erected the three great pylons in front of the sanctuary, and rebuilt part of the latter. Some years later, King Thothmes III made considerable additions to the buildings and sculptures, and erected the great columnar edifice at the extreme east of the enclosure of the Great Temple. He also built the two pylons facing towards the South."

"The Sanctuary, destroyed by the Persians, and since rebuilt by Philip Aridaeus, was also of the same Pharaoh, who seems to have been the first to build it of red granite, and a block of that stone which now forms part of the ceiling, and bears the name of the 3rd Thothmes, belonged most probably to the sanctuary he rebuilt."

"At the close of his reign the temple only extended to the smaller obelisks; before which were added, by Amenhotep III, the towers of the propylon, whose recesses for the flagstaffs, proving them to have been originally the front towers of the temple, are still visible on the West face."

"The Great Hall was added by Sethi I, the 2nd King of the XIXth Dynasty; and besides the innumerable bas-reliefs that adorn its walls, historical scenes, in the most finished and elegant style of Egyptian sculpture, were designed to the exterior of the North side."

WHERE ARE THE KAMITE KINGS?

Where are the Kamite Kings Photo. Illustration.
284. Bust of Rameses IV and his father Rameses III. How African they both look!

"In the reign of Sethi's (Seti's) son, Rameses II, great additions were made. He completed the sculptures on the South side of the Great Hall, and on the exterior of the wall of circuit. He also built the area in front, with massive propyla, preceded by granite colossi and an avenue of sphinxes. It may be worth noting in connection with this part of the building than on a statue in the Munich Museum is an inscription giving an account of the career of the person represented Bekenkhonsu, 'skilled in art, and the first prophet of Amen,' in which the following passage occurs: - "I performed the best I could for the people of Amen, as architect of my lord. I executed the pylon 'of Rameses II, the friend of Amen, who listens to those who pray to him' (thus he is named), at the first gate of the Temple of Amen. I placed obelisks at the same made of granite. Their height reached to the vault of heaven. A propylon is before the same in sight of the city of Thebes, and ponds and gardens, with flourishing trees. I made two great double doors of gold. Their height reaches to heaven. I caused to be made a double pair of great masts. I set them up in the splendid court in sight of his temple."

"Succeeding monarchs continued to display their piety, to gratify their own vanity, or to court the goodwill of the priesthood, by making additions to the buildings erected by their predecessors; and the several isolated monuments, becoming attached to the principal pile, formed at length one immense whole, connected either by great avenues of sphinxes, or by crude brick enclosures."

"The principal edifices united to the main temple by the successors of the 2nd Rameses are the three chambers below the front pro-pylon, and the small but complete temple (L) on the West side of the large area; the latter by Rameses III, the former by his second predecessor, Sethi, or Osirei II. Several sculptures were added, during the XXIInd Dynasty, at the western corner of the same area. The columns in this court, one alone of which is now standing, bear the name of Taharka, Psammetichus II, and of Ptolemy Philopator; and the gateway between them and the grand hall having been altered by Ptolemy Physcon, additional sculptures, bearing his name, were inserted amidst those of the 2nd Rameses. On the left, as you enter, he wears a Greek helmet." "It will be seen from the above account that the earliest name found on any of the buildings of the Great Temple is that of Osirtasen I, and the latest that of Alexander II, whose name appears in one of the small chambers belonging to the columnar edifice of Thothmes III."

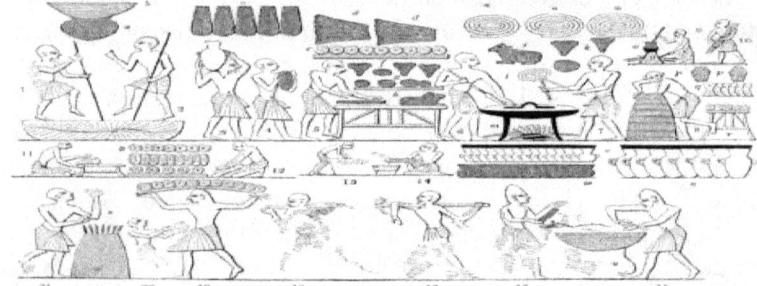

Where are the Kamite Kings Photo. Illustration. 295. In the tomb of Rameses III at Thebes. 1, 2. Kneading the dough with their feet; 3,4. carrying it to the confectioner (5), who rolls out the paste, which is afterwards made like cakes of various forms, *d, e, f, g, h*. 6, 7, 9 making a sort of (*l, m, n, o*) on a pan over the fire, m. 8. Preparing the oven. 9. Cooking Lentils, which are in the baskets *p, p*. 11, 12. Making cake of bread sprinkled with seeds. 13, 14. Kneading paste with the hands. 15. Carrying the cakes to the oven y, which is now lighted. At *a, b*, the dough is probably left to ferment in a basket, as is now done at Cairo.

WHERE ARE THE KAMITE KINGS?

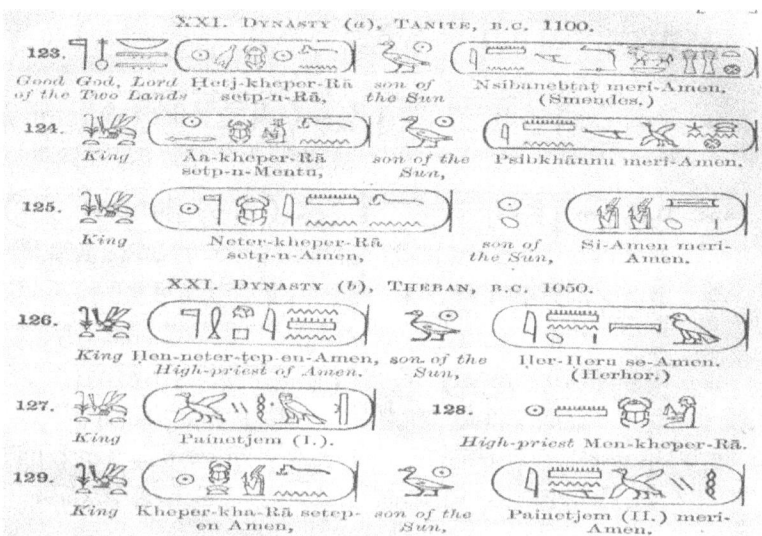

Kamite Kings Cartouche/Shennus 19. Contemporary Kings of the Twenty-First Dynasty, with one set ruling from Tanis and the other ruling from Thebes.

14. The Temple of Luxor

Murray's *Handbook for Egypt* (1888) provides the following description of the Temple of Luxor.

The site of Luxor was called *Waset* by the ancient Egyptians. For the Greeks it was a part of *Diospolis Parva* and in Arabic it was called *El Uksor*, or *Aboo l'Haggag*. The name, Luxor, or *El Kosoor*, signifies "the Palaces," from the temple there erected by Amenhotep III and Rameses II.

"*The Temple of Luxor.* The original sanctuary and the adjoining chambers, with the addition of the large colonnade and the pylon before it, were built by Amenhotep III. Rameses II afterwards added the great court, the pyramidal towers, and the obelisks and statues. The whole plan of the Temple is very irregular, from its having been built on the bank of the river, and following the direction of the quay."

"The excavations made by M. Maspero have exposed the Temple to view: it had previously been so covered with rubbish and modern buildings that it was difficult to trace the plan. It would appear that when first constructed, it was not separated from the Nile as it is at present, but rose direct from the water's edge."

"The parts built by Rameses II, though last in the order of antiquity, necessarily form the present commencement of the temple, which, like many others belonging to different epochs, is not two separate edifices, but one and the same building."

"A *dromos*, connecting it with Karnak, extended in front of the two beautiful Obelisks of red granite (only one of which now remains *in situ*), the other being in the Place de la Concorde at Paris), whose four sides are covered with a profusion of hieroglyphics, no less admirable for the style of their execution than for the depth to which they are cut, which in many instances exceed 2 inches. It is to be regretted that the companion obelisk has been removed, especially now that the excavation of the temple is carried out. The remaining obelisk is 84 feet in height .... The obelisk in Paris is 77 feet in height. Behind the remaining obelisk are two sitting *Statues of Rameses* II, one on either side of the pylon or gateway; ..."

"Near the North-West extremity of the *Propyla* .... Interesting battle-scenes on the front of the towers. Many of these are very spirited. On the western tower is the camp, surrounded by a wall, represented by Egyptian shields, with a guard posted at the gate."

"Within are chariots, horses, and the spoil taken from the enemy, as well as the holy place that held the Egyptian ark in a tent. There are instances of this found on other monuments such as at Abu Simbel and the Ramesseum."

"There is also the King's chariot, shaded by a large umbrella or parasol."

WHERE ARE THE KAMITE KINGS?

Where are the Kamite Kings Illustration. Usertesen III and Thutmose III at Gebel Dosha, from Lepsius' *Denkmaler*.

"At the doorway itself is the name of Sabaco, and on the abacus of the columns beyond, that of Ptolemy Philopator, both added at a later epoch."

"The *Hall* within, whose dimensions are about 190 feet by 170 feet, is surrounded by a Peristyle, consisting of two rows of columns, … [the east row interrupted by] the mosque of the village. The line of direction no longer continues the same behind this court, the Ramessean front having been turned eastward; which was done in order to facilitate its connection with the great temple of Karnak, as well as to avoid the vicinity of the river."

"Passing through the pylon of Amenhotep, you arrive at the great Colonnade, where the names of this Pharaoh and of Amen-Toonkh are sculptured. The latter, however, has been effaced as is generally the case whenever it is met with and those of Horus and of Sethi are introduced in its stead. The length of the colonnade to the next court is about 170 feet. To this succeeds an area of 155 feet by 167 feet, surrounded by a Peristyle of 12 columns in length and the same in breadth, terminating in a covered portico of 32 columns, 57 feet by 111."

FREDERICK MONDERSON

Where are the Kamite Kings Photo. Cairo Museum of Egyptian Antiquities. Pharaoh makes a double-handed Presentation to Thoth wearing moon and crescent headdress.

"Behind this is a space occupying the whole breadth of the building, divided into chambers of different dimensions, the center one leading to a hall supported by four columns, immediately before the entrance to the isolated sanctuary."

"On the East of the hall is a chamber containing some curious sculpture, representing the accouchement of Queen Maut-m-Shoi, the mother of Amenhotep. Two children nursed by the deity of the Nile are presented to Amen, the presiding divinity of Thebes. Several other subjects relate to the triad worshiped in this temple."

WHERE ARE THE KAMITE KINGS?

Where are the Kamite Kings Photo. Two "Ladies in the Egyptian House" at the Cairo Museum of Antiquities.

Where are the Kamite Kings Illustration. Amenhotep II with horns of the Nubian Ram sacred to Amen.

Where are the Kamite Kings Illustration. Pa-Her-Pet and Anonymous; the right lid covers the decorated coffin.

"The original Sanctuary was perhaps destroyed by the Persians; but the present one was rebuilt by Alexander (the son of Alexander, Ptolemy being the Governor of Egypt), and bears his name in the following dedicatory formula: 'This work (?) made he, the King of men, lord of the regions, Alexander, for his father Amen-ra, president of Tape (Thebes); he erected to him the sanctuary, a grand mansion, with repairs of sandstone, hewn, good, and hard stone, in lieu of? (that made by?) his majesty, the King of men, Amenhotep.'"

"Behind the sanctuary are two other sets of apartments, the larger ones supported by columns and ornamented with rich sculpture, much of which appears to have been gilded."

WHERE ARE THE KAMITE KINGS?

"Between this part and the great columnar hall is one of the old chambers, measuring 34 feet 6 inches by 57 feet 1 inch, with a semicircular niche. The walls are covered with frescoes of late Roman time; and it was evidently a court of law with the usual tribunal, in which are painted three figures larger than life wearing the toga and sandals. The center one holds a staff or Scepter (Scipio) in the right hand and a globe in the left; and near him was some object now defaced."

"The two other figures have each a scroll in one hand. On the walls to the right and left are the traces of figures, which are interesting from their costume; and on the sidewall to the East are several soldiers with their horses, drawn with great spirit. The colors are much damaged by exposure, and the frescoes can hardly be distinguished. They probably date after the age of Constantine. The costumes are remarkable; and some of the men wear embroidered upper garments, tight hose, and laced boots, or shoes tied over the instep. The false wainscot, or dado, below, is richly colored in imitation porphyry and other stones incrusted in patterns, and is better preserved than the frescoes of the upper part, where the old Gods of Egypt in bas-relief have outlived the paintings that once concealed them. There appears to be traces of a small cross-painted at one side of the tribune, and the figures have a nimbus round their heads, but without any of the character of Christian saints. Nor was the nimbus confined to saints by the early Christians."

"Behind the temple is a stone *Quay,* apparently of the late era of the Ptolemies or Caesars, since blocks bearing the sculpture of the former have been used in its construction. Opposite the corner of the temple, it takes a more easterly direction, and points out the original course of the river, which continued across the plain now lying between it and the ruins of Karnak, and which may be traced by the descent of the surface of that ground it gradually deserted. The southern extremity of the quay is of brick (probably a Roman addition), and indicates in like manner the former direction of the stream. When the temple was first built, the river seems to have flowed close under its walls."

FREDERICK MONDERSON

15. THE RAMESSEUM

Murray's *Handbook for Egypt* (1888) supplies the following description of the Ramesseum, Mortuary Temple of Rameses II.

"The RAMESEUM or Temple of Rameses II was erroneously called the MEMNONIUM, and the tomb of Osymandyas. There is, however, reason to suppose that it was the Memnonium of Strabo, attached to the name of Rameses II, being corrupted by the Greeks into Memnon, became the origin of the words Memnonium or Memnonia."

Where are the Kamite Kings Illustration. Thutmose IV slaying his enemies in the presence of the Gods.

PLAN

For symmetry of architecture and elegance of sculpture the Memnonium, may vie with any other Egyptian monument. No traces are visible of the dromos that probably existed before the pyramidal towers (A), which form the facade of its first area (CC) - court whose breadth of 180 feet, exceeding the length by nearly 13 yards, was reduced to a more just proportion by the introduction of

WHERE ARE THE KAMITE KINGS?

a double avenue of columns on either side, extending from the towers to the North wall. In this area, on the right of a flight of steps leading to the next court, was a stupendous Syenite STATUE OF RAMESES II (D), seated on a throne, in the usual attitude of Egyptian figures, the hands resting on his knees, indicative of that tranquility which he had returned to enjoy in Egypt after the fatigues of victory."

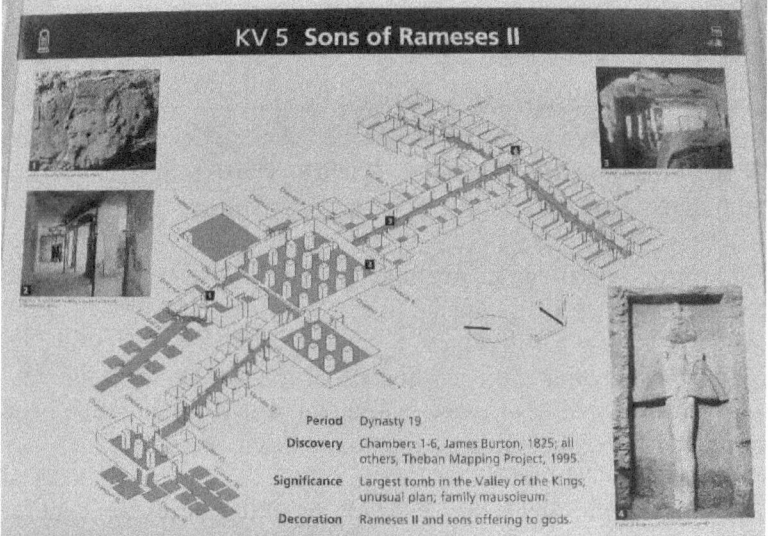

Where are the Kamite Kings Photo. KV 5 - Tomb of the Sons of Rameses II. Largest tomb in the Valley of the Kings. Notice the lips of the image of Ptah.

"The hands of the destroyer have leveled this monument of Egyptian grandeur; whose colossal fragments lie scattered round the pedestal: and its shivered throne evinces the force used for its destruction. It is a matter of surprise how the Egyptians could transport and erect a mass of such dimensions; the means employed for its ruin are scarcely less wonderful. We should not hesitate to account for the shattered appearance of the lower part by attributing it to the explosive force of powder, had that composition been known at the supposed period of its destruction. But is this early destruction certain?"

FREDERICK MONDERSON

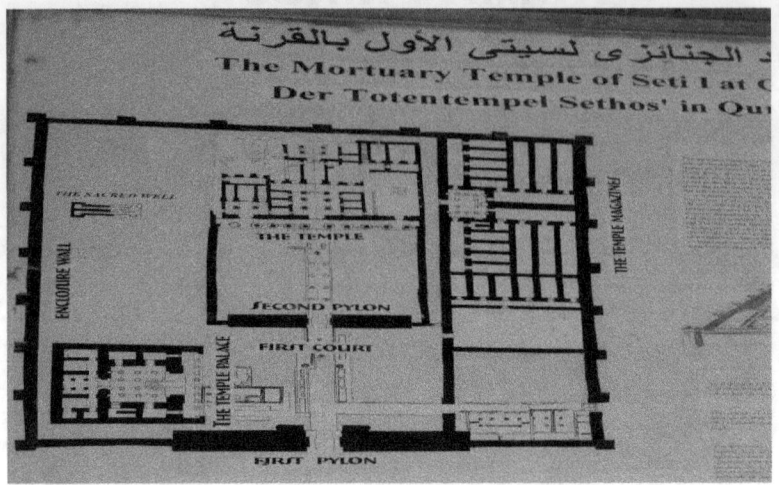

Where are the Kamite Kings Photo. Plan of the Mortuary Temple of Seti I at Kurneh, 19th Dynasty.

"The throne and legs are completely destroyed, and reduced to comparatively small fragments, while the upper part, broken at the waist, is merely thrown back upon the ground, and lies in that position which was the consequence of its fall; nor are there any marks of the wedge or other instrument which should have been employed for reducing those fragments to the state in which they now appear. The fissures seen across the head and in the pedestal are the work of a later period, when some of the pieces were cut for millstones by the Arabs. To say that this is the largest statue in Egypt will convey no idea of the gigantic size or enormous weight of a mass which, from an approximate calculation, exceeded, when entire, nearly three times the solid contents of the great obelisk of Karnak, and weighed over 1000 tons."

"No building in Thebes corresponds exactly with the description given of the tomb of Osymandyas by Hecataeus. Diodorus, who quotes his work, gives the dimensions of the first or outer court, 2 plethra (181 feet 8 inches English), agreeing very nearly with the breadth, but not with the length, or that now before us."

"The succeeding court, of 4 plethra, neither agrees with this, nor can agree with that of any other Egyptian edifice, since the plan of an Egyptian building invariably requires a diminution, but no increase, of dimensions, from the entrance to the inner chambers. The body

WHERE ARE THE KAMITE KINGS?

of the temple, behind the portico, retained one uniform breadth, the areas in front, and frequently the portico itself, exceeded the inner portion of it by their projecting sides."

"The Peristyle and 'columns in the form of living beings,' roofed colonnade, sitting statues, and triple entrance to a chamber supported by columns, agree well with the approach to the great hall of this temple: and the largest statue in Egypt can only be in the building before us. Yet the sculptures to which he alludes remind us rather of those of Medinet Haboo; and it is possible that either Hecataeus or Diodorus may have united or confounded the details of the two edifices. The second area (G G) is about 140 feet by 170 feet, having on the South, and North sides a row of Osiride pillars (H H) connected with each other by two lateral corridors of circular columns. Three flights of steps lead to the northern corridor (which may be called the portico), behind the Osiride pillars, the center one having on each side a black granite statue of Rameses II, the base of whose throne is cut to fit the talus of the ascent."

Where are the Kamite Kings Photo. Tomb of Rameses V/VI. Valley of the Kings. Individual controlling serpent with six heads face off against Red Crown (left) and White Crown (right). To control such an animal takes an extraordinary individual.

FREDERICK MONDERSON

Where are the Kamite Kings Photo. Cairo Museum of Egyptian Antiquities. One of two life-like statues of Tutankhamon dressed in royal attire.

"Behind the columns of the northern corridor, and on either side of the central door of the great hall, is a limestone pedestal, which, to judge from the space left in the sculptures, must have once supported the sitting of a figure of a lion, or perhaps a statue of the King. Three entrances (N O P) open into the grand hall (Q), each with a sculptured doorway of black granite: and between the two first columns of the central avenue, two pedestals (R S) supported (one on either side) two other statues of the King. Twelve massive columns, 32 feet 6 inches high, without the abacus, and 21 feet 3 inches circumference, form a double line along the center of this hall, and 18 of smaller dimensions (17 feet 8 inches circumference), to the right and left, complete the total of 48, which supported its solid roof studded with stars on an azure ground. To the hall, which measures 100 feet by 133 feet, succeeded 3 central (U V Z) and 6

WHERE ARE THE KAMITE KINGS?

lateral chambers (Y Y Y Y Y), indicating by a small flight of steps the gradual ascent of the rock on which this edifice is constructed. Of 9, 2 only (UV) of the central apartments now remain, each supported by 8 columns, and each measuring about 30 feet by 55 feet. The vestiges of their walls, and the appearance of the rock, which has been leveled to form an area around the exterior of the building, point out their original extent."

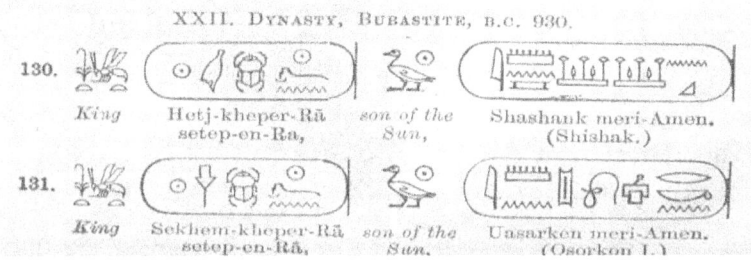

Kamite Kings Cartouche/Shennu (1). Kings of the Twenty-Second Dynasty.

Where are the Kamite Kings Photo. King wearing the Red Crown and Anonymous in a family portrait.

FREDERICK MONDERSON

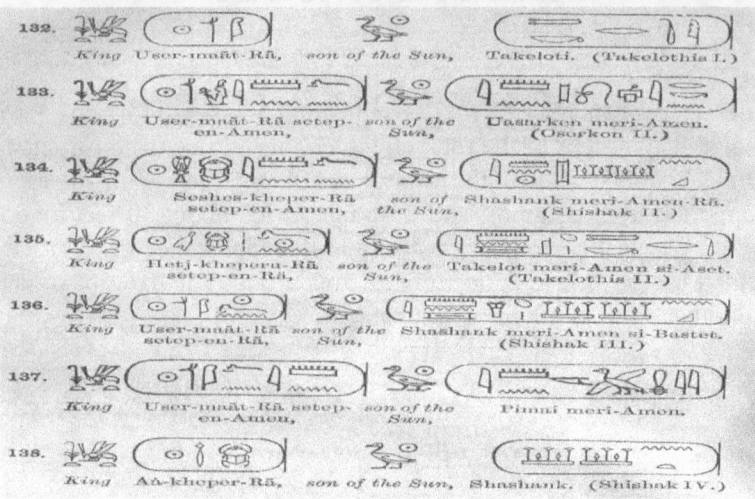

Kamite Kings Cartouche/Shennu (2). Kings of the Twenty-Second Dynasty.

"In the scene before us, an insolent soldier pulls the beard of his helpless captive, while others wantonly beat a supplicant. The display of this principle is the more striking, as the Egyptians on other occasions have recorded their humane treatment of an enemy in distress. Beyond these is a corps of infantry in close array, flanked by a strong body of chariots; and a camp, indicated by a rampart of Egyptian shields, with a wicker gate-way, guarded by four companies of sentries, who are on duty in the inner side, forms the most interesting object in the picture. Here the booty taken from the enemy is collected; oxen, chariots, plaustra, horses, asses, sacks of gold, represent the confusion incident after a battle. The richness of the spoil is expressed by the weight of a bag of gold, under which an ass is about to fall. One chief is receiving the salutation of a foot soldier; another, seated amidst the spoil, strings his bow; and a subtler suspends a water-skin on a pole he has fixed in the ground. Below this a body of infantry marches homewards; and beyond them the King, attended by his fan-bearers, holds forth his hand to receive the homage of the priests and principal persons, who approach his throne to congratulate his return. His charioteer is also in attendance, and the high-spirited horses of his car are with difficulty restrained by three grooms who hold them."

WHERE ARE THE KAMITE KINGS?

"Two captives below this are doomed to be beaten by four Egyptian soldiers; while they in vain, with outstretched hands, implore the clemency of their heedless conqueror."

"The sculptures on the gateway refer to the panegyrics, or assemblies, of the King, to whom different divinities are said to 'give life and power' (or 'pure life'). Over this gate passes a staircase, leading to the top of the building, whose entrance lies on the exterior of the East side."

"Upon the West tower is represented a battle in which the King discharges his arrows on the broken lines and flying chariots of the enemy; and his figure and car are again introduced, on the upper part, over the smaller sculptures. In a small compartment beyond these, which is formed by the end of the corridor of the area, he stands armed with a battle-axe, about to slay the captives he holds beneath him, who, in the hieroglyphics above, are called 'the chiefs of the foreign countries.' In the next compartment, still wearing his helmet, he approaches the temple attended by his sons, whose names are enumerated, the fan-bearers being Amenip Khepskhef, Rameses, and Prahiamentef, followed by the others to the number in all of 23, of whom the 13th is Merneptah, his successor; and to this the hieroglyphics before him allude."

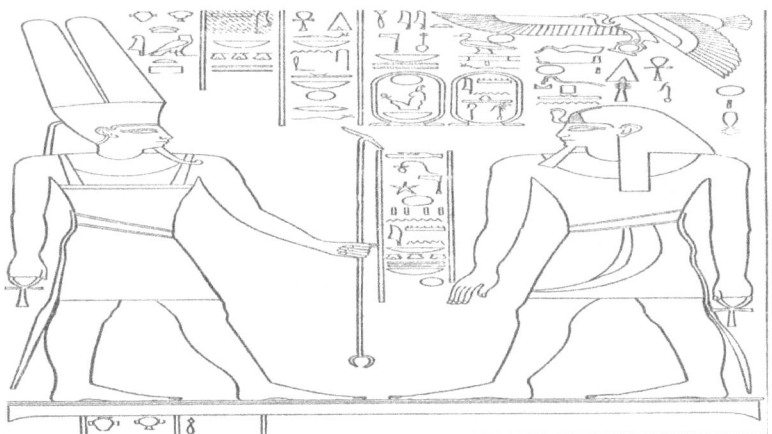

Where are the Kamite Kings Illustration. Amenhotep III adoring Amen, dweller in Kha-em-Ma'at. The God sports a curved beard, Amenhotep a straight beard.

FREDERICK MONDERSON

"On the North face of the South East wall of the 2nd Area - (G G), is another historical subject (K), representing Rameses II pursuing an enemy, whose numerous chariots, flying over the plain, endeavor to regain the river, and seek shelter under the fortified walls of their city, which is called in the accompanying hieroglyphs Ma-pu-li, a fort of the Khetas. And so forcibly do the details of this picture call to mind the battles of the Iliad, that some of them might serve as illustrations to that poem. In order to check the approach of the Egyptians, the enemy has crossed the river, whose stream, divided into a double fosse, surrounded the towered walls of their fortified city, and opposed their advance by a considerable body of chariots; while a large reserve of infantry, having crossed the *bridges*, is posted on the other bank, to cover the retreat or second their advance. But, routed by the Egyptians, they are forced to throw themselves back upon the town, and many, in re-crossing the river, are either carried away by the stream, or fall under the arrows of the invaders. Those who have succeeded in reaching the opposite bank are rescued by their friends, who, drawn up in three phalanxes (described in the hieroglyphics as 8000 strong); witness the defeat of their comrades, and the flight of the remainder of their chariots. Some carry to the rear the lifeless corpse of their chief, who has been drowned in the river, and in vain endeavor to restore life, by holding his head downwards to expel the water; and others implore the clemency of the victor, and acknowledge him their conqueror and lord."

"As in the sculpture on the propylon, the enemy is called *Khetas*, the name given by the Egyptians to the great nation of Hittites, whose Kings established a powerful empire to the north of Syria. The scene in which Rameses is represented charging the enemy by himself, and forcing them to cross the river, is the subject of a long historical poem, carved on one of the exterior walls of Karnak, and on the North face of the pylon of the temple of Luxor. It is known as the Poem of Pentaur, and has been translated by M. de Rouge; and into English by Mr. Lushington (*Records of the Past*, 11, 65) Eber in his well-known story, 'Warda,' has given an able description of this remarkable campaign."

"Above these battle scenes is a procession of priests, bearing the figures of the *Theban* ancestors of Rameses II. The first of these is

WHERE ARE THE KAMITE KINGS?

Menes; then a King of the XIth Dynasty; and after him those of the XVIIIth Dynasty. The intermediate monarchs are omitted. The remaining subjects are similar to those in the coronation of the King at Medinet Habu, where the flight of the four carrier pigeons; the

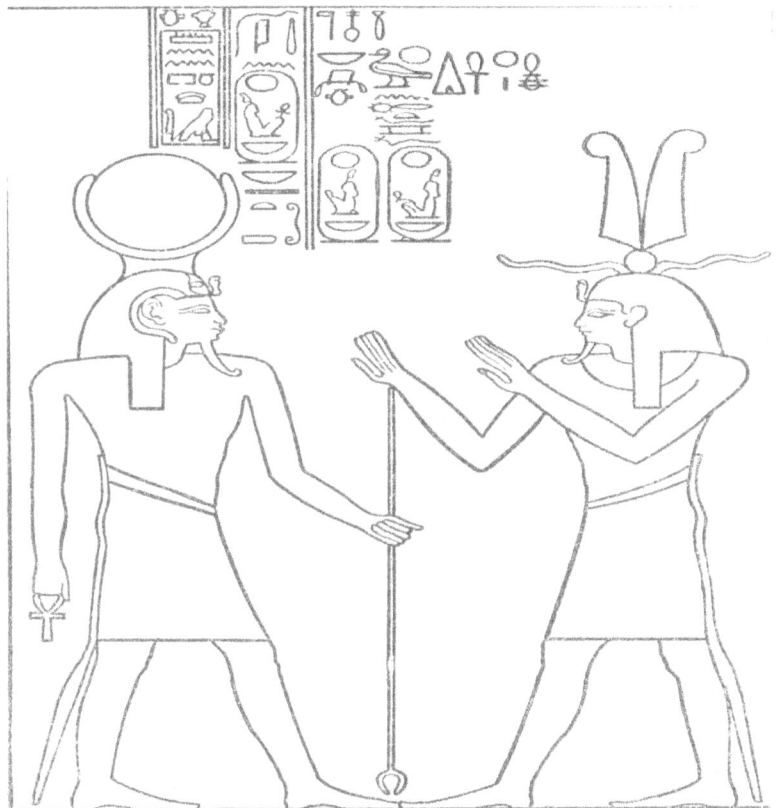

Where are the Kamite Kings Illustration. Amenhotep III worshipping himself under the form of the Lord of Kenset. Both images sport curved beards.

King cutting ears of corn, afterwards offered to the God of generation; the queen; the sacred bull; and the figures of his ancestors, placed before the God, are more easily traced from the greater preservation of that building."

FREDERICK MONDERSON

"Beyond the West staircase of the North corridor, the King is before Amen-Ra, Maut, and Khons or Khonsu. Thoth notes his palm-branch the years of the panegyrics; and the Gods do and Atum introduced Rameses into the presence of that triad of deities."

"On the other side, forming the South wall of the Great Hall (Q) is a small but interesting battle (T), where the use of the ladder and of the testudo throws considerable light on the mode of warfare at that early period. The town, situated on a lofty rock, is obstinately defended, and many are hurled headlong from its walls by spears, arrows, and stones of the besieged. They, however, on the nearer approach of the Egyptian King, are obliged to sue for peace, and send heralds with presents to deprecate his fury. His infantry, commanded by his sons, are putting to the sword the routed enemy they have overtaken beneath the walls, where they had in vain looked for refuge, the gates being already beset by Egyptian troops."

"One of the architraves in the Great Hall presents a long inscription, purporting that Amenmai Rameses has made the sculptures (or the work) for his father Amen-Ra, King of the Gods, and that he has erected the hall ... of hewn stone, good and hard blocks, supported by fine columns (Alluding, from their form, to those of the central colonnade) in addition to (the side) columns (being similar to those of the lateral colonnades). At the upper end of this hall, on the northwest wall, the King receives the falchion and Scepters from Amen-Ra, who is attended by the Goddess Maut. In the hieroglyphics mention is made of this palace of Rameses, of which the deity is said to be the guardian. We also learn from them that the King is to smite the heads of his foreign enemies with the former, and with the latter to defend or rule his country, Egypt. On the corresponding wall he receives the emblems of life and power from Amen-Ra, attended by Khons, in the presence of the lion-headed Goddess. Below these compartments, on either wall, is a procession of the twenty-three sons of the King; and on the west corner are three of his daughters, but without their names."

"On the ceiling of the next chamber (U) is an astronomical subject. On the upper side of it are the twelve Egyptian months, and at the end of Mesore a space seems to be left for the five days of the epact opposite which is the rising of the Dog-star, under the figure of Isis-Sothis. In the hieroglyphics of the border of this picture, mention is

WHERE ARE THE KAMITE KINGS?

made of the columns and of the building of this chamber with "hard stone," where apparently were deposited the 'Books of Thoth.'"

"On the walls are sculptured sacred arks, borne in procession by the priests; and at the base of the door leading to the next apartment is an inscription, purporting that the King had dedicated it to Amen, and mention seems to be made of its being beautified with gold and precious ornaments. The door itself was of two folds, turning on bronze pins, which moved in circular groves of the same metal, since removed from the stones in which they were fixed."

"On the North wall of the next and last room that now remains, the King is making offerings and burning incense, on one side to Ptah and the lion-headed Goddess; on the other to Ra (the sun), whose figure is gone. Large tablets before him mention the offerings he has made to different deities. It has been conjectured that Rameses II was actually buried in this temple. The tomb in the Biban el-Moluk which bears his name seems to have been abandoned incomplete."

"About 120 feet to the East of the outer court and the front towers of the Memnonium is the tank cased with stone usually attached to the Egyptian temples."

16.   MEDINET HABU

Murray's *Handbook for Egypt* (1888) provides the description for the temple of Medinet Habu, mortuary structure of Rameses III of the Twentieth Dynasty.

"The sculptures on the walls of this temple are very interesting. Some of them have referred to in passing through it, but others merit a more detailed description. We will begin with those on the

Interior of the Second Court -

FREDERICK MONDERSON

"The upper compartments of the North, South, East, and West sides of this court are occupied with what may be called *Ceremonial Scenes*."

"Beginning with the East or rather North East side (to the right on entering), Rameses is borne in his shrine, or canopy, seated on a throne ornamented by the figures of a lion, and a sphinx which is preceded by a hawk. Behind him stand two figures of Truth and Justice, with outspread wings. Nine Egyptian princes, whose names are above them, sons of the King, bear the shrine; officers wave flabella around the monarch; and others, of the sacerdotal order, attend on either side, carrying his arms and insignia. Four others follow: then six of the sons of the King, behind whom are two scribes and eight attendants of the military class, bearing stools and the steps of the throne. In another line are members of the sacerdotal order, four others of the King's sons, fan-bearers, and military scribes; a guard of soldiers bringing up the rear of the procession. Before the shrine, in one line, march six officers, bearing Scepters and other insignia; in another, a scribe reads aloud the contents of a scroll he holds unfolded in his hands, preceded by two of the King's sons and two distinguished persons of the military and priestly orders. The rear of both these lines is closed by a pontiff, who, turning round towards the shrine, burns incense before the monarch; and a band of music, composed of the trumpet, drum, double pipe, and Crotola, or clappers, with choristers, forms the van of the procession. The King, alighted from his throne, officiates as priest before the statue of Amen-Khem, or Amen-ra Generator; and, still wearing his helmet, he presents libations and incense before the altar, which is loaded with flowers and other suitable offering. The statue of the God, attended by officers bearing flabella, is carried on a palanquin, covered with rich drapery, by twenty-two priests; and behind it follows others, bringing the table and the altar of the deity. Before the statue is a sacred bull, followed by the King on foot, wearing the cap of the 'Lower Country.' Apart from the procession itself, stands the queen as a spectator of the ceremony; and before her a scribe reads a scroll he has unfolded. A priest turns round to offer incense to the white bull, and another, clapping his hands, brings up the rear of a long procession of hieraphori, carrying standard, images, and other sacred emblems; and the foremost bear the statues of the King's ancestors. This part of the picture refers to the *Coronation* of the King, who, in the hieroglyphics, is said to have "put on the crown of the upper and lower countries," which the

WHERE ARE THE KAMITE KINGS?

carrier-pigeons, flying to the four sides of the world, are to announce to the Gods of the south, north, east and west."

"In the next compartment the president of the assembly reads a long invocation, the contents of which are contained in the hieroglyphic inscription above; and the six ears of corn which the King, once more wearing his helmet, has cut with a golden sickle, are held out by a priest towards the deity. The white bull and the images of the King's ancestors are deposited in his temple, in the presence of Amen-Khem, the queen still witnessing the ceremony, which is concluded by an offering of incense and libation made by Ramesses to the statue of the God."

"In the lower compartment on this side is a procession of the arks of Amen-ra, Maut, and Khonoso, which the King, whose ark is also carried before him, comes to meet. In another part the Gods Seth and Hor-Hat pour alternate emblems of life and power (or purity) over the King; and on the south wall he is introduced by several divinities into the presence of the patron deities of the temple."

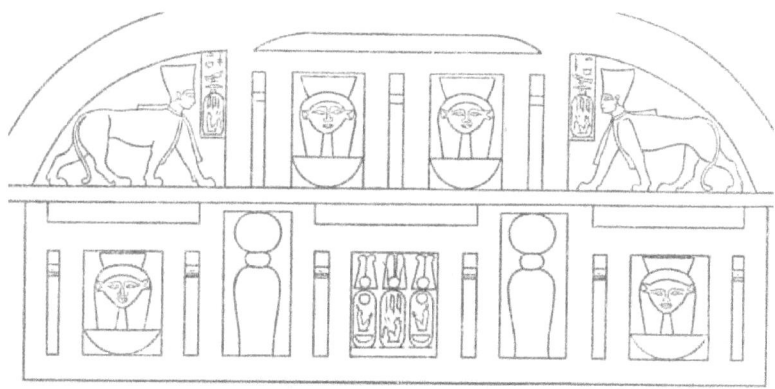

Where are the Kamite Kings Illustration. Entablature inscribed with the Prenomen of Amenhotep III and the name of his wife Queen Tiy.

"In the upper part of the West wall Rameses makes offerings to Ptah-Sokri and to Kneph; in another compartment he burns incense to the ark of Sokari; and near this is a tablet relating to the offering made to the same deity. The ark is then borne by 16 priests, with a pontiff and another of the sacerdotal order in attendance. The King then joins in another procession formed by eight of his sons and four chiefs, behind whom two priests turn round to offer incense to the monarch. The hawk, the emblem of the King or of Horus precedes them, and 18 priests carry the sacred emblem of the God Notre-Atmoo, which usually accompanies the ark of Sokari."

"On the South wall marches a long procession, composed of hieraphori, bearing different standards, thrones, arks and insignia, with musicians who precede the King and his attendants. The figure of the deity is not introduced perhaps intimating that this forms part of the religious pomp of the corresponding wall and from the circumstance of the King wearing the *pshent*, it is not improbable it may also allude to his coronation."

"On the North wall the King presents offerings to different Gods, and below is an ornamental kind of border, composed of a procession of the King's sons and daughters. Four of the former, his immediate successors, bear the asp or basilisk, the emblem of majesty, and have the Kingly ovals added to their names."

"The lower compartments of the North, South, East, and West sides of the court are filled with Historical or Battle scenes. They commence on the South West wall (to the left on entering)."

"Here Rameses standing in his car which his horses at full speed carry into the midst of the enemy's ranks, discharges his arrows on their flying infantry. The Egyptian chariots join in pursuit, and a body of their allies assists in slaughtering those who oppose them, or bind them as captives. The right hand on the slain are then cut off as trophies of victory."

"The sculptures on the lower part of West wall are a continuation of the scene. The Egyptian princes and generals conduct 'captive chiefs' into the presence of the King. He is seated at the back of the car, and the spirited horses are held by his attendants on foot. Besides other trophies, large heaps of hands are placed before him that an officer counts one by one as the other notes down their number on scroll, each heap containing 3000, and the total indicating the returns of the enemy's slain."

WHERE ARE THE KAMITE KINGS?

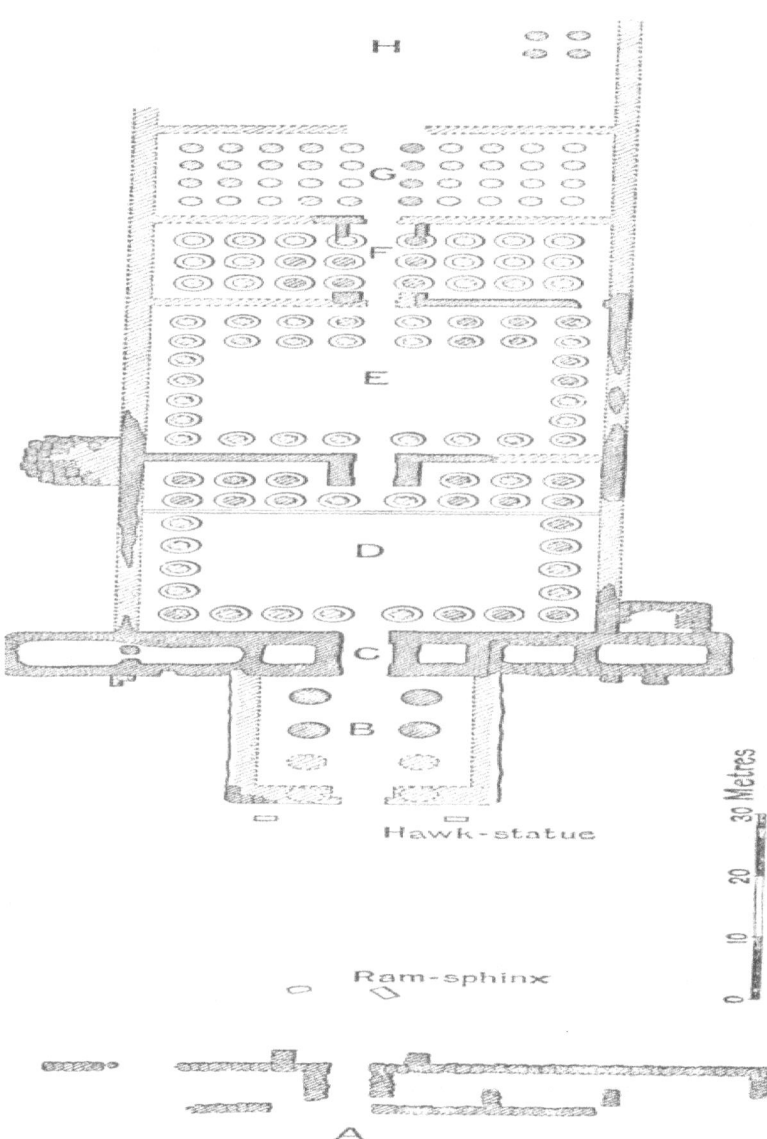

Where are the Kamite Kings Illustration. Plan of the Temple of Amenhotep III at Soleb in Nubia.

FREDERICK MONDERSON

Where are the Kamite Kings Photo. Both **Erik Monderson** (left); and his dad, **Dr. Fred Monderson** (right) stands beside Nebhepetra, Mentuhotep II of the 11th Dynasty, in the Cairo Museum of Egyptian Antiquities.

"The number of captives reckoned 1000 in each line is also mentioned in the hieroglyphic above, where the name of the Liboo (Libyans) or Rebo points out the nation against whom this war was carried on. A long hieroglyphic inscription is placed over the King, and a still longer tablet, occupying a great part of the wall, refers to the exploits of the Egyptian conqueror, and bears the date of his fifth year."
[This is where from James H. Breasted argued for the Processional Colonnade as "a new form of Egyptian architecture." Dieter Arnold argued otherwise! The Processional Colonnade is a hallmark of the Temple of Luxor built by Amenhotep III and rests within the temple's second Pylon. This King built the Third Pylon at Karnak and while this Processional Colonnade is west of the monumental pylon, we must credit him with constructing it, given his architect Amenhotep, Son of Hapu's name is all over the Karnak Temple. Thus, if Soleb and Luxor; then, in all probability, Karnak!]

"The suite of historical subject continues on the South wall. The King, returning victory to Egypt, proceeds slowly in his car, conducting in triumph the prisoners he has made, who walk beside and before it, three others being bound to the axle. Two of his sons attend as fan-bearers and several regiments of Egyptian infantry, with a corps of their allies, under the command of three other of these princes, marching in regular step and in close array of

WHERE ARE THE KAMITE KINGS?

disciplined troops, accompany their King. He arrives at Thebes and presents his captives to Amen-ra and Maut, the deities of the city, who compliment him as usual, on the victory he has gained and the overthrow of the enemy he has 'trampled beneath his feet.'"

"Exterior of the Building. But if the sculptures of the area arrest the attention of the antiquary or excite the admiration of the traveler, those of the exterior of the building are no less wonderful and the north and east walls are covered with a profusion of the most varied and interesting subjects which may also be divided into ceremonial and historical."

"The Ceremonial Scenes are on the West wall which is entirely covered with a list of the Festivals celebrated during the year in the temple by Rameses III, and on the upper part of the North wall where the King is making suitable offering to the Gods."

"The Historical or Battle Scenes are on the North and East walls. Beginning at east and of the West wall, there a succession of 10 pictures arranged in compartments, illustrating the history of a war waged by Rameses III against the Libyans or Rebo, and the Takkaro or Tochari. 1st Picture: A trumpeter assembles the troops who salute the King as he passes in his car. Rameses advances at a slow pace in his chariot, attended by fan-bearers and preceded by his troops: and a lion running at the side of the horses reminds us of the account given of Osymandyas who was said to have been accompanied in war by that animal."

"Other instances of it are met with in Nubia, among the sculpture of the second Rameses.

2nd Picture: The enemy is the Tamahoo, a Libyan tribe, who await the Egyptian invaders in the open field; the King presses forwards in his car, and bends his bow against the enemy. Several regiments of Egyptian archers in close array advance on different points, and harass them with showers of arrows. The chariots rush to the charge and a body of allies maintains the combat, hand to hand, with the enemy, who is at length routed and fly before their victorious aggressors.

FREDERICK MONDERSON

3rd Picture: Some thousands are left dead on the field, whose tongues and hands, being cut off, are brought by the Egyptian soldier as proofs of their success."

"Three thousand five hundred and thirty-five hands and tongues form part of the registered returns; and two heaps and a third of tongues containing each a somewhat larger number, are 'brought: under the superintendence of the chief officers,' like David's trophies, 'to the King' (Cf. 1 *Sam* xviii. 27 and 2 *Kings* x. 8)."

"4th Picture: The monarch then alights from his chariot and distributes rewards to his troops, and harangues the generals, while his military secretaries draw up an account of the number of spears, bows, swords and other arms taken from the enemy, which are laid before them; and mention seems to be made in the hieroglyphics of the horses that have been captured."

"5th Picture: Rameses then proceeds in his car, having his bow and sword in one hand and his whip in the other, indicating that his march still lies through an enemy's country. The van of his army is composed of a body of chariots; the infantry, in close order, preceding the royal car, constitute the center, and other similar corps forms the wings and rear. The hieroglyphic text contains little but praises addressed to the King and thanks the Gods."

"6th Picture: The troops are again summoned by sound of trumpet to the attack of another enemy, the Takkaro, and the Egyptian monarch gives order for charging the hostile army drawn up in the open plain. The troops of the enemy, after a short conflict, are routed, and retreat in great disorder. The women endeavor to escape with their children on the first approach of the Egyptians and retire in plausters drawn by oxen. The flying chariots denote the greatness of the general panic."

"7th Picture: The conquering Egyptians advance into the interior of the country. Here, while passing a large morass, the King is attacked by several lions, one of which, transfixed with darts and arrows, he lays breathless beneath his horse's feet; another attempts to fly towards the jungle, but receiving a last and fatal wound, writhes in the agony of approaching death. A third springs up from behind his car, and the hero prepares to receive and check its fury with his spear. It was, perhaps, in this country that Amenhotep III

WHERE ARE THE KAMITE KINGS?

killed the 110 lions, which according to the inscription on a scarabaeus in the Booklak Museum, he boasts of having slain in the first 10 years of his reign. Below this group is represented the march of the Egyptian army, with their allies the Shairetana, the Shaso or Shos (supposed to be Arabs), and a third corps, armed with clubs, whose form and character are very imperfectly preserved."

"8th Picture: Here we have the only representation existing in Egypt of a naval engagement. The Egyptians attack the hostile ships with fleet of galleys, which in their shapes differ essentially from those used on the Nile. The general form of the vessels of both combatants is very similar: a raised gunwale, protecting the rowers from the missiles of the foe, extends from the head to the stern, and a lofty poop and forecastle contains each a body of archers; but the head of a lion, which ornaments the prows of the Egyptian galleys, serves to distinguish them from those of the enemy. The former bear down their opponents, and succeed in boarding them and taking several prisoners. One of the hostile galleys is upset, and the slingers in shrouds, with the archers and spearmen on the prows, spear dismay among the few who resist. The King, trampling on the prostate bodies of the enemy, and aided by a corps of bowmen, discharges from the shore a continued shower of arrows: and his attendants stand at a short distance with his chariots and horses, awaiting his return."

"The scene of the engagement is doubtful, but it is evident that it took place either close to the coast or at the mouth of a river."

"9th Picture: The conquering army leads in triumph the prisoners captured in the naval fight, and the amputated hands of the slain are laid in heaps before the military chiefs. Though this custom savor of barbarism, the humanity of the Egyptians is very apparent in the above conflict; where the soldiers on the shore and in the ship do their utmost to rescue their enemies from a watery grave. The King distributes rewards to his victorious troops; and then commences the march back to Egypt. On the way, he stops at a town called in the hieroglyphics, Migdol-en-Ramese-hakou."

FREDERICK MONDERSON

"10th Picture: Triumphal return of the King to Thebes conducting his prisoners in triumph, and making offering to the Theban triad, Amen-ra, Maut, and Khons. The text contains the address to the divinities, and their response, and also an address to the prisoners of the King imploring his clemency, in order that they may live and celebrate his courage and virtues. On the remaining part of the East wall, to the South of the second propylon, another war is represented. In the first picture the King, alighted from his chariot, armed with his spear and shield, and trampling on the prostrate bodies of the slain, besieges the fort of an Asiatic enemy, whom he forces to sue for peace. In the next, he attacks a large town surrounded by water. The Egyptians fell the trees in the woody country which surrounds it, probably to form Testudos and ladders for the assault. Some are already applied by their comrades to the wall and while they reach their summit, the gates are driven from the ramparts, or precipitated over the parapet, by the victorious assailants, who announce by sound of trumpet the capture of the place."

"In the third compartment, on the North face of the first propylon, Rameses attacks two large towns, the upper one of which is taken with little resistance as the Egyptian troops have entered it and gained possession of the citadel. In the lower one, the terrified inhabitants are engaged in rescuing their children from the approaching danger, by hurrying them into the ramparts of the outer wall. The last Picture occupies the upper or North end of the East side, where the King presents his prisoners to the Gods of the temple."

"Other Ruins. Six hundred and fifty feet South West of the pavilion of Medinet Haboo is a small Ptolemaic Temple, built of sandstone, dedicated to Thoth. In the adytum are some curious hieroglyphical subjects, which have thrown great light upon the names and succession of the Ptolemies who preceded Physcon, or Euergetes II."

"This monarch is here represented making offering to four of his predecessors, Soter, Philadelphus, Philopator and Epiphanes, each name being accompanied by that of their respective queens. It is here, in particular, that the position of the Ptolemaic cognomen, as Soter, Philadelphus and others, satisfactorily proves that it is after and not in the name, that we must look for the title which

WHERE ARE THE KAMITE KINGS?

distinguished each of these Kings; nor will any one conversant with hieroglyphics fail to remark the adoption of these cognomens in each Prenomen of a succeeding Ptolemy; a circumstance analogous to the more ancient mode of borrowing; or quartering, from the Prenomen of an earlier Pharaoh some of the characters that composed that of a later King."

"The building, whose total length does not exceed 48 ft., consists of a transverse outer court, and three smaller successive chambers, communicating with each other."

"Near it, to the West, was an artificial basin, now forming a mound of irregular shape during the inundation, and surrounded on three sides by mimosas beyond which, to the North West and West, are the traces of some ruins, the remains of Egyptian and Copt tombs, and the limited enclosure of a modern church."

Where are the Kamite Kings Photo. Erik Monderson sits for a spell in the shop of Kitchener Garden at Aswan, Egypt.

FREDERICK MONDERSON

Where are the Kamite Kings Illustration. The Ram of Amen made by Amenhotep III and placed by him in the Temple of Kha-em-Maat (Soleb).

"A low plain, once a lake, extends from the South West of this temple to the distance of 7300 ft. by a breadth of 3000 ft., whose limits are marked by high mounds of sand and alluvial soil; on one series of which stands the modern village of Kom el-Byrat, the two southernmost presenting the vestiges of tombs, and the relics of human skeletons. This lake is called Birket Haboo. That the tradition which makes this a real lake is founded on fact, is evident from the appearance of the mounds of alluvial soil around it, which are taken from its excavated bed; and if required, we might find an additional proof in the upper part of the mounds on the desert side having on their summit some of the stones that form the substratum beneath the alluvial deposit."

"The excavation was evidently made after the mud of inundation had accumulated considerably upon the Theban plain: and though a smaller lake had probably been made there before, this larger one may not date till after the age of Amenhotep III, his colossi being based on the stony soil of the desert, which the inundation did not then reach. The lake was intended for the same purpose as that of Memphis and it is not impossible that the tombs on its southern

WHERE ARE THE KAMITE KINGS?

shores may have been of those offenders who were doomed to be excluded from participation in the funeral honors which the pious enjoyed in the consecrated mansions of the dead on the North side of this Acherusian lake: "Contum errant annos." Three thousand feet South West of the western angle of the lake is a small temple of Roman date, bearing the name of Hadrian and of Antoninus Pius, who completed it, and added the pylon in front. Its total length is 45 ft., and breadth 53; with an isolated sanctuary in the center two small chambers on the North East and three on the South West side; the first of which contains a staircase leading to the roof. In front stand two pylons, the outermost one being distant from the door of the temple about 200 ft."

Where are the Kamite Kings Photo. Cairo Museum of Egyptian Antiquities. Jewelry. A wide assortment of gold, silver and precious stones.

THE TOMB OF RAMESES III

Murray's *Handbook for Egypt* (1888) provides the description of the Tomb of Rameses III.

"The Tomb of Rameses III is commonly called Bruce's Tomb. It was discovered by the Traveler Bruce. It is also called *The Harper's Tomb*. This name is derived from the famous picture in one of the chambers of the men playing the harp. The execution of the sculpture is inferior to that in No. 17 [Sethi] but the nature of the subjects of this tomb is more interesting."

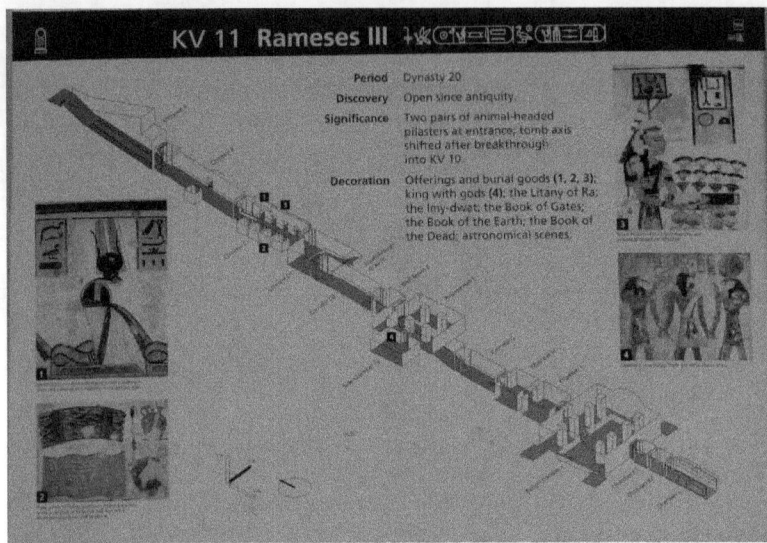

Where are the Kamite Kings Photo. Tomb of Rameses III, 20th Dynasty. Offerings and burial goods; king with gods; litany of the Imy-dwat; Book of Gates; Book of the Earth; Book of the Dead; astronomical scenes.

PLAN

The line of direction in this catacomb, after the first 130 feet is interrupted by the vicinity of the adjoining tomb, and makes, in consequence, a slight deviation to the right of 13 feet. Then it resumes the same direction again for another 275 feet. Its plan differs from that of Seti 1, and the rapidity of its descent is considerably less, being perpendicularly only 31 feet. Beyond the grand hall of the sarcophagus are three successive passages, in the last of which are benches intended apparently for the same purpose as those of the lateral chamber in Seti's tomb. They are also inferior in point of taste. The large granite sarcophagus was removed by Mr. Salt."

"*Sculpture* - This tomb is much defaced, and the nature of the rock is unfavorable for sculpture."

WHERE ARE THE KAMITE KINGS?

"The subjects in the first passage, after the recess to the right, are similar to those of Seti's and are supposed to relate to the descent to Amenta. The figure of Truth and the other groups in connection with that part of them are placed in a square niche. The character of the four people in the first hall differs slightly from those of the former tomb."

"Four blacks, clad in African dresses, being substituted instead of the Egyptians, though the same name, *Rot*, is introduced before them."

"The most interesting sculptures are in the small chambers on either side of the first two passages, since they throw considerable light on the style of the furniture and arms, and consequently on the manners and customs of the Egyptians."

"Left Side (on entering), Ist *Chamber*. Here we have kitchen scenes. The principal groups, though much defaced, may yet be recognized. Some are engaged in slaughtering oxen, and cutting up the joints, which are put into cauldrons on a tripod placed over a wood fire. In the lower line a man is employed in cutting a leather strap he holds with his feet."

Where are the Kamite Kings Photo. Tomb of Rameses IX. A huge serpent with three heads, two tails and four feet. Don't try to meet this fellow at night.

"Another man pounds something in the kitchen in a large mortar. Another apparently minces the meat. A pallet, suspended by ropes running in rings fastened to the roof, is raised from the ground, to guard against the intrusion of rats and other predators. On the opposite side, in the upper line, two men knead a substance with their feet; others cook meat, pastry, and broth, probably of lentils, which fill some baskets beside them. Sufficient of the frescoes in the lower line remain to show that others are engaged in drawing off, by means of syphons, a liquid from vases before them. On the end wall is the process of making bread. The dough is kneaded by hand. Commentaries made by both Herodotus and Strabo noted that dough was kneaded by feet. Small black seeds are sprinkled on the surface of the cakes. They are then carried on a wooded pallet to the oven."

Where are the Kamite Kings Illustration. Red granite lion made by Amenhotep III and usurped by the Nubian King Amen-Asru.

"The *2nd Chamber* merely contains emblems and deities. In the *3rd Chamber* are birds, and some productions of Egypt, as geese and quails, eggs, pomegranates, grapes, with other fruits and herbs, among which last is the *ghulga*, or *Periploca sycamore* of Linnaeus' classification. This plant resembles a form of ivy, which is unknown in Egypt. The figures in the lower line are of the God Nilus."

WHERE ARE THE KAMITE KINGS?

"The principal figures of the *Last Chamber* are two harpers playing on instruments of not inelegant form before the God Moui, or Hercules of the Greek. From these the tomb receives its name. One (if not both) of the minstrels is blind."

"*Right side* (on entering), *1st Chamber*. Several boats are seen with squared checkered sails. Some have spacious cabins and others only a seat near the mast. They are richly painted, and loaded with ornaments. Those in the lower lines have the mast and yarn lowered over the cabin."

"The 2nd Chamber contains various arms and warlike implements of the Egyptians. These include knives, quilted helmets, spears, daggers, quivers, bows, arrows, falchions, coats of mail, darts, clubs, and standards. On either side of the door is a black cow with the headdress of Hathor, one accompanied by hieroglyphics signifying the North, the other those of the South. These symbols intimate that these are the legends of Upper and Lower Egypt. The blue color of some of the weapons suffices to prove them to have been of steel."

"The 3rd Chamber has chairs of the most elegant form, covered with rich drapery, rightly ornamented, and in admirable taste. The beauty of Egyptian furniture is demonstrated here. It shows that at the time of the XXth Dynasty the Egyptians were greatly advanced in the arts of civilization and the comforts of domestic life. Displayed here are sofas, couches, vases of porcelain and pottery, copper utensils, caldrons, rare woods, printed stuffs, leopard-skins, baskets of a very neat and graceful shape, and basins and ewers, whose designs vie with the productions of the cabinet-maker, complete the interesting series of these paintings."

"The *4th Chamber* contains agricultural scenes. It shows the inundation of the Nile passing through the canals, sowing and reaping wheat, and a grain which from its height and round head appears to be the *doora* or sorghum, as well as the flowers of the country. Still, however successful the Egyptians may have been in seizing the character of animals, they failed in the art of drawing trees and flowers, and their colored plants would perplex the most profound botanist."

"In the *5th Chamber* are different forms for the God Osiris having various attributes."

"In the *6th Chamber* are rudders and sacred emblems."

"Each of these small apartments has a pit, now closed, where it is probable that some of the officers of the King's household were buried. In that case, the subjects on the walls refer to the station they held. These include the chief cook, the superintendent of the royal boats, the armor-bearer, the stewards of the household, and of the royal demesne, the priest of the King, the gardener, hieraphoros, and minstrel."

"In this tomb are several Greek graffiti, a fact which shows that it was one of those open during the reign of the Ptolemies."

Where are the Kamite Kings Photo. Valley of the Kings. Tomb of Tausert and Setnakht. Luis Casado of Brooklyn, New York stands before Anubis and Setnakht as he presents his name as Ma'at to the Goddess.

WHERE ARE THE KAMITE KINGS?

17. THE TOMB OF SETI I

Murray's *Handbook for Egypt* (1888) also provides a description of the Tomb of Seti I. This tomb of Seti I is located in the Valley of the Kings at Thebes. The Arabic title for this location is Bab or *Biban el-Moluk* which means 'gate' or 'Gates of the Kings.' Seti's tomb is commonly called Belzoni's Tomb after the strong man who discovered it in 1818. This tomb, No. 17, is in a remarkable state of preservation and its sculpture is of a high quality.

PLAN

"*Plan* - This is far from being well regulated, and the deviation from one line of direction greatly injures its general effect; nor does the rapid descent by a staircase of 24 feet in perpendicular depth on a horizontal length of 29, convey so appropriate an idea of the entrance to the abode of death as the gradual talus of others of these sepulchers. To this staircase succeeds a passage 18 1/2 feet by 9 feet, including the jambs. Passing another door, a second staircase descends in horizontal length 25 feet. Beyond, 2 doorways and a passage of 29 feet bring you to an oblong chamber 12 feet by 14 feet, where a pit, filled up by Belzoni, once appeared to form the utmost limit of the tomb."

"Part of its inner wall was composed of blocks of hewn stone, closely cemented together, and covered with a smooth coat of stucco, like the other walls of this excavated catacomb, on which was painted a continuation of those subjects that still adorn its remaining sides."

"Independent of the main object another advantage was thought of by the architect. The preservation of the inferior part of the tomb was effectually guaranteed from the destructive in-road of the rain-water, whose torrents its depth completely intercepted ...."

FREDERICK MONDERSON

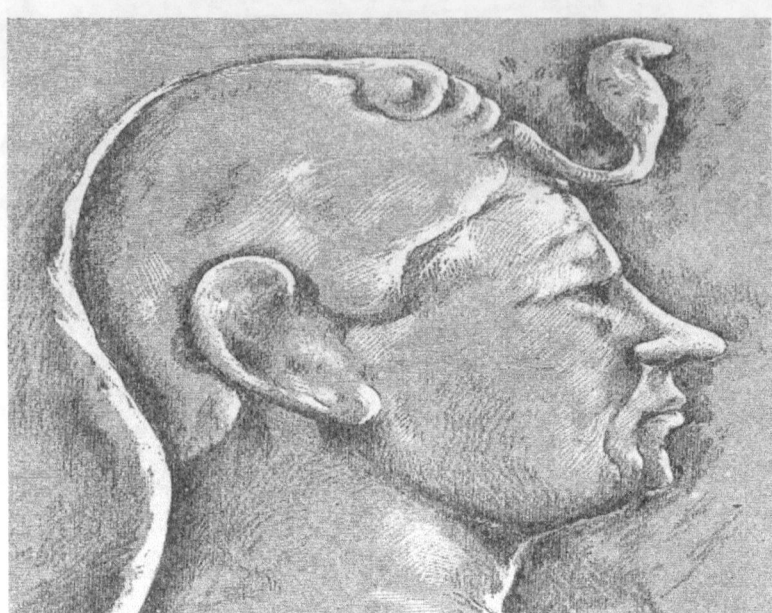

Where are the Kamite Kings Illustration. Illustrated bust of Psammetichus, Late Period Pharaoh of Egypt. His uraeus is prominent and so is his nose, that is not broken.

"The hollow sound of the wall of masonry above mentioned, and a small aperture, betrayed to Belzoni the secret of its hidden chambers; and a palm-tree, supplying the place of more classic ram, soon forced the intermediate barrier. The breach displayed the splendor of the succeeding hall, at once astonishing and delighting its discoverer, whose labors were so gratefully repaid. But this was not the only part of the tomb that had been closed. The outer door was also blocked up with masonry; and the staircase before it was concealed by accumulated fragments, and by the earth that had fallen from the hill above. And it was the sinking of the ground at this part, from the water that had soaked through into the tomb that led the peasants to suspect the secret of its position, which was revealed by them to Belzoni."

"The four pillars of the first hall beyond the pit, which supported a roof about 26 feet square, are decorated, like the whole of the walls, with highly-finished and well-preserved sculptures. From their vivid colors they appear to be the work of only yesterday. Near the center of the inner wall a few steps lead to a second hall, of similar dimensions, supported by two pillars, but left in an unfinished state.

WHERE ARE THE KAMITE KINGS?

The sculptors had not yet commenced the outline of the figures the draughts-men had just completed. It is here that the first deviation from the general line of direction occurs; which are still more remarkable in the staircase that descends at the southern corner of the first hall."

"To this last succeed two passages and a chamber 17 feet by 14, communicating by a door, not quite in the center of its inner wall, with the grand hall, which is 27 ft. square, and supported by six pillars. On either side of this hall is a small chamber, opposite the angle of the first pillars. The upper end terminates in a vaulted saloon, 19 feet by 30 feet."

"In the center stood an alabaster sarcophagus, that's now in the Soane Museum. It was upon the immediate summit of an inclined plane, which, with a staircase on either side, descends into the heart of the argillaceous rock at a distance of 150 ft. When Belzoni opened this tomb, it extended much farther; but the rock, which from its friable nature could only be excavated by supporting the roof with scaffolding, has since fallen, and curtailed a still greater portion of its original length. The inscriptions on the sarcophagus have been translated. The mummy of Sethi I is in the Boolak Museum."

"This passage, like the entrance of the tomb and the first hall, was closed and concealed by a wall of masonry, which, coming even with the base of the sarcophagus, completely masked the staircase, and covered it with an artificial floor."

"This part of the grand hall. At the upper end a step leads to an unfinished chamber. This room is 17 feet by 43 feet and supported by a row of four pillars. On the South West are other niches, and a room about 25 feet square, ornamented with two pillars and a broad bench (hewn, like the rest of the tomb, in the rock) around three of its sides, 4 feet high, with four shallow recesses on each face, and surmounted by an elegant Egyptian cornice. It is difficult to understand the purport of it, unless its level summit served as a repository for the mummies of the inferior persons of the King's household; but it is more probable that these were also deposited in pits."

FREDERICK MONDERSON

"The total horizontal length of this catacomb is 320 feet, without the inclined descent below the sarcophagus, and its perpendicular depth 90 feet. But, including that part, it measures 470 feet, and in depth about 180 feet to the spot where it is closed by the fallen rock."

SCULPTURES

"Although when this tomb was discovered by Belzoni it had already, at some remote period, been opened and violated, possibly at the time when the mummy of the King was removed to Deir el-Bahari, no injury had been done to the sculptures on the walls, and when he first saw it, every bas-relief was perfect, and the paintings as vivid and fresh as the day they were done. A century and a half exposure to the tender mercies of the savant, the antiquity-monger, and the tourist, has considerably spoilt its original beauty, and the thoughtful visitor cannot fail to mark with respect the spoliations and defacements to which it had been subjected."

"The sculptures in the *First Passage* consist of lines of hieroglyphics relating to the King Sethi I, or Osirei, "the beloved of Ptah," who was the father of Rameses II, and the occupant of this tomb. In the staircase which succeeds it are on one side 37, on the other 39 genii of various forms; among which a figure represented with a stream of tears issuing from his eyes is remarkable from having the (Coptic) word rimi, "lamentation," in the hieroglyphic above."

"In the *Second Passage* are the boats of Kneph; and several descending planes, on which are placed the valves of doors, probably referring to the descent of Amenti. The Goddess of Truth or Justice stands at the lower extremity. In the small chamber over the pit the King makes offerings to different Gods, Osiris being the principal deity. Hathor, Horus, Isis, and Anubis, are also introduced."

WHERE ARE THE KAMITE KINGS?

Where are the Kamite Kings Illustration. The Mayor of Thebes, Mentuemhat, during time of XXVth Ethiopian Dynasty.

"On the pillars of the *First Hall* the monarch stands in the presence of various divinities, who seem to be receiving him after his death. One of the most interesting subjects here is a procession of four different people, of red, white, black, and again white complexions, four by four, followed by Ra, "the sun." The four red figures are Egyptians, designated under the name *rot*, meaning "mankind;" the next, a white race, with blue, long bushy beards, and clad in a short dress, are a northern nation, with whom the Egyptians were long at war, and appear to signify the nations of the north; as the Negroes (called *Nehsi*,) the south; and the four others, also a white people, with a pointed beard, blue eyes, feathers in their hair, eyes and crosses or other devices about their persons, and dressed in long flowing robes, the east."

"These then are not in the character of prisoners, but a typification of the four divisions of the world, or the whole human race, and are introduced among the sculptures of these sepulchers in the same abstract sense as the trades of the Egyptians in the tombs of private individuals. The sculptures found in private tombs represent an epitome of human life, whereas these in this royal tomb refer to inhabitants of the whole world."

FREDERICK MONDERSON

"On the end wall of this hall is a fine group, which is remarkable as well for the elegance of its drawing as for the richness and preservation of the coloring. The subject is the introduction of the King, by Horus, into the presence of Osiris and Hathor."

"Though not the most striking, the most interesting drawings in this tomb are those of the *Second Hall*, which was left unfinished. These figures demonstrate freedom of outline by the draftsman. In preparing the wall to receive the bas-reliefs it was sometimes customary to portion it out into squares. However, this was not the method universally adopted for drawing Egyptian figures."

In this and other places that they sketched were without that prescribed measurement. It is probable that this was principally used when a copy was made of an original drawing. This method is presently used by modern artists. Here we find that the position of the figures was first traced with a red color by the draughtsman. This was then submitted to the inspection of the master artist. Then those parts he deemed deficient in proportion or correctness of attitude were altered by him in black ink (as appears to have been the case in the figures here designed). In that state they were left for the chisel of the sculptor."

"On this occasion the death of the King or some other cause prevented their completion. Still, their unfinished condition affords a satisfactory opportunity to appreciate the skill of the Egyptian draughtsman. We see here the bold decided line which was the aim of all antique drawing. In these figures some of the lines are a foot or a foot and a quarter in length; as from the shoulder to the elbow, or the knee to the instep; and done at a single stroke; while the red lines of the inferior artist, and his *pentimenti*, show, that, though he occasionally failed in the perfect use of his pencil, he was instructed in the same bold style of drawing, and in the importance of one long-continuous outline."

"In the sculptures critically examined, the handiwork of several artists can be traced."

"The subjects in the succeeding *Passages* refer mostly to the liturgies or ceremonies performed to the deceased monarch. In the *Square Chamber* beyond them the King is seen in the presence of

WHERE ARE THE KAMITE KINGS?

the deities Hathor, Horus, Anubis, Isis, Osiris, Nephthys and Ptah. The 'Liturgy of Ra,' which occurs on the passage of walls of this top, as well as in other royal tombs in this valley, has been translated, and is worthy of study."

"The Grand Hall contains numerous subjects, among which are a series of mummies, each in its own repository, whose folding-doors are thrown open. It is probable that all the parts of these catacombs refer to different states through which the deceased passed, and the various mansions of Hades or Amenta."

"The representations of the door-valves at their entrance tend to confirm this opinion. Many of the subjects relate to the life and actions of the deceased and many are similar to those in the 'Book of the Dead.' In the *Side Chambers* are some mysterious ceremonies connected with fire, and various other subjects."

"*The Transverse Vaulted Part of the Great Hall, or Saloon of the Sarcophagus* ornamented with a profusion of sculpture, is a termination worthy of the rest of this grand sepulchral monument. In the chamber on the left, with the broad bench, are various subjects; some of which, especially those appearing to represent human sacrifices, may refer to the initiation into the higher mysteries, by the supposed death and regeneration of the Neophyte."

Where are the Kamite Kings Photo. Image depicts King Tutankhamen in his chariot, shooting his arrows and trampling adversaries.

FREDERICK MONDERSON

Where are the Kamite Kings Photo. Kashida Maloney of Brooklyn, New York, stands beside a broken statue before the Temple of Luxor.

18. TOMB OF REKHMARA

Murray's *Handbook for Egypt* (1888) supplies a most complete graphic description of the classic tomb that depicts a great many individuals involved in a wide-range of technical crafts. This, like so many tombs, is off-limits to cameras. Those writers who had taken photographs previously find this a remarkable tomb and a treat to their readers.

"The Tomb of Rekhmara-is by far the most curious of all the private tombs in Thebes, since it throws more light on the manners and customs of the Egyptians than any hitherto discovered."

"In the Outer Chambers on the left hand (entering) is a grand procession of Ethiopian and Asiatic chiefs, bearing a tribute to the Egyptian monarch, Thothmes III. (See Wilkinson's *Ancient Egyptians*, vol. i. pl. ii). They are arranged in five lines. The first of the uppermost consists of blacks, and others of a red color from

WHERE ARE THE KAMITE KINGS?

the country of Pount (Punt), who bring ivory, apes, leopard skins, and dried fruits."

"Their dress is short, similar to that of the Asiatic tribes, who are represented at Medinet Habu. In the second line are people of a lighter hue, with long black hair descending in ringlets over their shoulders, but without beards: their dress also consists of a short apron thrown round the lower part of the body, meeting and folding over in front, and they wear scandals richly worked. Their presents are vases of elegant form, ornamented with flowers, necklaces, and other costly gifts, which according to the hieroglyphics, they bring as 'chosen (offerings) of the chief of the Gentiles of Kufa.'"

"In the third line are Ethiopians, who are styled 'Gentiles of the South.' The leaders are dressed in the Egyptian costume; the others have a girdle of skin, with the hair, as usual, outwards. They bring gold rings, and bags of precious stones or rather gold-dust, hides, apes, leopards, ebony, ivory, ostrich eggs and plumes, a camel-leopard, hounds with handsome collars, and a drove of long-horned oxen."

"The fourth line is composed of men of northern nations, clad in long white garments with a blue border tied at the neck, and ornamented with a cross or other devices. On their head is either a close cap, or their natural hair, short, and of a red color, and they have a small beard. Some bring long gloves, which with their close sleeves indicate as well as their white color, that they are the inhabitants of a cold climate."

"Among other offering are vases, similar to those of the Kufa, a chariot and horses, a bear, elephant, and ivory. Their name is Rotennoo, which reminds us of the Rateni of Arabia Petrea; but the style of their dress and the nature of their offering require them to have come from a richer and more civilized country, probably much farther to the north. Xenophon mentions gloves in Persia."

"In the fifth line Egyptian leads van, and are followed by women of Ethiopia (Cush), 'the Gentiles of the South,' carrying theirs in a pannier suspended from their head."

FREDERICK MONDERSON

"Behind these are the wives of the Rotennoo, who are dressed in long robes, divided into three sets of ample flounces."

"The offering being placed in the presence of the monarch, who is seated on the throne on the upper part of the picture, an inventory is taken of them by the Egyptian scribes. Those opposite the upper line consist of baskets of dried fruits, gold rings, and two obelisks."

"On the second lines are ingots and rings of silver, gold, and silver vases of elegant form, several heads of animal of the same metal."

"On the third are ostrich eggs and feathers, ebony, precious stones and rings of gold, an ape, several silver cups, ivory, leopard skins, ingots and rings of gold, sealed bags of precious stones or gold-dust, and other objects; and on the porcelain, with rare woods and various other rich presents."

"The inner chambers contain subjects of the most interesting and diversified kind. Among them, on the left wall (entering), are cabinetmakers, carpenters, rope-makers, and sculptors, some of whom are engaged in leveling and squaring a stone and others in finishing a sphinx, with two colossal statutes of the King."

"The whole process of Brick-making is also introduced. Their bricks were made with a simple mold; the stamp (for they bore the name of a King or of some high-priest) was not on the pallet, but was apparently impressed on the upper surface previous to their drying."

"The makers are not however, Jews, as some have supposed; but of the countries mentioned in the sculptures."

"It is sufficiently interesting to find a subject illustrating so completely the description of the Jews and their taskmasters given in the Bible, without striving to give it an importance to which it has no claim. (See Wilkinson's *Ancient Egyptians*, vol. i. p. 344, woodcut 112.)"

"Others are employed in heating liquid over a charcoal fire, to which are applied, on either side, a pair of feet, the operator standing and

WHERE ARE THE KAMITE KINGS?

pressing them alternately, while he pulls up each exhausted skin by a string he holds in his hand."

"In one instance the man has left the bellows, but they are raised, as if full of air, which would imply a knowledge of the valve."

Egyptian Name.	Meaning.	Civil Year.	In the Sacred Year the Month begins	In the Alexandrian year the Month begins
	1st month of Spring	Thoth	July 25	August 29.
	2nd " " "	Paophi	August 19	September 28.
	3rd " " "	Athyr	September 18	October 28.
	4th " " "	Cheiak	October 18	November 27.
	1st " " Summer or Ploughing Season	Tybi	November 17	December 27.
	2nd " " "	Mechir	December 17	January 26.
	3rd " " "	Phamenoth	January 16	February 25.
	4th " " "	Pharmuthi	February 15	March 27.
	1st " " Inundation	Pachons	March 17	April 26.
	2nd " " "	Payni	April 16	May 26.
	3rd " " "	Epiphi	May 16	June 25.
	4th " " "	Mesore	June 15	July 25.

Where are the Kamite Kings Illustration. The Egyptian Calendar, consisting of 3 Seasons of 4 Months each, with the name of each month, compared with the date of each month's beginning and its comparison in the Alexandrian year.

Where are the Kamite Kings Photo. Erik Monderson tries his hand at sculpturing under the watchful eye of a master at a workshop at Deir el Medina, Luxor, Egypt.

FREDERICK MONDERSON

Where are the Kamite Kings Photo. A King and a God in the Cairo Museum of Antiquities.

Where are the Kamite Kings Photo. Kashida Maloney of Brooklyn, New York, beside a stone Hathor Head statue on the grounds of the Cairo Museum of Egyptian Antiquities.

WHERE ARE THE KAMITE KINGS?

"Another singular fact is learnt from these paintings - their acquaintance with the use of glue - which is heated on the fire, and spread with a thick brush on a level piece of board. One of the workmen then applies two pieces of different-colored wood to each other, and this circumstance seems to decide that glue is here intended to be represented rather than a varnish or color of any kind."

"On the right wall (entering) the attitude of a maid-servant pouring out some wine to a lady, one of the guests, and returning an empty cup to a black slave who stands behind her, is admirably portrayed; nor does it offer the stiff position of an Egyptian figure. And the manner in which the slave is drawn, holding a plate with her arm and hand reversed, is very characteristic of a custom peculiar to the blacks. The guests are entertained by music, and the women here sit apart from the men."

"Among the other subjects on this wall worthy of notice may be mentioned a garden where the personage of the tomb is introduced in his boat, towed by his servants on a lake surrounded by Theban palms and date-trees. Numerous liturgies (or parentaila) are performed to the mummy of the deceased. At the upper end of the tomb a list of offerings is registered, with their names and number, in separate columns."

Where are the Kamite Kings Illustration. The *Sekhet-Hetepu* or "Elysian Fields," from *Papyrus of Ani*, British Museum No. 10,470, sheet 35, in E.A.W. Budge's *the Mummy* (1925).

FREDERICK MONDERSON

"The form of this inner chamber is singular, the roof ascending at a considerable angle towards the end wall; from below which the spectator, in looking toward the door, may observe a striking effect of a false perspective. In the upper part is a niche, or recess, at a considerable height above the pavement."

"In the Tomb of Neferhotep, a royal scribe, immediately below the isolated hill to the west of the entrance of the Assasif, is some very curious sculptures. In the Outer Chambers is the most complete procession of boats of any met with in the catacombs of Thebes. Two of them contain the female relatives of the deceased, his sister being chief mourner."

"One has on board the mummy, deposited in a shrine, to which a priest offers incense; in the other several women seated, or standing on the roof of the cabin, beat their heads in token of grief. In a third boat are the men, who make a similar lamentation, with two of the aged matrons of the family; and three others contain the flowers and offering furnished by the priests for the occasion, several of whom are also in attendance. (See Wilkinson's *Ancient Egyptians*, vol. iii. pl. lxvi.)"

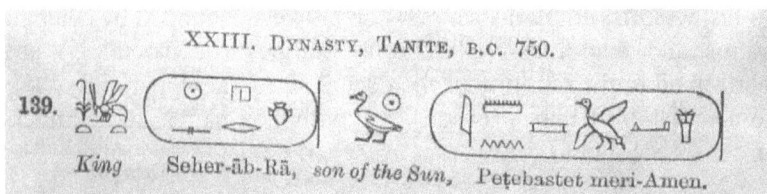

Kamite Kings Cartouche/Shennu. Kings of the Twenty-Third Dynasty.

"The Egyptians could not even here resist their turn for caricature. A small boat owing to the retrograde movement of a large one that had grounded and was pushed off the bank is struck by the rudder, and a large table, is overturned on the boatmen as they row."

"The procession arrives at the opposite bank, and follows the officiating priest along the sandy plain. The 'sister' of the deceased, embracing the mummy, addresses her lost relatives: flower, cakes, incense, and various offering are presented before the tomb; the

WHERE ARE THE KAMITE KINGS?

salutation of the men and women continues without; and several females, carrying their children in shawls suspended from their shoulders join in the lamentation."

Where are the Kamite Kings Illustration. Rameses II in battle. Notice the orderly nature of the Egyptian chariots and the chaos in the enemy ranks.

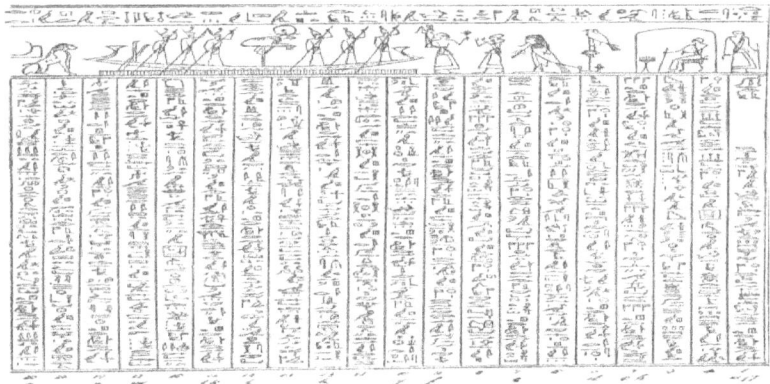

Where are the Kamite Kings Illustration. A chapter from *Book of the Dead*, with Gods sailing in their Barque overhead.

"On the corresponding wall, men and women, with the body exposed above the waist, throw dust on their heads, cover their faces with mud, - a custom recorded by Herodotus and Diodorus, and still retained in the funeral ceremonies of the Egyptian peasants to the present day. The former states that: "the females of the family cover their heads and faces with mud, and wander through the city beating themselves, wearing a girdle, and having their bosoms bare, accomplished by all their intimate friends; the men also make similar lamentations in a separate company."

"Besides other interesting groups on this wall are the figures of the mother, wife, and daughter of the deceased, following a funeral sledge drawn by oxen, where the character of the three ages is admirably portrayed."

"In the inner chambers are the Egyptian house and garden, the cattle, and a variety of the subjects, among which may be traced the occupations of the weaver, and of the gardener drawing water with the pole and bucket, the shadoof of the present day."

"Statues in high relief are seated at the upper end of this part of the tomb, and on the square pillars in its center are the names of Amenhotep I and queen Ames-Nofrit-are."

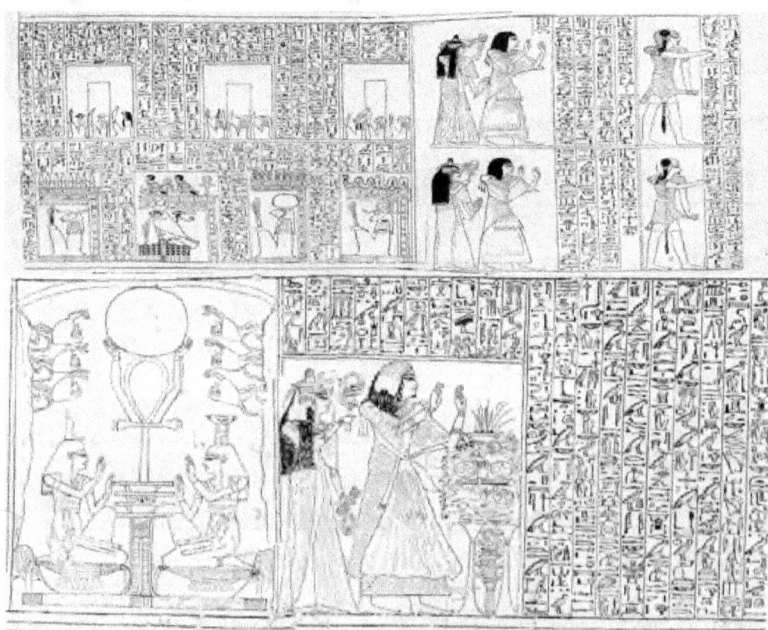

Where are the Kamite Kings Illustration. *Book of the Dead* in the XVIIIth Dynasty from the *Papyrus of Ani* in the British Museum No. 10,470, sheet 2 in E.A.W. Budge's *the Mummy* (1925).

WHERE ARE THE KAMITE KINGS?

"Tombs of Koornet Murraee - South West of the cemetery just described, after passing the temple of Dyre el-Medeeneh, are some more tombs, similar in their character to those on the hill of Sheykh Abd el-Koorneh, and known by the name above."

"Among them is one of two interesting ones, especially the Tomb of Hooi, a great functionary of the XVIIIth Dynasty."

Where are the Kamite Kings Illustration. *Book of the Dead* in the XIXth Dynasty from the *Papyrus of Hunefer* in the British Museum No. 9,901 in E.A.W. Budge's *the Mummy* (1925).

FREDERICK MONDERSON

"It is covered with painting, which, unfortunately, as in the case of so many of the tombs, is fast disappearing. In one of the pictures the King is represented on his throne, within a richly ornamented canopy, attended by a fan-bearer, who also holds his Scepter. - A procession advances in four lines into his presence."

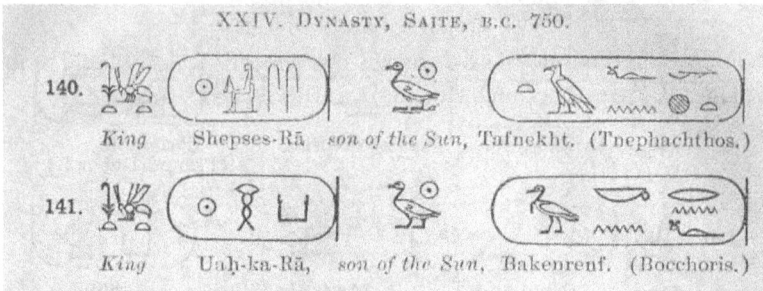

Kamite Kings Cartouche/Shennu. Kings of the Twenty-Fourth Dynasty

"The lower consists of Egyptians of the sacerdotal and military classes, some ladies of consequence, and young people bring bouquets and boughs of trees. They have just entered the royal court, and are preceded by a scribe, and others of the priestly order, who do obeisance before the deputy of his majesty, as he stands to receive them."

"This officer appears to have been the person of the tomb, and it is remarkable that he is styled "Royal Son," and prince of "Cush," or Ethiopia. In the second line black "chiefs of Cush" bring presents of gold rings, copper, skins, fans, or umbrellas of feather-work, and an ox, bearing on its horns an artificial garden and a lake of fish."

"Having placed their offerings, they prostrate themselves before the monarch. A continuation of these presents follows in the third line, where besides rings of gold, and bags of precious stones or gold-dust, are the leopard, panther's skins, and long-horned cattle, whose heads and horns are strangely ornamented with the heads and hands of Negroes."

WHERE ARE THE KAMITE KINGS?

"In the upper line, the queen of the same people arrives in a chariot drawn by oxen, and over shadowed by an umbrella, accompanied by her attendants, some of whom bear presents of gold. (See Wilkinson's *Ancient Egyptians*, vol. i. p. 235). She alights preceded and followed by the principal persons of her suite, and advances to the presence of the King."

"This may refer to a marriage that was contracted between the Egyptian monarch and a princess of Ethiopia, or merely annual tribute paid by the people. Among the different presents are a chariot, shields covered with bulls' hides bound with metal borders and studded with pins, chairs, couches, head-stools, and other objects."

"The dresses of the Negroes differ in the upper line from those below, the latter having partly the costume of the Egyptians, with the plaited hair of their national headdress; but those who follow the car of the princess are clad in skins, whose projecting tail, while it heightens the caricature the artist doubtless intended to indulge in, proves them to be persons of an inferior station, who were probably brought as slaves to the Egyptian monarch."

"Behind these are women of the same nation, bearing their children in a kind of basket suspended to their back. Many other interesting subjects cover the walls of the tombs, which throw much light on the customs of the Egyptians."

"In another catacomb, much unfortunately ruined, is a spirited chase, in which various animals of the desert are admirably designed. The fox, hare, gazelle, ibex, eriel (Antelope oryx), ostrich, and wild ox fly before the hounds; and the porcupine and hyena retire to the higher part of the mountains."

"The female hyena alone remains, but most of the dogs are represented in pursuit of the gazelles, or in the act of seizing those they have overtaken in the plain. (See Wilkinson's *Ancient Egyptians*, vol. ii. p. 92). The chasseur follows, and discharges his arrows among them as they fly. These arrows are very light, being made of reed, feathered, and tipped with stone."

FREDERICK MONDERSON

"They have been found in the tombs, together with those having metal points; both being used as the sculptures show, at the same period for the chase."

"In observing the accuracy with which the general forms and characters of their animals are drawn, one cannot but feel surprised that the Egyptians should have had so imperfect a knowledge of the art of representing the trees and flowers of their country, which, with the exception of the lotus, palms, and dom, can scarcely ever be identified; unless the fruit, as in the pomegranate and sycamore is present to assist us."

Where are the Kamite Kings Illustration. From the *Book of the Dead* in the XXIInd Dynasty in the British Museum No. 10,479, Sheet 7 in E.A.W. Budge's *The Mummy* (1925).

WHERE ARE THE KAMITE KINGS?

Where are the Kamite Kings Photo. African-Americans take time to admire the Step-Pyramid at Sakkara while Cherise Maloney of Brooklyn, New York, faces the camera.

19. THE ETHIOPIAN ASCENDENCY

A fundamental dilemma facing young African Americans is how they should regard the legacy, progenitors and heritage of the ancient African culture along the Nile River. Interestingly, if the intellectual pursuits and life's work of some of the most credible black scholars are yardsticks, we can thus pose this most profound question that certainly needs consideration. This is particularly significant if we begin to assess the seriousness or the meaning of the archaeological excavation and resulting anthropological synthesis that is now in its centenary and that we should consider its ramifications for the Twenty-First Century. The question then is this!

"Why have African American scholars, African Caribbean scholars and a number of African scholars, all interested in ancient African history and particularly the people and culture of ancient Kemet (Egypt) come up with essentially the same conclusions?" They all seem, after lengthy careers of research, teaching and writing, to be convinced that the ancient Egyptians/Kamites were black people and that modern European and American scholars have falsified the historical record. Further, how do we accept the work of scholars the likes of John H. Clarke, Yosef ben-Jochannan, Ivan Van Sertima, Maulana Karenga, Jacob Carruthers, J. E. Harris, John Jackson, Lester Brooks, Stanlake Samkange, George G.M. James, Carter G. Woodson, J.A. Rogers, W.E.B. Du Bois, Marcus Garvey, Duse Mohammed, Caseley Hayford, Cheikh Anta Diop, Martin Delaney, etc., who have all wrestled with the question of 'Who were these ancient Africans, the Egyptians?' and why have they concluded that these Nile Valley inhabitants were black while demonstrating that the historical record proves European imperialist and colonialist machinations have not simply raped Africa but purposefully distorted her history and deprived her descendants of their proper place in the respective order and narrative of human experience.

It is expected that after a lifetime of work, scholars ought to be able to modify positions they have taken earlier on in their careers. However, this has not been the case with those involved in the archaeological excavations and interpretations of the data at the turn of the twentieth century. Therefore, we must oftentimes wallow in the mud to understand how the pig finds such joy in this disgusting place.

I beg indulgence of those who may read this because I need to make a particular point. I also apologize beforehand to those righteous black minds out there who have proscribed but must understand the use of the disgusting descriptive employed here. I wish to quote from the work of a "well respected English scholar," who, after decades of gaining fame in the imperial rape of Africa's intellectual heritage could write in his book *Flights into Antiquity*, a chapter entitled: "The Exploits of a Nigger King." Here he speaks of the "grandiloquent and deeply religious annals left by King Piankhy, the most famous of the Nigger Kings, ..." Further on he writes of the "life of the court at Napata was an imitation of that of the Egyptian Pharaohs, Egypt being Ethiopia's northern neighbor; and Amon, the great Egyptian God, was the patron deity of the Nigger realm, while many other Pharaonic Gods were worshiped."

WHERE ARE THE KAMITE KINGS?

An even further quote underscores the seemingly unintentional manner, or should I say the intentional manner, in which that writer had systematically and maliciously maligned Africa and distorted the historical record, helping to ossify the issue in the minds of Europeans and Americans for generations. Writing of his influence, he states: "My dispatches from Egypt in the early spring of 1923 were printed in so many newspapers that they were daily read, I am told, by nearly a hundred million people, not more than a negligible fraction of which number would have troubled to read such matter at an earlier date. Previous to 1922, I delivered an occasional lecture, but it was only to a small audience of students; in 1923, however, I addressed, I suppose, well over a hundred thousand people in Great Britain and America, and the limit was only set by my laziness or lack of time. These personal experiences show how clearly the surprising change which has taken place that I will perhaps be pardoned for recording them here."

Where are the Kamite Kings Illustration. Tomb plans of the XXVth to the XXXth Dynasties.

FREDERICK MONDERSON

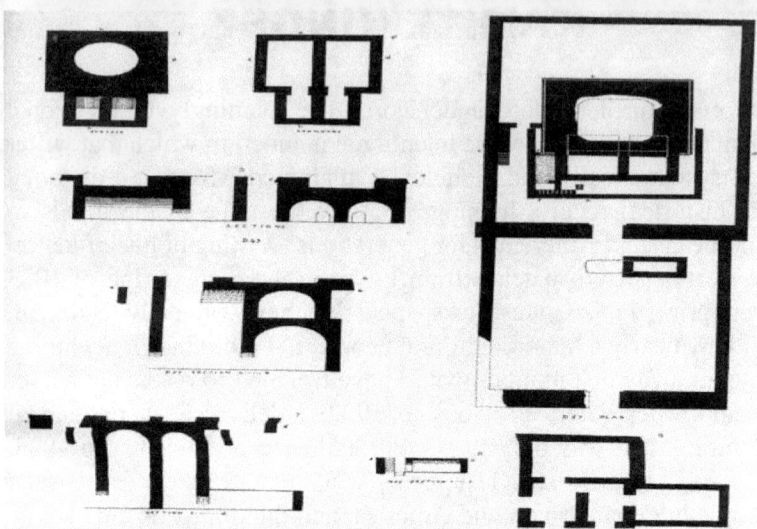

Where are the Kamite Kings Illustration. Tomb plans of the XXVth to the XXXth Dynasties.

The above quoted text, that most scholars mention, is completely devoid of references because the writer had produced more than a dozen books on, at the time, Ancient Egypt, since he had spent the previous decades involved in the excavation, or should I say the rape and colonization of Africa's magnificent and enlightening reservoir of ancient knowledge. He also became Editor of the Journal of Egyptian Archaeology. However, his contempt for Africa, its people and heritage is also mirrored in the same putrid disrespect shown by many of his contemporaries. This tainted outlook stained the western perception about Africa and Africans for generations to come. An important note here is the impact one man could have on the minds of so many. Now, multiply this by one hundred times for one hundred years and we begin to see the gravity of the problem.

Nonetheless, and in that regard, with this as a backdrop, we again ask, "How could credible black scholars spend their lengthy careers only in the end to disprove the insidious, pernicious and destructive legacy of the likes of Arthur Weigall and his 'partners in crime,' desecration and falsification?" Obviously European scholars and their American counterparts who were bent on perpetuating a false view of history, systematically orchestrated untruths designed to conceal and pillage, but these were later unmasked.

WHERE ARE THE KAMITE KINGS?

To elucidate this, some rather timely insights into the works of great African minds would highlight their findings as a point of departure for a basis to evaluate some of the data that will be presented in this section. It may be best to arrange the commentaries in chronological order that allows the reader to see the growing sophistication in black scholarship that continued to reveal findings of falsification, distortion and omission. In addition, these scholars' conclusions have in unison agreed, the people we call ancient Egyptians, were in fact, and by today's standards in America, must be considered black!

European scholars, beginning with the classical scholars, Herodotus, Diodorus Siculus, and the moderns, Count Volney, Baron Denon, Sir Godfrey Higgins, Kersey Graves, Gerald Massey, Albert Churchward, Raymond Dart, etc., all made contributions that have served to complement the work of their black counterparts, whose works are so essential. After all, Diop has maintained the African historian who refuses to challenge the cultural genocide and reclaim Egypt as the foundation of Africa is a neurotic.

Martin Delaney (1879: 64) can be considered one of the pioneers of the black intellectual movement. Troubled by European dominance and distortion, he wrote, the "hieroglyphic representations to be found on the temples and monuments of Egypt of the advanced status of the Negro race, settles at once the controversy, and leaves only to be proven the fact, that the earliest settlers, builders of the pyramids, sculptors of the sphinxes, and original God-Kings, were blacks of the Negro race." This is two decades after the pseudo-scientific writings of Samuel Cartwright previously mentioned. Bishop Samuel Crowther and most importantly Mr. Blyden also wrestled with the question as part of the African intellectual movement during the later years of the 19th Century.

FREDERICK MONDERSON

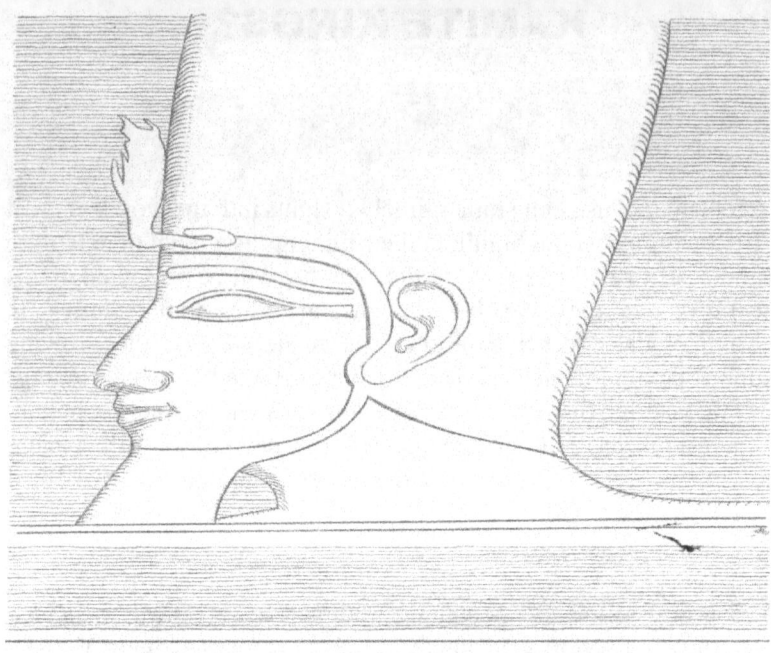

Where are the Kamite Kings Illustration. Portrait of Shabaka, XXVth Ethiopian Dynasty, from Lepsius' *Denkmaler*.

W.E.B. DuBois (1970: 18-19) was one of the first black voices in the twentieth century who produced a work in 1915 that challenged the systematic denigration of the Negro. In this book, *The Negro*, he held: "The ethnic history of Northeast Africa would seem, therefore, to have been this: pre-dynastic Egypt was settled by Negroes from Ethiopia. There were of varied type: the broad-nosed, woolly-haired type to which the word "Negro" is sometimes confined; the black, curly-haired, sharper featured type, which must be considered an equally Negroid variation. These Negroes met and mingled with the invading Mediterranean race from North Africa and Asia. Thus, the blood of the sallower race spread south and that of the darker race north. Black priests appear in Crete three thousand years before Christ, and Arabia is to this day thoroughly permeated with Negro blood. Perhaps, as Chamberlain says, "one of the prime reasons why no civilization of the type of that of the Nile arose in other parts of the continent, if such a thing were at all possible, was that Egypt acted as a sort of channel by which the genius of Negro-land was drafted off into the service of

WHERE ARE THE KAMITE KINGS?

Mediterranean and Asiatic culture. To one familiar with the striking and beautiful types arising from the mingling of Negro with Latin and Germanic types in America, the puzzle of the Egyptian type is easily solved. It was unlike any of its neighbors and a unique type until one view the modern mulatto; then the faces of Rahotpe and Nefert, of Khafra and Amenemhat I, of Aahmes and Nefertari, and even of the great Ramessu II, become curiously familiar."

Where are the Kamite Kings Photo. Entrance to Seti I's Temple of Osiris at Abydos. The famed "42 steps" are shown.

Still, in the even more compelling work designed to depict the relationship of *The World and Africa*, DuBois (1971: 90-91) further explained, the "name 'Negro' originally embraced a clear conception of ethnology - the African with dark skin, so-called 'woolly' hair, thick lips and nose; but it is one of the achievements of modern science to confine this type to a small district even in Africa. Gallas, Nubians, Hottentots, the Congo races, and the Bantus are not 'genuine' Negroes from this view, and thus we find that the continent of Africa is peopled by races other than the 'genuine' Negro."

FREDERICK MONDERSON

Again, Dubois (1971: 91) pointed out: "We find that the hideous Negro-type, which the fancy of observers once saw all over Africa, but which, as Livingstone says, is really to be seen only as a sign in front of tobacco-shops, has on closer inspection evaporated from almost all parts of Africa, to settle no one knows how in just this region. If we understand that an extreme case may have been taken for genuine and pure form, even so we do not comprehend the ground of its geographical limitation and location. We are here in presence of a refinement of science which to an unprejudiced eye will hardly hold water."

Additionally, and quoting Palgrave, Dubois (1971: 91) believed: "As to faces, the peculiarities of the Negro countenance are well known in caricature; but a truer pattern may be seen by those who wish to study it any day among the statues of the Egyptian room in the British Museum: the large gentle eye, the full but not over-protruding lips, the rounded contour, and the good-natured, easy, sensuous expression. This is the genuine African model; one not often to be met with in European or American through-fares, where the plastic African too readily acquires the careful look and even the irregularity of the features that surround him; but which is common enough in the villages and fields where he dwells after his own fashion among his own people; most common of all in the tranquil seclusion and congenial climate of Surinam plantations. There you may find, also, a type neither Asiatic nor European, but distinctly African; with much of independence and vigor in the male physiognomy and something that approaches, if it does not quite reach, beauty in the female. Rameses and his queen were cast in no other mold."

Even more significantly, Dubois (1971: 106) asserted: "We conclude, therefore, that the Egyptians were Negroids, and not only that, but by tradition they believed themselves descended not from the whites or the yellows, but from the black peoples of the south. Thence they traced their origin, and toward the south in earlier days they turned the faces of their buried corpses."

WHERE ARE THE KAMITE KINGS?

Where are the Kamite Kings Photo. Temple of Osiris at Abydos. Seti I, in Red Crown, drags a Barque before Thoth and another deity. King and the Gods are on the same plane or line.

Rogers (1970: 21) in an interesting pamphlet has provided the following: "The portrait of Cheops shows his Negro strain. See reproduction in Flinders Petrie: *Abydos*, Pl. XIV, Pt. II., London, 1903."

"In the Ethiopian hall of the old Boston Museum, I saw in 1924 a bust with the inscription, 'Negro princess of the Cheops family.'" The new museum there has two limestone busts, one of a Negro prince and the other a Negro princess of this family. See also, G. H. Beardsley, *The Negro in Greek and Roman Civilization*, p. 12, Baltimore, 1929."

"The testimony of eye-witnesses as well as that of modern science is that the Egyptians were Negroid, that is to say, largely mulatto, and the Ethiopians, unmixed Negroes."

Herodotus, (484-425 B.C.) very distinctly says that the Egyptians had black skin and woolly hair.

FREDERICK MONDERSON

Aristotle, 384-322 B.C., still ranks as a great scientist who clearly held that the Egyptians were "very black" and the Ethiopians, "woolly-haired." (*Physiognomy* Chap. VI). He also held that the "Egyptians were cowards because they were black!" Some scholars have contended Aristotle was both right and wrong. Sure, they were black but certainly not cowards.

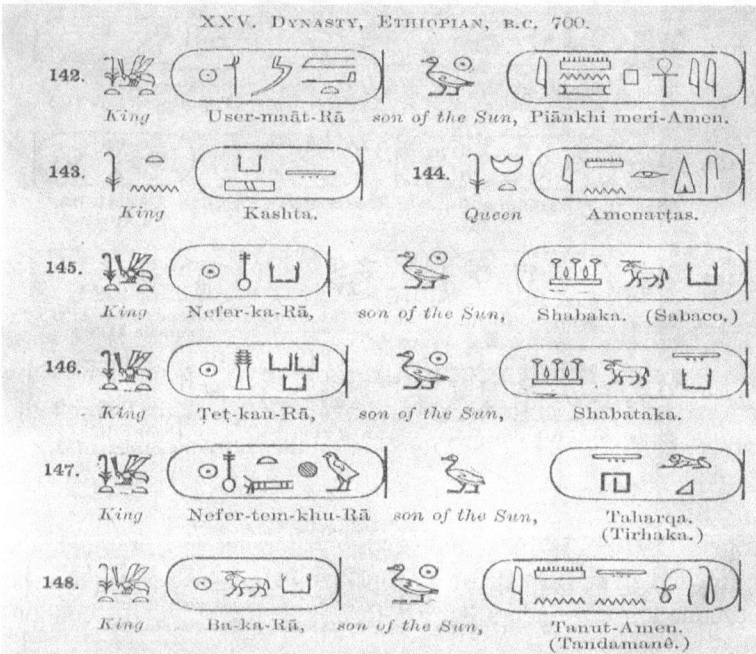

Kamite Kings Cartouche/Shennu. Kings of the Twenty-Fifth Dynasty.

Again, Rogers (1967: 37) in the first of a trilogy has written: "Some writers use the terms, Hamite and Semite, to describe the Egyptians, but these terms, like Aryan, have to do with language and nothing at all with race. A Hamite or a Semite might be white or coal-black just as one who speaks English or French may be of any color. Again, when a European speaks of Negro, he generally means an unmixed black man of primitive type, says the Chankalla; when an American does, he might be including someone who is even fairer than himself.... Instructions to the 1940 census-takers in America were that anyone with Negro strain, however slight, was to be set down as Negro. Someone has rightly described a Negro in America as one not light enough in color to ride in a white coach in America-

WHERE ARE THE KAMITE KINGS?

except, of course, that he happens to speak a foreign language, in which case, no matter how dark, he is classed as white."

Rogers (1967: 46) further states, while quoting Diodorus Siculus, the classical historian of the first century B.C., the: "'Ethiopians likewise say that the Egyptians are a colony drawn from them,' and that 'Egypt was made out of the mud and slime of Ethiopia,' meaning the rich silt brought down by the Nile. They further declared, according to this ancient writer, that the Egyptians got their laws, their customs, their burial rites, their statues, and their system of writing from Ethiopia."

In terms of cosmology, though of a late period, Jackson (1970: 93) mentioned: "The Edfu Text is an important source document on the early history of the Nile Valley. This famous inscription, found in the Temple of Horus at Edfu, gives an account of the origin of Egyptian civilization. According to this record, civilization was brought from the south by a band of invaders under the leadership of King Horus. This ruler, Horus, was later deified and became ultimately the Egyptian Christ. The followers of Horus were called 'the Blacksmiths,' because they possessed iron implements. This early culture has been traced back to Somaliland; although it may have originated in the Great Lakes region of Central Africa .... The ancestry of the South Egyptians came originally from this region that they entered the Nile Valley through Nubia, and brought with them a well-developed civilization. It is estimated that this migration must have occurred long before 5,000 B.C."

FREDERICK MONDERSON

Where are the Kamite Kings Illustration. Portrait of Shabataka, Beloved of Amen of the XXVth Ethiopian Dynasty, from Lepsius' *Denkmaler*.

Samkange (1971: 49) echoes essentially the same sentiments as the previous writers. He has written that distortion and degradation was: "Europe's attitude to the Hamites until Napoleon invaded Egypt in 1798, and his archaeologists and scientists found ancient monuments, well-preserved mummies, evidence of the beginnings of science and art. They came to realize that the origins of Western Civilization were much earlier than the Greeks or Romans. Even though the population which Frenchmen found in the country was racially mixed, Napoleon's scientists came to the conclusion that the ancient Egyptians were Negroid. One member of that expedition, Baron Denon, described the people as having 'a broad and flat nose, very short, a large flattened mouth ... thick lips, etc."

WHERE ARE THE KAMITE KINGS?

In addition, Samkange (1971: 50-51) has queried and responded: "But what race were Ancient Egyptians? Negro-of course! Even though there were Caucasians in Egypt at this time, there is nothing to suggest that they were more numerous than, or drove away, the native black population they found in the country. On the contrary, all the evidence points to the black population as having remained dominant. This was not only the opinion of Napoleon's scientists; it was also the view of contemporaries like Diodorus, Strabo, Pliny, Tacitus, and Herodotus, who visited the country."

A little further on Samkange (1971: 51) enlightened us: "Diop charges that many Negro skeletal remains and mummies were destroyed by white scholars because the facts were too disconcerting, and it was necessary to make them confirm to previously fixed assumptions. Those that have survived, together with paintings and reliefs, confirm the views of ancient writers that the Ancient Egyptians were Negro."

Murphy (1972: 18) has argued: "Until recent years it was frequently claimed that the Egyptian civilization was not truly 'African,' on the ground that both its people and their cultural affinities were more related to those of the Near East. While it is true that the Egyptians were a racially mixed people, with fewer Negroid genes than their Nubian neighbors to the south, they were fundamentally an African people. The history of Africa is the history of the migrations and intermingling of peoples; the further back one trace the history of Egypt, the more evident is the deep commonality of cultural roots over all of northern Africa, regardless of the facial composition of the peoples in various regions."

FREDERICK MONDERSON

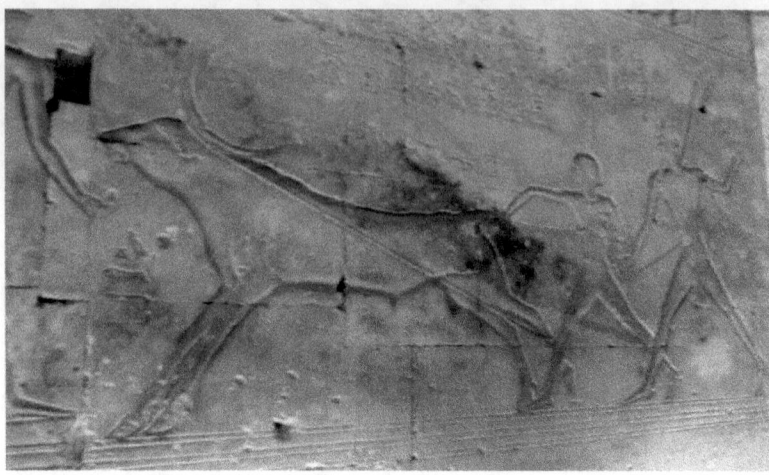

Where are the Kamite Kings Photo. Temple of Osiris at Abydos. In Red Crown, Rameses teaches young Merenptah how to lasso the Bull.

Again Murphy (1972: 19-21) has indicated: "Judging from the rock paintings in the central and eastern Sahara, and from skeletal remains, they included physical types that were ancestral to modern Berbers in the northern zone and to modern Negroes in the southern zones, with a great deal of mixture in between .... The Egyptians of this time were racially mixed, with the balance of Caucasoid and Negroid traits varying from time to time and region to region. The Caucasoid traits tended to be stronger in the delta area, the Negroid in Upper Egypt. In the delta close contact between the Libyans and the Egyptians blurred the differences between the two, while in the far south the Upper Egyptians shared many similarities with the neighboring Nubians."

Brooks (1971: 28-29), in a way best posed the question he subsequently answered. "Egyptian civilization has been considered a thing apart from the continent which gave rise to it and which provided its greatest achievements. Located on the African continent, peopled by human beings with dark skin, ancient Egypt and its culture have never been thought of as the products of African genius."

WHERE ARE THE KAMITE KINGS?

But the facts, the records, the archaeological evidence, Egyptian art and legend give us ample proof that they were. To begin at the beginning:

"Who were the people of ancient Egypt?"

"From the cemeteries dating back before 3200 B.C., anthropologists have identified remains they label 'Europoid' (including those of Cro-Magnon types), 'Negroid' and some Asian types, with the 'Europoid' predominating in the north and the 'Negroids' predominating in the south. As one expert puts it, 'the races were fused on the banks of the Nile well before pharaonic civilization came into being.' These people were black by the operating definition of skin color as well as by the general physical characteristics they had then."

Where are the Kamite Kings Photo. Temple of Osiris at Abydos. The Hypostyle Hall with its massive decorated columns. Notice the elevation from one level to the next as one enters further into all such temples.

The Greeks were surprised twenty-five hundred years ago to discover that the Egyptians were the darkest skinned peoples of the so-called Near East. Typically, they were - and are today - not homogeneous. Their skin color ranges from red-black to yellow. Their hair is black and wavy, curly or woolly; their eyes are bright and black; their bodies are lean and muscular, generally tending to tallness. Egyptian noses usually are large and straight, but frequently aquiline; their jaws generally tend to thrust forward with fleshy lips, often curled back. We can say without the slightest hesitation that the ancient Egyptians would have been considered Negroes by American standards, and until the passage of the Civil Rights Act of 1964 not one of the Egyptian Pharaohs could have bought a cup of coffee in a white drug store in the Southern states of the U.S.A."

Williams (1974: 77) held the belief that: "The recent revival of 'Black is beautiful' is no more than that - a revival. The great majority of ancient blacks took great pride in their color; and their resistance to amalgamation may be so interpreted. For one thing they had observed in Egypt was that a dynasty, beginning as all-black, could remain unbroken over generations and still in the end become near-white in color with not a black face in the royal lineage."

Again, Chancellor Williams (1974: 77-78) continued: "Reference was made to the 'Egyptians' race' of their mothers. For in Egypt, as elsewhere, it was a one-way sexual process. The 'master race' always kept its own women 'sacred' and secluded behind the walls of their homes. They were not allowed to go outside except under guard. African women had no such restrictions or protection. They were fair game for the men of all races, and for them it was always open season. Many black women preferred death by suicide. Of these, too, history does not sing. The 'master race,' then, while loudly proclaiming a strange doctrine of 'racial purity' for itself, has been the world's leader in bastardizing other peoples. So, it has been on a grand scale in the United States, in South America, in East and South Africa - and so it was in Egypt. The evolution of the Egyptians as a nationality group is as interesting as their anti-African attitude, although the latter differs not at all from that of many mixed breeds with African blood elsewhere. It has been stated that the original Egyptians were black, half-African and half-Asian. This general racial pattern changed, however, as the centuries passed along and more and more white conquerors, their followers and the other whites were attracted to the 'bread Basket on the Nile' - Canaanites, Jews, Syrians, Hittites, Persians,

WHERE ARE THE KAMITE KINGS?

Babylonians, Assyrians, Greeks, Turks, Arabs, Romans, et. al. Intermarriage between conquerors and conquered continued along with concubinage as a national institution. The direct result was that more and more Egyptians became lighter and near white in complexion. In short, they did in fact, become more Asian in blood than African. Yet this upper ruling class of near-whites was at no time more than a fourth of the population; for until the Islamic 'flood' which began in the middle of the seventh century A.D., the vast majority of the Egyptians were what modern scholars like to characterize as 'Negroid.'"

The XXVth Dynasty is special for a number of reasons but one of the most important implications is that they continued a tradition of infusing the wherewithal for uniting the nation of Kemet and supplying additional stimulus for cultural development. This connection can be tied to Bruce Williams' discovery of the earliest monarchy at Qustul in Nubia, with evidence of pharaonic paraphernalia, viz., stone incense burner, palace facade, falcon, enthroned pharaoh, Nile boat, white crown, whip and flail, etc. This dynamic was manifested in subsequent warfare and cultural ramifications unleashed by Menes, and continued by Zoser, Mentuhotep, Kamose and Ahmose, and now Piankhy and his successors. It should be remembered as Ivan Van Sertima has pointed out, Keith Seele the discoverer of this important find, when nations were asked to excavate in Nubia on eve of the Aswan High Dam being constructed, never revealed this information. It was packed away in the basement of the University of Chicago's Museum and he hoped to carry this secret to his grave. This is clearly an indication of the continued omission and distortion that has characterized the subject under discussion. Who knows what else is hidden in addition to the enormous amounts that have been destroyed, doctored, most likely purposeful?

Nevertheless, extensive architectural work was credited to this XXVth Dynasty as well as innovations in art style. Sculpture in the form of statuary showed bold realism and lasting innovations, as part of the revival that peaked in the XXVIth Dynasty.

FREDERICK MONDERSON

Karenga's (1992: 57) assessment of Egypt's gift to the world, can easily be credited to these rulers and their ancestors who were pioneers in monarchical rule, and religious belief and practice where he mentioned and gave them credit for: "... among other things a calendar, mathematics, astronomy, the alphabet, paper, ink, pen, geography, literature, art, surgery and magnificent and monumental architecture, represented in the pyramids, which have astronomical, mathematical and scientific value." Equally, the new information of Bauval and Brophy in *Black Genesis* is showing the astronomical, calendar, pastoral nature, early science of the people of Nabta Playa as forerunners of the pharaohs, in consternation with the old tired arguments of Wortham that the ancient Egyptians were Caucasians. From the western desert of southern Egypt, these black Africans, when their region started to dry up, migrated to the Nile Valley south of Aswan and started it all at a time ending contemporary with Bruce Williams' Qustol discovery.

Even more significant was the ancient African development of the multi-disciplinary approach to problem solving on the human experience plane that was essential as analytic tools, to young students initiating bold new approaches to learning. Karenga (1992: 57) continued that the history of Egypt was really, "... an attempt to settle the problems of living together - of government, defense, religion, family, property, science and art." Therefore, to meet the challenges of nature and society: "African Egypt ... made the beginning and set the pace ... in these seven lines of human endeavor."

Likewise, the application of the interdisciplinary approach to the study of African history is very important for young scholars. Utilizing the 8 major social sciences, of geography, archaeology, anthropology, history, sociology, economics and psychology, as stated earlier, this method becomes even more crucial at this time. They complement Karenga's "endeavors." Even more significant, however, and mirroring Diop's call for systematic study, Carruthers (1984: 17-18) emphasized, the "formulation of an African world-view." Similarly, he held that such an approach is the "... essential beginning point for all research which is based on the interests of African people. There can be no African history, no African social science without an African world-view. By African I do not mean merely a history or social science of Africa but a world history and a universal method of analysis designed by and for Africans."

WHERE ARE THE KAMITE KINGS?

Therefore, the work of such individuals must be considered seriously valid, in view of the historical and current degradation of Africa - culturally, socially and educationally. These great black minds have spent lifetimes exposing the distortion of western scholarship; this done through their research, teaching, writing, educational tours to Africa, Egypt and elsewhere on the continent that gave birth to the cradle of mankind and civilization. These researches have proved especially fruitful in the museums of Europe and America. Their successes are exemplary because their methodology and perseverance were organized and unrelenting. This consciousness, considered from an Afrocentric perspective, is crucial in the reconstruction of African historiography, as we progress in this new century that also forces us to look-back over the past centenary.

Following the collapse of the New Kingdom at the end of the Twentieth Dynasty, the state apparatus slipped into a period of instability that similarly had characterized the First Intermediate Period and the Second Intermediate Period. Some modern scholars have considered the Third Intermediate Period or Late Period appropriate for this time since the same characterization applied but more particularly because "foreigners" invaded the country.

The Ethiopians never really considered themselves "foreigners" and their domination of Kemet seems to have begun with Piankhy I, Khasta and his son Piankhy II.

Menkheperra, Piankhy I *Nile Year* 3362-3402 (Murnane c. 753-713 B.C.) founded the XXVth Dynasty that began ruling in a time of which the XXIInd and XXIIIrd Dynasties ruled rather contemporaneously. It seems Piankhy may have overthrown the XXIInd Dynasty late in his reign from Napata, in Nubia. His famous stele seems to have been erected at the end of the XXIInd Dynasty.

Piankhy, son of Khasta is really Piankhy II. His Protocol included the following:

FREDERICK MONDERSON

Horus	Sma-Taui
Two Ladies	Mes-Hen
Golden Horus	Sasht-Qennu
Suten Bat	Ra-Men-Kheper
Son of Ra	Piankhy, Son of Amen, born of Mut.

Not much Evidence of his reign has survived, though we know of him, according to Petrie III (1905: 268) from the great triumphal stele of grey granite: "... 6 feet in height and in width, and inscribed on both faces and edges with 159 lines of text." Found at Napata, today's Gebel Barkal, it is now in the Cairo Museum. At this site was also found a door lintel. In the Paris Museum is a bronze figure of Bast and the Cairo Museum also has a bronze-door hinge with his name. His Queen was Kenensat.

Yoyote (1962: 82) said of this Pharaoh: "Piankhy of Napata, the first Sudanese to become famous in history, conquered Upper Egypt and received the nominal submission of Lower Egypt. He was the perfect model of his dynasty: a devotee of Amen, a lover of horses, a strict observer of taboos (he refused to receive Egyptian princes who transgressed the sexual laws or ate fish)."

Where are the Kamite Kings Illustration. Head of statue of Taharka, XXVth Ethiopian Dynasty.

WHERE ARE THE KAMITE KINGS?

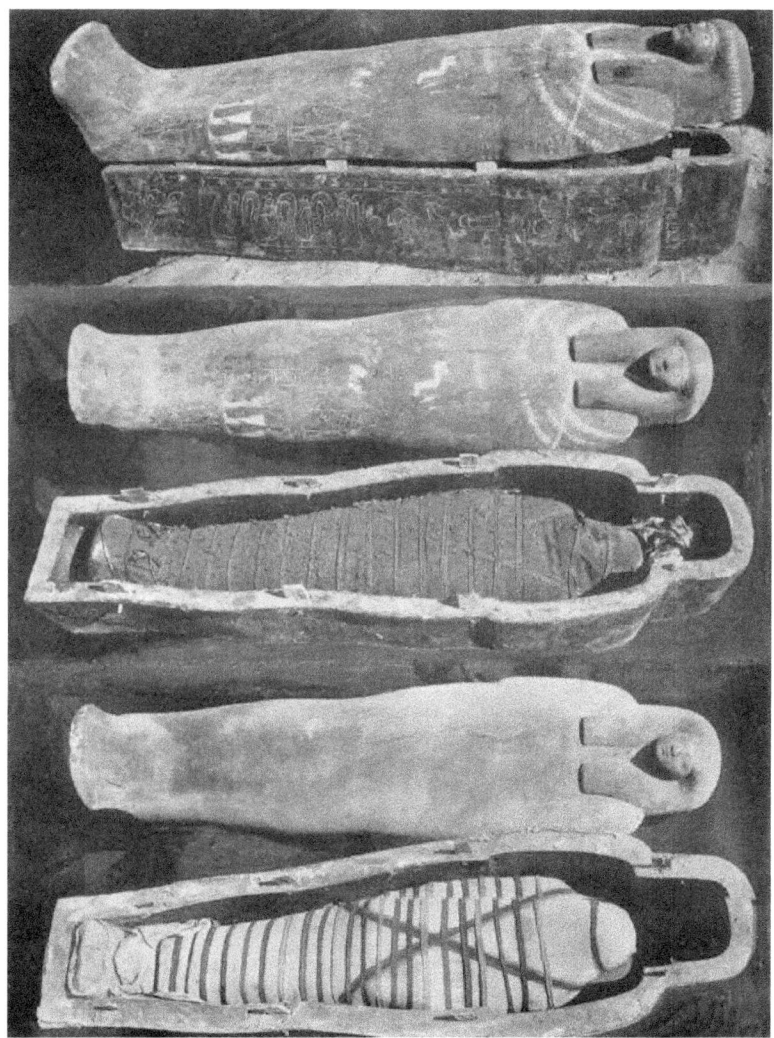

Where are the Kamite Kings Illustration. Coffins of the XXVth Dynasty found at Qurneh. These coffins show the lid, the mummy resting within and removal would show the decoration beneath the deceased.

FREDERICK MONDERSON

Where are the Kamite Kings Photo. Karnak Temple of God Amon-Ra. Great Court. The Taharka Column and stumps of other columns in Taharka's Kiosk.

What is interesting about this King is that he considered his invasion and unification of Kemet in aid of the "ancestors." This important ancestral connection has been a serious issue of contention among writers who offered any number of explanations as to its precise meaning. Remarkably, such writers refuse to see the connection between this monarch from the south of Egypt, whose homeland has contributed materially and spiritually to the growth of their fellow African cultural development further down the Nile. After all, Horus is thought to have come from a proximate area in interior Africa. Furthermore, during periods of internal instability, these lands to the south have always supplied the essential ingredients that reunited the land, provided the military backbone, material resources, craftsmanship, and cultural ethos that so successfully reunited and revivified the nation. Again, Bruce Williams' discoveries at Qustul in Nubia of the fundamental regalia of pharaonic rule, two centuries before they appear full blown at the start of dynastic rule at 3200 B.C., *Nile Year* 1040, may be the "ancestral connection" Piankhy spoke about.

WHERE ARE THE KAMITE KINGS?

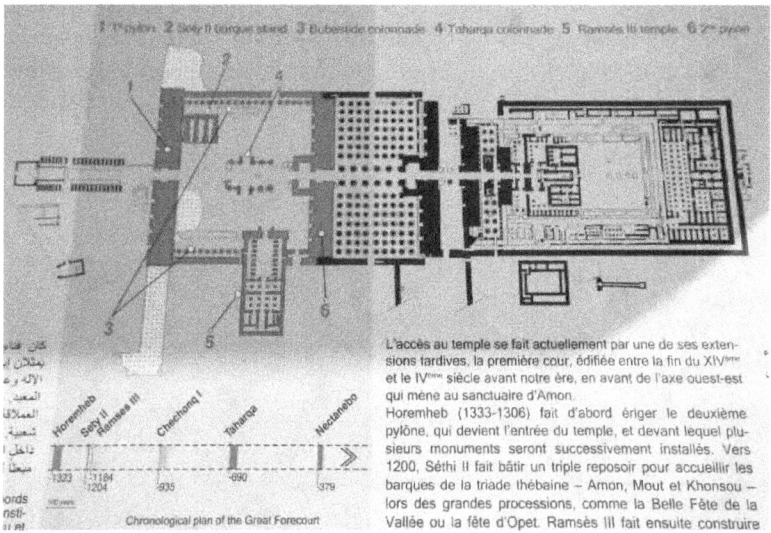

Where are the Kamite Kings Photo. Temple of Karnak with the Great Court Highlighted. 1. 1st Pylon; 2. Sety II barque stand; 3. Bubastide Colonnade; 4. Taharka Colonnade or Kiosk; 5. Ramesses III's Temple; 6. 2nd Pylon.

Ruffle (1977: 93) supplied a succinct, three paragraph summary of this important period which characterizes the seeming disdain some scholars hold for these Kings. He wrote: "'Between 725 and 716 the Assyrian threat was renewed.' So, King of Egypt (II *Kings*, 17, 4), probably to be identified with Osorkon IV, last King of the XXIInd dynasty, proved a useless support for Hosea of Israel, who was defeated by Shalmaneser V, and in 716 Osorkon IV himself had to buy off Sargon II, who had advanced to within 120 miles of Tanis."

"The XXIInd and XXIIIrd dynasties petered out in the face of this aggression and Tefnakht's successor, Barenrenef, was deposed by Piankhy's successor, Shabaka, who now occupied the whole country. Shabaka maintained an uneasy peace with the Assyrians but his successor Shebitku, sent a force under Taharka to attack Sennacherib during his unsuccessful siege of Jerusalem in 701 B.C. Taharka succeeded to the throne in c. 690 and was in turn attacked by Esarhaddon in 674 and 671, when Memphis was temporarily captured. In 667 Ashurbanipal again occupied the Delta and

FREDERICK MONDERSON

appointed Necho, Prince of Sais, as a vassal. After Taharka's death, Tanutemon recaptured the Delta and executed Necho, but Assurbanipal retaliated in strength and even captured and looted Thebes (*Nahum* 3, 8-10). Tantamani withdrew permanently to Nubia, and Necho's son Psammetichus was appointed a new Assyrian vassal in Sais and Memphis, although Upper Egypt was more or less independent under the mayor of Thebes, Montuemhat."

Where are the Kamite Kings Photo. Temple of Osiris at Abydos. In Blue or War Crown, Seti incenses enthroned Horus wearing the Double Crown. The King is not on the same plane or line as the God. An interesting observation is that the King and God never seem to be depicted wearing the same crown in any one frame.

WHERE ARE THE KAMITE KINGS?

Rogers I (1972: 92) who provides one of the better Biographies of this Piankhy, the great African, tells: "When he reached Heliopolis, King Osorkon and all the lords of the Delta, fifteen in number, surrendered without resistance." An inscription reads: "He came into the house of Ra and entered into the temple with great praise. The chief ritual prayed to the God that the rebels might be repelled from the King. The Dewat chamber was visited that the sedat-garment might be fastened on; he was purified with incense and libations; garlands from the pyramidion-house were presented to him; and flowers were brought to him. He ascended the steps of the front window to behold Ra in the pyramidion-house. The King himself stood alone, he broke through the bolts, opened the double doors, applied the clay and sealed them with the King's own seal. He charged the priests: 'I have proved the seal; no other shall enter therein of all the Kings who shall rise.' They threw themselves upon their bellies before his majesty saying: 'To abide, to endure without perishing, O Horus, Beloved of Heliopolis.'"

Now, for the likes of Weigall, et al., this was too much!

Kashta, *Nile Year* 3515-3525 (Murnane 725-715 B.C.), whose relationship with Piankhy I is purely conjectural, may have been a co-regent with Piankhy II. He had two sons, two daughters and two Queens. He is identified with his first daughter Peksather on an Abydos lintel, as father of Peksather and at Wadi Hammamat as the father also of Amenardus. Both these two princesses were sisters to Shabaka and Piankhy II.

Neferkara, Shabaka *Nile Year* 3400-3408 (Murnane 715-707 B.C.) followed Piankhy II as King of Egypt. According to Budge (1908: 70-72) his protocol included:

Horus	Seqeb-Taui
Two Ladies	Seqeb-Taui
Golden Horus	Seqeb-Taui
Suten-Bat	Ra-Nefer-Ka-Meri-Amen
Son of Ra	Shabaka

FREDERICK MONDERSON

More evidence of his reign has been found than that of his predecessor. Petrie III (1905: 281) tells of the impression of a seal, now in the British Museum, that came from Kouyunjik. Bubastis supplied a sistrum handle now in Berlin (8,181), and Athribis contained a limestone frieze, now in Cairo.

The mythological text of Shabaka, found at the Temple of Ptah at Memphis, is now in the British Museum. From this site also comes a scarab in Cairo and a Demotic papyrus found buried along the avenue. A stele of the Apis was found in year 2 at the Apis Serapeum. Hammamat inscriptions are dated to year 12, when he may have shared a co-regency with his father or brother from as early as 725 B.C.

Where are the Kamite Kings Illustration. Head of Shabaka, 25th Dynasty Ethiopian Pharaoh.

At Karnak, his name is on the door of the Temple of Ptah. It is also on chapel B, north of the Temple of Ptah, as well as door jambs here. At the great temple proper, he added to the work of Thutmose IV. On the Quay his name is inscribed in his second year. At Luxor, there is an added inscription on the Pylon. He is mentioned on the

WHERE ARE THE KAMITE KINGS?

inner pylon of the small temple at Medinet Habu. He is also on both pylons there. From Esneh comes a black granite shrine now in the Cairo Museum.

A Portrait of him is known. A white limestone statuette is in the Anastasi Collection. A beryl figure of Osiris now in Billa Albani bears his name. A black granite Naos is in Cairo. Demotic Papyri of year VII is in the Paris Museum and another of Pharmuthi 30, year X is known. A gold amulet was stolen from the Paris Museum. His Queen was Amenardus, a daughter of Piankhy. Shabataka was his son by an unknown Queen.

Where are the Kamite Kings Photo. Carmen Monderson leaves Karnak Temple as do other visitors. Note the Ram-Headed Sphinxes on both sides of the Sphinx Avenue.

Djedkaura, Shabataka, Shabitka reigned from *Nile Year* 3408-3422 (Murnane: 707-693 B.C.) following his father. Budge (1908: 71-72) provided his protocol.

Horus	Tet-Kha	
Golden Horus	He-Her-Nekht	Aa-Khefesh II
Nebu		

FREDERICK MONDERSON

Suten Bat   Ra-Tet-Khau
Son of Ra   Shabataka-Meri-Amen

Not much is known of his reign. According to Petrie III (1905: 286-87) a green basalt statue of him was found at Memphis. The end of a painted Cartouche/Shennu or Shennu at the Serapeum identified him. At Karnak, his name is in the Temple of Osiris and in a Chapel to the S. E. of the Sacred Lake. It is also on Quay No. 33, having been placed there during the third year of his reign. Lepsius's *Denkmaler* III, 301 contains a portrait of this King. A bronze shrine is in the British Museum, No. 26 a. A limestone bowl fragment and a glass heart and pottery bead are in the Flinders Petrie Collection. Plaques with feathers and scarabs also identify Shabataka.

Amenardus was the daughter of Khasta and wife of Piankhy II. Her name was found on Bronze plaques at Memphis and on an inscription at Wadi Hammamat. At Karnak, she is mentioned in Chapel B., N. of the Temple of Ptah. One large and a smaller Alabaster statue were also found here. A piece of an alabaster vase is in the Ashmolean Museum, Oxford. The Temple of Osiris at Karnak also contains her name. This Queen is in a Chapel at Medinet Habu, on an official Cone at Thebes and rock inscriptions at Aswan.

A grey granite statue of Amenardus is in the British Museum, No. 36,444. This Museum also has a Bronze door pivot, No. 36,301 and a Serpentine vase, No. 4,701. A Stone fragment is in the Berlin Museum, No. 2,107. Brown Serpentine ushabtis are in the Flinders Petrie Collection and the Paris Museum. A granite Osiris statue is in the Sabatier Collection. An Alabaster vase in is the British Museum, No. 24,709 and a glazed roll, British Museum, No. 29,212. Maspero's *Art in Egypt* has a colored photograph of Amenardus.

The Queen is associated with a number of other individuals such as Amenaru whose coffins Nos. 6,688 and 6,689 are in the British Museum. A diorite statue Amenaru (same as previous) is in the Paris Museum No. A. 85. An altar in connection with Gem-ast-pen-hor is in the Berlin Museum. Prince Horua's tomb was located at Thebes. A pendant identifies this individual and a granite figure is in the Cairo Museum. Three statuettes were found at Karnak, a seated figure is in the British Museum, No. 32,555 and a diorite

WHERE ARE THE KAMITE KINGS?

statue in the Paris Museum, No. A. 84. An inscription was discovered at Aswan.

Nefertemkhue, Taharka, *Nile Year* 3414-3448 (Murnane c. 701-667 B.C.) was one of the most renowned Ethiopian monarchs who ruled Kemet. He built extensively, particularly at Karnak, and has left ample evidence of his reign.

Petrie III (1905) informs that from Palmyra, a clay impress of seal is in the British Museum. Tanis has supplied a granite stele and his name is on a statue of Usertesen III. A granite weight from Memphis is in the Cairo Museum. The Serapeum has supplied an ink stele, Hotep-her-amen, of Year X, Apis I.A., and Senbf, Apis II., Year XXIV. A Cartouche/Shennu or Shennu was found in the Wadi Hammamat.

His extensive building at Karnak begins with the columns of the forecourt. It has been reasoned, the 'Taharka Column' that still stands in the forecourt of the Great Temple is the single survivor of ten in a Hypostyle Hall, planned for this space. While Sir Bannister Fletcher presented a plan of the temple showing 12 columns in the Taharka kiosk, Browder (1992: 117) shows a plan of Karnak Temple and 14 columns in Taharka's colonnade in the Great Court. The line of this structure is observed from the bases of remaining ones. There is a list of captured cities in the temple's forecourt. Near the E. Gate, there are 5 bases with his name. The Chapel of Osiris, Neb Ankh also bears his name. He is represented on a Building South of the Temple of Amen. Also, on Pylon X, South East of the Temple of Osiris Ptah, his name is there. Taharka's name is shown in the 2nd Court and on the door of the Temple of Ptah. It is on the Door of the 2nd Chapel of Mentu and it is also on the entrance pylon to the Great Hall. His name is on Quay, Nos. 34-37. The Base of a statuette contains a list of cities and in the Temple of Mut, the official Mentu-em-hat, recorded the King's name.

At Medinet Habu, this King constructed 'Shabaka's Pylon,' where a lintel also bears his name. From this temple, his *Stele of*

FREDERICK MONDERSON

Restoration in Year III is in the Cairo Museum. He also did restorations at Deir el Bahari. Elsewhere at Thebes, the Cone of Rameses bears his name, so too does a reused block at Ibrim. At Gebel Barkal, a Pedestal in the great temple bears his name, which is also represented in the smaller temple B.

The head of a statue bought at Luxor and another head of a red granite statue are both in the Cairo Museum. A bronze statuette portrait of this King is in the Cairo Collection. A bronze sphinx is in the Paris Museum. Two bronze plates are in the British Museum, Nos. 5,310 and 5,311. A Hieratic fragment is in the Cairo Museum, No. 6,337. Also, Demotic Papyri of years III-XVI are in the Cairo and Paris Museums. Scarabs of this King are rare.

His Queen and Sister were Amendukehat (Duk-hat-amen) and Shepenapt II. His Daughter was Amenardus II. Officials of his reign were Montuemhat, who was Governor of Thebes and whose Tomb was located in this city. Cones of this official identify the King. Three of the official's statues are in the British Museum. Ushabtis are in the Benson and Gourlay Collections. Inscriptions of his work of restorations exist. Another official was Nesishutefnut whose statue was found at Karnak. Peduamenapt's Assasif tomb was located. His name is on a door at Medinet Habu and a Karnak statue also bears his name. The coffin of Thes-ra-perau, a nurse of the King's daughter, is in the Florence Museum.

Where are the Kamite Kings Illustration. "Tables of Offerings" of the XXVIth Dynasty.

WHERE ARE THE KAMITE KINGS?

Where are the Kamite Kings Photo. Temple of Osiris at Abydos. Horus pours a libation to Osiris depicted with all his powers in his Shrine.

Tanutemen, *Nile Year* N.Y. 3448-3451 (Murnane: 667-664 B.C.) is listed in the Annals of Ashurbanipal. At Karnak his name is in the Temple of Osiris-Ptah. At Luxor was found evidence of a visit of Pedukhonsusenb in year III that is now in the Berlin Museum, No. 2,096. At Jebel Barkal, he is mentioned in the "Dream Stele," that's now in the Cairo Museum. His Queens were Qelhatat and Gerarheni.

Where are the Kamite Kings Illustration. Coffins and wooden canopic box of the XXVIth to XXXth Dynasties from Abydos in *Abydos* Part I by Flinders Petrie with a Chapter by A.E. Weigall (1902).

Some years ago, on an educational trip to the Holy Land of ancient Kemet, we visited the Temple of Luxor, as a group, early in the day. Later that afternoon, three of us returned to the revered site to take pictures of the play of the setting sun on this magnificent structure. As we waited in line, I noticed then the sign read "Admission Six Egyptian Pounds," and "Three Pounds for Students." As a student myself I tried to pay the lesser fee! The attendant in the booth would not accept my college ID from Hunter College, City University of New York, unless I had an approved International Student

WHERE ARE THE KAMITE KINGS?

Identification Card. Behind me stood a young Egyptian man of Arab ancestry. As I paid my Six Pounds and turned away, I noticed he only paid 25 Piasters! I reasoned and wondered, as for example: "Why did I pay 'six dollars' and he only paid 'twenty-five cents?'" I queried him about disparities in admission fees. He responded: "I pay this small amount because it is my ancestral culture."

How wrong could he be! In years past when I visited Egypt or Kemet, with the esteemed Dr. Yosef ben-Jochannan he always taught us to pay reverence to, respect for and cherish the ancient Kemetic culture as people of African-ancestry would. He also made us aware, that as African-Americans who visited the ancient "holy land," we were some of the most sophisticated, well-schooled, intellectually prepared and intelligent of all visitors to "the land of the ancestors" because of the world-view we take to it. African-Americans always seem to know more than the average visitor. That is, most African-Americans, in searching for their cultural heritage, have done or should always do background research to be aware and to discern when individuals, whether guides, other tourists or misinformed others as the young man, either disrespect or are misinformed about this ancient culture. The young man probably did not know the Arab invasion of Egypt came in 640 A.D., millennia after the "ancestors" had built the pyramids, domesticated the Nile, created theologies, cosmogonies, philosophic and ethical ideas, standards and practice, and had erected the most lasting and imposing architectural structures in praise to their ancestral deities.

As such, the descendants of these once great Africans must study any and every facet of this cultural history to benefit all people but especially people of African heritage worldwide.

FREDERICK MONDERSON

Where are the Kamite Kings Photo. Native Egyptian guide "Shawki" Abdel Rady and other "Kings" at the Sonesta Hotel.

Where are the Kamite Kings Photo. Abydos Temple of Rameses II. The King makes a Presentation to Osiris in White Crown as he holds Scepter, crook and flail.

WHERE ARE THE KAMITE KINGS?

Where are the Kamite Kings Photo. Abydos Temple of Rameses II. The King offers a vase to enthroned Thoth who does his work of writing.

Where are the Kamite Kings Photo. Abydos Temple of Rameses II. View of the temple's ruins from the Court of Rameses.

FREDERICK MONDERSON

Where are the Kamite Kings Photo. Above the Cartouche/Shennu of the King, symbol for eternity and long life.

20. Tombs in the Valley of the Kings

. Those marked Uninscribed means the tomb was unidentified at the time of discovery and remains so today, with some minor adjustments. Many of the Kings' mummies were moved, as in the case of the "Deir el Bahari Cache" and the "Amenhotep II tomb" discovery.

WHERE ARE THE KAMITE KINGS?

1. Rameses VII
2. Rameses IV
3. Rameses III (Unused)
4. Ramese XI
5. Sons of Rameses II
6. Rameses IX
7. Rameses II
8. Merenptah
9. Rameses V, VI
10. Amenemenes
11. Rameses III
12. Mummy Pit Children of Rameses II?
13. The Vizier Bai (Bay)
14. Tausert and Setnakht
15. Seti II
16. Rameses I
17. Seti I
18. Rameses X
19. Mentuherkhepshef
20. Queen Hatshepsut
21. Mummy Pit
22. Amenhotep III (Western Valley)
23. Ay (Ai) (Western Valley)
24. Uninscribed (Western Valley)
25. Uninscribed
26. Uninscribed
27. Uninscribed
28. Uninscribed
29. Uninscribed
30. Uninscribed
31. Uninscribed
32. Uninscribed
33. Uninscribed
34. Thutmose III
35. Amenhotep II
36. Lord Maherpra
37. Uninscribed
38. Thutmose I
39. Uninscribed
40. Mummy Pit
41. Uninscribed
42. Sennefer
43. Thutmose IV
44. Lady Tentkareu
45. Lord Userhat
46. Yuya and Tuya
47. Siptah
48. Vizier Amenemapt
49. Uninscribed
50. Uninscribed (Animals)
51. Uninscribed (Animals
52. Uninscribed (Animals)
53. Uninscribed
54. Uninscribed
55. Uninscribed
56. Uninscribed
57. Queen Tiy (Tii, Tiye) (Akhenaten?)
58. Uninscribed
59. Horemheb
60. Sitre In
61. Uninscribed
62. Tutankhamon

FREDERICK MONDERSON

21. TABLE OF EGYPTIAN
DYNASTIES
MYTHICAL PERIOD (From Manetho)

1. Gods   2. Gods   3. Gods   4. Gods

HISTORIAL PERIOD
(From Manetho and the Monuments)

I.	Thinite	This	Harabat el	253
	Madfouneh			
	II. Thinite	This	Harabat el	302
	Madfouneh			
III.	Memphite	Memphis	Mit-Rahyneh	214
IV.	Memphite	Memphis	Mit-Rahyneh	284
VI.	Elephantine	Elephantine	Geiret-Assouan	203
VI.	Memphite	Memphis	Mit-Rahyneh	284
VII.	Memphite	Memphis	Mit-Rahyneh	70
VIII.	Memphis	Memphis	Mit-Rahyneh	142
IX.	Heracleopolitan	Heracleopolis	Ahnas Medineh	109
X.	Heracleopolitan	Heracleopolis	Ahnas Medineh	
XI.	Diospolitan	Theban	Medinat Abu	213
XII.	Diospolitan	Theban	Medinat Abu	453
XIII.	Diospolitan	Theban	Medinat Abu	184
XIV.	Xiote	Xois	Sakha	511
XV.	Shepherds	Tanis	San (Hyksos)	
XVI.	Shepherds	Tanis	San	
XVII.	Diospolitan	Theban	Medinat Abu	241
XVIII.	Diospolitan	Theban	Medinat Abu	174
XIX.	Diospolitan	Theban	Medinat Abu	178
XX.	Diospolitan	Theban	Medinat Abu	
XXI.	Tanite	Tanis	San	130
XXII.	Bubasite	Bubastis	Tel Basta	170
XXIII.	Tanite	Tanis	San	89
XXIV.	Saite	Sais	Sa-el-Hagar	6
XXV.	Ethiopian	Napata	Mt. Barkal	50
XXVI.	Saite	Sais	Sa-el-Hagar	138
XXVII.	Persian	Persopolis		121
XXVIII.	Saite	Sais	Sa-el-Hagar	7
XXIX.	Mendesian	Mendes	Ashmun-er-Ruman	
XXX.	Sebennyte	Sebennytis	Samanhoud	38
XXXI.	Persian	Persopolis	Takt-i-Jemshid	8

WHERE ARE THE KAMITE KINGS?

22. CHRONOLOGY

Encyclopedia Britannica 11th Edition (1910) provides the following list. Chronology has always been an issue of contention by different scholars who either proffer or prefer the "Long Chronology" or "Short Chronology," depending upon the "flavor of the times," and this shows great differences in these lists. This work, however, utilizes the "Short Chronology" of William Murnane, contrasted with that of Dr. Yosef A.A. ben-Jochannan and the inverted *Nile Year*, absolute chronology of Cheikh Anta Diop and the Association for Study of Classical African Civilization (**ASCAC**).

Dynasty.	Meyer 1887 (minimum date).	Petrie 1894, &c.	Meyer 1904–1908.	Sethe 1905.	Breasted 1906.	Petrie 1906.
I.	3180	4777	3315	3360	3400	5510
II.		4514		3110		5247
III.		4212	2895	2810	2980	4945
IV.	2830	3998	2840	2720	2900	4731
V.		3721	2680	2630	2750	4454
VI.	2530	3503	2540	2480	2625	4206
VII.		3322		2300	2475	4003
VIII.		3252				3933
IX.		3106	2360		2445	3787
X.		3006				3687
XI.		2821	2160	2100	2160	3502
XII.	2130	2778	2000	2000	2000	3459
XIII.	1930	2565	1791		1788	3246
XIV.		2112				2793
XV.	1780		1680[1]			2533
XVI.		1928				2249
XVII.		1738				1731
XVIII.	1530	1587	1580		1580	1580
XIX.	1320	1327	1321		1350	1322

Dynasty.	Wiedemann 1884.	Meyer 1884.	Petrie 1905-1906.	Breasted 1906.	Maspero 1904.
XIX.	1490	1320	(1328), 1322	1350	
XX.	1280	1180	1202	1200	
XXI.	1100	1060	1102	1090	
XXII.	975	930	952	945	
XXIII.	810		755	745	
XXIV.	720		721	718	
XXV.	715	728	715	712	
XXVI.	664	663	664	663	
XXVII.	525	525	525	525	
XXVIII.	415		405		425
XXIX.	408		399		c. 405
XXX.	387		378		399
Ochus	350		342		380
					342

Where are the Kamite Kings Illustration. Scholars' views of the times of the dynasties.

FREDERICK MONDERSON

23. The Alphabet

Sign.	Description.	Name.	Word-sign Value.	Phonetic Value.	Determinative Value.
	child	ḥrd (khrod)			youth
	face	ḥr (ḥor)	ḥr	[ḥr]	
	eye	ír.t (yori.t)	ír	ír	see, &c.
	mouth	r (ro)	r	r	
	forearm	·(·ei)	·	·	[action of hand or arm]
	arm with stick	nḫt "be strong"	nḫt		violent action
	man with stick	nḫt "be strong"	nḫt		violent action
	lungs and windpipe	smȝ	smȝ		
	heart	íb			heart
	heart and windpipe	?	nfr		
	sparrow	?	šr		evil, worthlessness, smallness
	widgeon	sȝ.t	sȝ	sȝ	
	bolti-fish	ín.t	ín	ín	
	tusk	(1) íbḥ "tooth" (2) ḥw "taste"	bḥ ḥw	bḥ	bite, &c.
	cut branch	ḫt	ḫt	[ḫt]	wood, tree
	threshing-floor	sp.t	sp		
	sun	(1) r· "sun" (2) hrw "day"			(1) sun (2) division of time
	chamber, house	pr	pr		
	flat land	t·	t·	t·	(boundless horizon, eternity
	libation vase	ḥs.t	ḥs	ḥs	
	cord on stick	wz	wz	wz	
	basket	nb.t	nb		
	looped basket	?	k	k	
	sickle	?	m·	m·	
	composite hoe	[mr ?]	mr	mr	tillage
	fire-drill	z·.t(?)	z·	z·	
	attendant's equipment	šmś "follow"	šmś		
	knife	dś	dś		cut, prick, cutting instrument

Where are the Kamite Kings Illustration. The Egyptian/Kamite alphabet can provide the basis for young scholars to explore this important language of ancient Africa.

WHERE ARE THE KAMITE KINGS?

Where are the Kamite Kings Photo. Erik Monderson assumes the Royal Position with arms crossed in a tomb on El Kab Mountains.

24. INDEX

Aahmes I, King – 352, 477, 703
Aahmes-Nefertari – 476
Abolitionists – 27, 28, 35
Abu Simbel – 155, 572, 584, 585, 601, 603, 617, 642
Abydos – 6, 85, 86, 87, 89, 91, 94, 96, 107, 108, 111, 112, 114, 116, 118, 119, 120, 121, 125, 126, 127, 129, 130, 141, 178, 181, 182, 212, 213, 219, 238, 240, 242, 244, 251, 252, 256, 260, 267, 268, 270, 272, 273, 286, 325, 364, 381, 382, 386, 387, 389, 392, 398, 402, 440, 450, 476, 478, 482, 485, 489, 492, 498, 508, 516, 517, 521, 553, 557, 562, 563, 565, 568, 571, 608, 610, 721
    Abydos List (Table) – 252, 256,
    Second Abydos List (Tablet) – 381-382
African-American youth's interest in Egypt – 295
Afrocentric scholarship – 26, 67, 715
Agriculture, origins – 49, 50, 72, 144, 178, 269, 294
    Products – 294
    Types of – 294
Amenardus – 722, 723, 724
Amenemhat I (*Sehotpeibre*) – 376, 378, 380, 382, 383
Amenemhat II (*Nebkeure*) – 386, 388, 389, 390, 391,
Amenemhat III (N*emacre*) – 310, 342, 369, 379, 397, 398, 401, 414,
Amenemhat IV (*Mackherure*) – 402
Amenhotep I (*Thoserkere*) – 215, 370, 477, 478, 571, 571, 692
Amenhotep II (*Oekheperure*) – 215, 435, 437, 456, 497, 507, 509, 512, 514, 572, 616
Amenhotep III (*Nebmaere*) – 215, 224, 414, 437, 453, 454, 514, 520, 523, 526, 530, 531, 534, 572, 583, 584, 603, 617, 625, 638, 641, 664, 666, 670,
Amenhotep IV (*Neferkheperure*) (Akhenaton, Ikhnaton) – 437, 531, 533, 534, 553, 572
    Queen Nefertiti – 528, 529
Amon, Amun, Amen – 20, 21, 178, 276, 359, 382, 440, 447, 465, 540, 589, 590, 628, 646, 658, 660, 661, 665, 668,
    Variations of the name (Amon-Ra, Amun-Ra, Amen-Ra)
Amrah – 74, 201, 207
    Strongly curled hair – 204
Amratian Period – 67, 74, 75, 76, 142, 215,
    Features of the culture – 7 4

WHERE ARE THE KAMITE KINGS?

Ancient writers – 41, 709
Anezib – 85, 125
Antef I – 404
Antef II – 332, 333
Antef – 333
Antef IV – 332
Antef V – 310, 317, 332, 333
Antef VI – 332, 333
Anubis – 125
Archaeologists – 18, 69, 74, 116, 143, 171, 238, 266, 708
Archaic Period, Summary of – 80, 85, 130, 142, 144, 145, 196, 420
Aye (*Kheperkheperure*) – 261, 438, 552, 553,
Babylonian Talmud and "Noah's Curse" – 60
Badarian – 68, 69, 72
Battle of Kadesh – 591
ben-Jochannan, Dr. A.A. – 16, 19, 67, 80, 155, 288, 340, 729, 735
Blessing – 98
Book of the Dead – 124,
Breasted, James Henry – 19, 22, 31, 55, 67, 148, 213, 226, 244, 259,
    260, 264, 273, 274, 279, 285, 306, 307, 308, 317, 322, 383,
    493, 494, 497, 524, 664
British Association for Advancement of Science – 30
Brown, John – 28
Bruce Williams' Qustol discoveries – 46, 713, 714, 718
Calendar – 55, 56, 68, 80-81,
Champollion, Cheronnet the Younger – 22
Champollion, Jean Jacques – 28, 29, 186, 346, 388
Chapel for apotheosis of King Sankh-Ka-Ra – 334
Chronology – 63, 66, 67, 81, 148, 283, 334, 735
    "long" – 63, 735
    "short" – 63, 67, 735
Cities housing Egyptian collection – 17
Clarke, John Henrik – 4, 19, 32, 46, 50, 263, 348, 698
    "Colonization of African knowledge" – 263, 334, 348, 700
Classical scholars – 401
    Diodorus – 41, 229, 232, 243, 400, 637, 651, 701, 707
    Herodotus – 226, 232, 242, 399, 401, 587, 674, 691,
    Josephus – 41, 263
    Manetho – 22, 42, 111, 120, 131, 198, 213, 226, 255,
    Pliny – 230, 232, 243, 400

Strabo – 387, 399, 674,
Coffins – 91, 92, 93, 116, 205, 206, 207, 217, 251, 276, 277, 278, 333, 334, 348, 367, 377, 404, 407, 410, 411, 420, 445, 456, 476, 478, 479, 483, 485, 491, 532, 533, 534, 562, 577, 616, 622, 724, 726
Coffin, Levi – 28
Colonnade – 309, 353, 354, 356, 357, 360, 361, 362, 364, 402, 523, 525, 606, 617, 641, 643, 664, 725
Commentators, ancient, on Egypt – 226, 263,
Conspiracy against Ancient Egypt – 278, 285, 374, 383,
Cooking vessels of Amratians – 739
Crafts – 44, 269
Dancing before the God – 122
Den (Ten, Udimu, Sempti) – 120, 122, 123,
Denon, Count – 39, 41
Diop, Cheikh Anta – 3, 4, 19, 21, 50, 53, 55, 56, 59, 63, 78, 80, 81, 143, 155, 197, 226, 257, 338, 350, 454, 698, 701, 709, 714, 735,
    and the Calendar – 80-81
    (1974) *African Origins of Civilization* –
    (1992) *Civilization or Barbarism* –
Divisions or Periods of Egyptian history – 67, 219, 280, 368, 718
Djedefre – 243
Djedkare-Isesi – 264
DuBois, W.E.B. – 19, 702, 703, 704,
Dynamics of early Egyptian culture – 29, 40, 96, 177, 338, 348,
Dynasties –
    Division by Manetho – 42
    Division by modern scholars – 42
    Badarian, Amratian, Gerzean – 68-76
    Beginning of Dynastic or Pharaonic rule – 63-64, 68
    First (Thinite) – 79, 80
        List of Kings' names – 80, 128
        Monument set on fire –
    Second (Thinite) –
        List of Kings' names – 141
        Monuments –
    Third (Memphite) – 180, 181
        Names for Old Kingdom I – 255
    Fourth (Memphite) – 194, 213, 218
        Names for Old Kingdom II - 270
    Fifth (Elephantine) – 256

WHERE ARE THE KAMITE KINGS?

       List of Kings' names 257
  Sixth (Memphite) – 269
  Seventh (Memphite) – 307
  Eighth (Memphite) – 308
  Ninth (Heracleopolite) – 309
  Tenth (Heracleopolite) – 309
  Eleventh (Theban) – 321
  Twelfth (Theban) – 373
      Names – 366
  Seventeenth (Theban) – 433
      Names – 366
  Eighteenth (Theban) – 431, 472,
      Pharaohs – 433-434
      Names – 433, 434
  Nineteenth (Theban) – 561
      Pharaohs – 438
      Names – 438
  Twentieth (Theban) – 622
      Pharaohs – 455
      Names – 455
  Twenty-Fifth (Ethiopian) – 697
Educational Tour – 224-225
Egypt, Predynastic – 77, 254
Egyptian accomplishments – 22, 163, 168, 173, 295, 321, 341,
    451
Egyptian art – 711
Egyptian, origins, argument – 19, 21, 49, 59, 143, 155,
    170, 201, 252, 573, 708,
    Diop's arguments for and against – 59
Egyptology scholars who laid the foundation – 29, 63
Ethiopia's "eldest daughter Egypt" – 339, 340, 341, 414, 479, 684,
    705, 725
"Eurocentric conspiracy" – 35, 63, 143, 188, 197
"European Afrocentrists" – 39, 41, 63, 701
"Eve, African" – 55
Fagan, Brian – 52R
    (1975) *Rape of the Nile* – 52
Falsity regarding Ancient Egypt, scholars – 22, 39,
First Intermediate Period – 293, 306, 714
Food/trade exports – 76, 105, 131, 142, 144, 164, 165, 177, 178,

219, 254, 264, 269, 293, 294, 322, 448, 450, 631, 681
Garstang, John – 79, 126, 145, 181, 191, 192, 195-196, 198, 343, 403, 406, 411, 417, 419, 424
Gerzean – 67, 76, 142
Graeco-Roman temples – 45, 211, 360, 378
Hall – 309, 582, 589, 610, 637, 639, 652, 658, 678, 679, 682, 683, 725
Hall, H.R. – 309, 343, 361, 424,
Hatshepsut, Queen (*Ma'at-Ka-Ra*) – 22, 264, 361, 414, 436, 437, 486, 489, 493, 494, 496, 497, 498, 502, 503, 572
Hawass, Zahi – 3, 245, 246, 247
"Hebrew Myth" and "Noah's curse" –
Hen-Nekht – 126, 198, 199,
    "Negroid features" – 198
    "Bones of Hen-Nekht" – 198
    Merkhet (Semempses, Hen-Nekht) –
Hetepheres – 217
Hierakonpolis, Painted Tomb – 82, 140, 321, 416,
"Holy Land" Educational Tour –
Hor-Aha – 85, 94, 107, 108
Horemheb (Horemhab) (*Thoserkheperure*) – 556, 557
Horus Huni (Nefer-Ka-Ra) – 213, 214,
Hotepsekhemwy (Boethos, Buzau) – 128
Hyksos – 22, 23, 65, 337, 358, 417, 422, 432, 433, 472
    Pharaoh – 358, 432
Intef VI (Antef VI) – 278, 310, 317, 321, 322, 332,
Iron, Question of (H.R. Hall) – 50, 77, 229, 231, 232, 234, 235, 236, 237, 238, 239, 240, 241, 242, 297, 706
Kara, Nomarch – 292,
Karnak List (Tablet) –
Karnak Temple –
Khasta – 14, 715, 722
    Daughter, Amenardus I –
Khafre – 190, 218, 244, 249
Khasekhem (Sesochris, Huxefa) –
Khasekhmuwi (Cheneres, Zazai) –
Khufu – 217, 219, 223, 224, 226, 243, 247, 248, 270
Khufu, Khafre and Menkaure – 46
Kings'/Queen's attire – 260, 434
Kings' names (titles) – 117, 213
Kings, tombs at Abydos – 85,
Luxor Temple –224, 451, 454, 517, 544, 557, 558, 641, 664, 726,

WHERE ARE THE KAMITE KINGS?

    727,
Ma'at – 184, 301,
Manetho – 22, 42, 111, 120, 131, 198, 213, 226, 255, 270,
Medinet Habu, Temple of – 483, 527, 558, 582, 584, 614, 617, 622,
    627, 630, 631, 726,
Meryet-Nit, Queen – 85, 111, 128
Menkaure – 46, 190, 249, 279
Metternich, Age of – 27
Mentuhotep I (*Senkhibtoui*) – 318, 322, 332, 334, 346
Mentuhotep II (*Nebheptre*) – 215, 318, 322, 323, 324, 325, 330, 331,
    332, 333, 334, 336, 350, 353, 354, 356, 357, 360, 370, 376,
    414, 477, 492, 553,
Mentuhotep III (*Nebhapetre*) – 322, 323, 325, 332, 333, 334
Mentuhotep IV (*Senkhkere*) – 322, 333, 338
Merenptah (*Bienre Hotpehermae*) – 606, 607, 608, 610, 611, 612,
    613, 617,
    Queen Astnefert – 611
Meren-Ra – 283, 284
Methodology I – 150, 154,
Methodology II – 175, 715
Middle Kingdom – 22, 42, 224, 235, 236, 239, 317, 318, 321, 338,
    355, 371, 406, 447, 632
Min – 276, 440,
Mummification, *History of*, G. Elliot Smith – 24, 172, 336, 377,
    446, 456, 457, 470
Mu'Min – 184
    Dedication – 184
    Poem – 184-185
Narmer – 80, 81, 82, 83, 85, 94, 96, 105, 141, 142, 178, 215, 280,
    424,
    Names – 83, 94
    Palette and Macehead – 81, 82
    Tomb – 85, 96
    Unification – 339
    Victims at his tomb – 141
Naville, Edouard and H.R. Hall – 31, 309, 346, 350, 361, 364, 371,
    500
    Excavation at Deir el Bahari I – 346, 350,
    Excavation at Deir el Bahari II – 309, 361-364
Neferefre – 264, 280

FREDERICK MONDERSON

Neferirkare-Kakai – 260, 264,
Neferkara (Nephercheres) – 128, 136, 142, 317, 721
Negative Confessions – 290
Negro countries – 285
Neteren (Binothris) – 131
Neterka (Chaires) – 128, 135,
Neterkhet (Tosorthus) – 181
New Kingdom – 20, 321, 369, 431, 447, 448, 450, 627, 715,
    Accomplishments – 224,
    Art of – 448
    Cultural developments – 449
"New Race" – 74
Niuserre – 264, 265, 266, 280
    Sun Temple – 265, 266
Old Kingdom – 22, 87, 144, 177, 208, 221, 235, 237, 244, 246, 264, 269, 276, 286, 293, 321, 360, 433, 448
    Duration – 177
Osiris – 100, 105, 112, 178, 184, 295, 300, 334, 440, 447, 463, 466, 468, 469, 492, 568, 608, 612, 676, 680, 682, 723, 724, 725,
Palermo Stone – 126, 179, 214, 252
Pepi I – 123, 232, 249, 271, 273, 274, 278, 280, 283, 285
    Name – 123
Pepi II – 179, 285, 286, 288, 293, 306, 433
    Temple – 249
    Tomb of – 286, 288
Personality, Egyptian – 226, 433, 446, 476
    3 Entities – 446
Petrie, William Matthew Flinders – 30, 83, 87, 88, 90, 91, 92, 93, 112, 116, 118, 125, 126, 195, 201, 230, 232, 235, 236, 239, 240, 243, 317, 333, 334, 339, 340, 342, 382, 386, 389, 392, 398, 427, 428, 447, 476, 479, 481, 483, 484, 486, 491, 496, 497, 499, 503, 508, 517, 523, 531, 538, 540, 543, 544, 553, 557, 559, 563, 565, 577, 591, 604, 623, 630, 716, 722, 724, 725
    "Friends of" – 30, 31
    Sequence dating – 88
Physicians – 290,
Piankhy I and II – 698, 713, 715, 716, 718, 721, 724, 360, 444,
Plunderers – Belzoni, Drovetti, Salt - 186
Precession – 56
Prehistoric and historic periods – 74, 87,
Priests – 143, 145, 248, 259, 287, 446, 448, 449, 654, 662, 690, 702

WHERE ARE THE KAMITE KINGS?

     Functions – 445,
     Grade – 445
Priesthood, Wealth of – 83, 178, 291, 438, 439, 440, 447, 632
Pyramid Complex – 233, 288

Where are the Kamite Kings Photo. Erik Monderson stands beside the In Situ Altar dedicated to Ra-Horakhty in Queen Hatshepsut's Temple at Deir el Bahari.

Pyramids – 80, 127, 148, 165, 177, 179, 180, 199, 226, 229, 238,
     239, 245, 289, 295, 376, 450, 701, 714, 729
     Diodorus on – 400-401
     Herodotus – 399
     Pliny on – 399
     Measurement –
     "Bent" – 213
     "Layer" or "Step" – 214
     "Silt" – 288
     "Step" – 46, 180, 190, 191, 214, 225, 256, 260, 288,
     "True" – 46
"Pyramid Texts" – 237, 267, 291
     King Teti's – 291
Qaya – 85
Queen – 23, 531, 532, 660

FREDERICK MONDERSON

    Aah-Hotep (Sekenenra-Tao) – 477
    Nefertari (Aahmes) – 436, 486
    Aam (Mentuhotep II) – 333
    Achthoes (Antef) – 333
    Amenardus (Shabataka) – 723
    Amendukehat (Duk-hat-amen) (Taharka) – 726
    Anhapi (Amenhotep I) – 477
    Ankhesenamon (Tutankhamon) –
    Ast-amasereth (Rameses III) – 630
    Astnefert (Merenptah) – 613
    Berner-Ib (Hor-Aha) – 111
    Hatshepsut (Thutmose II) – 224
    Hetep-Heres (Snefru) – 216
    Humazery (Rameses III) – 630
    Isis, Aset (Thutmose I) – 480, 486
    Kasmat (Aahmes) – 477
    Kenensat (Piankhy) – 716
    Khenthawes (Shepsekaf) – 252
    Mert-Aten (Smenkhare) – 542
    Meryta-Hatshepsut (Thutmose III) – 496
    Maut-m-Shoi (Tuthmose IV) – 644
    Nebtu (Tuthmose III) – 497
    Nefertari II (Rameses II) 590
    Nefertiti (Amenhotep IV, Akhenaten) – 541
    Nefert (Senusert II) – 392
    Neith-Hotep (Narmer) – 105
    Nexem-Mut (Horemheb) – 559
    Sebek-Neferi-Ra (Usertesen IV) – 403
    Sistra – (Rameses I)
    Ta-Aa (Amenhotep II) – 512
    Teni-Hapi (Amenhotep I) – 477
    Tetashera (Teti-Sheri) – 364, 433
    Tiy (Tiye) (Amenhotep III) – 437
    Tuaa (Seti I) – 572
    Ty (Rameses III) – 553
    Weret-Yamtes (Pepi I) – 278
Quibell at Hierakonpolis – 81, 195, 280,
Ra, God – 80, 447, 585
Rameses I – 215, 561, 562, 563, 634
Rameses II – 21, 66, 215, 224, 236, 317, 343, 370, 439, 453, 498,
       553, 568, 572, 573, 574, 577, 579, 580, 582, 584, 585, 586,
       588, 589, 601, 604, 607, 611, 612, 613, 619, 632, 633, 635,

WHERE ARE THE KAMITE KINGS?

639, 640, 641, 642, 648, 649, 651, 656, 658, 659, 680, 704,
Rameses III – 66, 224, 236, 267, 439, 443, 444, 447, 453, 582, 622, 625, 627, 628, 629, 630, 632, 633, 640, 659, 661, 662, 665, 666, 671,

Where are the Kamite Kings Photo. Geniuses in the Cairo Museum of Egyptian Antiquities. Jean-Jacques Champollion and Erik Monderson.

Rameses IV – 464, 514, 631
Rameses VI – 419, 514, 546, 624
Rameses VIII – 514,
Rameses IX – 532,
Rameses XI – 631
Ramesseum – 360, 439, 572, 583, 601, 610,
Randall-MacIver – 209, 211, 252
    Among the Berbers –
    "Strongly curled hair" –
Reisner, George – 217, 246
Reqaqnah – 145, 192, 411
Revolutions - 41
Sahure – 260, 261, 264, 266, 279,
    Name – 260
Sakkara List (Tablet) – 85, 125, 126, 137, 213, 264, 267, 270, 273, 284, 382, 402, 457, 478,

FREDERICK MONDERSON

Sa-Nekht (Necherophes) Neb-Ka-Ra –
Science – 3, 24, 30, 49, 55, 164, 167, 169, 170, 175, 239, 259, 342, 437, 449, 456, 703, 704, 705, 708, 714,
"Scorpion King" – 83
Scott-Moncrieff – 494
Sebek-Neferi-Ra, Queen – 403
Sekhemib (Perabsen, Has, Uazmes) – 13, 4532, 495
Seti I (*Menmaere*) – 123, 215, 224, 439, 498, 553, 563, 564, 565, 566, 567, 568, 570, 571, 572, 573, 583, 609, 610, 624, 672, 677 -
Seti II (*Userkheperure*) – 453, 514,
Seven Wonders of the World – 224
Shabaka – 719, 721,
Shabataka – 215, 723, 724
Shepsekaf – 249, 252, 279
Sinai Expedition – 339, 412, 413-417
Smenkhare – 553
Smerkhet (Semerkha) hen-nekht – 126, 196, 741,
Snefru – 65, 192, 213, 214, 288, 414,
Sothic cycle – 55
Sphinx, beard on "permanent loan" – 39, 56, 74, 226, 245, 249, 289, 386, 398, 452, 495, 496, 516, 523, 529, 557, 570, 579, 580, 601, 604, 612, 616, 617, 632, 639, 640, 660, 686, 701, 726
    Age – 56
    Beard – 39
Sudanese dolls – 746
"Table of Offerings" – 286,
    Pepi II –
Taharka – 215, 478, 718, 724,
Tanutemon (Tanutemen) – 215, 718
Tarkhan – 90, 92,
Temples –
    Dendera – 45, 224, 272, 324, 360, 451, 491, 625,
    Edfu – 291, 292, 293, 418, 502, 707
    Esneh – 360, 486, 580, 723
    Kalabsha – 45, 224, 360
Teti I – 270, 278, 289, 291, 476,
Teti-Sheri (Tetashera) – 364,
Thebes – Temples, tombs, archaeologists – 23, 317, 318, 334, 336, 339, 346, 353, 370, 376, 387, 388, 419, 426, 438, 440, 447, 450, 479, 540, 601, 632, 637, 650, 665, 668, 720, 724, 726
Thoth – 103, 614, 658

WHERE ARE THE KAMITE KINGS?

Thutmose I (*Ockheperkere*) – 483, 484, 485
    Children – 484
    Officials – 484-485
    Queens, 3 – 484
    Tomb – 485
Thutmose II (*Ockheperker*) –476, 484, 485, 486, 494
    Children – 486
    Coffin – 485
    Queens – 486
Thutmose III (*Menkheperre*) – 215, 436, 437, 442, 454, 484, 486, 489, 490, 491, 494, 496, 497, 507, 512, 567, 572, 582, 612, 617, 627
    Annals – 442
    Children – 490,
    Coffin – 491
    Gifts to Amon 442
    Mother – 489
    Mummy – 491
    Obelisks, Lateran, Karnak –
    Queen, 3 – 489, 490
    Temple *Akh Menu* –
Thutmose IV (*Menkhepurure*) – 436, 494, 512, 513, 517, 542, 617, 721-722
    Tablet or Stele of the Sphinx – 516
Tombs –
    Officials –450
    Pharaohs – 450
Tools, materials of – 69, 72, 74, 88, 116, 145, 165, 172, 217, 218, 229, 232, 235, 240, 241, 242, 358, 414, 503, 714,
Tutankhamon (*Nebkheperure*) –, 438, 503, 553,
    Restoration, Stele – 322, 324, 341, 557, 726
Unis (Unas) – 126, 129, 131, 141, 267, 268, 273, 279, 289,
Usertesen I (Senusert I) – 123, 376, 378, 384, 385, 386, 387,
Usertesen II (Senusert II) – 310, 391, 392, 397,
Usertesen III (Senusert III) – 221, 310, 368, 394, 397, 725
Usertesen IV – 403
Van Sertima, Ivan – 4, 19, 32, 39, 50, 78, 145, 155, 698, 713
Von Luschan's "confusion on racc" – 60, 63
War of Liberation – 22, 434,

FREDERICK MONDERSON

Weni, lengthy Autobiography – 255, 278, 279, 284
White, Bull, Crown, Egyptologists, "Europeans," supremacy Wall, "vested interest," etc. – 4, 16, 22, 28, 32, 42, 46, 50, 56, 59, 60, 63, 67, 83, 85, 100, 107, 121, 127, 131, 138, 153, 155, 184, 197, 253, 257, 280, 318, 330, 338, 355, 357, 363, 402, 403, 404, 407, 422, 462, 494, 526, 532, 548, 601, 606, 660, 661, 681, 685, 706, 709, 712, 713, 723
Year, types, length, variations in – 22, 55, 45, 68, 81, 132, 139, 144, 177, 181, 195, 197, 213, 215, 216, 217, 219, 243, 244, 249, 252, 256, 260, 264, 265, 267, 270, 273, 280, 282, 283, 285, 286, 293, 315, 316, 321, 368, 370, 371, 372, 373, 376, 378, 383, 385, 386, 387, 388, 389, 390, 391, 392, 394, 397, 402, 403, 406, 424, 431, 438, 451, 472, 473, 478, 482, 485, 486, 491, 497, 502, 507, 512, 514, 520, 534, 542, 552, 553, 556, 559, 563, 564, 567, 571, 574, 584, 589, 601, 602, 603, 604, 613, 614, 616, 618, 621, 622, 628, 631, 632, 665, 715, 718, 721, 722, 723, 724, 725, 726, 727

Where are the Kamite Kings Photo. Erik Monderson on the grounds, before the entrance to Cairo Museum of Egyptian Antiquities, 2018.

Zer – 85, 111, 112, 114, 116, 118, 128, 141,
    Subsidiary graves –
Zet (Uadji, Djet) – 85, 88, 92, 119

WHERE ARE THE KAMITE KINGS?

Zoser (Neter-Kha) – 180, 181, 197, 225, 260, 265,

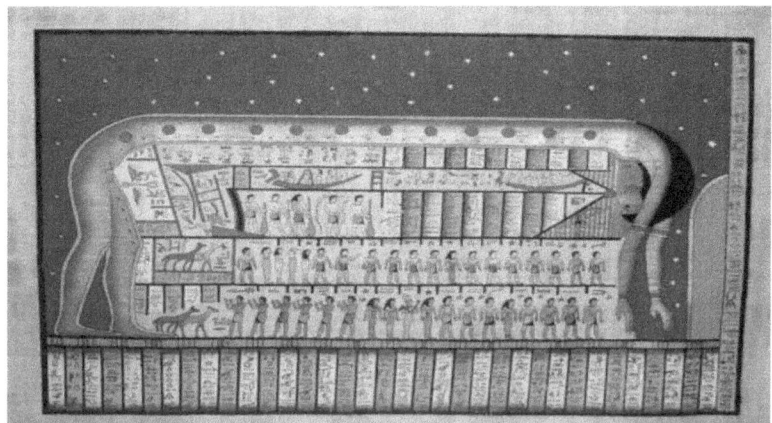

Where are the Kamite Kings Photo. Papyrus depiction of the Goddess Mut and the drama of the heavens as evidenced at Dendera Temple of Goddess Hathor.

Where are the Kamite Kings Photo. Shawki Abdel Rady and Erik Monderson leave Hathor's Temple at Dendera after a very enlightening visit.

FREDERICK MONDERSON

Where are the Kamite Kings Photo. Dr. Fred Monderson, author and lecturer sits with some of his earlier books.

www.ingramcontent.com/pod-product-compliance
Lightning Source LLC
Chambersburg PA
CBHW050319020526
44117CB00031B/1249